OXFORD STUDENT ATLAS

Editorial Adviser
Dr Patrick Wiegand

OXFORD
UNIVERSITY PRESS

Great Clarendon Street, Oxford OX2 6DP

Oxford University Press is a department of the University of Oxford.
It furthers the University's objective of excellence in research, scholarship,
and education by publishing worldwide in

Oxford New York

Auckland Bangkok Buenos Aires Cape Town Chennai
Dar es Salaam Delhi Hong Kong Istanbul Karachi Kolkata
Kuala Lumpur Madrid Melbourne Mexico City Mumbai Nairobi
São Paulo Shanghai Singapore Taipei Tokyo Toronto

with an associated company in Berlin

Oxford is a registered trade mark of Oxford University Press
in the UK and in certain other countries

© Oxford University Press 2002

First published 2002

© Maps copyright Oxford University Press

ISBN 0 19 831877 4 (hardback)
ISBN 0 19 831878 2 (paperback)

Printed in Italy

2 Contents

page

Maps and satellite images _____ 4

Map projections and graphics _____ 5

British Isles   Topographic maps

British Isles _____ 6
Orkney and Shetland Islands _____ 7
Scottish Highlands and Islands _____ 8–9
Northern Ireland   Southern Scotland _____ 10–11
Northern England _____ 12–13
Wales   West and East Midlands _____ 14–15
South East England _____ 16–17
South West England _____ 18–19
Ireland _____ 20–21

topographic maps of the British Isles

British Isles   Thematic maps

Political	22–23	Employment	33
Physical	24	Population	34–35
Geology	25	Sport Tourism	36
Climate	26–27	Quality of life	37
Land use	28	Conservation	38
Farming	29	Pollution	39
Water Minerals	30	Transport	40
Energy	31	Trade	41
Manufacturing industry	32		

Europe   Thematic maps

Physical _____ 42
Climate   Ecosystems _____ 43
Political _____ 44
Population   Wealth _____ 45
Economy _____ 46
Tourism _____ 47

Europe   Topographic maps

Benelux and the Ruhr _____ 48
Scandinavia and Iceland _____ 49
France _____ 50
Spain and Portugal _____ 51
Middle Europe _____ 52–53
Italy and the Balkans _____ 54–55
East Europe and Turkey _____ 56–57

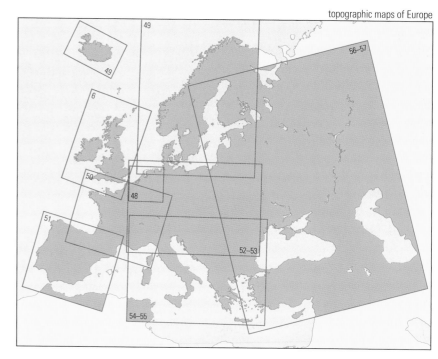

topographic maps of Europe

Asia   Thematic maps

Physical _____ 58
Political _____ 59
Climate   Ecosystems _____ 60
Economy   Population _____ 61

Asia   Topographic maps

Northern Eurasia _____ 62–63
Middle East _____ 64–65
South Asia _____ 66–67
China _____ 68–69
Japan _____ 70
South East Asia _____ 71

topographic maps of Asia

Oceania   Topographic map

Australia and
New Zealand _____ 72–73

Oceania   Thematic maps

Climate   Ecosystems
Population   Economy _____ 74

topographic map of Oceania

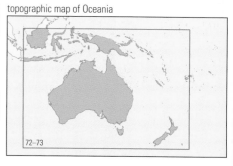

© Oxford University Press

Contents 3

Africa   Thematic maps

Physical Political	75
Satellite images	76
Climate Ecosystems	77
Economy Population	78
Tourism	79

Africa   Topographic maps

Northern Africa	80–81
Southern Africa	82
East Africa	83

North America   Thematic maps

Physical Political	84
Climate Ecosystems	85
Economy Population	86
Tourism	87

North America   Topographic maps

Canada	88–89
United States of America	90–91
Great Lakes	92–93
Mexico, Central America, and the Caribbean	94–95

South America   Topographic map

South America	96–97

South America   Thematic maps

Political	97
Climate Ecosystems	98
Economy Population	99

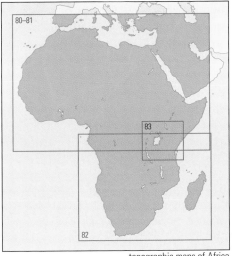
topographic maps of Africa

topographic maps of North America

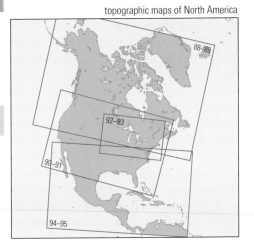

topographic map of South America

World   Thematic maps   *page*

Political	102–103
Physical	104–105
Earthquakes and volcanoes	106–107
Temperature and ocean currents	108
Pressure, winds, and precipitation	109
Climate regions	110–111
Climate data	112
Climate hazards	113
Ecosystems	114–115
Population	116–117
Population trends	118
Population migration	119
Quality of life	120–121
Economic activity	122
Development	123
Energy	124
Trade Transport	125
Environmental issues	126–127
Tourism	128–129
Time and distance	130
Cyberspace	131
Flags	132–133
Datasets	134–141

Index   142–160

Oceans and Poles   Topographic maps

Pacific Ocean	100
Arctic Ocean Antarctica	101

topographic map of the Poles

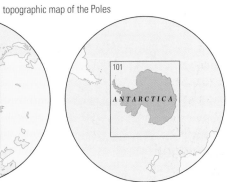

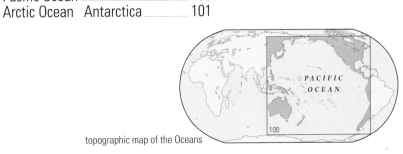
topographic map of the Oceans

4 Maps and satellite images

Satellite scanners 'read' the Earth's radiation. The data can be organised by computer to form a visual image. In this image the colours are not real but have been arranged to show how the land is used.

Orange: rough pasture
Red: forest and woodland
Green: improved pasture
Dark blue: urban areas

Topographic maps show the main features of the physical landscape as well as settlements, communications, and boundaries. Background colours show the height of the land.

Greens: low land
Browns: high land

Thematic maps show information about special topics such as agriculture, industry, population, the environment, and quality of life. This map shows land use.

Dark green: forest and woodland
Purple: built-up area

Symbols on thematic maps

Point symbols

Dot map
Each black dot represents 100 000 sheep.
From p29

Economic map
Blue squares represent a main centre of the motor vehicle industry.
From p32

Proportional symbols
The size of the circles is proportional to the amount of greenhouse gas emission.
From p127

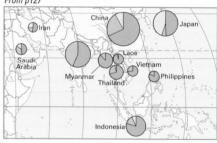

Line symbols

Isopleth map
Lines join places with equal amounts of sunshine.
From p27

Isotherm map
Some isopleths have special names. Isotherms join places with equal temperature.
From p26

Flowline map
The thickness of the line is proportional to the amount of internet traffic.
From p131

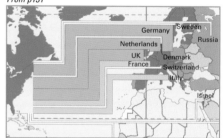

Area symbols

Choropleth map
Darker colours show areas with a higher percentage of land used for growing potatoes.
From p29

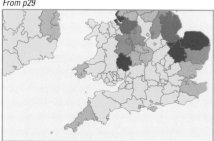

Environmental map
Each colour represents an ecosystem. Purple stands for mountains.
From p115

Political map
Colours have no meaning but are simply used to show where one country ends and another begins.
From p102

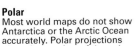

This map has been made by unpeeling strips from the Earth's surface. It would be difficult to use because gaps are left in the land and sea.

Parallels of latitude and meridians of longitude form a grid. Different grid patterns, called projections, can be used to turn the spherical surface of the Earth into a flat world map. It is impossible to make a world map in which both the sizes and shapes of the Earth's land masses are shown accurately. All world maps are distorted in some way.

There are many map projections. It is important that the projection used for a world map is suitable for the information shown on it.

Polar
Most world maps do not show Antarctica or the Arctic Ocean accurately. Polar projections give a better view of the poles.

Eckert IV
Equal area. The land masses are the correct size in relation to each other but there is some distortion in shape.

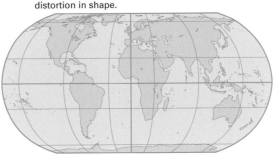

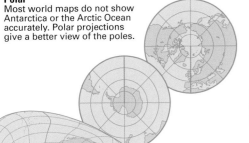

Mercator
Conformal. The shape of the land masses is correct but their size becomes larger further away from the equator.

Oblique Aitoff
Equal area. The arrangement of the land masses allows a good view of the northern hemisphere.

Graphical representation of data

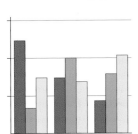

Clustered column
Compares values across categories
See example p35

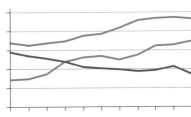

Line
Shows trend over time across categories
See example p33

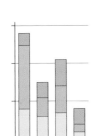

Stacked column
Compares the contribution of each value to a total across categories
See example p32

Pie
Shows the contribution of each value to a total
See example p124

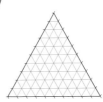

Triangular
Compares trios of values
See example p123

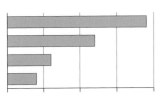

Simple bar
Length of bar is proportional to each value
See example p128

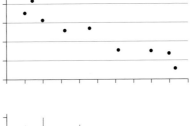

Scatter
Compares pairs of values
See example p61

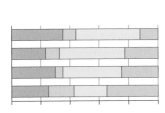

100% stacked bar
Compares the percentage each value contributes to a total across categories
See example p116

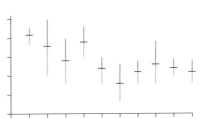

Line and whisker
Shows highest, average, and lowest values
See example p30

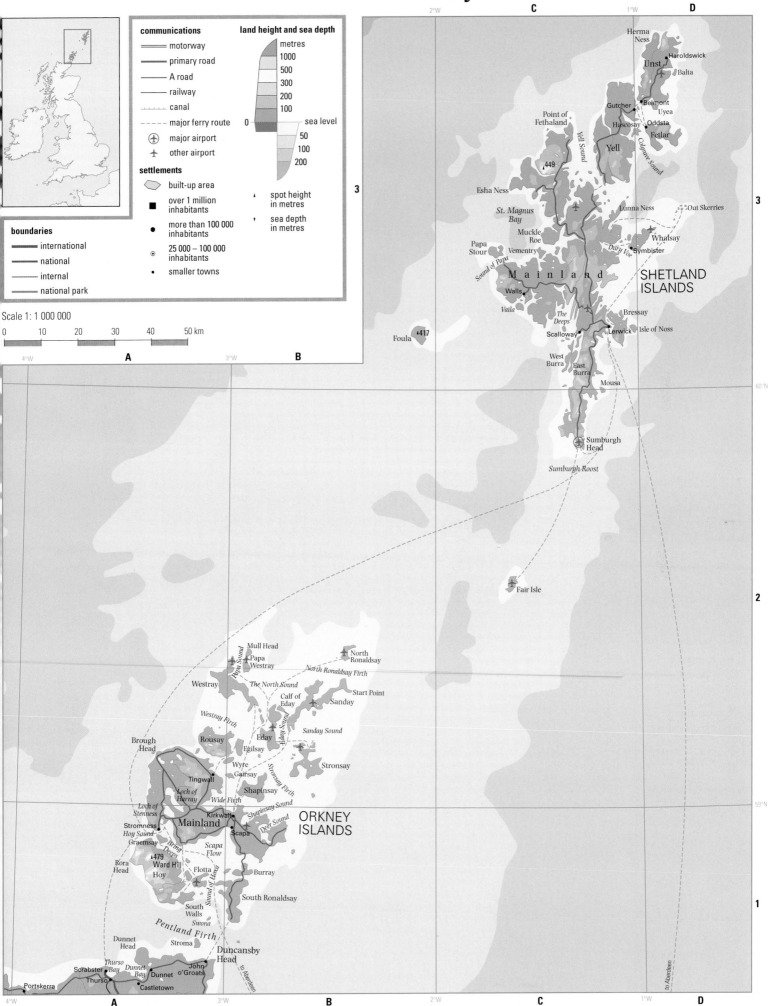

communications
- ═══ motorway
- ━━━ primary road
- ─── A road
- ─── railway
- ┼┼┼┼ canal
- ----- major ferry route
- ✈ major airport
- ✈ other airport

settlements
- built-up area
- ■ over 1 million inhabitants
- ● more than 100 000 inhabitants
- ◉ 25 000 – 100 000 inhabitants
- • smaller towns

land height and sea depth

metres
1000
500
300
200
100
0 — sea level
50
100
200

▲ spot height in metres
▼ sea depth in metres

boundaries
- ═══ international
- ━━━ national
- ─── internal
- ━━━ national park

Scale 1: 1 000 000

0   10   20   30   40   50 km

SHETLAND ISLANDS

Herma Ness
Haroldswick
Unst
Balta
Gutcher
Belmont
Uyea
Hascosay
Oddsta
Point of Fethaland
Yell
Fetlar
Colgrave Sound
Yell Sound
449
Esha Ness
Lunna Ness
Out Skerries
St. Magnus Bay
Muckle Roe
Whalsay
Papa Stour
Vementry
Dury Voe
Symbister
Sound of Papa
Mainland
Walls
Vaila
The Deeps
Bressay
Scalloway
Lerwick
Isle of Noss
West Burra
East Burra
Mousa
Foula ▲417

Sumburgh Head
Sumburgh Roost

Fair Isle

ORKNEY ISLANDS

Mull Head
Papa Westray
North Ronaldsay
North Ronaldsay Firth
Westray
The North Sound
Start Point
Calf of Eday
Sanday
Westray Firth
Eday Sound
Sanday Sound
Rousay
Eday
Egilsay
Stronsay
Wyre
Gairsay
Stronsay Firth
Brough Head
Tingwall
Shapinsay
Loch of Harray
Wide Firth
Loch of Stenness
Kirkwall
Shapinsay Sound
Stromness
Mainland
Scapa
Deer Sound
Hoy Sound
Graemsay
Bring Deeps
Scapa Flow
▲479 Ward Hill
Rora Head
Hoy
Flotta
Burray
Sound of Hoxa
South Ronaldsay
South Walls
Swona

Pentland Firth
Dunnet Head
Stroma
Duncansby Head
Thurso Bay
Scrabster
Dunnet Bay
Dunnet
John o'Groats
Portskerra
Thurso
Castletown
to Aberdeen

8 Scottish Highlands and Islands

8°W
B
7°W
C
6°W
D
A
3
2
1
57°N
Butt of Lewis
Port of Ness
Cellar Head
Barvas
Tolsta Head
Flannan Isles
Carloway
Gallan Head
Great Bernera
Lewis
Broad Bay
Tiumpan Head
Portnaguran
Eye Peninsula
Stornoway
Loch Roag
574
Loch Erisort
The Minch
Scarp
Loch Langavat
Kebock Head
Loch Seaforth
Loch Shell
799
Clisham
West Loch Tarbert
Taransay
Tarbert
Sound of Shiant
Shiant
Sound of Taransay
Scalpay
Toe Head
Harris
East Loch Tarbert
Pabbay
Leverburgh
Sound of Harris
Berneray
Rodel
Little Minch
Outer Hebrides
WESTERN ISLES
St. Kilda
North Uist
230
Lochmaddy
Sound of Monach
Waternish Point
Rubha Hunish
Kilmaluag
Uig
Loch Snizort
Heisker
Baleshare
Trotternish
Dunvegan Head
Ronay
719
The Storr
Benbecula
Dunvegan
Portree
Sound of Raasay
Inner Sound
Rona
Wiay
Skye
Raasay
East Suisnish
Idrigill Point
Loch Bracadale
Scalpay
Sconser
606
South Uist
620
Rubha Ardvule
Loch Eynort
Cuillin Hills
993
Sgurr Alasdair
Lochboisdale
Loch Boisdale
Loch Slapin
Broadford
Soay
Elgol
Loch Eishort
Sound of Barra
Eriskay
Fuday
Canna
Sanday
Sound of Canna
Rhum
Kinloch
Point of Sleat
Armadale
Ardvasar
Calligarry
Sound of Sleat
Mallaig
Barra
Castlebay
Askival
812
Vatersay
Sound of Rhum
Sandray
Eigg
393
Pabbay
Muck
Mingulay
Berneray
Barra Head
Inner Hebrides
Point of Ardnamurchan
Kilchoan
Coll
Arinagour
Tobermory
Scarinish
Tiree
Treshnish Isles
Ulva
Staffa
Sound of Mull
Salen
Lochaline
Craignure
Mull
Ben More
967
Lochdon
Kerrera
Iona
Fionnphort
Loch Scridain
Ross of Mull
Firth of Lorn
to Colonsay
Scour
Point of Stoer
Eddrac Ba
Lochinver
Rubha Coigeach
Enard Bay
Loch Broom
Greenstone Point
Ullapo
Gruinard Bay
Little Loch Broom
Rubha Reidh
Loch Ewe
Poolewe
Fionn Loch
Loch Gairloch
Gairloch
Loch Maree
Kinlochewe
Loch Torridon
1053
Torridon
Upper Loch Torridon
Shieldaig
NORTH WEST
HIG
Strathcarron
Lochcarron
Loch Carron
Stromeferry
Plockton
Kyle of Lochalsh
Kyleakin
Loch Alsh
Dornie
Loch Duich
Shiel
Loch Hourn
Loch Quoich
Loch Nevis
Loch Morar
Arisaig
Lochailort
Glenfinnan
Kinloch
Sound of Arisaig
Loch Eil
Loch Shiel
Salen
Loch Sunart
Strontian
North Ballachulis
South Ballachulis
Ballach
Loch Linnhe
Achnacroish
Lismore
Loch Creran
Oban
Taynuilt
Cruac
boundaries
international
national
internal
national park
communications
motorway
primary road
A road
railway
canal
major ferry route
major airport
other airport
settlements
built-up area
over 1 million inhabitants
more than 100 000 inhabitants
25 000 – 100 000 inhabitants
smaller towns
land height and sea depth
metres
1000
500
300
200
100
0
sea level
50
100
200
spot height in metres
sea depth in metres
Scale 1: 1 000 000
0
10
20
30
40
50 km

© Oxford University Press

Pentland Firth

Dunnet Head   Stroma   Duncansby Head
to Stromness
Scrabster Thurso Bay Dunnet Bay Dunnet John o'Groats
Strathy Strathy Point Thurso Castletown
Portskerra Melvich
Durness Whiten Head Loch Watten Sinclair's Bay
Kyle of Durness Bettyhill Halkirk Noss Head
Loch Hope Tongue Dyke Mybster Wick
Ben Hope Ben Loyal Loch Loyal Halladale Wick
927 764 Naver Strathy
Loch Meadie Loch nan Clàr
Reay Forest Loch More Thurso
Altnaharra Ben Klibreck Dunbeath Water Lybster
961 Berriedale Water Latheron
Unapool Kinbrace Morven Dunbeath
Loch Shin 705
Ben More Assynt Loch Naver Berriedale
998
Camisp Helmsdale
847 Helmsdale
Ledmore
Lairg Brora
Ogkel Brora
58°N
Shin Golspie
Beinn Dearg Evelix Bonar Bridge
1081 Carron Dornoch
Tarbat Ness
Dornoch Firth
Tain Portmahomack
Sgurr Mòr Nigg Bay
1109 Ben Wyvis Glass Alness Invergordon Lossiemouth Findochty Portknockie Troup Head Rosehearty Kinnaird Head
Loch Fannich 1046 Cromarty Moray Burghead Burghead Buckie Cullen Portsoy Whitehills Gardenstown Fraserburgh
Evanton Firth Bay Findhorn Elgin Fochabers Banff Macduff Loch of Strathbeg
Garve Black Isle Findhorn Kinloss Rattray Head
Loch Luichart Dingwall Fortrose Nairn Forres Aberchirder
Strathpeffer Conon Bridge Fort George MORAY Keith Deveron Turriff New Deer Mintlaw
Loch Meig Tore Rothes Craigellachie Peterhead
Muir of Ord North Kessock Charlestown Buchan Ness
Orrin Reservoir Beauly of Aberlour Huntly Boddam
Beauly Firth Dufftown Deveron Oldmeldrum Pitmedden Hatton
Farrar Inverness Ythan
Cannich Beauly Rhynie Inverurie Newmachar
Affric Glass Tomatin Strathspey 518 Ellen
Loch Ness Grantown-on-Spey Don Alford Kintore Dyce
Drumnadrochit Carrbridge Spey Kemnay Bridge of Don
Invermoriston Loch Mhòr Avon Tomintoul ABERDEENSHIRE Aberdeen
Moriston Monadhliath Aviemore Don Westhill ABERDEEN CITY
Fort Augustus Mountains Cairngorms Petercutter Nigg Bay
Invergarry Newtonmore Cairn Gorm Dee Cove Bay
Loch Oich Kingussie 1244 Aboyne Banchory Portlethen
935 Ben Macdui Balmoral Crathie Ballater Water of Feugh
Spey 1310 Braemar Cowie Water
Dalwhinnie Bridge of Dee Stonehaven
57°N
Loch Laggan Lochnagar
1130 1155 North Esk Fettercairn
Spean Bridge Glas Maol Inverbervie
Loch Ericht 1068 South Esk Laurencekirk
Ben Alder Tilt Glen Shee Prosen Water Milton Ness
Ben Nevis 1148 ANGUS
1344 Blair Atholl Glen Brechin Montrose Basin
Blackwater Reservoir Garry Inverquharity Montrose
Kinlochleven Rannoch Station Tummel Bridge Pitlochry Ardle Kirriemuir South Esk Lunan Bay
Loch Tummel Isla Forfar Lunan Water
150 Bridge of Ericht Dunalastair Reservoir Tay Alyth Arbroath
Loch Rannoch Kinloch Rannoch Rattray
Glen Etive Aberfeldy Blairgowrie Carnoustie
1108 Ben Lawers Dunkeld Coupar Monifieth
Rannoch Moor 1214 Isla Angus DUNDEE CITY Broughty Ferry
Loch Tulla Loch an Daimh Loch Tay Sidlaw Hills Buddon Ness
Bridge of Orchy Ben More Lyon Tay Dundee Tayport
Orchy 1174 Lochay Newport-on-Tay
Dochart Killin Almond New Scone Leuchars
Lochan Shira Dalmally Tyndrum Lochearnhead PERTH AND KINROSS Eden Mouth
Crianlarich Loch Earn Perth Firth of Tay St. Andrews Bay
Comrie Crieff Earn Newburgh Cupar St. Andrews

communications

- motorway
- primary road
- A road
- railway
- canal
- - - - major ferry route
- ✈ major airport
- ✈ other airport

settlements

- built-up area
- ■ over 1 million inhabitants
- ● more than 100 000 inhabitants
- ◉ 25 000 – 100 000 inhabitants
- • smaller towns

land height and sea depth

metres
1000
500
300
200
100
0 sea level
50
100
200

- ▲ spot height in metres
- ▼ sea depth in metres

boundaries

- international
- national
- internal
- national park

Scale 1: 1 000 000

0   10   20   30   40   50 km

© Oxford University Press

Transverse Mercator Projection

to Stavanger, Haugesund and Bergen
to Göteborg

horsley
Ashington   Newbiggin-by-the-Sea
Morpeth   Guide Post
Bedlington   Blyth
Blyth   Cramlington
teland   Seaton Delaval
Dudley   Whitley Bay
Gosforth Longbenton   Tynemouth
Newcastle Wallsend   North Shields
upon Tyne   South Shields
wburn   Jarrow   Marsden
Ryton Whickham Felling Boldon   Whitburn
ands Gateshead   TYNE AND WEAR
Gill   Washington   Sunderland
nnfield Stanley   Houghton-le-Spring
ett   Chester-   Hetton-   Seaham
le-Street   le-Hole   Murton
chester   Sacriston   Easington
Ushaw Moor   Durham   Peterlee
Law   Brandon   Blackhall Colliery
Crook   Willington   Wingate
gham   Spennymoor   Ferryhill
Bishop   Shildon   Hartlepool
Auckland Newton Aycliffe   HARTLEPOOL
Billingham Redcar   REDCAR AND CLEVELAND
DARLINGTON   STOCKTON-ON-TEES   Marske-by-the-Sea
Stockton-   South Bank   Saltburn-by-the-Sea
on-Tees   Eston   Brotton
Darlington Eaglescliffe Middlesbrough Skelton Loftus
Thornaby on Tees Guisborough
MIDDLESBROUGH
Stokesley   Whitby
ichmond   Great   Sleights
Broughton Cleveland Hills Esk   Robin Hood's Bay
Catterick ▲454   North York
Garrison   Northallerton   Moors
Leyburn   NORTH YORK MOORS NATIONAL PARK   Cloughton
Bedale   Kirkbymoorside   Scalby
N O R T H   Hambleton Hills   Helmsley Pickering   Scarborough
Masham   Thirsk   Eastfield
Y O R K S H I R E   Vale of   Filey
Ripon   Hovingham   Pickering Derwent   Hunmanby
Pateley   Easingwold   Malton   Staxton
Bridge   Boroughbridge   Norton   Flamborough
Nidd   Yorkshire   Head
Knaresborough   Shipton   Wolds   Sledmere Flamborough Bridlington
Harrogate   Haxby   Burton   Bridlington
246   Agnes   Bay
Great Driffield
Burley in Otley   York   Stamford Bridge Middleton- Hutton
Wharfedale   YORK   Wilberfoss   on-the- Cranswick
ley Guiseley Wetherby   Wolds
ingley Yeadon WEST   Boston Spa   Pocklington   Hornsea
orth Shipley Horsforth Tadcaster   EAST RIDING OF YORKSHIRE Leven
Baildon YORKSHIRE   Cawood   Aldbrough
dford   Garforth Riccall   Market
Leeds   Rothwell Kippax Selby   Weighton
sbury Pudsey   Linthouse   Holme-on-   South Cave   CITY OF
ax Morley   Gate Stanley   Spalding-Moor   Howden   KINGSTON UPON HULL
Cleckheaton Castleford   Welton   Kingston upon
Liversedge Batley   Knottingley   Brough   Hull   Hedon
by Dewsbury Normanton   Goole   Whitton   New Holland   Withernsea
Mirfield   Aire and Calder   Barton-upon-   Holderness
Wakefield Featherstone   Hessle Humber   Patrington
Huddersfield Horbury Crofton Ackworth   Humber   Easington
Clayton Royston Hemsworth Moor Top   Thorne   Crowle   Immingham
len West   Darton Cudworth   South Kirkby   Askern   NORTH LINCOLNSHIRE   Grimsby
Skelmanthorpe   Grimethorpe   Hatfield   Scunthorpe   Great Coates Cleethorpes
ham   Denby   Adwick   Kirk Sandall   NORTH EAST LINCOLNSHIRE
Barnsley le Street Bentley   Armthorpe   Humberston
Worsbrough   Doncaster Bessacarr   Brigg
Penistone Wombwell Wath Mexborough   Epworth   Caistor   North Somercotes
Hoyland   New Rossington   Saltfleet
Stocksbridge Rawmarsh Swinton Conisbrough   Trent   ▲168
Chapeltown   Tickhill   Lincoln
SOUTH   Rotherham   Bawtry   Wolds   Louth
Derwent YORKSHIRE   Maltby Harworth   Gainsborough
eservoir   Thurcroft Blyth   Market Rasen Mablethorpe
he Peak   Dinnington Carlton in   North   Sutton on Sea
Ladybower Sheffield   Anston Lindrick   Wheatley Till   Dunholme Wragby
636 Reservoir Beighton Killamarsh   Saxilby
Hathersage   Mosborough   Worksop   Retford   Lincoln Horncastle
el en-th Dronfield Eckington   East   Washingborough Alford
xton   Clowne   Markham   Heighington   Chapel
Eyam   Staveley Creswell   Birchwood   North Hykeham   St. Leonards
Chesterfield   Bolsover   Ollerton   Spilsby Burgh le Marsh
K DISTRICT DERBYSHIRE   NOTTINGHAMSHIRE Warsop Carlton- Metheringham Woodhall   Skegness
ONAL PARK   Clay Cross North   Mansfield Woodhouse on-Trent   Spa   Wainfleet
Hartington   Wingfield Shirebrook Mansfield   Waddington   All Saints
Sutton in   Rainworth Sherwood Forest   Navenby Wrangle
Matlock   Ashfield   Blidworth   Southwell   LINCOLNSHIRE
Bakewell Wingerworth South Normanton Ravenshead   Calverton   Newark- Sleaford Heckington   Boston
Wirksworth   Alfreton   Kirkby in   on-Trent   Kirton
Ashbourne Belper   Ripley Ashfield   Witham   Wrangle
th Duffield Heanor Hucknall   Bingham   Hunstanton
Eastwood Kimberley Arnold
Brailsford   Ilkeston Carlton
NOTTINGHAM   Sleaford
Nottingham   CITY

to Hamburg
to Amsterdam
to Rotterdam and Zeebrugge

Bridlington Bay
Flamborough Head
Humber
Spurn Head

Scale 1 : 1 000 000

0   10   20   30   40   50 km

boundaries
— international
— national
— internal
— national park

communications
═ motorway
— primary road
— A road
— railway
┼┼┼┼ canal
- - - major ferry route
✈ major airport
✈ other airport

settlements
⬡ built-up area
■ over 1 million inhabitants
● more than 100 000 inhabitants
⊙ 25 000 – 100 000 inhabitants
• smaller towns

land height and sea depth
metres
1000
500
300
200
100
0 sea level
50
100
200
▲ spot height in metres
▼ sea depth in metres

Scale 1: 1 000 000

0   10   20   30   40   50 km

boundaries
━━━ international
━━━ national
─── internal
─── national park

communications
═══ motorway
━━━ primary road
─── A road
─── railway
┼┼┼ canal
- - - major ferry route
⊕ major airport
✈ other airport

settlements
▱ built-up area
■ over 1 million inhabitants
● more than 100 000 inhabitants
⊙ 25 000 – 100 000 inhabitants
• smaller towns

land height and sea depth
metres
1000
500
300
200
100
sea level
50
100
200

▲ spot height in metres
▼ sea depth in metres

E 2°E F

to Göteborg
to Esbjerg
to Hamburg

Norfolk

Blakeney Point
Burnham Market
Wells-next-the-Sea
Sheringham
Cromer
Holt
Hunstanton
Heacham
Docking
Mundesley
Saxthorpe
North Walsham
Dersingham
Sandringham
Fakenham
Aylsham
Winterton-on-Sea
Reepham
Coltishall
King's Lynn
East Dereham
Taverham
Wroxham
Acle
Caister-on-Sea
Norwich
BROADS AUTHORITY
Great Yarmouth
Downham Market
Watton
Wymondham
Belton
Swaffham
Loddon
Hopton on Sea
Feltwell
Attleborough
Littleport
Breckland
Bungay
Lowestoft
Ely
Brandon
Thetford
Harleston
Beccles
Kessingland
Lakenheath
Diss
Isleham
Mildenhall
Halesworth
Southwold
Soham
Fordham
Eye
Yoxford
Kentford
Ixworth
Debenham
Leiston
Saxmundham
Newmarket
Bury St. Edmunds
Framlingham
Aldeburgh
Waterbeach
Burwell
Stowmarket
Wickham Market
Needham Market
Claydon
Orford
Orford Ness
SUFFOLK
Lavenham
Woodbridge
Haverhill
Long Melford
Sudbury
Ipswich
Hadleigh
Bawdsey
Sawston
Linton
Stour
Orwell
Deben
Alde
Blyth
Waveney

the Wash

KENT

Sevenoaks
Tonbridge
Maidstone
Bearsted
Charing
Wye
Ashford
Kennington
Brabourne Lees
Lyminge
Deal
Whitfield
St. Margaret's at Cliffe
South Foreland
Dover
Folkestone
Hythe
Dymchurch
New Romney
Romney Marsh
Dungeness
Lydd

EAST SUSSEX
Battle
Hailsham
Polegate
Eastbourne
Beachy Head
Hastings
Bexhill
Pevensey

FRANCE
NORD-PAS-DE-CALAIS
Calais
Dunkerque
Boulogne-sur-Mer
Cap Gris-Nez
Wimereux
Marquise
Slack
Ardres
Guines
Marck
Gravelines
Malo-les-Bains
Bray-Dunes
Bergues
Bourbourg
Esquelbecq
Wormhout
Cassel
Watten
St-Omer
Hazebrouck
Aire-sur-la-Lys
Thérouanne
Samer
Desvres
Hardelot-Plage

Strait of Dover (Pas de Calais)

to Oostende
to Hook of Holland
52°N
51°N

ESSEX
Chelmsford
Braintree
Colchester
Harwich
Felixstowe
Manningtree
Clacton-on-Sea
Frinton-on-Sea
Walton-on-the-Naze
The Naze
Brightlingsea
Wivenhoe
Mersea Island
Maldon
Southminster
Burnham-on-Crouch
Southend-on-Sea
SOUTHEND
Shoeburyness
Canvey Island
Basildon
Billericay
Brentwood
Grays
Tilbury
THURROCK
Chatham
Gillingham
MEDWAY
Gravesend
Rochester
Dartford
Bexley
Havering

Scale 1 : 1 000 000

0   10   20   30   40   50 km

© Oxford University Press Transverse Mercator Projection

boundaries
— international
— national
— internal
— national park

communications
— motorway
— primary road
— A road
— railway
+++ canal
--- major ferry route
✈ major airport
✈ other airport

settlements
⬡ built-up area
■ over 1 million inhabitants
● more than 100 000 inhabitants
◉ 25 000 – 100 000 inhabitants
• smaller towns

land height and sea depth
metres
1000
500
300
200
100
0 sea level
50
100
200

▲ spot height in metres
▼ sea depth in metres

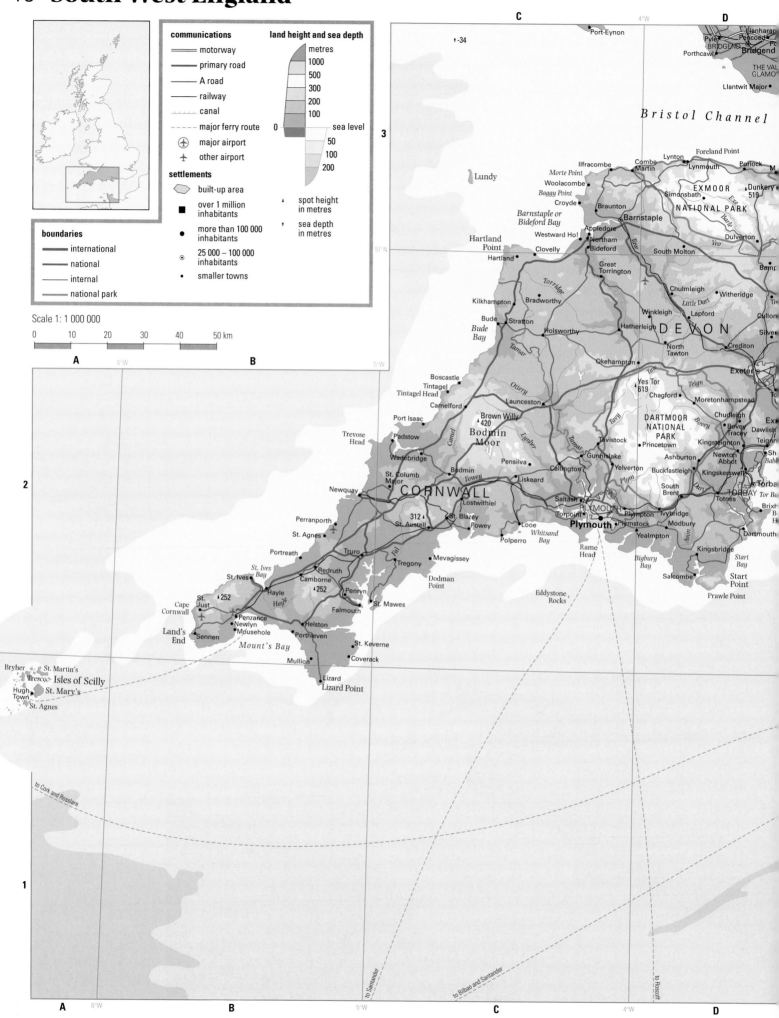

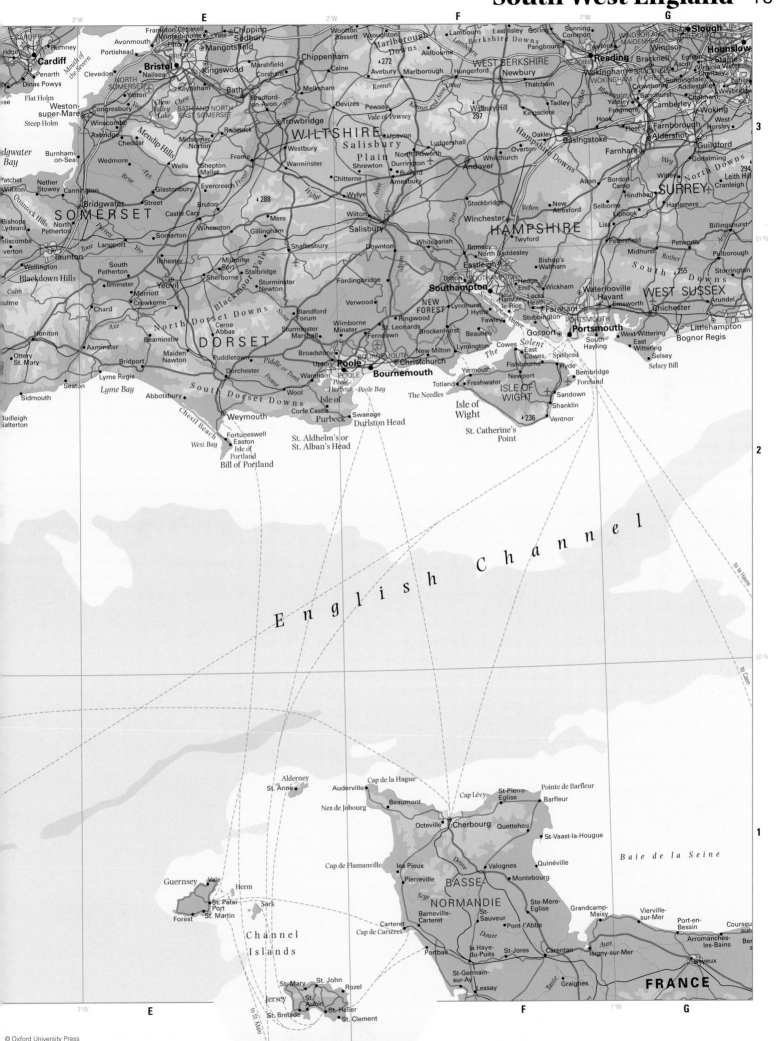

South West England

Cardiff
Rumney
Penarth
Dinas Powys
Flat Holm
Steep Holm
Weston-super-Mare
Burnham-on-Sea
Watchet
Williton
Nether Stowey
Cannington
Bridgwater
Bishops Lydeard
Wellington
Taunton
Blackdown Hills
Honiton
Ottery St. Mary
Sidmouth
Seaton
Budleigh Salterton

Portishead
Clevedon
Nailsea
Congresbury
Winscombe
Axbridge
Cheddar
Wedmore
Mendip Hills
Wells
Glastonbury
Street
Castle Cary
Bruton
Somerton
Langport
Ilchester
South Petherton
Ilminster
Chard
Merriott
Crewkerne
Axminster
Bridport
Beaminster
Maiden Newton

Avonmouth
Winterbourne
Frampton Cotterell
Yate
Chipping Sodbury
Mangotsfield
Filton
Bristol
Kingswood
Keynsham
Marshfield
Corsham
Bath
Bradford-on-Avon
Radstock
Midsomer Norton
Shepton Mallet
Evercreech
SOMERSET
Wincanton
Gillingham
Shaftesbury
Mere
Sherborne
Stalbridge
Sturminster Newton
Blandford Forum
Cerne Abbas
Yeovil
Milborne Port

Chippenham
Calne
Melksham
Devizes
Trowbridge
Westbury
Warminster
Chitterne
WILTSHIRE
Salisbury Plain
Shrewton
Amesbury
Bulford
Durrington
Wilton
Salisbury
Downton
Fordingbridge
Verwood
Ringwood
Wimborne Minster
Blackmoor Vale
North Dorset Downs
DORSET
Puddletown
Dorchester
Broadstone
Wareham
Wool
Isle of Purbeck
Corfe Castle
Swanage
Durlston Head
St. Aldhelm's or St. Alban's Head

Marlborough Downs
Avebury
Marlborough
Pewsey
Vale of Pewsey
Upavon
Ludgershall
Andover
Whitchurch
Stockbridge
Winchester
Romsey
North Baddesley
Eastleigh
Southampton
HAMPSHIRE
Totton
NEW FOREST
Lyndhurst
Brockenhurst
Lymington
New Milton
Christchurch
BOURNEMOUTH
Poole
Bournemouth
Poole Harbour
Poole Bay
The Needles
Isle of Wight

Lambourn
Berkshire Downs
Hungerford
Newbury
Thatcham
WEST BERKSHIRE
Kennet and Avon Canal
Watbury Hill 297
Oakley
Basingstoke
Overton
Hampshire Downs
Hook
Alton
Bordon Camp
Selborne
Liphook
Petersfield
Midhurst
Bishop's Waltham
Wickham
Fareham
Gosport
Portsmouth
South Hayling
Spithead
Fishbourne
Ryde
Bembridge
Foreland
Sandown
Shanklin
Ventnor
St. Catherine's Point
ISLE OF WIGHT
Newport
Yarmouth
Cowes
East Cowes
Totland
Freshwater

Eastllsley
Goring
Sonning Common
Pangbourne
Twyford
READING
Reading
Wokingham
WOKINGHAM
Crowthorne
Yateley
Sandhurst
Camberley
Farnborough
Aldershot
Farnham
Godalming
Witley
Haslemere
Liss
SURREY
North Downs
Leith Hill
Cranleigh
Guildford
Woking
West Horsley
Billingshurst
Petworth
WEST SUSSEX
South Downs 255
Storrington
Pulborough
Arundel
Littlehampton
Bognor Regis
Chichester
Emsworth
Havant
Waterlooville

Slough
SLOUGH
Windsor
WINDSOR AND MAIDENHEAD
Bracknell
BRACKNELL FOREST
Ascot
Sunningdale
Addlestone
Chobham
Weybridge
Esher
Hounslow
Staines
Egham
Virginia Water
Chertsey

ENGLISH CHANNEL
English Channel

to le Havre
to Caen

Alderney
St. Anne
Auderville
Cap de la Hague
Beaumont
Nez de Jobourg
Octeville
Cherbourg
Cap Lévy
St-Pierre-Eglise
Pointe de Barfleur
Barfleur
Quettehou
St-Vaast-la-Hougue
Baie de la Seine
Valognes
Quinéville
Montebourg
Ste-Mère-Eglise
Grandcamp-Maisy
Vierville-sur-Mer
Port-en-Bessin
Arromanches-les-Bains
Courseulles-sur-Mer
Bayeux
BASSE-NORMANDIE
FRANCE

Guernsey
Vale
Herm
St. Peter Port
Sark
St. Martin
Forest
Channel Islands

Jersey
St. Mary
St. John
Rozel
St. Aubin
St. Helier
St. Brelade
St. Clement
to St. Malo

Cap de Flamanville
les Pieux
Pierreville
Cap de Carteret
Carteret
Barneville-Carteret
St-Sauveur
la Haye-du-Puits
Portbail
Lessay
St-Germain-sur-Ay
Pont-l'Abbé
St-Jores
Carentan
Graignes
Isigny-sur-Mer
Douve
Taute
Aure

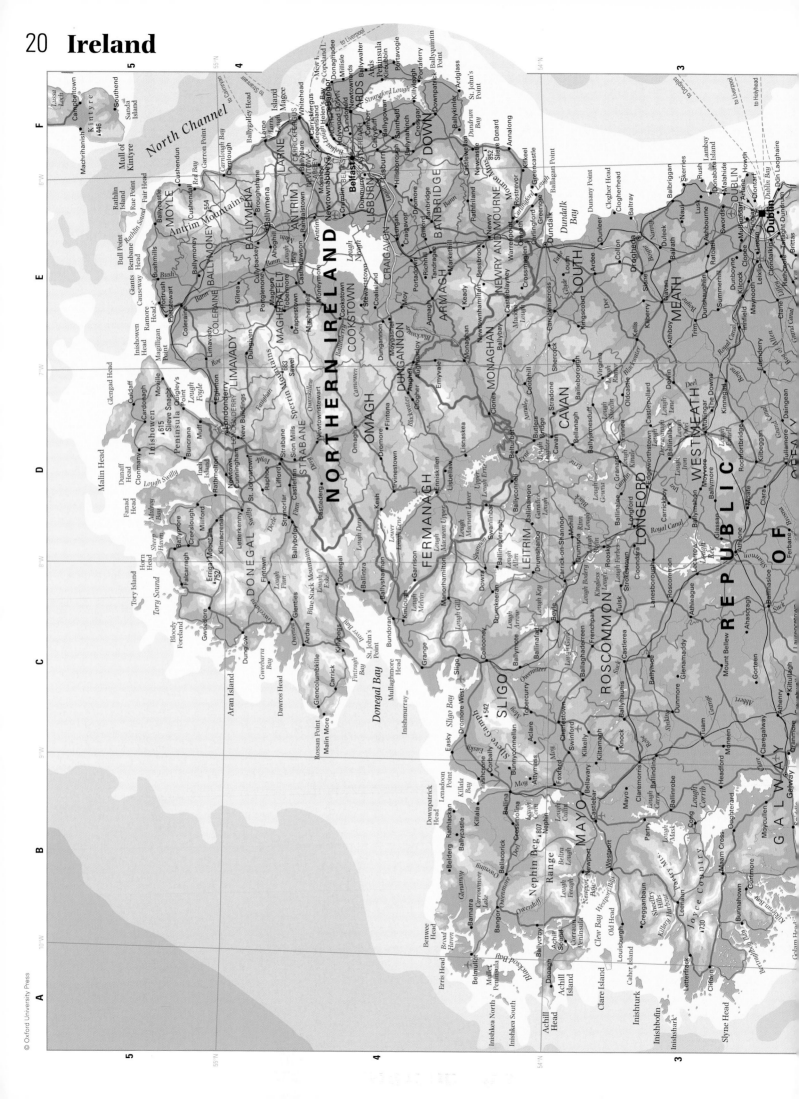

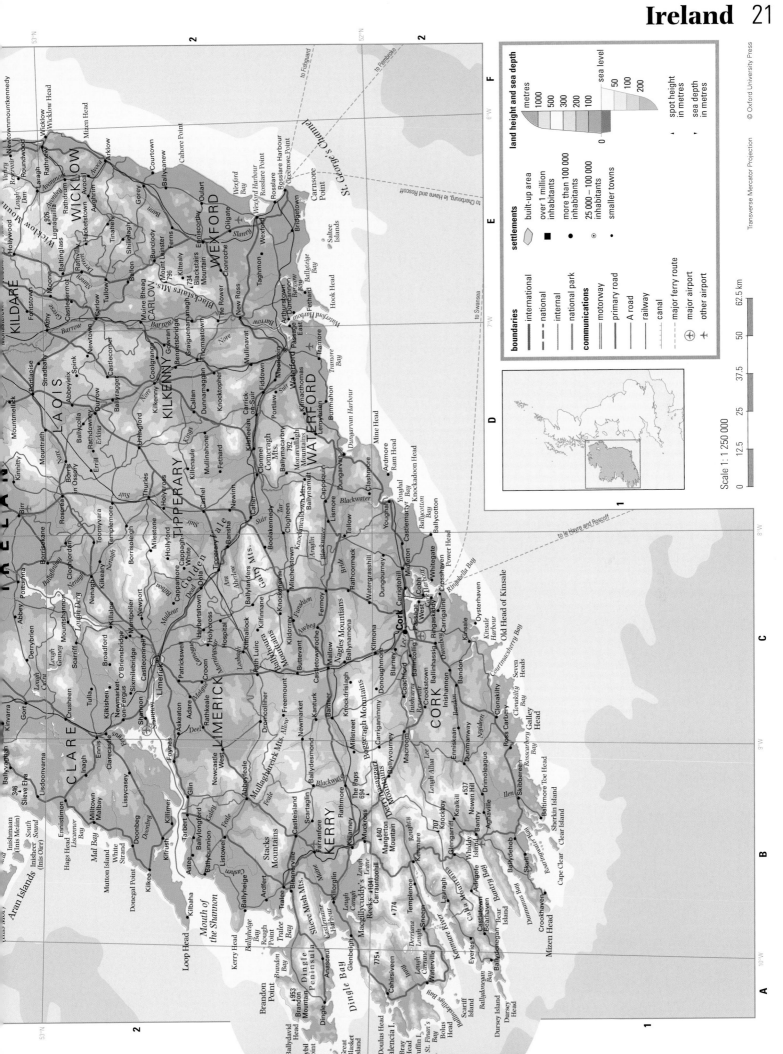

Transverse Mercator Projection

land height and sea depth

metres	
1000	
500	
300	
200	
100	
sea level	

sea level
50
100
200

▲ spot height in metres
▼ sea depth in metres

settlements

built-up area	
■	over 1 million inhabitants
●	more than 100 000 inhabitants
⊙	25 000 – 100 000 inhabitants
·	smaller towns

boundaries

international
national
internal
national park

communications

motorway
primary road
A road
railway
canal
⊕ major ferry route
✈ major airport
✈ other airport

Scale 1: 1 250 000

0   12.5   25   37.5   50   62.5 km

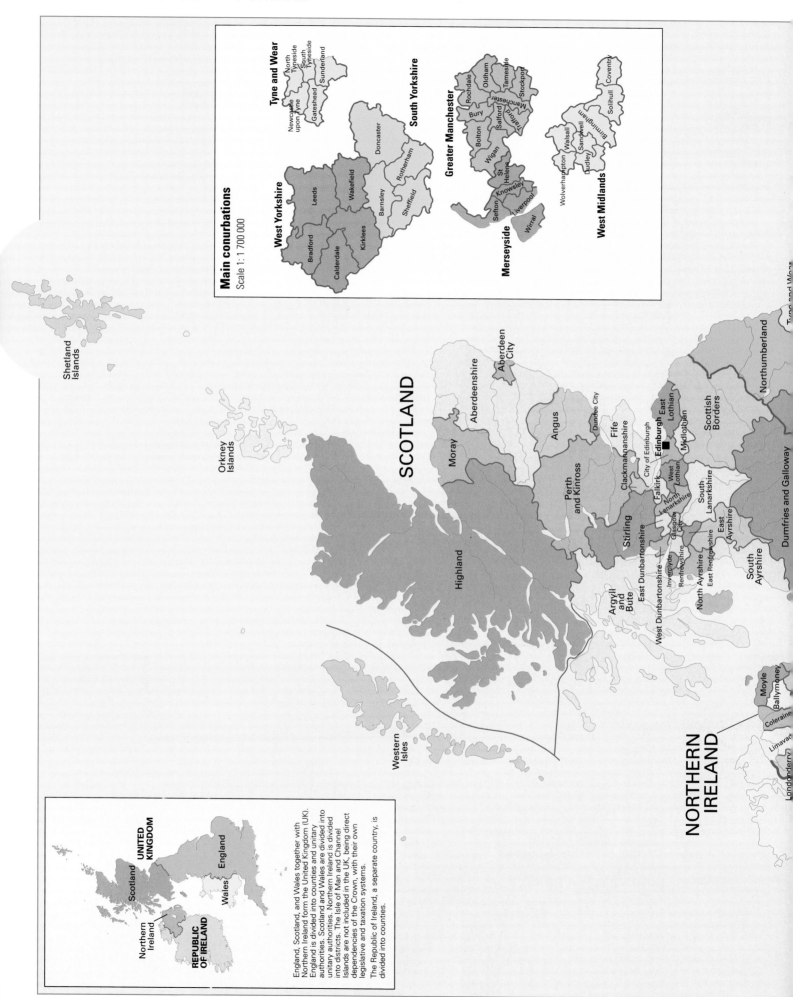

Main conurbations

Scale 1 : 1 700 000

Tyne and Wear
Newcastle upon Tyne
North Tyneside
South Tyneside
Gateshead
Sunderland

South Yorkshire
Doncaster
Rotherham
Barnsley
Sheffield

West Yorkshire
Leeds
Bradford
Calderdale
Kirklees
Wakefield

Greater Manchester
Rochdale
Oldham
Bury
Tameside
Trafford
Manchester
Salford
Stockport
Bolton
Wigan
St Helens

Merseyside
Sefton
Knowsley
Liverpool
Wirral

West Midlands
Wolverhampton
Walsall
Sandwell
Dudley
Birmingham
Solihull
Coventry

Shetland Islands

Orkney Islands

SCOTLAND

Highland

Western Isles

Moray

Aberdeenshire

Aberdeen City

Angus

Perth and Kinross

Dundee City

Fife

Clackmannanshire

City of Edinburgh

Edinburgh

East Lothian

Midlothian

Scottish Borders

Northumberland

Tyne and Wear

Falkirk

West Lothian

North Lanarkshire

Glasgow City

Stirling

Argyll and Bute

East Dunbartonshire

West Dunbartonshire

Inverclyde

Renfrewshire

East Renfrewshire

South Lanarkshire

South Ayrshire

North Ayrshire

East Ayrshire

Dumfries and Galloway

NORTHERN IRELAND

Moyle

Ballymoney

Coleraine

Limavady

Londonderry

UNITED KINGDOM

Scotland

Northern Ireland

England

Wales

REPUBLIC OF IRELAND

England, Scotland, and Wales together with Northern Ireland form the United Kingdom (UK). England is divided into counties and unitary authorities. Scotland and Wales are divided into unitary authorities. Northern Ireland is divided into districts. The Isle of Man and Channel Islands are not included in the UK, being direct dependencies of the Crown, with their own legislative and taxation systems.

The Republic of Ireland, a separate country, is divided into counties.

Scale 1 : 3 000 000 (main map)

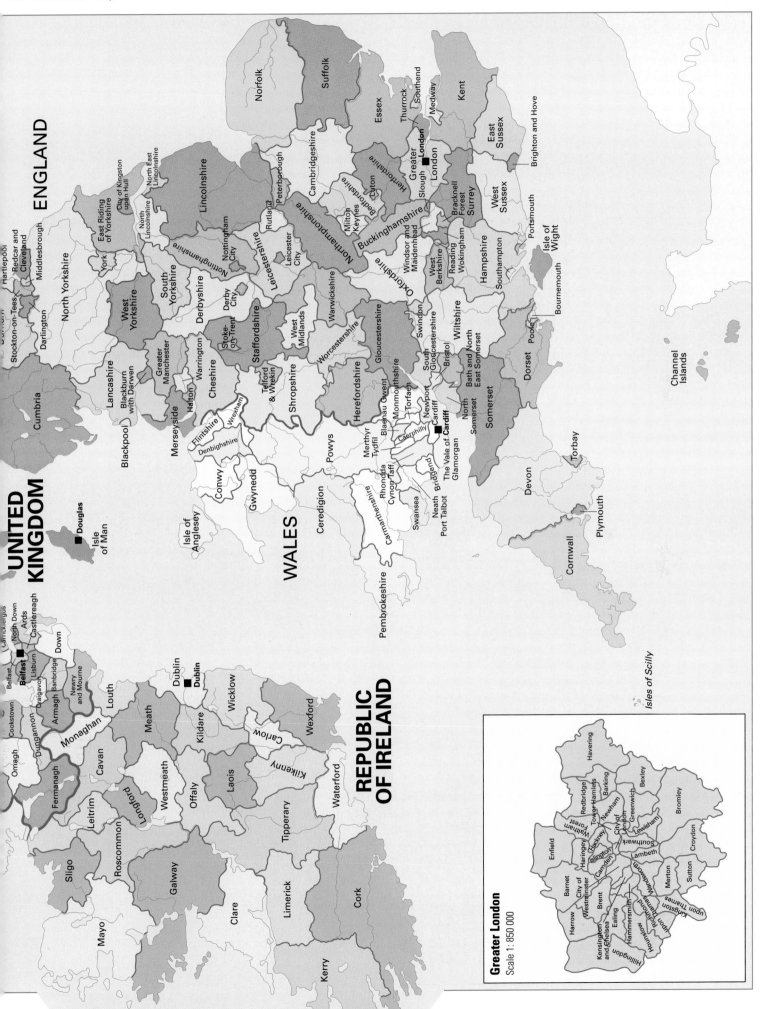

ENGLAND

UNITED KINGDOM

WALES

REPUBLIC OF IRELAND

Channel Islands

Norfolk

Suffolk

Essex

Thurrock

Southend

Kent

Medway

Cambridgeshire

Peterborough

Hertfordshire

Greater London

Slough

London

East Sussex

Brighton and Hove

West Sussex

Surrey

Bracknell Forest

Wokingham

Reading

West Berkshire

Portsmouth

Southampton

Hampshire

Isle of Wight

Bournemouth

Lincolnshire

City of Kingston upon Hull

North East Lincolnshire

North Lincolnshire

East Riding of Yorkshire

York

Nottinghamshire

Nottingham City

Rutland

Leicestershire

Leicester City

Northamptonshire

Milton Keynes

Bedfordshire

Luton

Buckinghamshire

Oxfordshire

Windsor and Maidenhead

Redcar and Cleveland

Hartlepool

Stockton-on-Tees

Middlesbrough

Darlington

North Yorkshire

Cumbria

West Yorkshire

South Yorkshire

Derbyshire

Derby City

Staffordshire

Stoke-on-Trent

Warwickshire

West Midlands

Worcestershire

Gloucestershire

Swindon

Wiltshire

South Gloucestershire

Bristol

Bath and North East Somerset

Dorset

Poole

Torbay

Lancashire

Blackpool

Blackburn with Darwen

Greater Manchester

Warrington

Halton

Cheshire

Merseyside

Telford & Wrekin

Shropshire

Herefordshire

Monmouthshire

Torfaen

Blaenau Gwent

Newport

Cardiff

Cardiff

North Somerset

Somerset

Devon

Cornwall

Plymouth

Wrexham

Flintshire

Denbighshire

Conwy

Gwynedd

Powys

Ceredigion

Merthyr Tydfil

Caerphilly

Rhondda Cynon Taff

Carmarthenshire

Bridgend

The Vale of Glamorgan

Swansea

Neath Port Talbot

Pembrokeshire

Isle of Anglesey

Douglas

Isle of Man

Isles of Scilly

Carrickfergus

Belfast

North Down

Ards

Castlereagh

Down

Lisburn

Craigavon

Banbridge

Newry and Mourne

Armagh

Dungannon

Cookstown

Omagh

Fermanagh

Monaghan

Louth

Meath

Dublin

Dublin

Wicklow

Wexford

Kildare

Carlow

Kilkenny

Waterford

Leitrim

Cavan

Longford

Westmeath

Offaly

Laois

Tipperary

Sligo

Roscommon

Galway

Clare

Limerick

Cork

Kerry

Mayo

Greater London
Scale 1 : 850 000

Havering

Redbridge

Barking

Newham

Tower Hamlets

Bexley

Greenwich

Lewisham

Bromley

Croydon

Sutton

Merton

Kingston upon Thames

Richmond upon Thames

Wandsworth

Lambeth

Southwark

City of London

Hackney

Islington

Camden

City of Westminster

Haringey

Enfield

Barnet

Harrow

Brent

Ealing

Hillingdon

Hounslow

Hammersmith

Kensington and Chelsea

Waltham Forest

Scale 1: 4 500 000

Land height and sea depth

metres
1000
500
300
200
100
0 — sea level
50
100
200

▲ spot height in metres

The British Isles consists of the two large islands of Great Britain and Ireland and a number of smaller islands.

Ireland

Great Britain

Shetland Islands

Herma Ness
Unst
Yell
Fetlar
Mainland
Whalsay
Bressay
Foula
Mull
Head
Sumburgh
Head
Fair Isle

North Ronaldsay
Westray
Rousay
Sanday
Stronsay
Shapinsay
Mainland
Orkney Islands
Hoy
South Ronaldsay
Pentland Firth
Duncansby Head

Rona

Butt of Lewis
Lewis
Cape Wrath
The Minch
Thurso
Loch Shin
Dornoch Firth

St. Kilda
Harris
▲799
Clisham
Ben Wyvis
▲1046
Moray Firth

Kinnairds Head

Buchan Ness

Outer Hebrides
North Uist
Benbecula
Skye
Cuillin Hills
▲1009
Carn Eige
▲1183
Loch Ness
Great Glen
Monadhliath Mountains
Spey
Deveron
Don

South Uist
Barra
Mallaig
Eigg
Rhum
▲1344
Ben Nevis
Cairngorms
▲1310
Ben Macdhui
Dee
N. Esk

Coll
Loch Linnhe
▲1818
Loch Awe
Grampian Mountains
S. Esk
Tay

Little Minch
Inner Hebrides
Tiree
Iona
Mull
Firth of Lorn
Loch Tay
Earn
Sidlaw Hills
Firth of Tay

Colonsay
Jura
Loch Fyne
Loch Lomond
Forth
Ochil Hills
Fife Ness
Firth of Forth

NORTH SEA

Islay
Sound of Jura
Bute
Arran
Central Lowlands
Clyde
Ayr
Lammermuir Hills
St. Abb's Head

Mull of Kintyre
North Channel
Firth of Clyde
Merrick
▲843
Southern Uplands
Broad Law
▲840
Teviot
Tweed
The Cheviot
▲815
Holy Island

Malin Head
Rathlin Island
Nith
Esk
Cheviot Hills
Coquet

Bloody Foreland
Errigal Mt.
▲752
Antrim Mtns.
▲554
Sawel
▲683
Dee
Solway Firth
Tyne

Aran Island
Donegal Mountains
Sperrin Mountains
Bann
Mourne
Lough Neagh
St. Bees Head
Cross Fell
▲893
Wear

Donegal Bay
Lower Lough Erne
Blackwater
Belfast Lough
Strangford Lough
Mull of Galloway
Cumbrian Mtns.
▲978
Scafell Pike
Tees
▲454
North York Moors

Erris Head
Upper Lough Erne
Mourne Mtns.
▲852
Slieve Donard
Isle of Man
▲621
Snaefell
Yorkshire Dales Natl.
Swale
Yorkshire Wolds

Rossan Point
Achill Island
Lough Conn
Mourne
Dundalk Bay
IRISH SEA
Morecambe Bay
Lune
Pennines
Wharfe
Derwent
Flamborough Head

Lough Mask
Lough Allen
Erne
Boyne
Ribble
Aire
Ouse
Holderness
Spurn Head
Humber

Slyne Head
Lough Corrib
Clare
Lough Ree
Anglesey
Liverpool Bay
Mersey
Don
Lincoln Wolds

Aran Islands
Galway Bay
Central Plain
Bog of Allen
Barrow
Dublin Bay
Holy Island
Caernarfon Bay
Cheshire Plain
The Peak
▲636
Trent
The Wash

Lough Derg
Nore
Wicklow Mtns.
▲926
Lugnaquillia
Conwy
▲1085
Snowdon
▲690
Dee
Welland
The Fens
Wensum
Norfolk Broads

Loop Head
Shannon
Suir
Wexford Bay
Wicklow Head
Cardigan Bay
▲892
Cader Idris
▲517
Cambrian Mtns.
Severn
Soar
Nene
Great Ouse
▲-1
Breckland
Waveney

Tralee Bay
▲953
Galty Mtns.
▲920
Blackwater
Carnsore Point
St. George's Channel
St. David's Head
▲330
Cotswold Hills
Avon
Orford Ness

Dingle Bay
▲1041
Carrauntoohill
Lee
Teifi
Black Mtns.
Brecon Beacons
▲886
Usk
Wye
The Naze

Caha Mtns.
Bantry Bay
Old Head of Kinsale
St. Bride's Bay
Carmarthen Bay
Gower
Swansea Bay
Bristol Channel
Mendip Hills
Salisbury Plain
▲297
Chiltern Hills
Lea
Thames
North Foreland

Mizen Head
Cape Clear
CELTIC SEA
Lundy
Quantock Hills
▲519
Exmoor Hills
Parrett
Frome
Hampshire Downs
▲294
Test
Wey
Thames
North Downs
Medway
Romney Marsh
The Weald

Hartland Point
Taw
Exe
Tamar
▲619
Dartmoor
Bodmin Moor
Lyme Bay
Portland Bill
The Solent
▲255
Arun
South Downs
Isle of Wight
Beachy Head
Dungeness
Strait of Dover

ATLANTIC OCEAN

Land's End
Isles of Scilly
Lizard Point
Start Point
English Channel
North Foreland

FRANCE

Alderney
Cap de la Hague

Guernsey
Channel Islands
Sark
Jersey
Baie de la Seine

Sedimentary | Periods | Eras | Approximate dates
in millions of years before present

Sedimentary	Periods	Eras	Approximate dates
Alluvium	Pleistocene and Recent	Quaternary	2
Sands and clays	Pliocene, Oligocene and Eocene	Tertiary	
London Clay, Reading and Thanet Beds	Eocene		70
Chalk	Cretaceous		
Greensand and Gault Clay			
Weald Clays and Sandstones		Mesozoic	
Purbeck and Portland Beds/ Kimmeridge and Oxford Clays	Jurassic		
Oolitic Limestone			
Liassic and Rhaetic Beds			
Keuper Marl and Sandstone	Triassic		
Bunter Sandstone			220
Permian Marl	Permian		
Magnesian Limestone			
Coal Measures	Carboniferous	Upper Palaeozoic	
Millstone Grit and Culm Measures			
Carboniferous Limestone			
Old Red Sandstone	Devonian		
Slates and shales	Silurian		
Slates and volcanic rocks	Ordovician	Lower Palaeozoic	
Hard grits, shales and slates	Cambrian		600
Rough sandstones and volcanic rocks	Pre-Cambrian		

Metamorphic
Schist, gneiss, quartzite

Igneous
Extrusive rocks (volcanic)
Intrusive rocks
— major faults

Quaternary glaciation
Southern limits of ice sheets

– – Devensian (last glaciation, 94 000 to 10 000 years before present)

⋯ Anglian (maximum glaciation, 660 000 to 420 000 years before present)

This map shows solid geology. Surface deposits of peat, gravels, clays, and alluvium were added during late Pleistocene times and recently.

Moine Thrust · Great Glen Fault · Highland Boundary Fault · Southern Uplands Fault · Pennine Fault · Craven Fault · Church Stretton Fault

Scale 1: 10 000 000

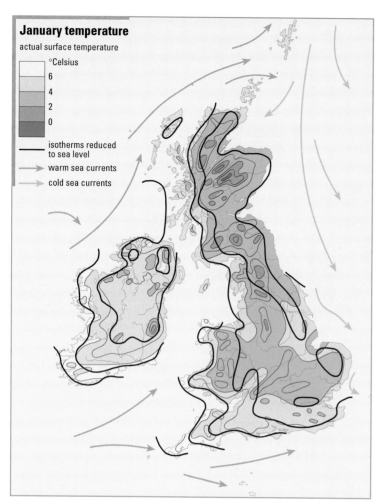

January temperature

actual surface temperature

°Celsius
6
4
2
0

——— isotherms reduced to sea level

→ warm sea currents

→ cold sea currents

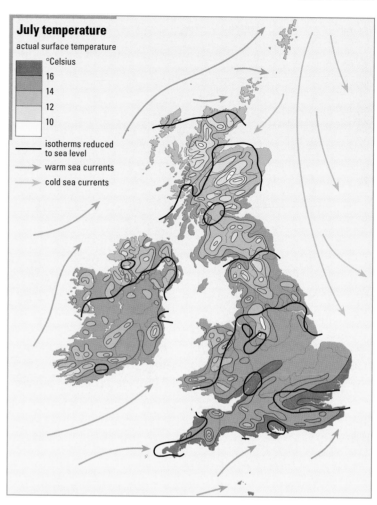

July temperature

actual surface temperature

°Celsius
16
14
12
10

——— isotherms reduced to sea level

→ warm sea currents

→ cold sea currents

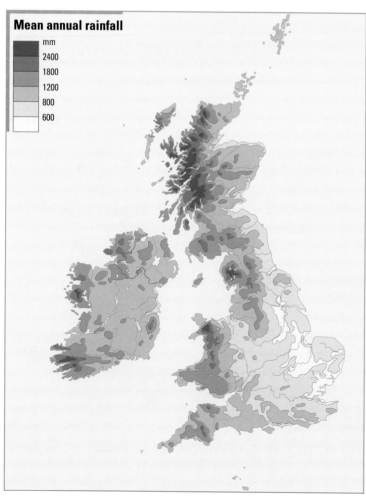

Mean annual rainfall

mm
2400
1800
1200
800
600

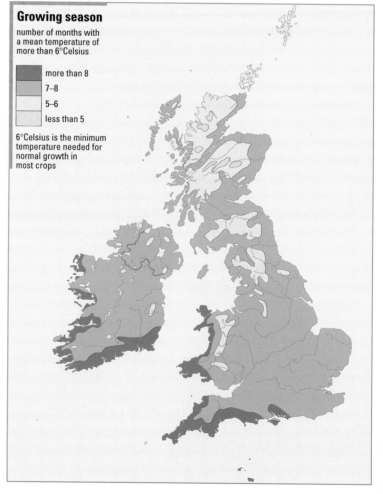

Growing season

number of months with a mean temperature of more than 6°Celsius

more than 8
7–8
5–6
less than 5

6°Celsius is the minimum temperature needed for normal growth in most crops

Transverse Mercator Projection   © Oxford University Press

Snow

average number of
mornings per year with
snow cover

- more than 60
- 40–60
- 30–40
- 20–30
- 10–20
- less than 10
- no data

Sunshine

average daily duration of
bright sunshine, in hours

- more than 5.0
- 4.5–5.0
- 4.0–4.5
- 3.5–4.0
- 3.0–3.5
- less than 3.0

© Oxford University Press

Climate graphs for selected British stations

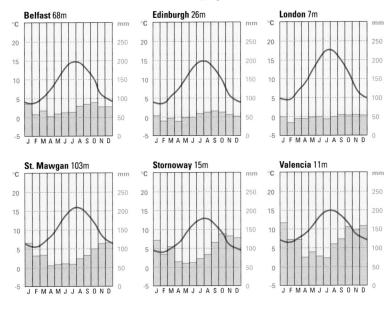

Belfast 68m

Edinburgh 26m

London 7m

St. Mawgan 103m

Stornoway 15m

Valencia 11m

Climate stations

Climate data

averages are for 1961–1990

Anglesey (Valley) 10m — climate station and its height above sea level

Temperature (°C)	high	average daily maximum temperature
	mean	average monthly temperature
	low	average daily minimum temperature
Rainfall (mm)		average monthly precipitation
Sunshine (hours)		average daily duration of bright sunshine

Climate stations map: Stornoway, Braemar, Tiree, Edinburgh, Belfast, Anglesey, Valencia, Cambridge, St. Mawgan, London, Exeter

		Jan	Feb	Mar	Apr	May	Jun	Jul	Aug	Sep	Oct	Nov	Dec	YEAR
Anglesey (Valley) 10m														
Temperature (°C)	high	7.7	7.7	9.1	11.4	14.4	16.9	18.4	18.5	16.7	14.2	10.6	8.7	12.8
	mean	5.5	5.1	6.5	8.3	11.1	13.6	15.3	15.4	13.9	11.6	8.1	6.4	10.0
	low	3.2	2.5	3.8	5.1	7.7	10.3	12.2	12.3	11.0	8.9	5.6	4.1	7.2
Rainfall (mm)		83	56	65	53	49	52	53	74	74	91	99	94	843
Sunshine (hours)		1.8	3.0	4.0	5.9	7.2	7.0	6.4	6.0	4.7	3.3	2.2	1.6	4.4
Braemar 339m														
Temperature (°C)	high	3.8	3.9	6.0	9.2	12.8	16.2	17.5	16.9	14.0	10.8	6.3	4.6	10.1
	mean	0.8	0.6	2.7	4.9	8.1	11.4	13.0	12.5	10.2	7.3	3.2	1.8	6.3
	low	-2.2	-2.7	-0.7	0.6	3.4	6.5	8.4	8.0	6.3	3.8	0.1	-1.0	2.5
Rainfall (mm)		106	62	72	48	66	58	54	71	81	93	87	91	889
Sunshine (hours)		0.8	2.0	3.1	4.6	5.2	5.6	5.1	4.8	3.5	2.2	1.2	0.6	3.2
Cambridge 26m														
Temperature (°C)	high	6.4	6.8	9.7	12.5	16.4	19.6	21.5	21.5	18.8	14.9	9.7	7.3	13.7
	mean	3.7	3.9	6.0	8.2	11.6	14.6	16.6	16.5	14.3	11.0	6.6	4.6	9.8
	low	1.0	0.9	2.2	3.9	6.7	9.6	11.7	11.5	9.8	7.1	3.5	1.8	5.8
Rainfall (mm)		43	32	42	43	49	50	44	53	46	49	51	49	551
Sunshine (hours)		1.8	2.5	3.5	4.7	6.2	6.5	6.0	5.7	4.8	3.5	2.2	1.5	4.1
Exeter 32m														
Temperature (°C)	high	8.0	8.0	10.2	12.7	15.8	19.1	21.0	20.8	18.4	15.0	11.0	9.0	14.0
	mean	5.0	5.0	6.6	8.6	11.5	14.6	16.5	16.3	14.2	11.4	7.8	6.0	10.2
	low	2.0	2.0	2.9	4.4	7.1	10.1	12.0	11.7	9.9	7.7	4.1	2.9	6.4
Rainfall (mm)		93	71	61	50	54	47	45	54	57	73	72	87	764
Sunshine (hours)		1.7	2.4	3.5	5.1	6.0	6.3	6.2	5.6	4.4	2.9	2.3	1.6	4.0
Tiree 12m														
Temperature (°C)	high	7.3	7.1	8.3	10.1	12.6	14.7	15.8	16.0	14.5	12.5	9.5	8.1	11.3
	mean	5.1	4.9	5.8	7.3	9.7	11.9	13.3	13.5	12.2	10.3	7.2	5.6	8.9
	low	2.9	2.6	3.3	4.4	6.7	9.1	10.8	10.9	9.8	8.1	4.8	3.8	6.4
Rainfall (mm)		127	79	96	59	59	61	78	95	129	140	122	120	1165
Sunshine (hours)		1.3	2.4	3.5	5.7	6.9	6.5	5.1	5.0	3.7	2.5	1.6	1.0	3.8
		Jan	Feb	Mar	Apr	May	Jun	Jul	Aug	Sep	Oct	Nov	Dec	YEAR

Land use

- rough grazing
- improved pasture
- cereals
- mixed farming
- · market gardening
- forest and woodland
- built-up area

Number of farms in the UK

	1950	1970	1999
England	316 485	192 700	147 220
Scotland	74 792	37 576	33 213
Wales	56 289	37 252	28 018
N. Ireland	86 287	61 124	31 132

Average size of farms in the UK (hectares)

	1950	1970	1999
England	33.3	51.4	62.2
Scotland	82.9	165.8	156.2
Wales	28.5	44.0	53.3
N. Ireland	14.0	17.8	34.5

Quantity of crops harvested in the UK, 2000

million tonnes   **total 45 million tonnes**

- vegetables 2.9
- fruit 0.3
- other crops 11.2
- cereals 24.0
- potatoes 6.6

Livestock in the UK, 2000

millions   **total 214.9 million**

- poultry 155.0
- cattle and calves 11.1
- sheep and lambs 42.3
- pigs 6.5

Agricultural employment in the UK

number of workers (thousands)

seasonal workers
- male
- female

regular part-time workers
- male
- female

regular full-time workers
- male
- female

(bar chart: 350, 300, 250, 200, 150, 100, 50 — years 1984, 1992, 2000)

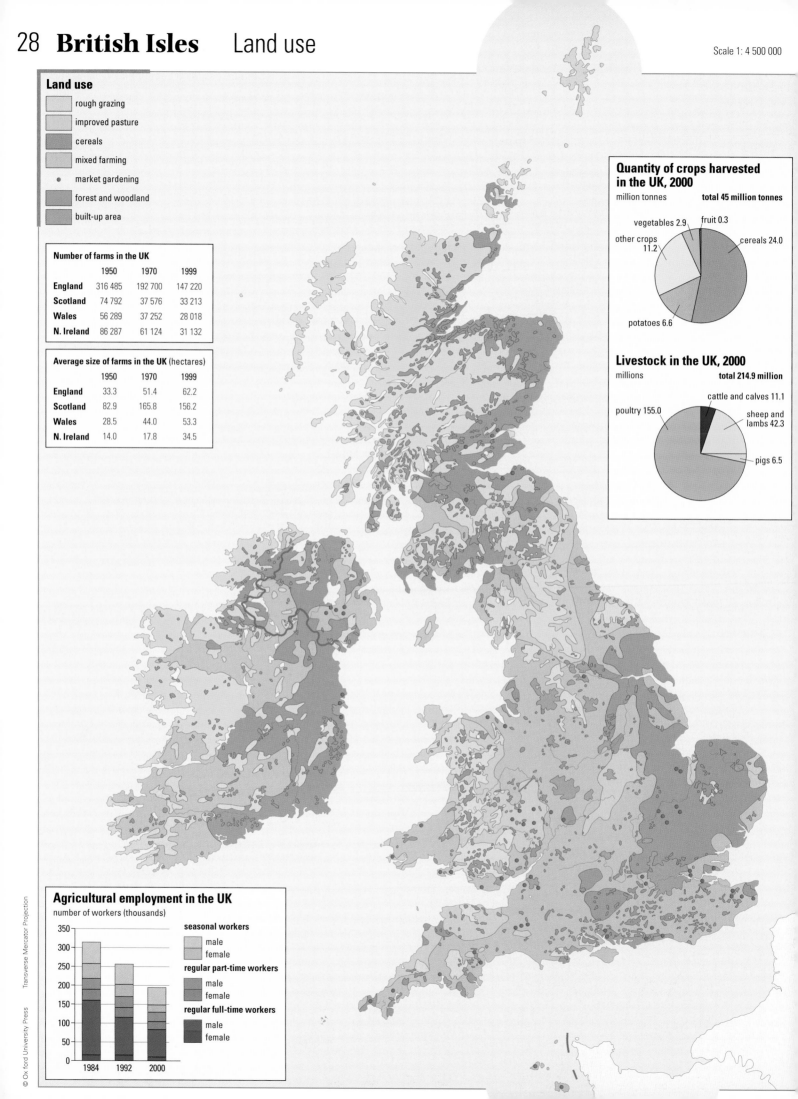

Scale 1: 12 500 000

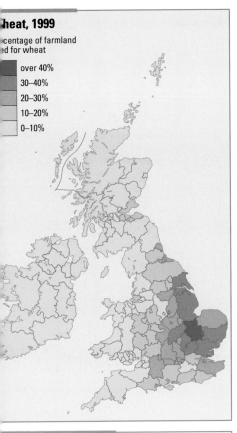

Wheat, 1999

percentage of farmland used for wheat

- over 40%
- 30–40%
- 20–30%
- 10–20%
- 0–10%

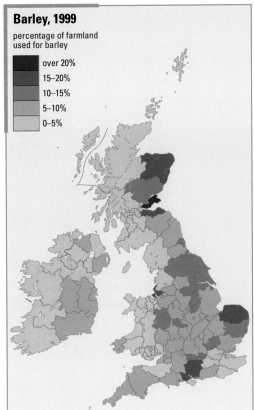

Barley, 1999

percentage of farmland used for barley

- over 20%
- 15–20%
- 10–15%
- 5–10%
- 0–5%

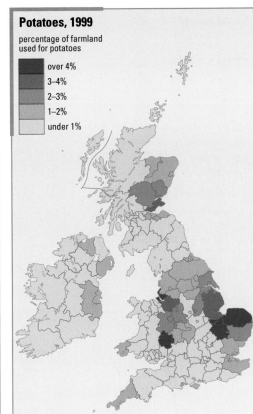

Potatoes, 1999

percentage of farmland used for potatoes

- over 4%
- 3–4%
- 2–3%
- 1–2%
- under 1%

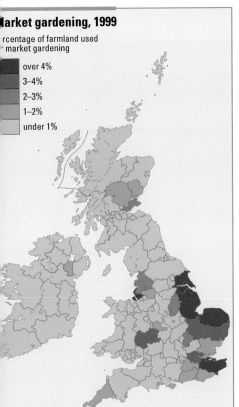

Market gardening, 1999

percentage of farmland used for market gardening

- over 4%
- 3–4%
- 2–3%
- 1–2%
- under 1%

Dairy and beef cattle, 1999

one dot represents 10 000 animals

- dairy cattle
- beef cattle

Sheep and Pigs, 1999

one dot represents 100 000 animals

- sheep
- pigs

© Oxford University Press

Transverse Mercator Projection

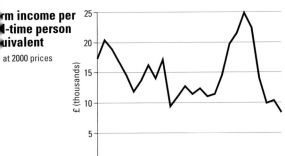

Farm income per full-time person equivalent

at 2000 prices

£ (thousands)

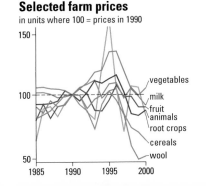

Selected farm prices

in units where 100 = prices in 1990

vegetables, milk, fruit, animals, root crops, cereals, wool

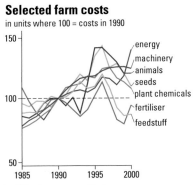

Selected farm costs

in units where 100 = costs in 1990

energy, machinery, animals, seeds, plant chemicals, fertiliser, feedstuff

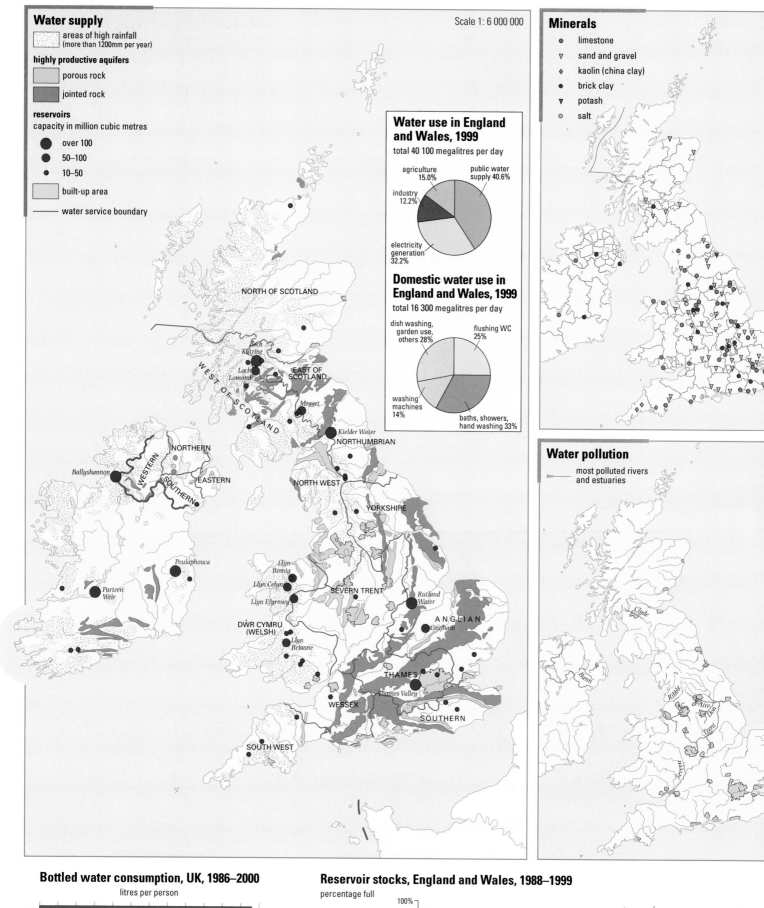

Water supply

areas of high rainfall (more than 1200mm per year)

highly productive aquifers

porous rock

jointed rock

reservoirs
capacity in million cubic metres

- over 100
- 50–100
- 10–50

built-up area

water service boundary

Scale 1: 6 000 000

Minerals

- limestone
- sand and gravel
- kaolin (china clay)
- brick clay
- potash
- salt

Water use in England and Wales, 1999
total 40 100 megalitres per day

- agriculture 15.0%
- public water supply 40.6%
- industry 12.2%
- electricity generation 32.2%

Domestic water use in England and Wales, 1999
total 16 300 megalitres per day

- dish washing, garden use, others 28%
- flushing WC 25%
- washing machines 14%
- baths, showers, hand washing 33%

Water pollution

most polluted rivers and estuaries

NORTH OF SCOTLAND

WEST OF SCOTLAND

Loch Katrine

Loch Lomond

EAST OF SCOTLAND

Megget

Kielder Water

NORTHUMBRIAN

Ballyshannon

WESTERN

NORTHERN

SOUTHERN

EASTERN

NORTH WEST

YORKSHIRE

Poulaphouca

Parteen Weir

Llyn Brenig

Llyn Celyn

SEVERN TRENT

Rutland Water

ANGLIAN

Grafham

Llyn Efyrnwy

DWR CYMRU (WELSH)

Llyn Brianne

THAMES

Thames Valley

WESSEX

SOUTHERN

SOUTH WEST

Clyde

Bann

Ribble

Aire

Don

Trent

Severn

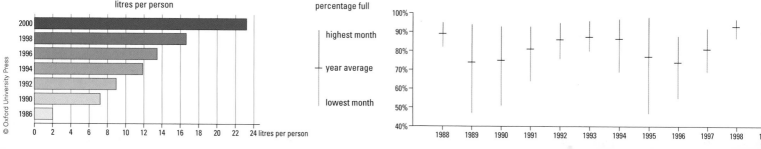

Bottled water consumption, UK, 1986–2000
litres per person

2000
1998
1996
1994
1992
1990
1986

0 2 4 6 8 10 12 14 16 18 20 22 24 litres per person

Reservoir stocks, England and Wales, 1988–1999
percentage full

- highest month
- year average
- lowest month

100%
90%
80%
70%
60%
50%
40%

1988 1989 1990 1991 1992 1993 1994 1995 1996 1997 1998 19

Scale 1: 6 000 000 (main map)

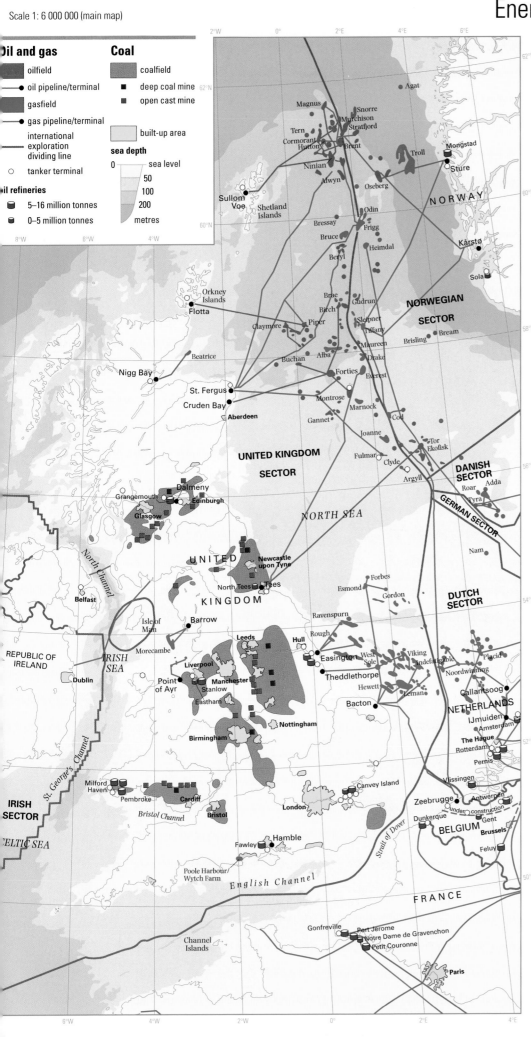

Oil and gas
- oilfield
- ● oil pipeline/terminal
- gasfield
- ● gas pipeline/terminal
- international exploration dividing line
- ○ tanker terminal

Oil refineries
- 5–16 million tonnes
- 0–5 million tonnes

Coal
- coalfield
- ■ deep coal mine
- ■ open cast mine
- built-up area

sea depth

0	sea level
50	
100	
200	
metres	

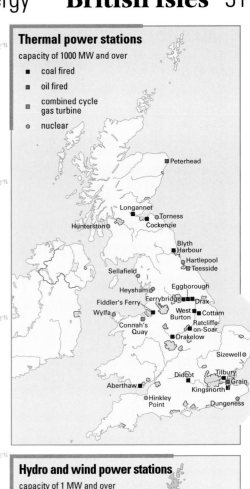

Thermal power stations
capacity of 1000 MW and over
- ■ coal fired
- ■ oil fired
- ■ combined cycle gas turbine
- ● nuclear

Peterhead, Longannet, Torness, Hunterston, Cockenzie, Blyth Harbour, Hartlepool, Teesside, Sellafield, Heysham, Eggborough, Fiddler's Ferry, Ferrybridge, Drax, Wylfa, West Burton, Cottam, Connah's Quay, Ratcliffe-on-Soar, Drakelow, Sizewell, Aberthaw, Didcot, Tilbury, Grain, Hinkley Point, Kingsnorth, Dungeness

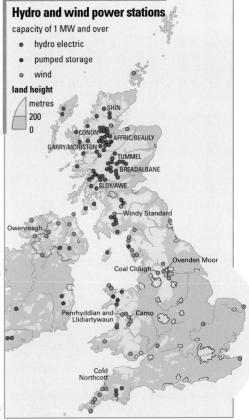

Hydro and wind power stations
capacity of 1 MW and over
- ● hydro electric
- ● pumped storage
- ● wind

land height

metres	200
	0

SHIN, CONON, AFFRIC/BEAULY, GARRY/MORISTON, TUMMEL, BREADALBANE, SLOY/AWE, Windy Standard, Owenreagh, Coal Clough, Ovenden Moor, Penrhyddlan and Llidiartywaun, Carno, Cold Northcott

Renewable energy, 1992–2000

biofuels · hydro · wind

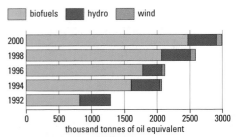

2000	
1998	
1996	
1994	
1992	

0   500   1000   1500   2000   2500   3000
thousand tonnes of oil equivalent

Oxford University Press   Transverse Mercator Projection

Scale 1: 4 500 000

Manufacturing industry

the map shows only the main centres of selected industries

- ▽ chemicals
- ● steel
- ○ non-ferrous metal smelting
- ● metal working
- ■ motor vehicles
- ■ railway vehicles
- ☐ aircraft and aerospace
- ■ shipbuilding and repair
- ▲ mechanical engineering
- ▲ electrical engineering
- △ electronics and computers
- ◆ clothing and footwear
- ◆ textiles and carpets

Regional aid to industry

Assisted areas, eligible under European Union law for grants to increase employment opportunities

- tier 1 and Northern Ireland (higher level of assistance)
- tier 2 (lower level of assistance)

UK employment

millions of people

[bar chart: 1981, 1991, 2001 — scale 0 to 30]

- agriculture, forestry, and fishing
- energy and water
- manufacturing
- transport and communications
- services

UK manufacturing production, 2000

Total value of output £472 734 million

[pie chart]

- other 3.5%
- food; drink 15.6%
- transport equipment 13.1%
- textiles; leather 3.5%
- wood products 1.3%
- electrical; optical equipment 14.6%
- paper; printing; publishing 9.7%
- machinery 7.3%
- fuels; refining 5.7%
- metals 8.9%
- chemicals 10.1%
- non-metallic mineral products 2.6%
- rubber; plastics 4.2%

Map labels:

Fort William

Dundee, Kinross, Markinch, Grangemouth, Kirkcaldy, Coatbridge, Leith, Glasgow, Broxburn, Edinburgh, Motherwell, Irvine, Kilmarnock, Prestwick, Mauchline, Selkirk, Galashiels, Cumnock, Hawick, Girvan

Donegal, Killala, Westport, Ballieborough, Dundalk, Dunleer, Delvin, Navan, Longford, Athlone, Clane, Dublin, Galway, Ballinasloe, Tullamore, Rathcoole, Bray, Dún Laoghaire, Holyhead, Ennis, Newmarket-on-Fergus, Limerick, Thurles, Arklow, Askeaton/Foynes, Tralee, Clonmel, Waterford, Killarney, Cork, Kinsale

Belfast, Newtownards, Craigavon, NORTHERN IRELAND

Whitehaven, Kendal, Lynemouth, Newcastle upon Tyne/Gateshead, South Shields, Prudhoe, Sunderland, Washington, Billingham, Teesside, Middlesbrough, Wilton

Nelson/Burnley, Halifax, Bradford, Brough, Kingston upon Hull, Blackburn, Preston, Leeds, Wakefield, Immingham, Grimsby, Bolton, St Helens, Huddersfield, Oldham, Scunthorpe, Liverpool, Rotherham, Sheffield, MERSEYSIDE, Manchester, SOUTH YORKSHIRE, Ince, Northwich, Sandbach, Newark, Wrexham, Crewe, Derby, Nottingham, Burnaston, Castle Donington, Stafford, Rugeley, Loughborough, Wolverhampton, Ibstock, Walsall, Leicester, Peterborough, Birmingham, Solihull, Coventry, Kettering, Norwich, Kidderminster, Rugby, Rushden, Redditch, Longbridge, Northampton, Wellingborough, Cambridge, Banbury, Milton Keynes, Ipswich, Cowley, Luton, Borehamwood, Chelmsford, Watford, Northfleet, Velindre, Swindon, Bracknell, WEST WALES AND THE VALLEYS, Ebbw Vale, Cwmbran, Reading, London, Baglan Bay, Newport, Newbury, Swansea, Port Talbot, Llanwern, Bristol, Farnborough, Guildford, Bridgend, Avonmouth, Godalming, Appledore, Street, Southampton, Yeovil, CORNWALL, ISLES OF SCILLY

© Oxford University Press — Transverse Mercator Projection

Employment in primary activity, 2000

percentage of the workforce employed in agriculture, forestry,
fishing, mining, and quarrying, by administrative area

- over 20%
- 10–20%
- 2.5–10%
- 1–2.5%
- under 1%

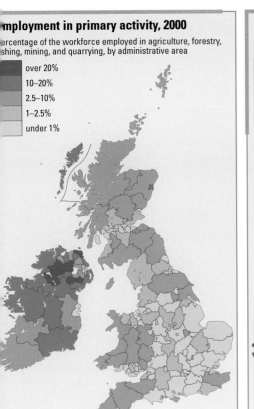

Employment in secondary activity, 2000

percentage of the workforce employed in manufacturing,
construction, and utilities, by administrative area

- over 30%
- 25–30%
- 20–25%
- 15–20%
- under 15%

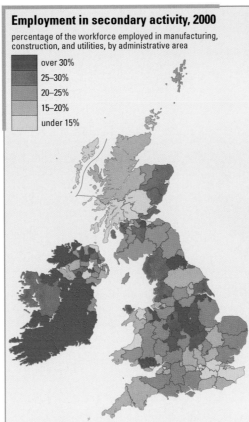

Employment in tertiary activity, 2000

percentage of the workforce employed in services, transport,
finance, and administration, by administrative area

- over 85%
- 80–85%
- 75–80%
- 70–75%
- 65–70%
- under 65%

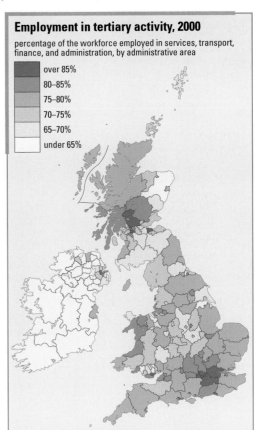

Unemployment, 2000

percentage of the workforce unemployed,
by administrative area

- over 6%
- 5–6%
- 4–5%
- 3–4%
- 2–3%
- under 2%

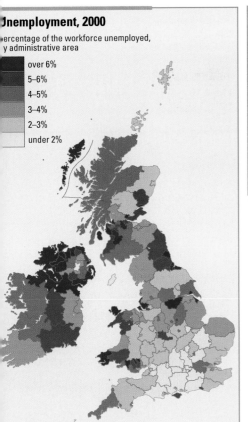

Change in manufacturing employment, 1991–2000

percentage change in the number of people employed in
manufacturing, by administrative area

gain
- over 20%
- 10–20%
- 0–10%

loss
- 0–10%
- 10–20%
- over 30%

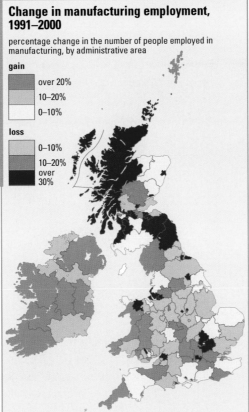

Net jobs gains and losses, 1986–2000

thousands of jobs by former Standard Statistical Region

gains
300
200
100
0

losses
0
100
200

activity
- primary
- secondary
- tertiary

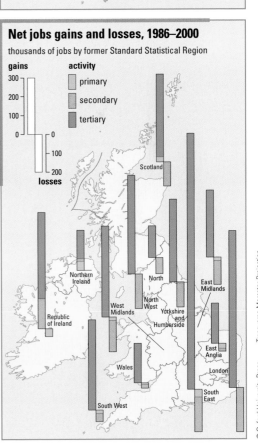

Scotland

Northern Ireland

North

East Midlands

Republic of Ireland

West Midlands

North West

Yorkshire and Humberside

East Anglia

Wales

London

South East

South West

UK workforce structure, 2000

Total workforce 29 412 000

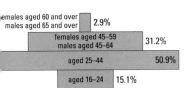
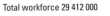

females aged 60 and over
males aged 65 and over — 2.9%

females aged 45–59
males aged 45–64 — 31.2%

aged 25–44 — 50.9%

aged 16–24 — 15.1%

UK employment rates, 1960–2000

percentage of people of working age

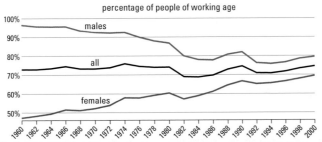

males

all

females

100%
90%
80%
70%
60%
50%

1960 1962 1964 1966 1968 1970 1972 1974 1976 1978 1980 1982 1984 1986 1988 1990 1992 1994 1996 1998 2000

UK unemployment structure, 2000

percentage of all economically active people

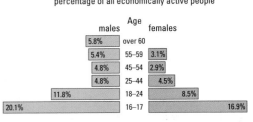

males	Age	females
5.8%	over 60	
5.4%	55–59	3.1%
4.8%	45–54	2.9%
4.8%	25–44	4.5%
11.8%	18–24	8.5%
20.1%	16–17	16.9%

Transverse Mercator Projection

© Oxford University Press

Population density, 1999

people per square kilometre

- over 1000
- 500–1000
- 250–500
- 100–250
- 50–100
- 10–50
- under 10

Major cities and towns

number of people

- ☐ over 1 000 000
- ○ 400 000–1 000 000
- ◉ 100 000–400 000
- • 25 000–100 000

Young people, 1999

percentage of the population under 16 years old, by administrative area

- over 24%
- 22–24%
- 21–22%
- 20–21%
- 19–20%
- under 19%

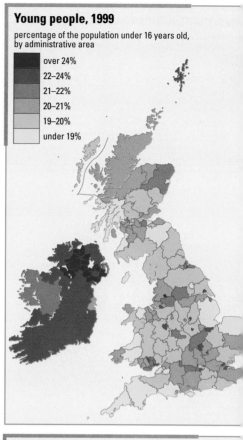

Retired people, 1999

percentage of the population over retirement age*, by administrative area

- over 22%
- 20–22%
- 18–20%
- 16–18%
- 14–16%
- under 14%

*65 for men
60 for women

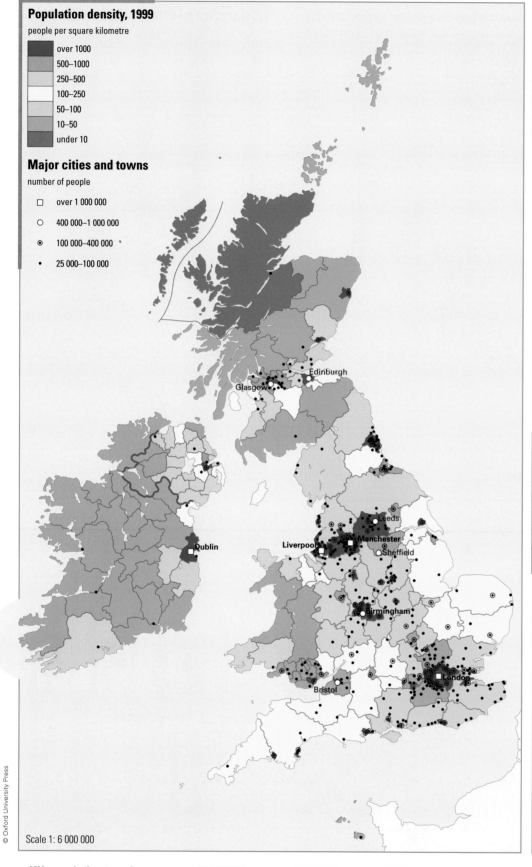

Scale 1: 6 000 000

© Oxford University Press

UK population trends	1901	1911	1921	1931	1941	1951	1961	1971	1981	1991	2001	2011	2021
Total population (millions)	38.24	42.08	44.03	46.04	48.22	50.23	52.81	55.93	56.35	57.65	59.62	60.93	63.64
Infant mortality (deaths per 1000 live births)	138.0	110.0	76.0	62.0	50.0	27.0	21.0	17.9	11.0	7.4	5.6	5.5	5.5
Birth rate (births per 1000 people)	28.6	24.5	22.8	16.3	14.4	15.9	17.9	16.1	13.0	13.8	12.0	11.5	11.5
Death rate (deaths per 1000 people)	16.5	14.3	11.9	12.5	13.0	12.6	12.0	11.5	11.6	11.3	10.5	10.0	10.3
Life expectancy (years)	47.0	52.2	57.3	60.0	61.0	68.5	70.9	71.9	73.8	76.0	77.5	79.5	80.5

projected

Scale 1: 12 500 000 (smallest maps)

opulation change, 1981–1999

rcentage change in the number of people,
administrative area

crease
- over 20%
- 15–20%
- 10–15%
- 5–10%
- 0–5%

crease
- 0–10%
- 10–16%

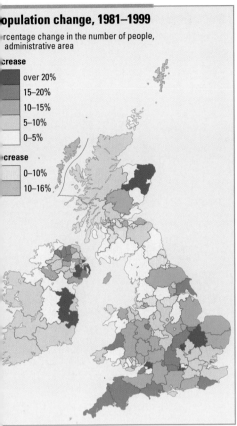

Natural population change, 1999

difference between births and deaths per 1000 people,
by administrative area

more births than deaths
- more than 6
- 4–6
- 2–4
- 0–2

**more deaths
than births**
- 0–2
- 2–5
- more
  than 4

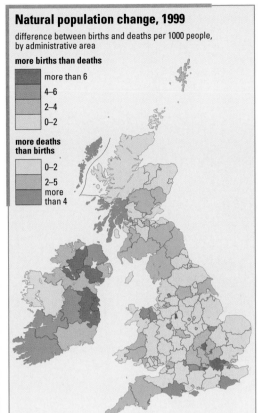

Internal migration, 1999–2000

difference between the number moving in and the number
moving out per 1000 people, by administrative area

more people moved in than out
- more than 6
- 3–6
- 0–3

**more people
moved out
than in**
- 0–3
- 3–6
- more
  than 6
- no data

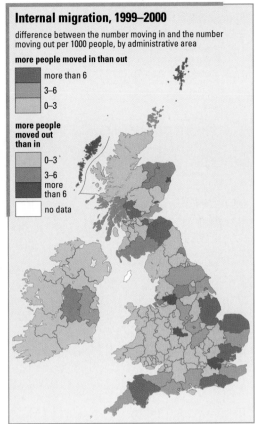

Population structure of the UK

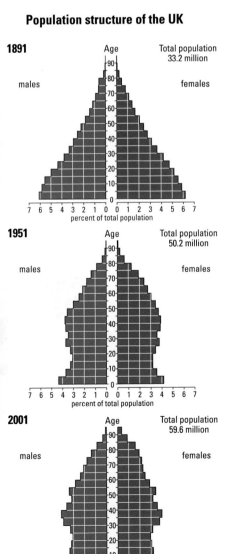

1891

Age

Total population
33.2 million

males   females

7 6 5 4 3 2 1 0 1 2 3 4 5 6 7
percent of total population

1951

Age

Total population
50.2 million

males   females

7 6 5 4 3 2 1 0 1 2 3 4 5 6 7
percent of total population

2001

Age

Total population
59.6 million

males   females

7 6 5 4 3 2 1 0 1 2 3 4 5 6 7
percent of total population

Ethnic minority groups, 2000

members of all ethnic minority groups as a percentage
of population, by administrative area
- over 16%
- 8–16%
- 4–8%
- 2–4%
- 0–2%
- no data

thousands of people

500
400
300
200
100
0

- Black (including
  Caribbean and African)
- South Asian (Indian,
  Pakistani, and Bangladeshi)
- Chinese and other

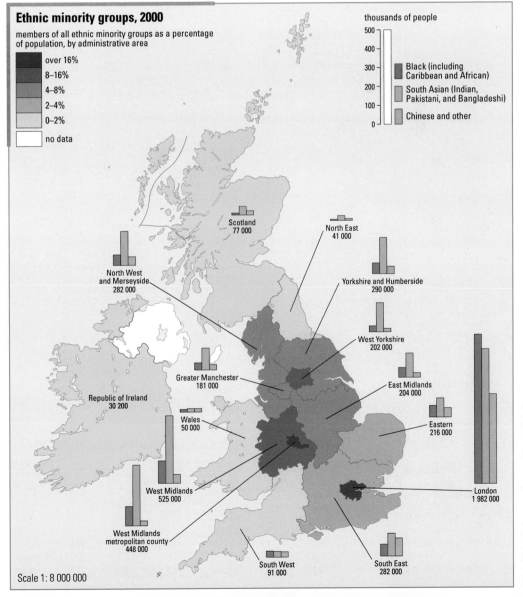

Scotland
77 000

North East
41 000

North West
and Merseyside
282 000

Yorkshire and Humberside
290 000

West Yorkshire
202 000

Greater Manchester
181 000

East Midlands
204 000

Republic of Ireland
30 200

Eastern
216 000

Wales
50 000

West Midlands
525 000

West Midlands
metropolitan county
448 000

London
1 982 000

South West
91 000

South East
282 000

Scale 1: 8 000 000

© Oxford University Press

Transverse Mercator Projection

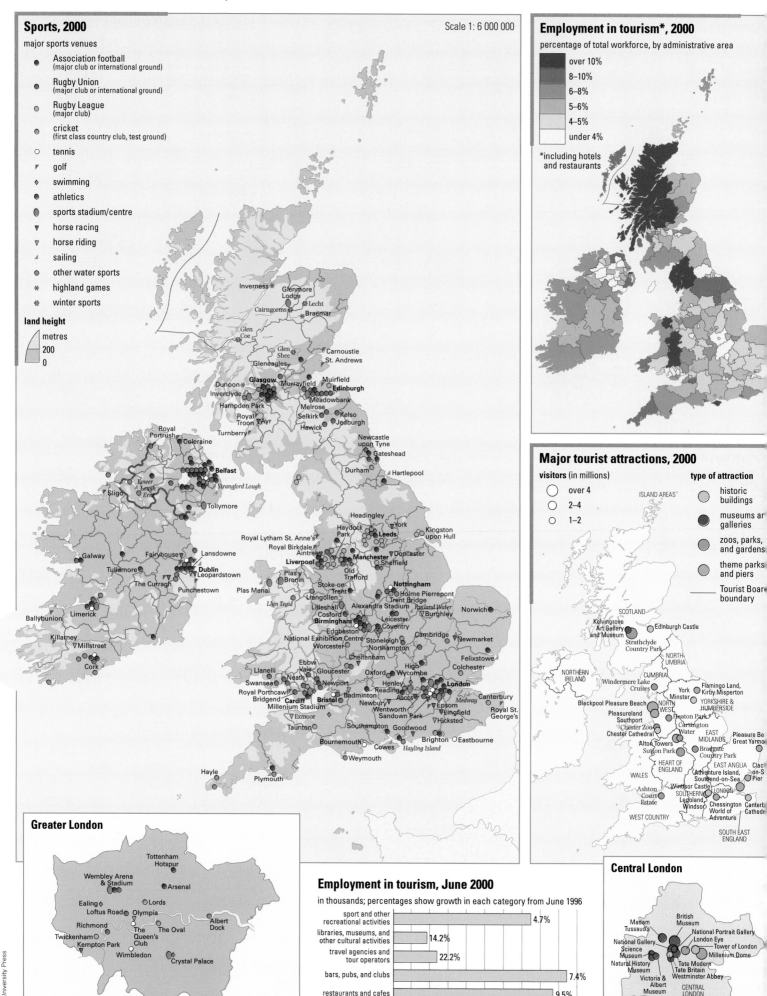

Sports, 2000

major sports venues

- Association football (major club or international ground)
- Rugby Union (major club or international ground)
- Rugby League (major club)
- cricket (first class country club, test ground)
- ○ tennis
- golf
- swimming
- athletics
- sports stadium/centre
- horse racing
- horse riding
- sailing
- other water sports
- highland games
- winter sports

land height

metres
200
0

Scale 1: 6 000 000

Greater London

- Tottenham Hotspur
- Wembley Arena & Stadium
- Arsenal
- Ealing
- Loftus Road
- Olympia
- Lords
- Richmond
- Albert Dock
- Twickenham
- The Queen's Club
- The Oval
- Kempton Park
- Wimbledon
- Crystal Palace

Employment in tourism* , 2000

percentage of total workforce, by administrative area

over 10%
8–10%
6–8%
5–6%
4–5%
under 4%

*including hotels and restaurants

Major tourist attractions, 2000

visitors (in millions)
○ over 4
○ 2–4
○ 1–2

type of attraction
- historic buildings
- museums and galleries
- zoos, parks, and gardens
- theme parks and piers
— Tourist Board boundary

SCOTLAND
Kelvingrove Art Gallery and Museum
Edinburgh Castle
Strathclyde Country Park
NORTHERN IRELAND
ISLAND AREAS
NORTH UMBRIA
CUMBRIA
Windermere Lake Cruises
York Minster
Flamingo Land, Kirby Misperton
YORKSHIRE & HUMBERSIDE
Blackpool Pleasure Beach
NORTH WEST
Pleasureland Southport
Heaton Park
Carsington Water
EAST MIDLANDS
Pleasure Beach Great Yarmouth
Chester Zoo
Chester Cathedral
Alton Towers
Sutton Park
Bradgate Country Park
HEART OF ENGLAND
EAST ANGLIA
WALES
Adventure Island, Southend-on-Sea
Clacton-on-Sea Pier
Windsor Castle
Ashton Court Estate
Legoland Windsor
SOUTHERN
LONDON
Chessington World of Adventure
Canterbury Cathedral
WEST COUNTRY
SOUTH EAST ENGLAND

Central London

Madam Tussaud's
British Museum
National Portrait Gallery
National Gallery
London Eye
Science Museum
Tower of London
Millennium Dome
Natural History Museum
Tate Modern
Tate Britain
Victoria & Albert Museum
Westminster Abbey
CENTRAL LONDON

Employment in tourism, June 2000

in thousands; percentages show growth in each category from June 1996

Category	Growth
sport and other recreational activities	4.7%
libraries, museums, and other cultural activities	14.2%
travel agencies and tour operators	22.2%
bars, pubs, and clubs	7.4%
restaurants and cafes	9.5%
hotels and other tourist accommodation	2.2%

0 50 100 150 200 250 300 350 400 450 500

Income, 2000

average gross weekly earnings of workers in full-time employment, by administrative area

- over £475
- £425–£475
- £400–£425
- £375–£400
- £350–£375
- under £350
- no data

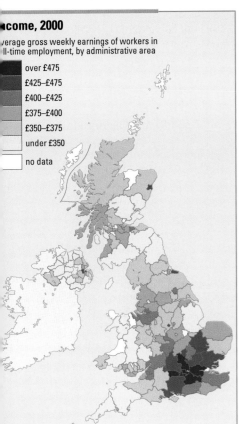

Education, 2000

percentage of 16 year olds entering further or higher education, by administrative area

- over 90%
- 85–90%
- 80–85%
- 75–80%
- 70–75%
- under 70%

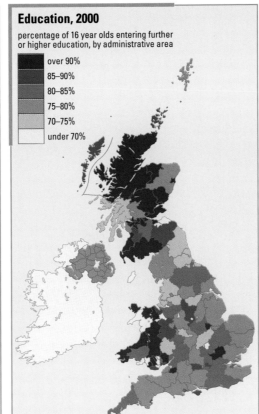

Index of Multiple Deprivation (IMD), 2000

IMD is calculated from a number of indicators including low income, unemployment, poor health, disability, lack of education, unsatisfactory housing, and poor access to services. The map shows the 10% most deprived areas within each part of the UK.

- England
- Wales
- Scotland
- Northern Ireland

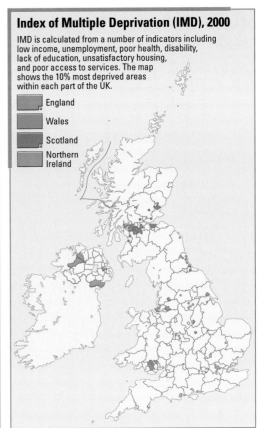

Burglaries, 2000

per 1000 households, by administrative area

- over 40
- 30–40
- 20–30
- 10–20
- under 10

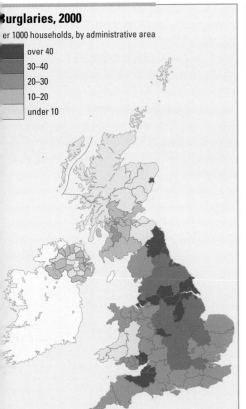

Coronary heart disease, 1992–1996

age-standardised death rates per 100 000 people, by administrative area

- over 130
- 112–129
- 97–111
- 82–96
- under 81

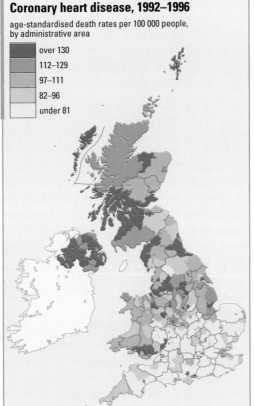

House prices, 2001

comparative prices for similar size and style of house in similar neighbourhoods

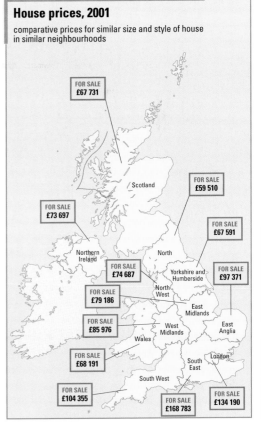

FOR SALE £67 731
FOR SALE £59 510
FOR SALE £73 697
FOR SALE £67 591
FOR SALE £74 687
FOR SALE £97 371
FOR SALE £79 186
FOR SALE £85 976
FOR SALE £68 191
FOR SALE £104 355
FOR SALE £168 783
FOR SALE £134 190

Scotland
Northern Ireland
North
Yorkshire and Humberside
North West
East Midlands
West Midlands
East Anglia
Wales
South East
London
South West

Consumer goods, 1970–2000

percent of UK households having use of each product

- car
- central heating
- washing machine
- dishwasher
- microwave oven
- video
- PC
- CD player
- ooo no data

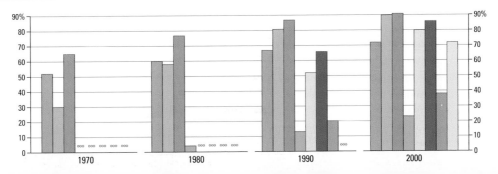

1970   1980   1990   2000

Conservation

- **National Parks***
- Areas of Outstanding Natural Beauty (England, Wales, and Northern Ireland) National Scenic Areas (Scotland)
- Heritage Coast (England and Wales) Coastal Conservation Zone (Scotland)
- internationally recognized sites (including Special Protection Areas, 'Ramsar' Sites, and Biosphere Reserves)
- ✳ Natural Heritage Sites
- ✳ Cultural Heritage Sites
- built-up area

*National parks are designated to conserve the natural beauty and cultural heritage of areas of outstanding landscape value. There are 10 national parks in England and Wales, all designated in the 1950's following the National Parks and Access to the Countryside Act, 1949. The Broads is not officially a national park but is considered as such by the government and has had its own authority since 1989. In 2002 the government was consulting on proposals to establish the New Forest and South Downs as national parks. The National Parks (Scotland) Act was passed in July 2000, and it is expected that the Cairngorms and Loch Lomond and the Trossachs will become Scotland's first national parks in 2002/3.

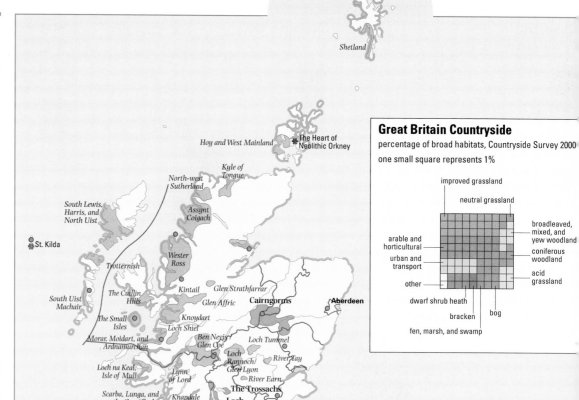

Great Britain Countryside
percentage of broad habitats, Countryside Survey 2000
one small square represents 1%

National Parks, 2000
area and visitor numbers

Acid rain

Environmental damage is more likely where acid deposition is high and soils (particularly those that are already acid) are more sensitive.

areas where potential damage to vegetation from nitrogen in acid rain is

- very high
- high
- moderate
- low

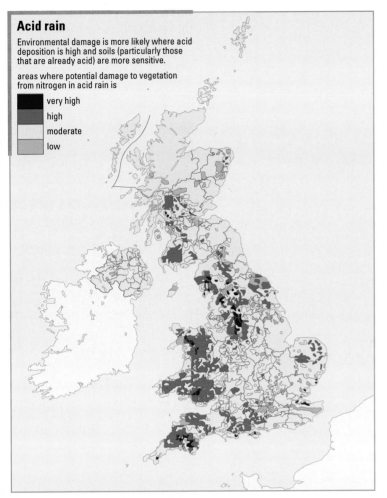

Ozone, 1996

Number of days when ozone concentration exceeded 50 parts per billion, used to assess the potential for effects on human health.

days per year

- over 45
- 35–45
- 30–35
- 25–30
- under 25

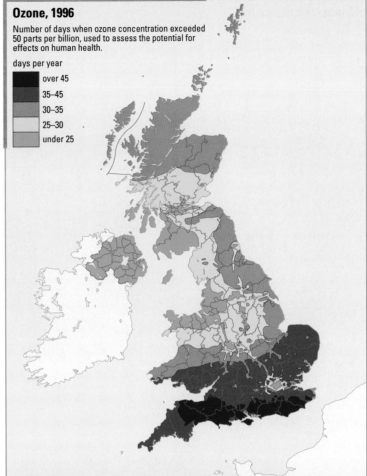

Coastal and offshore pollution

— bathing beaches heavily polluted by sewage, 1997

oil spills within UK waters, 1989–1998

tonnes

- over 5000
- 50–5000
- 0–50

Braer 86 248 tonnes
5 January 1993

ATLANTIC OCEAN

NORTH SEA

Sea Empress 72 000 tonnes
15 February 1996

English Channel

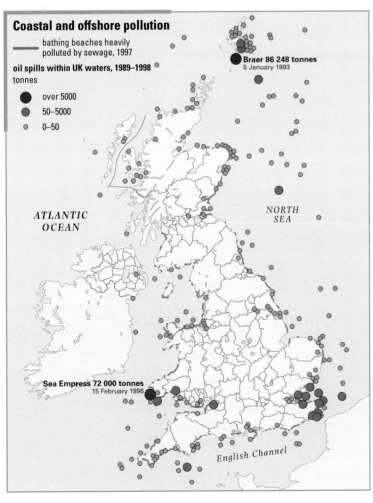

Light pollution

Image of the British Isles at night showing city lights. The patches of light in the North Sea are flares from oil rigs.

Scale 1: 7 500 000

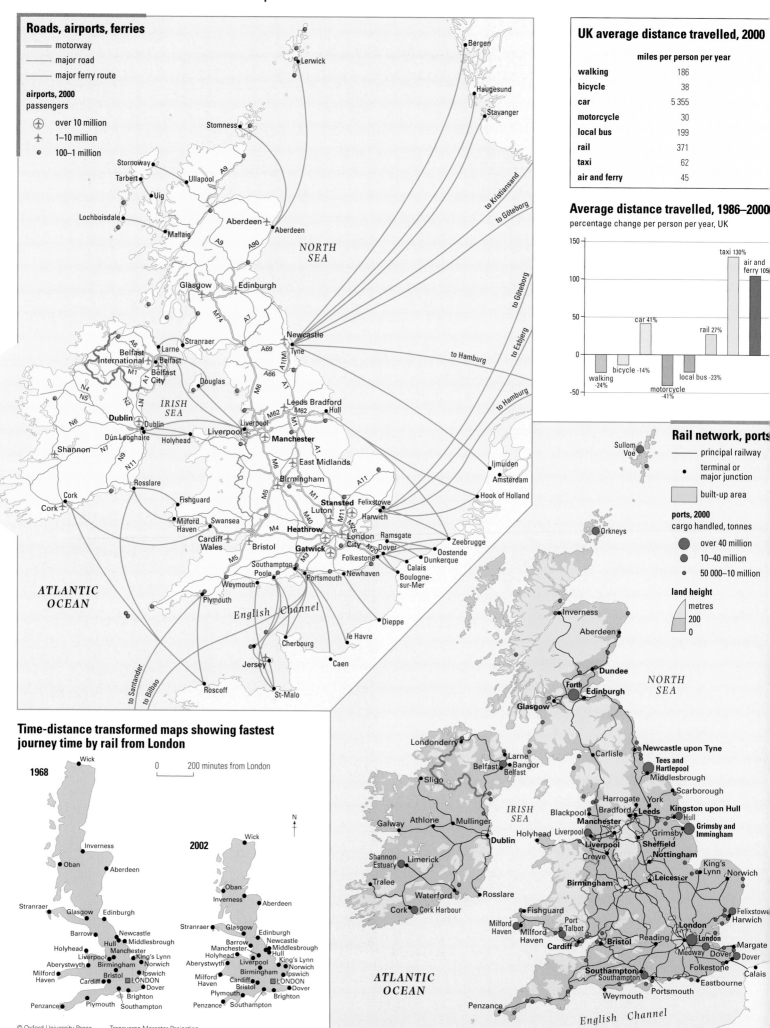

Roads, airports, ferries

— motorway
— major road
— major ferry route

airports, 2000
passengers
⊕ over 10 million
✈ 1–10 million
• 100–1 million

UK average distance travelled, 2000

miles per person per year

walking	186
bicycle	38
car	5 355
motorcycle	30
local bus	199
rail	371
taxi	62
air and ferry	45

Average distance travelled, 1986–2000

percentage change per person per year, UK

walking −24%
bicycle −14%
car 41%
motorcycle −41%
local bus −23%
rail 27%
taxi 130%
air and ferry 105

Rail network, ports

— principal railway
• terminal or major junction
▢ built-up area

ports, 2000
cargo handled, tonnes
● over 40 million
● 10–40 million
• 50 000–10 million

land height
metres
200
0

Time-distance transformed maps showing fastest journey time by rail from London

0 — 200 minutes from London

1968

2002

© Oxford University Press   Transverse Mercator Projection

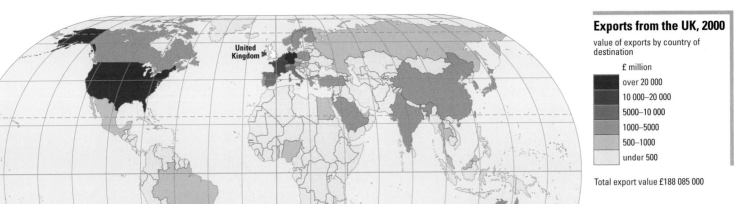

Exports from the UK, 2000

value of exports by country of destination

£ million

- over 20 000
- 10 000–20 000
- 5000–10 000
- 1000–5000
- 500–1000
- under 500

Total export value £188 085 000

Imports to the UK, 2000

value of exports by country of origin

£ million

- over 20 000
- 10 000–20 000
- 5000–10 000
- 1000–5000
- 500–1000
- under 500

Total import value £218 108 000

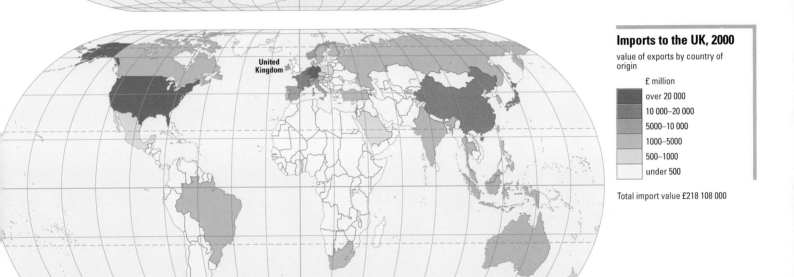

Major goods exported, 2000
percentage of total value of exports

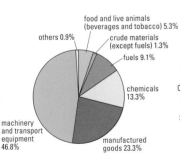

others 0.9%
food and live animals (beverages and tobacco) 5.3%
crude materials (except fuels) 1.3%
fuels 9.1%
chemicals 13.3%
machinery and transport equipment 46.8%
manufactured goods 23.3%

Major trading partners, 2000
percentage of total value of exports

others 23.4%
USA 15.6%
Germany 12.1%
France 9.9%
Netherlands 8.1%
Republic of Ireland 6.6%
Belgium and Luxembourg 5.5%
Italy 4.5%
Spain 4.4%
Sweden 2.2%
China 2.2%
Japan 2.0%
Canada 1.9%
Switzerland 1.6%

Major goods imported, 2000
percentage of total value of imports

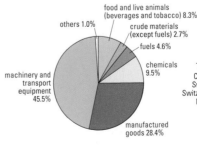

others 1.0%
food and live animals (beverages and tobacco) 8.3%
crude materials (except fuels) 2.7%
fuels 4.6%
chemicals 9.5%
machinery and transport equipment 45.5%
manufactured goods 28.4%

Major trading partners, 2000
percentage of total value of imports

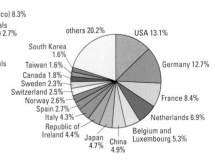

others 20.2%
USA 13.1%
Germany 12.7%
France 8.4%
Netherlands 6.9%
Belgium and Luxembourg 5.3%
China 4.9%
Japan 4.7%
Republic of Ireland 4.4%
Italy 4.3%
Spain 2.7%
Norway 2.6%
Switzerland 2.5%
Sweden 2.3%
Canada 1.8%
Taiwan 1.6%
South Korea 1.6%

UK Balance of Trade, 1988–2000
the difference in value between exports and imports

	1988	1989	1990	1991	1992	1993	1994	1995	1996	1997	1998	1999	2000
Value of exports (£ million)	80 711	92 611	102 313	103 939	107 863	122 039	135 260	153 577	167 196	171 923	164 056	166 198	188 085
Value of imports (£ million)	102 264	117 335	121 020	114 162	120 913	135 358	146 351	165 600	180 918	184 265	185 869	193 722	218 108

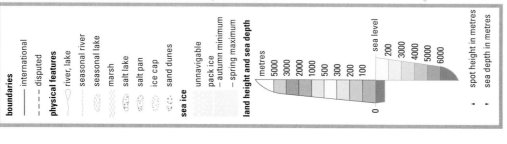

URAL MOUNTAINS

Ural

Pechora

Severnaya (N.) Dvina

Volga

Oka

Don

Kola Peninsula

WHITE SEA

Lake Onega

Rybinsk Reservoir

Lake Ladoga

Central Russian Uplands

Caspian Sea

Volga

Tsimlyansk Reservoir

Caucasus

5123 Mt Ararat

5642 Mt Elbrus

Lake Urmia

Lake Van

Tigris

Euphrates

Dnieper

Gulf of Finland

Lake Peipus

Daugava

Pripet Marshes

Pripet

Dniester

SEA OF AZOV

Crimea

BLACK SEA

Anatolian Plateau

Toros Daglari

Kizil Irmak

Lake Tuz

Iivarajoki

Kemi

Lappland

Torne

Salpausselkä

Neman

Vistula

CARPATHIANS

2548

Danube

Balkan Mts.

Rodopi Planina

Bosporus

SEA OF MARMARA

Dardanelles

2917 Mt Olympus

Pindhos Mountains

AEGEAN SEA

Cyclades

Rhodes

Cyprus

Crete

Indalsälven

Lake Mälaren

Gulf of Bothnia

Åland

BALTIC SEA

Gotland

Öland

Vistula

North European Plain

Oder

Bohemian Massif

Hungarian Basin

Tisza

Drava

Sava

Dinaric Alps

Tauern

Corfu

Peloponnese

IONIAN SEA

-5121

Loften Islands

Skellefte

Dal

Klar

Lake Vänern

Lake Vättern

Bornholm

Skåne

Elbe

1603

Erzgebirge

Schwäbische Alb

Danube

Bodensee

Drau

ADRIATIC SEA

APPENNINI

1277

Mt Etna 3323

Sicily

Malta

MEDITERRANEAN

Jostedalsbreen

Hardanger vidda

Kattegat

Skagerrak

Jylland

Fyn

Sjaelland

Harz Mts.

Weser

Rhine

Vosges

Vesuvius

C. Bon

G. of Gabes

TYRRHENIAN SEA

Vejlefjorden

Scandinavia

Arctic Circle

36

Frisian Islands

Rhine

Ardennes

Marne

Alpes Maritimes

ALPS

4807 Mont Blanc

Pb

Po

LIGURIAN SEA

Corsica

Sardinia

Jan Mayen

Norwegian Basin

3970

Prime Meridian

NORTH SEA

Texel

Waal

Aâas

Meuse

Seine

Paris Basin

Loire

L. Geneva

Rhône

Central Massif

Gulf of Lyons

Balearic Islands

Menorca

Mallorca

Ibiza

GREENLAND SEA

Iceland

Vatnajökull

1491 Hekla

Faroe Islands

Shetland Islands

Orkney Islands

C. Wrath

British Isles

Southern Uplands

1344 Ben Nevis

Great Britain

Pennines

Cambrian Mts.

The Wash

Thames

Str. of Dover

English Channel

Channel Islands

Cotentin

Brittany Pen.

Dordogne

Garonne

Pyrénées

3404

Ebro

ATLANTIC OCEAN

Rockall Bank

Outer Hebrides

Malin Head

Central Plain

Ireland

Shannon

St. George's Channel

Scilly Is.

Bay of Biscay

C. Finisterre

Cantabrian Mts.

Duero

Central Cordilleras

Douro

Tagus

La Mancha

Sierra Morena

Guadiana

Guadalquivir

Betican Cordilleras

Str. of Gibraltar

ATLAS MOUNTAINS

Grand Hrg Occidental

West European Basin

C. de São Vicente

boundaries
— international
- - - disputed

physical features
river, lake
seasonal river
seasonal lake
marsh
salt lake
salt pan
ice cap
sand dunes

sea ice
unnavigable
pack ice — autumn minimum
— spring maximum

land height and sea depth

metres
5000
3000
2000
1000
500
300
200
100
0

sea level
200
3000
4000
5000
6000

metres

▲ spot height in metres
▼ sea depth in metres

Scale 1: 22 000 000

0   220   440   660   880   1100 km

Scale 1: 50 000 000

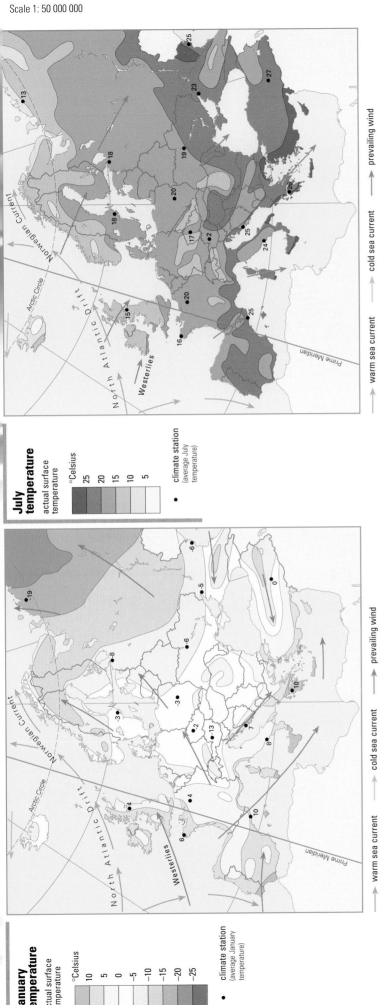

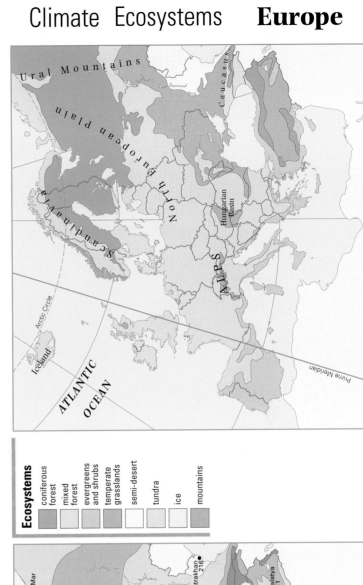

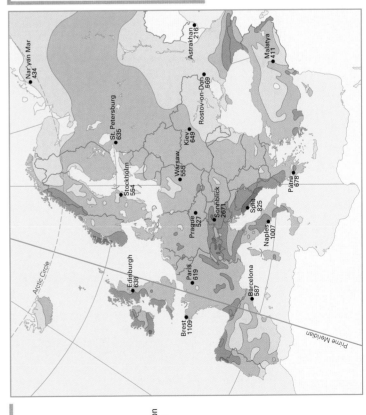

July temperature

actual surface temperature

°Celsius
25
20
15
10
5

● climate station (average July temperature)

Ecosystems

coniferous forest
mixed forest
evergreens and shrubs
temperate grasslands
semi-desert
tundra
ice
mountains

January temperature

actual surface temperature

°Celsius
10
5
0
-5
-10
-15
-20
-25

● climate station (average January temperature)

Precipitation

average annual precipitation

mm
2000
1000
500
250
0

● climate station (average annual precipitation)

Conical Orthomorphic Projection

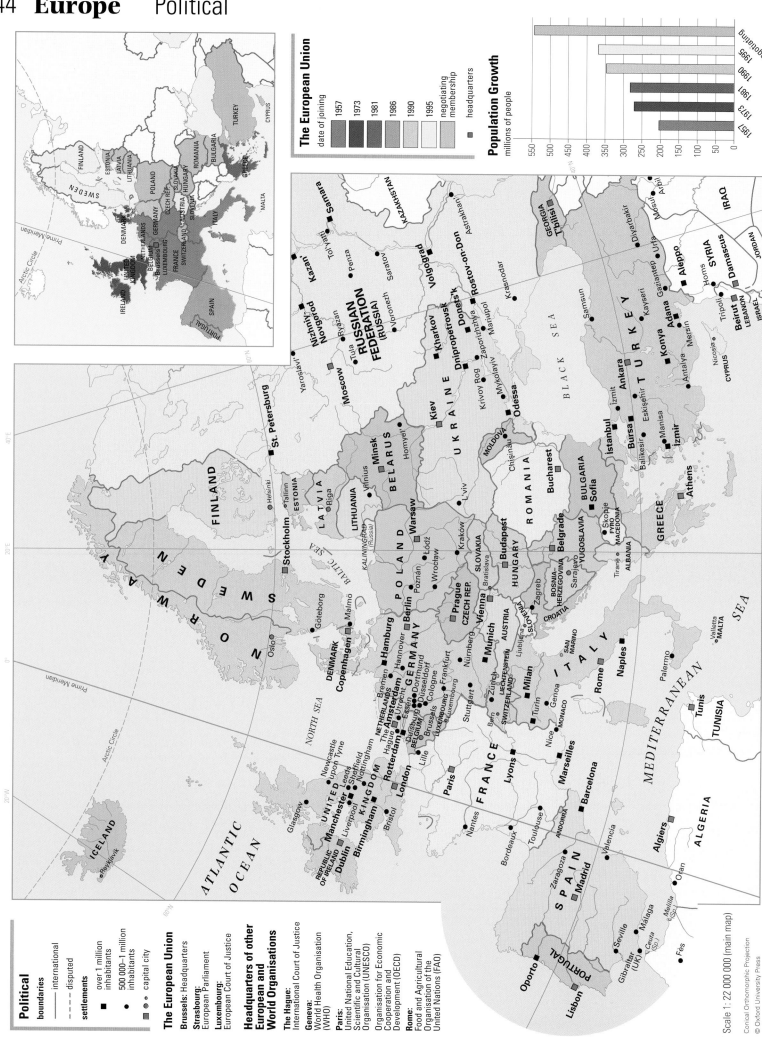

The European Union

date of joining

- 1957
- 1973
- 1981
- 1986
- 1990
- 1995
- negotiating membership
- ■ headquarters

Population Growth
millions of people

negotiating
1995
1990
1981
1973
1957

550 500 450 400 350 300 250 200 150 100 50 0

Political

boundaries
— international
--- disputed

settlements
- ■ over 1 million inhabitants
- ■ 500 000–1 million inhabitants
- ● capital city

The European Union
Brussels: Headquarters

Strasbourg:
European Parliament

Luxembourg:
European Court of Justice

Headquarters of other European and World Organisations

The Hague:
International Court of Justice

Geneva:
World Health Organisation (WHO)

Paris:
United National Education, Scientific and Cultural Organisation (UNESCO)
Organisation for Economic Cooperation and Development (OECD)

Rome:
Food and Agricultural Organisation of the United Nations (FAO)

Scale 1 : 22 000 000 (main map)

Conical Orthomorphic Projection
© Oxford University Press

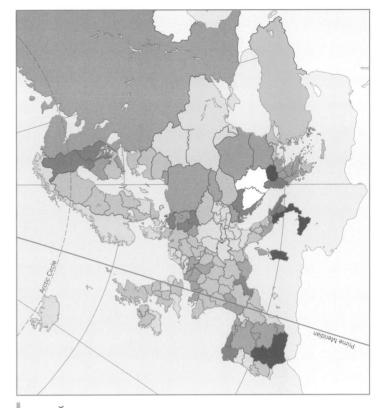

European Union budget, 2000

net contributions to and receipts from (in pounds)

contributions

- over 5 billion
- 1–5 billion
- 0–1 billion

receipts

- 0–1 billion
- 1–5 billion

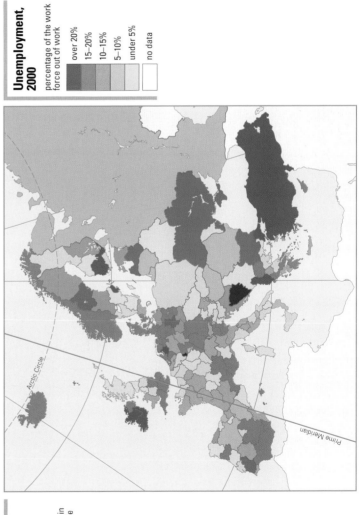

Unemployment, 2000

percentage of the work force out of work

- over 20%
- 15–20%
- 10–15%
- 5–10%
- under 5%
- no data

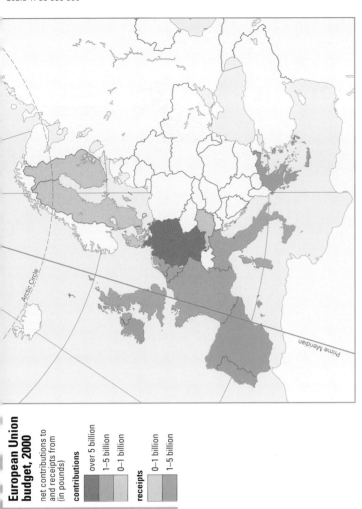

Yekaterinburg
Perm
Ufa
Samara
Kazan
Nizhniy Novgorod
Volgograd
Rostov-na-Donu
St Petersburg
Moscow
Kharkiv
Donets'k
Minsk
Kiev
Dnipropetrovsk
Odessa
Istanbul Ankara
Adana
Konya
Bursa
Izmir
Athens
Stockholm
Warsaw
Bucharest
Copenhagen
Vienna
Budapest
Belgrade
Sofia
Berlin
Prague
Hamburg
Amsterdam
Munich
Milan
Rome
Manchester
Rotterdam
Paris
Lyons
Naples
Marseilles
Dublin
Liverpool
Birmingham
London
Barcelona
Madrid
Oporto
Lisbon

Population density

people per square kilometre

- over 200
- 100–200
- 10–100
- 1–10
- under 1

Major cities

population in millions

- ■ over 3
- □ 1–3
- ● 0.5–1
- · 0.1–0.5

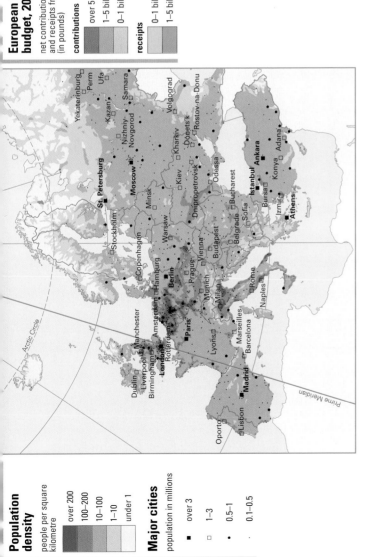

Population change, 1995–2000

percentage change in the number of people

increase

- over 8%
- 4–8%
- 2–4%
- 1–2%
- 0–1%

decrease

- 0–1%
- 1–2%
- 2–4%
- over 4%

Conical Orthomorphic Projection

Scale 1: 22 000 000

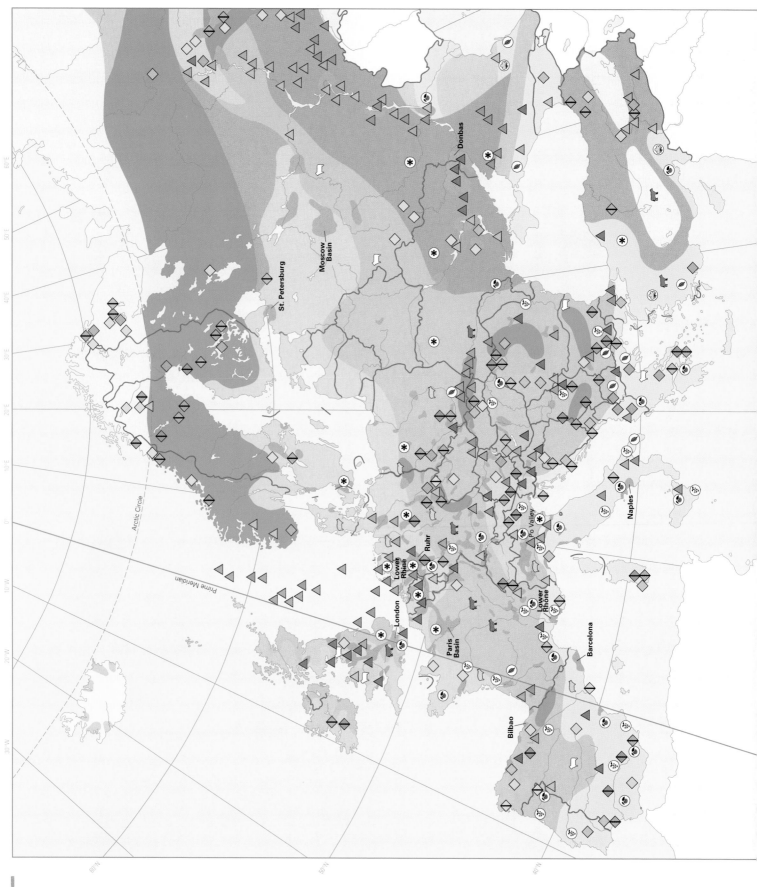

St. Petersburg

Moscow Basin

Donbas

London

Lower Rhine

Ruhr

Paris Basin

Po Valley

Lower Rhône

Bilbao

Barcelona

Naples

Arctic Circle

Prime Meridian

Conical Orthomorphic Projection

Land use

rough grazing
shifting cultivation
mixed subsistence
grazing and stock rearing
mixed farming
grain farming
Mediterranean farming
dairy farming
specialized horticulture
forestry
industrial areas
unproductive land

Livestock

sheep
cattle
pig

Crops

wine grapes
tobacco
fruit
sugar
cotton

Minerals

iron ore
manganese
chromium
nickel
tin
lead
zinc
copper
bauxite

Energy

coal
oil
gas
hydro

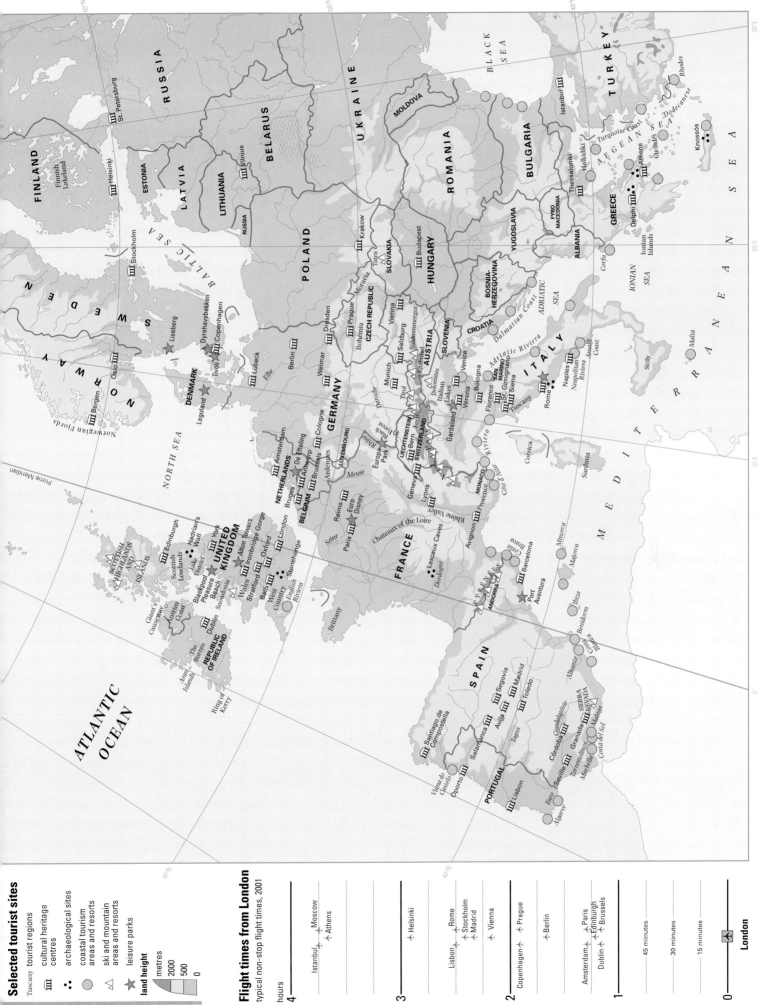

Scale 1: 17 000 000

Selected tourist sites

Tuscany tourist regions

- 𝄞 cultural heritage centres
- ∴ archaeological sites
- ⬤ coastal tourism areas and resorts
- △ ski and mountain areas and resorts
- ★ leisure parks

land height

metres
2000
500
0

Flight times from London

typical non-stop flight times, 2001

hours

4 — Istanbul ✈ Moscow
  ✈ Athens

3 — ✈ Helsinki
  Lisbon ✈ Rome
  ✈ Stockholm
  ✈ Madrid
  ✈ Vienna

2 — Copenhagen ✈ Prague
  ✈ Berlin

  Amsterdam ✈ Paris
  ✈ Edinburgh
1 — Dublin ✈ Brussels

  45 minutes

  30 minutes

  15 minutes

0 — ✈ London

© Oxford University Press   Conical Orthomorphic Projection

NORTH SEA

Waddeneilanden (West Frisian Islands)

Ostfriesische Inseln (East Frisian Islands)

NETHERLANDS

Amsterdam

Rotterdam

BELGIUM

Brussels (Bruxelles)

GERMANY

LUXEMBOURG

FRANCE

Scale 1: 2 500 000

0   25   50   75   100   125 km

Conical Orthomorphic Projection

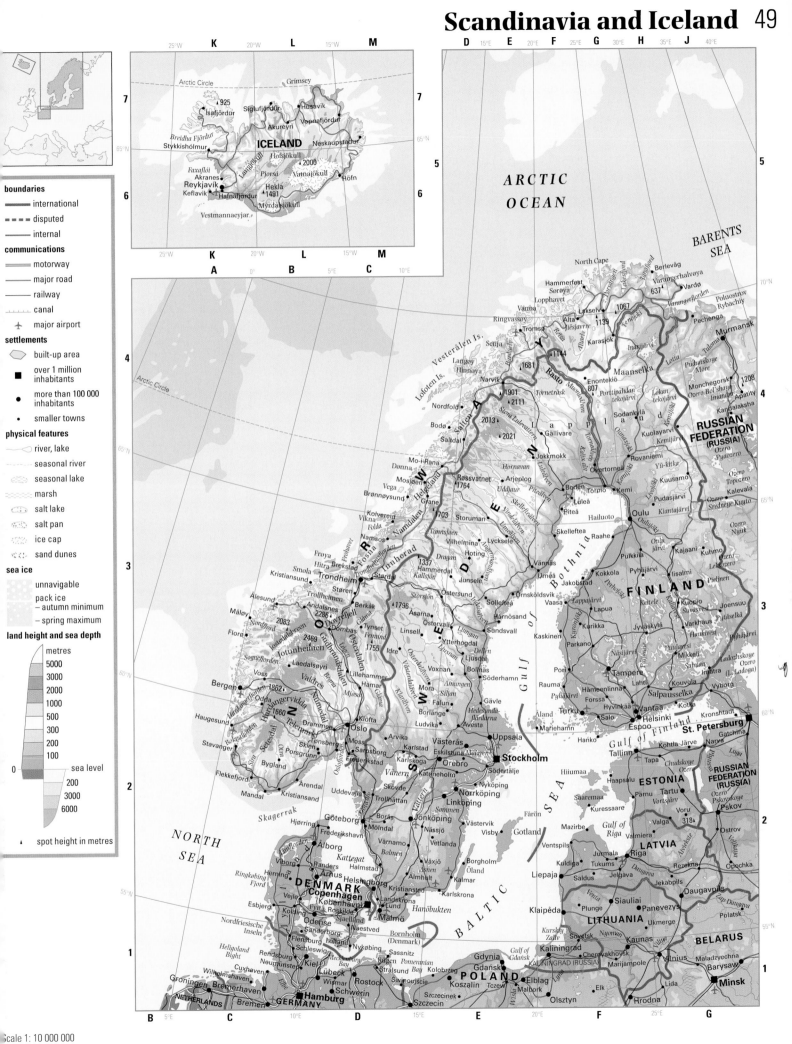

ICELAND

boundaries
- international
- disputed
- internal

communications
- motorway
- major road
- railway
- canal
- major airport

settlements
- built-up area
- over 1 million inhabitants
- more than 100 000 inhabitants
- smaller towns

physical features
- river, lake
- seasonal river
- seasonal lake
- marsh
- salt lake
- salt pan
- ice cap
- sand dunes

sea ice
- unnavigable
- pack ice
  – autumn minimum
  – spring maximum

land height and sea depth

metres
5000
3000
2000
1000
500
300
200
100
0 sea level
200
3000
6000

- spot height in metres

Scale 1: 10 000 000

100   200   300   400   500 km

Conical Orthomorphic Projection
© Oxford University Press

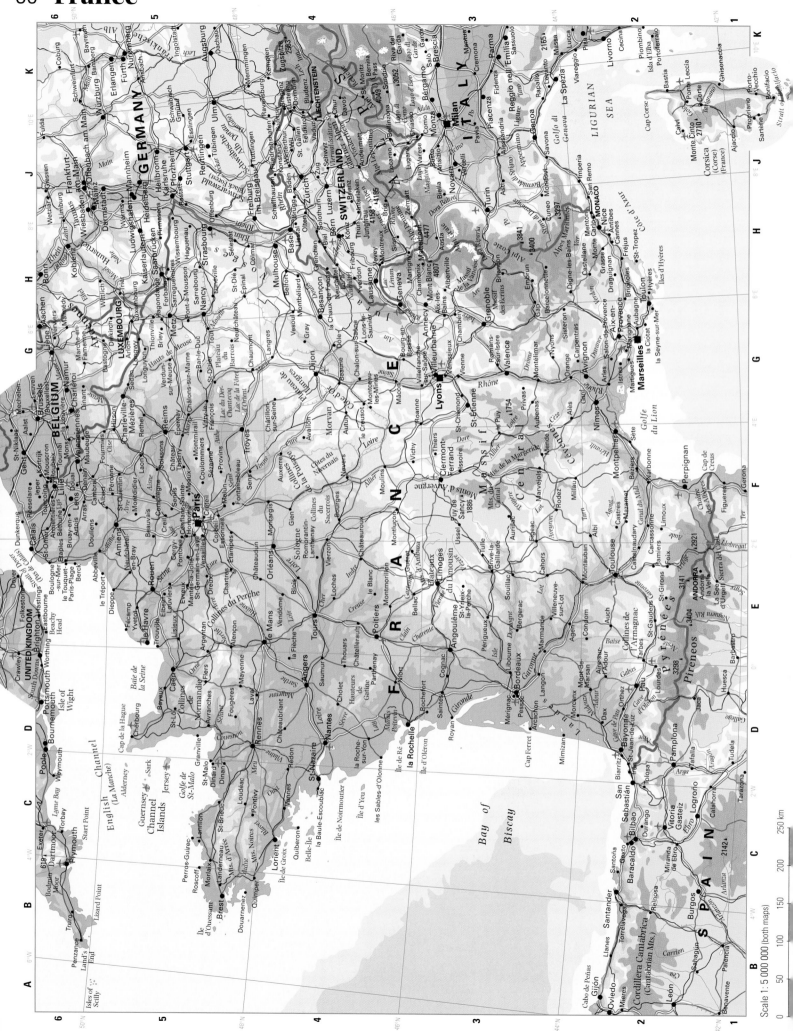

Scale 1: 5 000 000 (both maps)

0   50   100   150   200   250 km

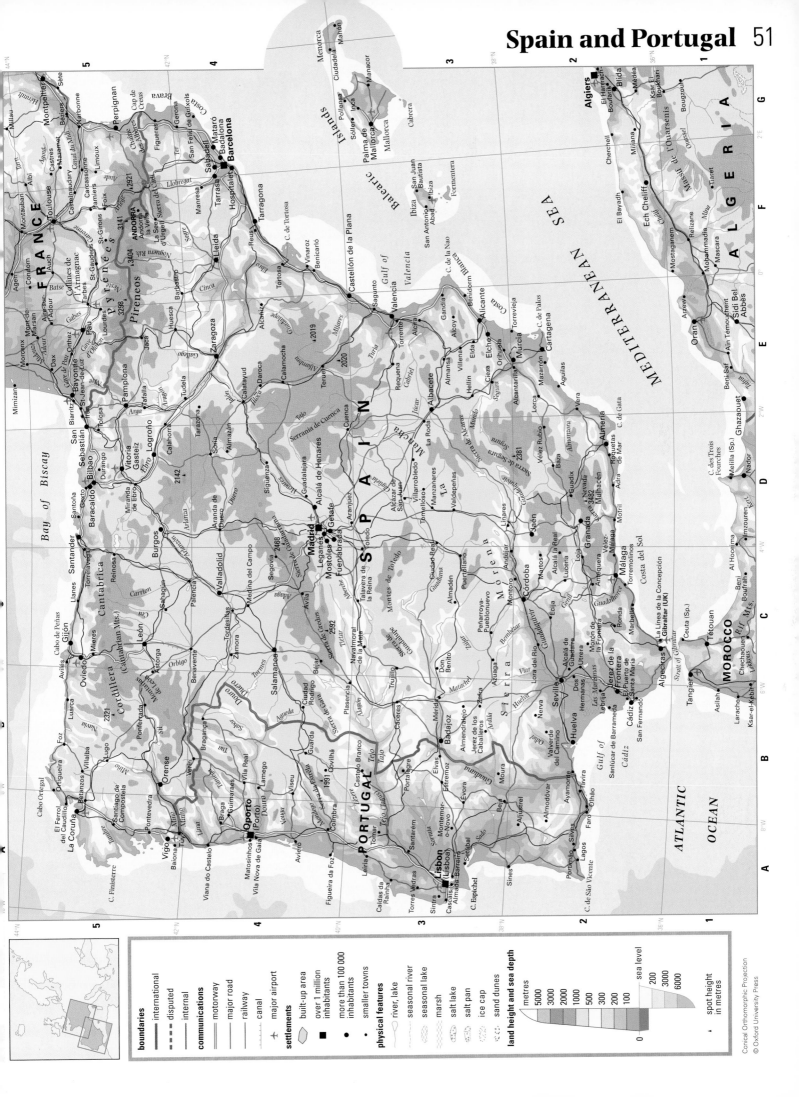

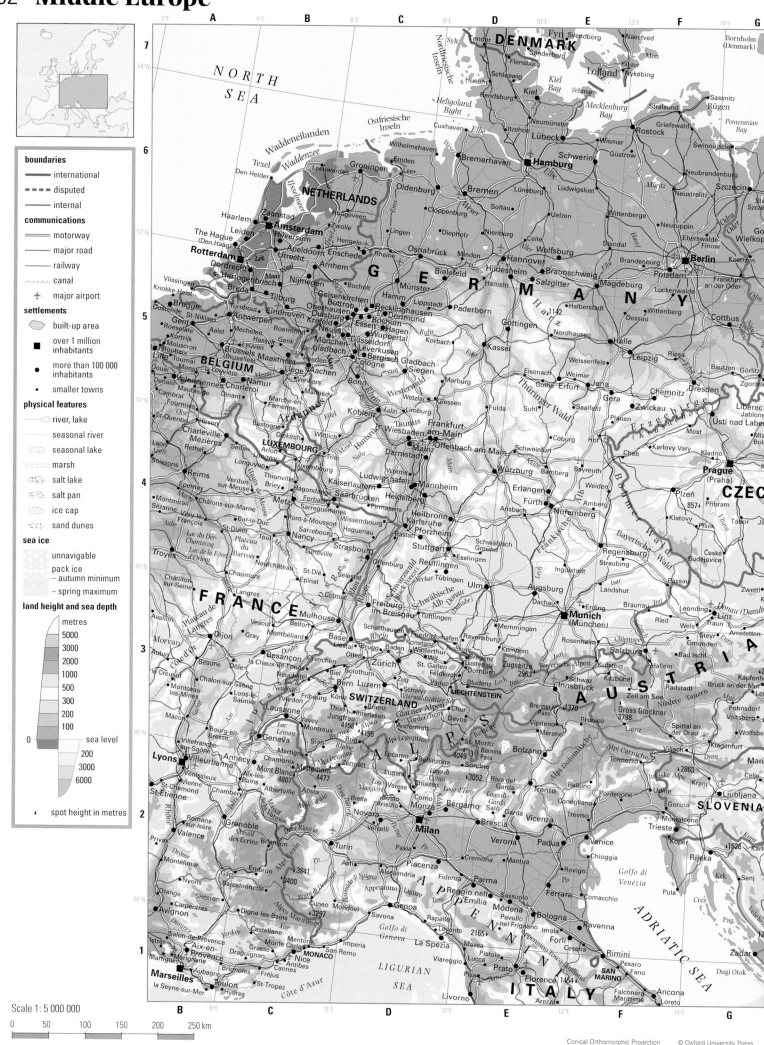

Conical Orthomorphic Projection

BALTIC SEA

Gulf of Gdansk

Kurskiy Zaliv

LITHUANIA

BELARUS

POLAND

UKRAINE

SLOVAKIA

HUNGARY

ROMANIA

CROATIA

BOSNIA-HERZEGOVINA

YUGOSLAVIA

BULGARIA

MOLDOVA

UKRAINE

REPUBLIC

CARPATHIANS

Meridionali

Carpatii

Beskidy Zachodnie

Jura Krakowska

Tatry

Nízke Tatry

Dinara Planina

Darłowo, Wejherowo, Gdynia, Sopot, Słupsk, Gdańsk, Koszalin, Elbląg, Tczew, Malbork, Starogard Gdański, Ostróda, Iława, Chojnice, Grudziądz, Olsztyn, Szczecinek, Wałcz, Jastrowie, Piła, Bydgoszcz, Toruń, Inowrocław, Gniezno, Poznań, Kościan, Leszno, Jarocin, Kalisz, Konin, Koło, Kutno, Włocławek, Płock, Ciechanów, Krotoszyn, Zgierz, Łódź, Pabianice, Zduńska Wola, Łowicz, Skierniewice, Żyrardów, Pruszków, Warsaw (Warszawa), Ostrów Wielkopolski, Głogów, Nowa Sól, Legnica, Zielona Góra, Wrocław, Brzeg, Częstochowa, Opole, Piotrków Trybunalski, Tomaszów Mazowiecki, Radom, Puławy, Myszków, Kielce, Radomsko, Włoszczowa, Kłodzko, Nysa, Bytom, Zabrze, Sosnowiec, Gliwice, Katowice, Racibórz, Rybnik, Kraków, Tarnów, Rzeszów, Przeworsk, Wisłok, Nowy Sącz, Nowy Targ, Jasło, Krosno, Przemyśl

Sovetsk, Neman, Kaliningrad, KALININGRAD (RUSSIA), Chernyakhovsk, Gusev, Marijampolé, Kaunas, Vilnius, Suwałki, Ełk, Ketrzyn, Hrodna, Lida, Maladzyechna, Barysaw, Mahilyow, Dzyarzhynsk, Minsk, Babruysk, Zhlobin, Szczytno, Jezioro Śniardwy, Łomża, Biebrza, Ostrołęka, Narew, Białystok, Słonim, Baranavichy, Slutsk, Soligorsk, Homyel', Mława, Ostrów Mazowiecka, Bielsk Podlaski, Pinsk, Luninyets, Pripyat, Ptsich, Mazyr, Rechitsa, Siedlce, Łuków, Biała Podlaska, Brest, Kobryn, Ratno, Sarny, Uhor', Korosten, Kalinkavichy, Nowy Dwór Mazowiecki, Chornobyl', Pilica, Wieprz, Chełm, Lublin, Zamość, Vladimir Volynskiy, Kovel', Novograd Volynskiy, Starachowice, Ostrowiec Świętokrzyski, Stalowa Wola, Chervonograd, Luts'k, Rivne, Zhytomyr, Fastov, Kiev, Bila Tserkva, Tarnobrzeg, Brody, Dubno, Kremenets, Berdychiv, Kazatin, L'viv, Zolochev, Ternopil', Khmel'nyts'kyy, Vinnytsya, Sambor, Drohobych, Borislav, Stryy, Dnestr, Kopychintsy, Zhmerynka, Zakopane, Poprad, Prešov, Uzhgorod, Ivano-Frankivs'k, Kam"yanets'-Podil's'kyy, Mohyliv-Podil's'kyy, Bug, Dolina, Kolomyya, Khotin, Nistru (Dnestr), Košice, Žilina, Ružomberok, Martin, Trenčín, Prievidza, Banská Bystrica, Zvolen, Rožňava, Mukachevo, Beregovo, Chernivtsi, Prut, Dorohoi, Floresti, Balta, Soroca, Bălţi, Olomouc, Přerov, Brno, Zlín, Znojmo, Stockerau, Klosterneuburg, Wien (Vienna), Schwechat, Eisenstadt, Wiener Neustadt, Sopron, Mosonmagyaróvár, Neusiedler See, Bratislava, Nitra, Levice, Komárno, Esztergom, Vác, Gödöllő, Salgótarján, Balassagyarmat, Eger, Miskolc, Nyíregyháza, Satu Mare, Carei, Baia Mare, Sighetu Marmaţiei, Borşa, Vatra Dornei, Rădăuţi, Suceava, Paşcani, Iaşi, Chişinău, Tighina, Tiraspol', Cimişlia, Comrat, Roman, Vaslui, Bârlad, Sarata, Bolhrad, Izmayil, Győr, Tatabánya, Pápa, Szombathely, Veszprém, Székesfehérvár, Budapest, Cegléd, Szolnok, Gyöngyös, Karcag, Debrecen, Zalău, Bistrita, Dej, Cluj-Napoca, Toplita, Piatra Neamţ, Bacău, Buhuşi, Oneşti, Adjud, Tecuci, Galaţi, Ianca, Brăila, Tulcea, Lacul Razim, Zalaegerszeg, Nagykanizsa, Kaposvár, Čakovec, Varaždin, Pécs, Szekszárd, Baja, Kecskemét, Kiskunfélegyháza, Kiskunhalas, Hódmezővásárhely, Makó, Szeged, Arad, Oradea, Beiuş, Ciucea, Turda, Târgu Mureş, Sighişoara, Mediaş, Comăneşti, Miercurea-Ciuc, Sfântu Gheorghe, Focşani, Râmnicu Sărat, Buzău, Salonta, Békéscsaba, Subotica, Kikinda, Sombor, Timişoara, Lugoj, Deva, Hunedoara, Brad, Alba Iulia, Sebeş, Făgăraş, Braşov, Sibiu, Câmpulung, Râmnicu Vâlcea, Târgovişte, Ploieşti, Câmpina, Titu, Bucharest, Urziceni, Slobozia, Călăraşi, Constanţa, Eforie, Mangalia, Zagreb, Sisak, Virovitica, Osijek, Slavonski Brod, Vinkovci, Vukovar, Zrenjanin, Novi Sad, Drava, Sava, Caransebeş, Reşiţa, Oraviţa, Vršac, Petroşani, Târgu Jiu, Orşova, Drobeta-Turnu-Severin, Vidin, Montana, Piteşti, Slatina, Caracal, Alexandria, Roşiori de Vede, Giurgiu, Ruse, Razgrad, Şumen, Varna, Dobrich, Prijedor, Banja Luka, Doboj, Tuzla, Loznica, Valjevo, Šabac, Belgrade, Smederevo, Pančevo, Craiova, Olt, Turnu Măgurele, Zenica, Sarajevo, Split, Neretva, Titovo Užice, Čačak, Kragujevac, Kraljevo, Kruševac, Kralj, Vidin, Pavlikeni, Türgovishte, Pleven, Iskŭr, Drina

Neman, Łyna, Wisła, Notec, Warta, Oder, Odra, Morawa, Vah, Hron, Tisza, Duna (Danube), Dunav (Danube), Dunărea (Danube), Mureş, Dobrogea, Siret, Bistrita, Moldova, Prut, Someş, Crişul, Tisza, Barcau, Kriva, Balaton

1490, 2663, 2043, 1074, 1836, 2058, 2102, 1827, 2548, 1336, 2107, 1015

© Oxford University Press

HUNGARY

Tatabánya · Budapest · Karcag · Zalău · Dej · Bistrița · 2102 · Roman · MOLDOVA · Cimislia
Pápa · Ceglёd · Szolnok · Ciucea · Toplita · Piatra Neamț · Buhuşi · Vaslui · Comrat
Szombathely · Székesfehérvár · Veszprém · Kecskemét · Oradea · Cluj-Napoca · Bacău · Comănești · Onești · Bârlad · Sarata
Kiskunfélegyháza · Salonta · Beiuş · Turda · Târgu Mureş · Miercurea-Ciuc · Comănești · Adjud · Tecuci · Belhrad
Nagykanizsa · Kiskunhalas · Hódmezovasarhely · 1827 · Medias · Sighişoara · Baraolt · Sfântu Gheorghe · Focşani · Galați · Izmayil · UKRAINE
Kaposvár · Szekszárd · Szeged · Makó · Arad · Brad · Sebeş · Alba Iulia · Sibiu · Făgăraş · Braşov · Tulcea · Lacul Razim
Pécs · Baja · Lipova · Deva · Hunedoara · ROMANIA · 2548 · Râmnicu Sărat · Brăila · Ilanca
Barcs · Subotica · Timişoara · Caransebeş · Lugoj · Meridionali · Câmpulung · Câmpina · Buzău · Dobrogea
CROATIA · Virovitica · Sombor · Kikinda · Reşita · Carpaţii · Râmnica Vâlcea · Târgovişte · Ploieşti · Urziceni · Lacul Razim
Osijek · Zrenjanin · Vršac · Oravita · Târgu Jiu · Piteşti · Titu · Slobozia · Constanța
Slavonski Brod · Vukovar · Novi Sad · Petroşani · Costeşti · Bucharest · Călăraşi · Eforie · Silistra
Doboj · Vinkovci · Pančevo · Orşova · Drobeta-Turnu-Severin · Slatina · Dunărea (Danube) · Mangalia
BOSNIA-HERZEGOVINA · Loznica · Šabac · Belgrade · Smederevo · Craiova · Caracal · Alexandria · Giurgiu · Ruse · Dobrich
Zenica · Valjevo · YUGOSLAVIA · Turnu Măgurele · Roşiori de Vede · Oltenița
2107 · Tuzla · Čačak · 1336 · Kragujevac · Vidin · Dunav (Danube) · Rezgrad · Varna
Sarajevo · Titovo Užice · Kraljevo · Kruševac · Montana · Vratsa · Pleven · Veliko Tŭrnovo · Tŭrgovishte · Shumen
Mostar · 2522 · Novi Pazar · Niš · Lovech · Gabrovo · Sliven · Karnobat · BLACK SEA
Metković · Nikšić · Kosovska Mitrovica · Leskovac · BULGARIA · Kazanlŭk · Stara Zagora · Yambol · Burgas
Trebinje · MONTENEGRO · 2382 · Priština · Vranje · Pernik · Sofia · Pazardzhik · Planina · Dimitrovgrad · Kŭrlkareli
Dubrovnik · Podgorica · 2682 · Peć · Uroševac · Kyustendil · 2925 · Plovdiv · Khaskovo · Edirne · Kirklareli
Skadarsko ezero · Prizren · Blagoevgrad · Asenovgrad · Svilengrad · Lüleburgaz · Kilyos
Shkodër · Drin · Kukës · Tetovo · Kumanovo · Štip · Arda · Smolyan · Rodopi Planina · Corlu · İstanbul
Lezhe · 2702 · Skopje · 2915 · Pirin Planina · Komotini · Ergene · Tekirdağ · SEA OF MARMARA
ALBANIA · Gostivar · Titov Veles · FYRO MACEDONIA · Xanthi · Keşan · Gelibolu · Bandirma
Tiranë · Prilep · Gevgelija · Kilkís · Sérres · Dráma · Kavála · Alexandroúpoli · 1767 · Biga · Mustafakemalpaşa
Durrës · Kavajë · Elbasan · Bitola · Yiannitsá · Strimonas · Amfipoli · 1045 · Thásos · Samothráki · Çanakkale · TURKEY
Lushnjë · Prespansko ezero · Édessa · Thessaloníki · Chalkidikí · Gökçeada · Balikesir
Fier · Berat · 2379 · Flórina · Véroia · Polýgyros · Áthos 2033 · Edremit · Kirkağaç
Vlorë · Korçë · Kastoriá · Katerini · Thermaïkós Kólpos · Límnos · Bergama · Akhisar · Manisa
Gjirokastër · 2633 · Kozáni · Ólympos 2917 · AEGEAN SEA · Lésvos · Mytilíni · Salihli
Strait of Otranto · Ioánnina · Lárisa · Vólos · Vórei oi Sporádes (Northern Sporades) · Skýros · İzmir · Ödemiş
Kérkyra (Corfu) · Trikala · Chíos · Torbalı · Nazilli
Corfu · GREECE · Skýros · Chíos · Büyük Menderes · Çine
Árta · 2128 · Karpenísi · Évvoia (Euboea) · Sámos · Milas
Iónia Nisiá (Ionian Islands) · Préveza · Lamía · Parnassós 2457 · Chalkída · Ándros · Çine
Lefkáda · Agrínio · Leivadiá · Thíva · Ákra Kafiréas · Tínos · Íkaria · Muğla
Mesolóngi · Kefalloniá · Korinthiakós Kólpos · Aígio · Thíva · Ákra · Kéa · Kýthnos · Kyklades (Cyclades) · Kálymnos · Gökova Körfezi
Patras · Kórinthos · Piraeus · Athens · Sé[r]ifos · Páros · Náxos · Amorgós · Kós
IONIAN SEA · Zákynthos · Pýrgos · Náfplio · Kýthnos · Sífnos · Íos · Astypálaia · Dodekánisos (Dodecanese)
Peloponnísos · Trípoli · MIRTOAN SEA · Milos · Thíra (Santoríni) · Anáfi · 1215
Kyparissiakós Kólpos · Alfeiós · Kalamáta · Spárti · Monemvasía · Milos · Ródos (Rhodes)
Ákra Akrítas · 2407 · Neápoli · Ákra Maléas · SEA OF CRETE · Kárpathos
Kýthira · Kásos
Gávdos · Chaniá · Iráklion · Réthymno · 2456 · Agios Nikólaos · Kríti (Crete) · Pýrgos

Bari · Monopoli · Bríndisi · Lecce · Táranto · Golfo di Táranto · Gallipoli · Otranto · Capo Santa Maria di Leuca · Ciro Marina · Crotone · Golfo di Squillace

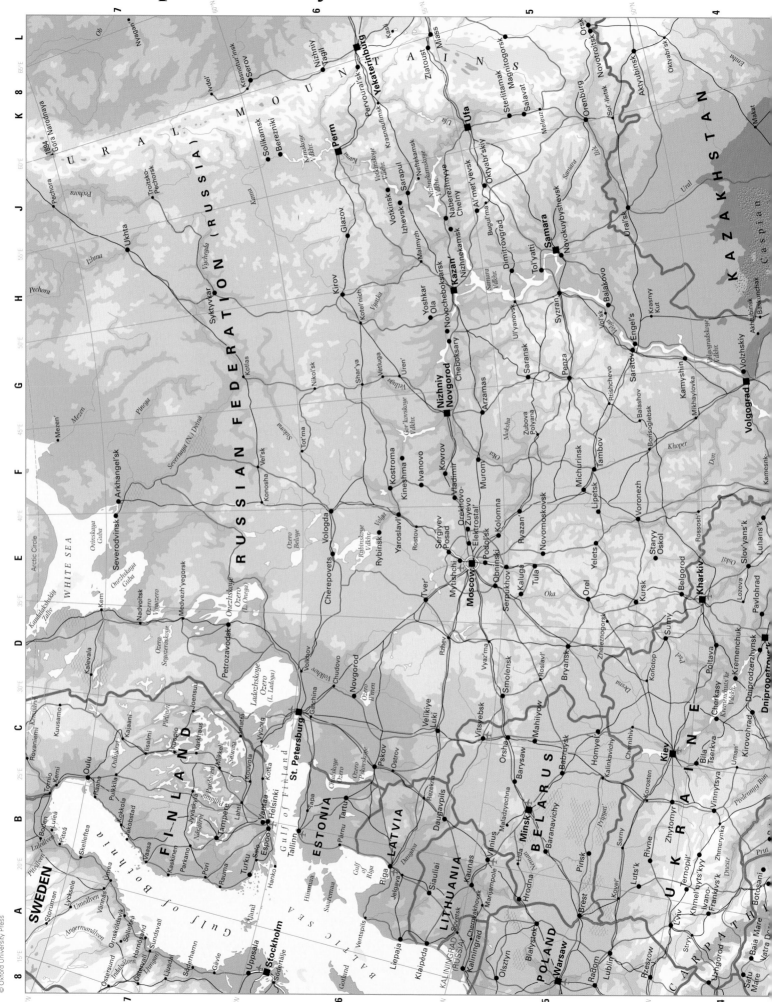

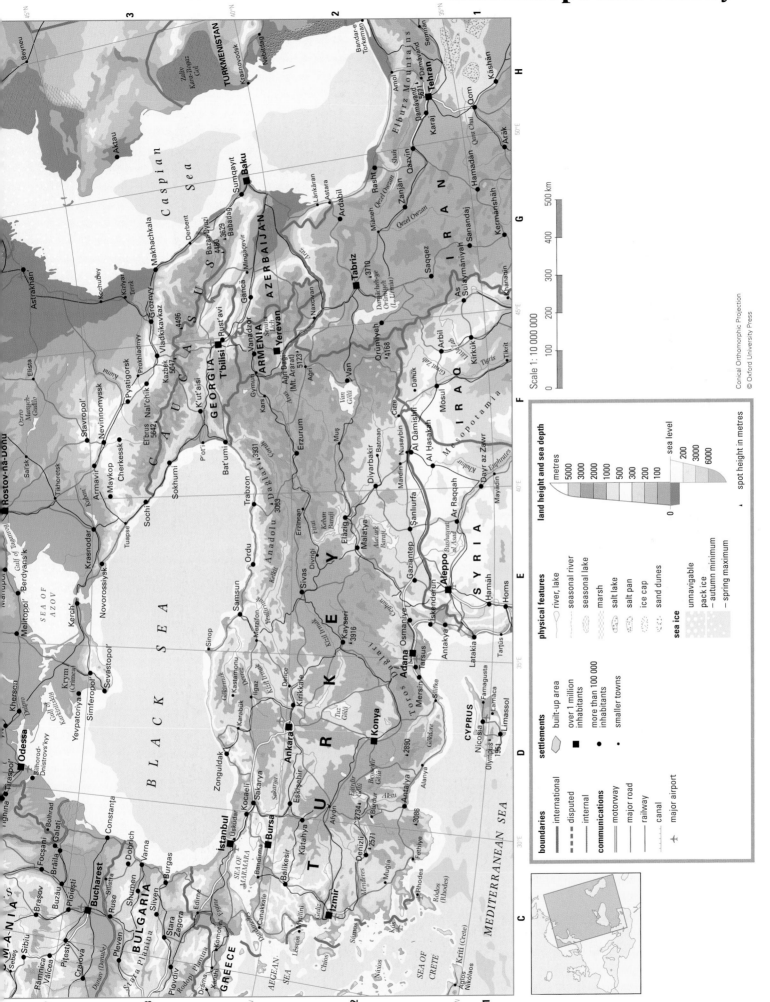

Scale 1: 10 000 000

0   100   200   300   400   500 km

Conical Orthomorphic Projection

© Oxford University Press

boundaries
— international
--- disputed
— internal

communications
— motorway
— major road
— railway
— canal
✈ major airport

settlements
⬡ built-up area
■ over 1 million inhabitants
● more than 100 000 inhabitants
• smaller towns

physical features
river, lake
seasonal river
seasonal lake
marsh
salt lake
salt pan
ice cap
sand dunes

sea ice
unnavigable
pack ice
– autumn minimum
– spring maximum

land height and sea depth
metres
5000
3000
2000
1000
500
300
200
100
sea level
200
3000
6000
▴ spot height in metres

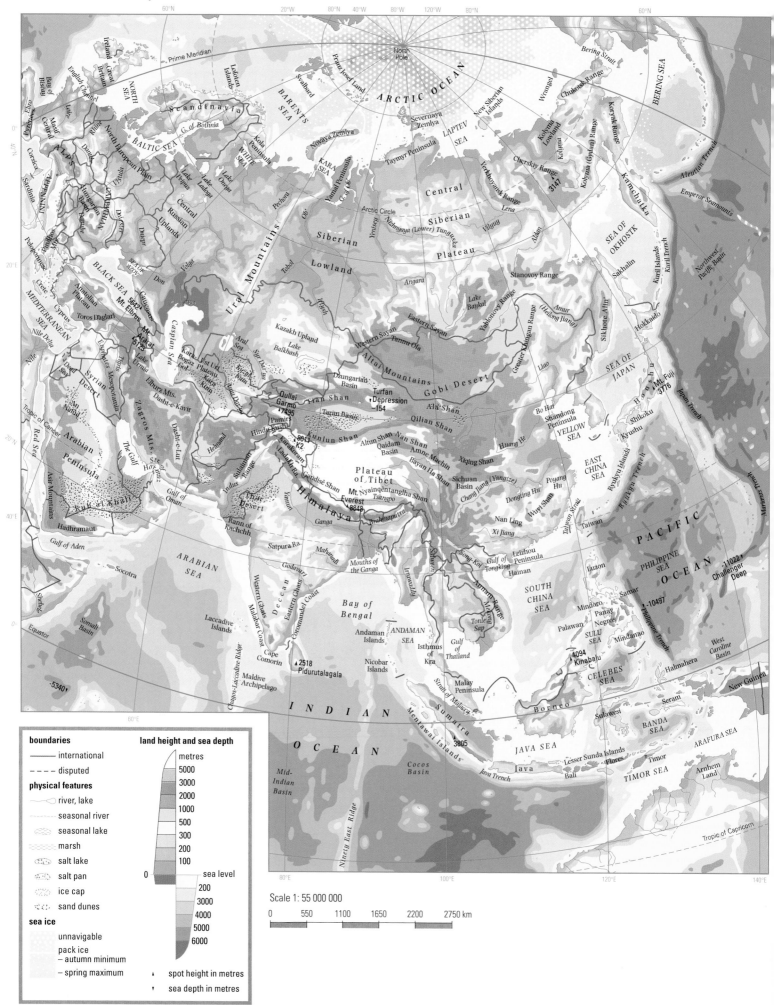

boundaries

——	international
- - -	disputed

physical features

river, lake
seasonal river
seasonal lake
marsh
salt lake
salt pan
ice cap
sand dunes

sea ice

unnavigable

pack ice
— autumn minimum
— spring maximum

land height and sea depth

metres
5000
3000
2000
1000
500
300
200
100
0   sea level
200
3000
4000
5000
6000

▲ spot height in metres
▼ sea depth in metres

Scale 1: 55 000 000

0   550   1100   1650   2200   2750 km

Zenithal equal Area Projection   © Oxford University Press

Scale 1: 60 000 000

EUROPE

UNITED
KINGDOM

FRANCE
GERMANY
POLAND
BELARUS
UKRAINE

ITALY
ROMANIA

NORWAY
SWEDEN
FINLAND

Kaliningrad
(part of Russian
Federation)

Moscow

ARCTIC OCEAN

North
Pole

Prime Meridian

Arctic Circle

RUSSIAN FEDERATION
(RUSSIA)

Kuril
Islands
(Russia)

Administered by Russia
Claimed by Japan

GREECE
Ankara
TURKEY
GEORGIA
ARMENIA
Tbilisi
Yerevan
AZERBAIJAN
Baku

KAZAKHSTAN
Astana

LEBANON
Beirut
ISRAEL
Jerusalem
SYRIA
Damascus
Amman
JORDAN
IRAQ
Baghdad

UZBEKISTAN
Tashkent
TURKMENISTAN
Ashgabat
Bishkek
KIRGYZSTAN
Dushanbe
TAJIKISTAN

Ulan Bator
MONGOLIA

NORTH
KOREA
Pyongyang
Seoul
SOUTH
KOREA

Tokyo
JAPAN

EGYPT

KUWAIT
Kuwait
Tehran
IRAN

Kabul
AFGHANISTAN
Jammu &
Kashmir
Islamabad

Beijing

CHINA

Tropic of Cancer

Riyadh
BAHRAIN
Manama
QATAR
SAUDI
ARABIA
Doha
UNITED
ARAB
EMIRATES
Abu Dhabi
Muscat
OMAN

PAKISTAN

New
Delhi

NEPAL
Kathmandu
BHUTAN
Thimphu

Ryukyu
Islands
(Japan)

Taibei
TAIWAN

Sana
YEMEN
REPUBLIC

DJIBOUTI

SOMALIA

Socotra
(Yemen Rep.)

Equator

INDIA

Lakshadweep
(India)

Dhaka
BANGLADESH
MYANMAR

Yangon

LAOS
Hanoi
Vientiane

PACIFIC
OCEAN

MALDIVES

Malé

Colombo
SRI LANKA

Andaman
Islands
(India)

Nicobar
Islands
(India)

THAILAND
Bangkok
CAMBODIA
VIETNAM
Phnom Penh

Manila
PHILIPPINES

BRUNEI
Bandar
Seri Begawan

MALAYSIA

Kuala Lumpur
SINGAPORE

INDIAN
OCEAN

INDONESIA

Jakarta

Dili
EAST
TIMOR

international boundary
disputed boundary
capital city

Asian urban and rural population, 2000

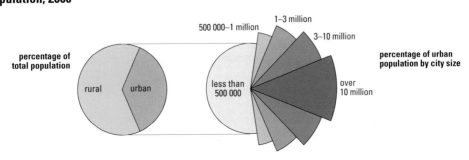

percentage of
total population

rural urban

500 000–1 million
1–3 million
3–10 million

less than
500 000

over
10 million

percentage of urban
population by city size

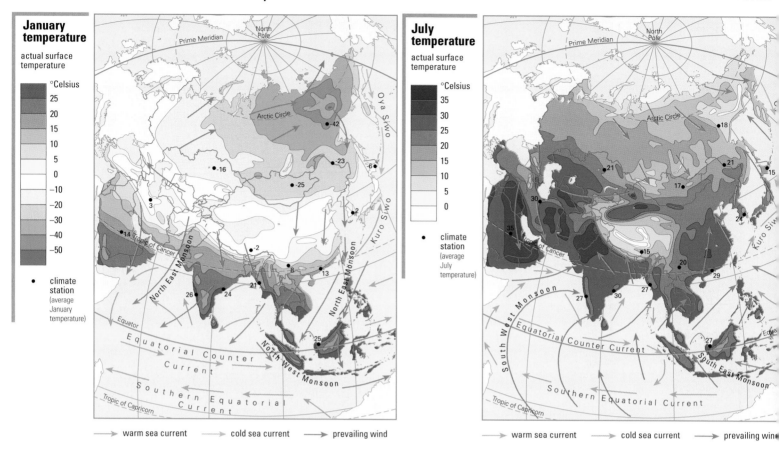

January temperature

actual surface temperature

°Celsius
25
20
15
10
5
0
−10
−20
−30
−40
−50

● climate station
(average January temperature)

→ warm sea current   → cold sea current   → prevailing wind

July temperature

actual surface temperature

°Celsius
35
30
25
20
15
10
5
0

● climate station
(average July temperature)

→ warm sea current   → cold sea current   → prevailing win

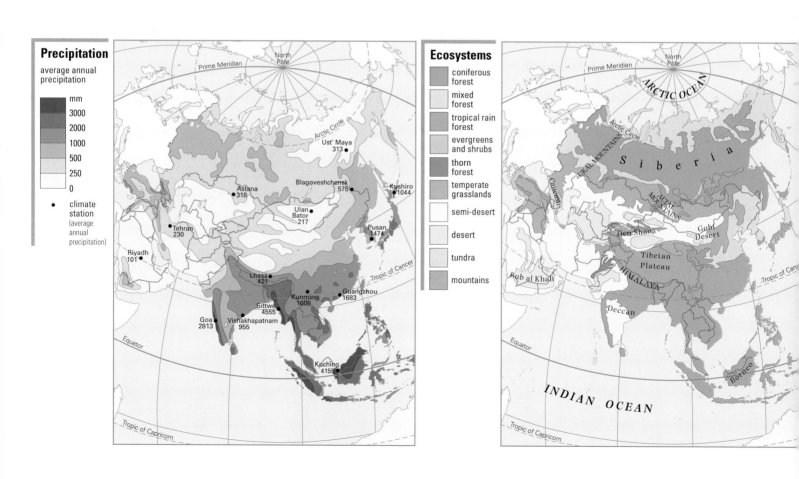

Precipitation

average annual precipitation

mm
3000
2000
1000
500
250
0

● climate station
(average annual precipitation)

Ust' Maya 313
Astana 318
Blagoveshchensk 575
Kushiro 1044
Ulan Bator 217
Tehran 230
Pusan 1474
Riyadh 101
Lhasa 421
Kunming 1008
Guangzhou 1683
Sittwe 4555
Goa 2813
Vishakhapatnam 955
Kuching 4155

Ecosystems

- coniferous forest
- mixed forest
- tropical rain forest
- evergreens and shrubs
- thorn forest
- temperate grasslands
- semi-desert
- desert
- tundra
- mountains

ARCTIC OCEAN
URAL MOUNTAINS
Siberia
ALTAI MOUNTAINS
Caucasus
Tien Shan
Gobi Desert
Tibetan Plateau
HIMALAYA
Rub al Khali
Deccan
INDIAN OCEAN
Borneo

Scale 1: 75 000 000

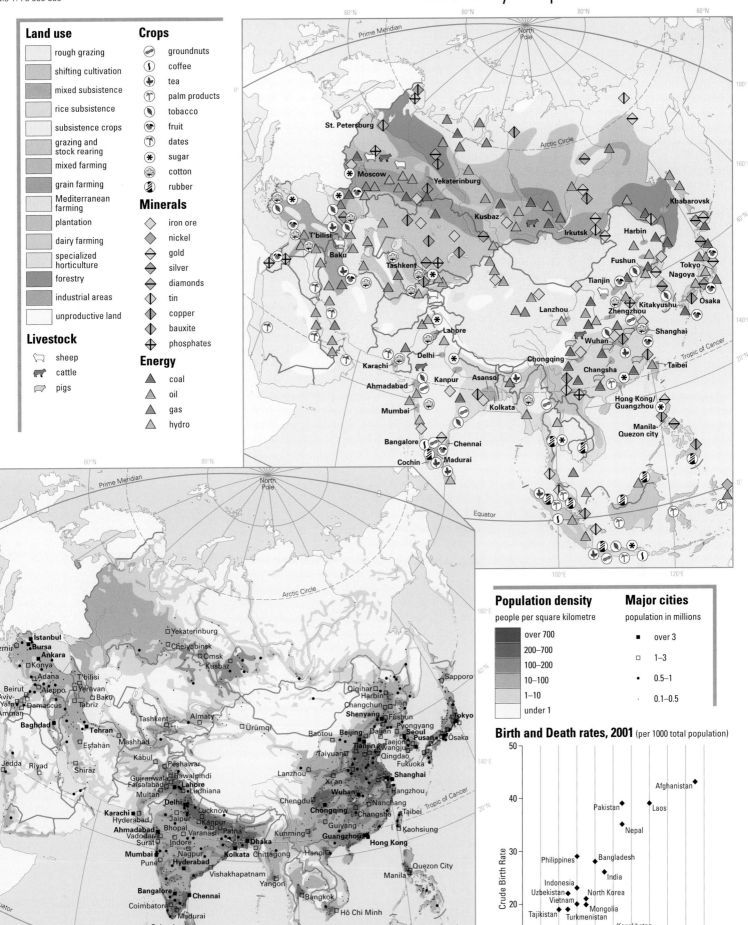

Land use

- rough grazing
- shifting cultivation
- mixed subsistence
- rice subsistence
- subsistence crops
- grazing and stock rearing
- mixed farming
- grain farming
- Mediterranean farming
- plantation
- dairy farming
- specialized horticulture
- forestry
- industrial areas
- unproductive land

Livestock

- sheep
- cattle
- pigs

Crops

- groundnuts
- coffee
- tea
- palm products
- tobacco
- fruit
- dates
- sugar
- cotton
- rubber

Minerals

- iron ore
- nickel
- gold
- silver
- diamonds
- tin
- copper
- bauxite
- phosphates

Energy

- coal
- oil
- gas
- hydro

Population density

people per square kilometre

- over 700
- 200–700
- 100–200
- 10–100
- 1–10
- under 1

Major cities

population in millions

- over 3
- 1–3
- 0.5–1
- 0.1–0.5

Birth and Death rates, 2001 (per 1000 total population)

Crude Birth Rate

Crude Death Rate

Afghanistan
Laos
Pakistan
Nepal
Philippines   Bangladesh
Indonesia   India
Uzbekistan   North Korea
Vietnam
Tajikistan   Mongolia
Turkmenistan
Kazakhstan
South Korea   Azerbaijan/China
Japan   Russia

Zenithal Equal Area Projection

© Oxford University Press

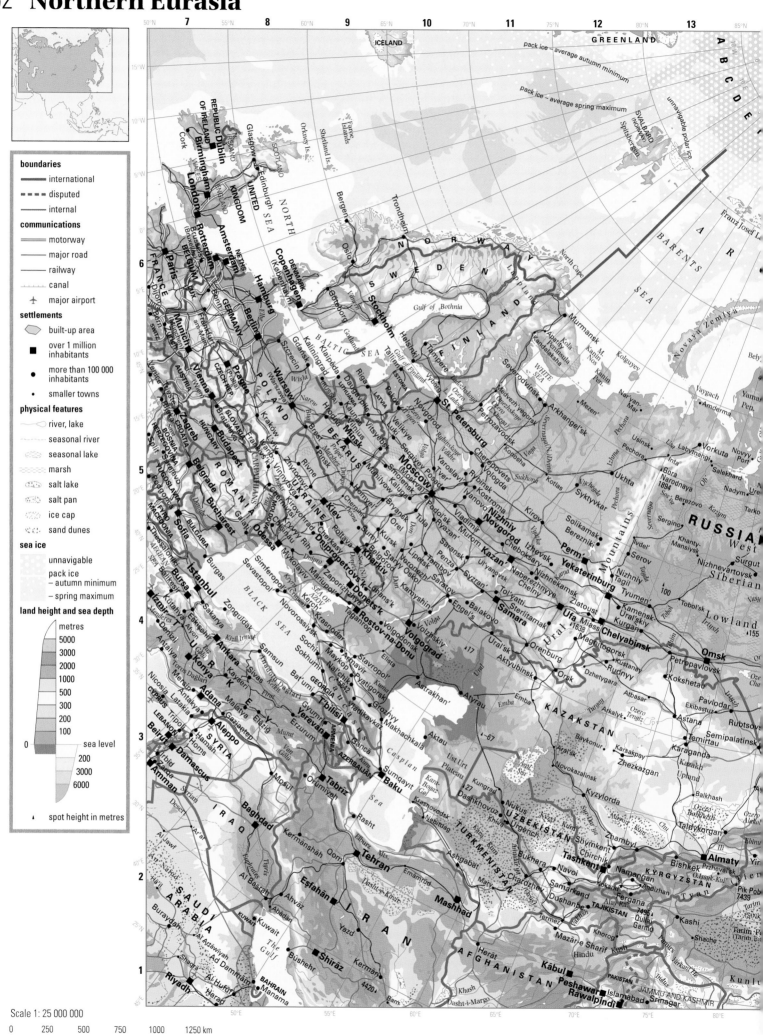

boundaries

	international
▬▬▬	disputed
────	internal

communications

	motorway
	major road
	railway
	canal
✈	major airport

settlements

⬡	built-up area
■	over 1 million inhabitants
●	more than 100 000 inhabitants
•	smaller towns

physical features

	river, lake
	seasonal river
	seasonal lake
	marsh
	salt lake
	salt pan
	ice cap
	sand dunes

sea ice

	unnavigable
	pack ice – autumn minimum – spring maximum

land height and sea depth

metres
5000
3000
2000
1000
500
300
200
100
sea level
200
3000
6000

▲ spot height in metres

Scale 1: 25 000 000

0   250   500   750   1000   1250 km

Conical Orthomorphic Projection

© Oxford University Press

Israel and Lebanon

Scale 1: 4 000 000

| 0 | 40 | 80 | 120 | 160 | 200 km |

Scale 1: 12 500 000

| 0 | 125 | 250 | 375 | 500 | 625 km |

© Oxford University Press

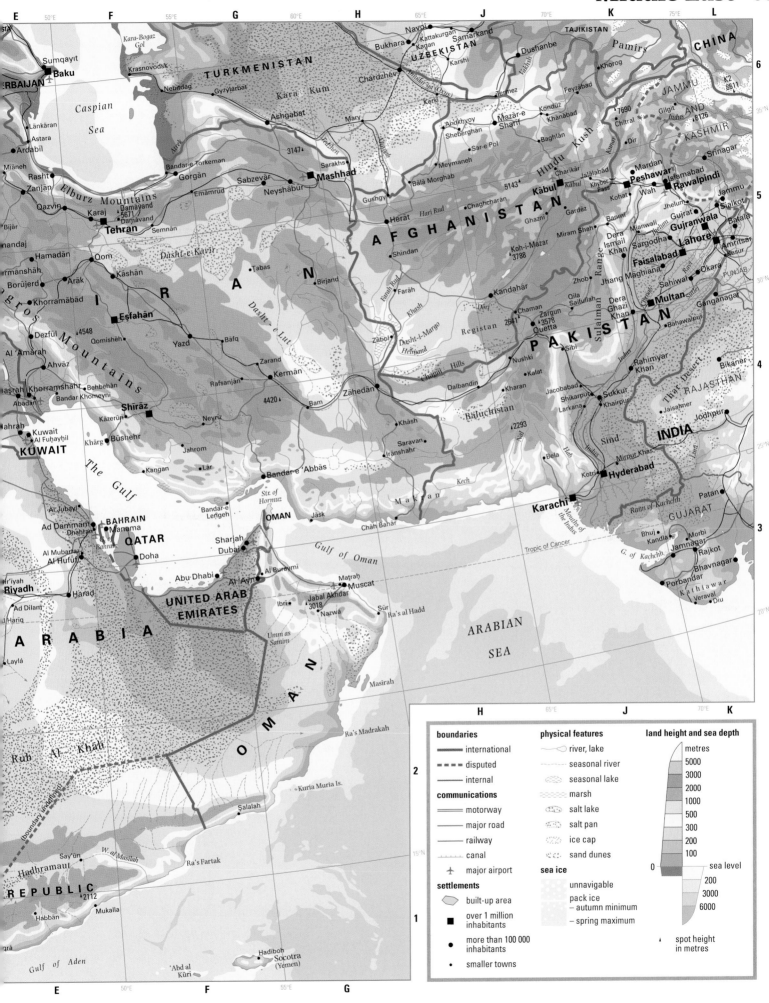

E   50°E   F   55°E   G   60°E   H   65°E   J   70°E   K   75°E   L

CHINA

TAJIKISTAN

Navoi
Bukhara   Samarkand
Kagan   Dushanbe
Kattakurgan
UZBEKISTAN   Khorog
Chārdzhev   K2
Kerki   Termez   8611
Karshi   Feyzābad   7690   Gilgit   Indus   8126
Chardzhou (Oxus)   Kondūz   JAMMU
Andkhvoy   Mazār-e   Khānabād   Chitral   Dir   AND
Sheberghān   Sharīf   Baghlān   Srinagar
Sar-e Pol   Hindu Kush   KASHMIR
Meymaneh   Charikar   Jalālābād   Mardan   Peshawar   Rawalpindi
Bālā Morghāb   5143   Kābul   Kābul   Khyber   Wah   Islāmābād   Jammu
Pass   Kohat   Jhelum   Sialkot
Herāt   Hari Rud   Ghazni   Gardēz   Bannu   Mianwali   Gujrat   Gujranwala
Chaghcharān   Koh-i-Mazar   Miram Shah   Dera   Sargodha   Lahore   Amritsar
Shindan   3788   Ismail   Jhelum   Faisalabad   Kasur
Khan   Jhang Maghiana   Sahiwal   Okara   PUNJAB

A F G H A N I S T A N

Koh-i-Mazar
Dōrī   Qila
Zhob   Saifullah   Dera
Chaman   Zargun   Ghazi   Multan
Kandahār   2641   3578   Khan   Bahawalpur
Farāh   Quetta   Sulaiman   Rahimyar
Khash   Sibi   Khan
Zābol   Dasht-i-Margo   Registan   Nushki   Kalat   Jacobabad   Bikaner
Helmand   Chagai Hills   Dalbandin   Khārān   Shikarpur   Sukkur   Thar Desert   RAJASTHAN
Khāsh   Baluchistan   Larkana   Khairpur   Jaisalmer   Jodhpur
Saravan   2293   Bela   Sind   INDIA

I R A N

Damāvand
5671   Tabas
Damāvand   Dasht-e Kavir
Tehran   Birjand
Qom   Semnān   Farāh
Arāk   Kāshān   Yazd   Dasht-e Lut   Zāhedān
Esfahān   Bāfq
Dezful   4548   Qomishēh   Zarand   4420   Bam
Yazd   Rafsanjān   Kermān
Ahvāz   Behbehān   Shirāz   Neyrīz   Khāsh
Kāzerūn   Saravan
Bushehr   Jahrom   Īrānshahr
Khārg   Lār   Kech
Kangan   Makran
Bandar-e Abbās   Jāsk   Chāh Bahār
Bandar-e   Str. of
Lengeh   Hormuz

Raht
Zanjan
Qazvin
Karaj
Borūjerd
Khorramābād
Hamadān
Dezful
Al 'Amārah
Ahvāz
Abādān
Basrah   Khorramshahr
Bandar Khomeyni
Bandar Khomeyni
KUWAIT
Al Fuhayhil
Kuwait
The Gulf

Jamnagar
Rajkot   Morbi
Patan
GUJARAT
Hyderabad   Bhuj   Kandla
Kotri   Rann of Kachchh
Karachi   Mirpur Khas   Bhavnagar
Mouths of   Kathiawar   Diu
the Indus   Porbandar   Veraval
G. of Kachchh

Ad Dammam   BAHRAIN
Dhahran   Manama   QATAR
Al Mubarraz   Doha
Al Hufūf   Abu Dhabi
Sharjah
Dubai
UNITED ARAB   Al Ayn   Al Buraymi
EMIRATES   Ibri   Maṭraḥ
Abu Dhabi   Muscat
Ṣāḥār   Jabal Akhdar
Umm as   3018   Sūr
Samim   Nazwā   Ra's al Hadd

Riyadh   O M A N
Harad
Ad Dilam
Al Hariq

A R A B I A
Laylá

Rub Al Khālī
boundary undefined

Masirah

**A R A B I A N
S E A**

Tropic of Cancer

20°N

Salalah   Kuria Muria Is.

15°N

REPUBLIC   Hadhramaut
2112   Say'ūn   Ra's Fartak
W. al Masīlah
Mukalla

Gulf of Aden   Hadiboh   Socotra   (Yemen)
Abd al Kūri

H   65°E   J   70°E   K

boundaries	physical features	land height and sea depth
⎯⎯⎯ international	⎯◯ river, lake	metres
▬ ▬ ▬ disputed	⌁⌁⌁ seasonal river	5000
⎯⎯ internal	⌁⌁⌁ seasonal lake	3000
communications	≋≋≋ marsh	2000
═══ motorway	salt lake	1000
⎯⎯ major road	salt pan	500
⎯⎯ railway	ice cap	300
＋＋＋ canal	sand dunes	200
✈ major airport	**sea ice**	100
settlements	unnavigable	0 sea level
⬡ built-up area	pack ice	200
■ over 1 million	– autumn minimum	3000
inhabitants	– spring maximum	6000
● more than 100 000 inhabitants		
• smaller towns		▴ spot height in metres

TURKMENISTAN
Kara-Bogaz   Krasnovodsk
Gol   Nebitdag   Gyzylarbat   Ashgabat
3147   Sarakhs
Bandar-e Torkeman   Gorgān   Sabzevār   Neyshābūr   Mashhad
Atrek   Pedkhen   Mary   Gushgy   Bālā Morghāb

Sumqayit
Baku
Lānkāran
Astara
Ardabīl
Miāneh
Caspian Sea
Elburz Mountains
AZERBAIJAN
Bijār
mandaj
Borūjerd

ḥrah
Kuwait

Riyadh

boundaries
━━━ international
╌╌╌ disputed
─── internal

communications
═══ motorway
─── major road
─── railway
┼┼┼ canal
✈ major airport

settlements
⬡ built-up area
■ over 1 million inhabitants
● more than 100 000 inhabitants
• smaller towns

physical features
～ river, lake
╌╌ seasonal river
seasonal lake
marsh
salt lake
salt pan
ice cap
sand dunes

sea ice
unnavigable
pack ice
– autumn minimum
– spring maximum

land height and sea depth
metres
5000
3000
2000
1000
500
300
200
100
0 sea level
200
3000
6000

▲ spot height in metres

Scale 1: 12 500 000

0   125   250   375   500   625 km

© Oxford University Press

TAJIKISTAN
Khorog
Korki
Termez
Andkhvoy
Feyzabad
Sheberghän
Kondūz
Khānābād
Sar-e Pol
Baghlan
Meymaneh
Bāla Morghāb
K2 (Qogir Feng, Godwin Austen)
Hindu Kush
7690
Chitral
Gilgit
8611
Mazar-e Sharif
8126
Karakoram Pass
Herāt
Charikār
Jalālābad
Ladakh Range
Kunlun
Shindan
Kābul
Khyber Pass
Mardan
Srinagar
Leh
Rutog
Aling Kangri
Kabul
Peshawar
Islamabad
JAMMU AND KASHMIR
7315
AFGHANISTAN
Wah
Kohat
Rawalpindi
Jammu
Shiquan (Indus)
Hari Rud
Ghaznī
Banmi
7755
Barga
Gardez
Mianwali
Jhelum
Gujrat
Sialkot
Pathankot
Manali
Garyarsa
Farāh
Miram Shah
Sargodha
Guiranwala
HIMACHAL
Rampur
Kamet
Zābol
Chenab
Lahore
PRADESH
7816
Nanda Devi
Kandahār
Dera Ismail Khan
Jhang
Batala
Amritsar
Shimla
Dehra Dun
Dhaulag
Kharan
Faisalabad
Ravi
Jalandhar
Maghiana
Ludhiana
CHANDIGARH
UTTARANCHAL
Zhob
Sahiwal
Kasur
Chandigarh
816
Chaman
Sutlej
Okara
Ambala
Quetta
Qila Saifullah
Multan
Bathinda
PUNJAB
Saharanpur
Dera Ghazi Khan
Patiala
Yamunanagar
Muzaffarnagar
Nushki
Bahawalpur
Ganganagar
HARYANA
Meerut
Moradabad
Dalbandin
Sibi
Hisar
Panipat
Rampur
Bareilly
Kalat
Rahimyar Khan
PAKISTAN
New Delhi
Delhi
Shahjahanpur
Baluchistan
Jacobabad
Ghaziabad
Khāsh
Shikarpur
Bikaner
Alwar
Faridabad
Aligarh
Bahraich
Saravan
Larkana
Sukkur
Sikar
Bharatpur
Agra
Mathura
Firozabad
Lucknow
Gorakh
Nad
RAJASTHAN
Jaipur
Etawah
Faizabad
Sind
Bela
Jodhpur
Ajmer
Gwalior
Jhansi
Kanpur
UTTAR PRADE
Mirpur Khas
Bhilwara
Kota
Jaun
Kech
Hab
Hyderabad
Luni
Chambal
Varanas
Karachi
Kotri
Udaipur
Lalitpur
Allahabad
Mirz
Gandhi Sagar
Satna
Rewa
Mouths of the Indus
Govind Ballash Pant Sagar
Tropic of Cancer
Patan
Ratlam
Ujjain
Sagar
Murwara
INDIA
Rann of Kachchh
Bhuj
Sabarmati
Godhra
Jabalpur
Shahdol
Bilaspur
Raiga
GUJARAT
Ahmadabad
Vindhya Range
Bhopal
CHATTISGARH
Hi
Gulf of Kachchh
Rajkot
Nadiad
Indore
Mahadeo Hills
Res
Jamnagar
Kandla
Khambhat
MADHYA PRADESH
Balaghat
Kathiawar
Vadodara
Narmada
Raipur
Durg-Bhilai
Porbandar
Bhavnagar
Bharuch
Satpura Range
Khandwa
Nagpur
Gondia
Junagadh
Tapi
Bhusawal
Veraval
Diu
Surat
Jalgaon
Burhanpur
Amravati
Bhandara
Navsari
Wardha
DAMMAN AND DIU
Daman
Dhule
Akola
Chandrapur
DADRA AND NAGAR HAVELI
Nashik
Malegaon
Godavari
Aurangabad
ARABIAN SEA
Thane
Ulhasnagar
MAHARASHTRA
Nanded
Jagdalpur
Mumbai
Ahmadnagar
Balaghat Range
Nizamabad
Pune
Latur
Warangal
Vizianagara
Deccan
Solapur
Bhima
Gulbarga
Hyderabad
Vishakhapatn
WESTERN GHATS
Kolhapur
Sangli
Bijapur
ANDHRA PRADESH
Khammam
Kakina
Ichalkaranji
Raichur
Krishna
Eluru
Rajahmun
Belgaum
Kurnool
Guntur
Vijayawada
Dharwad
Adoni
Tenali
Hospet
Bellary
Karwar
Anantapur
Penner
EASTERN GHATS
GOA
Davangere
Cuddapah
Nellore
Shimoga
Bhadravati
Tumkur
Chittoor
Tirupati
Mangalore
KARNATAKA
Bangalore
Kolar Gold Fields
Vellore
Chennai
Kasaragod
Mysore
Coromandel Coast
Cannanore
PONDICHERRY
Amindivi Islands
Salem
TAMIL NADU
Pondicherry
Kavaratti
Calicut
Nilgiri Hills
Erode
Cuddalore
Cannanore Islands
Palghat
Tiruppur
Kumbakonam
LAKSHADWEEP
Trichur
Coimbatore
Tiruchchirappali
PONDICHERRY
Malabar Coast
Cochin
Dindigul
Thanjavur
Nine Degree Channel
KERALA
Anai Mudi
Madurai
2695
Cardamom Hills
Jaffna
Minicoy Island
Alleppey
Rajapalaiyam
Manna
SRI LANKA
Eight Degree Channel
Quilon
Tuticorin
Palk Strait
Trivandrum
Tirunelveli
Gulf of Mannar
Trincomalee
Ihavandiffulu Atoll
Nagercoil
Puttalam
Anuradhapura
Hanimadu Island
Batticaloa
Negombo
Matale
Kandy
Colombo
2524
Badulla
Moratuwa
Pidurutalagala
Galle
Matara
Hambantota

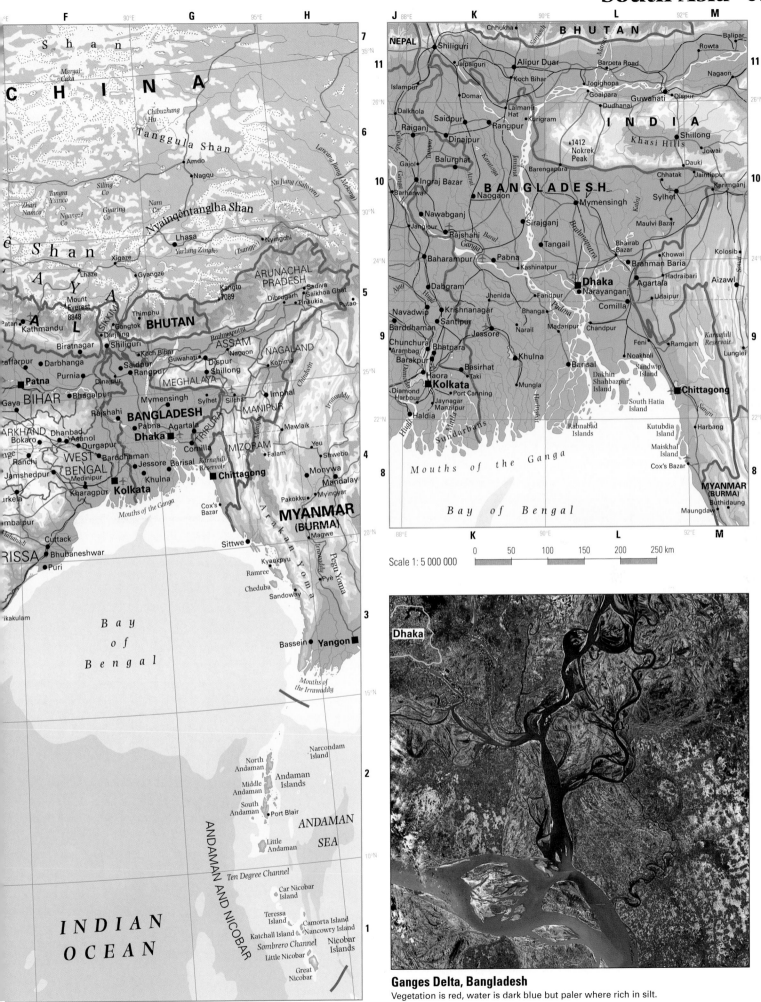

Left map

F 90°E **G** 95°E **H** 7 35°N

S h a n

Margai Caka

C H I N A

Chibuzhang Hu

T a n g g u l a   S h a n

Lancang Jiang (Mekong)

ê
S h a n

Tangra Yumco *Siling Co* *Gyaring Co*

Zhari Namco *Ngangzê Co*

Nam Co

Amdo

Nagqu

Nu Jiang (Salween)

N y a i n q ê n t a n g l h a   S h a n

Lhasa • Nyingchi

Xigaze *Yarlung Zangbo (Tsangpo)* 30°N 6

Lhaze • Gyangze

H   A   L   A   Y   A

Mount Everest 8848

Kangto 7089

ARUNACHAL PRADESH

Sadiya • Saikhoa Ghat
Dibrugarh • Tinsukia
Putao

Patan • Kathmandu

SIKKIM
Thimphu
Gangtok • Darjiling

BHUTAN

5

Biratnagar Shiliguri

Brahmaputra

ASSAM

NAGALAND

affurpur Darbhanga Koch Bihar Guwahati Dispur
Saidpur Rangpur Shillong Nageon Kohima

25°N

Purnia Dinajpur

MEGHALAYA

Patna Bhagalpur

BIHAR

Rajshahi Mymensingh Sylhet Silchar Imphal

MANIPUR

Gaya

Dhanbad Asanol Durgapur

BANGLADESH

Pabna Agartala **TRIPURA**

Dhaka

Comilla **MIZORAM**

Mawlaik Yeu

Chindwin

Irrawaddy

RKHAND Bokaro

WEST BENGAL

Barddhaman Jessore Barisal

Falam Shwebo

Ranchi Medinipur Khulna

Karnafuli Reservoir

Jamshedpur

Kolkata

Chittagong

Monywa Mandalay

4

rkela Kharagpur

Mouths of the Ganga

Cox's Bazar

Pakokku • Myingyan

MYANMAR (BURMA)

mbalpur

Cuttack

RISSA Bhubaneshwar
• Puri

A r a k a n   Y o m a

Sittwe

Magwe

Pegu Yoma

Irrawaddy

20°N 3

ikakulam

*B a y
o f
B e n g a l*

Kyaukpyu
Ramree
Cheduba
Sandoway

Pye

Mouths of the Irrawaddy

Bassein **Yangon**

15°N

**I N D I A N
O C E A N**

North Andaman
Middle Andaman
South Andaman • Port Blair

Andaman Islands

Narcondam Island

ANDAMAN SEA

Little Andaman

10°N 2

Ten Degree Channel

Car Nicobar Island

ANDAMAN AND NICOBAR

Teressa Island
Katchall Island • Camorta Island
Nancowry Island

Sombrero Channel **Nicobar Islands**

Little Nicobar
Great Nicobar

1

85°E **F** 90°E **G** 95°E

Right map

J 88°E **K** 90°E **L** 92°E **M**

NEPAL Chhukha **B H U T A N**

Shiliguri *Sankosh* Balipar

Jaipaiguri Alipur Duar Barpeta Road Rowta 11

Islampur Koch Bihar Jogighopa Nagaon

Domar Goalpara Guwahati Dispur 26°N

Dalkhola Lalmani Hat Dudhanai

Raiganj Saidpur Rangpur Kurigram **I N D I A**

Dinajpur Shillong 6

Gajol Balurghat Barengapara 1412 Nokrek Peak *Khasi Hills* Jowai

Barharwa Ingraj Bazar Chhatak Jaintipur 10

B A N G L A D E S H Karimganj

Naogaon Mymensingh Sylhet

Nawabganj Maulvi Bazar 24°N

Jangipur Rajshahi Sirajganj Kolosib

Baharampur Pabna Tangail Bhairab Bazar Khowai

Kashinatpur Brahman Baria Aizawl

Dabgram **Dhaka** Agartala Hadraibari 5

Atrai Jhenida Narayanganj Udaipur

Navadwip Krishnanagar Faridpur Bhanga *Padma* Comilla

Barddhaman Santipur Narail Madaripur Chandpur Feni Ramgarh *Karnafuli Reservoir*

Chunchura Bhatpara Jessore Noakhali Lunglei 9

Arambag Barakpur Basirhat Khulna Barisal Sandwip Island

Haora **Kolkata** Taki Mungla Dakhin Shahbazpur Island

Diamond Harbour Port Canning South Hatia Island **Chittagong**

Jaynagar Manzilpur Kutubdia Island Harbang 22°N

Haldia *Sundarbans* Rabnabad Islands Maiskhal Island

Cox's Bazar 8

Hugli

M o u t h s   o f   t h e   G a n g a **MYANMAR (BURMA)**

Buthidaung

B a y   o f   B e n g a l Maungdaw

88°E **K** 90°E **L** 92°E **M**

Scale 1 : 5 000 000

0 50 100 150 200 250 km

Inset photo

Dhaka

Ganges Delta, Bangladesh
Vegetation is red, water is dark blue but paler where rich in silt.

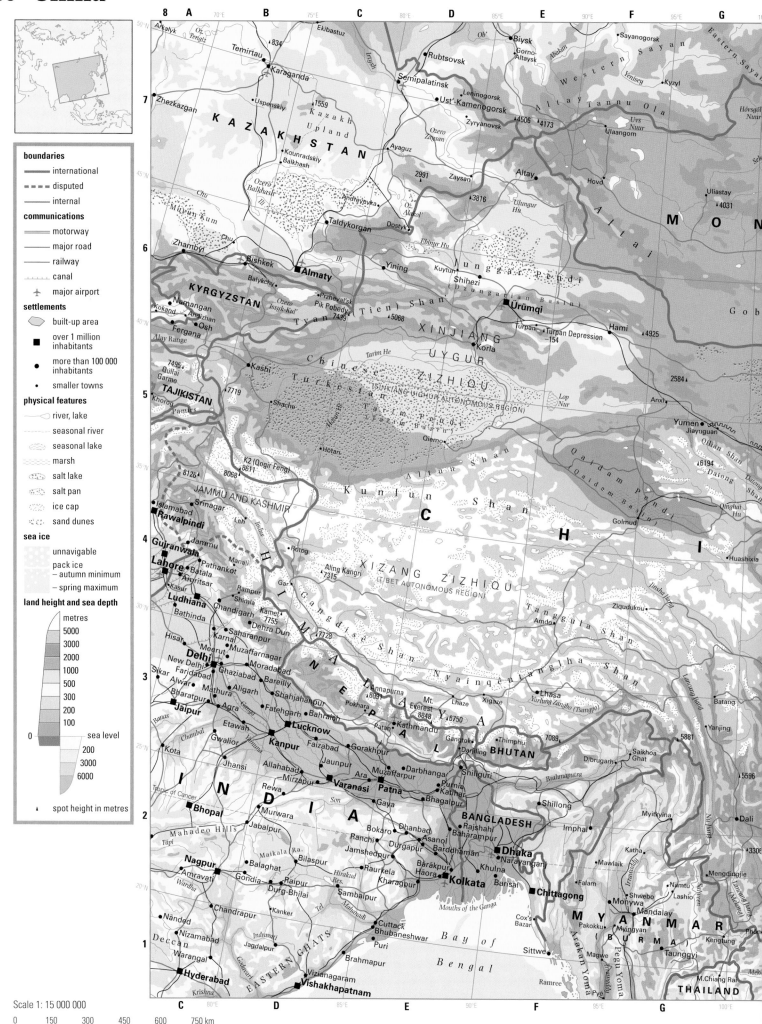

Scale 1: 15 000 000

0   150   300   450   600   750 km

Conical Orthomorphic Projection

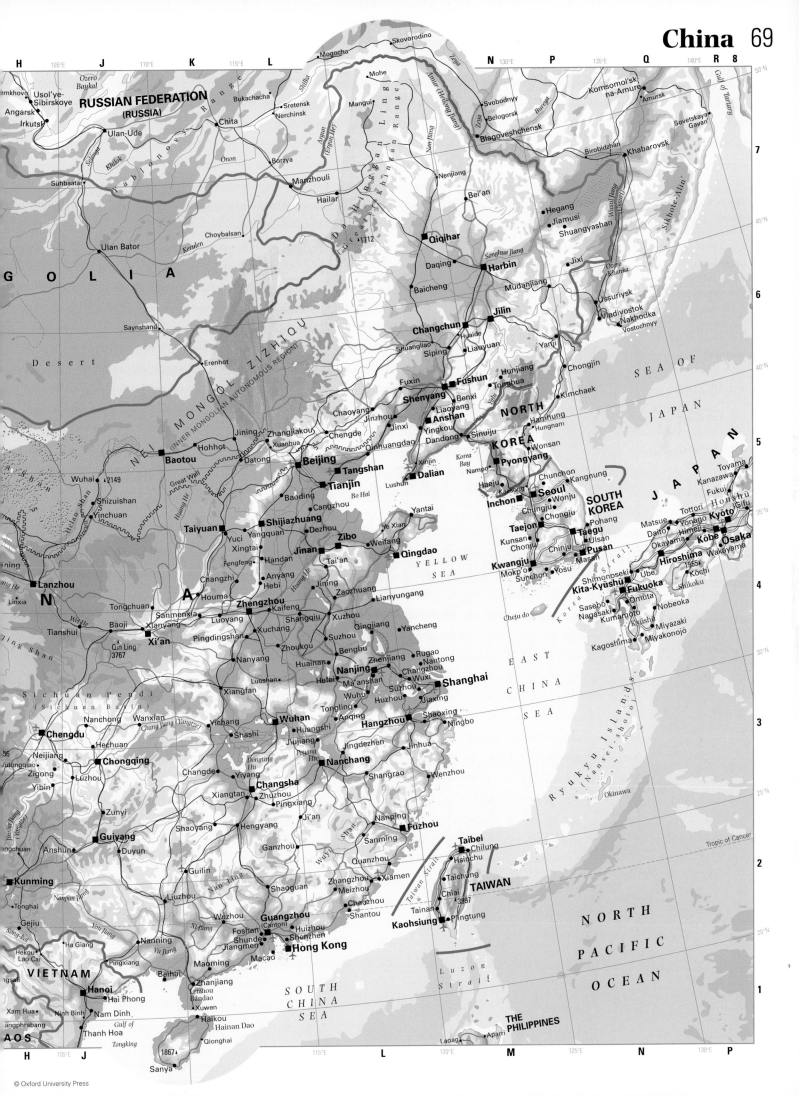

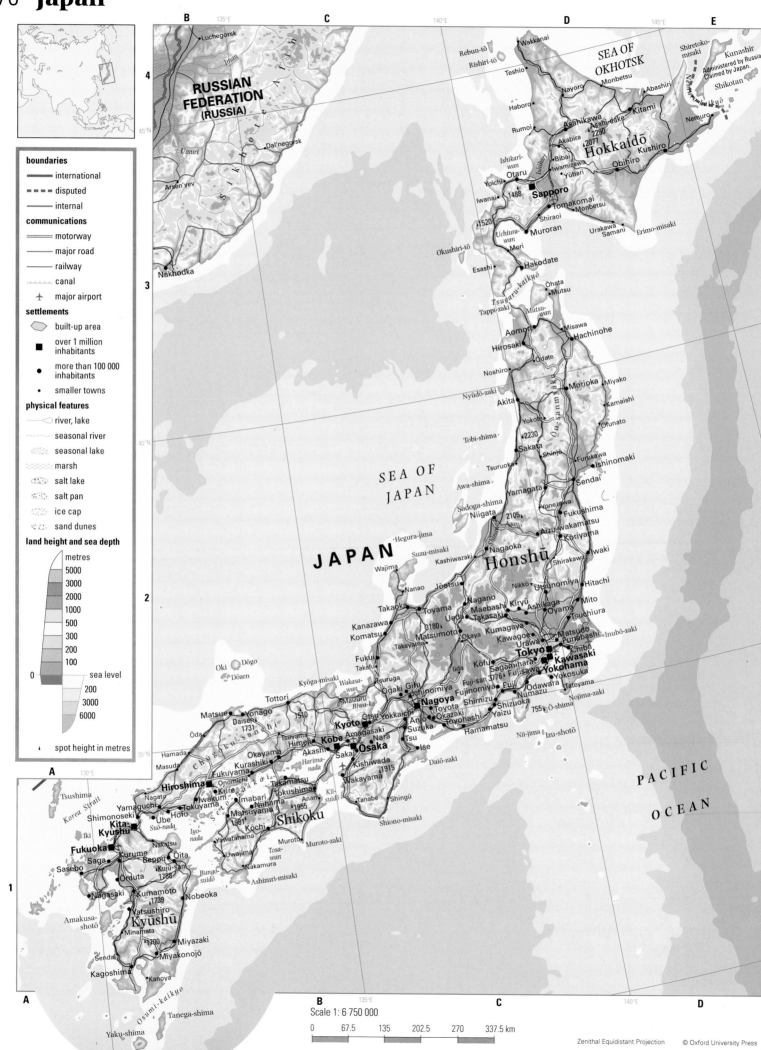

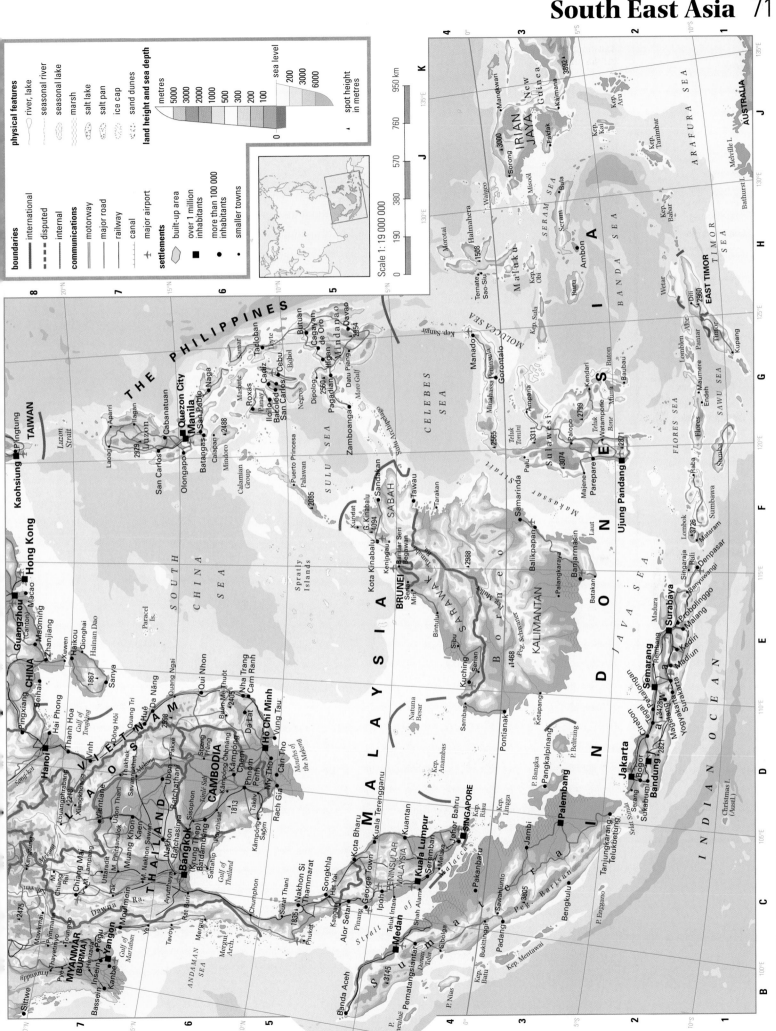

Conical Orthomorphic Projection

physical features
- river, lake
- seasonal river
- seasonal lake
- marsh
- salt lake
- salt pan
- ice cap
- sand dunes

boundaries
- international
- disputed
- internal

communications
- motorway
- major road
- railway
- canal
- major airport

settlements
- built-up area
- over 1 million inhabitants
- more than 100 000 inhabitants
- smaller towns

land height and sea depth

metres
5000
3000
2000
1000
500
300
200
100
sea level
200
3000
6000

spot height in metres

Scale 1: 19 000 000

0   190   380   570   760   950 km

THE PHILIPPINES

TAIWAN

Kaohsiung
P'ingtung

Luzon Strait

Aparri
Laoag
Ilagan
2929
Luzon
San Carlos
Cabanatuan
Quezon City
Manila
San Pablo
Olongapo
2488
Batangas
Calapan
Mindoro
Naga
Masbate
Calamian Group
Roxas
Panay
Iloilo
Bacolod
San Carlos
Cadiz
Cebu
Tacloban
Samar
Leyte
Negros
Bohol
Dipolog
2560
Cagayan de Oro
Butuan
Iligan
Mindanao
2954
Davao
Pagadian
Datu Piang
Zamboanga
Moro Gulf

Puerto Princesa
Palawan
2085
SULU SEA

Kundat
Sandakan
G. Kinabalu 4094
Kota Kinabalu
Tawau
Tarakan
SABAH

SOUTH CHINA SEA

Spratly Islands

Paracel Is.

Hainan Dao
1867
Sanya
Qionghai
Haikou
Xuwen
Zhanjiang

CHINA
Guangzhou (Canton)
Macao
Hong Kong
Beihai
Maoming
Pingxiang
1248

VIETNAM
Hanoi
Hai Phong
Thanh Hoa
Vinh
Dong Hoi
Quang Tri
Hue
2598
Da Nang
Quang Ngai
Qui Nhon
2405
Nha Trang
Buon Me Thuot
Da Lat
Cam Ranh
Ho Chi Minh
Vung Tau

LAOS
Luangprabang
Xiangkhoang
Vientiane
Thakhek
Savannakhet
Pakxe

Song-koi
2475

CAMBODIA
Stoeng Treng
Kampong Cham
Phnom Penh
Kampong Saom
Takev
Tonle Sap
1813
Battambang
Sisophon

Rach Gia
Can Tho
My Tho
Mouths of the Mekong

THAILAND
Chiang Rai
Chiang Mai
M. Lampang
Uttaradit
M. Phitsanulok
Tak
M. Nakhon Sawan
Udon Thani
Khon Kaen
Nakhon Ratchasima
Ubon Ratchathani
Krung Thep (Bangkok)
Ayutthaya
Rat Buri
Chon Buri
Chanthaburi
Chumphon
Surat Thani
Nakhon Si Thammarat
1835
Songkhla
Hat Yai

MYANMAR (BURMA)
Sittwe
Mawmai
Pyinmana
Taunggyi
Thayetmyo
Pyè
Henzada
Pegu
Yangon
Insein
Kanbe
Bassein

Salween
Dawna Ra.
Moulmein
Gulf of Martaban
Ye
Tavoy
Mergui
Mergui Arch.

ANDAMAN SEA

Gulf of Thailand

PENINSULAR MALAYSIA
Kangar
Alor Setar
Pinang
George Town
Ipoh
Teluk Intan
Kuala Terengganu
Kota Bharu
Kuantan
Kuala Lumpur
Shah Alam
Seremban
Melaka
Johor Bahru
SINGAPORE

MALAYSIA

Gulf of Tongking

BRUNEI
Bandar Seri Begawan
Miri
Seria
Bintulu
SARAWAK
Sibu
Kuching
Sibas
1468
Serian
Sambas
Pontianak
Ketapang

BORNEO
KALIMANTAN
2988
Samarinda
Balikpapan
Banjarmasin
Palangkaraya
Laut

Natuna Besar
Kep. Anambas
Kep. Riau
Kep. Lingga
P. Bangka
Pangkalpinang
P. Belitung
Tanjungkarang
Telukbetung

S U M A T R A
Banda Aceh
3745
Pematangsiantar
Medan
Sibolga
Tanjungbalai
Danau Toba
Teluk Dalam
Bukittinggi
Padang
Sawahlunto
Pakanbaru
Jambi
Pangkalpinang
Palembang
Bengkulu
Peg. Barisan
3805

INDIAN OCEAN

P. Nias
P. Batu
Kep. Mentawai
P. Enggano
Simeulue

SERETO
Selat Sunda

INDONESIA
Jakarta
Serang
Bogor
Sukabumi
Bandung
2821
Cirebon
Tegal
Pekalongan
Semarang
3428
Yogyakarta
Surakarta
Magelang
Madiun
Kediri
Surabaya
Malang
Probolinggo
Madura
Rembang

JAVA SEA

Bali
Singaraja
Denpasar
Banyuwangi
Lombok
3726
Mataram
Sumbawa
Baba
Flores
Sumba
Ende
Maumere

FLORES SEA
SAWU SEA

Kupang
Timor
EAST TIMOR
Dili
2960
TIMOR SEA

Wetar
Alor
Pantar
Lomblen

BANDA SEA

Ambon
1508
Buru
Seram
Bula
SERAM SEA
Obi
Kep. Obi
Kep. Sula
Misoöl
Waigeo

MOLUCCA SEA

Ternate
Sao-Siu
Manado
Gorontalo
Mihabassa Peninsula
Tampana
Teluk Tomini
2565
Palu
1311
Teluk Tolo
3074
SULAWESI (CELEBES)
Majene
Mamuju
Parepare
Palopo
2799
Watampone
Teluk Bone
Ujung Pandang
2871
Kendari
Buton
Baubau
Muna

CELEBES SEA

Kep. Sangir

MAKASSAR Strait

Halmahera
Morotai

IRIAN JAYA
New Guinea
Sorong
3000
Manokwari
Kaimana
3892
Faktak
Kep. Kai
Kep. Aru

ARAFURA SEA

Kep. Tanimbar
Kep. Babar
Waigeo

AUSTRALIA
Melville I.
Bathurst I.

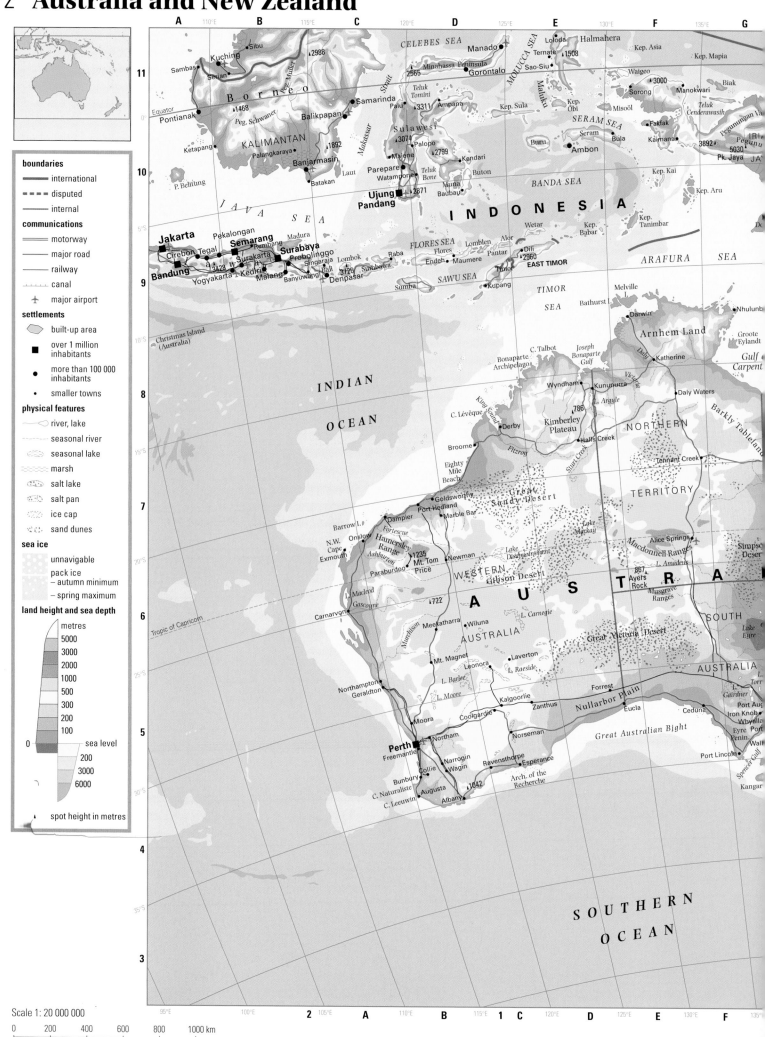

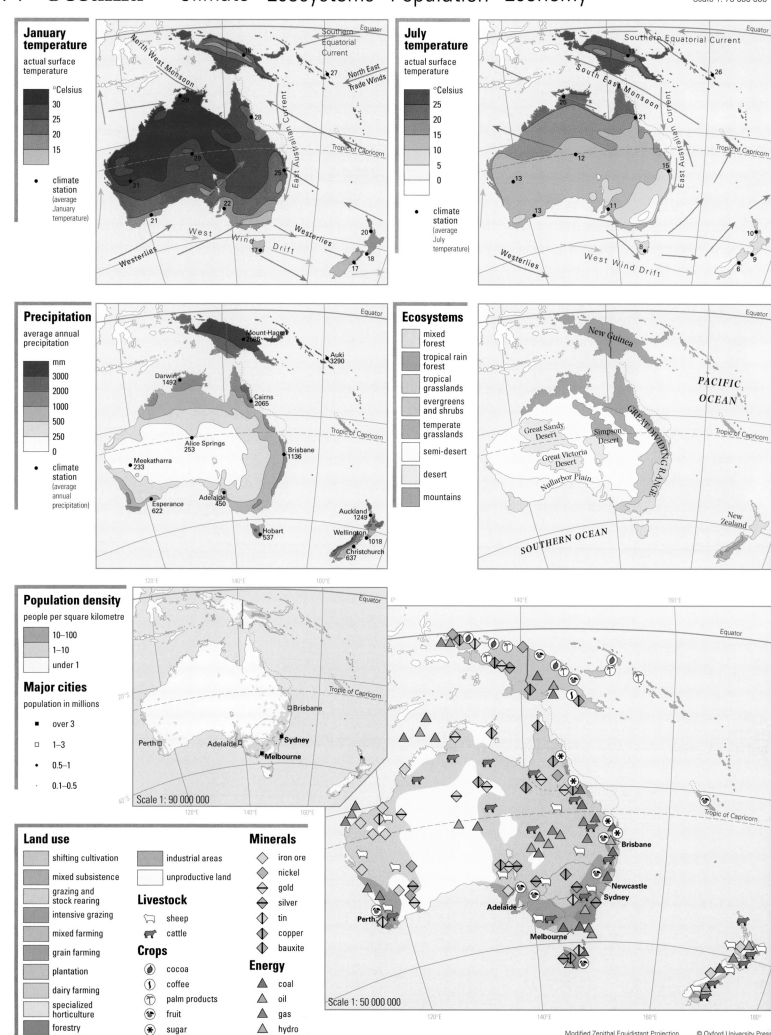

January temperature

actual surface temperature

°Celsius
30
25
20
15

● climate station (average January temperature)

Southern Equatorial Current
North West Monsoon
North East Trade Winds
East Australian Current
Tropic of Capricorn
West Wind Drift
Westerlies

18 27 29 28 25 29 31 22 21 20 17 18 17

July temperature

actual surface temperature

°Celsius
25
20
15
10
5
0

● climate station (average July temperature)

Southern Equatorial Current
South East Monsoon
East Australian Current
Tropic of Capricorn
Westerlies
West Wind Drift

17 26 25 21 12 15 13 13 11 8 10 9 6

Precipitation

average annual precipitation

mm
3000
2000
1000
500
250
0

● climate station (average annual precipitation)

Mount Hagen 2586
Auki 3290
Darwin 1492
Cairns 2065
Alice Springs 253
Brisbane 1136
Meekatharra 233
Esperance 622
Adelaide 450
Auckland 1249
Hobart 537
Wellington 1018
Christchurch 637

Equator
Tropic of Capricorn

Ecosystems

- mixed forest
- tropical rain forest
- tropical grasslands
- evergreens and shrubs
- temperate grasslands
- semi-desert
- desert
- mountains

New Guinea
PACIFIC OCEAN
Great Sandy Desert
Simpson Desert
Great Victoria Desert
GREAT DIVIDING RANGE
Nullarbor Plain
New Zealand
SOUTHERN OCEAN
Equator
Tropic of Capricorn

Population density

people per square kilometre
- 10–100
- 1–10
- under 1

Major cities

population in millions
■ over 3
□ 1–3
● 0.5–1
· 0.1–0.5

120°E 140°E 160°E
Equator
Tropic of Capricorn
20°S
40°S

Brisbane
Perth Adelaide Sydney Melbourne

Scale 1: 90 000 000

Land use

- shifting cultivation
- mixed subsistence
- grazing and stock rearing
- intensive grazing
- mixed farming
- grain farming
- plantation
- dairy farming
- specialized horticulture
- forestry
- industrial areas
- unproductive land

Livestock

🐑 sheep
🐄 cattle

Crops

🥥 cocoa
☕ coffee
🌴 palm products
🍎 fruit
✳ sugar

Minerals

◇ iron ore
◆ nickel
◆ gold
◆ silver
◈ tin
◈ copper
◈ bauxite

Energy

▲ coal
▲ oil
▲ gas
▲ hydro

Brisbane
Newcastle
Sydney
Adelaide
Melbourne
Perth

Scale 1: 50 000 000

120°E 140°E 160°E 180°

Modified Zenithal Equidistant Projection   © Oxford University Press

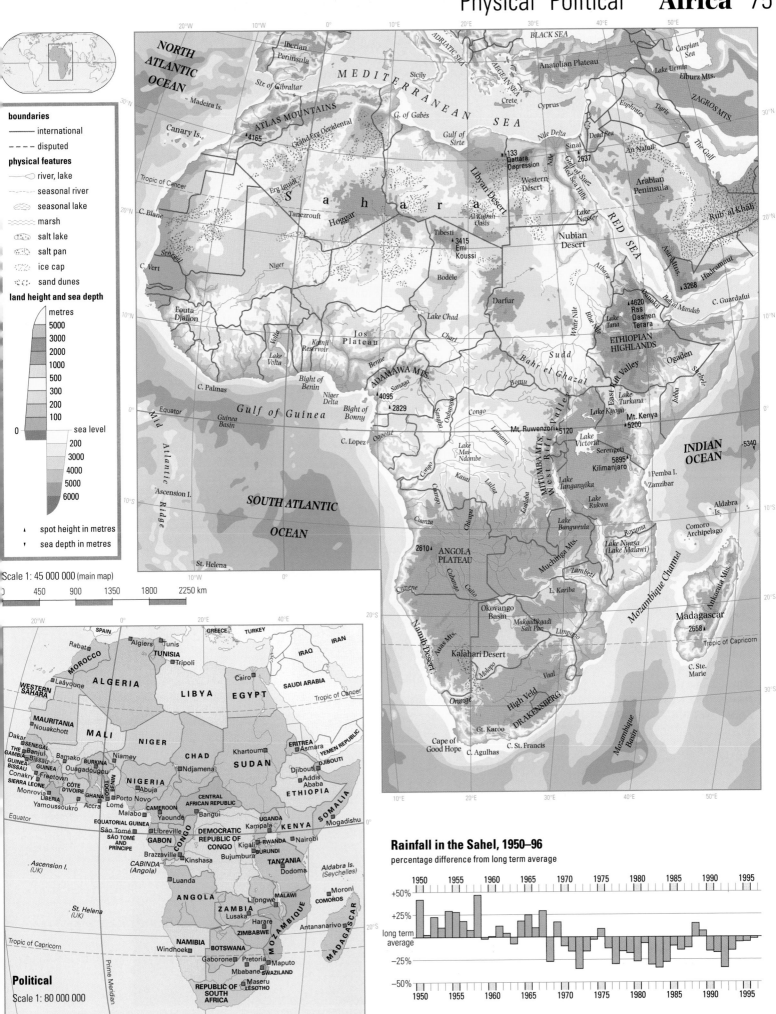

boundaries
— international
--- disputed

physical features
~ river, lake
⋯ seasonal river
⬭ seasonal lake
≈ marsh
⬭ salt lake
⬭ salt pan
⬭ ice cap
⬭ sand dunes

land height and sea depth
metres
5000
3000
2000
1000
500
300
200
100
0 — sea level
200
3000
4000
5000
6000

▲ spot height in metres
▼ sea depth in metres

Scale 1: 45 000 000 (main map)

0   450   900   1350   1800   2250 km

Political
Scale 1: 80 000 000

© Oxford University Press   Zenithal Equal Area Projection

Rainfall in the Sahel, 1950–96
percentage difference from long term average

1950   1955   1960   1965   1970   1975   1980   1985   1990   1995

+50%
+25%
long term average
−25%
−50%

1950   1955   1960   1965   1970   1975   1980   1985   1990   1995

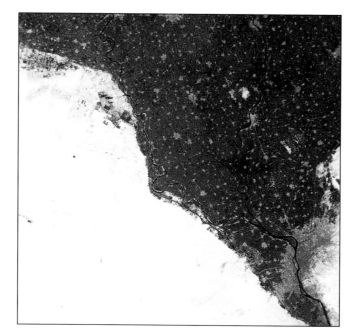

Nile River Delta

Cairo is shown by the blue/grey area to lower right of the image. The city has grown in size from 1.5 million people in 1947 to more than 6 million in 1991. Other blue areas show rapid urban development in the delta. Yellow areas at top left of the image show the spread of agriculture in the desert, assisted by centre pivot irrigation.

Kenya crop cover

Remote sensing can be used to predict food shortages. Dark green areas on the satellite image of Kenya for April, 2000 show the newly sown 'long rains' cereal crop. However, gaps in the dark green pattern indicate a poor harvest and in June, $88 million of international food aid was agreed. By August, low rainfall had led to widespread crop failure in the south, shown as light green, and spread of bare soil in the north, shown as orange and yellow.

April, 2000

August, 2000

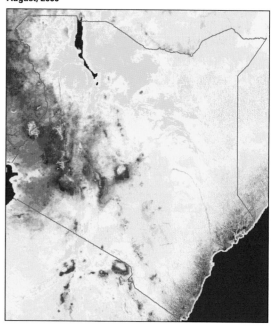

Mozambique floods

Before flooding, August, 1999.

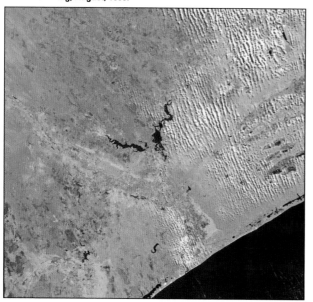

After flooding, March 2000.

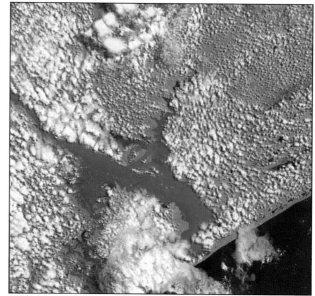

These images from the Landsat 7 satellite show the Limpopo river before and after flooding. Torrential rain between 4 and 7 February, 2000 added to already high levels of seasonal rainfall. Tropical cyclone Eline hit the southern coast of Mozambique on 21 February bringing even more rain. Over a million people were made homeless and 100 000 hectares of agricultural land flooded. 620 miles of roads were swept away.

Scale 1: 90 000 000

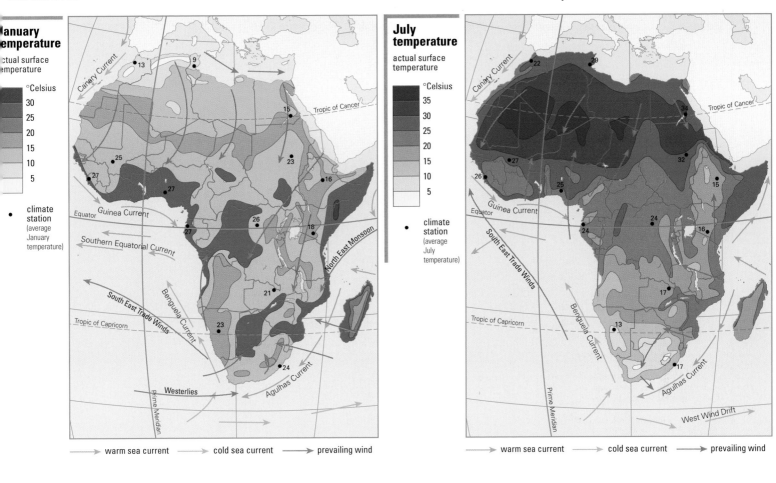

January temperature

ctual surface emperature

°Celsius
30
25
20
15
10
5

● climate station
(average January temperature)

Canary Current

Tropic of Cancer

13

9

15

25

27

27

23

16

26

27

18

North East Monsoon

Equator

Guinea Current

Southern Equatorial Current

South East Trade Winds

Benguela Current

21

23

Tropic of Capricorn

24

Westerlies

Prime Meridian

Agulhas Current

→ warm sea current → cold sea current → prevailing wind

July temperature

actual surface temperature

°Celsius
35
30
25
20
15
10
5

● climate station
(average July temperature)

Canary Current

22

29

34

Tropic of Cancer

27

32

26

25

15

Equator

Guinea Current

24

24

16

South East Trade Winds

Benguela Current

17

Tropic of Capricorn

13

17

Agulhas Current

Prime Meridian

West Wind Drift

→ warm sea current → cold sea current → prevailing wind

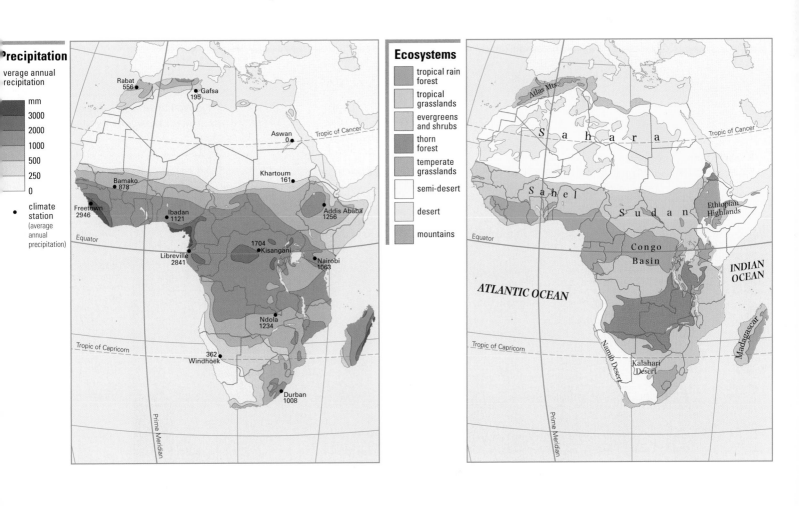

Precipitation

verage annual recipitation

mm
3000
2000
1000
500
250
0

● climate station
(average annual precipitation)

Rabat 556

Gafsa 195

Aswan 0

Tropic of Cancer

Khartoum 161

Bamako 878

Freetown 2946

Ibadan 1121

Addis Ababa 1256

Equator

Libreville 2841

Kisangani 1704

Nairobi 1063

Ndola 1234

Tropic of Capricorn

Windhoek 362

Durban 1008

Prime Meridian

Ecosystems

tropical rain forest

tropical grasslands

evergreens and shrubs

thorn forest

temperate grasslands

semi-desert

desert

mountains

Atlas Mts.

S a h a r a

Tropic of Cancer

S a h e l

S u d a n

Ethiopian Highlands

Equator

Congo Basin

INDIAN OCEAN

ATLANTIC OCEAN

Tropic of Capricorn

Namib Desert

Kalahari Desert

Madagascar

Prime Meridian

Scale 1: 55 000 000

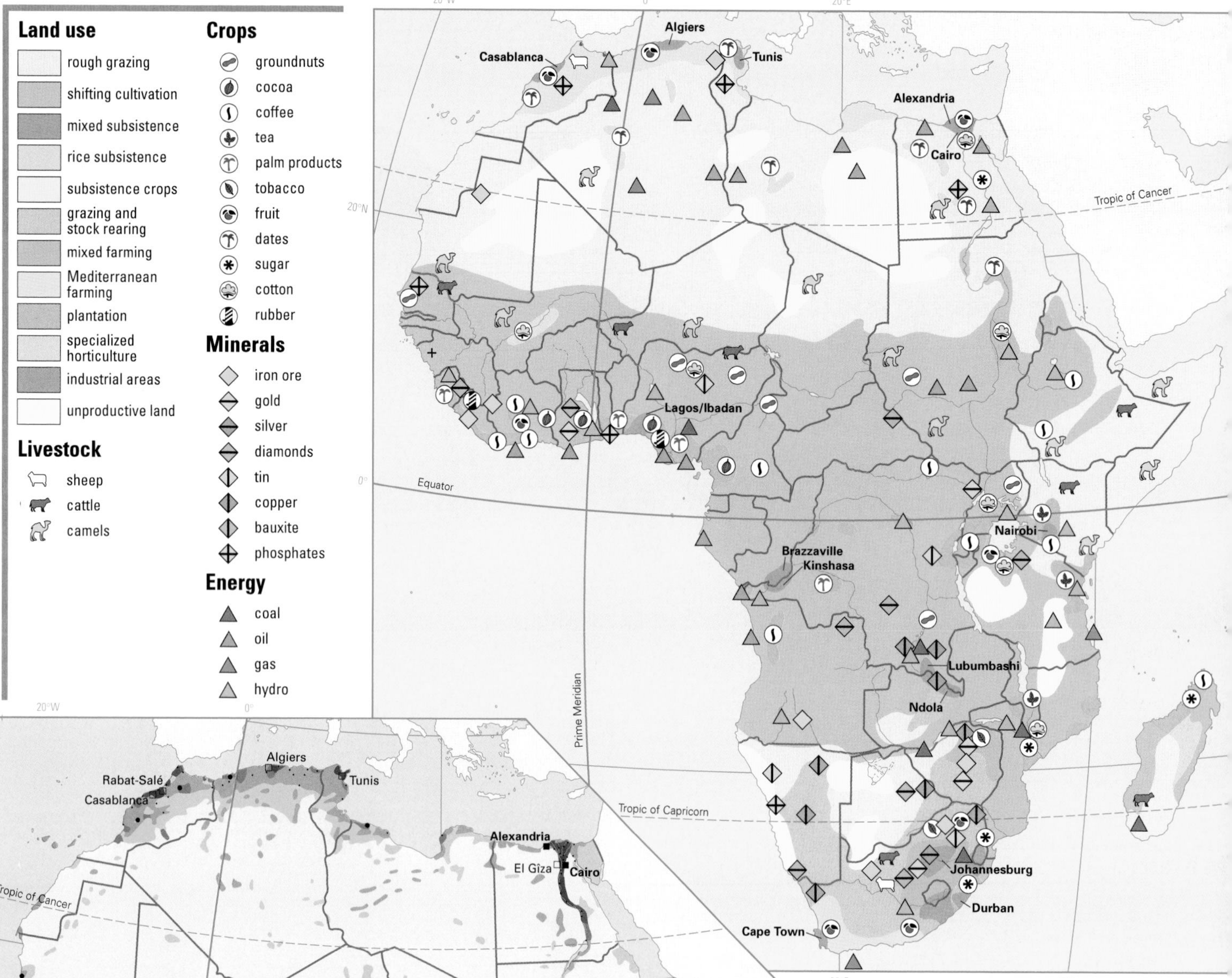
Land use
rough grazing
shifting cultivation
mixed subsistence
rice subsistence
subsistence crops
grazing and stock rearing
mixed farming
Mediterranean farming
plantation
specialized horticulture
industrial areas
unproductive land
Livestock
sheep
cattle
camels
Crops
groundnuts
cocoa
coffee
tea
palm products
tobacco
fruit
dates
sugar
cotton
rubber
Minerals
iron ore
gold
silver
diamonds
tin
copper
bauxite
phosphates
Energy
coal
oil
gas
hydro
Algiers
Casablanca
Tunis
Alexandria
Cairo
Tropic of Cancer
Lagos/Ibadan
Equator
Nairobi
Brazzaville
Kinshasa
Lubumbashi
Ndola
Prime Meridian
Tropic of Capricorn
Johannesburg
Durban
Cape Town
20°W
0°
20°E
40°E
20°N

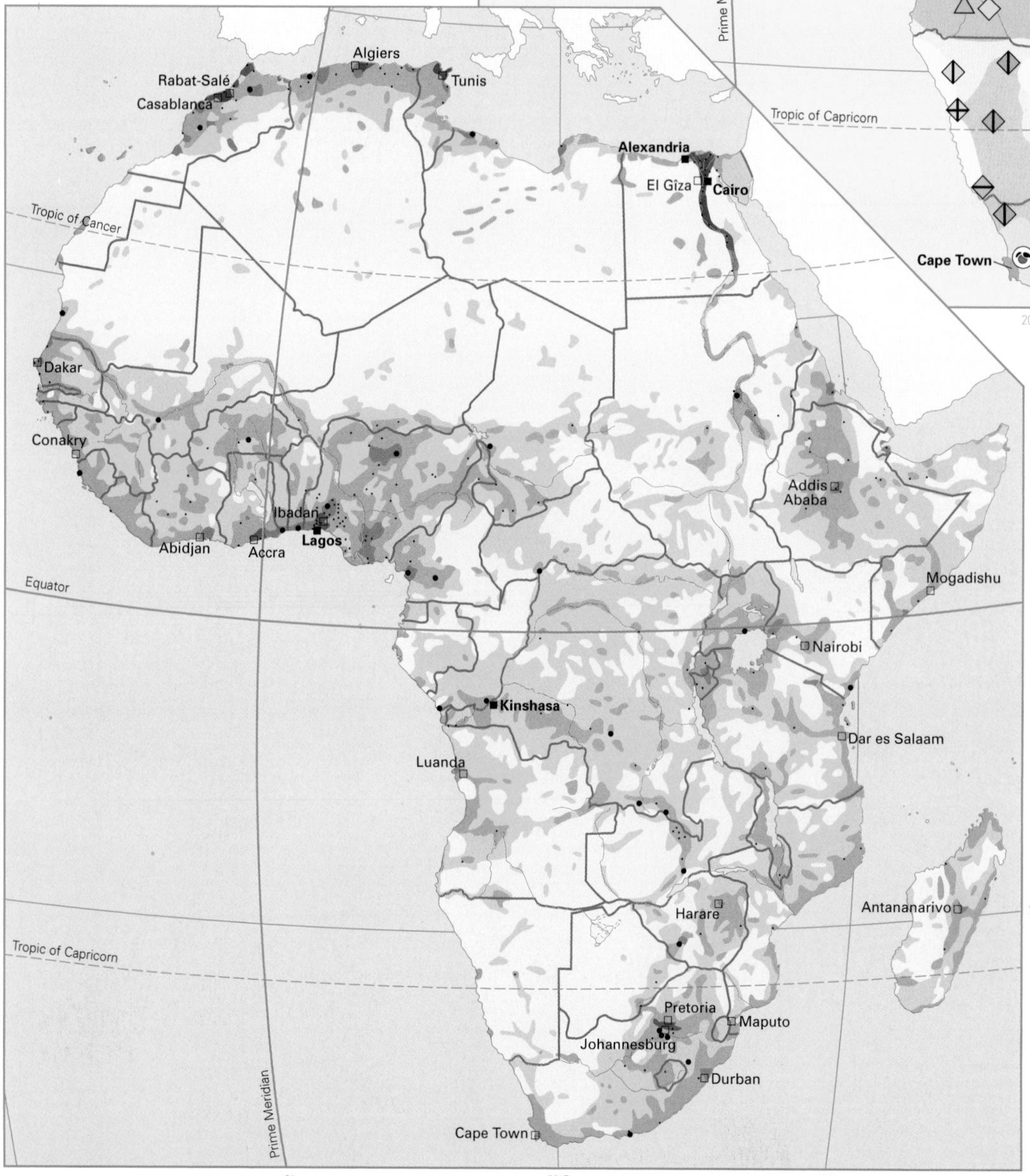
Algiers
Rabat-Salé
Casablanca
Tunis
Alexandria
El Gîza
Cairo
Tropic of Cancer
Dakar
Conakry
Ibadan
Lagos
Abidjan
Accra
Addis Ababa
Mogadishu
Equator
Nairobi
Kinshasa
Dar es Salaam
Luanda
Harare
Antananarivo
Tropic of Capricorn
Pretoria
Maputo
Johannesburg
Durban
Cape Town
Prime Meridian
20°W
0°
20°E
40°E
20°N
20°S
Population density
people per square kilometre
over 700
200–700
100–200
10–100
1–10
under 1
Major cities
population in millions
over 3
1–3
0.5–1
0.1–0.5

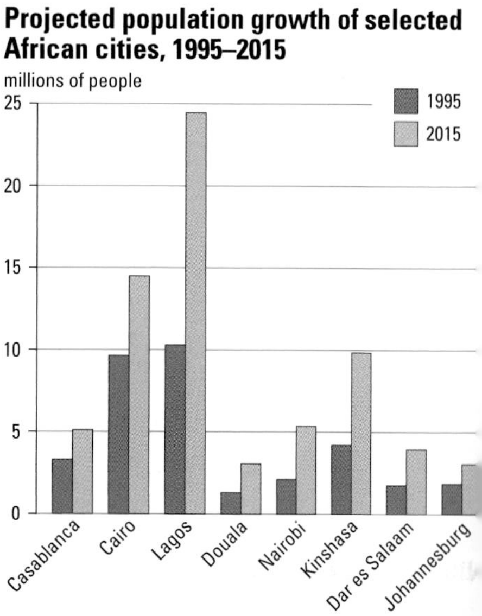
Projected population growth of selected African cities, 1995–2015
millions of people
1995
2015
25
20
15
10
5
0
Casablanca
Cairo
Lagos
Douala
Nairobi
Kinshasa
Dar es Salaam
Johannesburg

Zenithal Equal Area Projection

© Oxford University Press

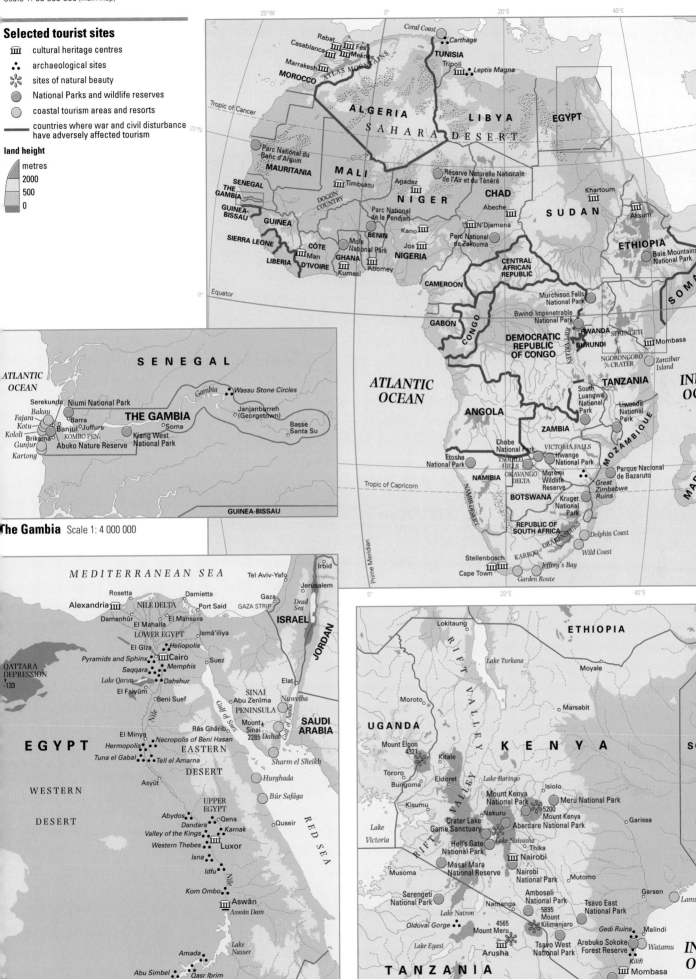

Scale 1: 55 000 000 (main map)

The Gambia Scale 1: 4 000 000

Nile Valley and Eastern Egypt Scale 1: 10 000 000

Kenya Scale 1: 10 000 000

Zenithal Equal Area Projection

© Oxford University Press

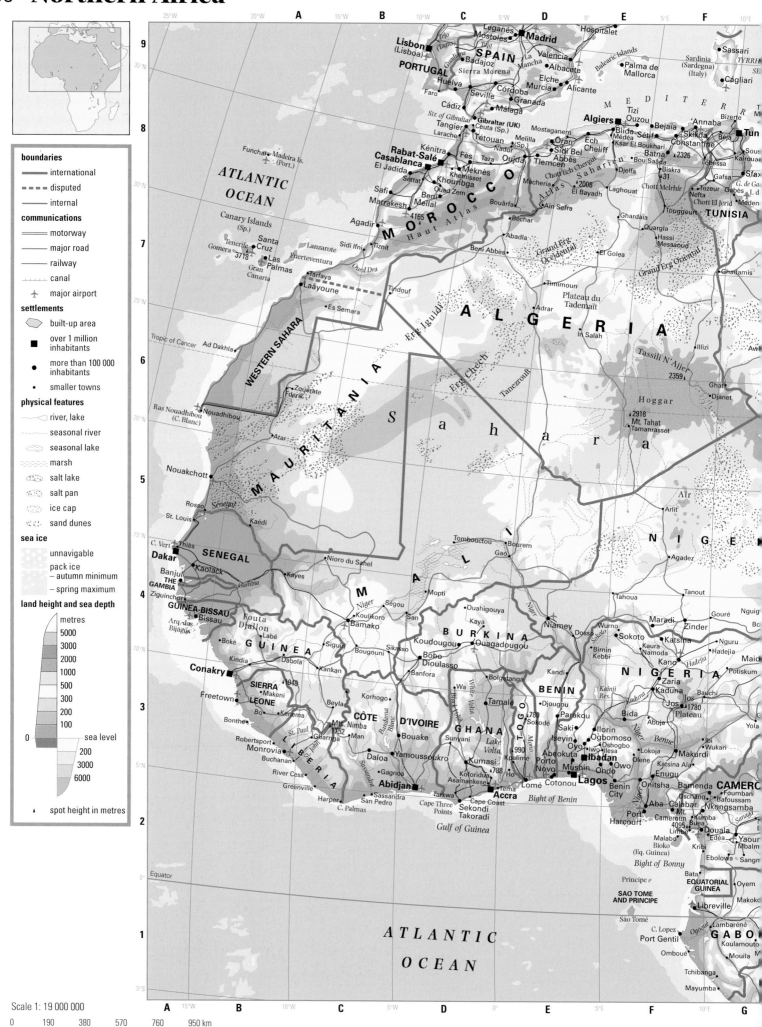

Zenithal Equal Area Projection

boundaries
international
disputed
internal

communications
motorway
major road
railway
canal
major airport

settlements
built-up area
over 1 million inhabitants
more than 100 000 inhabitants
smaller towns

physical features
river, lake
seasonal river
seasonal lake
marsh
salt lake
salt pan
ice cap
sand dunes

sea ice
unnavigable
pack ice
– autumn minimum
– spring maximum

land height and sea depth
metres
5000
3000
2000
1000
500
300
200
100
sea level
200
3000
6000
▲ spot height in metres

Scale 1: 19 000 000

0   190   380   570   760   950 km

ATLANTIC OCEAN

SPAIN
PORTUGAL
MOROCCO
WESTERN SAHARA
MAURITANIA
ALGERIA
Sahara
TUNISIA
SENEGAL
THE GAMBIA
GUINEA-BISSAU
GUINEA
SIERRA LEONE
LIBERIA
MALI
CÔTE D'IVOIRE
BURKINA
GHANA
TOGO
BENIN
NIGER
NIGERIA
CAMEROON
EQUATORIAL GUINEA
SAO TOME AND PRINCIPE
GABON

Madrid
Lisbon (Lisboa)
Algiers
Rabat-Salé
Casablanca
Dakar
Conakry
Accra
Ibadan
Lagos

ATLANTIC OCEAN
Gulf of Guinea
Bight of Benin
Bight of Bonny
Equator
Tropic of Cancer

ITALY

Naples, Vesuvio, 1277, Bari, Táranto, Cosenza, Catanzaro, Reggio di Calabria, Messina, Palermo, Catania, Siracusa, Etna 3323, Mt, Sicily, MALTA, Valletta

GREECE — Tiranë, ALBANIA, FYRO MACEDONIA, Thessaloníki, Ólympos 2917, Lárisa, Athens, Patras, Pelopónnisos, Ionian Sea, Aegean Sea, Dodekánisos (Dodecanese), Sea of Crete, Kríti (Crete), Iráklion

TURKEY — Istanbul, Sea of Marmara, Izmit, Bursa, Eskişehir, Balikesir, Izmir, Zonguldak, Kizil Irmak, Ankara, Sivas, Erzurum, Ağri Daği (Mt. Ararat) 5123, Van Gölü, Malatya, Kayseri, Konya, Denizli, Antalya, Adana, Mersin, Iskenderun, Gaziantep, Urfa, Diyarbakir

Nicosia, CYPRUS, Limassol, LEBANON, Beirut, Latakia, Homs

SYRIA — Aleppo, Damascus, IRAQ, Mosul, Kirkük, Baghdad, Tigris, Euphrates, An Nāsiriyah, Al Başrah

Caspian Sea — Gorgan, Rasht, Damāvand 5671, Sabzevar, Dasht-e Kavir, Tabriz, Daryācheh-ye Orümiyeh (L. Urmia), Orümiyeh, Tehran, Qom, Kermānshāh, Zagros Mountains, Eşfahān 4548, Yazd, Shirāz

IRAN

Haifa, ISRAEL, Tel Aviv-Yafo, Jerusalem, Dead Sea, Amman, JORDAN, Ma'ān, Elat, Aqaba, Sinai 2637, Tabūk 2579, Aynūnah

KUWAIT, Kuwait, Al Fuhayhil, Al Jawf, Sākākah, An Nafūd, Ha'il, Tayma', Khaybar, Al Jubayl, Ad Dammām, BAHRAIN, Manama, QATAR, Doha, Al Hutūf, Ad Dahnā, UNITED ARAB EMIRATES, Bandar-e Lengeh

SAUDI ARABIA — Buraydah, 'Unayzah, Shaqra, Riyadh, Ad Dilam, Al Hariq, Layla, Medina, Yanbu' al Bahr, Jedda, Mecca, At Tā'if, Al Lith, Al Qunfudhah, Abhā, Sabyā, Jizān, Najrān, Rub Al Khali

RED SEA, Râs Banâs, Halaib, Port Sudan, Suakin, Jaza'ir Farasān, Massawa, Arch. Kamarān, Dehalak

LIBYA — Al Khums, Misratah, Gulf of Sirte, Benghazi, Sirte, Ajdabiya, Al Bayda, Darnah, Sidi Barrani, Sirte Desert, Ras Lanuf, Jālū, Zaltan, Sabhā, Murzuq, Jabal as Sawdā' 840, 1200, Sarīr Calanscio, Great Sand Sea, Libyan Desert

EGYPT — Alexandria (El Iskandariya), Damietta, Port Said, Suez Canal, Isma'iliya, El Mahalla el Kubra, El Giza, Cairo (El Qâ'hira), Suez, El Faiyûm, Beni Suef, El Minya, Asyût, Sohâg 2187, Girga, Luxor, El Khârga, Idfu, Aswân, Aswân Dam 1st Cataract, Lake Nasser, Qattara Depression -133, Siwa, Qasr Farâfra, Farâfra Oasis, Dakhla Oasis, Al Kufra Oasis, Al Jawf, Libyan Plateau, Hurghada, Bûr Safâga, Quseir, Tubruq, Jabal al Akhdar

CHAD — Lake Chad, Ndjamena, Ati, Abéché, Geneina, Jebel Marra 3071, El Fasher, Faya-Largeau, Fada, Zouar, Tibesti 3265, Emi Koussi 3415, Aozou Strip, Plateau du Ennedi, Dépression du Mourdi, Bodélé, Bahr el Ghazal, Chari, Bousso, Bongor, Koumra, Sarh, Moundou, Am Timan, Birao

SUDAN — Wadi Halfa, 2nd Cataract, Selima Oasis, Nubian Desert 2260, Dongola, 3rd Cataract, 4th Cataract, Abu Hamed, Merowe, 5th Cataract, Berber, Atbara, Ed Debba, Ed Damer, el Milk, Jebel Abyad Plateau, Khartoum, Omdurman, White Nile Dam, Wad Medani, Sabaloka Cataract, Sennar, El Obeid, En Nahud, Umm Ruwaba, Kosti, Er Roseires, Gedaref, Kassala, Teseney, El Muglad, Talodi, Kodok, Radom, Bahr el Arab, Malakal, Lol, Wau, Nyala, Ayod, Akobo, Sobat, Jur, Sue, Amadi, Juba, Nimule 3187, Yambio, Bahr el Jebel (White Nile), Bahr el Azraq (Blue Nile)

CENTRAL AFRICAN REPUBLIC — Massif des Bongos 1055, Ouadda, Bria, Batangafo, Bambari, Sibut, Bangui, Berbérati, Carnot, Nola, Mbaiki, Bossangoa, Bozoum, Bouar, Ndélé, Bangassou, Mobaye, Ubangi

ETHIOPIA — Gonder, Lake Tana, Ras Dashen Terara 4620, Debre Tabor 3556, Choke Mts 4153, Abai (Blue Nile), Debre Mark'os, Addis Ababa, Nek'emte 3298, Dembi Dolo, Gore, Jima, Sodo, Yirga Alem, Gidole, Negele, Dolo Odo, Mega, Moyale, Awash, Dese 4000, Dire Dawa, Harer, Ahmar Mts, Degeh Bur, Ginir 4307, Mendebo Mts, Imi, K'elafo, Shebele, Genale, Lake Chamo, Maji 1548, Omo, Awash

ERITREA — Asmara, Keren, Adwa -116, Adigrat, Mekele, Teseney

DJIBOUTI, Djibouti 150, Saylac, Assab, Bab el Mandab

YEMEN REPUBLIC — Sana 3760, Hodeida, Ta'izz 3268, Dhamār, Habbān, Mukalla, Al Mukhā, Hadhramaut, Say'ūn, W. al Masilah, Madinat ash Sha'b, Aden, Little Aden, Shuqrā, Gulf of Aden

SOMALIA — Boosaaso, Raas Caseyr, Dharoor, Xaafuun, Ceerigaabo 2408, Berbera, Hargeysa, Boorama, Laascaanood, Bender Bayla, Haud, Ogaden, Buulobarde, Baydhabo, Luuq, Wajir, Hobyo, Gaalkacyo, Mogadishu, Marka, Ibba

UGANDA — Lake Albert, Fort Portal, Owen Falls Dam, Kampala, Kasese, Jinja, Lake Kyoga, Masindi, Gulu, Soroti, Tororo, Mt. Elgon 4321, Mambasa, Bunia, Arua, Moroto

KENYA — Lake Turkana, 2805, Marsabit, Mado Gashi, Eldoret, Nanyuki, Mt. Kenya 5200, Nakuru 2777, Nairobi, Thika, Machakos, Garissa, Kismaayo, Pate I., Lamu, Mombasa, Voi, Equator

DEMOCRATIC REPUBLIC OF CONGO — Mbandaka, Boyoma Falls, Kisangani, Buta, Aketi, Bondo, Isiro, Mungbere, Niangara, Uele, Bumba, Lake Edward, Mt. Karisimbi 4507, Lake Kivu, RWANDA, Kigali, Butare, BURUNDI 2685, Bujumbura, Bukavu, Kindu, Kibombo, Kasai, Lomela, Ikela, Opala, Ubundu, Dekese

Lake Victoria — Bukoba, Mwanza, Biharamulo, Shinyanga, L. Eyasi 3418, L. Natron, Mt. Kilimanjaro 5895, Arusha, Moshi, Pemba I.

INDIAN OCEAN

Congo, Owando, Ouesso, Impfondo, Dongou, Budjala, Libenge, Mbaiki

Lac Mai-Ndombe, Djambala, Bandundu, Lac Fitri

East Rift Valley

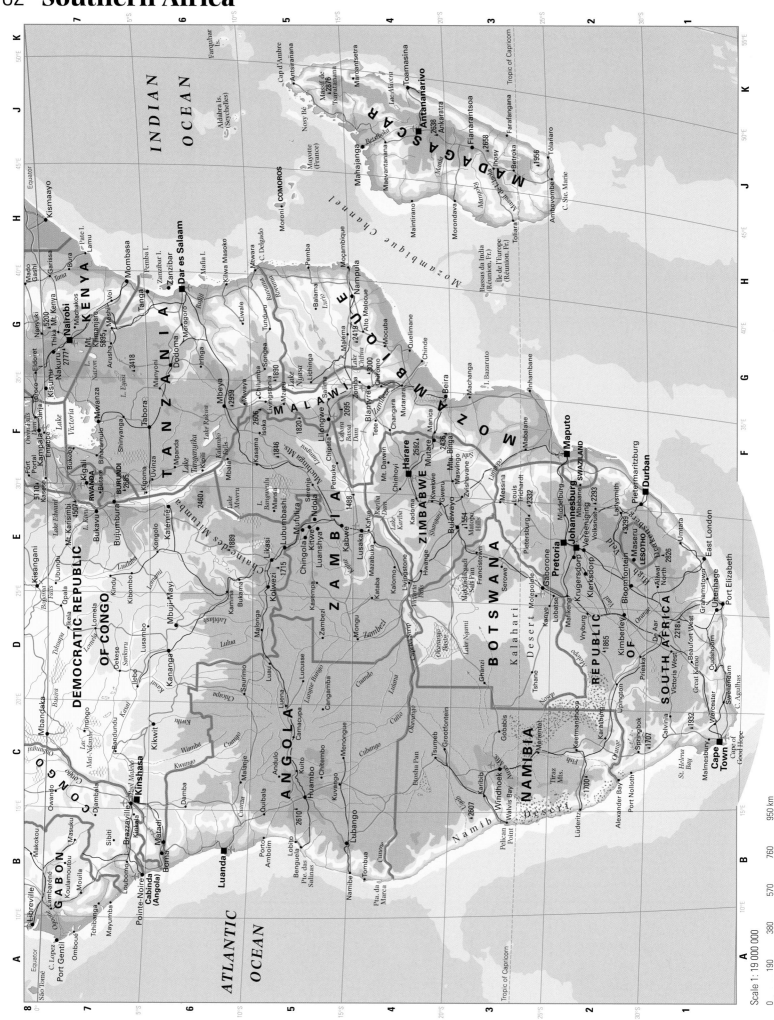

INDIAN
OCEAN

ATLANTIC
OCEAN

Scale 1 : 19 000 000

0   190   380   570   760   950 km

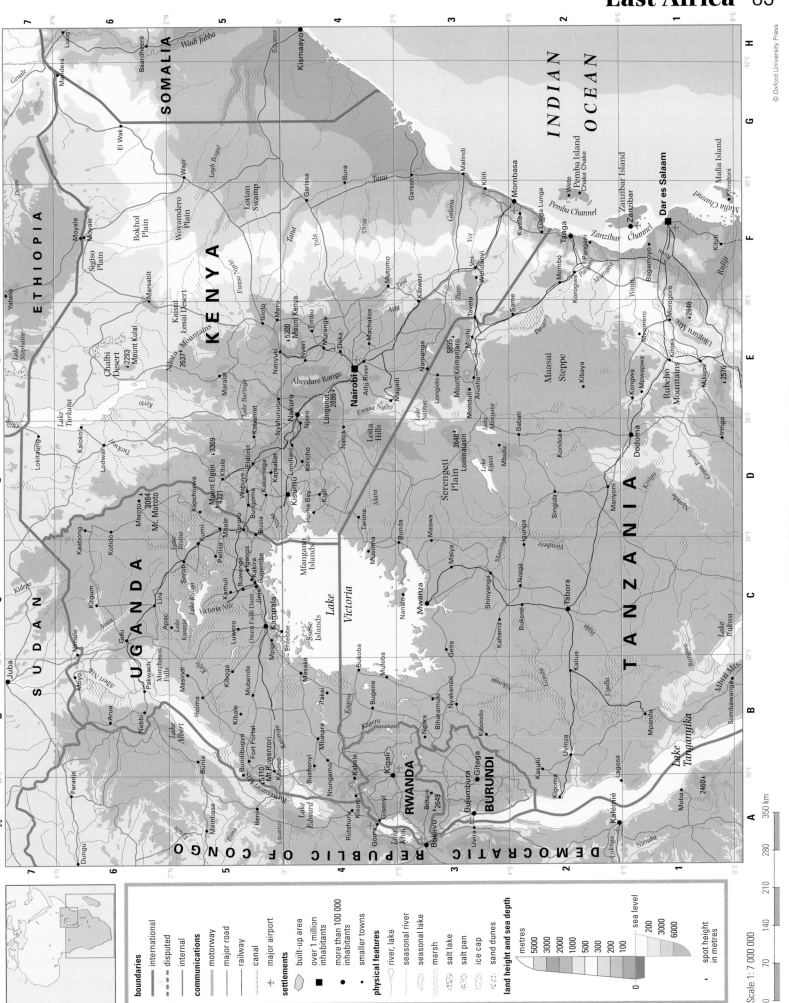

Scale 1 : 7 000 000

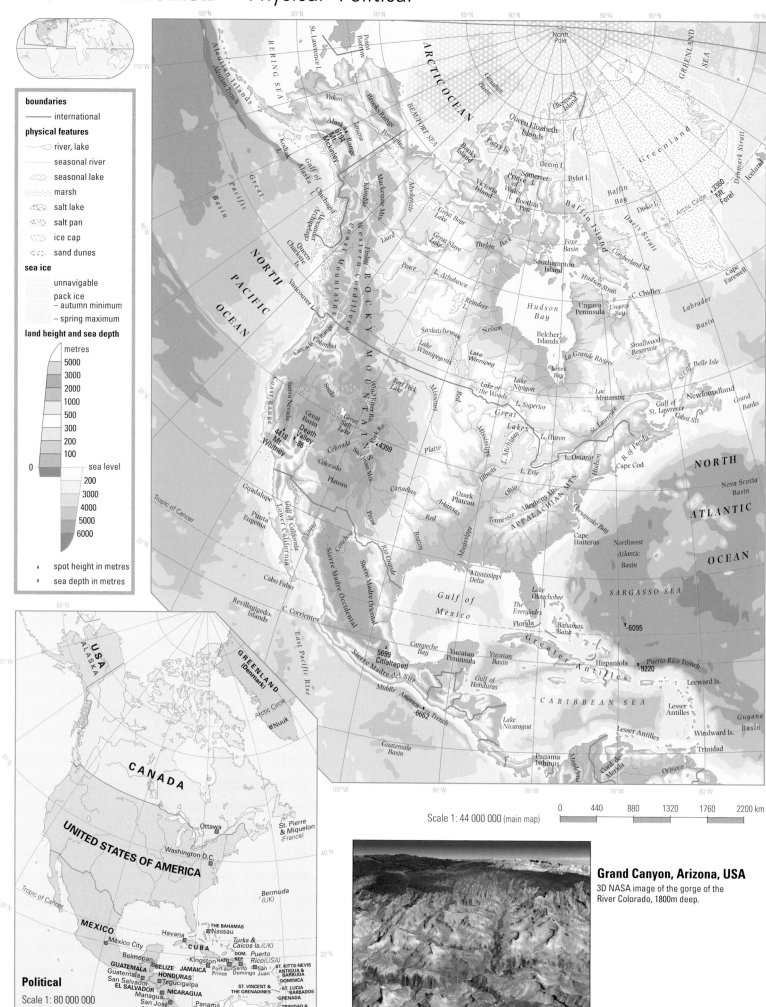

boundaries
— international

physical features
— river, lake
--- seasonal river
~ seasonal lake
~ marsh
~ salt lake
~ salt pan
~ ice cap
~ sand dunes

sea ice
unnavigable
pack ice
– autumn minimum
– spring maximum

land height and sea depth
metres
5000
3000
2000
1000
500
300
200
100
0   sea level
200
3000
4000
5000
6000

▲ spot height in metres
▼ sea depth in metres

Political
Scale 1 : 80 000 000

Scale 1 : 44 000 000 (main map)

0   440   880   1320   1760   2200 km

Oblique Mercator Projection   © Oxford University Press

Grand Canyon, Arizona, USA
3D NASA image of the gorge of the
River Colorado, 1800m deep.

Scale 1: 80 000 000

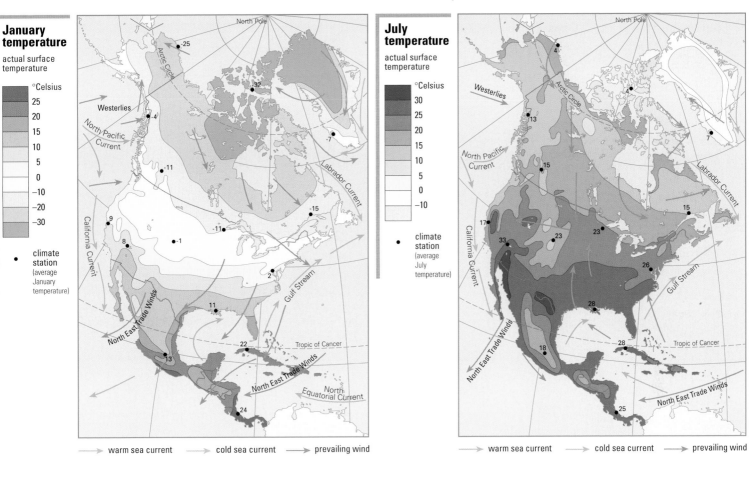

January temperature

actual surface temperature

°Celsius
25
20
15
10
5
0
−10
−20
−30

climate station (average January temperature)

North Pole
Arctic Circle
−25
32
Westerlies
−4
−7
North Pacific Current
−11
−15
California Current
9
−11
8
−1
2
Gulf Stream
11
22
13
Tropic of Cancer
North East Trade Winds
24
North East Trade Winds
North Equatorial Current

→ warm sea current   → cold sea current   → prevailing wind

July temperature

actual surface temperature

°Celsius
30
25
20
15
10
5
0
−10

climate station (average July temperature)

North Pole
4
Westerlies
4
Arctic Circle
13
North Pacific Current
15
7
California Current
17
33
23
23
15
Labrador Current
26
28
Gulf Stream
North East Trade Winds
18
28
Tropic of Cancer
25
North East Trade Winds

→ warm sea current   → cold sea current   → prevailing wind

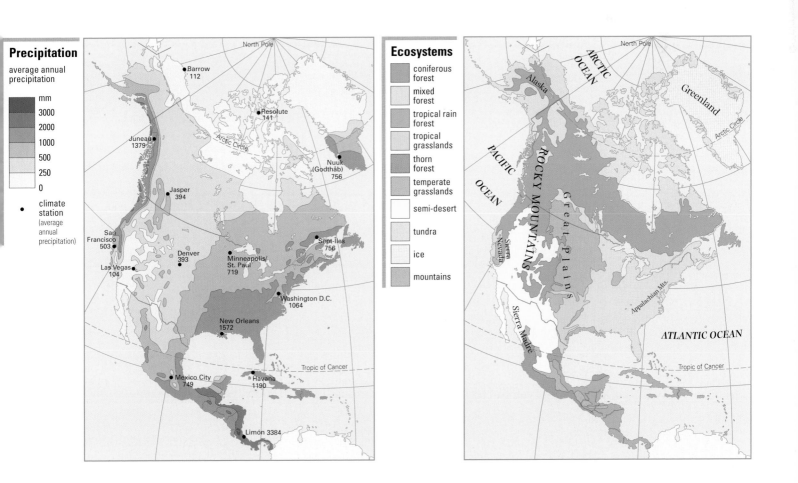

Precipitation

average annual precipitation

mm
3000
2000
1000
500
250
0

climate station (average annual precipitation)

North Pole
Barrow 112
Resolute 141
Juneau 1379
Arctic Circle
Nuuk (Godthåb) 756
Jasper 394
San Francisco 503
Denver 393
Minneapolis/ St. Paul 719
Sept-Îles 756
Las Vegas 104
Washington D.C. 1064
New Orleans 1572
Tropic of Cancer
Mexico City 749
Havana 1190
Limón 3384

Ecosystems

coniferous forest
mixed forest
tropical rain forest
tropical grasslands
thorn forest
temperate grasslands
semi-desert
tundra
ice
mountains

North Pole
ARCTIC OCEAN
Alaska
Greenland
PACIFIC OCEAN
ROCKY MOUNTAINS
Sierra Nevada
Great Plains
Arctic Circle
Appalachian Mts.
Sierra Madre
ATLANTIC OCEAN
Tropic of Cancer

    Oblique Mercator projection

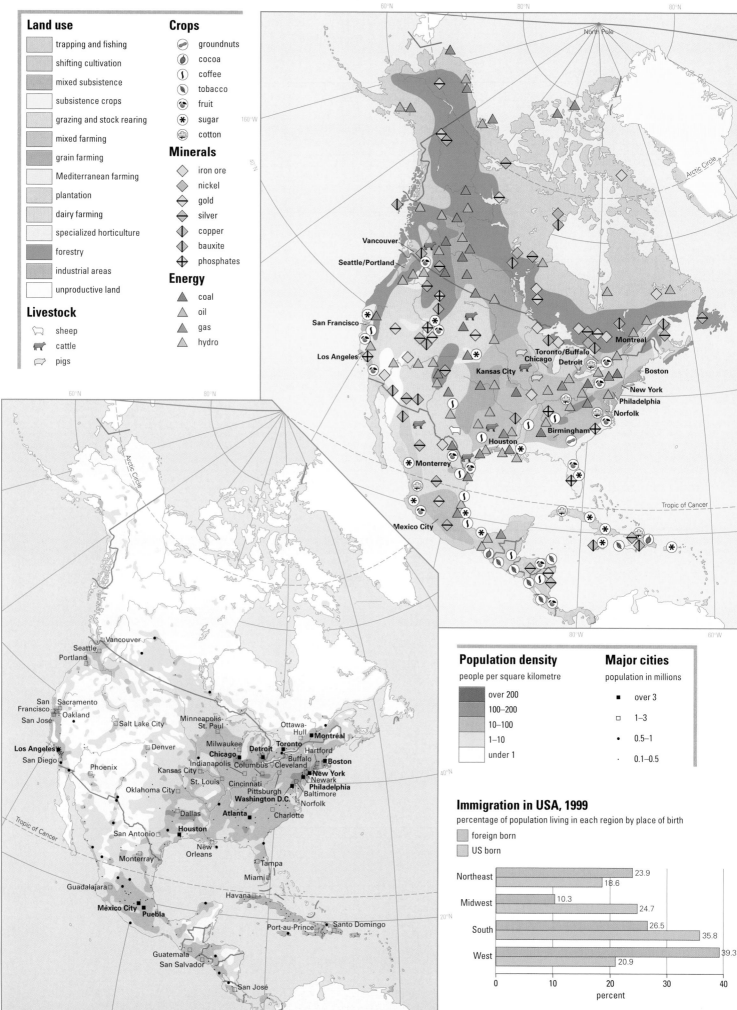

Land use

- trapping and fishing
- shifting cultivation
- mixed subsistence
- subsistence crops
- grazing and stock rearing
- mixed farming
- grain farming
- Mediterranean farming
- plantation
- dairy farming
- specialized horticulture
- forestry
- industrial areas
- unproductive land

Livestock

- sheep
- cattle
- pigs

Crops

- groundnuts
- cocoa
- coffee
- tobacco
- fruit
- sugar
- cotton

Minerals

- iron ore
- nickel
- gold
- silver
- copper
- bauxite
- phosphates

Energy

- coal
- oil
- gas
- hydro

Population density

people per square kilometre

- over 200
- 100–200
- 10–100
- 1–10
- under 1

Major cities

population in millions

- over 3
- 1–3
- 0.5–1
- 0.1–0.5

Immigration in USA, 1999

percentage of population living in each region by place of birth

- foreign born
- US born

Region	foreign born	US born
Northeast	23.9	18.6
Midwest	10.3	24.7
South	26.5	35.8
West	39.3	20.9

percent

Scale 1 : 40 000 000 (main map)

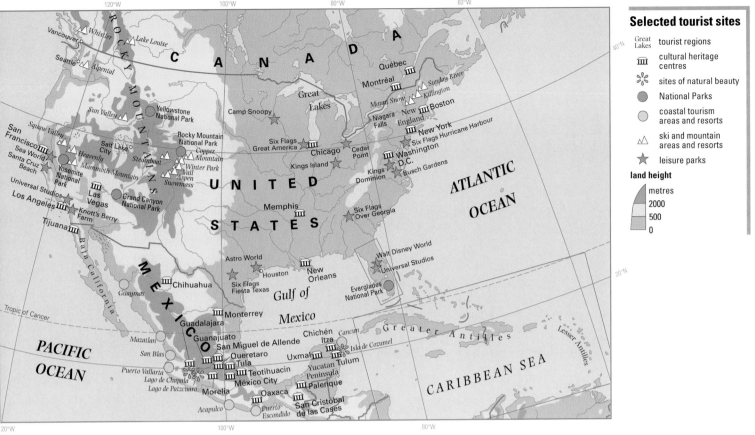

Selected tourist sites

- tourist regions
- cultural heritage centres
- sites of natural beauty
- National Parks
- coastal tourism areas and resorts
- ski and mountain areas and resorts
- leisure parks

land height

metres
2000
500
0

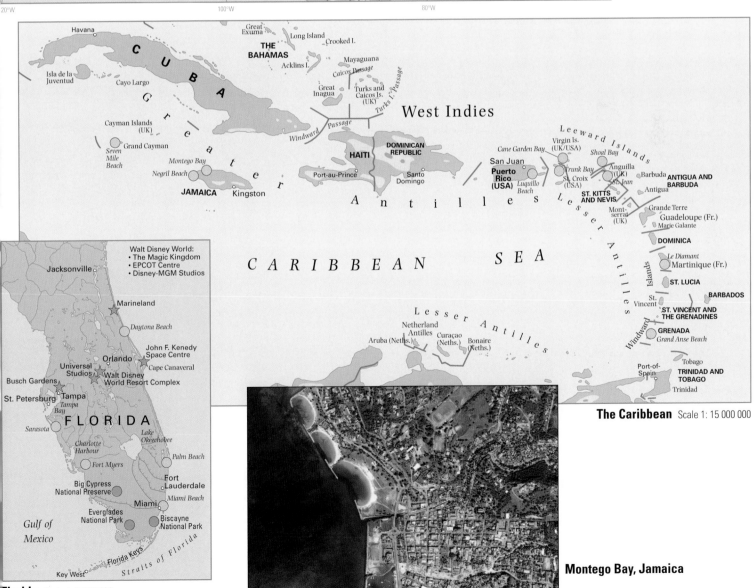

The Caribbean Scale 1 : 15 000 000

Walt Disney World:
- The Magic Kingdom
- EPCOT Centre
- Disney-MGM Studios

Florida Scale 1 : 8 000 000

Montego Bay, Jamaica

Oblique Mercator Projection   © Oxford University Press

88 Canada

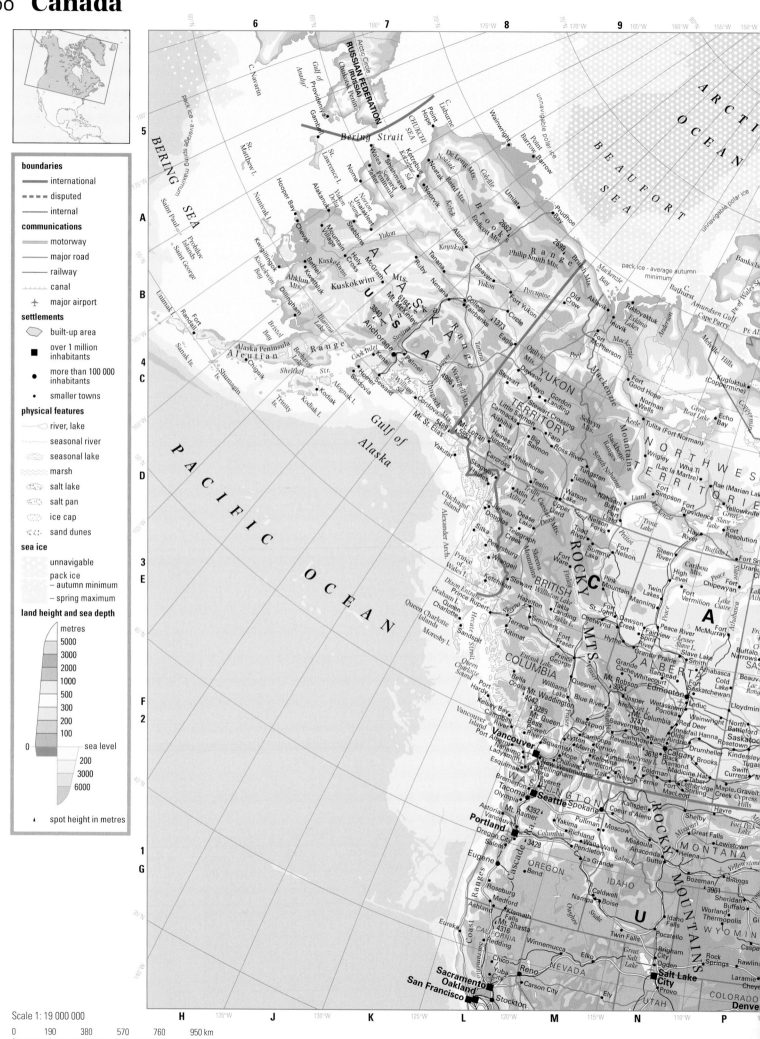

Scale 1: 19 000 000

Zenithal Equidistant Projection   © Oxford University Press

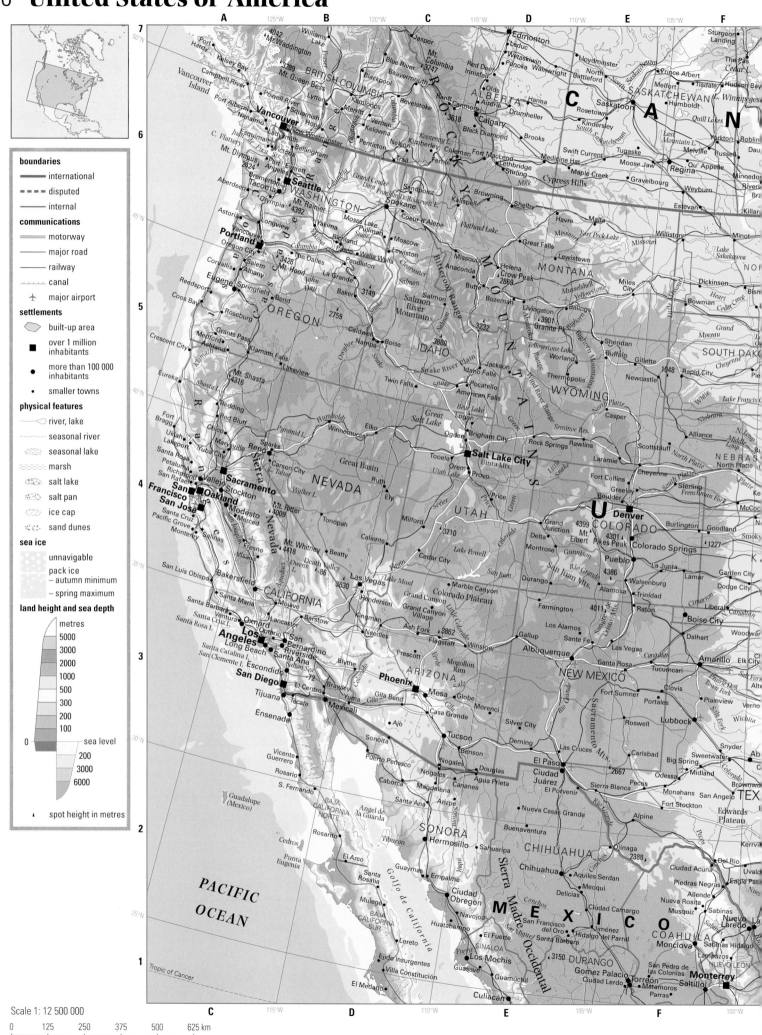

boundaries
━━━ international
╌╌╌ disputed
──── internal

communications
motorway
major road
railway
canal
✈ major airport

settlements
built-up area
■ over 1 million inhabitants
● more than 100 000 inhabitants
• smaller towns

physical features
river, lake
seasonal river
seasonal lake
marsh
salt lake
salt pan
ice cap
sand dunes

sea ice
unnavigable
pack ice
– autumn minimum
– spring maximum

land height and sea depth

metres
5000
3000
2000
1000
500
300
200
100
0 — sea level
200
3000
6000

▲ spot height in metres

Scale 1: 12 500 000

0   125   250   375   500   625 km

G
H
J
K
L
M
N
P
7
6
5
4
3
2
1
95°W
90°W
85°W
80°W
75°W
70°W
65°W
45°N
40°N
35°N
30°N
25°N
C A N A D A
ONTARIO
QUÉBEC
NEW BRUNSWICK
NOVA SCOTIA
MANITOBA
MINNESOTA
WISCONSIN
MICHIGAN
IOWA
ILLINOIS
INDIANA
OHIO
PENNSYLVANIA
NEW YORK
VERMONT
NEW HAMPSHIRE
MAINE
NEW JERSEY
DELAWARE
MARYLAND
WEST VIRGINIA
VIRGINIA
KENTUCKY
TENNESSEE
NORTH CAROLINA
SOUTH CAROLINA
GEORGIA
ALABAMA
MISSISSIPPI
LOUISIANA
ARKANSAS
MISSOURI
OKLAHOMA
FLORIDA
THE BAHAMAS
ATLANTIC
OCEAN
Gulf of Mexico
James Bay
Hudson Bay
Lake Superior
Lake Michigan
Lake Huron
Lake Erie
Lake Ontario
Georgian Bay
Lake of the Woods
Lake Nipigon
Lake Winnipeg
Lake Manitoba
Lac Seul
Lac St. Jean
Lac Mistassini
Gulf of St. Lawrence
Honguedo Passage
Bay of Fundy
Chesapeake Bay
Delaware Bay
Straits of Florida
Florida Keys
Florida Bay
Mississippi Delta
Appalachian Mts.
Ozark Plateau
Ouachita Mts.
Adirondack Mts.
Catskill Mts.
Boston Mts.
L. Okeechobee
The Everglades
Tropic of Cancer
Cape Hatteras
Cape Cod
C. Canaveral
C. Sable
Nantucket I.
Akimiski I.
Manitoulin I.
Ile d'Anticosti
Mississippi
Missouri
Ohio
Tennessee
Cumberland
Arkansas
Red
Ouachita
Yazoo
Alabama
Tombigbee
Savannah
Altamaha
Pearl
Sabine
Trinity
Brazos
Colorado
Connecticut
Hudson
Albany
Moose
Abitibi
Missinaibi
Harricana
Winnipeg
Norway House
Big Trout Lake
Island Lake
Sandy Lake
Winisk L.
Attawapiskat
Lansdowne House
Fort Hope
Pickle Lake
Moosonee
Eastmain
Waskaganish
Chibougamau
Matagami
Mingan
Sept-Îles
Manicouagan
Baie-Comeau
Matane
Rimouski
Gaspé
Chandler
Campbellton
Bathurst
Miramichi
Chicoutimi
Jonquière
Roberval
Dolbeau
Rivière-du-Loup
Edmundston
Grand Falls
Moncton
Amherst
Saint John
Fredericton
Woodstock
Presque Isle
Digby
Yarmouth
Clark's Harbour
Québec
Lévis
Montmagny
La Tuque
Shawinigan
Trois-Rivières
Drummondville
Sherbrooke
Coaticook
Montréal
Ottawa
Hull
Cornwall
Hawkesbury
Pembroke
Renfrew
Arnprior
Maniwaki
Mont-Laurier
Val-d'Or
Rouyn-Noranda
Timmins
Kirkland Lake
New Liskeard
Cochrane
Kapuskasing
Hearst
Coral
Foleyet
Chapleau
Wawa
White River
Michipicoten
Terrace Bay
Nipigon
Thunder Bay
Geraldton
Longlac
Nakina
Auden
Sioux Lookout
Dryden
Kenora
Atikokan
Fort Frances
Winnipeg
Selkirk
Riverton
Morden
Sudbury
North Bay
Mattawa
Parry Sound
Huntsville
Midland
Owen Sound
Kincardine
Hanover
Guelph
Kitchener
Hamilton
St. Catharines
Niagara Falls
Toronto
Oshawa
Peterborough
Kingston
Smiths Falls
London
Sarnia
Windsor
Chatham
Blind River
Sault Ste. Marie
Manitoulin I.
Duluth
Superior
Ironwood
Ontonagon
Copper Harbor
Keweenaw Peninsula
Marquette
Escanaba
St. Ignace
Mackinaw City
Traverse City
Green Bay
Door Penin.
Wausau
Eau Claire
Appleton
Oshkosh
Manitowoc
Sheboygan
Fond du Lac
Milwaukee
Madison
Waukesha
Janesville
Kenosha
Waukegan
Chicago
Rockford
Dubuque
Cedar Rapids
Waterloo
Davenport
Clinton
Iowa City
Rock Island
Des Moines
Fort Dodge
Mason City
Albert Lea
Rochester
Winona
La Crosse
St. Paul
Minneapolis
Mankato
New Ulm
Red Wing
Worthington
St. Cloud
Willmar
Brainerd
Little Falls
Bemidji
Grand Rapids
Virginia
Crookston
Fergus Falls
Moorhead
Fargo
Wahpeton
Sioux City
Sioux Falls
Council Bluffs
Omaha
Lincoln
Grand Island
Kansas City
Topeka
Lawrence
Manhattan
St. Joseph
Atchison
Salina
Emporia
Wichita
McPherson
Hutchinson
Joplin
Springfield
Columbia
Jefferson City
St. Louis
Hannibal
Quincy
Kirksville
Peoria
Bloomington
Galesburg
Champaign
Decatur
Danville
Kankakee
Gary
South Bend
Elkhart
Fort Wayne
Kokomo
Muncie
Lafayette
Anderson
Indianapolis
Terre Haute
Evansville
Bloomington
Louisville
Lexington
Frankfort
Owensboro
Bowling Green
Paducah
Hopkinsville
Clarksville
Nashville
Knoxville
Oak Ridge
Johnson City
Kingsport
Chattanooga
Memphis
Jackson
Huntsville
Decatur
Florence
Birmingham
Tuscaloosa
Anniston
Gadsden
Montgomery
Mobile
Dothan
Selma
Tupelo
Meridian
Jackson
Vicksburg
Hattiesburg
Biloxi
Gulfport
Pascagoula
New Orleans
Baton Rouge
Lafayette
Lake Charles
Alexandria
Shreveport
Monroe
Natchez
Little Rock
Hot Springs
Pine Bluff
Fort Smith
Fayetteville
Jonesboro
Texarkana
El Dorado
Tulsa
Oklahoma City
Muskogee
McAlester
Ardmore
Dallas
Fort Worth
Irving
Waco
Temple
Austin
San Antonio
Houston
Galveston
Beaumont
Port Arthur
Pasadena
Bay City
Freeport
Victoria
Corpus Christi
Kingsville
Brownsville
Matamoros
Harlingen
Tyler
Longview
Lufkin
Nacogdoches
Detroit
Flint
Saginaw
Lansing
Grand Rapids
Kalamazoo
Muskegon
Jackson
Toledo
Cleveland
Akron
Canton
Youngstown
Columbus
Dayton
Cincinnati
Springfield
Mansfield
Pittsburgh
Erie
Altoona
Johnstown
Harrisburg
Lancaster
York
Reading
Allentown
Scranton
Wilkes-Barre
Williamsport
State College
Philadelphia
Trenton
Newark
New York
Paterson
Buffalo
Rochester
Syracuse
Utica
Schenectady
Albany
Binghamton
Elmira
Poughkeepsie
Hartford
New Haven
Bridgeport
Springfield
Worcester
Boston
Providence
Fall River
New Bedford
Lowell
Manchester
Nashua
Concord
Portsmouth
Portland
Lewiston
Augusta
Bangor
Burlington
Plattsburgh
Rutland
Barre
Baltimore
Washington D.C.
Annapolis
Dover
Wilmington
Atlantic City
Salisbury
Cumberland
Hagerstown
Frederick
Winchester
Fredericksburg
Richmond
Charlottesville
Staunton
Lynchburg
Roanoke
Norfolk
Virginia Beach
Hampton
Newport News
Portsmouth
Chesapeake
Charleston
Huntington
Parkersburg
Clarksburg
Wheeling
Morgantown
Beckley
Bluefield
Winston-Salem
Greensboro
Durham
Raleigh
Charlotte
Asheville
Fayetteville
Wilmington
Rocky Mount
Goldsboro
Wilson
New Bern
Jacksonville
Elizabeth City
Greenville
Spartanburg
Columbia
Florence
Charleston
Rock Hill
Anderson
Atlanta
Athens
Augusta
Macon
Columbus
Savannah
Albany
Valdosta
Waycross
Brunswick
Jacksonville
Tallahassee
Panama City
Pensacola
Gainesville
Ocala
Orlando
Tampa
St. Petersburg
Clearwater
Lakeland
Sarasota
Bradenton
Fort Myers
Naples
Melbourne
Ft. Pierce
West Palm Beach
Fort Lauderdale
Miami
Homestead
Key West
Daytona Beach
St. Augustine
Freeport
Grand Bahama
Great Abaco
Marsh Harbour
Nassau
New Providence I.
Andros
Andros Town
Eleuthera
Governor's Harbour
Cat I.
San Salvador
Long Island
Great Exuma
853
472

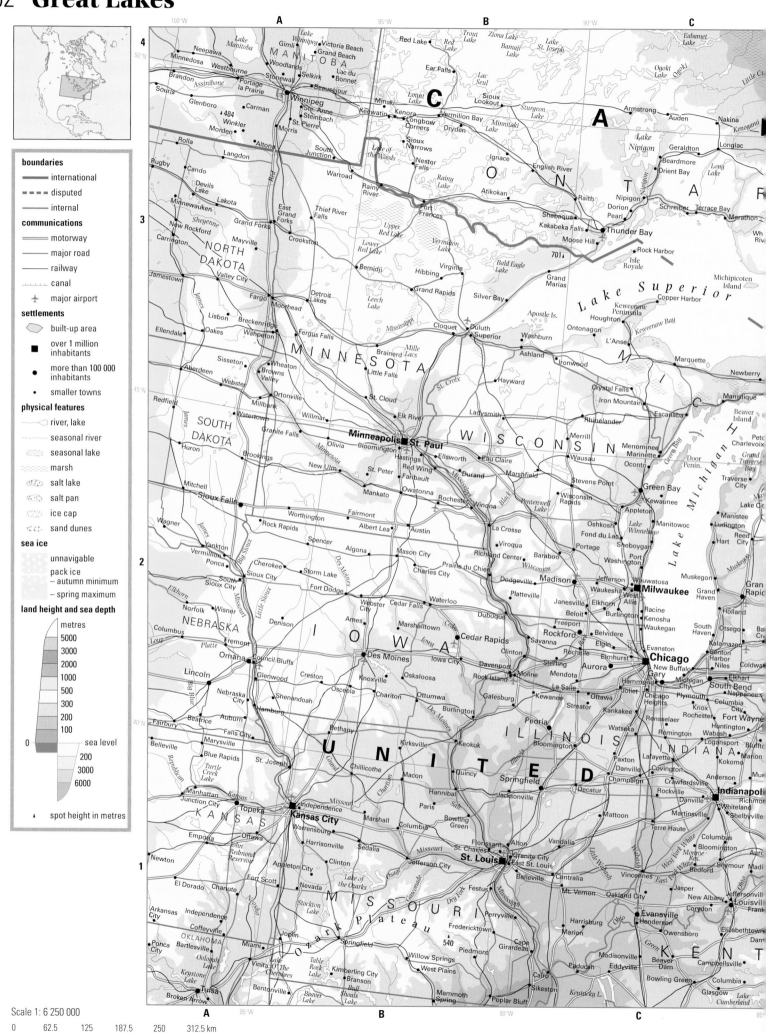

Conical Orthomorphic Projection

Scale 1: 6 250 000

0   62.5   125   187.5   250   312.5 km

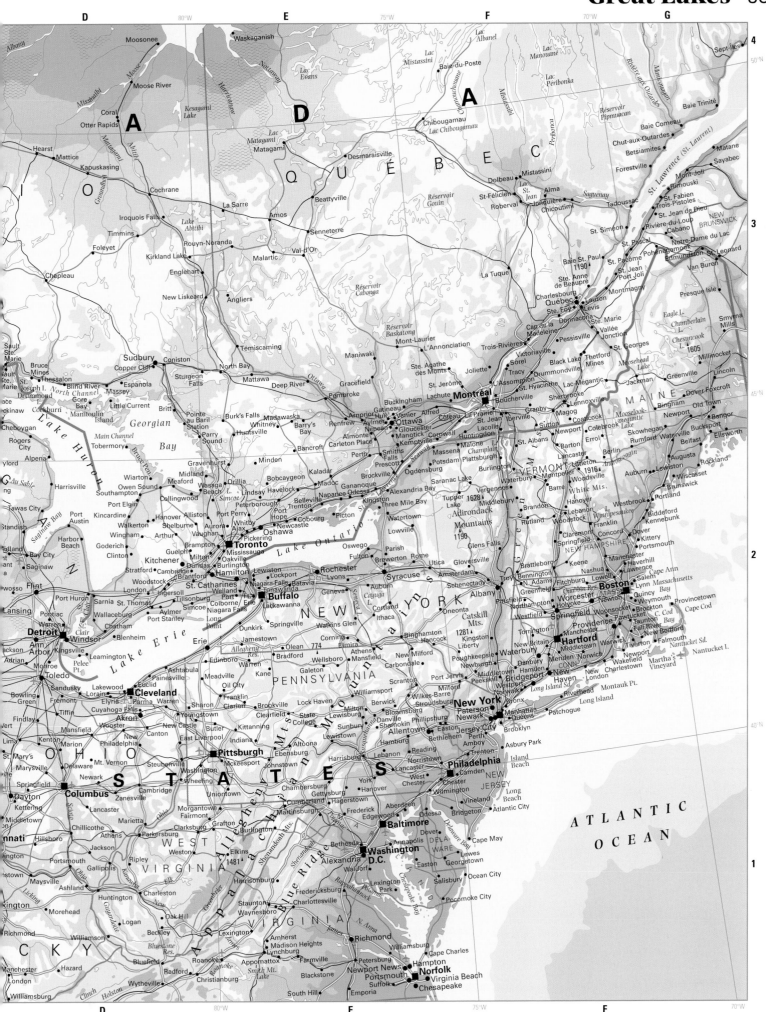

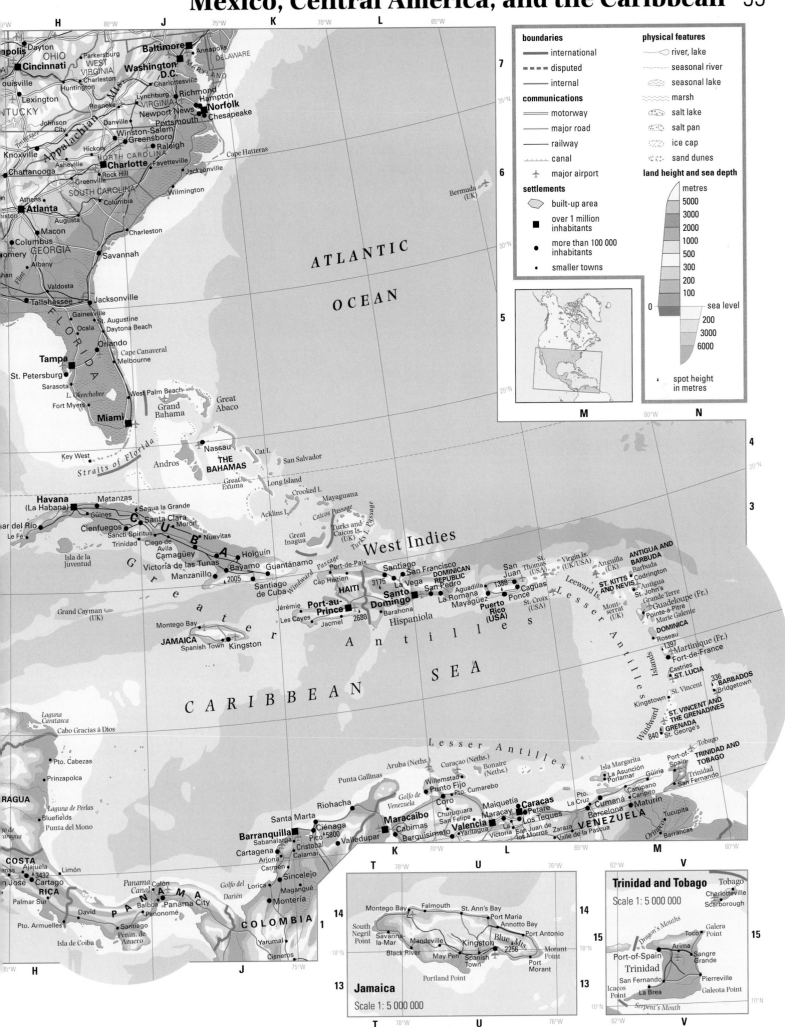

boundaries
— international
--- disputed
— internal

communications
— motorway
— major road
— railway
+-+-+ canal
✈ major airport

settlements
⬡ built-up area
■ over 1 million inhabitants
● more than 100 000 inhabitants
• smaller towns

physical features
river, lake
seasonal river
seasonal lake
marsh
salt lake
salt pan
ice cap
sand dunes

land height and sea depth
metres
5000
3000
2000
1000
500
300
200
100
0 — sea level
200
3000
6000
● spot height in metres

ATLANTIC OCEAN

OHIO
WEST VIRGINIA
KENTUCKY
VIRGINIA
NORTH CAROLINA
SOUTH CAROLINA
GEORGIA
FLORIDA

Dayton
Parkersburg
Baltimore
Annapolis
DELAWARE
Cincinnati
Washington D.C.
Charlottesville
MARYLAND
Louisville
Charleston
Richmond
Lexington
Lynchburg
Hampton
Newport News
Norfolk
Johnson City
Huntington
Roanoke
Portsmouth
Chesapeake
Knoxville
Danville
Winston-Salem
Greensboro
Raleigh
Chattanooga
Hickory
Fayetteville
Asheville
Rock Hill
Cape Hatteras
Greenville
Charlotte
Athens
Columbia
Wilmington
Atlanta
Augusta
Macon
Columbus
montgomery
Albany
Savannah
Flint
Valdosta
Jacksonville
Tallahassee
Gainesville
St. Augustine
Ocala
Daytona Beach
Orlando
Cape Canaveral
Tampa
Melbourne
St. Petersburg
L. Okeechobee
Sarasota
West Palm Beach
Fort Myers
Miami
Key West
Straits of Florida
Nassau
Cat I.
San Salvador
Andros
THE BAHAMAS
Grand Bahama
Great Abaco
Great Exuma
Long Island
Crooked I.
Mayaguana
Acklins I.
Great Inagua
Caicos Passage
Turks and Caicos Is. (UK)
Bermuda (UK)

Havana (La Habana)
Matanzas
Sagua la Grande
Santa Clara
Morón
Pinar del Río
Güines
CUBA
Cienfuegos
Sancti Spíritus
Nuevitas
Le Fé
Trinidad
Ciego de Avila
Camagüey
Holguín
Isla de la Juventud
Victoria de las Tunas
Bayamo
Guantánamo
Manzanillo
2005
Windward Passage
Santiago de Cuba
Grand Cayman (UK)
Greater
Montego Bay
JAMAICA
Spanish Town
Kingston

West Indies
Cap Haïtien
Port-de-Paix
Santiago
San Francisco
DOMINICAN REPUBLIC
Jérémie
Les Cayes
Jacmel
Port-au-Prince
HAITI
3175
La Vega
Santo Domingo
San Pedro
2680
Barahona
Hispaniola
Antilles

San Juan
St. Thomas (USA)
Virgin Is. (UK/USA)
Anguilla (UK)
ANTIGUA AND BARBUDA
Barbuda
Codrington
Aguadilla
1388
Caguas
Antigua
St. John's
Mayagüez
Puerto Rico (USA)
Ponce
La Romana
St. Croix (USA)
Leeward Is.
ST. KITTS AND NEVIS
Montserrat (UK)
Grande Terre
Pointe-à-Pitre
Guadeloupe (Fr.)
Marie Galente
DOMINICA
Roseau
1397
Martinique (Fr.)
Fort-de-France
Castries
ST. LUCIA
336
BARBADOS
Bridgetown
Kingstown
St. Vincent
ST. VINCENT AND THE GRENADINES
840
GRENADA
St. George's
Lesser Antilles Islands
Windward

CARIBBEAN SEA

Laguna Caratasca
Cabo Gracias á Dios
Pto. Cabezas
Prinzapolca
RAGUA
Laguna de Perlas
Bluefields
Punta del Mono
o de
aragua
COSTA
Ajajuela
3432
Limón
RICA
San José
Cartago
Palmar Sur
David
Santiago
Penín. de
Azuero
Isla de Coiba
Pto. Armuelles
Panama Canal
Colón
Balboa
PANAMA
Penonomé
Panama City
Golfo del Darién
COLOMBIA

Lesser Antilles
Aruba (Neths.)
Curaçao (Neths.)
Bonaire (Neths.)
Isla Margarita
Tobago
Punta Gallinas
Willemstad
Punto Fijo
Pto. Cumarebo
La Asunción
Porlamar
Port-of-Spain
TRINIDAD AND TOBAGO
Punta Gallinas
Coro
Güiria
Riohacha
Golfo de Venezuela
Churuguara
Maiquetía
Carúpano
Caripito
Trinidad
Santa Marta
Ciénaga
Maracaibo
San Felipe
Caracas
Cumaná
Maturín
San Fernando
Barranquilla
Pico
5800
Cabimas
Barquisimeto
Valencia
Petare
Los Teques
Barcelona
VENEZUELA
Tucupita
Sabanalarga
Valledupar
Yaritagua
La Cruz
Cartagena
Cristobal
Victoria
San Juan de los Morros
Zaraza
Orinoco
Barrancas
Arjona
Calamar
Barinas
Valle de la Pascua
Carmen
Sincelejo
Magangué
Lorica
Montería

COSTA
RICA
PANAMA

Jamaica (inset) — Scale 1: 5 000 000
Montego Bay
Falmouth
St. Ann's Bay
Port Maria
Annotto Bay
Port Antonio
South Negril Point
Savanna-la-Mar
Mandeville
Blue Mts.
2256
Morant Point
Kingston
Black River
May Pen
Spanish Town
Portland Point
Port Morant

Trinidad and Tobago (inset) — Scale 1: 5 000 000
Tobago
Charlotteville
Scarborough
Dragon's Mouths
Galera Point
Toco
Port-of-Spain
Arima
Sangre Grande
Trinidad
San Fernando
Pierreville
Icacos Point
La Brea
Galeota Point
Serpent's Mouth

© Oxford University Press

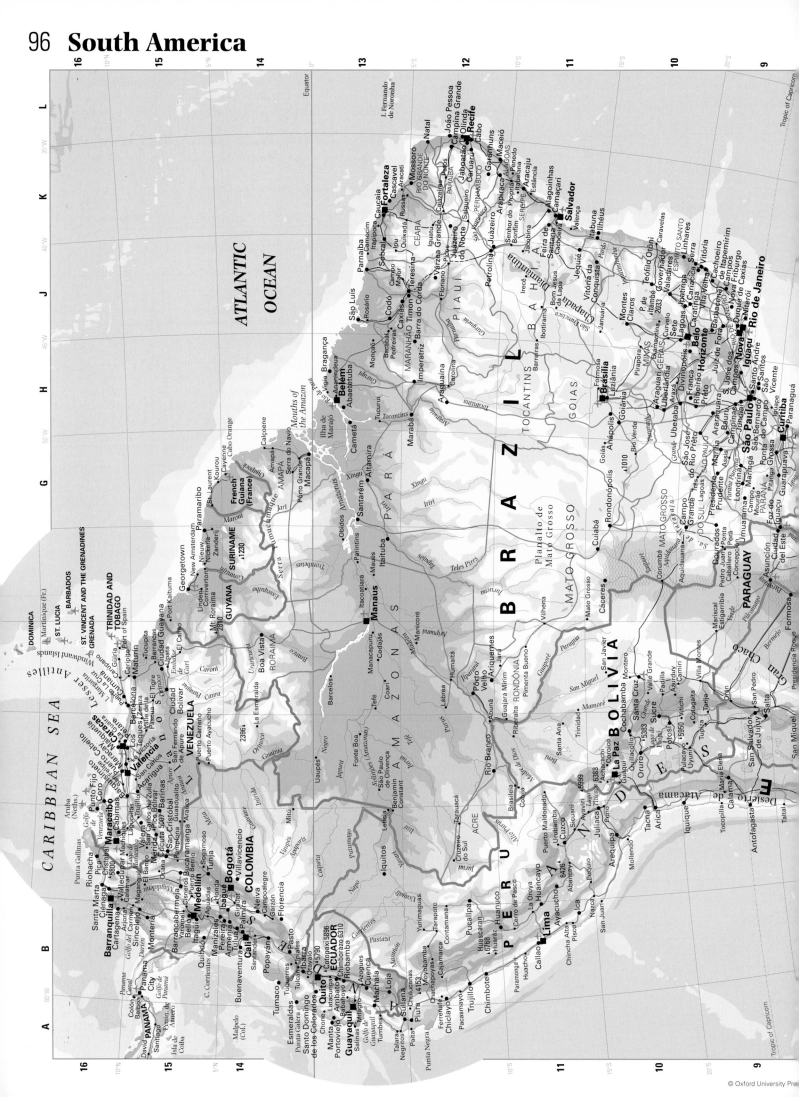

Political

Scale 1: 70 000 000

PANAMA
VENEZUELA
Caracas
COLOMBIA
Bogotá
GUYANA Georgetown
SURINAME Paramaribo
Cayenne
French Guiana (France)
Quito
ECUADOR
PERU
Lima
La Paz
BOLIVIA
B R A Z I L
Brasília
PARAGUAY
Asunción
URUGUAY Montevideo
Buenos Aires
ARGENTINA
C H I L E
Santiago
Juan Fernández Isl. (Chile)
Stanley
Falkland Islands (UK)
South Georgia (UK)

Rocas Island (Brazil)
Fernando de Noronha (Brazil)
Equator
Tropic of Capricorn

Deforestation in the Brazilian rain forest

Grey colour shows areas of forest loss with a characteristic 'fishbone' pattern.

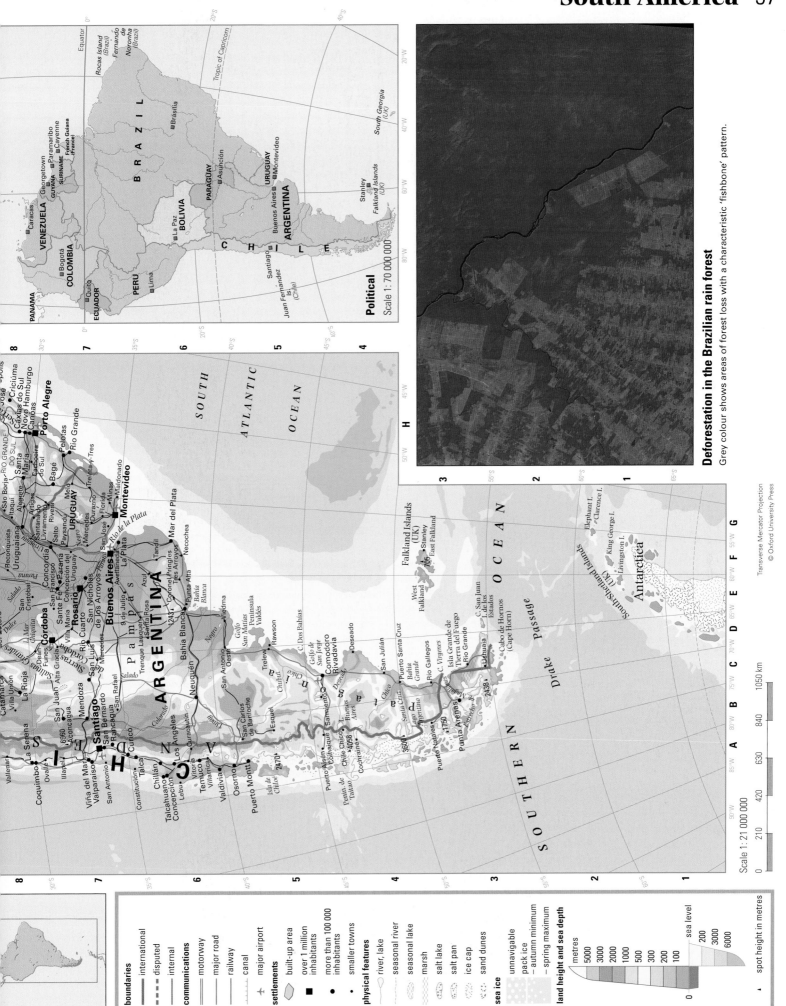

Transverse Mercator Projection
© Oxford University Press

Scale 1: 21 000 000

0   210   420   630   840   1050 km

S O U T H   A T L A N T I C   O C E A N

S O U T H E R N   O C E A N

ARGENTINA
P a m p a s
P a t a g o n i a
CHILE

Buenos Aires
Montevideo
URUGUAY
Rosario
Córdoba
Santiago
Valparaíso
Mendoza
Mar del Plata
Porto Alegre
Bahía Blanca
Comodoro Rivadavia
Puerto Montt
Punta Arenas
Ushuaia
Río Gallegos
Falkland Islands (UK)
Stanley
West Falkland
East Falkland
Cabo de Hornos (Cape Horn)
Tierra del Fuego
Isla Grande de Tierra del Fuego
Drake Passage
Antarctica
South Shetland Islands (UK)
Elephant I.
Clarence I.
King George I.
Livingston I.

Legend

boundaries
international
disputed
internal

communications
motorway
major road
railway
canal
✈ major airport

settlements
built-up area
⬡ over 1 million inhabitants
■ more than 100 000 inhabitants
● smaller towns

physical features
river, lake
seasonal river
seasonal lake
marsh
salt lake
salt pan
ice cap
sand dunes

sea ice
unnavigable
pack ice
— autumn minimum
— spring maximum

land height and sea depth

metres	
5000	
3000	
2000	
1000	
500	
300	
200	
100	
sea level	
200	
3000	
6000	

▲ spot height in metres

Scale 1 : 70 000 000

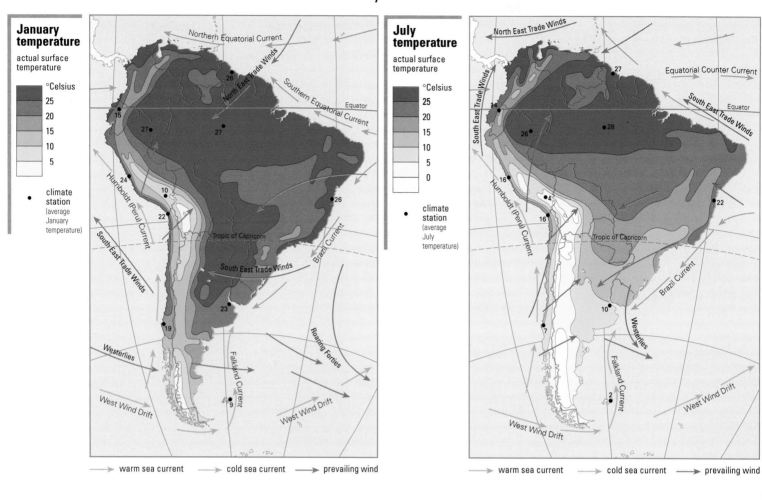

January temperature

actual surface temperature

°Celsius
25
20
15
10
5

climate station (average January temperature)

Northern Equatorial Current
North East Trade Winds
Southern Equatorial Current
Equator
26
15
27
27
Humboldt (Peru) Current
24
10
22
Tropic of Capricorn
South East Trade Winds
South East Trade Winds
Brazil Current
26
23
19
Westerlies
Falkland Current
Roaring Forties
West Wind Drift
West Wind Drift
9

July temperature

actual surface temperature

°Celsius
25
20
15
10
5
0

climate station (average July temperature)

North East Trade Winds
South East Trade Winds
Equatorial Counter Current
27
14
26
28
South East Trade Winds
Equator
Humboldt (Peru) Current
16
4
22
16
Tropic of Capricorn
Brazil Current
10
Westerlies
7
Falkland Current
West Wind Drift
West Wind Drift
2

→ warm sea current   → cold sea current   → prevailing wind

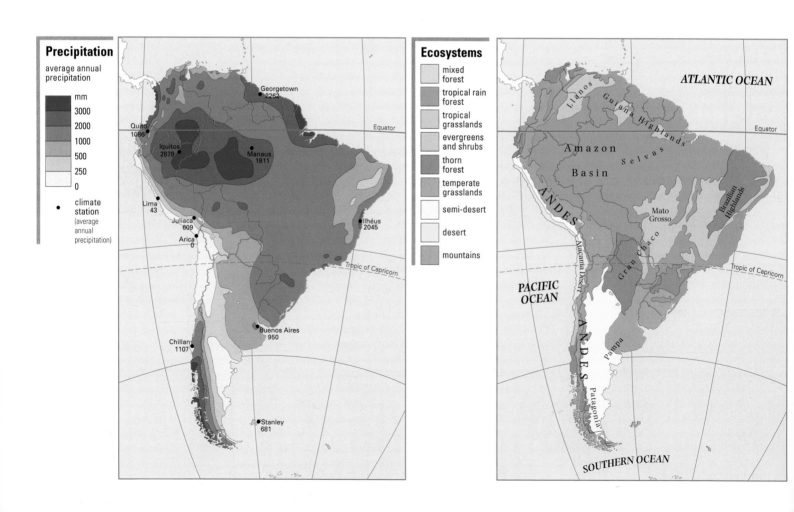

Precipitation

average annual precipitation

mm
3000
2000
1000
500
250
0

climate station (average annual precipitation)

Georgetown 2262
Quito 1086
Iquitos 2879
Manaus 1811
Equator
Lima 43
Juliaca 609
Arica 0
Ilhéus 2045
Tropic of Capricorn
Chillan 1107
Buenos Aires 950
Stanley 681

Ecosystems

mixed forest
tropical rain forest
tropical grasslands
evergreens and shrubs
thorn forest
temperate grasslands
semi-desert
desert
mountains

ATLANTIC OCEAN
Llanos
Guiana Highlands
Equator
Amazon Basin
Selvas
ANDES
Mato Grosso
Brazilian Highlands
Atacama Desert
Gran Chaco
Tropic of Capricorn
PACIFIC OCEAN
ANDES
Pampa
Patagonia
SOUTHERN OCEAN

Oblique Mercator Projection   © Oxford University Pre

Scale 1: 45 000 000

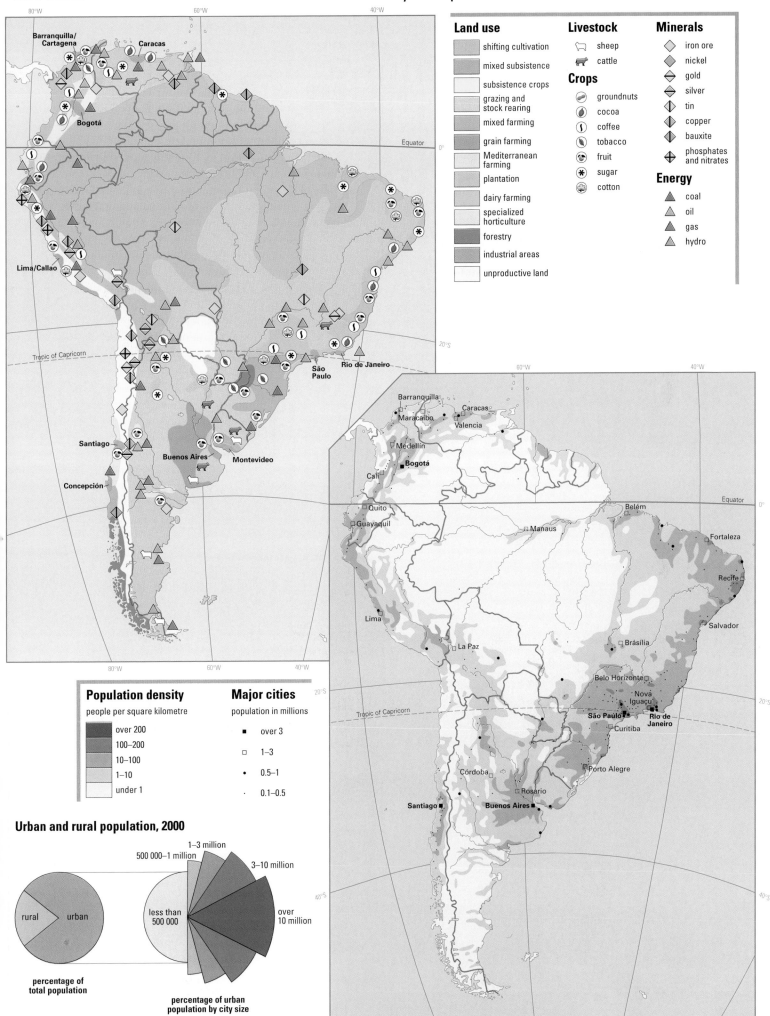

Land use

- shifting cultivation
- mixed subsistence
- subsistence crops
- grazing and stock rearing
- mixed farming
- grain farming
- Mediterranean farming
- plantation
- dairy farming
- specialized horticulture
- forestry
- industrial areas
- unproductive land

Livestock

- sheep
- cattle

Crops

- groundnuts
- cocoa
- coffee
- tobacco
- fruit
- sugar
- cotton

Minerals

- iron ore
- nickel
- gold
- silver
- tin
- copper
- bauxite
- phosphates and nitrates

Energy

- coal
- oil
- gas
- hydro

Equator
0°

Tropic of Capricorn

20°S

São Paulo
Rio de Janeiro

Santiago
Concepción
Buenos Aires
Montevideo

Lima/Callao

Bogotá

Barranquilla/Cartagena
Caracas

Population density

people per square kilometre

- over 200
- 100–200
- 10–100
- 1–10
- under 1

Major cities

population in millions

- over 3
- 1–3
- 0.5–1
- 0.1–0.5

Urban and rural population, 2000

rural urban

less than 500 000
500 000–1 million
1–3 million
3–10 million
over 10 million

percentage of total population

percentage of urban population by city size

Barranquilla
Maracaibo
Caracas
Valencia
Medellín
Bogotá
Cali
Quito
Guayaquil
Manaus
Belém
Fortaleza
Recife
Salvador
Lima
La Paz
Brasília
Belo Horizonte
Nova Iguaçu
São Paulo
Rio de Janeiro
Curitiba
Córdoba
Porto Alegre
Rosário
Santiago
Buenos Aires

Equator
0°

Tropic of Capricorn
20°S

40°S

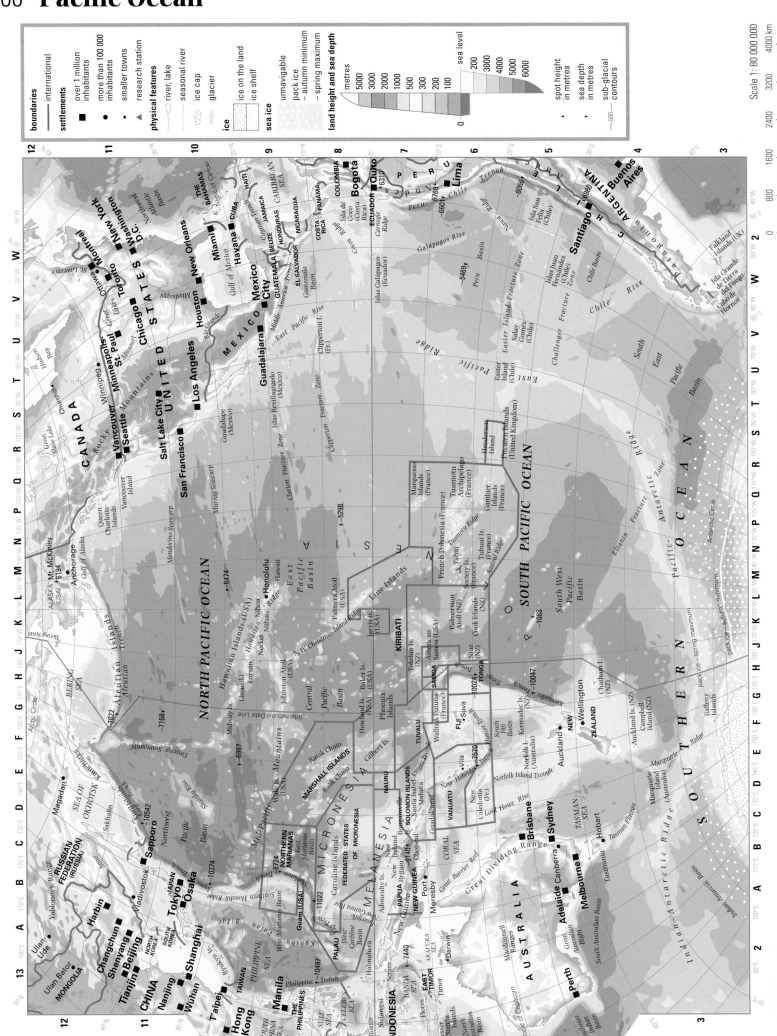

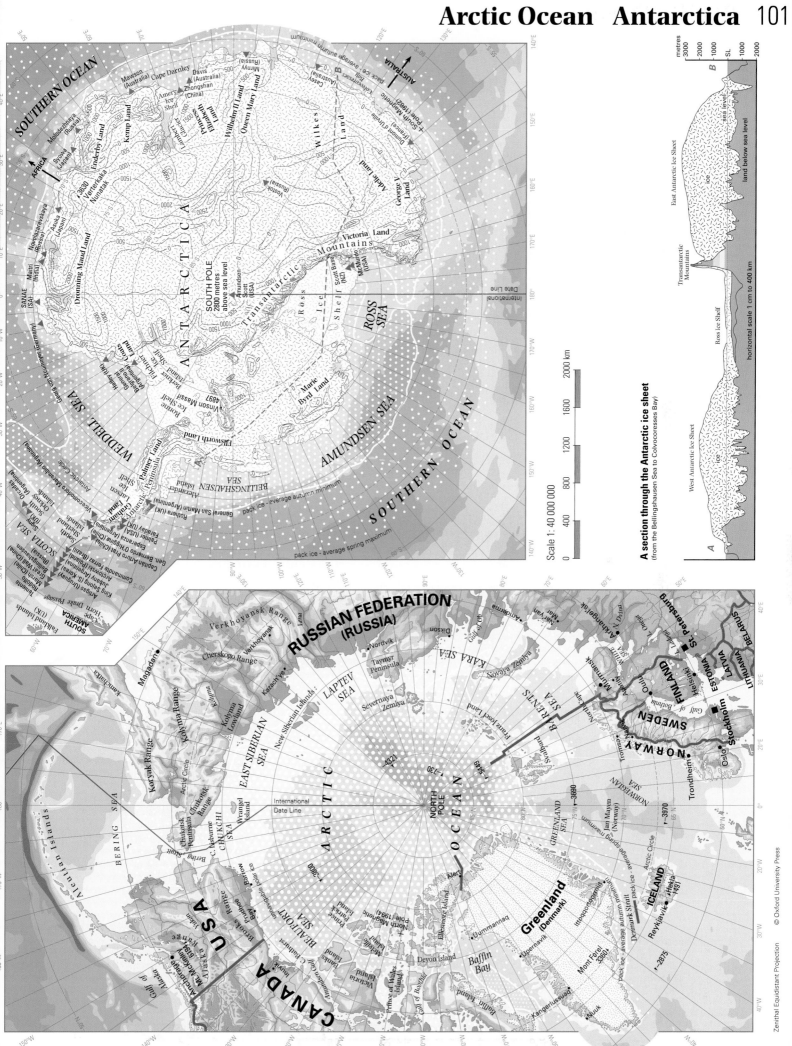

Equatorial scale 1: 95 000 000 (main map)

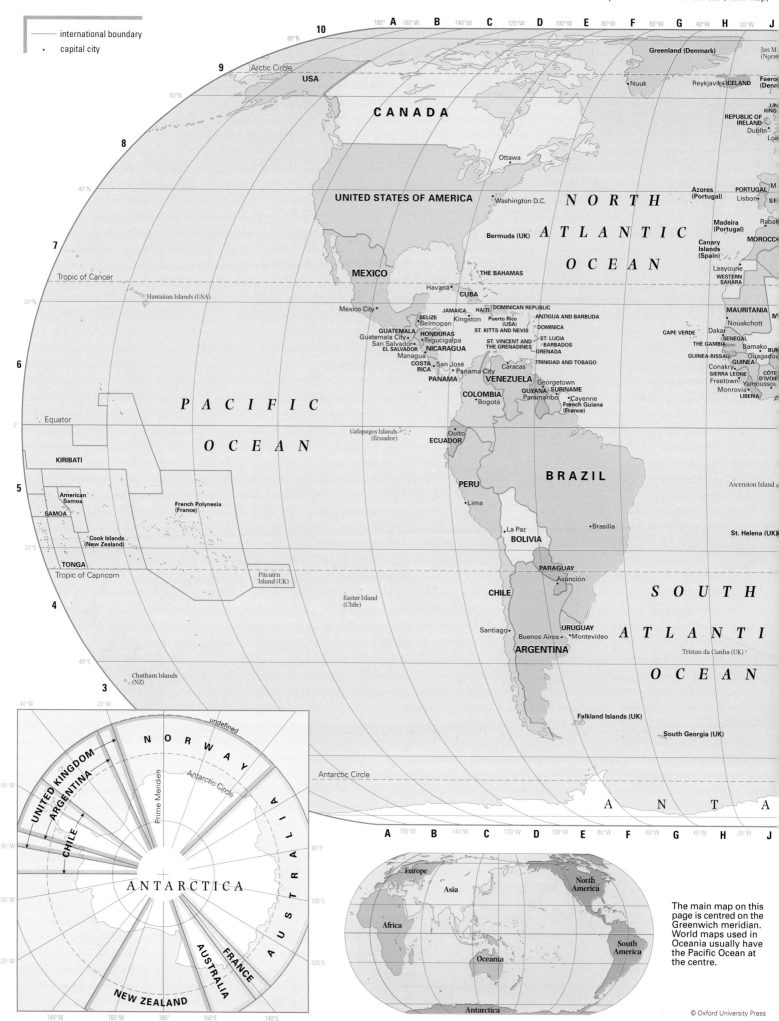

international boundary
• capital city

10
9 Arctic Circle
8
180° **A** 160°W **B** 140°W **C** 120°W **D** 100°W **E** 80°W **F** 60°W **G** 40°W **H** 20°W **J**
80°N
60°N
40°N
Tropic of Cancer
20°N
0° Equator
20°S
Tropic of Capricorn
40°S

7
6
5
4
3

USA
CANADA
Ottawa
UNITED STATES OF AMERICA
Washington D.C.
Bermuda (UK)
MEXICO
Hawaiian Islands (USA)
Mexico City
Havana
THE BAHAMAS
CUBA
JAMAICA
Kingston
HAITI
DOMINICAN REPUBLIC
BELIZE
Belmopan
Puerto Rico (USA)
ANTIGUA AND BARBUDA
ST. KITTS AND NEVIS
DOMINICA
GUATEMALA
Guatemala City
San Salvador
HONDURAS
Tegucigalpa
ST. LUCIA
ST. VINCENT AND
THE GRENADINES
BARBADOS
GRENADA
EL SALVADOR
NICARAGUA
Managua
TRINIDAD AND TOBAGO
COSTA
RICA
San José
Panama City
Caracas
PANAMA
VENEZUELA
Georgetown
COLOMBIA
Bogotá
GUYANA
Paramaribo
SURINAME
Cayenne
French Guiana
(France)

Galapagos Islands
(Ecuador)
Quito
ECUADOR

PACIFIC
OCEAN

KIRIBATI
American
Samoa
SAMOA
Cook Islands
(New Zealand)
TONGA
French Polynesia
(France)
Pitcairn
Island (UK)
Easter Island
(Chile)
Chatham Islands
(NZ)

PERU
Lima
La Paz
BOLIVIA
BRAZIL
Brasília
PARAGUAY
Asunción
CHILE
URUGUAY
Santiago
Buenos Aires
Montevideo
ARGENTINA

NORTH
ATLANTIC
OCEAN

Greenland (Denmark)
Jan M
(Norv
Nuuk
Reykjavik
ICELAND
Faeroe
(Denn
UN
KING
REPUBLIC OF
IRELAND
Dublin
Lo
Azores
(Portugal)
PORTUGAL
Lisbon
M
SP
Madeira
(Portugal)
Canary
Islands
(Spain)
Rabat
MOROCC
Laayoune
WESTERN
SAHARA
MAURITANIA
Nouakchott
M
CAPE VERDE
Dakar
SENEGAL
THE GAMBIA
Bamako
BU
GUINEA-BISSAU
GUINEA
Ouagado
Conakry
SIERRA LEONE
Freetown
CÔTE
D'IVOIR
Yamoussou
Monrovia
LIBERIA
Ascension Island
St. Helena (UK)

SOUTH
ATLANTI
OCEAN
Tristan da Cunha (UK)
Falkland Islands (UK)
South Georgia (UK)
Antarctic Circle
A   N   T   A

180° **A** 160°W **B** 140°W **C** 120°W **D** 100°W **E** 80°W **F** 60°W **G** 40°W **H** 20°W **J**

40°W 20°W
undefined
N O R W A Y
UNITED KINGDOM
ARGENTINA
Antarctic Circle
CHILE
Prime Meridian
A U S T R A L I A
ANTARCTICA
FRANCE
AUSTRALIA
NEW ZEALAND
60°W
80°W
100°W
120°W
140°W
160°W
180°
160°E
140°E
40°E
60°E
80°E
100°E
120°E

Europe
Asia
North
America
Africa
Oceania
South
America
Antarctica

The main map on this
page is centred on the
Greenwich meridian.
World maps used in
Oceania usually have
the Pacific Ocean at
the centre.

© Oxford University Press

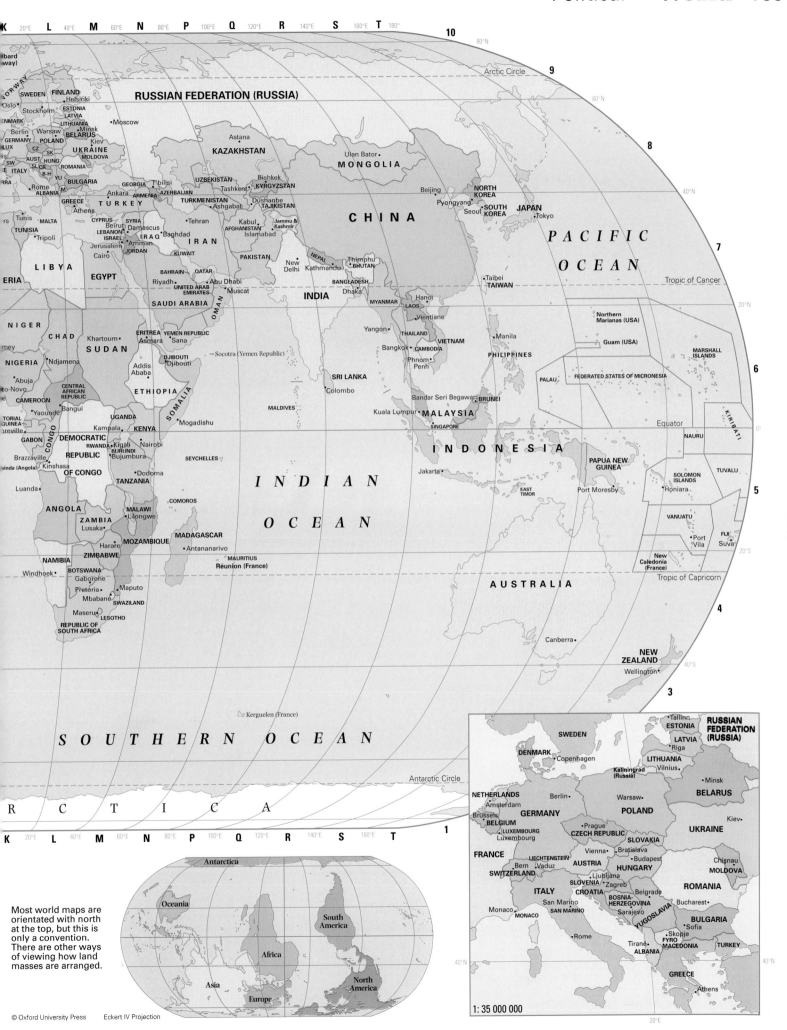

K 20°E L 40°E M 60°E N 80°E P 100°E Q 120°E R 140°E S 160°E T 180° 10

80°N

Arctic Circle 9

60°N

RUSSIAN FEDERATION (RUSSIA)

bard
way)

NORWAY
SWEDEN FINLAND
Helsinki
Oslo
Stockholm ESTONIA
ENMARK LATVIA
LITHUANIA
Moscow
8
GERMANY POLAND BELARUS Minsk
Berlin Warsaw
LUX CZ SK UKRAINE
AUST HUNG MOLDOVA
SLC R ROMANIA Kiev
ITALY B-H Astana
Rome VU **KAZAKHSTAN**
ALBANIA BULGARIA
M
GREECE GEORGIA T'bilisi UZBEKISTAN Bishkek
Athens Ankara ARMENIA AZERBAIJAN TURKMENISTAN Tashkent KYRGYZSTAN
rs Tunis TURKEY Ashgabat Dushanbe **MONGOLIA** Ulan Bator
MALTA CYPRUS SYRIA Damascus TAJIKISTAN
TUNISIA Beirut Tehran Kabul
LEBANON ISRAEL IRAQ Baghdad AFGHANISTAN Islamabad
Jerusalem Amman JORDAN IRAN **CHINA** 40°N
Cairo KUWAIT PAKISTAN New Delhi
ERIA BAHRAIN QATAR Delhi NEPAL Thimphu
LIBYA **EGYPT** Riyadh Abu Dhabi Kathmandu BHUTAN
UNITED ARAB Muscat **INDIA** BANGLADESH Beijing NORTH KOREA 7
EMIRATES Dhaka Pyongyang SOUTH **JAPAN**
SAUDI ARABIA MYANMAR KOREA Seoul Tokyo Tropic of Cancer

NIGER CHAD ERITREA YEMEN REPUBLIC Hanoi Taibei **TAIWAN**
SUDAN Khartoum Asmara Sana LAOS 20°N
NIGERIA Ndjamena DJIBOUTI Socotra (Yemen Republic) Yangon Vientiane
Abuja Djibouti THAILAND VIETNAM Manila Northern Marianas (USA)
to-Novo CENTRAL Addis SRI LANKA Bangkok CAMBODIA Guam (USA) MARSHALL
AFRICAN Ababa Phnom PHILIPPINES ISLANDS 6
CAMEROON REPUBLIC **ETHIOPIA** Colombo Penh FEDERATED STATES OF MICRONESIA
TORIAL Yaounde SOMALIA MALDIVES PALAU
GUINEA Bangui UGANDA Bandar Seri Begawan BRUNEI
reville GABON Kampala KENYA Kuala Lumpur **MALAYSIA**
CONGO DEMOCRATIC RWANDA Kigali Nairobi SINGAPORE Equator KIRIBATI
REPUBLIC BURUNDI NAURU
Brazzaville Bujumbura SEYCHELLES **INDONESIA**
inda (Angola) OF CONGO Dodoma PAPUA NEW TUVALU
Kinshasa TANZANIA Jakarta GUINEA SOLOMON
Luanda COMOROS EAST Port Moresby ISLANDS 5
I N D I A N TIMOR Honiara
ANGOLA MALAWI
ZAMBIA Lilongwe **O C E A N** VANUATU
Lusaka MADAGASCAR 20°S
NAMIBIA ZIMBABWE MOZAMBIQUE Antananarivo New Port FIJI
Harare MAURITIUS Caledonia Vila Suva
Windhoek BOTSWANA Réunion (France) (France) Tropic of Capricorn
Gaborone **AUSTRALIA** 4
Pretoria
Maputo
Mbabane SWAZILAND
Maseru LESOTHO
REPUBLIC OF
SOUTH AFRICA

**P A C I F I C
O C E A N**

Canberra **NEW
ZEALAND** 40°S
Wellington 3

Kerguelen (France)

S O U T H E R N   O C E A N

Antarctic Circle

R C T I C A 1

K 20°E L 40°E M 60°E N 80°E P 100°E Q 120°E R 140°E S 160°E T

Most world maps are
orientated with north
at the top, but this is
only a convention.
There are other ways
of viewing how land
masses are arranged.

Antarctica
Oceania
South America
Africa
Asia
North America
Europe

© Oxford University Press   Eckert IV Projection

Inset map (1:35 000 000):

Tallinn RUSSIAN FEDERATION (RUSSIA)
SWEDEN ESTONIA
LATVIA Riga
DENMARK Copenhagen LITHUANIA
Kaliningrad Vilnius
(Russia) Minsk
NETHERLANDS Berlin Warsaw BELARUS
Amsterdam
Brussels GERMANY POLAND
BELGIUM Prague Kiev
LUXEMBOURG CZECH REPUBLIC UKRAINE
Luxembourg SLOVAKIA
FRANCE LIECHTENSTEIN Vienna Bratislava Chişinău
Bern Vaduz AUSTRIA Budapest MOLDOVA
SWITZERLAND HUNGARY
Ljubljana Zagreb ROMANIA
SLOVENIA Belgrade
ITALY CROATIA BOSNIA- Bucharest
San Marino HERZEGOVINA
Monaco SAN MARINO Sarajevo YUGOSLAVIA BULGARIA
MONACO Sofia
Rome Skopje
Tiranë FYRO TURKEY
ALBANIA MACEDONIA
GREECE
Athens

Equatorial scale 1: 95 000 000

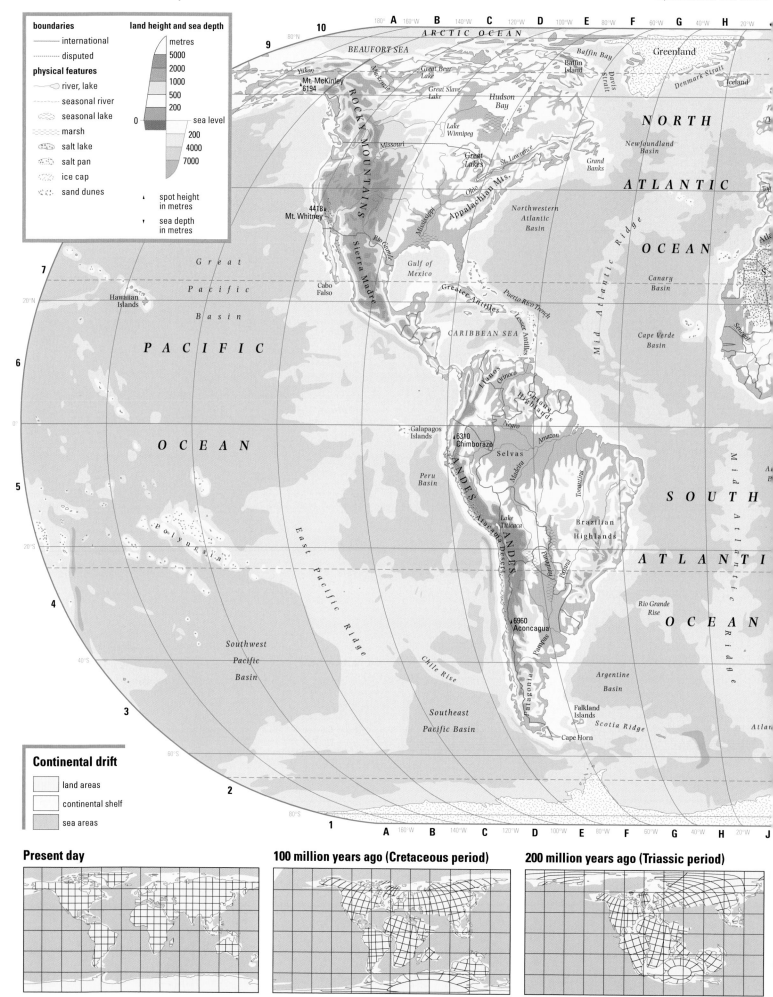

boundaries
international
disputed

land height and sea depth
metres
5000
2000
1000
500
200
0 ——— sea level
200
4000
7000

physical features
river, lake
seasonal river
seasonal lake
marsh
salt lake
salt pan
ice cap
sand dunes

▲ spot height in metres
▼ sea depth in metres

ARCTIC OCEAN
BEAUFORT SEA
80°N
Greenland
Baffin Bay
Baffin Island
Davis Strait
Denmark Strait
Iceland

Yukon
Mt. McKinley 6194
Mackenzie
Great Bear Lake
Great Slave Lake
Hudson Bay
Lake Winnipeg
NORTH
Newfoundland Basin
ROCKY MOUNTAINS
Missouri
Great Lakes
St. Lawrence
ATLANTIC
Grand Banks
Mt. Whitney 4418
Sierra Madre
Rio Grande
Ohio
Mississippi
Appalachian Mts.
Northwestern Atlantic Basin
OCEAN
Mid Atlantic Ridge

Great
Pacific
Basin
7
20°N
Hawaiian Islands
Cabo Falso
Gulf of Mexico
Greater Antilles
Puerto Rico Trench
Lesser Antilles
CARIBBEAN SEA
Canary Basin
Cape Verde Basin
Senegal

PACIFIC
6
OCEAN
0°
Galapagos Islands
Llanos
Orinoco
Guiana Highlands
Negro
Amazon
Madeira
6310 Chimborazo
Selvas
Peru Basin
SOUTH
Mid Atlantic

5
20°S
Polynesia
ANDES
Atacama Desert
Lake Titicaca
Tocantins
Brazilian Highlands
ATLANTIC
East Pacific Ridge
Parand
Paraguay
Rio Grande Rise
4
Southwest Pacific Basin
6960 Aconcagua
Pampas
OCEAN
Argentine Basin

3
Chile Rise
Patagonia
Falkland Islands
Scotia Ridge
Southeast Pacific Basin
Cape Horn
Atlan

Continental drift
land areas
continental shelf
sea areas

Present day

100 million years ago (Cretaceous period)

200 million years ago (Triassic period)

© Oxford University Press

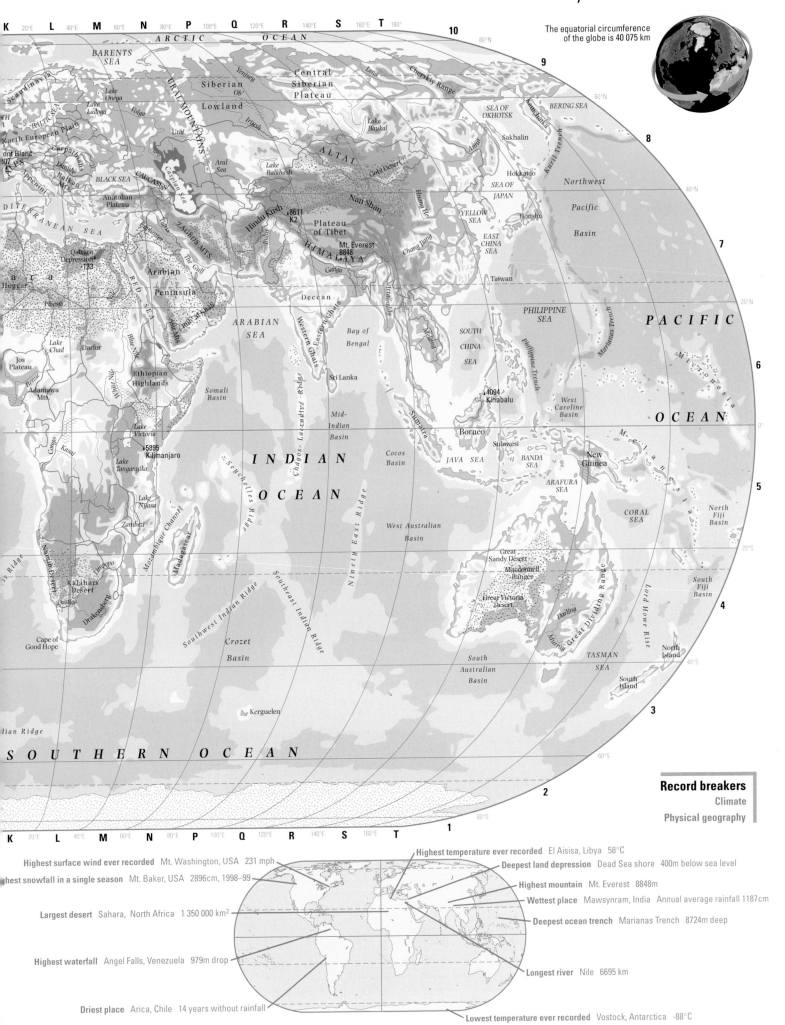

The equatorial circumference of the globe is 40 075 km

K 20°E **L** 40°E **M** 60°E **N** 80°E **P** 100°E **Q** 120°E **R** 140°E **S** 160°E **T** 180° **10**

ARCTIC OCEAN

BARENTS SEA

Scandinavia

Lake Onega

Lake Ladoga

URAL MOUNTAINS

Siberian Lowland

Yenisey

Ob

Irtysh

Central Siberian Plateau

Lena

Cherskiy Range

SEA OF OKHOTSK

Kamchatka

BERING SEA

80°N

9

60°N

8

BALTIC SEA

North European Plain

Volga

Ural

Caspian Sea

Aral Sea

Lake Balkhash

ALTAI

Gobi Desert

Amur

Sakhalin

Hokkaido

Kuril Trench

Northwest Pacific Basin

40°N

Mont Blanc 307

ALPS

Appenines

Carpathians

Dinaric Alps

Balkan Mts

BLACK SEA

CAUCASUS

Anatolian Plateau

ZAGROS MTS

Tigris

Euphrates

Indus

Hindu Kush 8611 K2

Nan Shan

Plateau of Tibet

Mt. Everest 8848

HIMALAYA

Huang He

Chang Jiang

SEA OF JAPAN

YELLOW SEA

EAST CHINA SEA

Honshu

Taiwan

7

MEDITERRANEAN SEA

Qattara Depression -133

Sahara

Hoggar

Tibesti

RED SEA

The Gulf

Arabian Peninsula

Nafud

Rub' al Khali

Ganga

Deccan

Western Ghats

Eastern Ghats

Bay of Bengal

Irrawaddy

Mekong

PHILIPPINE SEA

SOUTH CHINA SEA

Marianas Trench

PACIFIC

20°N

6

Jos Plateau

Lake Chad

Darfur

Blue Nile

White Nile

Nile

Ethiopian Highlands

Nile Mts

ARABIAN SEA

Sri Lanka

Chagos-Laccadive Ridge

Mid-Indian Basin

Sumatra

Kinabalu 4094

West Caroline Basin

Micronesia

OCEAN

0°

Benue

Adamawa Mts

Congo

Kasai

Lake Victoria

Kilimanjaro 5895

Lake Tanganyika

Somali Basin

INDIAN

Borneo

Sulawesi

JAVA SEA

BANDA SEA

New Guinea

Melanesia

5

Zambezi

Lake Nyasa

Mozambique Channel

Madagascar

Seychelles Ridge

OCEAN

Cocos Basin

ARAFURA SEA

CORAL SEA

North Fiji Basin

20°S

Namib Desert

Kalahari Desert

Limpopo

Orange

Drakensberg

Ninety East Ridge

West Australian Basin

Southeast Indian Ridge

Great Sandy Desert

Macdonnell Ranges

Great Victoria Desert

Great Dividing Range

Darling

Murray

Lord Howe Rise

South Fiji Basin

4

Is Ridge

Cape of Good Hope

Southwest Indian Ridge

Crozet Basin

South Australian Basin

TASMAN SEA

North Island

South Island

40°S

lian Ridge

Kerguelen

3

SOUTHERN OCEAN

60°S

2

80°S

1

K 20°E **L** 40°E **M** 60°E **N** 80°E **P** 100°E **Q** 120°E **R** 140°E **S** 160°E **T** 180°

Record breakers

Climate

Physical geography

Highest surface wind ever recorded Mt. Washington, USA 231 mph

Highest snowfall in a single season Mt. Baker, USA 2896cm, 1998–99

Largest desert Sahara, North Africa 1 350 000 km²

Highest waterfall Angel Falls, Venezuela 979m drop

Driest place Arica, Chile 14 years without rainfall

Highest temperature ever recorded El Aisisa, Libya 58°C

Deepest land depression Dead Sea shore 400m below sea level

Highest mountain Mt. Everest 8848m

Wettest place Mawsynram, India Annual average rainfall 1187cm

Deepest ocean trench Marianas Trench 8724m deep

Longest river Nile 6695 km

Lowest temperature ever recorded Vostock, Antarctica -88°C

© Oxford University Press   Eckert IV Projection

Equatorial scale 1: 130 000 000

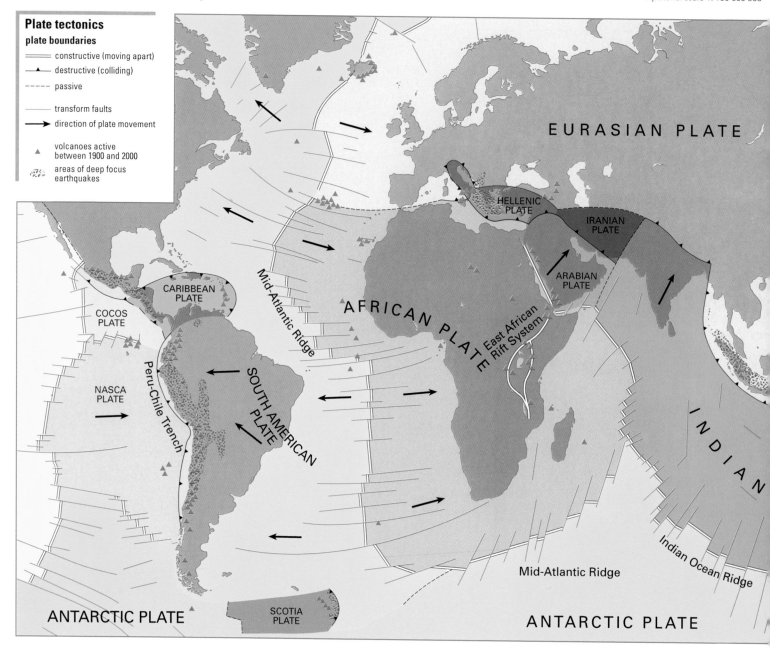

Plate tectonics

plate boundaries

———— constructive (moving apart)

—▲— destructive (colliding)

– – – passive

———— transform faults

——► direction of plate movement

▲ volcanoes active between 1900 and 2000

areas of deep focus earthquakes

EURASIAN PLATE

HELLENIC PLATE

IRANIAN PLATE

ARABIAN PLATE

CARIBBEAN PLATE

COCOS PLATE

Mid-Atlantic Ridge

AFRICAN PLATE

East African Rift System

NASCA PLATE

Peru-Chile Trench

SOUTH AMERICAN PLATE

INDIAN

Indian Ocean Ridge

Mid-Atlantic Ridge

ANTARCTIC PLATE

SCOTIA PLATE

ANTARCTIC PLATE

Structure of the Earth

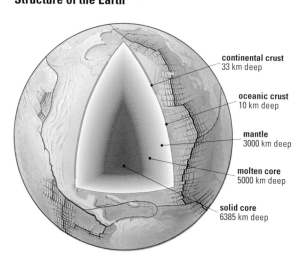

continental crust 33 km deep

oceanic crust 10 km deep

mantle 3000 km deep

molten core 5000 km deep

solid core 6385 km deep

Mt. St. Helens

A digital elevation model (DEM) of the stratovolcano which erupted on 18 May, 1980 in Washington State, USA.

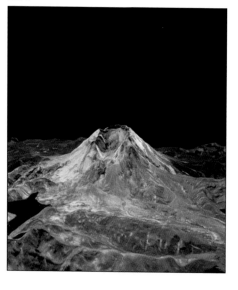

Deadliest earthquakes, 1990–2000

force measured on the Richter scale

Year	Place	Force	Deaths
1990	Northwestern Iran	7.7	37 000
1990	Luzon, Philippines	7.7	1660
1991	Afghanistan/Pakistan	6.8	1000
1991	Uttar Pradesh, India	6.1	1500
1992	Erzincan, Turkey	6.7	2000
1992	Flores Island, Indonesia	7.5	2500
1993	Maharashtra, India	6.3	9800
1994	Cauca, Colombia	6.8	1000
1995	Kobe, Japan	7.2	5500
1995	Sakhalin Island, Russia	7.6	2000
1997	Ardabil, Iran	unknown	>1000
1997	Khorash, Iran	7.1	>1600
1998	Takhar, Afghanistan	6.1	>3800
1998	Northeastern Afghanistan	7.1	>3000
1999	Western Colombia	6.0	1124
1999	Izmit, Turkey	7.4	>17 000
1999	Central Taiwan	7.6	2295
1999	Ducze, Turkey	7.2	>700

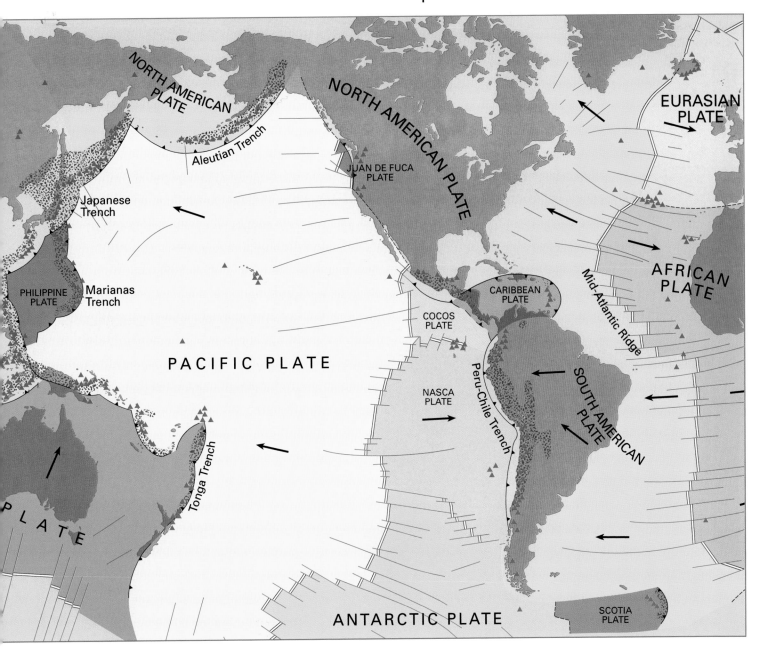

NORTH AMERICAN PLATE

NORTH AMERICAN PLATE

EURASIAN PLATE

Aleutian Trench

JUAN DE FUCA PLATE

Japanese Trench

AFRICAN PLATE

Mid-Atlantic Ridge

PHILIPPINE PLATE

Marianas Trench

CARIBBEAN PLATE

COCOS PLATE

PACIFIC PLATE

SOUTH AMERICAN PLATE

NASCA PLATE

Peru-Chile Trench

Tonga Trench

PLATE

ANTARCTIC PLATE

SCOTIA PLATE

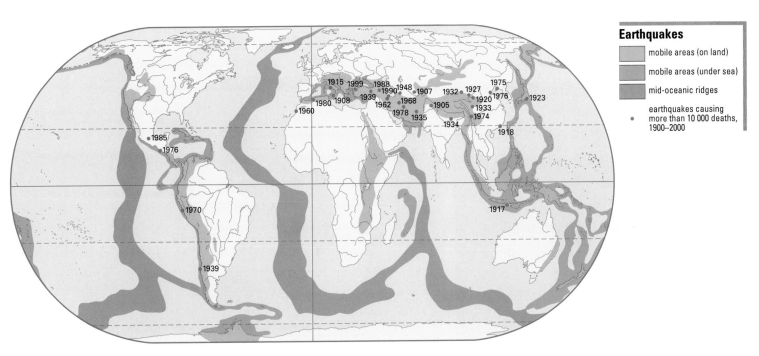

Earthquakes

- mobile areas (on land)
- mobile areas (under sea)
- mid-oceanic ridges
- · earthquakes causing more than 10 000 deaths, 1900–2000

1915
1999
1988
1948
1907
1932
1927
1975
1980
1908
1939
1990
1968
1905
1920
1976
1923
1960
1962
1978
1933
1935
1974
1934
1918
1985
1976
1970
1917
1939

Eckert IV Projection

Scale 1: 240 000 000

January temperature

actual surface temperature

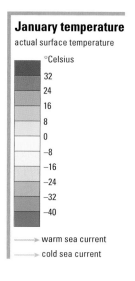

°Celsius

32
24
16
8
0
−8
−16
−24
−32
−40

→ warm sea current
→ cold sea current

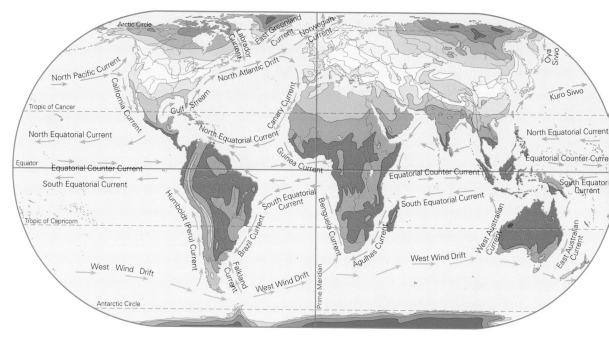

July temperature

actual surface temperature

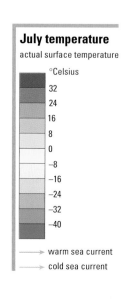

°Celsius

32
24
16
8
0
−8
−16
−24
−32
−40

→ warm sea current
→ cold sea current

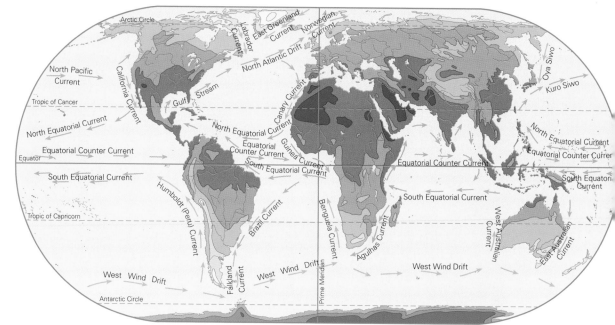

Antarctic ozone 'hole'

Three dimensional image of ozone depletion over Antarctica in September, 1998. The lowest ozone concentration is shown in blue.

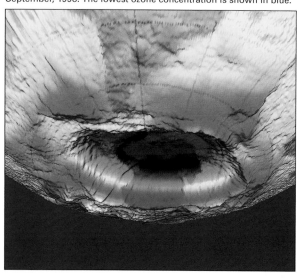

Global warming

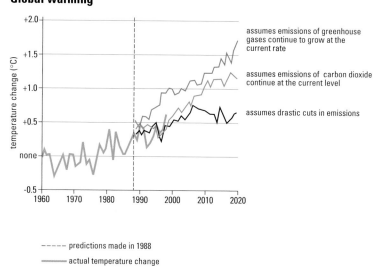

assumes emissions of greenhouse gases continue to grow at the current rate

assumes emissions of carbon dioxide continue at the current level

assumes drastic cuts in emissions

- - - - predictions made in 1988

—— actual temperature change

© Oxford University Press

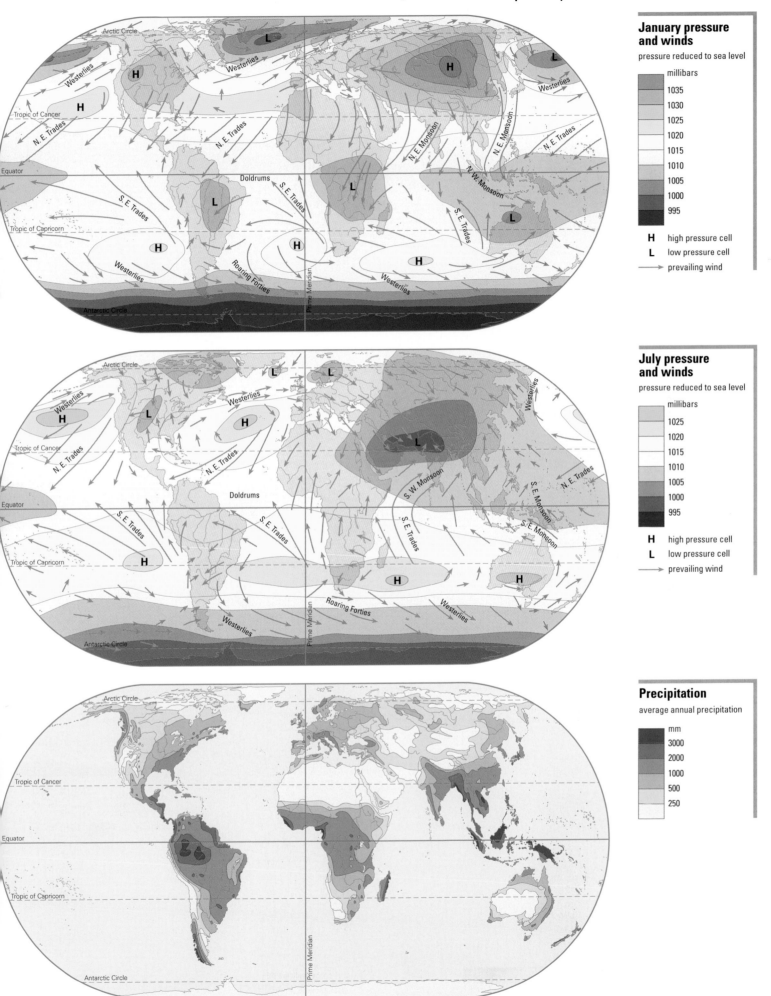

January pressure and winds

pressure reduced to sea level

millibars

- 1035
- 1030
- 1025
- 1020
- 1015
- 1010
- 1005
- 1000
- 995

H high pressure cell

L low pressure cell

→ prevailing wind

July pressure and winds

pressure reduced to sea level

millibars

- 1025
- 1020
- 1015
- 1010
- 1005
- 1000
- 995

H high pressure cell

L low pressure cell

→ prevailing wind

Precipitation

average annual precipitation

mm

- 3000
- 2000
- 1000
- 500
- 250

Equatorial scale 1: 95 000 000

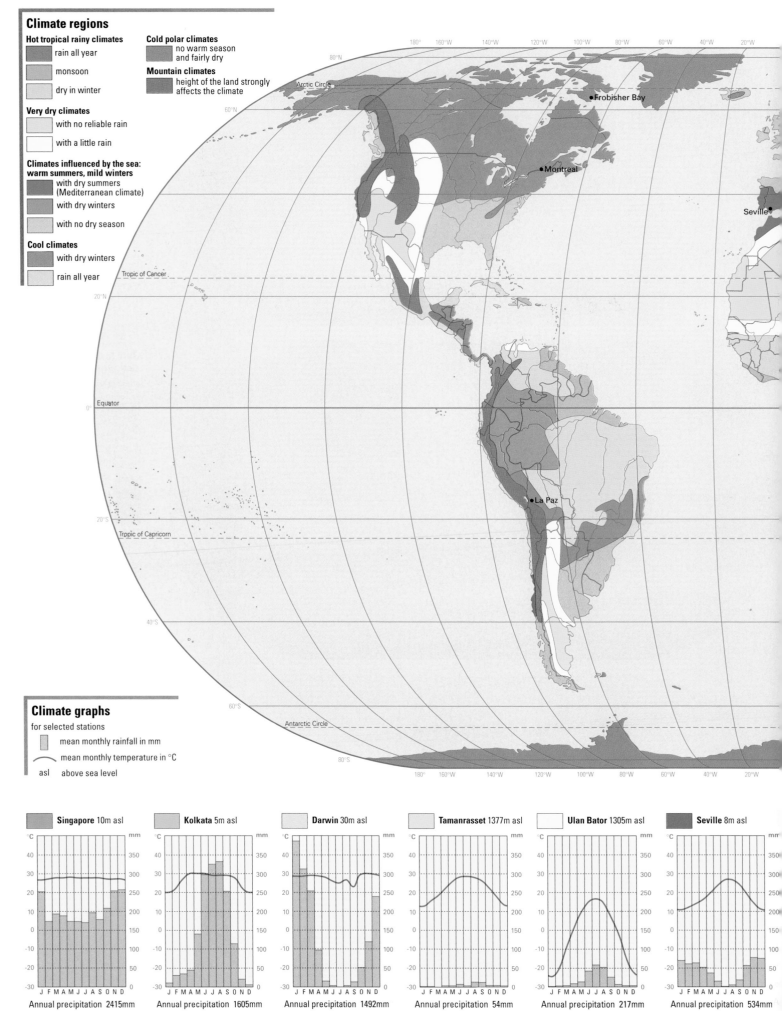

Climate regions

Hot tropical rainy climates
- rain all year
- monsoon
- dry in winter

Very dry climates
- with no reliable rain
- with a little rain

Climates influenced by the sea: warm summers, mild winters
- with dry summers (Mediterranean climate)
- with dry winters
- with no dry season

Cool climates
- with dry winters
- rain all year

Cold polar climates
- no warm season and fairly dry

Mountain climates
- height of the land strongly affects the climate

Climate graphs

for selected stations
- mean monthly rainfall in mm
- mean monthly temperature in °C
- asl above sea level

Singapore 10m asl
Annual precipitation 2415mm

Kolkata 5m asl
Annual precipitation 1605mm

Darwin 30m asl
Annual precipitation 1492mm

Tamanrasset 1377m asl
Annual precipitation 54mm

Ulan Bator 1305m asl
Annual precipitation 217mm

Seville 8m asl
Annual precipitation 534mm

Eckert IV Projection   © Oxford University Press

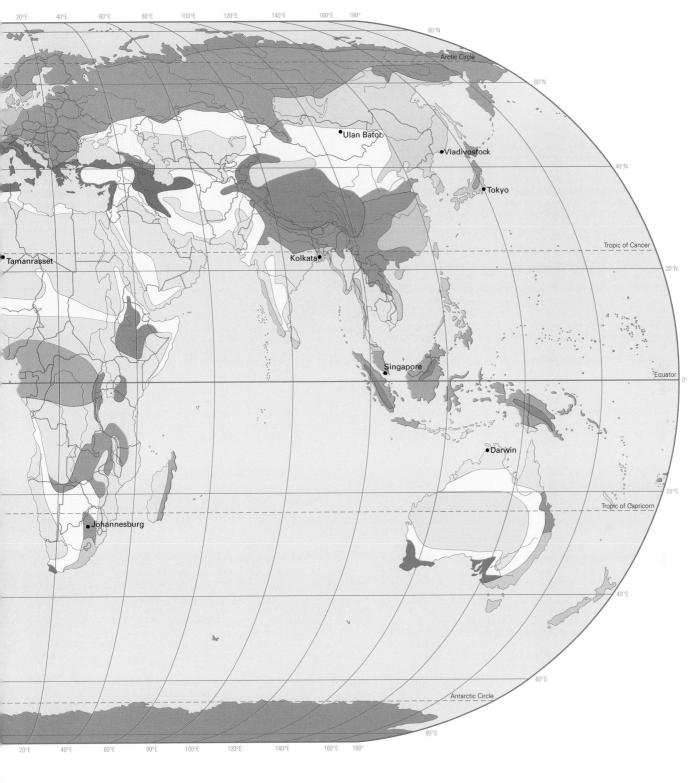

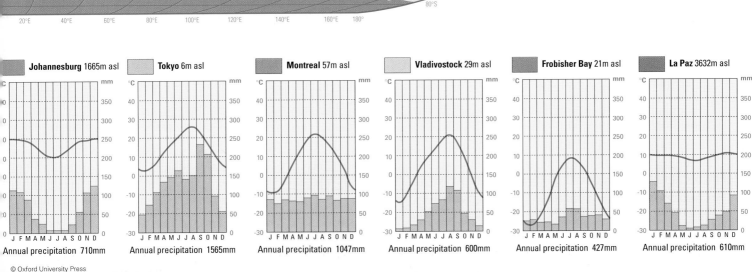

Johannesburg 1665m asl	Tokyo 6m asl	Montreal 57m asl	Vladivostock 29m asl	Frobisher Bay 21m asl	La Paz 3632m asl

Annual precipitation 710mm   Annual precipitation 1565mm   Annual precipitation 1047mm   Annual precipitation 600mm   Annual precipitation 427mm   Annual precipitation 610mm

Climate data

Averages are for 1961–1990

Denver 1626m climate station and its height above sea level

Temperature (°C) high average daily maximum temperature
mean average monthly temperature
low average daily minimum temperature

Rainfall (mm) average monthly precipitation

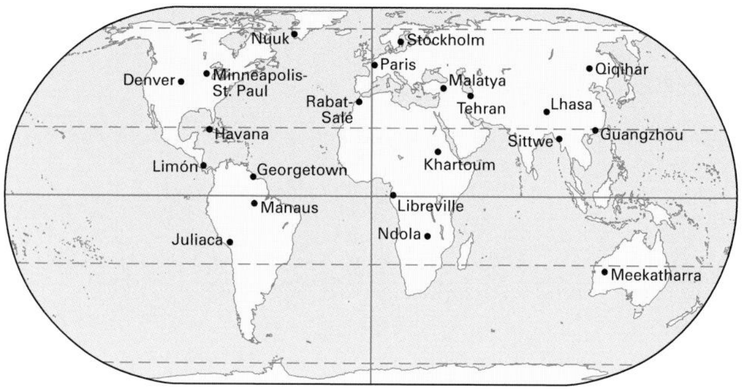

Denver 1626m

		Jan	Feb	Mar	Apr	May	Jun	Jul	Aug	Sep	Oct	Nov	Dec	YEAR
Temperature (°C)	high	6.2	8.1	11.2	16.6	21.6	27.4	31.2	29.9	24.9	19.1	11.4	6.9	17.9
	mean	-1.3	0.8	3.9	9.0	14.0	19.4	23.1	21.9	16.8	10.8	3.9	-0.6	10.1
	low	-8.8	-6.6	-3.4	1.4	6.4	11.3	14.8	13.8	8.7	2.4	-3.7	-8.1	2.4
Rainfall (mm)		13	15	33	43	61	46	49	38	32	25	22	16	393

Georgetown 2m

		Jan	Feb	Mar	Apr	May	Jun	Jul	Aug	Sep	Oct	Nov	Dec	YEAR
Temperature (°C)	high	28.6	28.9	29.2	29.5	29.4	29.2	29.6	30.2	30.8	30.8	30.2	29.1	29.6
	mean	26.1	26.4	26.7	27.0	26.8	26.5	26.6	27.0	27.5	27.6	27.2	26.4	26.8
	low	23.6	23.9	24.2	24.4	24.3	23.8	23.5	23.8	24.2	24.4	24.2	23.8	24.0
Rainfall (mm)		185	89	111	141	286	328	268	201	98	107	186	262	2262

Guangzhou 42m

		Jan	Feb	Mar	Apr	May	Jun	Jul	Aug	Sep	Oct	Nov	Dec	YEAR
Temperature (°C)	high	18.3	18.4	21.6	25.5	29.4	31.3	32.7	32.6	31.4	28.6	24.4	20.5	26.2
	mean	13.3	14.3	17.7	21.9	25.6	27.3	28.5	28.3	27.1	24.0	19.4	15.0	21.9
	low	5.0	6.6	10.7	16.1	20.7	23.5	25.7	25.2	22.6	17.6	11.9	6.5	16.0
Rainfall (mm)		43	65	85	182	284	258	228	221	172	79	42	24	1683

Havana 50m

		Jan	Feb	Mar	Apr	May	Jun	Jul	Aug	Sep	Oct	Nov	Dec	YEAR
Temperature (°C)	high	25.8	26.1	27.6	28.6	29.8	30.5	31.3	31.6	31.0	29.2	27.7	26.5	28.8
	mean	22.2	22.4	23.7	24.8	26.1	26.9	27.6	27.8	27.4	26.2	24.5	23.0	25.2
	low	18.6	18.6	19.7	20.9	22.4	23.4	23.8	24.1	23.8	23.0	21.3	19.5	21.6
Rainfall (mm)		64	69	46	54	98	182	106	100	144	181	88	58	1190

Juliaca 3827m

		Jan	Feb	Mar	Apr	May	Jun	Jul	Aug	Sep	Oct	Nov	Dec	YEAR
Temperature (°C)	high	16.7	16.7	16.5	16.8	16.6	16.0	16.0	17.0	17.6	18.6	18.8	17.7	17.1
	mean	10.2	10.1	9.9	8.7	6.4	4.5	4.3	5.8	8.1	9.5	10.2	10.4	8.2
	low	3.6	3.5	3.2	0.6	-3.8	-7.0	-7.5	-5.4	-1.4	0.3	1.5	3.0	-0.8
Rainfall (mm)		133	109	99	43	10	3	2	6	22	41	55	86	609

Khartoum 380m

		Jan	Feb	Mar	Apr	May	Jun	Jul	Aug	Sep	Oct	Nov	Dec	YEAR
Temperature (°C)	high	30.8	33.0	36.8	40.1	41.9	41.3	38.4	37.3	39.1	39.3	35.2	31.8	37.1
	mean	23.2	25.0	28.7	31.9	34.5	34.3	32.1	31.5	32.5	32.4	28.1	24.5	29.9
	low	15.6	17.0	20.5	23.6	27.1	27.3	25.9	25.3	26.0	25.5	21.0	17.1	22.7
Rainfall (mm)		0	0	0	0.5	4	5	46	75	25	5	1	0	161

Lhasa 3650m

		Jan	Feb	Mar	Apr	May	Jun	Jul	Aug	Sep	Oct	Nov	Dec	YEAR
Temperature (°C)	high	6.9	9.0	12.1	15.6	19.3	22.7	22.1	21.1	19.7	16.3	11.2	7.7	15.3
	mean	-2.1	1.1	4.6	8.1	11.9	15.5	15.3	14.5	12.8	8.1	2.2	-1.7	7.5
	low	-10.1	-6.8	-3.0	0.9	5.0	9.3	10.1	9.4	7.5	1.3	-4.9	-9.0	0.8
Rainfall (mm)		1	1	2	5	27	72	119	123	58	10	2	1	421

Libreville 15m

		Jan	Feb	Mar	Apr	May	Jun	Jul	Aug	Sep	Oct	Nov	Dec	YEAR
Temperature (°C)	high	29.5	30.0	30.2	30.1	29.4	27.6	26.4	26.8	27.5	28.0	28.4	29.0	28.6
	mean	26.8	27.0	27.1	26.6	26.7	25.4	24.3	24.3	25.4	25.7	25.9	26.2	26.0
	low	24.1	24.0	23.9	23.1	24.0	23.2	22.1	21.8	23.4	23.4	23.4	23.4	23.3
Rainfall (mm)		250	243	363	339	247	54	7	14	104	427	490	303	2841

Limón 3m

		Jan	Feb	Mar	Apr	May	Jun	Jul	Aug	Sep	Oct	Nov	Dec	YEAR
Temperature (°C)	high	27.9	28.6	29.6	29.6	28.5	27.5	27.7	27.7	27.2	27.0	27.1	27.7	28.0
	mean	24.0	24.3	25.0	25.8	26.1	25.9	25.2	25.6	25.7	25.4	25.1	24.3	25.2
	low	20.3	20.3	20.9	21.6	22.2	22.3	22.1	22.1	22.2	21.9	21.6	20.9	21.5
Rainfall (mm)		319	201	193	287	281	276	408	289	163	198	367	402	3384

Malatya 849m

		Jan	Feb	Mar	Apr	May	Jun	Jul	Aug	Sep	Oct	Nov	Dec	YEAR
Temperature (°C)	high	2.9	5.3	11.1	18.2	23.5	29.2	33.8	33.4	28.9	20.9	11.8	5.7	18.7
	mean	-0.4	1.5	6.9	13.0	17.8	22.9	27.0	26.5	22.0	14.8	7.6	2.4	13.5
	low	-3.2	-1.7	2.4	7.7	11.8	16.1	19.8	19.4	15.2	9.5	3.7	-0.3	8.4
Rainfall (mm)		42	36	60	61	50	22	3	2	6	40	47	42	411

Manaus 84m

		Jan	Feb	Mar	Apr	May	Jun	Jul	Aug	Sep	Oct	Nov	Dec	YEAR
Temperature (°C)	high	30.5	30.4	30.6	30.7	30.8	31.0	31.3	32.6	32.9	32.8	32.1	31.3	31.4
	mean	26.1	26.0	26.1	26.3	26.3	26.4	26.5	27.0	27.5	27.6	27.3	26.7	26.7
	low	23.1	23.1	23.2	23.3	23.3	23.0	22.7	23.0	23.5	23.7	23.7	23.5	23.3
Rainfall (mm)		260	288	314	300	256	114	88	58	83	126	183	217	2287

Meekatharra 518m

		Jan	Feb	Mar	Apr	May	Jun	Jul	Aug	Sep	Oct	Nov	Dec	YEAR
Temperature (°C)	high	38.1	36.5	34.5	29.2	23.6	19.7	18.9	21.0	25.4	29.4	33.1	36.5	28.8
	mean	31.2	30.1	28.0	23.2	17.8	14.3	13.2	14.8	18.4	22.2	25.9	29.3	22.4
	low	24.3	23.7	21.5	17.1	11.9	8.9	7.5	8.5	11.4	15.0	18.6	22.1	15.9
Rainfall (mm)		26	30	22	17	27	36	25	12	6	7	14	11	23

Minneapolis-St. Paul 255m

		Jan	Feb	Mar	Apr	May	Jun	Jul	Aug	Sep	Oct	Nov	Dec	YEAR
Temperature (°C)	high	-6.3	-3.0	4.0	13.6	20.8	26.0	28.9	27.1	21.5	14.9	5.0	-3.6	12.
	mean	-11.2	-7.8	-0.6	8.0	14.7	20.1	23.1	21.4	15.8	9.3	0.7	-7.8	7.
	low	-16.2	-12.7	-5.2	2.3	8.7	14.2	17.3	15.7	10.2	3.8	-3.8	-12.1	1.
Rainfall (mm)		24	22	49	62	86	103	90	92	69	56	39	27	71

Ndola 1270m

		Jan	Feb	Mar	Apr	May	Jun	Jul	Aug	Sep	Oct	Nov	Dec	YEAR
Temperature (°C)	high	26.6	26.9	27.4	27.5	26.6	25.1	25.2	27.5	30.5	31.5	29.4	27.0	27.
	mean	20.8	20.8	21.0	20.5	18.6	16.5	16.7	19.2	22.5	23.7	22.5	21.0	20.
	low	17.1	17.1	16.5	14.4	10.8	7.9	7.8	10.2	13.6	16.2	17.1	17.2	13.8
Rainfall (mm)		293	249	170	46	4	1	0	0	3	32	130	306	123

Nuuk 70m

		Jan	Feb	Mar	Apr	May	Jun	Jul	Aug	Sep	Oct	Nov	Dec	YEAR
Temperature (°C)	high	-4.4	-4.5	-4.8	-0.8	3.5	7.7	10.6	9.9	6.3	1.7	-1.0	-3.3	1.
	mean	-7.4	-7.8	-8.0	-3.9	0.6	3.9	6.5	6.1	3.5	-0.6	-3.6	-6.2	-1.
	low	-10.1	-10.6	-10.6	-6.1	-1.5	1.3	3.8	3.8	1.6	-2.5	-5.8	-8.7	-3.
Rainfall (mm)		39	47	50	46	55	62	82	89	88	70	74	54	75

Paris 65m

		Jan	Feb	Mar	Apr	May	Jun	Jul	Aug	Sep	Oct	Nov	Dec	YEAR
Temperature (°C)	high	6.0	7.6	10.8	14.4	18.2	21.5	24.0	23.8	20.8	16.0	10.1	6.8	15.
	mean	3.4	4.2	6.6	9.5	13.2	16.4	18.4	18.0	15.3	11.4	6.7	4.2	10.6
	low	0.9	1.3	2.9	5.0	8.3	11.2	12.9	12.7	10.6	7.7	3.8	1.7	6.6
Rainfall (mm)		54	46	54	47	63	58	84	52	54	56	56	56	650

Qiqihar 148m

		Jan	Feb	Mar	Apr	May	Jun	Jul	Aug	Sep	Oct	Nov	Dec	YEAR
Temperature (°C)	high	-12.7	-7.8	2.3	12.9	21.0	26.2	27.8	26.1	20.1	11.1	-1.3	-10.4	9.
	mean	-19.2	-14.8	-4.5	6.1	14.4	20.3	22.8	20.9	14.0	4.8	-7.1	-16.2	3.5
	low	-24.5	-20.9	-11.0	-0.9	7.3	14.2	17.9	16.2	8.5	-0.7	-12.0	-21.2	-2.3
Rainfall (mm)		1	2	5	15	31	64	138	94	45	19	4	3	421

Rabat Sale 75m

		Jan	Feb	Mar	Apr	May	Jun	Jul	Aug	Sep	Oct	Nov	Dec	YEAR
Temperature (°C)	high	17.2	17.7	19.2	20.0	22.1	24.1	26.8	27.1	26.4	24.0	20.6	17.7	21.9
	mean	12.6	13.1	14.2	15.2	17.4	19.8	22.2	22.4	21.5	19.0	15.9	13.2	17.2
	low	8.0	8.6	9.2	10.4	12.7	15.4	17.6	17.7	16.7	14.1	11.1	8.7	12.5
Rainfall (mm)		77	74	61	62	25	7	1	1	6	44	97	101	556

Sittwe 5m

		Jan	Feb	Mar	Apr	May	Jun	Jul	Aug	Sep	Oct	Nov	Dec	YEAR
Temperature (°C)	high	28.0	29.4	31.4	34.1	31.5	29.5	28.9	28.9	30.1	31.1	30.3	28.5	30.
	mean	21.4	22.7	24.8	28.9	28.3	27.1	26.8	26.7	27.4	27.6	25.7	22.6	25.8
	low	14.7	15.9	18.2	23.6	25.1	24.6	24.7	24.5	24.6	24.0	21.0	16.6	21.5
Rainfall (mm)		11	8	5	44	268	1091	1155	1025	537	289	105	17	4555

Stockholm 52m

		Jan	Feb	Mar	Apr	May	Jun	Jul	Aug	Sep	Oct	Nov	Dec	YEAR
Temperature (°C)	high	-0.7	-0.6	3.0	8.6	15.7	20.7	21.9	20.4	15.1	9.9	4.5	1.1	10.0
	mean	-2.8	-3.0	0.1	4.6	10.7	15.6	17.2	16.2	11.9	7.5	2.6	-1.0	6.6
	low	-5.0	-5.3	-2.7	1.1	6.3	11.3	13.4	12.7	9.0	5.3	0.7	-3.2	3.6
Rainfall (mm)		39	27	26	30	30	45	72	66	55	50	53	46	539

Tehran 1191m

		Jan	Feb	Mar	Apr	May	Jun	Jul	Aug	Sep	Oct	Nov	Dec	YEAR
Temperature (°C)	high	7.2	9.9	15.4	21.9	28.0	34.1	36.8	35.4	31.5	24.0	16.5	9.8	22.5
	mean	3.0	5.3	10.3	16.4	22.1	27.5	30.4	29.2	25.3	18.5	11.6	5.6	17.1
	low	-1.1	0.7	5.2	10.9	16.1	20.9	24.0	23.0	19.2	12.9	6.7	1.3	11.7
Rainfall (mm)		37	34	37	28	15	3	3	1	1	14	21	36	230

Wellington 8m

		Jan	Feb	Mar	Apr	May	Jun	Jul	Aug	Sep	Oct	Nov	Dec	YEAR
Temperature (°C)	high	21.3	21.1	19.8	17.3	14.8	12.8	12.0	12.7	14.2	15.9	17.8	19.6	16.6
	mean	17.8	17.7	16.6	14.3	11.9	10.1	9.2	9.8	11.2	12.8	14.5	16.4	13.5
	low	14.4	14.3	13.5	11.3	9.1	7.3	6.4	6.9	8.3	9.7	11.3	13.2	10.5
Rainfall (mm)		67	48	76	87	99	113	111	106	82	81	74	74	1018

Tropical revolving storms

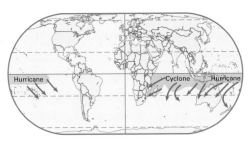

☐ temperature 27°C and over at mean sea level

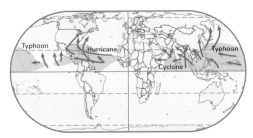

August–September
Maximum frequency in
northern hemisphere

January–March
Maximum frequency in
southern hemisphere

Hurricane Floyd, Florida

Winds in this hurricane reached 225km per hour and caused 40 deaths.
US NOAA satellite image, 15 September, 1999.

Drought and flood

☐ areas where severe drought may occur

— major river flood plains susceptible to flooding

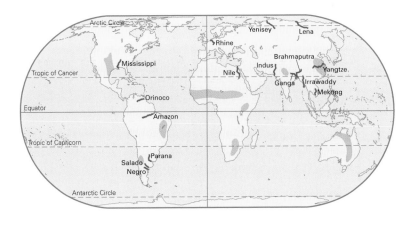

Dust storms, South West Africa

Dust streaming from SW African coastal
deserts into the Atlantic Ocean.
NASA SeaWiFS image, 6 June, 2000.

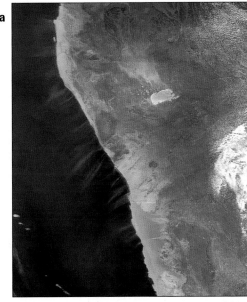

El Niño

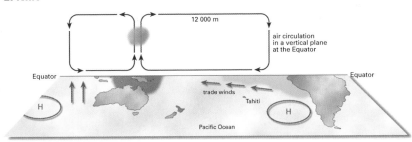

Normal year
The Humboldt current carries cold water north along the coast of Peru.
High temperatures in S.E. Asia draw in the S.E. Trade Winds which
push the surface waters west. Rainfall in S.E. Asia is high. Cold water
continues to flow north along the coast of S. America and this is rich in
plankton and fish.

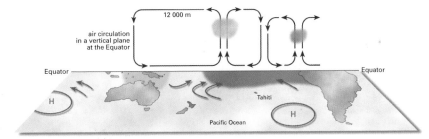

El Niño year
Weaker S.E. Trade Winds allow hot water from the western Pacific to
drift eastwards. Warm waters appear in Peru at about Christmas time.
Arid coastal areas in S. America suffer torrential rains. Coastal fish
stocks move to deeper cold water out of reach of small boats.
Drought occurs in S.E. Asia.

Equatorial scale 1: 105 000 000

Ecosystems

vegetation types are those which would occur naturally without interference by people

coniferous forest
cone bearing trees

deciduous and mixed forest
leaf shedding and coniferous trees

tropical rain forest
many species of lush, tall trees

tropical grasslands (savannah)
tall grass parkland with scattered trees

evergreen trees and shrubs
plants and small trees with leathery leaves

thorn forest
low trees and shrubs with spines or thorns

temperate grasslands
prairies, steppes, pampas, and veld

semi-desert
short grasses and drought-resistant scrub

desert
sand and stones, very little vegetation

tundra
moss and lichen, with few trees

ice
no vegetation

mountains
thin soils, steep slopes, and high altitude affects type of vegetation

ice
Aerial view of Jameson Land, towards Liverpool Land, Greenland

deciduous and mixed forest
Deciduous forest with scattered white pine, Blue Ridge Mountains, North Carolina, USA

temperate grasslands
Prairie, South Dakota, USA

tropical rain forest
Monteverde Cloud Forest Reserve, Costa Rica

thorn forest
Acacia thorns, Hwange, Zimbabwe

evergreen trees and shrubs
Coastal maquis vegetation,
Albufeira, Algarve, Portugal

coniferous forest
Forest track, Finland

tundra
Kolyma River Delta, Siberia, Russia

mountains
Mt. Everest and Sagarmatha
National Park, Nepal

semi-desert
Short grasses, Uluru National Park,
Northern Territory, Australia

desert
Waved sand dunes, Sahara Desert, Algeria

tropical grasslands (savannah)
Amboseli National Park, Kenya

20°E   40°E   60°E   80°E   100°E   120°E   140°E   160°E

80°N

Kolyma River Delta
Russia

Arctic Circle

60°N

Finland

ara Desert

Tropic of Cancer

20°N

Mt. Everest and
Sagarmatha National Park
Nepal

Equator   0°

Amboseli National Park
Kenya

Hwange
Zimbabwe

20°S

Tropic of Capricorn

Uluru National Park
Northern Territory
Australia

40°S

Antarctic Circle

20°E   40°E   60°E   80°E   100°E   120°E

Eckert IV Projection   © Oxford University Press

Population density

people per square kilometre

- over 200
- 100–200
- 50–100
- 5–50
- 1–5
- under 1

Major cities

population in millions

- ■ over 10
- ⊡ 5–10
- ▫ 1–5

Population structure, 2000

World

males   Age   females

percent of total population

Kenya

males   Age   females

percent of total population

Brazil

males   Age   females

percent of total population

Japan

males   Age   females

percent of total population

Italy

males   Age   females

percent of total population

China

males   Age   females

percent of total population

USA

males   Age   females

percent of total population

Population by continent, 2000   millions of people

Europe 729	Asia 3688	Africa 805	Oceania 31	North America 481	South America 347

Land area by continent   thousands of square kilometres

Europe 10 498	Asia 44 387	Africa 30 335	Oceania 8503	North America 24 241	South America 17 832	Antarctica 13 340

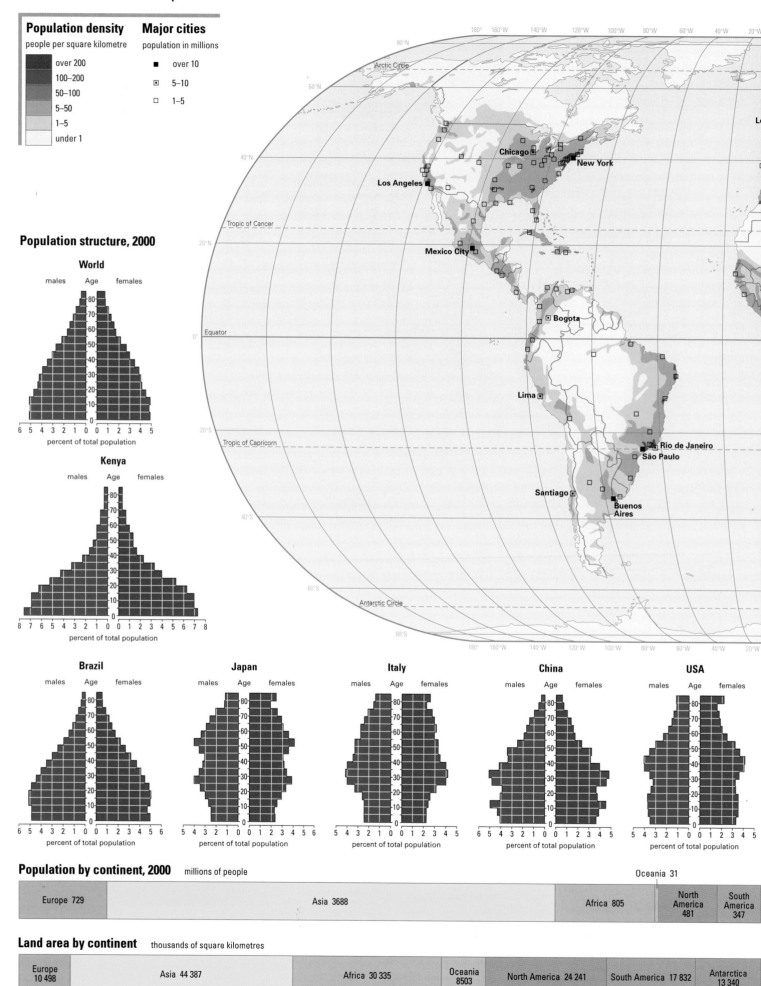

Eckert IV Projection   © Oxford University Press

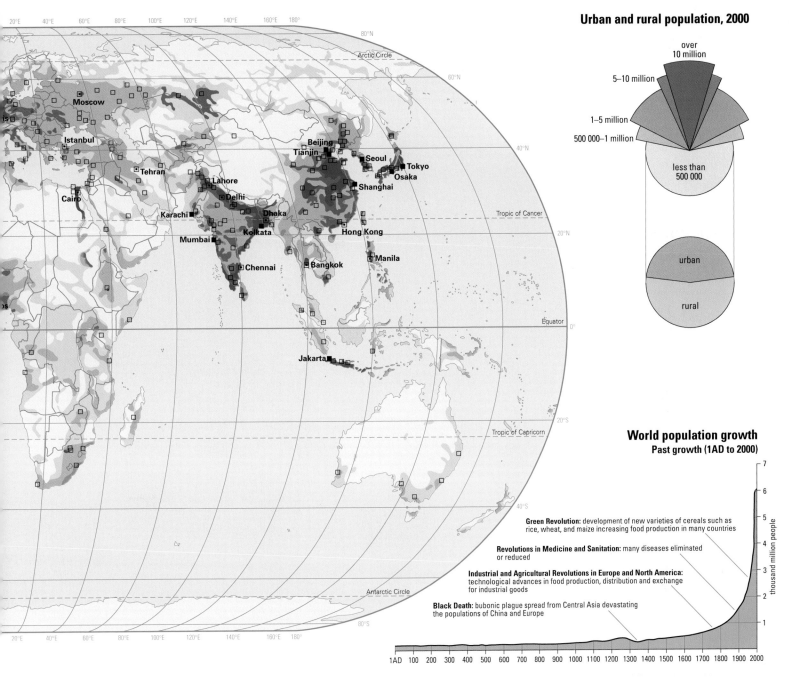

Urban and rural population, 2000

over 10 million

5–10 million

1–5 million

500 000–1 million

less than 500 000

urban

rural

World population growth
Past growth (1AD to 2000)

Green Revolution: development of new varieties of cereals such as rice, wheat, and maize increasing food production in many countries

Revolutions in Medicine and Sanitation: many diseases eliminated or reduced

Industrial and Agricultural Revolutions in Europe and North America: technological advances in food production, distribution and exchange for industrial goods

Black Death: bubonic plague spread from Central Asia devastating the populations of China and Europe

thousand million people

1AD 100 200 300 400 500 600 700 800 900 1000 1100 1200 1300 1400 1500 1600 1700 1800 1900 2000

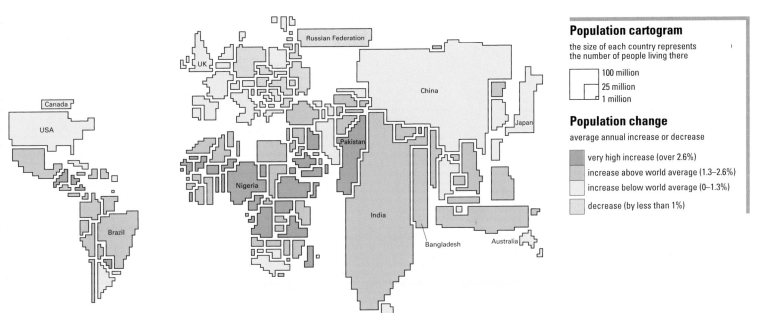

Population cartogram

the size of each country represents the number of people living there

100 million
25 million
1 million

Population change

average annual increase or decrease

very high increase (over 2.6%)

increase above world average (1.3–2.6%)

increase below world average (0–1.3%)

decrease (by less than 1%)

Population change, 1990–2000

percentage population gain or loss

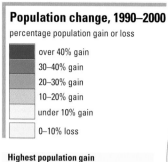

- over 40% gain
- 30–40% gain
- 20–30% gain
- 10–20% gain
- under 10% gain
- 0–10% loss

Highest population gain
Afghanistan 75.5%
Qatar 54.6%
Jordan 53.2%
French Guiana 48.9%
Marshall Islands 47.3%

United Kingdom 3.3%

Highest population loss
Kuwait -7.9%
Georgia -8%
Latvia -10%
Bulgaria -12.3%
Bosnia-Herzegovina -13.3%

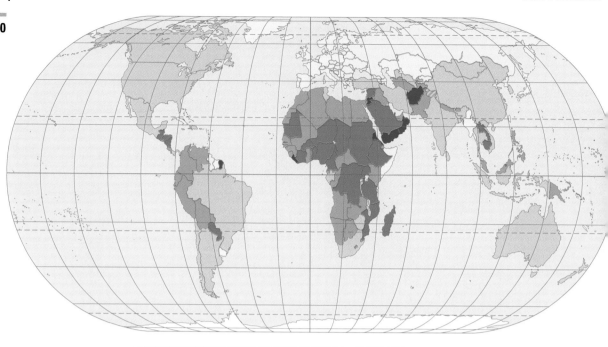

Urban population, 2000

percentage of the population living in urban areas

- over 80%
- 60–80%
- 40–60%
- 20–40%
- under 20%

Most urban
Kuwait 100%
Monaco 100%
Nauru 100%
Singapore 100%
Belgium 97%

United Kingdom 90%

Least urban
Bhutan 15%
Solomon Islands 13%
Nepal 11%
Burundi 8%
Rwanda 5%

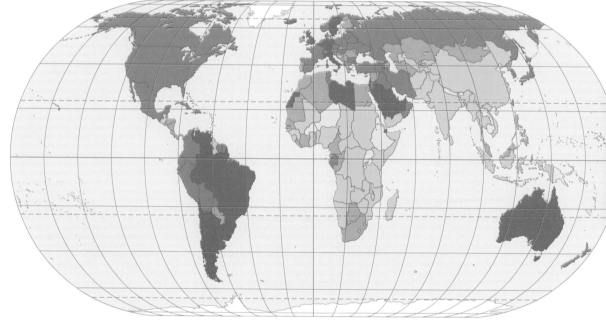

Fertility rate, 2000

average number of children born to childbearing women

- over 6 children
- 5–5.9 children
- 4–4.9 children
- 3–3.9 children
- 2–2.9 children
- 1–1.9 children

Largest families
Niger 7.5 children
Yemen 7.2 children
Mali 7.0 children
Angola 6.9 children
Uganda 6.9 children

United Kingdom 1.7 children

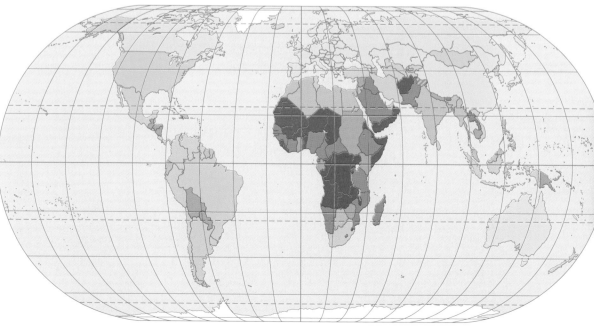

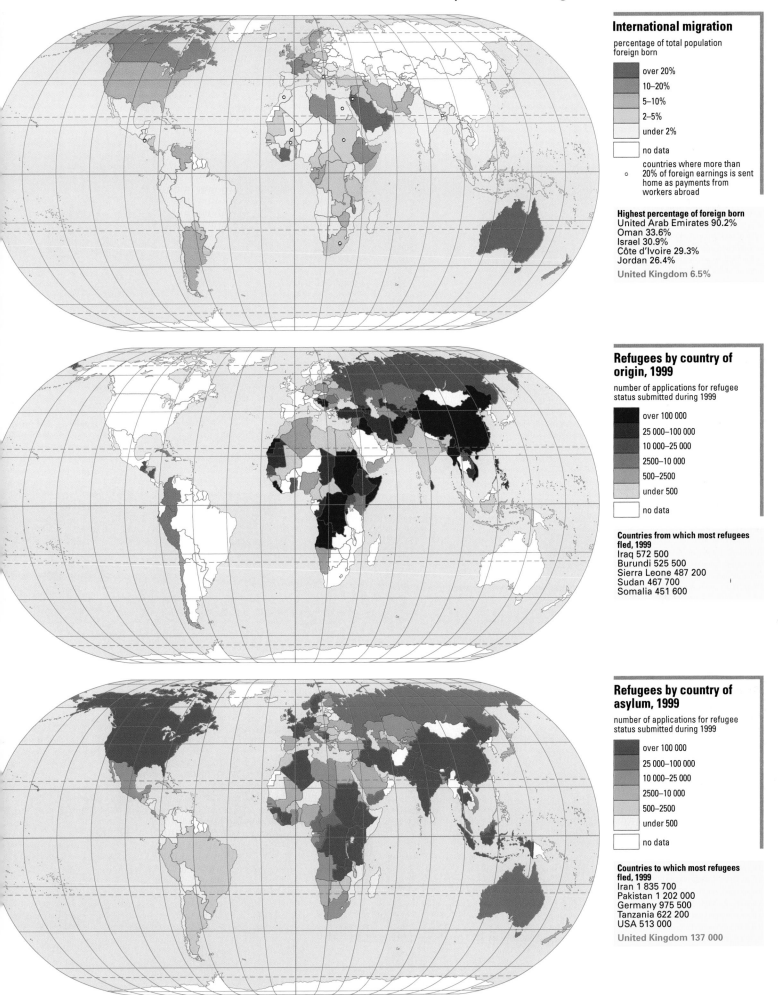

International migration

percentage of total population
foreign born

- over 20%
- 10–20%
- 5–10%
- 2–5%
- under 2%
- no data
- o countries where more than 20% of foreign earnings is sent home as payments from workers abroad

Highest percentage of foreign born
United Arab Emirates 90.2%
Oman 33.6%
Israel 30.9%
Côte d'Ivoire 29.3%
Jordan 26.4%

United Kingdom 6.5%

Refugees by country of origin, 1999

number of applications for refugee
status submitted during 1999

- over 100 000
- 25 000–100 000
- 10 000–25 000
- 2500–10 000
- 500–2500
- under 500
- no data

Countries from which most refugees fled, 1999
Iraq 572 500
Burundi 525 500
Sierra Leone 487 200
Sudan 467 700
Somalia 451 600

Refugees by country of asylum, 1999

number of applications for refugee
status submitted during 1999

- over 100 000
- 25 000–100 000
- 10 000–25 000
- 2500–10 000
- 500–2500
- under 500
- no data

Countries to which most refugees fled, 1999
Iran 1 835 700
Pakistan 1 202 000
Germany 975 500
Tanzania 622 200
USA 513 000

United Kingdom 137 000

Purchasing power, 1999

Purchasing Power Parity (PPP) in US$
Based on Gross Domestic Product (GDP)
per person, adjusted for the local cost
of living

- over 25 000
- 10 000–25 000
- 5000–10 000
- 2500–5000
- 1000–2500
- under 1000

Highest purchasing power
Luxembourg $42 769
United States $31 872
Norway $28 433
Iceland $27 835
Switzerland $27 171

United Kingdom $22 093

Lowest purchasing power
Ethiopia $628
Malawi $586
Burundi $578
Tanzania $501
Sierra Leone $448

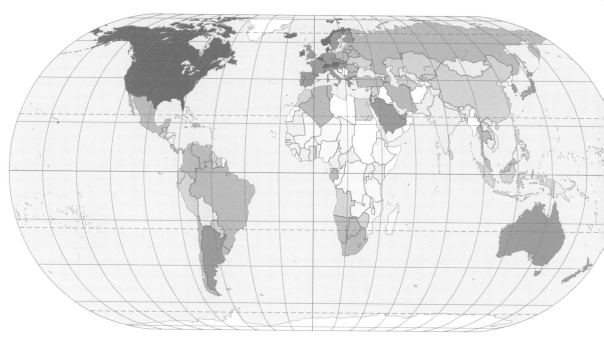

Literacy and schooling, 1999

percentage of the population over 15 years
able to read and write

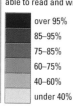

- over 95%
- 85–95%
- 75–85%
- 60–75%
- 40–60%
- under 40%

Highest literacy levels
Latvia 99.8%
Poland 99.7%
Georgia 99.6%
Slovenia 99.6%
Ukraine 99.6%

United Kingdom 99%

Lowest literacy levels
Gambia 35.7%
Guinea 35%
Sierra Leone 32%
Burkina 23%
Niger 15.3%

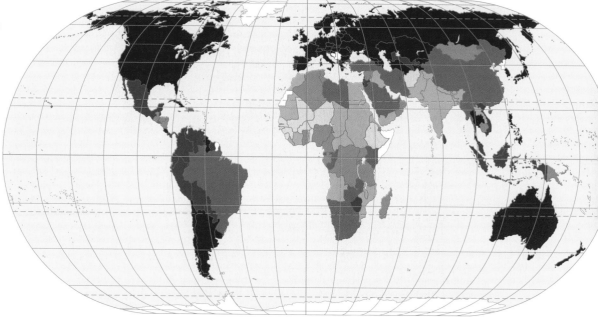

Life expectancy

average expected lifespan of babies
born in 2000

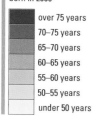

- over 75 years
- 70–75 years
- 65–70 years
- 60–65 years
- 55–60 years
- 50–55 years
- under 50 years

Highest life expectancy
Japan 81 years
San Marino 80 years
Sweden 80 years
Switzerland 80 years

United Kingdom 77 years

Lowest life expectancy
Malawi 39 years
Rwanda 39 years
Angola 38 years
Zambia 37 years

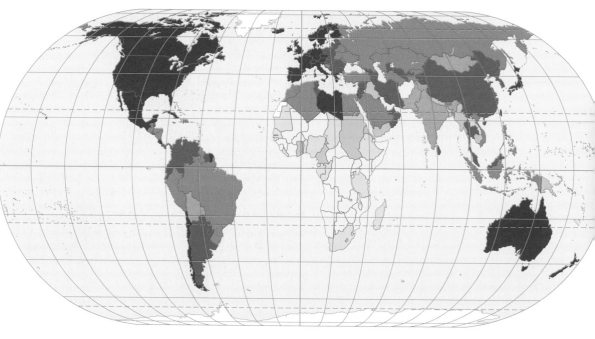

Eckert IV Projection   © Oxford University Press

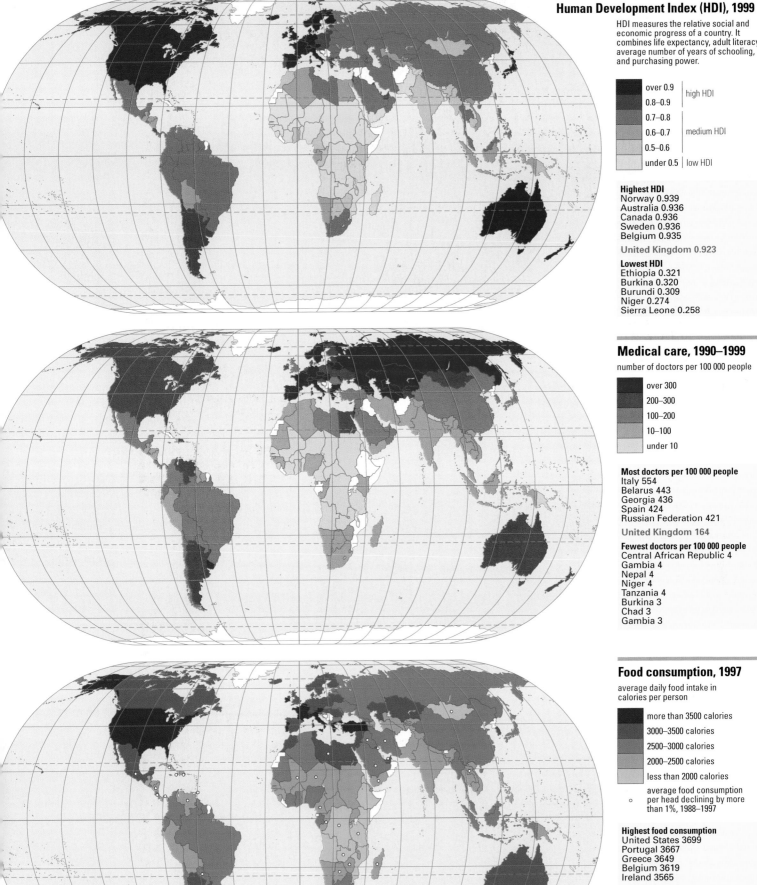

Human Development Index (HDI), 1999

HDI measures the relative social and economic progress of a country. It combines life expectancy, adult literacy, average number of years of schooling, and purchasing power.

over 0.9 — high HDI
0.8–0.9
0.7–0.8
0.6–0.7 — medium HDI
0.5–0.6
under 0.5 — low HDI

Highest HDI
Norway 0.939
Australia 0.936
Canada 0.936
Sweden 0.936
Belgium 0.935
United Kingdom 0.923

Lowest HDI
Ethiopia 0.321
Burkina 0.320
Burundi 0.309
Niger 0.274
Sierra Leone 0.258

Medical care, 1990–1999

number of doctors per 100 000 people

over 300
200–300
100–200
10–100
under 10

Most doctors per 100 000 people
Italy 554
Belarus 443
Georgia 436
Spain 424
Russian Federation 421

United Kingdom 164

Fewest doctors per 100 000 people
Central African Republic 4
Gambia 4
Nepal 4
Niger 4
Tanzania 4
Burkina 3
Chad 3
Gambia 3

Food consumption, 1997

average daily food intake in calories per person

more than 3500 calories
3000–3500 calories
2500–3000 calories
2000–2500 calories
less than 2000 calories

○ average food consumption per head declining by more than 1%, 1988–1997

Highest food consumption
United States 3699
Portugal 3667
Greece 3649
Belgium 3619
Ireland 3565

United Kingdom 3276

Lowest food consumption
Comoros 1858
Ethiopia 1858
Congo, Democratic Republic 1755
Burundi 1685
Eritrea 1622

Scale 1: 240 000 000

Employment in agriculture

percentage of the labour force

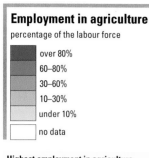

over 80%
60–80%
30–60%
10–30%
under 10%
no data

Highest employment in agriculture
Bhutan 94%
Nepal 94%
Burkina 92%
Burundi 92%
Rwanda 92%

Lowest employment in agriculture
Bahrain 2%
Brunei 2%
United Kingdom 2%
Kuwait 1%
Singapore 0%

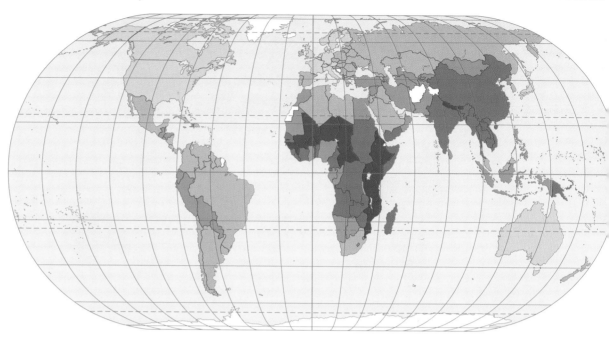

Employment in industry

percentage of the labour force

over 80%
60–80%
30–60%
10–30%
under 10%
no data

Highest employment in industry
Bulgaria 48%
Romaina 47%
Slovenia 46%
Czech Republic 45%
Armenia 43%
Mauritius 43%

United Kingdom 29%

Lowest employment in industry
Bhutan 2%
Burkina 2%
Ethiopia 2%
Guinea 2%
Guinea-Bissau 2%
Mali 2%
Nepal 0%

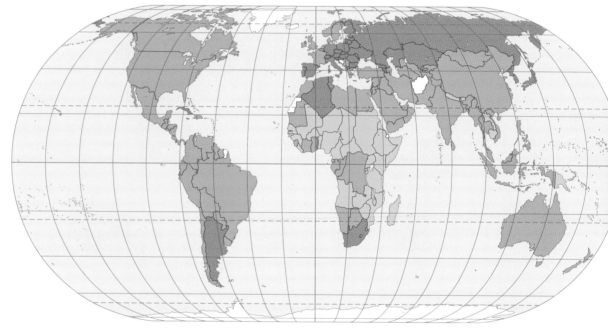

Employment in services

percentage of the labour force

over 80%
60–80%
30–60%
10–30%
under 10%
no data

Highest employment in service
Bahamas 79%
Brunei 74%
Kuwait 74%
Sweden 74%
Canada 72%

United Kingdom 69%

Lowest employment in services
Burkina 6%
Nepal 6%
Niger 6%
Burundi 5%
Rwanda 5%
Bhutan 4%

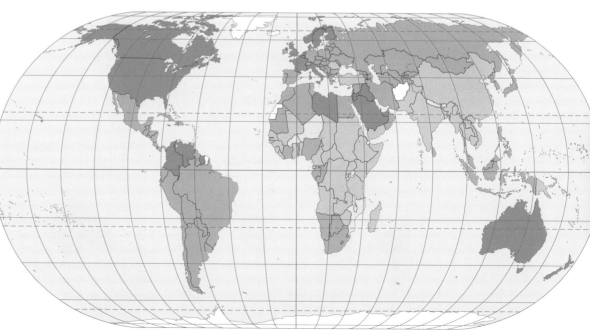

Eckert IV Projection   © Oxford University Press

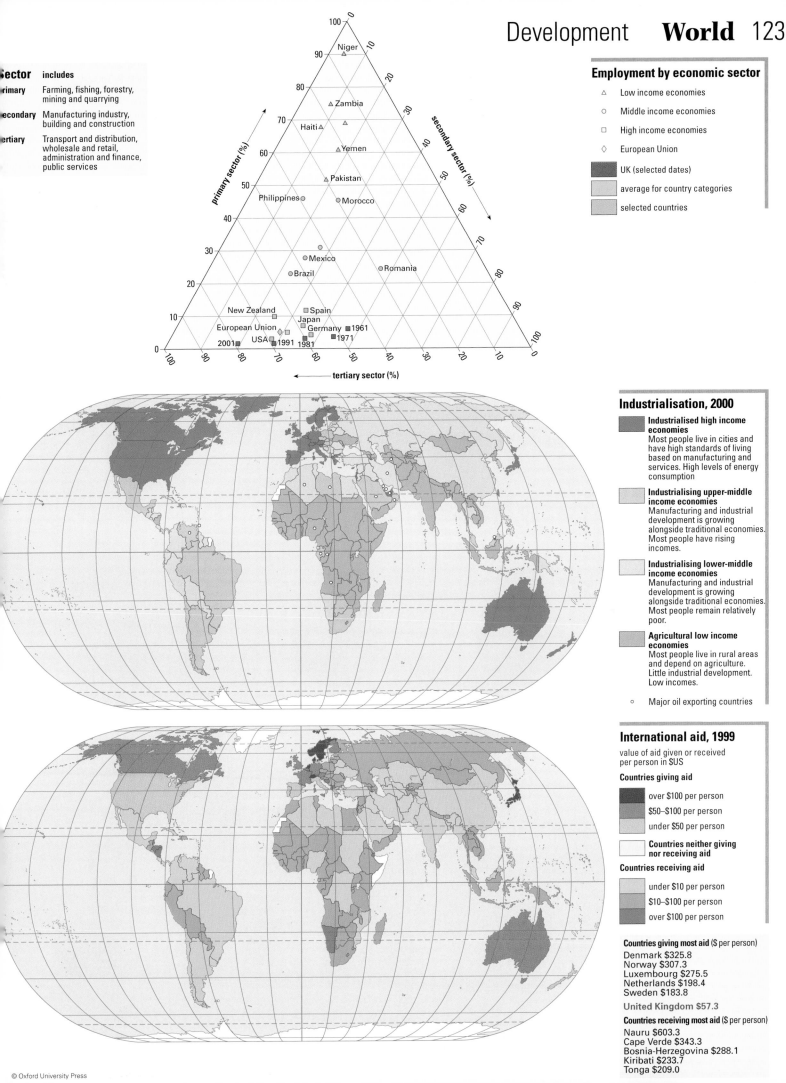

Sector | **includes**

Primary — Farming, fishing, forestry, mining and quarrying

Secondary — Manufacturing industry, building and construction

Tertiary — Transport and distribution, wholesale and retail, administration and finance, public services

Employment by economic sector

△ Low income economies

○ Middle income economies

□ High income economies

◇ European Union

UK (selected dates)

average for country categories

selected countries

Industrialisation, 2000

Industrialised high income economies
Most people live in cities and have high standards of living based on manufacturing and services. High levels of energy consumption

Industrialising upper-middle income economies
Manufacturing and industrial development is growing alongside traditional economies. Most people have rising incomes.

Industrialising lower-middle income economies
Manufacturing and industrial development is growing alongside traditional economies. Most people remain relatively poor.

Agricultural low income economies
Most people live in rural areas and depend on agriculture. Little industrial development. Low incomes.

○ Major oil exporting countries

International aid, 1999

value of aid given or received per person in $US

Countries giving aid

over $100 per person

$50–$100 per person

under $50 per person

Countries neither giving nor receiving aid

Countries receiving aid

under $10 per person

$10–$100 per person

over $100 per person

Countries giving most aid ($ per person)
Denmark $325.8
Norway $307.3
Luxembourg $275.5
Netherlands $198.4
Sweden $183.8

United Kingdom $57.3

Countries receiving most aid ($ per person)
Nauru $603.3
Cape Verde $343.3
Bosnia-Herzegovina $288.1
Kiribati $233.7
Tonga $209.0

Scale 1: 240 000 000

Energy production, 1999

kg oil equivalent per person

- over 25 000
- 2500–25 000
- 1000–2500
- 100–1000
- under 100

Highest energy producers
kg oil equivalent per person
Qatar 84 909
United Arab Emirates 67 071
Brunei 61 623
Kuwait 60 047
Norway 53 532

United Kingdom 5057

Lowest energy producers
these countries do not produce energy

Belize
Cyprus
Chad
Djibouti
Eritrea
Gambia

Guinea-Bissau
Lesotho
Liberia
Namibia
Sierra Leone
Somalia

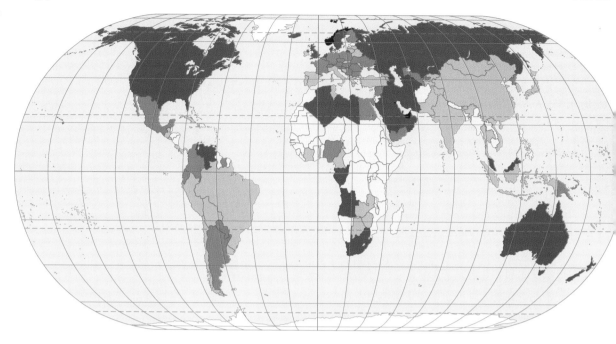

- North America
- Central and South America
- Europe
- former USSR
- Middle East
- Africa
- Asia Pacific

Oil reserves
Proven recoverable reserves
World total: 142 100 000 000 tonnes

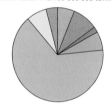

Gas reserves
Proven recoverable reserves
World total: 150 000 000 000 000 m³

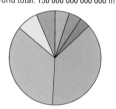

Coal reserves
Proven recoverable reserves
World total: 984 211 000 000 tonnes

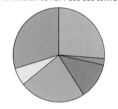

Oil consumption
World total: 3503 600 000 tonnes

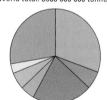

Gas consumption
World total: 2404 600 000 000 m³

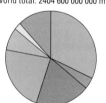

Coal consumption
World total: 2186 000 000 tonnes oil equivalent

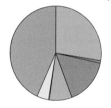

Energy consumption, 1999

kg oil equivalent per person

- over 10 000
- 2500–10 000
- 1000–2500
- 250–1000
- under 250

Highest energy consumers
kg oil equivalent per person
Qatar 24 222
United Arab Emirates 20 162
Bahrain 14 695
Iceland 11576
Luxembourg 10 888

United Kingdom 4177

Lowest energy consumers
kg oil equivalent per person
Afghanistan 25
Burkina 24
Ethiopia 22
Cambodia 16
Chad 8

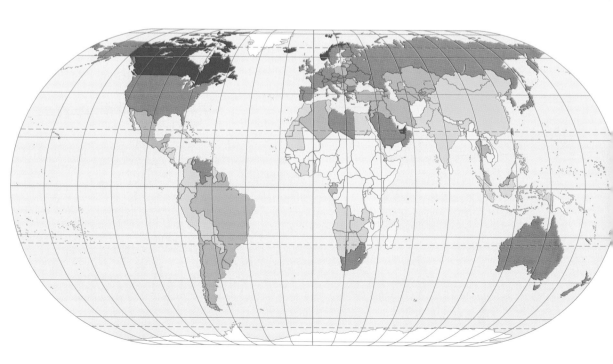

World trade cartogram, 1999

the size of each country represents its share of total world trade

☐ 1% of world trade

☐ 0.1% of world trade

Change in share of world trade, 1990–1999

over 50%	
5–50%	growth
0–5% growth or decline	little or no change
5–50	decline
over 50%	

Only those countries with more than 0.01% share in world trade are shown

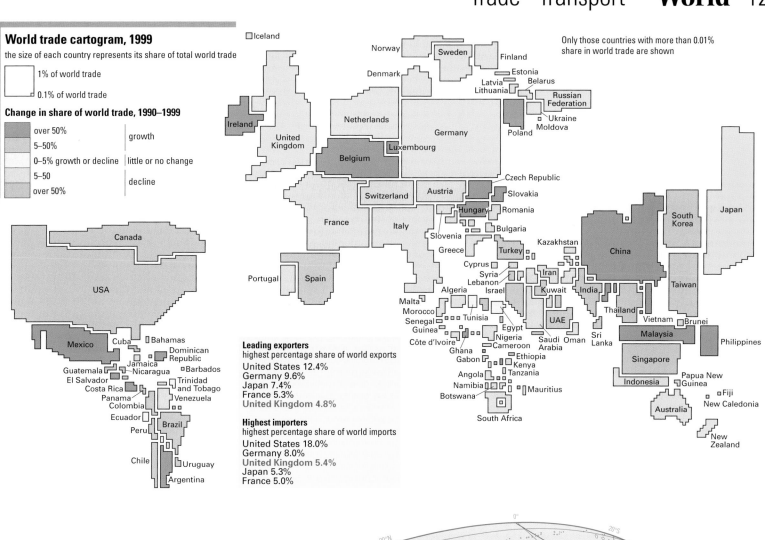

Leading exporters
highest percentage share of world exports

United States 12.4%
Germany 9.6%
Japan 7.4%
France 5.3%
United Kingdom 4.8%

Highest importers
highest percentage share of world imports

United States 18.0%
Germany 8.0%
United Kingdom 5.4%
Japan 5.3%
France 5.0%

Transport

Air transport

— major air route
• major airport

Sea transport

— major shipping lane
• major port

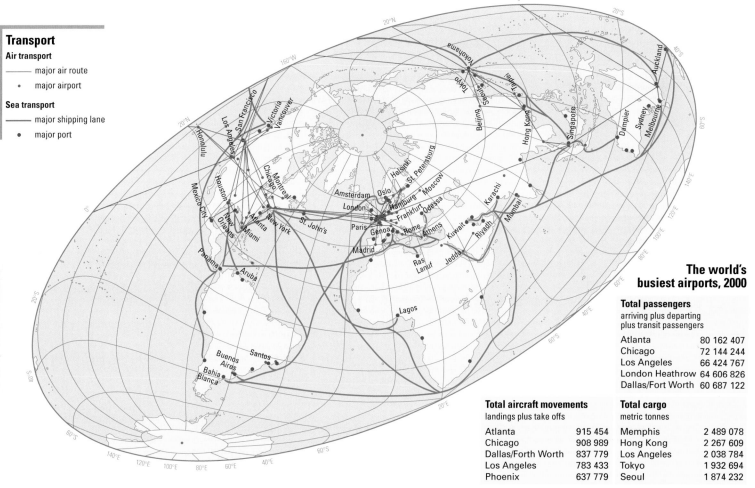

The world's busiest airports, 2000

Total passengers
arriving plus departing
plus transit passengers

Atlanta	80 162 407
Chicago	72 144 244
Los Angeles	66 424 767
London Heathrow	64 606 826
Dallas/Fort Worth	60 687 122

Total aircraft movements
landings plus take offs

Atlanta	915 454
Chicago	908 989
Dallas/Forth Worth	837 779
Los Angeles	783 433
Phoenix	637 779

Total cargo
metric tonnes

Memphis	2 489 078
Hong Kong	2 267 609
Los Angeles	2 038 784
Tokyo	1 932 694
Seoul	1 874 232

Desertification and tropical deforestation

existing areas of desert

areas with a high risk of desertification

areas with a moderate risk of desertification

existing areas of tropical rain forest

former areas of tropical rain forest

Countries losing greatest areas of forest ('000 hectares)

Brazil	2554
Indonesia	1084
Congo, Dem. Rep.	740
Bolivia	581
Mexico	508

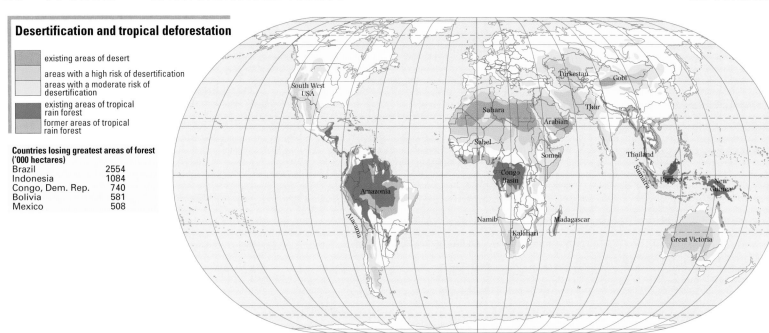

Lake Chad, West Africa, 1973–1997

Lake Chad was once the sixth-largest lake in the world, but persistent drought since the 1960's has shrunk it to about one tenth of its former size. Wetland marsh (shown on the satellite images as red) has now largely replaced open water (shown in blue). The lake is shallow and very responsive to the high variability on rainfall in the region. People living around Lake Chad do not have secure food supplies. Farming and irrigation projects have been affected by fluctuations in the level of the lake.

1973

1997

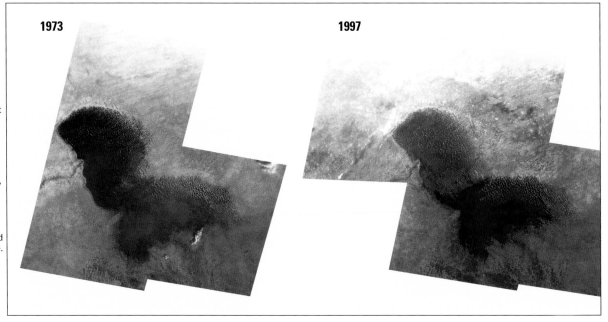

Acid rain

Sulphur and nitrogen emissions
Oxides of sulphur and nitrogen produced by burning fossil fuel react with rain to form dilute sulphuric and nitric acids

 areas with high levels of fossil fuel burning

• cities where sulphur dioxide emissions are recorded and exceed World Health Organization recommended levels

Areas of acid rain deposition
Annual mean values of pH in precipitation

 pH less than 4.2 (most acidic)

—— pH 4.2–4.6

— pH 4.6–5.0

⟨⟩ other areas where acid rain is becoming a problem

Lower pH values are more acidic. 'Clean' rain water is slightly acidic with a pH of 5.6. The pH scale is logarithmic, so that a value of 4.6 is ten times as acidic as normal rain.

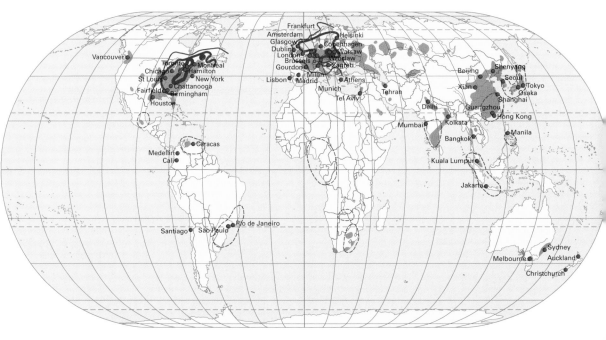

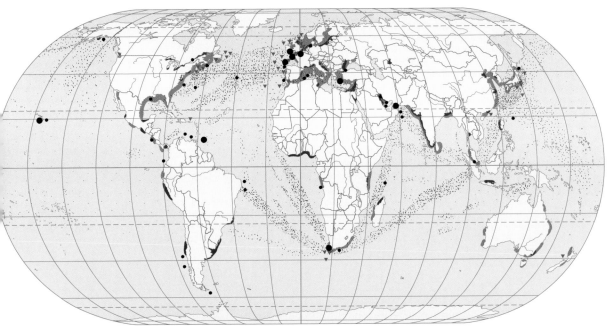

Sea pollution

Major oil spills

- ● over 100 000 tonnes
- · under 100 000 tonnes
- 🌫 frequent oil slicks from shipping

Other sea pollution

- ⬤ severe pollution
- ⬤ moderate pollution
- ▼ deep sea dump sites

Major oil spills ('000 tonnes)

1977	*Ekofisk* well blow-out, North Sea	270
1979	*Ixtoc 1* well blow-out, Gulf of Mexico	600
1979	Collision of *Atlantic Empress* and *Aegean Captain*, off Tobago, Caribbean	370
1983	*Nowruz* well blow-out, The Gulf	600
1991	Release of oil by Iraqi troops, *Sea Island* terminal, The Gulf	799

Phytoplankton in the Mediterranean Sea

Phytoplankton are micro-organisms that thrive in shallow, polluted sea areas. In this false colour satellite image red, orange, and yellow show the highest densities of phytoplankton. Green and blue show the lowest densities.

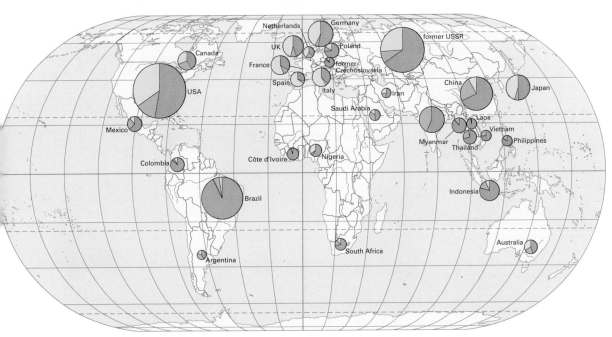

Greenhouse gases

Highest total emissions by country
thousand tonnes of carbon

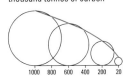

1000 800 600 400 200 20

Types of gas

- carbon dioxide
- methane
- chlorofluorocarbons (CFC's)

Scale 1: 125 000 000 (main map)

Selected tourist destinations

- 🏛 cultural heritage sites
- ❈ natural heritage sites
- ◯ resorts
- ⬤ tourist cities
- ── main cruise routes

land height

metres
2000
500
0

Top tourist destinations, 2000

	arrivals (000's)	% change 1999–2000
France	75 500	3.4
USA	50 900	4.9
Spain	48 200	3.0
Italy	41 200	12.8
China	31 200	15.5
United Kingdom	25 200	-0.8
Russian Federation	21 200	14.5
Mexico	20 600	8.4
Canada	20 400	4.9
Germany	19 000	10.9

Market share, 2000

percent of all international tourist arrivals

France	10.8%
USA	7.3%
Spain	6.9%
Italy	5.9%
China	4.5%
UK	3.6%
Russia	3.0%
Mexico	3.0%
Canada	2.9%
Germany	2.7%

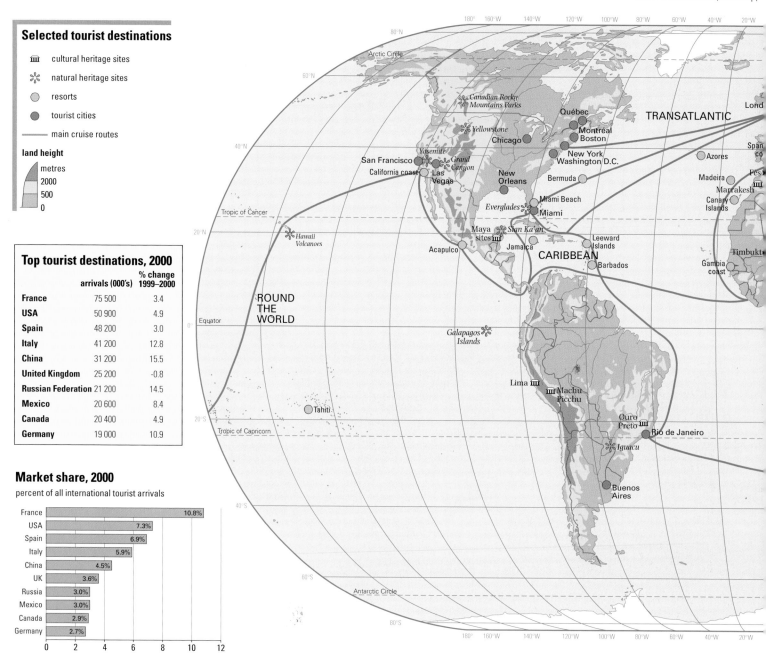

Earnings from tourism, 1998

tourist receipts in million $US

- over 5000
- 1000–5000
- 250–1000
- 100–250
- under 100
- no data

Highest tourist earnings (millions)
USA $71 250
France $29 931
Italy $29 866
Spain $29 737
United Kingdom $20 978

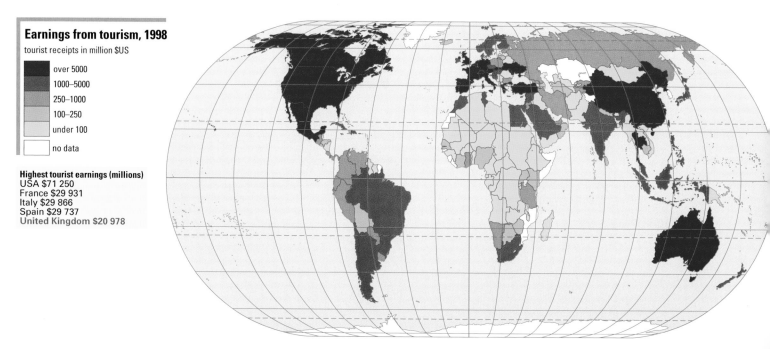

Eckert IV Projection   © Oxford University Press

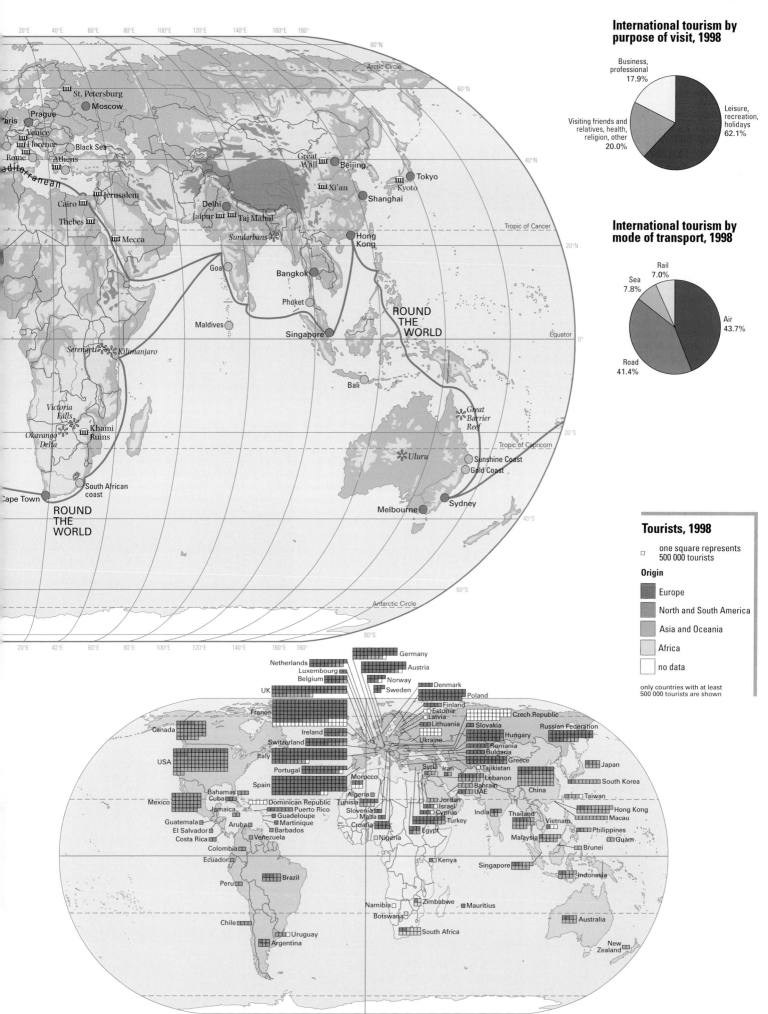

International tourism by purpose of visit, 1998

Business, professional
17.9%

Visiting friends and
relatives, health,
religion, other
20.0%

Leisure,
recreation,
holidays
62.1%

International tourism by mode of transport, 1998

Rail 7.0%

Sea 7.8%

Air 43.7%

Road 41.4%

Tourists, 1998

☐ one square represents 500 000 tourists

Origin

- Europe
- North and South America
- Asia and Oceania
- Africa
- no data

only countries with at least 500 000 tourists are shown

Time zones, 2001

Minus numbers show hours behind Greeenwich Mean Time (GMT).
Plus numbers show hours ahead of GMT.

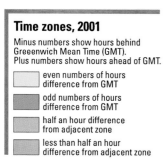

	even numbers of hours difference from GMT
	odd numbers of hours difference from GMT
	half an hour difference from adjacent zone
	less than half an hour difference from adjacent zone

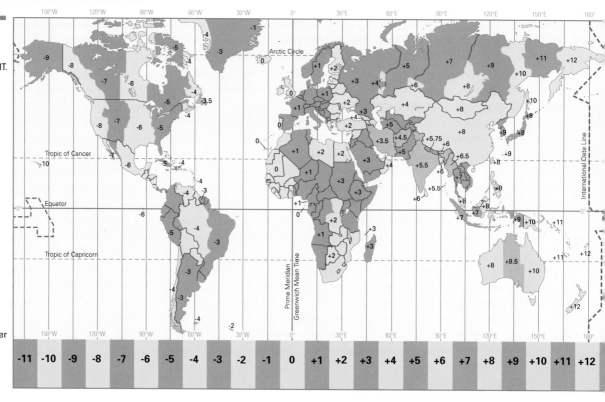

Longitude is measured from the **prime meridian** which passes through Greenwich. There are 24 standard time zones, each of 15° of longitude. The edges of these time zones usually follow international boundaries.

The **international date line** marks the point where one calendar day ends and another begins. A traveller crossing from east to west moves forward one day. Crossing from west to east the calendar goes back one day.

-11	-10	-9	-8	-7	-6	-5	-4	-3	-2	-1	0	+1	+2	+3	+4	+5	+6	+7	+8	+9	+10	+11	+12

Distance

Flight distance between cities in kilometres
to convert kilometres to miles multiply by 0.62

Beijing											
19 307	**Buenos Aires**										
1983	18 484	**Hong Kong**									
11 710	8088	10 732	**Johannesburg**								
8145	11 161	9645	9071	**London**							
10 081	9871	11 678	16 676	8774	**Los Angeles**						
12 468	7468	14 162	14 585	8936	2484	**Mexico City**					
4774	14 952	4306	8274	7193	14 033	15 678	**Mumbai**				
11 000	8548	12 984	12 841	5580	3951	3371	12 565	**New York**			
8226	11 097	9613	8732	338	9032	9210	7032	5839	**Paris**		
4468	15 904	2661	8860	10 871	14 146	16 630	3919	15 533	10 758	**Singapore**	
8949	11 800	7374	11 040	16 992	12 073	12 969	9839	15 989	16 962	6300	**Sydney**
2113	18 388	2903	13 547	9581	8823	11 355	6758	10 871	9726	5322	7823	**Tokyo**

The Earth rotates from west to east

The Earth rotates on its axis once in every 24 hours.

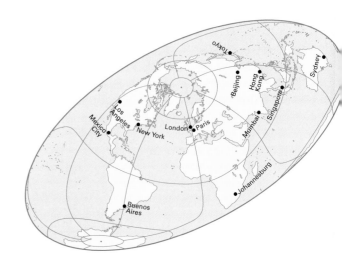

Flying time

Typical flight times by air between cities in hours and minutes
ooo means there is no direct flight available, early 2002

Beijing											
ooo	**Buenos Aires**										
3.00	ooo	**Hong Kong**									
ooo	ooo	13.00	**Johannesburg**								
10.25	14.50	13.30	10.50	**London**							
13.30	16.40	14.50	ooo	13.00	**Los Angeles**						
ooo	13.10	ooo	ooo	11.05	4.15	**Mexico City**					
ooo	ooo	7.45	20.15	10.30	ooo	ooo	**Mumbai**				
25.20	13.25	19.25	16.25	7.20	6.00	6.00	20.05	**New York**			
10.20	13.50	12.45	10.55	1.10	12.30	12.20	12.10	7.40	**Paris**		
6.15	ooo	4.05	10.30	14.40	18.45	ooo	6.30	22.05	14.15	**Singapore**	
12.55	16.35	8.50	14.30	22.45	14.35	ooo	14.40	21.45	22.25	8.55	**Sydney**
3.35	ooo	4.55	ooo	12.40	10.40	15.50	12.35	15.55	12.50	7.05	10.00	**Tokyo**

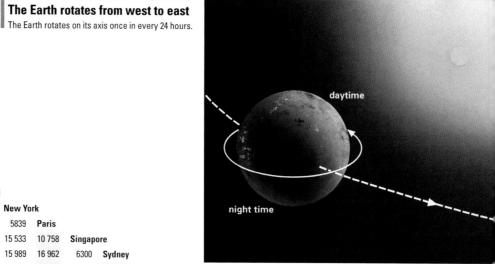

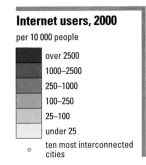

Internet users, 2000

per 10 000 people

	over 2500
	1000–2500
	250–1000
	100–250
	25–100
	under 25
○	ten most interconnected cities

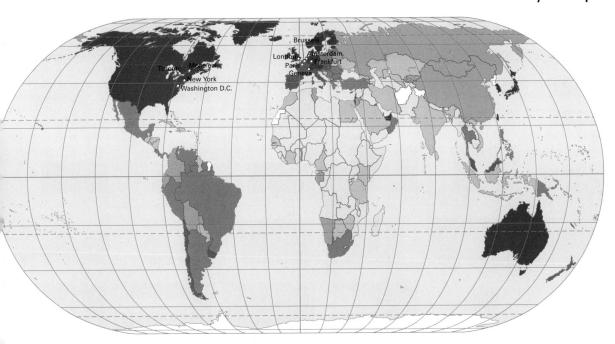

Brussels
London
Amsterdam
Paris Frankfurt
Geneva
Toronto Montreal
New York
Washington D.C.

Internet traffic, 2000

internet providers
per 10 000 people

	over 100
	10–100
	1–10
	under 1

internet bandwidth
megabits per second (Mbps)

	over 5000
	1000–5000
	under 1000

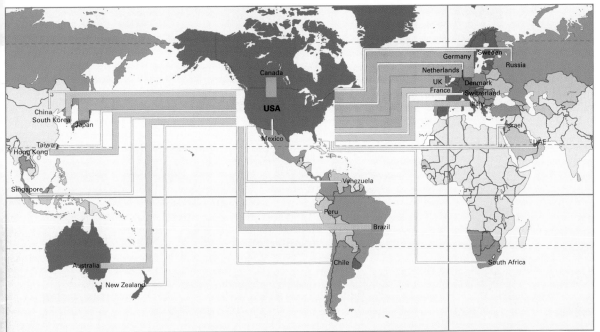

China
South Korea
Japan
Taiwan
Hong Kong
Singapore
Australia
New Zealand
Canada
USA
Mexico
Venezuela
Peru
Brazil
Chile
Germany Sweden
Netherlands Russia
UK Denmark
France Switzerland
Italy
Israel
UAE
South Africa

Internet traffic flow

The 'arc map' shows internet traffic between 50 countries. Arcs are coloured to show internet traffic between countries. The height of each arc is proportional to the volume of internet traffic flowing over a link, so the highest arcs represent the greatest volume of traffic.

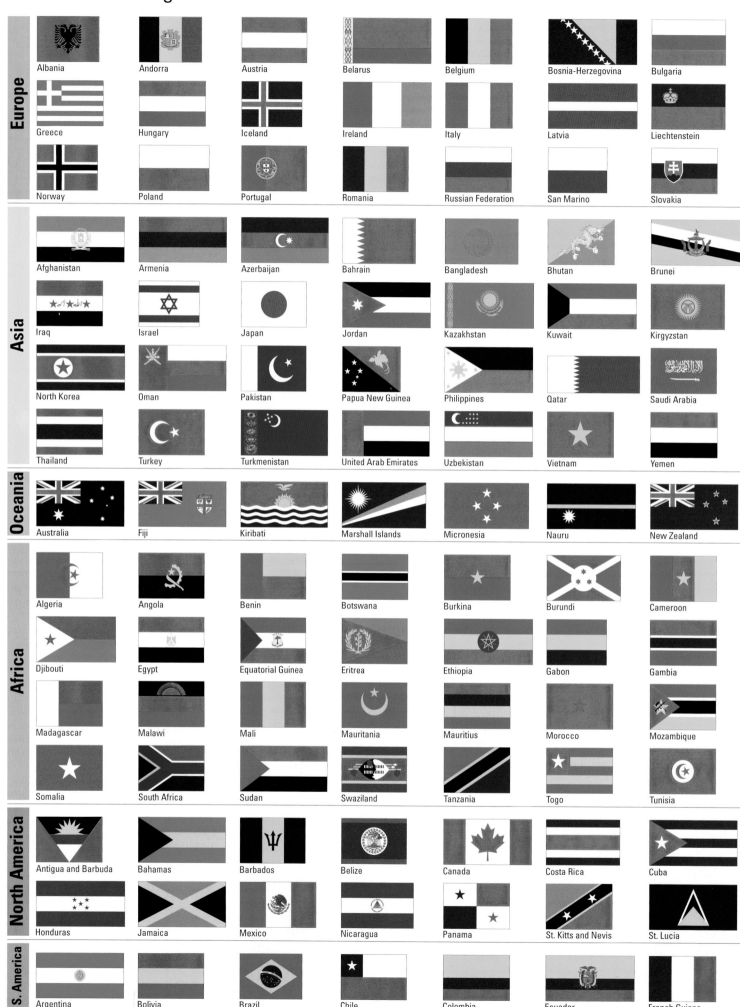

Europe

Albania · Andorra · Austria · Belarus · Belgium · Bosnia-Herzegovina · Bulgaria

Greece · Hungary · Iceland · Ireland · Italy · Latvia · Liechtenstein

Norway · Poland · Portugal · Romania · Russian Federation · San Marino · Slovakia

Asia

Afghanistan · Armenia · Azerbaijan · Bahrain · Bangladesh · Bhutan · Brunei

Iraq · Israel · Japan · Jordan · Kazakhstan · Kuwait · Kirgyzstan

North Korea · Oman · Pakistan · Papua New Guinea · Philippines · Qatar · Saudi Arabia

Thailand · Turkey · Turkmenistan · United Arab Emirates · Uzbekistan · Vietnam · Yemen

Oceania

Australia · Fiji · Kiribati · Marshall Islands · Micronesia · Nauru · New Zealand

Africa

Algeria · Angola · Benin · Botswana · Burkina · Burundi · Cameroon

Djibouti · Egypt · Equatorial Guinea · Eritrea · Ethiopia · Gabon · Gambia

Madagascar · Malawi · Mali · Mauritania · Mauritius · Morocco · Mozambique

Somalia · South Africa · Sudan · Swaziland · Tanzania · Togo · Tunisia

North America

Antigua and Barbuda · Bahamas · Barbados · Belize · Canada · Costa Rica · Cuba

Honduras · Jamaica · Mexico · Nicaragua · Panama · St. Kitts and Nevis · St. Lucia

S. America

Argentina · Bolivia · Brazil · Chile · Colombia · Ecuador · French Guiana

© Oxford University Press

Croatia

Czech Republic

Denmark

Estonia

Finland

France

Germany

Lithuania

Luxembourg

Macedonia, FYRO

Malta

Moldova

Monaco

Netherlands

Slovenia

Spain

Sweden

Switzerland

Ukraine

United Kingdom

Yugoslavia

Europe

Cambodia

China

Cyprus

Georgia

India

Indonesia

Iran

Laos

Lebanon

Malaysia

Maldives

Mongolia

Myanmar

Nepal

Seychelles

Singapore

South Korea

Sri Lanka

Syria

Taiwan

Tajikistan

Asia

Northern Marianas

Palau

Samoa

Solomon Islands

Tonga

Tuvalu

Vanuatu

Oceania

Cape Verde

Central African Republic

Chad

Comoros

Congo

Congo, Dem. Rep.

Côte d'Ivoire

Ghana

Guinea

Guinea-Bissau

Kenya

Lesotho

Liberia

Libya

Namibia

Niger

Nigeria

Rwanda

Sao Tomé and Pirncipe

Senegal

Sierra Leone

Uganda

Zambia

Zimbabwe

Africa

Dominica

Dominican Republic

El Salvador

Greenland

Grenada

Guatemala

Haiti

St. Vincent & the Grenadines

Trinidad and Tobago

United States of America

North America

Guyana

Paraguay

Peru

Suriname

Uruguay

Venezuela

S. America

The datasets below are explained on pages 140/1

	ooo	no data
	per capita	for each person

	Land		Population									Employment		
	Area	Arable and permanent crops	Total	Density	Change	Births	Deaths	Fertility	Infant mortality	Life expectancy	Urban	Agriculture	Industry	Services
			2001	2001	1990–2000	2000	2000	2000	1999	2000	2000	1990	1990	1990
	thousand km²	% of total	millions	persons per km²	%	births per 1000	deaths per 1000	children per mother	per 1000 live births	years	%	%	%	%
Afghanistan	652	12.4	22.5	34.5	75.5	43	19	6.0	165	45	22	ooo	ooo	ooo
Albania	29	24.3	3.2	110.4	7.1	17	5	2.8	29	72	46	55	23	22
Algeria	2382	3.5	30.8	12.9	23.1	25	6	3.1	36	69	49	26	31	43
Andorra	0.5	2.2	0.06	120.0	26.5	13	4	1.2	6	ooo	93	ooo	ooo	ooo
Angola	1247	2.8	13.5	10.8	25.9	50	25	6.9	172	38	32	75	8	17
Antigua and Barbuda	0.4	18.2	0.07	175.0	6.0	22	6	2.4	17	70	37	ooo	ooo	ooo
Argentina	2780	9.8	37.5	13.5	13.2	19	8	2.6	19	73	90	12	32	56
Armenia	30	18.8	3.8	126.7	-0.6	9	6	1.1	25	73	67	18	43	39
Australia	7741	6.2	19.3	2.5	12.6	13	7	1.7	5	79	85	6	26	68
Austria	84	17.6	8.1	96.4	5.4	10	9	1.3	4	78	65	8	38	54
Azerbaijan	87	22.9	8.1	93.1	7.6	15	6	2.0	35	72	51	31	29	40
Bahamas, The	14	0.7	0.3	21.4	14.7	21	5	2.4	18	72	84	5	16	79
Bahrain	0.7	8.7	0.7	1000.0	26.7	21	3	2.8	13	72	88	2	30	68
Bangladesh	144	58.6	140.4	975.0	17.6	28	8	3.3	58	59	21	65	16	19
Barbados	0.4	39.5	0.3	750.0	4.4	14	9	1.6	14	73	38	14	30	56
Belarus	208	30.4	10.2	49.0	1.5	9	14	1.3	23	68	70	20	40	40
Belgium	33	25.2	10.3	312.1	2.7	11	10	1.6	6	78	97	3	28	69
Belize	23	3.9	0.2	8.7	30.5	25	6	3.2	35	72	49	33	19	48
Benin	113	16.4	6.5	57.5	37.4	45	15	6.3	99	50	39	63	8	29
Bhutan	47	3.4	2.1	44.7	25.5	40	9	5.6	80	66	15	94	2	4
Bolivia	1099	2.0	8.5	7.7	24.0	32	9	4.2	64	62	63	47	18	35
Bosnia-Herzegovina	51	12.7	4.1	80.4	-13.3	12	8	1.6	15	68	40	ooo	ooo	ooo
Botswana	582	0.6	1.6	2.8	20.9	31	20	3.9	46	41	49	46	20	34
Brazil	8547	7.6	172.6	20.2	14.4	22	7	2.4	34	68	81	23	23	54
Brunei	6	1.2	0.3	50.0	30.3	22	3	2.7	8	74	67	2	24	74
Bulgaria	111	40.7	7.9	71.2	-12.3	9	14	1.2	14	72	68	13	48	39
Burkina	274	12.6	11.9	43.4	32.2	47	17	6.8	106	47	15	92	2	6
Burundi	28	39.5	6.5	232.1	14.6	42	17	6.5	106	47	8	92	3	5
Cambodia	181	21.0	13.4	74.0	36.2	28	11	4.0	86	56	16	74	8	18
Cameroon	475	15.1	15.2	32.0	31.1	39	12	5.2	95	55	48	70	9	21
Canada	9971	4.6	31.0	3.1	12.6	11	8	1.4	6	79	78	3	25	72
Cape Verde	4	10.2	0.4	100.0	14.9	37	7	4.0	54	68	53	30	30	40
Central African Republic	623	3.2	3.8	6.1	25.3	38	18	5.1	113	45	39	80	3	17
Chad	1284	2.8	8.1	6.3	40.0	49	16	6.6	118	50	21	83	4	13
Chile	757	3.0	15.4	20.3	15.4	18	5	2.3	11	75	86	19	25	56
China	9598	14.1	1292.4	134.7	10.8	15	6	1.8	33	71	36	72	15	13
Colombia	1139	3.8	42.8	37.6	20.8	24	6	2.6	26	71	71	27	23	50
Comoros	2	52.9	0.7	350.0	34.8	47	12	6.8	64	56	29	78	9	13
Congo	342	0.6	3.1	9.1	27.7	46	16	6.3	81	50	41	49	15	36
Congo, Dem. Rep.	2345	3.4	52.5	22.4	36.8	47	16	7.0	128	48	29	68	13	19
Costa Rica	51	9.9	4.1	80.4	22.6	22	4	2.6	13	77	45	26	27	47
Côte d'Ivoire	322	22.8	16.4	50.9	34.1	36	16	5.2	102	46	46	60	10	30
Croatia	57	28.1	4.7	82.5	-5.0	10	11	1.4	8	74	54	16	34	50
Cuba	111	40.3	10.9	98.2	5.7	14	7	1.6	6	75	75	19	30	51
Cyprus	9	15.5	0.8	88.9	11.3	13	8	1.8	7	77	66	14	30	56
Czech Republic	79	42.2	10.3	130.4	-0.4	9	11	1.1	5	75	77	11	45	44
Denmark	43	53.4	5.3	123.3	3.8	13	11	1.7	4	76	72	6	28	66
Djibouti	23	ooo	0.6	26.1	22.1	43	16	6.1	104	46	83	ooo	ooo	ooo
Dominica	0.8	20.0	0.08	100.0	-1.6	16	8	1.8	16	73	71	ooo	ooo	ooo
Dominican Republic	49	32.2	8.5	173.5	18.9	26	5	3.1	43	69	61	25	29	46
Ecuador	284	10.6	12.9	45.4	25.2	28	6	3.3	27	71	62	33	19	48
Egypt	1001	3.3	69.1	69.0	21.8	28	7	3.5	41	66	43	40	22	38
El Salvador	21	38.5	6.4	304.8	20.1	30	7	3.5	35	70	58	36	21	43
Equatorial Guinea	28	8.2	0.5	17.9	28.8	45	14	5.9	105	50	37	66	11	23
Eritrea	118	4.3	3.8	32.2	40.5	43	13	6.0	66	55	16	80	5	15

© Oxford University Press

Wealth   Energy and trade   Quality of life

GNP	Purchasing power	Growth of PP	Energy consumption	Imports	Exports	Aid received (given)	Human Development Index	Health care	Food consumption	Safe water	Illiteracy male	Illiteracy female	Higher education	Cars	
1999	1999	1990–1999	1997	1999	1999	1999	1999	1990–1999	1997	1999	1998	1998	1996	2000	
billion US$	US$	%	kg oil equivalent per capita	US$ per capita	US$ per capita	million US$		doctors per 100 000 people	daily calories per capita	% access	%	%	students per 100 000 people	people per car	
ooo	ooo	ooo	ooo	ooo	ooo	142	ooo	ooo	ooo	13	ooo	ooo	165	644	Afghanistan
2.9	3189	2.8	317	170	344	480	0.725	129	2961	76	9	24	1087	36	Albania
46.5	5063	-0.5	912	420	312	89	0.693	85	2853	94	24	46	1238	34	Algeria
ooo	ooo	ooo	ooo	ooo	ooo	ooo	ooo	ooo	ooo	100	ooo	ooo	ooo	2	Andorra
2.7	3179	-2.8	587	398	515	388	0.422	8	1903	38	ooo	ooo	ooo	111	Angola
ooo	10 225	ooo	ooo	ooo	ooo	11	ooo	ooo	2365	91	ooo	ooo	ooo	ooo	Antigua and Barbuda
77.9	12 277	3.6	1730	740	869	91	0.842	268	3093	79	3	3	3317	7	Argentina
1.9	2215	-3.9	476	101	242	209	0.745	316	2371	84	1	3	1886	1900	Armenia
380.8	24 574	2.9	5484	3801	4364	(982)	0.939	240	3224	100	ooo	ooo	5682	2	Australia
10.0	25 089	1.4	3439	11 719	11 840	(527)	0.921	302	3536	100	ooo	ooo	2988	2	Austria
4.4	2850	-10.7	1529	158	237	162	0.738	360	2236	ooo	ooo	ooo	2289	30	Azerbaijan
ooo	15 258	-0.1	ooo	ooo	ooo	12	0.820	152	2443	96	ooo	ooo	ooo	4	Bahamas, The
ooo	13 688	0.8	13 689	ooo	ooo	4	0.824	100	ooo	ooo	ooo	ooo	1402	5	Bahrain
47.0	1483	ooo	197	43	61	1203	0.470	20	2085	97	49	71	397	2808	Bangladesh
ooo	14 353	1.5	ooo	ooo	ooo	-2	0.864	125	3176	100	ooo	ooo	2535	7	Barbados
26.8	6876	-2.9	2449	655	685	24	0.782	443	3225	100	0	ooo	3168	9	Belarus
250.6	25 443	1.4	5611	18 856	17 811	(760)	0.935	395	3619	ooo	ooo	ooo	3551	2	Belgium
0.7	4959	0.7	ooo	ooo	ooo	46	0.776	55	2907	76	ooo	ooo	ooo	29	Belize
2.3	933	1.8	377	83	122	211	0.420	6	2487	63	46	77	256	260	Benin
0.4	1341	3.4	ooo	ooo	ooo	67	0.477	16	ooo	62	ooo	ooo	ooo	ooo	Bhutan
8.2	2355	1.8	548	154	234	569	0.648	130	2174	79	9	22	ooo	65	Bolivia
ooo	ooo	ooo	ooo	ooo	ooo	1063	ooo	ooo	ooo	ooo	ooo	ooo	ooo	34	Bosnia-Herzegovina
5.1	6872	1.8	ooo	1903	1570	61	0.577	24	2183	70	27	22	587	59	Botswana
742.8	7037	1.5	1051	323	369	184	0.750	127	2974	83	16	16	1424	11	Brazil
ooo	ooo	-0.5	6840	ooo	ooo	1	0.857	85	2857	ooo	ooo	ooo	516	2	Brunei
11.3	5071	-2.1	2480	733	830	265	0.772	345	2686	100	1	2	3110	5	Bulgaria
2.6	965	1.4	ooo	27	62	398	0.320	3	2121	ooo	68	87	83	744	Burkina
0.8	578	-5.0	ooo	9	20	74	0.309	ooo	1685	52	45	63	ooo	650	Burundi
3.0	1361	1.9	ooo	84	105	279	0.541	30	2048	30	43	80	85	788	Cambodia
8.5	1573	-1.5	413	148	151	434	0.506	7	2111	62	20	33	ooo	152	Cameroon
591.4	26 251	1.7	7930	8957	8354	(1699)	0.936	229	3119	100	ooo	ooo	5953	2	Canada
0.6	4490	3.2	ooo	ooo	ooo	136	0.708	17	3015	74	ooo	ooo	ooo	133	Cape Verde
1.0	1166	1.1	ooo	41	64	117	0.372	4	2016	60	43	68	ooo	422	Central African Republic
1.6	850	-0.3	ooo	38	61	188	0.359	3	2032	27	21	69	51	853	Chad
71.1	8652	5.6	1574	1260	1173	69	0.825	110	2796	94	4	5	2546	15	Chile
980.2	3617	9.5	907	169	147	2324	0.718	162	2897	75	9	25	473	369	China
93.6	5749	1.4	761	324	312	301	0.765	116	2597	91	9	9	1640	43	Colombia
0.2	1429	-3.1	ooo	ooo	ooo	22	0.510	7	1858	96	ooo	ooo	ooo	1	Comoros
1.9	727	-3.3	459	578	618	140	0.502	25	2143	51	14	29	ooo	119	Congo
ooo	801	-8.1	311	28	26	132	0.429	7	1755	45	29	53	212	525	Congo, Dem. Rep.
9.8	8860	3.0	769	1998	1752	-10	0.821	141	2649	98	5	5	2830	22	Costa Rica
10.4	1654	0.6	394	326	252	447	0.426	9	2610	77	47	64	568	88	Côte d'Ivoire
20.4	7387	1.0	1687	1727	2083	48	0.803	229	2445	95	1	3	1911	5	Croatia
ooo	ooo	ooo	1291	ooo	ooo	58	ooo	ooo	2480	95	ooo	ooo	1013	574	Cuba
9.1	19 006	2.8	2777	ooo	ooo	50	0.877	255	3429	100	ooo	ooo	1193	4	Cyprus
52	13 018	0.9	3938	3222	3300	318	0.844	303	3244	ooo	ooo	ooo	2009	3	Czech Republic
170.3	25 869	2.0	3994	12 394	10 959	(1773)	0.921	290	3407	100	ooo	ooo	3349	3	Denmark
0.5	ooo	-5.1	ooo	ooo	ooo	75	0.447	14	2084	100	ooo	ooo	26	55	Djibouti
0.2	5425	ooo	ooo	ooo	ooo	10	ooo	ooo	3059	97	ooo	ooo	ooo	23	Dominica
16.1	5507	3.9	673	940	1093	195	0.722	216	2288	79	17	17	2223	53	Dominican Republic
16.2	2994	0.3	713	408	317	146	0.726	170	2679	71	8	11	ooo	123	Ecuador
87.5	3420	2.4	656	196	306	1579	0.635	202	3287	95	35	58	1895	52	Egypt
11.8	4344	2.8	691	490	727	183	0.701	107	2562	74	19	25	1935	67	El Salvador
0.5	4676	16.3	ooo	ooo	ooo	20	0.610	25	ooo	43	ooo	ooo	ooo	143	Equatorial Guinea
0.8	881	2.2	ooo	17	157	149	0.416	3	1622	46	34	62	90	760	Eritrea

The datasets below are explained on pages 140/14

	no data
ooo	no data
per capita	for each person

	Land		Population									Employment		
	Area	Arable and permanent crops	Total	Density	Change	Births	Deaths	Fertility	Infant mortality	Life expectancy	Urban	Agriculture	Industry	Services
	2001	2001	2001	2001	1990–2000	2000	2000	2000	1999	2000	2000	1990	1990	1990
	thousand km²	% of total	millions	persons per km²	%	births per 1000	deaths per 1000	children per mother	per 1000 live births	years	%	%	%	%
Estonia	45	25.2	1.4	31.1	-9.0	9	13	1.3	17	71	69	14	41	45
Ethiopia	1104	9.7	64.5	58.4	32.7	44	15	5.9	118	52	15	86	2	12
Fiji	18	15.6	0.8	44.4	12.8	25	6	3.3	18	67	46	46	15	39
Finland	338	6.4	5.2	15.4	3.6	11	10	1.7	4	77	60	8	31	61
France	552	35.4	59.5	107.8	4.6	13	9	1.9	5	79	74	5	29	66
French Guiana	91	0.1	0.2	2.2	48.9	27	4	3.4	ooo	76	79	ooo	ooo	ooo
Gabon	268	1.8	1.3	4.9	13.0	32	16	4.3	85	52	73	51	16	33
Gambia, The	11	17.7	1.3	118.2	42.2	43	14	5.9	61	52	37	82	8	10
Georgia	70	15.3	5.2	74.3	-8.0	9	9	1.2	19	73	56	26	31	43
Germany	357	33.7	82.0	229.7	4.3	9	10	1.3	5	78	86	4	38	58
Ghana	239	22.2	19.7	82.4	27.2	32	10	4.3	63	58	37	59	13	28
Greece	132	29.3	10.6	80.3	4.4	10	10	1.3	6	78	59	23	27	50
Greenland	342	ooo	0.06	0.2	1.1	ooo	ooo	ooo	ooo	ooo	ooo	ooo	ooo	ooo
Grenada	0.3	32.4	0.09	300.0	-3.3	21	8	2.4	22	65	34	ooo	ooo	ooo
Guatemala	109	17.5	11.7	107.3	31.2	36	7	4.8	45	66	39	52	17	31
Guinea	246	6	8.3	33.7	25.8	41	19	5.5	115	45	26	87	2	11
Guinea-Bissau	36	9.7	1.2	33.3	29.1	42	20	5.8	128	45	22	85	2	13
Guyana	215	2.3	0.8	3.7	-6.0	21	8	2.5	56	65	36	22	25	53
Haiti	28	32.8	8.3	296.4	13.9	33	15	4.7	83	49	35	68	9	23
Honduras	112	16.3	6.6	58.9	31.0	33	6	4.4	33	66	46	41	20	39
Hungary	93	54.2	9.9	106.5	-2.3	10	14	1.3	9	71	64	15	38	47
Iceland	103	0.07	0.3	2.9	8.5	15	7	2.0	5	79	93	ooo	ooo	ooo
India	3288	51.6	1025.1	311.8	19.2	26	9	3.2	70	61	28	64	16	20
Indonesia	1905	16.3	214.8	112.8	19.2	23	6	2.7	38	67	39	55	14	31
Iran	1633	11.8	71.4	43.7	17.8	18	6	2.6	37	70	64	39	23	38
Iraq	438	12.2	23.6	53.9	25.0	37	10	5.3	104	59	68	16	18	66
Ireland	70	15.4	3.8	54.3	8.2	14	9	1.9	6	77	58	14	29	57
Israel	21	20.9	6.2	295.2	29.5	22	6	3.0	6	78	91	4	29	67
Italy	301	37.9	57.5	191.0	1.6	9	10	1.3	6	79	90	9	31	60
Jamaica	11	24.9	2.6	236.4	7.7	20	5	2.4	10	71	50	25	23	52
Japan	378	12.9	127.3	336.8	2.4	9	8	1.3	4	81	78	7	34	59
Jordan	89	4.3	5.1	57.3	53.2	27	5	3.6	29	70	79	15	23	62
Kazakhstan	2717	11.1	16.1	5.9	0.2	15	10	1.8	35	66	56	22	32	46
Kenya	580	7.8	31.3	54.0	27.7	34	14	4.4	76	48	20	80	7	13
Kiribati	0.7	50.7	0.08	114.3	28.9	32	8	4.5	53	62	37	ooo	ooo	ooo
Kuwait	18	0.4	2.0	111.1	-7.9	20	2	4.2	11	73	100	1	25	74
Kyrgyzstan	199	7.2	5.0	25.1	6.7	20	7	2.4	55	69	35	32	27	41
Laos	237	4.0	5.4	22.8	30.6	39	14	5.4	93	52	17	78	6	16
Latvia	65	29.1	2.4	36.9	-10.0	8	14	1.2	17	71	69	16	40	44
Lebanon	10	29.6	3.6	360.0	13.7	23	7	2.5	28	71	88	7	31	62
Lesotho	30	10.7	2.1	70.0	23.7	33	13	4.3	93	53	16	40	28	32
Liberia	111	2.9	3.1	27.9	44.5	49	17	6.6	157	50	45	ooo	ooo	ooo
Libya	1760	1.2	5.4	3.1	23.6	28	4	3.9	19	75	86	11	23	66
Liechtenstein	0.2	25.0	0.03	150.0	11.8	12	7	1.4	10	ooo	23	ooo	ooo	ooo
Lithuania	65	46.0	3.7	56.9	-2.2	9	11	1.3	18	73	68	18	41	41
Luxembourg	3	ooo	0.4	133.3	14.5	13	9	1.7	5	78	88	ooo	ooo	ooo
Macedonia, FYRO	26	24.7	2.0	76.9	7.8	14	8	1.9	22	73	60	21	40	39
Madagascar	587	5.3	16.4	27.9	34.6	43	13	5.8	95	54	22	78	7	15
Malawi	118	16.9	11.6	98.3	12.7	46	23	6.4	132	39	20	87	5	8
Malaysia	330	23.1	22.6	68.5	24.5	25	4	3.2	8	73	57	27	23	50
Maldives	0.3	10.0	0.3	1000.0	39.3	41	9	5.8	60	61	25	32	31	37
Mali	1240	3.8	11.7	9.4	29.9	50	20	7.0	143	46	26	86	2	12
Malta	0.3	28.1	0.4	1333.3	9.1	11	8	1.7	6	77	91	ooo	ooo	ooo
Marshall Islands	0.2	16.7	0.06	300.0	47.3	26	4	6.6	63	65	65	ooo	ooo	ooo
Mauritania	1026	0.5	2.8	2.7	34.4	43	15	6.0	120	51	54	55	10	35

Wealth | Energy and trade | Quality of life

GNP	Purchasing power	Growth of PP	Energy consumption	Imports	Exports	Aid received (given)	Human Development Index	Health care	Food consumption	Safe water	Illiteracy male	Illiteracy female	Higher education	Cars	
1999	1999	1990–1999	1997	1999	1999	1999	1999	1990–1999	1997	1999	1998	1998	1996	2000	
billion US$	US$	%	kg oil equivalent per capita	US$ per capita	US$ per capita	million US$		doctors per 100 000 people	daily calories per capita	% access	%	%	students per 100 000 people	people per car	
5.0	8355	-0.3	3811	2816	3034	83	0.812	297	2849	ooo	ooo	ooo	2965	3	Estonia
6.6	628	2.4	287	14	29	633	0.321	ooo	1858	24	58	70	74	1433	Ethiopia
1.8	4799	1.2	ooo	ooo	ooo	34	0.757	48	2865	47	ooo	ooo	757	17	Fiji
22.9	23 096	ooo	6435	9328	7279	(416)	0.925	299	3100	100	ooo	ooo	4418	3	Finland
27.2	22 897	1.1	4224	6420	5773	(5637)	0.924	303	3518	100	ooo	ooo	3541	2	France
ooo	ooo	ooo	ooo	ooo	ooo	ooo	ooo	ooo	ooo	ooo	ooo	ooo	ooo	7	French Guiana
4.0	6024	0.6	1419	2135	1489	48	0.617	ooo	2556	70	ooo	ooo	649	7	Gabon
0.4	1580	-0.6	ooo	189	240	33	0.398	4	2350	62	ooo	ooo	148	186	Gambia, The
3.4	2431	ooo	423	142	242	239	0.742	436	2614	76	ooo	ooo	3149	12	Georgia
79.2	23 742	1.0	4231	7635	7382	(5515)	0.921	350	3382	ooo	ooo	ooo	2603	2	Germany
7.4	1881	1.6	383	131	195	608	0.542	6	2611	64	22	40	ooo	214	Ghana
24.0	15 414	1.8	2435	1402	2415	194	0.881	392	3649	ooo	2	5	3138	4	Greece
ooo	ooo	ooo	ooo	ooo	ooo	ooo	ooo	ooo	ooo	ooo	ooo	ooo	ooo	ooo	Greenland
0.3	6817	ooo	ooo	ooo	ooo	10	ooo	ooo	2768	94	ooo	ooo	ooo	ooo	Grenada
18.4	3674	1.5	536	297	429	293	0.626	93	2339	92	25	40	804	84	Guatemala
3.7	1934	1.5	ooo	95	112	238	0.397	13	2231	48	ooo	ooo	112	488	Guinea
0.2	678	-1.9	ooo	47	67	52	0.339	17	2430	49	ooo	ooo	ooo	267	Guinea-Bissau
0.7	3640	5.2	ooo	ooo	ooo	27	0.704	18	2530	94	ooo	ooo	956	32	Guyana
3.6	1464	-3.4	237	70	152	263	0.467	8	1869	46	50	54	ooo	252	Haiti
4.8	2340	0.3	532	346	463	817	0.634	83	2403	90	27	27	985	165	Honduras
46.8	11 430	1.4	2492	2777	2859	248	0.829	357	3313	99	1	1	1903	4	Hungary
8.1	27 835	1.8	8566	ooo	ooo	0	0.932	326	3117	ooo	ooo	ooo	2918	2	Iceland
42.2	2248	4.1	479	53	66	1484	0.571	48	2496	88	33	57	638	218	India
19.5	2857	3.0	693	260	196	2206	0.677	16	2886	76	9	20	1157	86	Indonesia
10.5	5531	1.9	1777	283	218	161	0.714	85	2836	95	18	33	1763	44	Iran
ooo	ooo	ooo	1240	ooo	ooo	76	ooo	ooo	2619	85	ooo	ooo	ooo	35	Iraq
71.4	25 918	6.1	3412	21 493	18 128	(245)	0.916	219	3565	ooo	ooo	ooo	3702	3	Ireland
ooo	18 440	2.3	3014	5789	6538	906	0.893	385	3278	99	2	6	3571	5	Israel
36.0	22 172	1.2	2839	5083	4680	(1806)	0.909	554	3507	ooo	1	2	3299	2	Italy
6.0	3561	-0.6	1552	1291	1511	-23	0.738	140	2553	71	18	10	768	23	Jamaica
78.9	24 898	1.1	4084	3650	3107	(15 323)	0.928	193	2932	96	ooo	ooo	3131	3	Japan
7.0	3955	1.1	1081	690	976	430	0.714	166	3014	96	6	17	ooo	28	Jordan
18.9	4951	-4.9	2439	430	419	161	0.742	353	3085	91	ooo	ooo	2859	ooo	Kazakhstan
10.6	1022	-0.3	494	85	101	308	0.514	13	1976	49	12	27	ooo	174	Kenya
0.08	ooo	ooo	ooo	ooo	ooo	21	ooo	ooo	ooo	47	ooo	ooo	ooo	ooo	Kiribati
ooo	ooo	-1.5	8936	6982	6040	7	0.818	189	3096	100	17	22	1750	3	Kuwait
1.4	2573	-6.4	603	106	141	267	0.707	301	2447	77	ooo	ooo	1088	36	Kyrgyzstan
1.4	1471	3.8	ooo	87	107	294	0.476	24	2108	90	38	70	260	540	Laos
6.0	6264	-3.7	1806	1214	1502	96	0.791	282	2864	ooo	0	0	2248	5	Latvia
15.8	4705	5.7	1265	505	2421	194	0.758	210	3277	100	9	21	2712	5	Lebanon
1.2	1854	2.1	ooo	103	395	31	0.541	5	2243	91	29	7	234	350	Lesotho
ooo	ooo	ooo	ooo	ooo	ooo	94	ooo	ooo	ooo	ooo	ooo	ooo	ooo	310	Liberia
ooo	ooo	ooo	2909	1358	980	7	0.770	128	3289	72	ooo	ooo	ooo	11	Libya
ooo	ooo	ooo	ooo	ooo	ooo	ooo	ooo	ooo	ooo	ooo	ooo	ooo	ooo	2	Liechtenstein
9.7	6656	-3.9	2376	1145	1442	129	0.803	395	3261	ooo	0	1	2251	4	Lithuania
19.3	42 769	3.8	8052	ooo	ooo	(119)	0.924	272	ooo	ooo	ooo	ooo	640	2	Luxembourg
3.4	4651	-1.5	ooo	721	963	273	0.766	204	2664	99	ooo	ooo	1557	7	Macedonia, FYRO*
3.7	799	-1.2	ooo	57	76	358	0.462	11	2021	47	28	42	188	288	Madagascar
2.0	586	0.9	ooo	51	86	446	0.397	ooo	2043	57	27	56	58	644	Malawi
77.3	8209	4.7	2237	4247	3369	143	0.774	66	2977	95	9	18	1048	6	Malaysia
0.3	4423	3.9	ooo	ooo	ooo	31	0.739	40	2485	100	ooo	ooo	ooo	ooo	Maldives
2.6	753	1.1	ooo	55	80	354	0.378	5	2029	65	54	69	134	557	Mali
3.5	15 189	4.2	2515	ooo	ooo	25	0.866	261	3398	100	ooo	ooo	2183	2	Malta
0.1	ooo	ooo	ooo	ooo	ooo	63	ooo	ooo	ooo	ooo	ooo	ooo	ooo	ooo	Marshall Islands
1.0	1609	1.3	ooo	130	148	219	0.437	14	2622	37	48	69	365	280	Mauritania

The datasets below are explained on pages 140

		Land		Population										Employment		
		Area	Arable and permanent crops	Total	Density	Change	Births	Deaths	Fertility	Infant mortality	Life expectancy	Urban		Agriculture	Industry	Servic
				2001	2001	1990–2000	2000	2000	2000	1999	2000	2000		1990	1990	1990
		thousand km²	% of total	millions	persons per km²	%	births per 1000	deaths per 1000	children per mother	per 1000 live births	years	%		%	%	%
Mauritius		2	52.0	1.2	600.0	9.9	17	7	2.0	19	71	43		17	43	40
Mexico		1958	13.9	100.4	51.3	18.8	24	5	2.8	27	75	74		28	24	48
Micronesia, Fed. States		0.7	51.4	0.1	142.9	22.6	31	6	4.6	20	66	27		ooo	ooo	ooo
Moldova		34	64.4	4.3	126.5	0.8	11	11	1.4	27	68	46		33	30	37
Monaco		0.002	ooo	0.03	15 000	5.7	20	17	ooo	5	ooo	100		ooo	ooo	ooo
Mongolia		1567	0.8	2.6	1.7	18.0	20	7	2.2	63	63	57		32	22	46
Morocco		447	21.2	30.4	68.0	22.0	26	6	3.4	45	69	55		45	25	30
Mozambique		802	4.2	18.6	23.2	33.8	43	22	5.6	127	72	28		83	8	9
Myanmar		677	15.0	48.4	71.5	8.4	28	12	3.3	79	56	27		73	10	17
Namibia		824	1.0	1.8	2.2	25.7	36	17	5.0	56	46	27		49	15	36
Nauru		0.02	ooo	0.01	500.0	24.8	19	5	3.7	25	61	100		ooo	ooo	ooo
Nepal		147	20.2	23.6	160.5	27.8	35	11	4.8	75	57	11		94	0	6
Netherlands		41	22.9	15.9	387.8	6.3	13	9	1.7	5	78	62		5	26	69
New Zealand		271	12.1	3.8	14.0	13.7	15	7	2.0	6	77	77		10	25	65
Nicaragua		130	21.1	5.2	40.0	32.1	35	6	4.3	38	68	57		28	26	46
Niger		1267	4.0	11.2	8.8	32.1	53	24	7.5	162	41	17		90	4	6
Nigeria		924	33.3	116.9	126.5	33.4	41	14	5.8	112	52	36		43	7	50
Northern Marianas		0.5	17.4	0.04	80.0	6.3	ooo	ooo	ooo	ooo	ooo	ooo		ooo	ooo	ooo
North Korea		121	16.6	22.4	185.1	8.3	21	7	2.3	23	70	59		38	32	30
Norway		324	2.7	4.5	13.9	5.6	13	10	1.8	4	78	74		6	25	69
Oman		213	0.4	2.6	12.2	42.9	39	4	6.1	14	71	72		44	24	32
Pakistan		796	27.5	145.0	182.2	24.2	39	11	5.6	84	60	33		52	19	29
Palau		0.5	21.7	0.02	40.0	23.4	18	8	2.5	28	67	71		ooo	ooo	ooo
Panama		76	8.7	2.9	38.2	17.6	25	5	2.6	21	74	56		26	16	58
Papua New Guinea		463	1.5	4.9	10.6	28.8	34	11	4.8	79	56	15		79	7	14
Paraguay		407	5.6	5.6	13.8	31.9	32	5	4.3	27	73	52		39	22	39
Peru		1285	3.3	26.1	20.3	22.9	24	6	2.9	42	69	72		36	18	46
Philippines		300	33.5	77.1	257.0	24.8	29	6	3.5	31	67	47		46	15	39
Poland		323	44.6	38.6	119.5	1.4	10	10	1.4	9	73	62		27	36	37
Portugal		92	29.4	10.0	108.7	1.3	12	11	1.5	5	76	48		18	34	48
Qatar		11	1.9	0.6	54.6	54.6	31	4	3.9	12	72	91		3	32	65
Romania		238	41.3	22.4	94.1	-2.0	10	12	1.3	21	71	55		24	47	29
Russian Federation		17 075	7.4	144.7	8.5	-1.4	9	15	1.2	18	66	73		14	42	44
Rwanda		26	42.4	8.0	307.7	3.8	39	21	5.8	110	39	5		92	3	5
St. Kitts and Nevis		0.4	22.2	0.04	100.0	-6.3	20	11	2.5	24	69	43		ooo	ooo	ooo
St. Lucia		0.6	27.4	0.2	333.3	12.0	19	6	2.1	17	71	30		ooo	ooo	ooo
St. Vincent & the Grenadines		0.4	28.2	0.1	250.0	8.4	19	7	2.2	21	72	44		ooo	ooo	ooo
Samoa		3.0	43.0	0.2	66.7	5.3	30	6	4.5	21	68	33		ooo	ooo	ooo
San Marino		0.06	16.7	0.03	500.0	14.8	12	8	1.3	6	80	89		ooo	ooo	ooo
Sao Tome and Principe		1.0	42.7	0.1	100.0	33.9	43	8	6.2	59	65	44		ooo	ooo	ooo
Saudi Arabia		2150	1.8	21.0	9.8	39.0	35	6	5.7	20	67	83		19	20	61
Senegal		197	11.5	9.7	49.2	25.7	41	13	5.7	68	52	43		77	8	15
Seychelles		0.5	15.6	0.08	160.0	8.0	18	7	2.0	13	70	63		ooo	ooo	ooo
Sierra Leone		72	7.5	4.6	63.9	23.8	47	20	6.3	182	45	37		68	15	17
Singapore		1	1.6	4.1	4100.0	37.6	14	5	1.6	4	78	100		0	36	64
Slovakia		49	32.5	5.4	110.2	2.8	10	10	1.3	9	73	57		12	32	56
Slovenia		20	10.0	2.0	100.0	1.7	9	10	1.2	5	76	50		6	46	48
Solomon Islands		29	2.1	0.5	17.2	39.4	41	7	5.7	22	67	13		77	7	16
Somalia		638	1.7	9.2	14.4	8.7	48	19	7.3	125	46	28		ooo	ooo	ooo
South Africa		1221	12.9	43.8	35.9	13.7	25	14	2.9	54	53	54		14	32	54
South Korea		99	19.1	47.1	475.8	10.7	14	5	1.5	5	74	79		18	35	47
Spain		506	36.6	39.9	78.9	1.6	10	9	1.2	6	78	64		12	33	55
Sri Lanka		66	29.0	19.1	289.4	11.9	18	6	2.1	17	72	22		48	21	31
Sudan		2506	6.7	31.8	12.7	31.7	34	11	4.9	67	56	27		70	8	22
Suriname		163	0.4	0.4	2.5	9.2	26	7	3.0	27	71	69		21	18	61

Wealth | Energy and trade | Quality of life

NP	Purchasing power	Growth of PP	Energy consumption	Imports	Exports	Aid received (given)	Human Development Index	Health care	Food consumption	Safe water	Illiteracy male	Illiteracy female	Higher education	Cars	
99	1999	1990–1999	1997	1999	1999	1999	1999	1990–1999	1997	1999	1998	1998	1996	2000	
ion US$	US$	%	kg oil equivalent per capita	US$ per capita	US$ per capita	million US$		doctors per 100 000 people	daily calories per capita	% access	%	%	students per 100 000 people	people per car	
4.2	9107	3.9	ooo	2217	2331	42	0.765	85	2917	100	ooo	ooo	632	26	Mauritius
8.8	8297	1.0	1501	1475	1557	35	0.790	186	3097	86	7	11	1739	11	Mexico
0.2	ooo	ooo	ooo	ooo	ooo	108	ooo	ooo	ooo	ooo	ooo	ooo	ooo	ooo	Micronesia, Fed. States
1.6	2037	-10.8	1029	135	175	102	0.699	350	2567	100	1	2	2143	25	Moldova
ooo	ooo	ooo	ooo	ooo	ooo					100	ooo	ooo	ooo	2	Monaco
0.9	1711	-0.6	ooo	204	252	219	0.569	243	1917	60	28	49	1767	104	Mongolia
3.8	3419	0.4	340	350	393	678	0.596	46	3078	82	40	66	1167	29	Morocco
3.9	861	3.8	461	350	88	118	0.323	ooo	1832	60	42	73	40	233	Mozambique
ooo	ooo	ooo	296	24	37	73	0.551	30	2862	68	11	21	590	1274	Myanmar
3.2	5468	0.8	ooo	889	1072	178	0.601	30	2183	77	18	20	735	31	Namibia
ooo	ooo	ooo	ooo	ooo	ooo	7							ooo	ooo	Nauru
5.1	1237	2.3	321	49	63	344	0.480	4	2366	81	43	78	485	ooo	Nepal
4.3	24 215	2.1	4800	15 644	14 256	(3134)	0.931	251	3284	100	ooo	ooo	3018	3	Netherlands
2.7	19 104	1.8	4435	4454	4631	(134)	0.913	218	3395	ooo	ooo	ooo	3318	2	New Zealand
2.1	2279	0.4	551	161	387	675	0.635	86	2186	79	34	31	1209	98	Nicaragua
2.0	753	-1.0	ooo	26	38	187	0.274	4	2097	59	78	93	ooo	590	Niger
7.9	853	-0.5	753	119	103	152	0.455	19	2735	57	30	48	ooo	151	Nigeria
ooo	ooo	ooo	ooo	ooo	ooo	0	ooo	ooo	ooo	ooo	ooo	ooo	ooo	ooo	Northern Marianas
ooo	ooo	ooo	ooo	ooo	ooo	201	ooo	ooo	ooo	100	ooo	ooo	ooo	ooo	North Korea
6.4	28 433	3.2	5501	12 171	12 098	(1370)	0.939	413	3357	100	ooo	ooo	4239	3	Norway
ooo	ooo	0.3	3003	2783	2062	40	0.747	133	ooo	39	ooo	ooo	695	13	Oman
4.0	1834	1.3	442	61	81	732	0.498	57	2476	88	42	71	ooo	161	Pakistan
ooo	ooo	ooo	ooo	ooo	ooo	29	ooo	ooo	ooo	79	ooo	ooo	ooo	ooo	Palau
8.6	5875	2.4	856	2375	2655	14	0.784	167	2430	87	8	9	3025	15	Panama
3.7	2367	2.3	ooo	444	367	216	0.534	7	2224	42	29	45	ooo	136	Papua New Guinea
8.5	4384	-0.2	824	582	633	78	0.738	110	2566	79	6	9	948	66	Paraguay
60.3	4622	3.2	621	293	339	452	0.743	93	2302	77	6	16	3268	48	Peru
78.0	3805	0.9	520	506	477	690	0.749	123	2366	87	5	5	2958	110	Philippines
53.1	8450	4.4	2721	998	1353	984	0.828	236	3366	ooo	0	0	1865	5	Poland
05.9	16 064	2.3	2051	3405	4661	(276)	0.874	312	3667	82	6	11	3242	3	Portugal
ooo	ooo	ooo	18 335	ooo	ooo	5	0.801	126	ooo	ooo	ooo	ooo	1518	4	Qatar
34.2	6041	-0.5	1957	441	508	373	0.772	184	3253	58	1	3	1819	10	Romania
32.5	7473	-5.9	4019	587	363	1816	0.775	421	2904	99	0	1	3006	9	Russian Federation
2.1	885	-3.0	ooo	12	37	373	0.395	ooo	2056	41	29	43	ooo	889	Rwanda
0.3	11 596	ooo	ooo	ooo	ooo	5	ooo	ooo	2771	98	ooo	ooo	ooo	8	St. Kitts and Nevis
0.6	5509	ooo	ooo	ooo	ooo	26	ooo	ooo	2734	98	ooo	ooo	ooo	21	St. Lucia
0.3	5309	ooo	ooo	ooo	ooo	16	ooo	ooo	2472	93	ooo	ooo	ooo	16	St. Vincent & the Grenadines
0.2	4047	1.4	ooo	ooo	ooo	23	0.701	34	ooo	99	ooo	ooo	ooo	56	Samoa
ooo	ooo	ooo	ooo	ooo	ooo	ooo	ooo	ooo	ooo	ooo	ooo	ooo	ooo	1	San Marino
0.04	1977	ooo	ooo	ooo	ooo	28	ooo	ooo	2138	ooo	ooo	ooo	ooo	3	Sao Tome and Principe
ooo	10 815	-1.1	4906	2673	2123	29	0.754	166	2783	95	17	36	1455	11	Saudi Arabia
4.7	1419	0.6	315	136	168	534	0.423	8	2418	78	55	74	297	104	Senegal
0.5	9974	ooo	ooo	ooo	ooo	13	ooo	ooo	2487	ooo	ooo	ooo	ooo	12	Seychelles
0.7	448	-7.0	ooo	16	33	74	0.258	7	2035	28	ooo	ooo	ooo	131	Sierra Leone
95.4	20 767	4.7	8661	33 984	30 053	-1	0.876	163	ooo	100	4	12	2730	10	Singapore
19.4	10 591	1.6	3198	2241	2436	318	0.831	353	2984	100	ooo	ooo	1897	4	Slovakia
19.6	15 977	2.5	3213	5261	5702	31	0.874	228	3101	100	0	0	2657	3	Slovenia
0.3	1975	ooo	ooo	ooo	ooo	40	ooo	ooo	2122	71	ooo	ooo	ooo	ooo	Solomon Islands
ooo	ooo	ooo	ooo	ooo	ooo	ooo	ooo	ooo	ooo	ooo	ooo	ooo	ooo	876	Somalia
33.2	8908	-0.2	2636	761	685	539	0.702	56	2990	86	15	16	1841	11	South Africa
97.9	15 712	4.7	3834	3645	3057	-55	0.875	136	3155	92	1	14	6106	6	South Korea
51.6	18 079	2.0	2729	4119	4277	1363	0.908	424	3310	ooo	2	4	4254	2	Spain
15.7	3279	4.0	386	291	352	251	0.735	37	2302	83	6	12	474	87	Sri Lanka
9.4	ooo	ooo	414	26	49	243	0.439	9	2395	75	ooo	ooo	ooo	398	Sudan
ooo	4178	3.3	ooo	ooo	ooo	36	0.758	25	2665	95	ooo	ooo	ooo	8	Suriname

	○○○	no data
	per capita	for each person

	Land		**Population**									**Employment**		
	Area	Arable and permanent crops	Total	Density	Change	Births	Deaths	Fertility	Infant mortality	Life expectancy	Urban	Agriculture	Industry	Service
			2001	2001	1990–2000	2000	2000	2000	1999	2000	2000	1990	1990	1990
	thousand km²	% of total	millions	persons per km²	%	births per 1000	deaths per 1000	children per mother	per 1000 live births	years	%	%	%	%
Swaziland	17	10.4	0.9	52.9	27.1	41	20	5.9	62	40	25	40	22	38
Sweden	450	6.1	8.8	19.6	3.7	10	11	1.5	3	80	84	○○○	○○○	○○○
Switzerland	41	10.6	7.2	175.6	6.2	11	9	1.5	3	80	68	6	35	59
Syria	185	29.7	16.6	89.7	31.1	31	6	4.1	25	70	50	33	24	43
Taiwan	36	○○○	22.5	625.0	9.4	14	6	1.7	○○○	75	77	○○○	○○○	○○○
Tajikistan	143	6.0	6.1	42.7	20.8	19	4	2.4	54	68	27	41	23	36
Tanzania	945	4.9	36.0	38.1	34.6	41	13	5.6	90	53	22	84	5	11
Thailand	513	35.1	63.6	124.0	11.2	14	6	1.8	26	72	30	64	14	22
Togo	57	40.5	4.7	82.5	36.0	40	11	5.8	80	55	31	66	10	24
Tonga	0.8	64.0	0.1	125.0	11.1	27	6	4.2	18	71	32	○○○	○○○	○○○
Trinidad and Tobago	5	23.8	1.3	260.0	-1.9	14	8	1.7	17	71	72	11	31	58
Tunisia	164	31.2	9.6	58.5	16.9	19	6	2.3	24	72	62	28	33	39
Turkey	775	34.4	67.6	87.2	17.1	22	7	2.5	40	69	66	53	18	29
Turkmenistan	488	3.5	4.8	9.8	23.2	19	5	2.2	52	67	44	37	23	40
Tuvalu	0.02	○○○	0.01	500.0	18.2	30	9	3.1	40	67	18	○○○	○○○	○○○
Uganda	241	28.3	24.0	100.0	35.7	48	19	6.9	83	42	15	85	5	10
Ukraine	604	55.7	49.1	81.3	-4.9	8	15	1.1	17	68	68	20	40	40
United Arab Emirates	84	1.6	2.7	32.1	21.5	18	4	3.5	8	74	84	8	27	65
United Kingdom	245	24.6	59.5	242.9	3.3	12	11	1.7	6	77	90	2	29	69
United States of America	9364	18.6	285.9	30.5	10.3	15	9	2.1	7	77	75	3	28	69
Uruguay	177	7.4	3.4	19.2	7.4	16	10	2.3	15	74	92	14	27	59
Uzbekistan	447	10.8	25.3	16.6	20.0	22	5	2.7	45	70	38	34	25	41
Vanuatu	12	9.8	0.2	16.7	23.3	36	6	4.6	37	65	21	○○○	○○○	○○○
Venezuela	912	3.8	24.6	27.0	21.8	25	5	2.9	20	73	87	12	27	61
Vietnam	332	22.2	79.2	238.6	18.8	20	6	2.3	31	66	24	71	14	15
Western Sahara	252	0.008	0.3	1.2	28.1	46	17	6.8	○○○	○○○	95	○○○	○○○	○○○
Yemen	528	3.2	19.1	36.2	45.4	44	11	7.2	86	59	26	61	17	22
Yugoslavia	102	36.5	10.5	102.9	9.2	12	11	1.6	20	72	52	○○○	○○○	○○○
Zambia	753	7.0	10.7	14.2	22.1	45	22	6.1	112	37	38	75	8	17
Zimbabwe	391	8.6	12.9	33.0	12.3	29	20	4.0	60	40	32	68	8	24

Explanation of datasets

Land

Area does not include areas of lakes and seas

Arable and permanent crops percentage of total land area used for arable and permanent crops

Population

Total estimate for mid 2001

Density the total population of a country divided by its land area

Change percentage change in population between 1990 and 2000. Negative numbers indicate a decrease

Births number of births per one thousand people in one year

Deaths number of deaths per one thousand people in one year

Fertility average number of children born to child bearing women

Infant mortality number of deaths of children under one year per 1000 live births

Life expectancy number of years a baby born now can expect to live

Urban percentage of the population living in towns and cities

Employment

Agriculture percentage of the labour force employe in agriculture

Industry percentage of the labour force employe in industry

Services percentage of the labour force employe in services

Macedonia, FYRO*   Former Yugoslav Republic of Macedonia

Wealth | Energy and trade | Quality of life

GNP	Purchasing power	Growth of PP	Energy consumption	Imports	Exports	Aid received (given)	Human Development Index	Health care	Food consumption	Safe water	Illiteracy male	Illiteracy female	Higher education	Cars	
1999	1999	1990–1999	1997	1999	1999	1999	1999	1990–1999	1997	1999	1998	1998	1996	2000	
million US$	US$	%	kg oil equivalent per capita	US$ per capita	US$ per capita	million US$		doctors per 100 000 people	daily calories per capita	% access	%	%	students per 100 000 people	people per car	
1.4	3987	-0.2	ooo	ooo	ooo	29	0.583	15	2483	ooo	ooo	ooo	630	38	Swaziland
21.8	22 636	1.2	5869	12 213	10 735	(1630)	0.936	311	3194	100	ooo	ooo	3116	2	Sweden
73.1	27 171	-0.1	3699	16 526	14 843	(969)	0.924	323	3223	100	ooo	ooo	2072	2	Switzerland
15.2	4454	2.7	983	329	313	228	0.700	144	3351	80	13	42	1559	107	Syria
ooo	ooo	ooo		6034	5795	0	ooo	ooo	ooo	ooo	ooo	ooo	ooo	5	Taiwan
1.8	ooo	ooo	562	122	113	122	0.660	201	2001	69	1	1	1895	ooo	Tajikistan
8.0	501	-0.1	455	33	62	990	0.436	4	1995	54	17	36	57	735	Tanzania
21.0	6132	3.8	1319	1123	886	1003	0.757	24	2360	80	3	7	2252	37	Thailand
1.5	1410	-0.5	ooo	101	146	71	0.489	8	2469	54	28	62	315	174	Togo
0.2	ooo	ooo	ooo	ooo	ooo	21	ooo	ooo	ooo	100	ooo	ooo	ooo	19	Tonga
5.7	8176	2.0	6414	2611	2312	26	0.798	79	2661	86	ooo	ooo	787	6	Trinidad and Tobago
19.9	5957	2.9	738	916	963	245	0.714	70	3283	99	21	42	1341	24	Tunisia
86.3	6380	2.2	1142	676	721	-10	0.735	121	3525	83	7	25	2301	17	Turkey
3.2	3347	-9.6	2615	287	426	21	0.730	300	2306	58	ooo	ooo	2072	ooo	Turkmenistan
ooo	ooo	ooo	ooo	ooo	ooo	7	ooo	ooo	ooo	100	ooo	ooo	ooo	ooo	Tuvalu
6.8	1167	4.0	ooo	30	76	590	0.435	ooo	2085	50	24	46	179	923	Uganda
37.5	3458	-10.3	2960	347	310	480	0.742	229	2795	55	0	1	2996	10	Ukraine
ooo	18 162	-1.6	11 967	ooo	ooo	4	0.809	181	3390	ooo	ooo	ooo	801	7	United Arab Emirates
138.1	22 093	2.1	3863	6282	6687	(3401)	0.923	164	3276	100	ooo	ooo	3237	2	United Kingdom
8351	31 872	2.0	8076	3345	4272	(9145)	0.934	279	3699	100	ooo	ooo	5341	2	United States of America
19.5	8879	3.0	883	1055	1197	22	0.828	370	2816	98	3	2	2458	11	Uruguay
17.6	2251	-3.1	1798	125	121	134	0.698	309	2433	85	7	17	ooo	ooo	Uzbekistan
0.2	3108	ooo	ooo	ooo	ooo	37	ooo	ooo	2700	88	ooo	ooo	ooo	50	Vanuatu
87.0	5495	-0.5	2526	899	690	44	0.765	236	2321	84	7	9	ooo	13	Venezuela
28.2	1860	6.2	521	180	181	1421	0.682	48	2484	56	5	9	678	562	Vietnam
ooo	ooo	ooo	ooo	ooo	ooo	ooo	ooo	ooo	ooo	ooo	ooo	ooo	ooo	ooo	Western Sahara
5.9	8.6	-0.4	208	137	158	457	0.468	23	2051	69	34	77	419	101	Yemen
ooo	ooo	ooo	ooo	ooo	ooo	638	ooo	ooo	ooo	ooo	16	31	1625	5	Yugoslavia
3.2	756	-2.4	634	85	97	623	0.427	7	1970	64	8	17	238	107	Zambia
6.1	2876	0.6	866	196	180	244	0.554	14	2145	85	ooo	ooo	661	61	Zimbabwe

Explanation of datasets

Wealth

GNP Gross National Product (GNP) is the total value of goods and services produced in a country plus income from abroad.

Purchasing power Gross Domestic Product (GDP) is the total value of goods and services produced in a country. Purchasing power parity (PPP) is GDP per person, adjusted for the local cost of living

Growth of PP average annual growth (or decline, shown as a negative value in the table) in purchasing power. This figure shows whether people are becoming better or worse off

Energy and trade

Energy consumption consumption of energy per person shown as the equivalent in kilograms of oil

Imports total value of imports per person shown in US dollars

Exports total value of exports per person shown in US dollars

Aid received (given) amount of economic aid a country has received. Negative values indicate that the repayment of loans exceeds the amount of aid received. Figures in brackets show aid given

Quality of life

HDI Human Development Index (HDI) measures the relative social and economic progress of a country. It combines life expectancy, adult literacy, average number of years of schooling, and purchasing power. Economically more developed countries have an HDI approaching 1.0. Economically less developed countries have an HDI approaching 0.

Health care number of doctors in each country per 100 000 people

Food consumption average number of calories consumed by each person each day

Safe water percentage of the population with access to safe drinking water

Illiteracy percentage of men and women who are unable to read and write

Higher education number of students in higher education per 100 000 people

Cars the number of people for every car

How to use the index

To find a place on an atlas map use either the grid code or latitude and longitude.

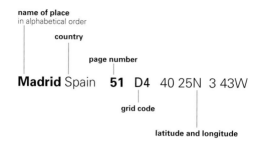

name of place
in alphabetical order

country

page number

Madrid Spain **51** D4 40 25N 3 43W

grid code

latitude and longitude

Grid code

Madrid Spain **51** D4 40 25N 3 43W

Madrid is in grid square D4

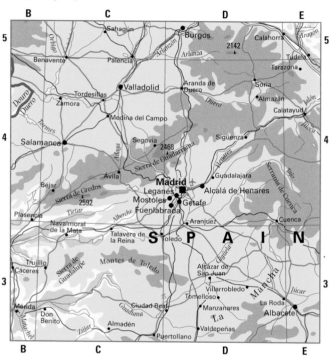

Latitude and longitude

Madrid Spain **51** D4 40 25N 3 43W

Madrid is at latitude 40 degrees, 25 minutes north and 3 degrees, 43 minutes west

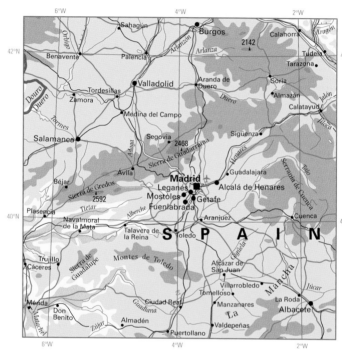

Geographical abbreviations

admin	administrative area
Arch.	Archipelago
b.	bay or harbour
c.	cape, point, or headland
can.	canal
co.	county
d.	desert
fj.	fjord
G.	Gunung; Gebel
g.	gulf
geog. reg.	geographical region
i.	island
is.	islands
Kep.	Kepulauan
l.	lake, lakes, lagoon
mt.	mountain, peak, or spot height
mts.	mountains
NP	National Park
P.	Pulau
p; pen	peninsula
Peg	Pegunungan
plat.	plateau
prov.	province
Pt.	Point
Pta.	Punta
Pte.	Pointe
Pto.	Porto; Puerto
r.	river
Ra.	Range
res.	reservoir
salt l.	salt lake
sd.	sound, strait, or channel
St.	Saint

Ste.	Sainte
Str.	Strait
sum.	summit
tn.	town or other populated place
v.	valley
vol.	volcano

Political abbreviations

Aust.	Australia
Bahamas	The Bahamas
CAR	Central African Republic
Col.	Columbia
CDR	Congo Democratic Republic
Czech Rep.	Czech Republic
Dom. Rep.	Dominican Republic
Eq. Guinea	Equatorial Guinea
Fr.	France
Med. Sea	Mediterranean Sea
Neths	Netherlands
NI	Northern Ireland
NZ	New Zealand
Philippines	The Philippines
PNG	Papua New Guinea
Port.	Portugal
RoI	Republic of Ireland
RSA	Republic of South Africa
Sp.	Spain
Switz.	Switzerland
UAE	United Arab Emirates
UK	United Kingom
USA	United States of America
W. Indies	West Indies
Yemen	Yemen Republic

A

Place	Page	Grid	Lat	Long
Aachen Germany	52	C5	50 46N	6 06E
Aalten Belgium	48	B4	51 56N	6 35E
Abādān Iran	65	C5	30 20N	48 15E
Abbeville France	50	E6	50 06N	1 51E
Abbey RoI	21	C3	53 06N	8 24W
Abbeyfeale RoI	21	B2	52 24N	9 18W
Abbeyleix RoI	21	D2	52 55N	7 20W
Abbeytown England	12	C3	54 51N	3 17W
Abbotsbury England	19	E2	50 40N	2 36W
Aberaeron Wales	14	B2	52 49N	44 43W
Abercarn Wales	14	C1	51 39N	3 08W
Aberchirder Scotland	9	G2	57 33N	2 38W
Aberdare Wales	14	C1	51 43N	3 27W
Aberdaron Wales	14	B2	52 49N	44 43W
Aberdeen Scotland	9	G2	57 10N	2 04W
Aberdeen USA	91	G6	45 28N	98 30W
Aberdeen City u.a. Scotland	9	G2	57 10N	2 00W
Aberdeenshire u.a. Scotland	9	G2	57 10N	2 50W
Aberdyfi Wales	14	B2	52 33N	4 02W
Aberfeldy Scotland	9	F1	56 37N	3 54W
Aberffraw Wales	14	B3	53 12N	4 28W
Aberfoyle Scotland	11	E3	56 11N	4 23W
Abergavenny Wales	14	C1	51 50N	3 00W
Abergele Wales	14	C3	53 17N	3 34W
Aberlady Scotland	11	G3	56 01N	2 51W
Aberporth Wales	14	B2	52 07N	4 34W
Abersoch Wales	14	B2	52 50N	4 31W
Abertillery Wales	14	C1	51 45N	3 09W
Aberystwyth Wales	14	B2	52 25N	4 05W
Abidjan Côte d'Ivoire	80	D3	5 19N	4 01W
Abilene USA	90	G3	32 27N	99 45W
Abingdon England	16	B2	51 41N	1 17W
Abington Scotland	11	F2	55 29N	3 42W
Aboyne Scotland	9	G2	57 05N	2 50W
Abu Dhabi UAE	65	F3	24 28N	54 25E
Abuja Nigeria	80	F3	9 10N	7 11E
Acapulco Mexico	94	E3	16 51N	99 56W
Accra Ghana	80	D3	5 33N	0 15W
Accrington England	12	D2	53 46N	2 21W
Achill Head RoI	20	A3	53 59N	10 13W
Achill Island RoI	20	A3	53 55N	10 05W
Achill Sound tn. RoI	20	B3	53 56N	9 54W
Achnacroish Scotland	8	D1	56 32N	5 30W
Achnasheen Scotland	9	D2	57 35N	5 06W
Ackworth Moor Top England	13	E2	53 39N	1 20W
Aclare RoI	20	C4	54 02N	8 54W
Acle England	17	E3	52 38N	1 33E
Adana Turkey	57	E2	37 00N	35 19E
Adare RoI	21	C2	52 34N	8 48W
Ad Dammām Saudi Arabia	65	F4	26 25N	50 06E
Addis Ababa Ethiopia	81	N3	9 03N	38 42E
Addlestone England	16	C2	51 22N	0 31W
Adelaide Australia	73	G4	34 56S	138 36E
Aden Yemen	64	E1	12 50N	45 03E
Aden, Gulf of Indian Ocean	65	E1	12 30N	47 30E
Adriatic Sea Med. Sea	54	F5	43 00N	15 00E
Adrigole RoI	21	B1	51 44N	9 42W
Adur r. England	16	C1	50 55N	0 20W
Adwick le Street England	13	E2	53 34N	1 11W
Aegean Sea Med. Sea	55	L3	39 00N	24 00E
AFGHANISTAN	66	A6/B6		
Agen France	50	E3	44 12N	0 38E
Aghaville RoI	21	B1	51 39N	9 21W
Agra India	66	D5	27 09N	78 00E
Ağri Daği mt. Turkey	57	F2	39 44N	44 15E
Agropoli Italy	54	F4	40 21N	14 59E
Ahascragh RoI	20	C3	53 24N	8 20W
Ahmadabad India	66	C4	23 03N	72 40E
Ahoghill NI	10	C1	54 51N	6 22W
Ailsa Craig i. Scotland	10	D2	55 16N	5 07W
Airdrie Scotland	11	F2	55 52N	3 59W
Aire r. England	12	E2	53 40N	1 00W
Aire-sur-l'Adour France	50	D2	43 42N	0 15W
Aix-en-Provence France	50	G2	43 31N	5 27E
Aix-les-Bains France	50	G3	45 41N	5 55E
Ajaccio France	50	J1	41 55N	8 43E
Ajmer India	66	C5	26 29N	74 40E
Akron USA	91	K5	41 04N	81 31W
Alabama state USA	91	J3	32 00N	87 00W
Åland is. Finland	49	E3	60 15N	20 00E
Alaska state USA	88	D6/F6	63 10N	157 30W
Alaska, Gulf of USA	88	F5/G5	58 00N	147 00W
Alaska Range USA	88	E6/G6	62 30N	152 30W
Albacete Spain	51	E3	39 00N	1 52W
ALBANIA	55	H4/J4		
Al Başrah Iraq	65	E5	30 30N	47 50E
Albert France	50	F6	50 00N	2 40E
Alberta prov. Canada	88	M4/N4	54 00N	117 30W
Albertville France	50	H3	45 40N	6 24E
Albi France	50	F2	43 56N	2 08E
Ålborg Denmark	49	C2	57 05N	9 50E
Albrighton England	15	D2	52 38N	2 16W
Albuquerque USA	90	E4	35 05N	106 38W
Alcalá de Henares Spain	51	D4	40 28N	3 22W
Alcantarilla Spain	51	E2	37 59N	1 12W
Alcázar de San Juan Spain	51	D3	39 24N	3 12W
Alcester England	15	E2	52 13N	1 52W
Alcira Spain	51	E3	39 10N	0 27W
Aldbourne England	16	B2	51 30N	1 37W
Aldbrough England	13	F2	53 50N	0 06W
Alde r. England	17	E3	52 10N	1 30E
Aldeburgh England	17	E3	52 09N	1 35E
Alderley Edge tn. England	12	D2	53 18N	2 15W
Alderney i. Channel Islands	19	E1	49 43N	2 12W
Aldershot England	16	C2	51 15N	0 47W
Aldridge England	15	E2	52 36N	1 55W
Aldsworth England	15	E1	51 48N	1 46W
Alençon France	50	E5	48 25N	0 05E
Aleppo Syria	64	C6	36 14N	37 10E
Alès France	50	G3	44 08N	4 05E
Alessándria Italy	54	C6	44 55N	8 37E
Ålesund Norway	49	C3	62 28N	6 11E
Aleutian Range USA	88	D5	56 30N	159 00W
Alexandria Egypt	81	L8	31 13N	29 55E
Alexandria Scotland	11	E2	55 59N	4 36W
Alexandroúpoli Greece	55	L4	40 51N	25 53E
Alford England	13	G2	53 17N	0 11E
Alford Scotland	9	G2	57 13N	2 42W
Alfreton England	13	E2	53 06N	1 23W
Algeciras Spain	51	C2	36 08N	5 27W
ALGERIA	80	D7/F7		
Algiers Algeria	80	E9	36 50N	3 00E
Alicante Spain	51	E3	38 21N	0 29W
Alice USA	91	G2	27 45N	98 06W
Alice Springs tn. Australia	72	F6	23 42S	133 52E
Alkmaar Neths	48	C5	52 38N	4 44E
Allahabad India	66	E5	25 27N	81 50E
Allegheny Mountains USA	93	E1/2	40 00N	79 00W
Allen r. England	12	D3	54 50N	2 20W
Allendale Town England	12	D3	54 54N	2 15W
Allentown USA	91	L5	40 37N	75 30W
Alloa Scotland	11	F3	56 07N	3 49W
Alma USA	93	D2	43 23N	84 40W
Almadén Spain	51	C3	38 47N	4 50W
Almansa Spain	51	E3	38 52N	1 06W
Almaty Kazakhstan	62	K5	43 19N	76 55E
Almería Spain	51	D2	36 50N	2 26W
Älmhult Sweden	49	D2	56 32N	14 10E
Aln r. England	11	H2	55 25N	1 45W
Alness Scotland	9	E2	57 41N	4 15W
Alnwick England	11	H2	55 25N	1 42W
Alpes Maritimes mts. France/Italy	50	H2	44 15N	6 45E
Alpi Dolomitiche mts. Italy	54	D7	46 00N	12 00E
Alpi Pennine mts. Italy/Switz.	52	C3	45 55N	7 30E
Alps mts. Europe	52	D3	46 00N	7 30E
Alsager England	12	D2	53 06N	2 19W
Alston England	12	D3	54 49N	2 26W
Altai mts. Mongolia	68	F7	47 00N	92 30E
Altamira Brazil	96	G13	3 13S	52 15W
Altnaharra Scotland	9	E3	58 16N	4 27W
Alton England	16	C2	51 09N	0 59W
Altrincham England	12	D2	53 24N	2 21W
Alyth Scotland	9	F1	56 37N	3 13W
Amarillo USA	90	F4	35 14N	101 50W
Amazonas r. Brazil	96	G13	2 00S	53 00W
Amble England	11	H2	55 20N	1 34W
Ambleside England	12	D3	54 26N	2 58W
Ambon Indonesia	71	H3	3 41S	128 10E
Amersfoort Neths	48	D5	52 09N	5 23E
Amersham England	16	C2	51 40N	0 38W
Amesbury England	16	B2	51 10N	1 47W
Amfípoli Greece	55	K4	40 48N	23 52E
Amiens France	50	F5	49 54N	2 18E
Amlwch Wales	14	B3	53 25N	4 20W
Amman Jordan	64	C5	31 04N	46 17E
Ammanford Wales	14	B1	51 48N	3 58W
Ampthill England	16	C2	52 02N	0 30W
Amritsar India	66	C6	31 35N	74 56E
Amsterdam Neths	48	C5	52 22N	4 54E
Amstetten Austria	52	G4	48 08N	14 52E
Amur r. Asia	69	N8	52 30N	126 30E
Anascaul RoI	21	A2	52 09N	10 04W
Anchorage USA	88	F6	61 10N	150 00W
Ancona Italy	54	E5	43 37N	13 31E
Ancroft England	11	G2	55 42N	2 00W
Andalsnes Norway	49	C3	62 33N	7 43E
Andaman Islands India	67	G2	12 00N	94 00E
Anderlecht Belgium	48	C3	50 50N	4 20E
Andermatt Switz.	52	D3	46 38N	8 36E
Andes mts. S. America	96/97	B14/C6	10 00S	77 00W
ANDORRA	50	E2		
Andorra la Vella Andorra	50	E2	42 30N	1 30E
Andover England	16	B2	51 13N	1 28W
Andreas Isle of Man	12	B3	54 22N	4 26W
Ándros i. Greece	55	L2	37 49N	24 54E
Andújar Spain	51	C3	38 02N	4 03W
Angara r. Russia	62	M8	58 00N	97 30E
Angers France	50	D4	47 29N	0 32W
Angle Wales	14	A1	51 41N	5 06W
Anglesey i. Wales	14	B3	53 18N	4 25W
Anglesey, Isle of u.a. Wales	14	B3	53 18N	4 25W
ANGOLA	82	C5		
Angoulême France	50	E3	45 40N	0 10E
Anguilla i. Leeward Islands	94	P10	18 14N	63 05W
Angus u.a. Scotland	9	G1	56 45N	3 00W
'Annaba Algeria	80	F9	36 55N	7 47E
Annalong NI	10	D1	54 06N	5 55W
Annan r. Scotland	11	F2	55 05N	3 20W
Annan Scotland	11	F1	54 59N	3 16W
Annapolis USA	91	L4	38 59N	76 30W
Annapurna mt. Nepal	66	E5	28 34N	83 50E
Annbank Scotland	11	E2	55 28N	4 30W
Annecy France	50	H3	45 54N	6 07E
Annfield Plain England	13	E3	54 52N	1 45W
Ansbach Germany	52	E4	49 18N	10 36E
Anshan China	69	M6	41 05N	122 58E
Anstey England	15	E2	52 40N	1 10W
Anston England	13	E2	53 22N	1 13W
Anstruther Scotland	11	G3	56 14N	2 42W
Antalya Turkey	57	D2	36 53N	30 42E
Antananarivo Madagascar	82	J4	18 52S	47 30E
Antarctica	101			
Antequera Spain	51	C2	37 01N	4 34W
Antibes France	50	H2	43 35N	7 07E
ANTIGUA & BARBUDA	94	Q9		
Antrim NI	10	C1	54 43N	6 13W
Antrim district NI	10	C1	54 40N	6 10W
Antrim Mountains NI	10	C2	55 00N	6 10W
Antwerpen Belgium	48	C4	51 13N	4 25E
Aosta Italy	54	B6	45 43N	7 19E
Apeldoorn Neths	48	D5	52 13N	5 57E
Appalachian Mountains USA	91	K4	37 00N	82 00W
Appennini mts. Italy	54	C6/F4	43 00N	12 30E
Appleby-in-Westmorland England	12	D3	54 36N	2 29W
Appledore England	18	C3	51 03N	4 12W
Appleton USA	91	J5	44 17N	88 24W
'Aqaba, Gulf of Middle East	64	D4	28 40N	34 40E
Arabian Sea Indian Ocean	65	H3	22 00N	63 00E
Aral Sea Asia	62	H5/J6	45 00N	60 00E
Aranda de Duero Spain	51	D4	41 40N	3 41W
Aran Fawddwy mt. Wales	14	C2	52 47N	3 41W
Aran Island RoI	20	C4	55 00N	8 40W
Aran Islands RoI	21	B3	53 10N	9 50W
Aranjuez Spain	51	D4	40 02N	3 37W
Arbil Iraq	64	D6	36 12N	44 01E
Arbroath Scotland	9	G1	56 34N	2 35W
Arcachon France	50	D3	44 40N	1 11W
Arctic Ocean	101			
Ardara RoI	20	C4	54 46N	8 25W
Ardbeg Scotland	10	C2	55 39N	6 05W
Ardee RoI	20	E3	53 52N	6 33W
Ardennes mts. Belgium	48	D3	50 10N	5 45E
Ardfert RoI	21	B2	52 20N	9 47W
Ardglass NI	10	D1	54 16N	5 37W
Ardle r. Scotland	9	F1	56 40N	3 30W
Ardminish Scotland	10	D2	55 42N	5 44W
Ardmore RoI	21	D1	51 57N	7 43W
Ardmore Point Scotland	10	C2	55 41N	6 01W
Ardnamurchan, Point of Scotland	8	C1	56 44N	6 14W
Ardrossan Scotland	11	E2	55 39N	4 49W
Ards district NI	10	D1	54 35N	5 35W
Ards Peninsula NI	10	D1	54 25N	5 30W
Ardvasar Scotland	8	D2	57 03N	5 55W
Arendal Norway	49	C2	58 27N	8 56E
Arezzo Italy	54	D5	43 28N	11 53E
Argentan France	50	D5	48 45N	0 01W
ARGENTINA	97	D5		
Argyll and Bute u.a. Scotland	10	D3	56 10N	5 00W
Århus Denmark	49	D2	56 15N	10 10E
Arinagour Scotland	8	C1	56 37N	6 31W
Arisaig Scotland	8	D1	56 51N	5 51W
Arisaig, Sound of Scotland	8	D1	56 50N	5 50W
Arizona state USA	90	D3	34 00N	112 00W
Arkansas state USA	91	H3	34 00N	93 00W
Arkansas r. USA	90	G4	36 00N	99 00W
Arkansas City USA	91	G4	37 03N	97 02W
Arkhangel'sk Russia	62	G9	64 32N	40 40E
Arklow RoI	21	E2	52 48N	6 09W
Arles France	50	G2	43 41N	4 38E
Arlon Belgium	48	D2	49 41N	5 49E
Armadale Highland Scotland	8	D2	57 05N	5 54W
Armadale West Lothian Scotland	11	F2	55 54N	3 41W
Armagh NI	10	C1	54 21N	6 39W
Armagh district NI	10	C1	54 20N	6 40W
ARMENIA	57	F3		
Armentières France	50	F6	50 41N	2 53E
Armthorpe England	13	E2	53 32N	1 03W
Arnhem Neths	48	D4	52 00N	5 53E
Arnold England	15	E2	53 00N	1 09W
Arran i. Scotland	10	D2	55 35N	5 15W
Arras France	50	F6	50 17N	2 46E
Artane RoI	20	E3	53 23N	6 12W
Arthur's Seat sum. Scotland	11	F2	55 57N	3 11W
Arthurstown RoI	21	E2	52 15N	6 57W
Aruba i. Neths	96	C16		
Arun r. England	16	C2	51 00N	0 30W
Arundel England	16	C1	50 51N	0 34W
Arvika Sweden	49	D2	59 41N	12 38E
Ascoli Piceno Italy	54	E5	42 52N	13 35E
Ascot England	16	C2	51 25N	0 41W
Ash England	17	E2	51 17N	1 16E
Ashbourne England	13	E2	53 01N	1 43W
Ashbourne RoI	20	E3	53 31N	6 24W
Ashburton England	18	D2	50 31N	3 45W
Ashby-de-la-Zouch England	15	E2	52 46N	1 28W
Ashford England	17	D2	51 09N	0 53E
Ash Fork USA	90	D4	35 13N	112 29W
Ashgabat Turkmenistan	62	H4	37 58N	58 24E
Ashington England	13	E4	55 11N	1 34W
Ashkirk Scotland	11	G2	55 29N	2 50W
Ashton-in-Makerfield England	12	D2	53 29N	2 39W
Ashton-under-Lyne England	12	D2	53 29N	2 06W
Ashwell England	16	C3	52 03N	0 09W
Askeaton RoI	21	C2	52 36N	8 58W
Askern England	13	E2	53 37N	1 09W
Askrigg England	12	D3	54 19N	2 04W
Asmara Eritrea	81	N5	15 20N	38 58E
Aspatria England	12	C3	54 46N	3 20W
Assisi Italy	54	E5	43 04N	12 37E
Astana Kazakhstan	62	K7	51 10N	71 28E
Astee RoI	21	B2	52 33N	9 34W
Asti Italy	54	C6	44 54N	8 13E
Astorga Spain	51	B5	42 27N	6 04W
Astoria USA	90	B6	46 12N	123 50W
Astrakhan' Russia	62	G6	46 22N	48 04E
Asunción Paraguay	96	F7	25 15S	57 40W
Aswân Egypt	81	M6	24 05N	32 56E
Athabasca Canada	88	N4	54 44N	113 15W
Athabasca, Lake Canada	88	P5	59 10N	109 30W
Athboy RoI	20	E3	53 37N	6 55W
Athenry RoI	20	C3	53 18N	8 45W
Athens Greece	55	K2	38 00N	23 44E
Atherstone England	15	E2	52 35N	1 31W
Athleague RoI	20	C3	53 34N	8 15W
Athlone RoI	20	D3	53 25N	7 56W
Áthos mt. Greece	55	L4	40 10N	24 19E
Athy RoI	21	E2	52 59N	6 59W
Atlanta USA	91	K3	33 45N	84 23W
Atlantic City USA	91	M4	39 23N	74 27W
Atlantic Ocean	104			
Attleborough England	17	E3	52 31N	1 01E
Attymass RoI	20	B4	54 03N	9 04W
Aubagne France	50	G2	43 17N	5 35E
Aubenas France	50	G3	44 37N	4 24E
Auch France	50	E2	43 40N	0 36E
Auchencairn Scotland	11	F1	54 51N	3 53W
Auchterarder Scotland	11	F3	56 18N	3 43W
Auchtermuchty Scotland	11	F3	56 17N	3 15W
Auckland NZ	73	P3	36 51S	174 46E
Audley England	12	D2	53 03N	2 20W
Augher NI	10	B1	54 26N	7 08W
Aughnacloy NI	10	C1	54 25N	6 59W
Aughrim RoI	21	E2	52 52N	6 20W
Aughton England	13	E2	53 22N	1 19W
Augsburg Germany	52	E4	48 21N	10 54E
Augusta USA	91	K3	33 29N	82 00W
Auldgirth Scotland	11	F2	55 12N	3 43W
Aurillac France	50	F3	44 56N	2 26E
AUSTRALIA	72/73			
AUSTRIA	52	E3/G3		
Autun France	50	G4	46 58N	4 18E
Auxerre France	50	F4	47 48N	3 35E
Avallon France	50	F4	47 30N	3 54E
Avebury England	16	B2	51 27N	1 51W
Aveiro Portugal	51	A4	40 38N	8 40W
Aveley England	17	D2	51 30N	0 15E
Avesta Sweden	49	E3	60 09N	16 10E
Avezzano Italy	54	E5	42 02N	13 26E
Aviemore Scotland	9	F2	57 12N	3 50W
Avignon France	50	G2	43 56N	4 48E
Avila Spain	51	C4	40 39N	4 42W
Avoca RoI	21	E2	52 52N	6 13W
Avon r. Warwickshire England	15	E2	52 10N	1 55W
Avon r. Hampshire England	16	B1	51 05N	1 55W
Avon r. Wiltshire England	16	A2	51 25N	2 05W
Avon r. Scotland	9	F2	57 27N	1 40W
Avonmouth England	19	E3	51 31N	2 42W
Avranches France	50	D5	48 42N	1 21W
Axbridge England	19	E3	51 18N	2 49W
Axe r. Somerset England	19	E3	51 11N	2 43W
Axe r. Dorset England	19	E2	50 50N	2 50W
Axminster England	19	E2	50 47N	3 00W
Ayamonte Spain	51	B2	37 13N	7 24W
Ayers Rock mt. Australia	72	F5	25 18S	131 18E
Aylesbury England	16	C2	51 50N	0 50W
Aylesford England	17	D2	51 18N	0 30E
Aylesham England	17	E2	51 12N	1 11E

Aylsham England 17 E3 52 49N 1 15E
Ayr r. Scotland 11 E2 55 30N 4 10W
Ayr Scotland 11 E2 55 28N 4 38W
Ayre, Point of
　Isle of Man 12 B3 54 25N 4 22W
Aysgarth England 12 E3 54 17N 2 00W
AZERBAIJAN 57 G3
Azov, Sea of Asia 57 E4 46 00N 36 00E
Azuaga Spain 51 C3 38 16N 5 40W

B
Babbacombe Bay
　England 18 D2 50 30N 3 30W
Bacup England 12 D2 53 42N 2 12W
Badajoz Spain 51 B3 38 53N 6 58W
Badalona Spain 51 G4 41 27N 2 15E
Baden Switz. 52 D3 47 28N 8 19E
Bad Ischl Austria 52 F3 47 43N 13 38E
Baffin Bay Canada/
　Greenland 89 X8/Z8 72 00N 65 00W
Baffin Island Canada 89 U8/W7 68 30N 70 00W
Baggy Point England 18 C3 51 09N 4 16W
Baghdad Iraq 64 D5 33 20N 44 26E
BAHAMAS, THE 95 J4
Bahia Blanca Argentina 97 E6 38 45S 62 15W
Bahia de Campeche
　Mexico 94 E4/F4 20 00N 95 00W
BAHRAIN 65 F4
Bahrain, Gulf of
　The Gulf 65 F4 25 55N 50 30E
Bahr el Abiad r. Sudan 81 M4 14 00N 32 20E
Bahr el Azraq r. Sudan 81 M4 13 30N 33 45E
Baia Mare Romania 53 L3 47 39N 23 36E
Baie de la Seine France 50 D5 49 40N 0 30W
Baildon England 13 E2 53 52N 1 46W
Bailieborough Rol 20 E3 53 54N 6 59W
Baja California p.
　Mexico 94 B5 27 30N 113 00W
Bakersfield USA 90 C4 35 25N 119 00W
Bakewell England 13 E2 53 13N 1 40W
Baku Azerbaijan 57 G3 40 22N 49 53E
Bala Wales 14 C2 52 54N 3 35W
Balaton l. Hungary 53 H3 47 00N 17 30E
Balbriggan Rol 20 E3 53 37N 6 11W
Balcombe England 16 C2 51 04N 0 08W
Baldock England 16 C2 51 59N 0 12W
Balearic Islands
　Med. Sea 51 F3/H3 40 00N 2 00E
Baleshare i. Scotland 8 B2 57 32N 7 22W
Bali i. Indonesia 71 E2/F2 8 30S 115 00E
Ballachulish Scotland 8 D1 56 40N 5 10W
Ballagan Point Rol 20 E4 54 00N 6 06W
Ballaghaderreen Rol 20 C3 53 55N 8 36W
Ballantrae Scotland 10 D2 55 06N 5 00W
Ballater Scotland 9 F2 57 03N 3 03W
Ballaugh Isle of Man 12 B3 54 18N 4 32W
Ballina Rol 20 B4 54 07N 9 09W
Ballinafad Rol 20 C4 54 02N 8 20W
Ballinagleragh Rol 20 C4 54 09N 8 01W
Ballinalack Rol 20 D3 53 38N 7 28W
Ballinalee Rol 20 D3 53 46N 7 39W
Ballinamore Rol 20 D4 54 03N 7 47W
Ballinasloe Rol 20 C3 53 20N 8 13W
Ballincollig Rol 21 C1 51 54N 8 35W
Ballindine Rol 20 C3 53 40N 8 57W
Ballingry Scotland 11 F3 56 11N 3 20W
Ballinhassig Rol 21 C1 51 49N 8 32W
Ballinrobe Rol 20 B3 53 37N 9 13W
Ballinskelligs Bay Rol 21 A1 51 46N 10 17W
Ballintra Rol 20 C4 54 35N 8 07W
Ballon Rol 21 E2 52 44N 6 46W
Ballybay Rol 20 E4 54 08N 6 54W
Ballybofey Rol 20 D4 54 48N 7 47W
Ballybunnion Rol 21 B2 52 31N 9 40W
Ballycanew Rol 21 E2 52 36N 6 18W
Ballycastle NI 10 C2 55 12N 6 15W
Ballycastle Rol 20 B4 54 17N 9 22W
Ballyclare NI 10 C1 54 45N 6 00W
Ballycolla Rol 21 D2 52 52N 7 26W
Ballyconnell Rol 20 D4 54 07N 7 35W
Ballycotton Rol 21 C1 51 50N 8 01W
Ballycotton Bay Rol 21 D1 51 51N 7 57W
Ballycroy Rol 20 B4 54 02N 9 49W
Ballydavid Head Rol 21 A2 52 14N 10 21W
Ballydehob Rol 21 B1 51 34N 9 28W
Ballydesmond Rol 21 B2 52 10N 9 13W
Ballydonegan Rol 21 A1 51 37N 10 12W
Ballydonegan Bay Rol 21 A1 51 29N 10 09W
Ballygalley Head NI 10 D1 54 54N 5 51W
Ballygowan NI 10 D1 54 30N 5 47W
Ballyhaunis Rol 20 C3 53 46N 8 46W
Ballyheige Rol 21 B2 52 24N 9 50W
Ballyheige Bay Rol 21 B2 52 23N 9 52W
Ballyhoura Mountains
　Rol 21 C2 52 17N 8 33W
Ballyjamesduff Rol 20 D3 53 52N 7 12W
Ballykinler NI 10 D1 54 17N 5 47W
Ballylanders Rol 21 C2 52 23N 8 21W
Ballylongford Rol 21 B2 52 33N 9 28W
Ballymacarbry Rol 21 D2 52 16N 7 12W
Ballymahon Rol 20 D3 53 34N 7 45W
Ballymena NI 10 C1 54 52N 6 17W
Ballymena district NI 10 C1 54 52N 6 20W
Ballymoe Rol 20 C3 53 42N 8 28W
Ballymoney NI 10 C2 55 04N 6 31W
Ballymoney district NI 10 C2 55 00N 6 30W

Ballymore Donegal Rol 20 D5 55 09N 7 56W
Ballymore
　Westmeath Rol 20 D3 53 29N 7 40W
Ballymote Rol 20 C4 54 06N 8 31W
Ballynahinch NI 10 D1 54 24N 5 54W
Ballynamona Rol 21 C2 52 05N 8 39W
Ballynamult Rol 21 D2 52 13N 7 40W
Ballyquintin Point NI 10 D1 54 19N 5 30W
Ballyragget Rol 21 D2 52 47N 7 20W
Ballyshannon Rol 20 C4 54 30N 8 11W
Ballyteige Bay Rol 21 E2 52 12N 6 45W
Ballyvaghan Rol 21 B3 53 07N 9 09W
Ballyvourney Rol 21 B1 51 56N 9 10W
Ballywalter NI 10 D1 54 33N 5 30W
Balmaclellan Scotland 11 E2 55 05N 4 07W
Balmoral Scotland 9 F2 57 02N 3 13W
Balrath Rol 20 E3 53 37N 6 29W
Baltic Sea Europe 49 E2/F2 55 15N 17 00E
Baltimore Rol 21 B1 51 29N 9 22W
Baltimore USA 91 L4 39 18N 76 38W
Baltinglass Rol 21 E2 52 55N 6 41W
Baltray Rol 20 E3 53 44N 6 16W
Bamako Mali 80 C4 12 40N 7 59W
Bamberg Germany 52 E4 49 54N 10 54E
Bamburgh England 11 H2 55 36N 1 42W
Bampton England 18 D2 51 00N 3 29W
Banagher Rol 21 D3 53 11N 7 59W
Banbridge Rol 10 C1 54 21N 6 16W
Banbridge district NI 10 C1 54 15N 6 20W
Banbury England 16 B3 52 04N 1 20W
Banchory Scotland 9 G2 57 30N 2 30W
Bandar Seri Begawan
　Brunei 71 F4 4 53N 115 00E
Bandon Rol 21 C1 51 45N 8 45W
Bandung Indonesia 71 D2 6 57S 107 34E
Banff Canada 88 M4 51 10N 115 34W
Banff Scotland 9 G2 57 40N 2 33W
Bangalore India 66 D2 12 58N 77 35E
Bangkok Thailand 71 C6 13 44N 100 30E
BANGLADESH 67 F4/G4
Bangor NI 10 D1 54 40N 5 40W
Bangor Rol 20 B4 54 09N 9 44W
Bangor Wales 14 B3 53 13N 4 08W
Bangui CAR 81 J2 4 23N 18 37E
Banja Luka
　Bosnia-Herzegovina 55 G6 44 47N 17 11E
Banjul The Gambia 80 A4 13 28N 16 39W
Bann r. Coleraine NI 10 C2 55 05N 6 40W
Bann r. Banbridge NI 10 C1 54 20N 6 11W
Bann r. Rol 21 E2 52 39N 6 24W
Bannockburn Scotland 11 F3 56 05N 3 56W
Bannow Bay Rol 21 E2 52 13N 6 48W
Bansha Rol 21 C2 52 28N 8 04W
Banstead England 16 C2 51 19N 0 12W
Banteer Rol 21 C2 52 08N 8 54W
Bantry Rol 21 B1 51 41N 9 27W
Bantry Bay Rol 21 B1 51 35N 9 40W
Baotou China 69 J6 40 38N 109 59E
Baracaldo Spain 51 D5 43 17N 2 59W
Baranavichy Belarus 53 N6 53 09N 26 00E
BARBADOS 94 S11
Barbastro Spain 51 F5 42 02N 0 07E
Barcelona Spain 51 G4 41 25N 2 10E
Barcs Hungary 53 H2 45 58N 17 30E
Bardsey Island Wales 14 B2 52 46N 4 48W
Barents Sea
　Arctic Ocean 101 75 00N 40 00E
Bargoed Wales 14 C1 51 43N 3 15W
Bari Italy 55 G4 41 07N 16 52E
Barisal Bangladesh 67 G4 22 41N 90 20E
Barking England 17 D2 51 33N 0 06E
Barle r. England 18 D3 51 05N 3 36W
Bar-le-Duc France 50 G5 48 46N 5 10E
Barletta Italy 54 G4 41 20N 16 17E
Barmouth Wales 14 B2 52 43N 4 03W
Barnard Castle England 13 E3 54 33N 1 55W
Barnatra Rol 20 B4 54 13N 9 50W
Barnet England 16 C2 51 39N 0 12W
Barnoldswick England 12 D2 53 56N 2 16W
Barnsley England 13 E2 53 34N 1 28W
Barnstaple England 18 C3 51 05N 4 04W
Barnstaple or Bideford
　Bay England 18 C3 51 05N 4 25W
Barquisimeto
　Venezuela 96 D16 10 03N 69 18W
Barra i. Scotland 8 B1/B2 57 00N 7 25W
Barra Head Scotland 8 B1 56 47N 7 36W
Barranquilla Colombia 96 C16 11 10N 74 50W
Barra, Sound of
　Scotland 8 B2 57 06N 7 22W
Barre USA 91 M5 44 13N 72 31W
Barreiro Portugal 51 A3 38 40N 9 05W
Barrhead Scotland 11 E2 55 48N 4 24W
Barrow r. Rol 21 E2 52 38N 6 58W
Barrow-in-Furness
　England 12 C3 54 07N 3 14W
Barry Wales 14 C1 51 24N 3 18W
Barton-upon-Humber
　England 13 F2 53 41N 0 27W
Barvas Scotland 8 C3 58 22N 6 32W
Barysaw Belarus 53 P7 54 09N 28 30E
Basel Switz. 52 C3 47 33N 7 36E
Basildon England 17 D2 51 34N 0 25W
Basingstoke England 16 B2 51 16N 1 05W
Bassenthwaite Lake
　England 12 C3 54 40N 3 13W
Bastia France 50 J2 42 14N 9 26E

Bastogne Belgium 48 D3 50 00N 5 43E
Bath England 19 E3 51 23N 2 22W
Bath and North East
　Somerset u.a. England 19 E3 51 25N 2 30W
Bathgate Scotland 11 F2 55 55N 3 39W
Bathurst Canada 89 X3 47 37N 65 40W
Batley England 13 E2 53 44N 1 37W
Baton Rouge USA 91 H3 30 30N 91 10W
Battle England 17 D1 50 55N 0 29E
Bat Yam Israel 64 N10 31 59N 34 45E
Bawdsey England 17 E3 52 01N 1 25E
Bawtry England 13 E2 53 26N 1 01W
Bayeux France 50 D5 49 16N 0 42W
Bayonne France 50 D2 43 30N 1 28W
Bayreuth Germany 52 E4 49 27N 11 35E
Bayston Hill tn.
　England 14 D2 52 40N 2 48W
Beachy Head England 17 D1 50 44N 0 16E
Beaconsfield England 16 C2 51 37N 0 39W
Beadnell Bay England 11 H2 55 32N 1 30W
Beaminster England 19 E2 50 49N 2 45W
Bear Island Rol 21 B1 51 40N 9 48W
Bearsden Scotland 11 E2 55 56N 4 20W
Bearsted England 17 D2 51 17N 0 35E
Beatrice USA 91 G5 40 17N 96 45W
Beaulieu England 16 B1 50 49N 1 27W
Beauly Scotland 9 E2 57 29N 4 29W
Beauly r. Scotland 9 E2 57 25N 4 33W
Beauly Firth Scotland 9 E2 57 30N 4 20W
Beaumaris Wales 14 B3 53 16N 4 05W
Beaune France 50 G4 47 02N 4 50E
Beauvais France 50 F5 49 26N 2 05E
Bebington England 12 D2 53 20N 2 59W
Beccles England 17 E3 52 28N 1 34E
Bedale England 13 E3 54 17N 1 35W
Bedford England 16 C3 52 08N 0 29W
Bedfordshire co.
　England 16 C2 52 08N 0 29W
Bedlington England 13 E4 55 08N 1 25W
Bedwas Wales 14 C1 51 35N 3 12W
Bedworth England 15 E2 52 29N 1 28W
Beeston England 15 E2 52 56N 1 12W
Beighton England 13 E2 53 21N 1 21W
Beijing China 69 L5 39 55N 116 26E
Beinn Dearg mt.
　Scotland 9 E2 57 47N 4 56W
Beira Mozambique 82 F4 19 49S 34 52E
Beirut Lebanon 64 C5 33 52N 35 30E
Beith Scotland 11 E2 55 45N 4 38W
Beja Portugal 51 B3 38 01N 7 52W
Bejaïa Algeria 80 F9 36 49N 5 03E
Béjar Spain 51 C4 40 24N 5 45W
BELARUS 56 B5/6
Beldelberg Rol 20 B4 54 18N 9 33W
Belém Brazil 96 H12 1 27S 48 29W
Belfast NI 10 D1 54 35N 5 55W
Belfast district NI 10 C1/D1 54 40N 6 05W
Belfast Lough est. NI 10 D1 54 40N 5 50W
Belford England 11 H2 55 36N 1 49W
Belfort France 50 H4 47 38N 6 52E
BELGIUM 48 B3/D3
Belgrade Yugoslavia 55 J6 44 50N 20 30E
BELIZE 94 G3
Bellac France 50 E4 46 07N 1 04E
Bellacorick Rol 20 B4 54 07N 9 34W
Bellanagh Rol 20 D3 53 56N 7 24W
Bellavary Rol 20 B3 53 53N 9 12W
Bellingham England 11 G2 55 09N 2 16W
Bellsbank Scotland 11 E2 55 19N 4 24W
Bellshill Scotland 11 E2 55 49N 4 02W
Belmont Scotland 7 D3 60 41N 0 58W
Belmopan Belize 94 G3 17 13N 88 48W
Belmullet Rol 20 B4 54 14N 10 00W
Belo Horizonte Brazil 96 J10 19 54S 43 54W
Belper England 13 E2 53 01N 1 29W
Belton England 17 E3 52 34N 1 40E
Beltra Lough Rol 20 B3 53 55N 9 25W
Belturbet Rol 20 D4 54 06N 7 28W
Belvoir, Vale of
　England 15 F2 52 08N 0 55W
Bembridge England 16 B1 50 41N 1 05W
Ben Alder mt. Scotland 9 E1 56 49N 4 28W
Benavente Spain 51 C4 42 00N 5 40W
Benbane Head NI 10 C2 55 14N 6 29W
Benbecula i. Scotland 8 B2 57 25N 7 20W
Ben Cleuch mt.
　Scotland 11 F3 56 11N 3 47W
Ben Cruachan mt.
　Scotland 9 D1 56 26N 5 09W
Benevento Italy 54 F4 41 08N 14 46E
Bengal, Bay of
　Indian Ocean 67 F3 17 00N 88 00E
Benghazi Libya 81 K8 32 07N 20 04E
Benicarló Spain 51 F4 40 25N 0 25E
Benidorm Spain 51 E3 38 33N 0 09W
BENIN 80 E4
Benin City Nigeria 80 F3 6 19N 5 41E
Ben Klibreck mt.
　Scotland 9 E3 58 14N 4 22W
Ben Lawers mt.
　Scotland 9 E1 56 33N 4 15W
Benllech Wales 14 B3 53 19N 4 15W
Ben Lomond mt.
　Scotland 11 E3 56 12N 4 38W
Ben Loyal mt. Scotland 9 E3 58 24N 4 26W

Ben Macdui mt.
　Scotland 9 F2 57 04N 3 40W
Ben More mt.
　Highland Scotland 8 C1 56 25N 6 02W
Ben More mt.
　Stirling Scotland 9 E1 56 23N 4 31W
Ben More Assynt mt.
　Scotland 9 E3 58 07N 4 52W
Bennettsbridge Rol 21 D2 52 35N 7 10W
Benson USA 90 D3 31 58N 110 19W
Bentley England 13 E2 53 33N 1 09W
Benwee Head Rol 20 B4 54 21N 9 48W
Ben Wyvis mt. Scotland 9 E2 57 40N 4 35W
Beppu Japan 70 B1 33 18N 131 30E
Bérgamo Italy 54 C6 45 42N 9 40E
Bergen Norway 49 C3 60 23N 5 20E
Bergerac France 50 E3 44 50N 0 29E
Bergisch Gladbach
　Germany 52 C5 50 59N 7 10E
Bering Sea
　Pacific Ocean 100 H12/J13 60 00N 175 00W
Bering Strait
　Russia/USA 88 B7 69 00N 169 00W
Berkeley England 15 D1 51 42N 2 27W
Berkhamsted England 16 C2 51 46N 0 35W
Berkshire Downs
　England 16 B2 51 30N 1 25W
Berlin Germany 52 F6 52 32N 13 25E
Bern Switz. 52 C3 46 57N 7 26E
Bernalda Italy 55 G4 40 24N 16 443
Berner Alpen mts.
　Switz. 52 C3/D3 46 25N 7 30E
Berneray i. Scotland 8 B2 57 45N 7 10W
Bernina Pass Switz. 52 D3 46 25N 10 02E
Berriedale Scotland 9 F3 58 11N 3 33W
Berry Head England 18 D2 50 24N 3 29W
Berwick-upon-Tweed
　England 11 G2 55 46N 2 00W
Besançon France 50 G4 47 14N 6 02E
Bessacarr England 13 E2 53 30N 1 05W
Bessbrook NI 10 C1 54 12N 6 24W
Betanzos Spain 51 A5 43 17N 8 13W
Bethersden England 17 D2 51 07N 0 45E
Bethesda Wales 14 B3 53 11N 4 03W
Bethlehem Middle East 64 C5 31 42N 35 12E
Béthune France 50 F6 50 32N 2 38E
Bettyhill Scotland 9 E3 58 32N 4 14W
Betws-y-Coed Wales 14 C3 53 05N 3 48W
Beverley England 13 F2 53 51N 0 26W
Bewdley England 15 D2 52 22N 2 19W
Bewl Water l. England 17 D2 51 02N 0 23E
Bexhill England 17 D1 50 50N 0 29E
Bexley England 17 D2 51 27N 0 09E
Béziers France 50 F2 43 21N 3 13E
Bharatpur India 66 D5 27 14N 77 29E
Bhopal India 66 D4 23 17N 77 28E
Bhubaneshwar India 67 F4 20 13N 85 50E
BHUTAN 67 G5
Białystok Poland 53 L6 53 09N 23 10E
Biarritz France 50 D2 43 29N 1 33W
Bicester England 16 B2 51 54N 1 09W
Biddeford USA 91 M5 43 29N 70 27W
Biddulph England 12 D2 53 08N 2 10W
Bideford England 18 C3 51 01N 4 13W
Biel Switz. 52 C3 46 27N 8 13E
Bielefeld Germany 52 D6 52 02N 8 32E
Bielsko-Biała Poland 53 J4 49 50N 19 00E
Bigbury Bay England 18 D2 50 17N 4 00W
Biggar Scotland 11 F2 55 38N 3 32W
Biggleswade England 16 C3 52 05N 0 17W
Bihać
　Bosnia-Herzegovina 54 F6 44 49N 15 53E
Bikaner India 66 C5 28 01N 73 22E
Bila Tserkva Ukraine 53 Q4 49 49N 30 10E
Bilbao Spain 51 D5 43 15N 2 56W
Billericay England 17 D2 51 38N 0 25E
Billinge England 12 D2 53 30N 2 42W
Billingham England 13 E3 54 36N 1 17W
Billingshurst England 16 C2 51 01N 0 28W
Bill of Portland c.
　England 19 E2 50 31N 2 27W
Bingham England 15 F2 52 57N 0 57W
Bingley England 13 E2 53 51N 1 50W
Birchwood tn. England 13 F2 53 14N 0 33W
Birkenhead England 12 C2 53 24N 3 02W
Birmingham England 15 E2 52 30N 1 50W
Birmingham USA 91 J3 33 30N 86 55W
Birr Rol 21 D3 53 05N 7 54W
Birstall England 15 E2 52 40N 1 08W
Biscay, Bay of
　Atlantic Ocean 50 C3 45 30N 2 50W
Bishkek Kyrgyzstan 62 K5 42 49N 74 46E
Bishop Auckland
　England 13 E3 54 40N 1 40W
Bishopbriggs Scotland 11 E2 55 54N 4 14W
Bishop's Castle tn.
　England 14 C2 52 29N 3 00W
Bishop's Cleeve
　England 15 D1 51 57N 2 04W
Bishop's Lydeard
　England 19 D3 51 04N 3 12W
Bishop's Stortford
　England 17 D2 51 53N 0 09E
Bishopston Wales 14 B1 51 35N 4 03W
Bishop's Waltham
　England 16 B1 50 58N 1 12W

Bishopton Scotland 11 E2 55 54N 4 31W
Bissau Guinea-Bissau 80 A4 11 52N 15 39W
Blaby England 15 E2 52 35N 1 09W
Black r. RoI 20 D3 53 55N 7 42W
Blackburn England 12 D2 53 45N 2 29W
Blackdown Hills
England 19 D2 50 55N 3 10W
Blackhall Colliery tn.
England 13 E3 54 43N 1 20W
Black Head RoI 21 B3 53 09N 9 16W
Blackhope Scar mt.
Scotland 11 F2 55 58N 3 07W
Black Isle Scotland 9 E2 57 35N 4 15W
Blackmoor Vale
England 19 E2 50 56N 2 19W
Black Mountains Wales 14 C1 51 55N 3 10W
Black Mountain Wales 14 C1 51 50N 3 55W
Blackpool England 12 C2 53 50N 3 03W
Black Sea Europe 57 D3/E3 43 00N 35 00E
Blacksod Bay RoI 20 A3/A4 54 05N 10 00W
Blackstairs Mountains
RoI 21 E2 52 33N 6 49W
Blackwater r.
Hampshire England 16 C2 51 22N 0 54W
Blackwater r.
Essex England 17 D2 51 45N 0 50E
Blackwater r.
Waterford RoI 21 D2 52 02N 7 51W
Blackwater r.
Meath RoI 20 E3 53 41N 6 44W
Blackwaterfoot
Scotland 10 D2 55 30N 5 19W
Blackwater r. NI 10 C1 54 20N 6 50W
Blackwood Wales 14 C1 51 41N 3 13W
Blaenau Ffestiniog
Wales 14 C2 52 59N 3 56W
Blaenau Gwent u.a.
Wales 14 C1 51 45N 3 10W
Blaenavon Wales 14 C1 51 48N 3 05W
Blagoveshchensk
Russia 63 Q7 50 19N 127 30E
Blaina Wales 14 C1 51 48N 3 11W
Blair Atholl Scotland 9 F1 56 46N 3 51W
Blairgowrie Scotland 9 F1 56 36N 3 21W
Blakeney Point England 17 E3 52 58N 1 00E
Blandford Forum
England 19 E2 50 52N 2 11W
Blantyre Malawi 82 F4 15 46S 35 00E
Blantyre Scotland 11 E2 55 47N 4 06W
Blarney RoI 21 C1 51 56N 8 34W
Blennerville RoI 21 B2 52 15N 9 43W
Blessington RoI 21 E3 53 10N 6 32W
Bletchley England 16 C3 52 00N 0 46W
Blidworth England 13 E2 53 09N 1 11W
Blithe r. England 15 E2 52 45N 1 50W
Blois France 50 E4 47 36N 1 20E
Bloody Foreland RoI 20 C5 55 10N 8 15W
Bludenz Austria 52 D3 47 10N 9 50E
Blue Stack Mountains RoI 20 C4 54 44N 8 03W
Blyth Nottinghamshire
England 13 E2 53 23N 1 03W
Blyth Northumberland
England 13 E4 55 07N 1 30W
Blyth r. England 13 E4 55 08N 1 45W
Blyth r. England 17 E3 52 28N 1 30E
Boa Vista Brazil 96 E14 3 23S 55 30W
Bocholt Germany 52 C5 51 49N 6 37E
Bochum Germany 52 C5 51 28N 7 11E
Boddam Scotland 9 H2 57 28N 1 48W
Boden Sweden 49 F4 65 50N 21 44E
Bodensee l. Switz. 52 D3 47 40N 9 30E
Bodmin England 18 C2 50 29N 4 43W
Bodmin Moor England 18 C2 50 35N 4 40W
Boggeragh Mountains
RoI 21 B2/C2 52 00N 8 50W
Bogie r. Scotland 9 G2 57 25N 2 50W
Bognor Regis England 16 C1 50 47N 0 41W
Bogotá Colombia 96 C14 4 38N 74 05W
Böhmer Wald mts.
Germany 52 F4 49 00N 13 00E
Boise City USA 90 F4 36 44N 102 31W
Boldon England 13 E3 54 57N 1 27W
BOLIVIA 96D10/E10
Bollington England 12 D2 53 18N 2 06W
Bologna Italy 54 E6 44 30N 11 20E
Bolsover England 13 E2 53 15N 1 26W
Bolton England 12 D2 53 35N 2 26W
Bolus Head RoI 21 A1 51 45N 10 10W
Bolzano Italy 54 E7 46 30N 11 22E
Bonar Bridge tn.
Scotland 9 E2 57 53N 4 21W
Bo'ness Scotland 11 F3 56 01N 3 37W
Bonifacio France 50 J1 41 23N 9 10E
Bonifacio, Strait of
France/Italy 50 J1 41 20N 8 45E
Bonn Germany 52 C5 50 44N 7 06E
Bonnybridge Scotland 11 F2 55 59N 3 54W
Bonnyrigg Scotland 11 F2 55 52N 3 08W
Boolakennedy RoI 21 C2 52 20N 8 03W
Bootle Cumbria England 12 C3 54 17N 3 23W
Bootle
Merseyside England 12 C2 53 28N 3 00W
Bordeaux France 50 D3 44 50N 0 34W
Bordon Camp England 16 C2 51 07N 0 53W
Borneo i.
Indonesia/Malaysia 71 D3/F5 1 00N 113 00E

Bornholm i. Denmark 49 D2 55 02N 15 00E
Boroughbridge
England 13 E3 54 05N 1 24W
Borris in Ossory RoI 21 D2 52 57N 7 37W
Borrisokane RoI 21 C2 53 00N 8 08W
Borrisoleigh RoI 21 D2 52 45N 8 00W
Borrowash England 15 E2 52 55N 1 24W
Borth Wales 14 B2 52 29N 4 03W
Boscastle England 18 C2 50 41N 4 42W
BOSNIA-
HERZEGOVINA 55 G6/H6
Boston England 13 F1 52 29N 0 01W
Boston USA 91 M5 42 20N 71 05W
Boston Spa England 13 E2 53 54N 1 21W
Bothnia, Gulf of
Finland/Sweden 49 E3/F3 61 00N 19 10E
Botoşani Romania 53 N3 47 44N 26 41E
BOTSWANA 82 D3/E3
Bottrop Germany 52 C5 51 31N 6 55E
Boulder USA 90 E5 40 02N 105 16W
Boulogne-sur-Mer
France 50 E6 50 43N 1 37E
Bourg-en-Bresse
France 50 G4 46 12N 5 13E
Bourges France 50 F4 47 05N 2 23E
Bourne England 15 F2 52 46N 0 23W
Bourne End England 16 C2 51 34N 0 42W
Bournemouth England 19 F2 50 43N 1 54W
Bournemouth u.a.
England 19 F2 50 43N 1 54W
Bourton-on-the-Water
England 15 E1 51 53N 1 46W
Bovey r. England 18 D2 50 40N 3 50W
Bovey Tracey England 18 D2 50 36N 3 40W
Bowes England 12 D3 54 30N 2 01W
Bowland, Forest of
England 12 D2/D3 54 00N 2 40W
Bowmore Scotland 10 C2 55 45N 6 17W
Bowness-on-
Windermere England 12 D3 54 22N 2 55W
Boxtel Neths 48 D4 51 36N 5 20E
Boyle RoI 20 C3 53 58N 8 18W
Boyne r. RoI 20 E3 53 45N 6 25W
Bozeman USA 90 D6 45 40N 111 00W
Brabourne Lees
England 17 D2 51 08N 1 00E
Brackley England 15 E2 52 02N 1 09W
Bracknell England 16 C2 51 26N 0 46W
Bracknell Forest u.a.
England 16 C1 51 25N 0 50W
Bradford England 13 E2 53 48N 1 45W
Bradford-on-Avon
England 16 A2 51 22N 2 15W
Bradwell-on-Sea
England 17 D2 51 44N 0 54E
Bradworthy England 18 C2 50 54N 4 24W
Braemar Scotland 9 F2 57 01N 3 23W
Braga Portugal 51 A4 41 32N 8 26W
Bragança Portugal 51 B4 41 47N 6 46W
Brahmaputra r.
India/Bangladesh 67 G5 26 40N 93 00E
Brăila Romania 53 N2 45 17N 27 58E
Brailsford England 15 E2 52 59N 1 36W
Braintree England 17 D2 51 53N 0 32E
Brampton England 12 D3 54 57N 2 43W
Brandenburg Germany 52 F6 52 25N 12 34E
Brandon
Durham England 13 E3 54 46N 1 38W
Brandon
Suffolk England 17 D3 52 27N 0 37E
Brandon Bay RoI 21 A2 52 15N 10 05W
Brandon Mountain RoI 21 A2 52 10N 10 10W
Brandon Point RoI 21 A2 52 15N 10 05W
Brant r. England 13 F2 53 05N 0 30W
Brásília Brazil 96 H10 15 45S 47 57W
Braşov Romania 53 M2 45 39N 25 35E
Bratislava Slovakia 53 H4 48 10N 17 10E
Braunau Austria 52 F4 48 16N 13 03E
Braunschweig
Germany 52 E6 52 15N 10 30E
Braunton England 18 C3 51 07N 4 10W
Bray RoI 20 E3 53 12N 6 06W
Bray Head RoI 21 A1 51 53N 10 25W
BRAZIL 96F11/H11
Brazzaville Congo 82 C7 4 14S 15 14E
Breaston England 15 E2 52 56N 1 12W
Brechin Scotland 9 G1 56 44N 2 40W
Brecon Wales 14 C1 51 57N 3 24W
Breda Neths 48 C4 51 35N 4 46E
Bregenz Austria 52 D3 47 31N 9 46E
Bremen Germany 52 D6 53 05N 8 48E
Bremerhaven Germany 52 D6 53 33N 8 35E
Brent r. England 16 C2 51 34N 0 17W
Brentwood England 17 D2 51 38N 0 18E
Brescia Italy 54 D6 45 33N 10 13E
Bressay i. Scotland 7 C3 60 08N 1 05W
Brest Belarus 56 B5 52 08N 23 40E
Brest France 50 B5 48 23N 4 30W
Briançon France 50 H3 44 53N 6 39E
Bridgend Wales 14 C1 51 31N 3 35W
Bridgend u.a. Wales 14 C1 51 32N 3 35W
Bridge of Dee tn.
Scotland 9 F1 56 59N 3 20W
Bridge of Don tn.
Scotland 9 G2 57 11N 2 05W
Bridge of Ericht tn.
Scotland 9 E1 56 44N 4 23W

Bridge of Orchy tn.
Scotland 9 E1 56 30N 4 46W
Bridge of Weir tn.
Scotland 11 E2 55 52N 4 35W
Bridgeport USA 91 M5 41 12N 73 12W
Bridgetown RoI 21 E2 52 14N 6 33W
Bridgnorth England 15 D2 52 33N 2 25W
Bridgwater England 19 D3 51 08N 3 00W
Bridgwater Bay
England 19 D3 51 15N 3 20W
Bridlington England 13 F3 54 05N 0 12W
Bridlington Bay
England 13 F3 54 03N 0 10W
Bridport England 19 E2 50 44N 2 46W
Brierfield England 12 D2 53 50N 2 14W
Brig Switz. 52 C3 46 19N 8 00E
Brigg England 13 F2 53 34N 0 30W
Brighouse England 13 E2 53 42N 1 47W
Brightlingsea England 17 E2 51 49N 1 02E
Brighton England 16 C1 50 50N 0 10W
Brighton and Hove u.a.
England 16 C1 50 51N 0 09W
Brignoles France 50 H2 43 25N 6 03E
Brindisi Italy 55 G4 40 37N 17 57E
Brisbane Australia 73 K5 27 30S 153 00E
Bristol England 19 E3 51 27N 2 35W
Bristol u.a. England 19 E3 51 30N 2 38W
Bristol Channel UK 18 C1/D1 51 20N 4 00W
British Columbia prov.
Canada 88 K4/K5 56 50N 125 30W
British Isles Europe 6
Briton Ferry tn. Wales 14 C1 51 38N 3 49W
Brittas RoI 20 E3 53 14N 6 27W
Brive-la-Gaillarde
France 50 E3 45 09N 1 32E
Brixham England 18 D2 50 23N 3 30W
Brno Czech Rep. 53 H4 49 13N 16 40E
Broad Bay Scotland 8 C3 58 15N 6 10W
Broadford RoI 21 C2 52 48N 8 38W
Broadford Scotland 8 D2 57 14N 5 54W
Broad Haven b. RoI 20 B4 54 18N 9 55W
Broadstairs England 17 E2 51 22N 1 27E
Broadstone England 19 E2 50 45N 2 00W
Broadway England 15 E2 52 02N 1 50W
Brockenhurst England 16 B1 50 49N 1 34W
Brodick Scotland 10 D2 55 35N 5 09W
Bromley England 16 D2 51 31N 0 01E
Bromsgrove England 15 D2 52 20N 2 03W
Bromyard England 15 D2 52 11N 2 30W
Brora Scotland 9 F3 58 01N 3 51W
Brora r. Scotland 9 E3 58 05N 4 00W
Broseley England 15 D2 52 37N 2 29W
Brotton England 13 F3 54 34N 0 56W
Brough East Riding of
Yorkshire England 13 F2 53 44N 0 35W
Brough
Cumbria England 12 D3 54 32N 2 19W
Brough Head Scotland 7 A2 59 09N 3 19W
Broughshane NI 10 C1 54 54N 6 12W
Broughton Wales 14 D3 53 10N 3 00W
Broughton in Furness
England 12 C3 54 17N 3 13W
Broughty Ferry tn.
Scotland 9 G1 56 28N 2 53W
Brownhills tn. England 15 E2 52 39N 1 55W
Broxburn Scotland 11 F2 55 57N 3 29W
Bruay-en-Artois France 50 F6 50 29N 2 33E
Brue r. England 19 E3 51 10N 2 59W
Brugg Switz. 52 D3 47 29N 8 13E
Brugge Belgium 48 B4 51 13N 3 14E
BRUNEI 71 E4/F4
Brunico Italy 54 D7 46 47N 11 57E
Brunswick USA 91 K3 31 09N 81 30W
Brussels Belgium 48 C3 50 50N 4 21E
Bruton England 19 E3 51 07N 2 27W
Bryher i. England 18 A1 49 57N 6 21W
Brymbo Wales 14 C3 53 05N 3 03W
Brynamman Wales 14 C1 51 49N 3 52W
Brynmawr Wales 14 C1 51 49N 3 11W
Bucharest Romania 53 N2 44 25N 26 07E
Buchan Ness Scotland 9 H2 57 28N 1 47W
Buckfastleigh England 18 D2 50 29N 3 46W
Buckhaven Scotland 11 F3 56 11N 3 03W
Buckie Scotland 9 G2 57 40N 2 58W
Buckingham England 16 C2 52 00N 1 00W
Buckinghamshire co.
England 16 C2 51 50N 0 50W
Buckley Wales 14 C3 53 10N 3 05W
Buckuden Ness Scotland 9 G1 56 28N 2 45W
Bude England 18 C2 50 50N 4 33W
Bude Bay England 18 C2 50 50N 4 40W
Budleigh Salterton
England 19 D2 50 38N 3 20W
Buenaventura
Colombia 96 B14 3 54N 77 02W
Buenos Aires Argentina 97 F7 34 40S 58 30W
Buffalo USA 91 L5 42 52N 78 55W
Builth Wells Wales 14 C2 52 09N 3 24W
Bujumbura Burundi 83 A3 3 22S 29 19E
Bulford England 16 B2 51 12N 1 46W
BULGARIA 55 K5/M5
Bulkington England 15 E2 52 28N 1 25W
Bull Point NI 10 C2 55 18N 6 16W
Bunclody RoI 21 E2 52 38N 6 40W
Buncrana RoI 20 D5 55 08N 7 27W
Bundoran RoI 20 C4 54 28N 8 17W

Bungay England 17 E3 52 28N 1 26E
Bunmahon RoI 21 D2 52 08N 7 23W
Bunnahown RoI 20 B3 53 24N 9 47W
Bunnyconnellan RoI 20 B4 54 06N 9 01W
Buraydah Saudi Arabia 64 D4 26 20N 43 59E
Bure r. England 17 E3 52 47N 1 20E
Burgas Bulgaria 55 M5 42 30N 27 29E
Burgess Hill tn.
England 16 C1 50 58N 0 08W
Burghead tn. Scotland 9 F2 57 42N 3 30W
Burghead Bay Scotland 9 F2 57 41N 3 31W
Burgh le Marsh
England 13 G2 53 10N 0 15E
Burgos Spain 51 D5 42 21N 3 41W
BURKINA 80 D4
Burley-in-Wharfedale
England 13 E2 53 55N 1 45W
Burnham Market
England 17 D3 52 57N 0 44E
Burnham-on-Crouch
England 17 D2 51 38N 0 49E
Burnham-on-Sea
England 19 D3 51 15N 3 00W
Burnley England 12 D2 53 48N 2 14W
Burnmouth Scotland 11 G2 55 50N 2 04W
Burnsall England 12 E3 54 03N 1 57W
Burntisland tn.
Scotland 11 F3 56 03N 3 15W
Burntwood England 15 E2 52 40N 1 56W
Burray i. Scotland 7 B1 58 51N 2 54W
Burrow Head Scotland 11 E1 54 41N 4 24W
Burry Port Wales 14 B1 51 42N 4 15W
Burscough Bridge tn.
England 12 D2 53 37N 2 51W
Burton Agnes England 13 F3 54 03N 0 19W
Burton Latimer
England 15 F2 52 22N 0 40W
Burton upon Trent
England 15 E2 52 48N 1 36W
BURUNDI 83 A3/B3
Burwell England 17 D3 52 16N 0 19E
Bury England 12 D2 53 36N 2 17W
Bury St. Edmunds
England 17 D3 52 15N 0 43E
Bush r. NI 10 C2 55 10N 6 30W
Bushey England 16 C2 51 39N 0 22W
Bushmills NI 10 C2 55 12N 6 32W
Bute i. Scotland 10 D2 55 50N 5 05W
Bute, Sound of
Scotland 10 D2 55 45N 5 10W
Butler's Bridge RoI 20 D4 54 03N 7 22W
Buttermere l. England 12 C3 54 32N 3 16W
Buttevant RoI 21 C2 52 14N 8 40W
Butt of Lewis c.
Scotland 8 C3 58 30N 6 20W
Buxton England 13 E2 53 15N 1 55W
Bydgoszcz Poland 53 H6 53 16N 18 00E
Byfield England 15 E2 52 11N 1 14W
Bytom Poland 53 J5 50 21N 18 51E

C

Cabo de Hornos Chile 97 D2 56 00S 67 15W
Cabo Finisterre Spain 51 A5 42 52N 9 16W
Cabrera i. Spain 51 G3 39 00N 2 59E
Cáceres Spain 51 B3 39 29N 6 23W
Cadair Idris mt. Wales 14 C2 52 42N 3 54W
Cádiz Spain 51 B2 36 32N 6 18W
Cádiz, Gulf of Spain 51 B2 36 30N 7 15W
Caen France 50 D5 49 11N 0 22W
Caerleon Wales 14 D1 51 37N 2 57W
Caernarfon Wales 14 B3 53 08N 4 16W
Caernarfon Bay Wales 14 B3 53 05N 4 30W
Caerphilly Wales 14 C1 51 35N 3 14W
Caerphilly u.a. Wales 14 C1 51 37N 3 5W
Caersws Wales 14 C2 52 31N 3 26W
Cágliari Italy 54 C3 39 13N 9 08E
Caha Mountains RoI 21 B1 51 40N 9 40W
Caher RoI 21 D2 52 21N 7 56W
Caher Island RoI 20 A3 53 43N 10 01W
Cahersiveen RoI 21 A1 51 57N 10 13W
Cahore Point RoI 21 E2 52 34N 6 11W
Cahors France 50 E3 44 28N 0 26E
Cairn Gorm mt.
Scotland 9 F2 57 07N 3 40W
Cairngorms mts.
Scotland 9 F2 57 10N 3 30W
Cairnryan Scotland 10 D2 54 58N 5 02W
Cairns Australia 73 J7 16 51S 145 43E
Cairo Egypt 81 M7 30 00N 31 15E
Caister-on-Sea England 17 E3 52 39N 1 44E
Caistor England 13 F2 53 30N 0 19W
Calahorra Spain 51 E5 46 19N 1 58W
Calais France 50 E6 50 57N 1 52E
Calamocha Spain 51 E4 40 54N 1 18W
Calatayud Spain 51 E4 41 21N 1 39W
Caldew r. England 12 C3 54 45N 3 00W
Caldey Island Wales 14 B1 51 38N 4 42W
Caldicot Wales 14 D1 51 36N 2 45W
Caldwell USA 90 C5 43 39N 116 40W
Calgary Canada 88 N4 51 05N 11 05W
Cali Colombia 96 B14 3 24N 76 30W
California state USA 90 C4 35 00N 119 00W
Callan RoI 21 D2 52 33N 7 23W
Callander Scotland 11 E3 56 15N 4 13W

Calligarry Scotland 8 D2 57 02N 5 58E
Callington England 18 C2 50 30N 4 18W
Calne England 16 A2 51 27N 2 00W
Calverton England 13 E2 53 03N 1 05W
Calvi France 50 J2 42 34N 8 44E
Cam r. England 17 D3 52 15N 0 11E
Camberley England 16 C2 51 21N 0 45W
CAMBODIA 71 C6/D6
Camborne England 18 B2 50 12N 5 19W
Cambrai France 50 F6 50 10N 3 14E
Cambrian Mountains
  Wales 14 C2 52 15N 3 45W
Cambridge England 17 D3 52 12N 0 07E
Cambridge USA 91 L4 38 34N 76 04W
Cambridgeshire co.
  England 16 C3 52 30N 0 00
Camel r. England 18 C2 50 31N 4 44W
Camelford England 18 C2C 50 37N 4 41W
CAMEROON 80 G3
Campbeltown Scotland 10 D2 55 26N 5 36W
Campina Grande Brazil 96 K12 7 15S 35 50W
Campinas Brazil 96 H9 22 54S 47 06W
Campobasso Italy 54 F4 41 33N 14 39E
Campsie Fells Scotland 11 E3 56 00N 4 15W
CANADA 88/89
Canadian r. USA 90 F4 35 00N 104 00W
Canary Islands Spain 80 A7/B7 28 30N 15 10W
Canaveral, Cape USA 91 K2 28 28N 80 28W
Canberra Australia 73 J3 35 18S 149 08E
Cancún Mexico 94 G4 21 09N 86 45W
Canisp mt. Scotland 9 D3 58 07N 5 03W
Canna i. Scotland 8 C2 57 05N 6 35W
Canna, Sound of
  Scotland 8 C2 57 00N 6 30W
Cannes France 50 H2 43 33N 7 00E
Cannich Scotland 9 E2 57 12N 4 46W
Cannington England 19 D3 51 09N 3 04E
Cannock England 15 D2 52 42N 2 01W
Cannock Chase
  England 15 D2/E2 52 45N 2 04W
Canonbie Scotland 11 G2 55 05N 2 57W
Canterbury England 17 E2 51 17N 1 05E
Canvey Island England 17 D2 51 32N 0 33E
Cap de la Hague France 50 D5 49 44N 1 56W
Cape Clear i. Rol 21 B1 51 30N 9 30W
Cape Cornwall England 18 B2 50 07N 5 44W
Capel i. Italy 16 C2 51 10N 0 20W
Cape Town RSA 82 C1 33 56S 18 28E
CAPE VERDE 102
Cape York Peninsula
  Australia 73 H8 12 30S 142 30E
Cap Ferret c. France 50 D3 44 42N 1 16W
Cappagh White Rol 21 C2 52 40N 8 10W
Cappamore Rol 21 C2 52 37N 8 20W
Cappoquin Rol 21 D2 52 08N 7 50W
Capri i. Italy 54 F4 40 33N 14 15E
Caprivi Strip Namibia 82 D4 17 30S 27 50E
Caracas Venezuela 96 D16 10 35N 66 56W
Carcassonne France 50 F2 43 13N 2 21E
Cardiff Wales 14 C1 51 30N 3 13W
Cardiff u.a. Wales 14 C1 51 32N 3 14W
Cardigan Wales 14 B2 52 06N 4 40W
Cardigan Bay Wales 14 B2 52 30N 4 30W
Cargenbridge Scotland 11 F2 55 05N 3 41W
Caribbean Sea
  Central America 95 J3/L3 15 00N 75 00W
Carlingford Rol 20 E4 54 02N 6 11W
Carlingford Lough
  NI/Rol 10 C1 54 05N 6 10W
Carlisle England 12 D3 54 54N 2 55W
Carlow Rol 21 E2 52 50N 6 55W
Carlow co. Rol 21 E2 52 40N 6 55W
Carloway Scotland 8 C3 58 17N 6 48W
Carlton in Lindrick
  England 13 E2 53 22N 1 06W
Carlton-on-Trent
  England 13 F2 53 10N 0 48W
Carluke Scotland 11 F2 55 45N 3 51W
Carmarthen Wales 14 B1 51 51N 4 20W
Carmarthen Bay Wales 14 B1 51 40N 4 30W
Carmarthenshire u.a.
  Wales 14 B1 51 55N 4 00W
Carmel Head Wales 14 B3 53 24N 4 34W
Carndonagh Rol 20 D5 55 15N 7 15W
Carn Eige mt. Scotland 9 D2 57 22N 5 07W
Carnforth England 12 D3 54 08N 2 46W
Carnlough NI 10 D1 54 59N 5 59W
Carnlough Bay NI 10 D1 54 59N 5 57W
Carnoustie Scotland 9 G2 56 30N 2 44W
Carnsore Point Rol 21 E2 52 10N 6 22W
Carpathians mts.
  Europe 53 J4/M3 49 00N 22 00E
Carpentras France 50 G3 44 03N 5 03E
Carradale Scotland 10 D2 55 35N 5 28E
Carrauntoohil mt. Rol 21 B2 52 00N 9 45W
Carrbridge Scotland 9 F2 57 17N 3 49W
Carrick Rol 20 C4 54 39N 8 38W
Carrickboy Rol 20 D3 53 37N 7 41W
Carrickfergus NI 10 D1 54 43N 5 49W
Carrickfergus district
  NI 10 D1 54 45N 5 50W
Carrickmacross Rol 20 E3 53 58N 5 49W
Carrick-on-Shannon
  Rol 20 C3 53 57N 8 05W
Carrick-on-Suir Rol 21 D2 52 21N 7 25W
Carrigaline Rol 21 C1 51 48N 8 24W
Carriganimmy Rol 21 B1 51 57N 9 02W

Carrigtohill Rol 21 C2 51 55N 8 16W
Carron r. Scotland 9 E2 57 53N 4 30W
Carronbridge Scotland 11 F2 55 16N 3 48W
Carrutherstown
  Scotland 11 F2 55 04N 3 24W
Carryduff NI 10 D1 54 31N 5 53W
Carsethorn Scotland 11 F1 54 55N 3 35W
Carsphairn Scotland 11 E2 55 13N 4 16W
Cartagena Colombia 96 B16 10 24N 75 33W
Cartagena Spain 51 E2 37 36N 0 59W
Carterton England 16 B2 51 45N 1 35W
Casablanca Morocco 80 C8 33 39N 7 35W
Cascade Range
  N. America 90 B5/6 48 00N 121 00W
Caserta Italy 54 F4 41 04N 14 20E
Cashel Rol 21 D2 52 31N 7 53W
Casper USA 90 E5 42 50N 106 20W
Caspian Sea Asia 57 G3/H3 41 00N 50 00E
Cassino Italy 54 E4 41 29N 13 50E
Castellane France 50 H2 43 50N 6 30E
Castellón de la Plana
  Spain 51 E3 39 59N 0 03W
Castelnaudary France 50 E2 43 18N 1 57E
Castelo Branco
  Portugal 51 B3 39 50N 7 30W
Castelvetrano Italy 54 E2 37 41N 12 47E
Castlebar Rol 20 B3 53 52N 9 17W
Castlebay Scotland 8 B1 56 57N 7 28W
Castleblaney Rol 20 E4 54 07N 6 44W
Castle Cary England 19 E3 51 06N 2 31W
Castlecomer Rol 21 D2 52 48N 7 12W
Castleconnell Rol 21 C2 52 43N 8 30W
Castledawson NI 10 C1 54 47N 6 33W
Castlederg NI 10 B1 54 42N 7 36W
Castledermot Rol 21 E2 52 55N 6 50W
Castle Donington
  England 15 E2 52 51N 1 19W
Castle Douglas
  Scotland 11 F1 54 57N 3 56W
Castlefin Rol 20 D4 54 47N 7 35W
Castleford England 13 E2 43 44N 1 21W
Castleisland Rol 21 B2 52 14N 9 27W
Castle Kennedy
  Scotland 10 E1 54 54N 4 57W
Castlemaine Harbour
  Rol 21 B2 52 08N 9 33W
Castlepollard Rol 20 D3 53 40N 7 17W
Castlerea Rol 20 C3 53 46N 8 29W
Castlereagh district NI 10 D1 54 35N 5 55W
Castletown Isle of Man 12 B3 54 04N 4 38W
Castletown Scotland 9 F3 58 35N 3 23W
Castletown Bearhaven
  Rol 21 B2 51 39N 9 55W
Castletownroche Rol 21 C2 52 10N 8 28W
Castlewellan NI 10 D1 54 16N 5 57W
Castres France 50 F2 43 36N 2 14E
Castrovillari Italy 54 G3 39 48N 16 12E
Catánia Italy 54 F2 37 31N 15 06E
Catanzaro Italy 55 G3 38 54N 16 36E
Caterham England 16 C2 51 17N 0 04W
Catlemartyr Rol 21 C1 51 55N 8 03W
Catrine Scotland 11 E2 55 30N 4 20W
Catshill tn. England 15 D2 52 22N 2 03W
Catterick Garrison
  England 13 E3 54 23N 1 40W
Caucasus mts. Asia 57 F3/G3 43 00N 43 00E
Cavan Rol 20 D3 53 58N 7 21W
Cavan co. Rol 20 D3/4 54 02N 7 10W
Cawood England 13 E2 53 50N 1 07W
Caxias Brazil 96 J13 4 53S 43 20W
Cayenne French Guiana 96 G14 4 55N 52 18W
Cedar Rapids tn. USA 91 H5 41 59N 91 39W
Cefalù Italy 54 F3 38 03N 14 03E
Cefn-mawr Wales 14 C2 52 59N 3 09W
Cellar Head Scotland 8 C3 58 25N 6 11W
Celle Germany 52 E6 52 37N 10 05E
Cemaes Wales 14 B3 53 24N 4 27W
Cemaes Head Wales 14 B2 53 10N 4 50W
CENTRAL AFRICAN
  REPUBLIC 81 J3/K3
Ceredigion u.a. Wales 14 B2/C2 52 14N 4 00W
Cergy-Pontoise France 50 F5 49 02N 2 04E
Cerignola Italy 54 F4 41 16N 15 54E
Cerne Abbas England 19 E2 50 49N 2 29W
Cesena Italy 54 E6 44 09N 12 15E
České Budějovice
  Czech Rep. 52 G4 48 58N 14 29E
Ceuta territory Spain 51 C1 35 53N 5 19W
Cévennes mts. France 51 F3 44 20N 3 30E
CHAD 81 J4/K4
Chadderton England 12 D2 53 33N 2 08W
Chad, Lake West Africa 81 G4 13 50N 14 00E
Chagford England 18 D2 50 41N 3 50W
Chalfont St. Giles
  England 16 C2 51 39N 0 35W
Chalkida Greece 55 K3 38 28N 23 36E
Chalkidikí p. Greece 55 K4 40 30N 23 00E
Chalmer r. England 17 D2 51 54N 0 21E
Châlons-sur-Marne
  France 50 G5 48 58N 4 22E
Chalon-sur-Saône
  France 50 G4 46 47N 4 51E
Chambéry France 50 G3 45 34N 5 55E
Chamonix France 50 H3 45 55N 6 52E
Champlain, Lake USA 93 F2 45 00N 73 00W
Chandigarh India 66 D6 30 44N 76 54E
Chang Jiang r. China 69 J4 31 00N 110 00E

Changsha China 69 K3 28 10N 113 00E
Chaniá Greece 55 L1 35 31N 24 01E
Channel Islands
  British Isles 19 E1 49 30N 2 30W
Chapel-en-le-Frith
  England 13 E2 53 20N 1 54W
Chapeltown England 13 E2 53 28N 1 27W
Chard England 19 E2 50 53N 2 58W
Charing England 17 D2 51 13N 0 48E
Charlbury England 16 B2 51 53N 1 29W
Charleroi Belgium 48 C3 50 25N 4 27E
Charleston USA 91 K4 38 23N 81 40W
Charlestown Rol 20 C3 53 58N 8 47W
Charlestown of
  Aberlour Scotland 9 F2 57 28N 3 14W
Charleville-Mézières
  France 50 G5 49 46N 4 43E
Charlotte USA 91 K4 35 03N 80 50W
Charlottesville USA 91 L4 38 02N 78 29W
Charlton Kings England 15 D2 51 53N 2 03W
Chartres France 50 E5 48 27N 1 30E
Châteaubriant France 50 D4 47 43N 1 22W
Châteaudun France 50 E5 48 04N 1 20E
Châteauroux France 50 E4 46 49N 1 41E
Château-Thierry
  France 50 F5 49 03N 3 24E
Châtellerault France 50 E4 46 49N 0 33E
Chatham England 17 D2 51 23N 0 32E
Chatham Canada 89 U2 42 24N 82 11W
Châtillon-sur-Seine
  France 50 G4 47 52N 4 35E
Chattanooga USA 91 J4 35 02N 85 18W
Chatteris England 16 D3 52 27N 0 03E
Chaumont France 50 G3 48 07N 5 08E
Cheadle Greater
  Manchester England 12 D2 53 24N 2 13W
Cheadle
  Staffordshire England 15 E2 52 59N 1 59W
Cheddar England 19 E3 51 17N 2 46W
Chelmsford England 17 D2 51 44N 0 28E
Chelyabinsk Russia 62 J8 55 12N 61 25E
Chemnitz Germany 52 F5 50 50N 12 55E
Chengdu China 69 H4 30 37N 104 06E
Chennai India 66 E2 13 05N 80 18E
Chepstow Wales 15 D1 51 39N 2 41W
Cherbourg France 50 D5 49 38N 1 37W
Cherkasy Ukraine 56 D4 49 27N 32 04E
Chernivtsi Ukraine 53 M4 48 19N 25 52E
Chertsey England 16 C2 51 23N 0 30W
Cherwell r. England 16 B2 51 55N 1 18W
Chesapeake USA 91 L4 36 45N 76 15W
Chesham England 16 C2 51 43N 0 38W
Cheshire co. England 12 D2 53 30N 2 30W
Cheshire Plain England 12 D2 53 12N 2 50W
Cheshunt England 16 C2 51 43N 0 02W
Chesil Beach England 19 E2 50 38N 2 50W
Chester England 12 D2 53 12N 2 54W
Chesterfield England 13 E2 53 15N 1 25W
Chester-le-Street
  England 13 E3 54 52N 1 34W
Cheviot Hills
  England/Scotland 11 G2 55 25N 2 30W
Cheviot, The mt.
  England 11 G2 55 29N 2 20W
Chew r. England 19 E3 51 21N 2 40W
Chiba Japan 70 D2 35 38N 140 07E
Chicago USA 91 J5 41 50N 87 45W
Chichester England 16 C1 50 50N 0 48W
Chieti Italy 54 F5 42 21N 14 10E
Chigwell England 16 D2 51 37N 0 05E
CHILE 96/97 C5/C8
Chiltern Hills England 16 B2/C2 51 40N 1 00W
Chimborazo mt.
  Ecuador 96 B13 1 29S 78 52W
CHINA 68/69
Chinnor England 16 C2 51 43N 0 56W
Chioggia Italy 54 E6 45 13N 12 17E
Chíos i. Greece 55 L3 38 00N 26 00E
Chippenham England 16 A2 51 28N 2 07W
Chipping Campden
  England 15 E2 52 03N 1 46W
Chipping Norton
  England 16 B2 51 56N 1 32W
Chipping Ongar
  England 17 D2 51 43N 0 15E
Chipping Sodbury
  England 15 D1 51 33N 2 24W
Chirk Wales 14 C2 52 66N 3 03W
Chisinău Moldova 81 P3 47 00N 28 50E
Chita Russia 63 P7 52 03N 113 35E
Chittagong Bangladesh 67 G4 22 20N 91 48E
Chobham England 16 C2 51 21N 0 37W
Cholet France 50 D4 47 04N 0 53W
Chongqing China 69 J3 29 30N 106 35E
Chorley England 12 D2 53 40N 2 38W
Chorleywood England 16 C2 51 40N 0 29W
Chornobyl Ukraine 53 Q5 51 17N 30 15E
Christchurch England 16 B1 50 44N 1 45W
Christchurch NZ 73 P2 43 32S 172 38E
Chudleigh England 18 D2 50 36N 3 45W
Chudskoye Ozero l.
  Russia/Estonia 56 C6 58 40N 27 30E
Chulmleigh England 18 D2 50 55N 3 52W

Chum r. England 15 D1 51 46N 1 58W
Chur Switz. 52 D3 46 52N 9 32E
Churchill Canada 89 S5 58 45N 94 00W
Church Stoke Wales 14 C2 52 32N 3 05W
Church Stretton
  England 14 D2 52 32N 2 49W
Chute-aux-Outardes
  Canada 93 G3 49 17N 67 57W
Cincinnati USA 91 K4 39 10N 83 30W
Cinderford England 15 D1 51 50N 2 29W
Cirencester England 15 E1 51 44N 1 59W
Citlaltépetl mt. Mexico 94 E3 19 00N 97 18W
City of Edinburgh u.a.
  Scotland 11 F2 55 55N 3 15W
City of Kingston upon
  Hull u.a. England 13 F2 53 45N 0 25W
Ciudad Bolívar
  Venezuela 96 E15 8 06N 63 36W
Ciudadela Spain 51 G3 40 00N 3 50E
Ciudad Guayana
  Venezuela 96 E15 8 22N 62 37W
Ciudad Juárez Mexico 94 C6 31 42N 106 29W
Ciudad Obregón
  Mexico 94 C5 27 28N 109 59W
Ciudad Real Spain 51 D3 38 59N 3 55W
Ciudad Rodrigo Spain 51 B4 40 36N 6 33W
Civitavecchia Italy 54 D5 42 05N 11 47E
Clachan Scotland 10 D2 55 45N 5 34W
Clackmannan Scotland 11 F3 56 05N 3 46W
Clackmannanshire u.a.
  Scotland 11 F3 56 10N 3 40W
Clacton on Sea
  England 17 E2 51 48N 1 09E
Clane Rol 20 E3 53 18N 6 41W
Claonaig Scotland 10 D2 55 46N 5 22W
Clara Rol 20 D3 53 20N 7 36W
Clare r. Rol 20 C3 53 20N 9 00W
Clare co. Rol 21 B2/C2 52 45N 9 00W
Clarecastle Rol 21 C2 52 49N 8 57W
Claregalway Rol 20 C3 53 21N 8 57W
Clare Island Rol 20 A3/B3 53 49N 10 00W
Claremorris Rol 20 C3 53 44N 9 00W
Clarksville USA 91 J4 36 31N 87 21W
Clashmore Rol 21 D2 52 00N 7 49W
Clay Cross England 13 E2 53 10N 1 24W
Claydon England 17 E3 52 06N 1 07E
Clay Head Isle of Man 12 B3 54 11N 4 25W
Clayton-le-Moors
  England 12 D2 53 47N 2 23W
Clayton West England 13 E2 53 36N 1 37W
Clear Island Rol 21 B1 51 26N 9 30W
Clearwater USA 91 K2 27 57N 82 48W
Cleator Moor England 12 C3 54 31N 3 30W
Cleckheaton England 12 E2 53 44N 1 43W
Cleethorpes England 13 F2 53 34N 0 02W
Cleobury Mortimer
  England 15 D2 52 23N 2 29W
Clermont-Ferrand
  France 50 F3 45 47N 3 05E
Clevedon England 19 E3 51 27N 2 51W
Cleveland USA 91 K5 43 15N 75 50W
Cleveland Hills England 13 E3 54 25N 1 15W
Cleveleys England 12 C2 53 53N 3 03W
Clew Bay Rol 20 B3 53 50N 9 50W
Clifden Rol 20 A3 53 29N 10 01W
Clinton USA 91 H5 41 51N 90 12W
Clisham mt. Scotland 8 C2 57 58N 6 50W
Clitheroe England 12 D2 53 53N 2 23W
Cloghan Rol 20 D3 53 13N 7 53W
Clogheen Rol 21 D2 52 17N 8 00W
Clogher NI 10 B1 54 25N 7 10W
Clogherhead Rol 20 E3 53 48N 6 15W
Clogher Head Rol 20 E3 53 48N 6 13W
Cloghjordan Rol 21 C2 52 57N 8 02W
Clonakilty Rol 21 C1 51 37N 8 54W
Clonakilty Bay Rol 21 C1 51 33N 8 50W
Clonaslee Rol 20 D3 53 09N 7 31W
Clondalkin Rol 20 E3 53 19N 6 24W
Clonee Rol 20 E3 53 25N 6 26W
Clones Rol 20 D4 54 11N 7 15W
Clonmany Rol 20 D5 55 16N 7 25W
Clonmel Rol 21 D2 52 21N 7 42W
Clonroche Rol 21 E2 52 27N 6 43W
Clontarf Rol 20 E3 52 02N 6 12W
Cloondara Rol 20 D3 53 43N 7 54W
Cloppenburg Germany 52 D6 52 52N 8 02E
Cloughton England 13 F3 53 20N 0 27W
Clovelly England 18 C2 51 00N 4 24W
Clowne England 13 E2 53 17N 1 15W
Cluj-Napoca Romania 53 L3 46 47N 23 37E
Clwydian Range Wales 14 C3 53 12N 3 20W
Clydach Wales 14 C1 51 42N 3 56W
Clyde r. Scotland 11 F2 55 40N 3 45W
Clydebank Scotland 11 E2 55 54N 4 24W
Clyde River tn. Canada 89 X8 70 30N 68 30W
Coachford Rol 21 C1 51 55N 8 47W
Coalisland NI 10 C1 54 32N 6 42W
Coalville England 13 E2 52 44N 1 20W
Coast Ranges USA 90 B4/6 41 00N 123 00W
Coatbridge Scotland 11 E2 55 52N 4 01W
Cobh Rol 21 C1 51 51N 8 17W
Coburg Germany 52 E5 50 16N 10 58E
Cochin India 66 D1 9 56N 76 15E
Cockburnspath
  Scotland 11 G2 55 56N 2 21W
Cockenzie Scotland 11 G2 55 58N 2 58W
Cockermouth England 12 C3 54 40N 3 21W

Place	Page	Grid	Lat.	Long.
Codsall England	15	D2	52 37N	2 12W
Coggeshall England	17	D2	51 52N	0 41E
Cognac France	50	D3	45 42N	0 19W
Coimbra Portugal	51	A4	40 12N	8 25W
Colchester England	17	D2	51 54N	0 54E
Coldingham Scotland	11	G2	55 53N	2 10W
Coldstream Scotland	11	G2	55 39N	2 15W
Coleford England	15	D1	51 48N	2 37W
Coleraine NI	10	C2	55 08N	6 40W
Coleraine *district* NI	10	C2	55 00N	6 40W
Coleshill England	15	E2	52 30N	1 42W
Colgrave Sound Scotland	7	D3	60 35N	0 55W
Colintraive Scotland	10	D2	55 56N	5 09W
Coll *i.* Scotland	8	C1	56 40N	6 35W
Collin Scotland	11	F2	55 04N	3 32W
Collon Rol	20	E3	53 47N	6 29W
Collooney Rol	20	C4	54 11N	8 29W
Colmar France	50	H5	48 05N	7 21E
Colmonell Scotland	10	E2	55 08N	4 55W
Coln *r.* England	15	E1	51 46N	1 50W
Colne England	12	D3	53 52N	2 09W
Colne *r.* England	17	D2	51 53N	0 45E
Cologne Germany	52	C5	50 56N	6 57E
COLOMBIA	96	C14		
Colombo Sri Lanka	66	D1	6 55N	79 52E
Colonsay *i.* Scotland	10	C3	56 05N	6 15W
Colorado *r.* N. America	90	D3	33 00N	114 00W
Colorado *state* USA	90	E4/F4	39 00N	106 00W
Colorado Springs USA	90	F4	38 50N	104 50W
Colsterworth England	15	F2	52 48N	0 37W
Coltishall England	17	E3	52 44N	1 22E
Columbia *r.* N. America	90	B6	46 00N	120 00W
Columbus USA	91	K5	39 59N	83 03W
Colwyn Bay *tn.* Wales	14	C3	53 18N	3 43W
Comacchio Italy	54	E6	44 42N	12 11E
Combe Martin England	18	C3	51 13N	4 02W
Comber NI	10	D1	54 33N	5 45W
Comeragh Mountains Rol	21	D2	52 19N	7 40W
Como Italy	54	C6	45 48N	9 05E
COMOROS	82	H5		
Compiègne France	50	F5	49 25N	2 50E
Comrie Scotland	9	F1	56 23N	4 00W
Conakry Guinea	80	B3	9 30N	13 43W
Concordia USA	91	G4	39 35N	97 39W
Condom France	50	E2	43 58N	0 23E
Conflans-Ste. Honorine France	50	F5	49 01N	2 09E
Cong Rol	20	B3	53 33N	9 16W
Congleton England	12	D2	53 10N	2 13W
CONGO	82	C7		
Congo *r.* Congo/CDR	82	J2	2 00S	17 00E
CONGO DEMOCRATIC REPUBLIC	82	D7/E7		
Congresbury England	19	E3	51 23N	2 48W
Conisbrough England	13	E2	53 29N	1 13W
Coniston England	12	C3	54 22N	3 05W
Coniston Water England	12	C3	54 20N	3 05W
Connah's Quay Wales	14	C3	53 13N	3 03W
Connecticut *state* USA	91	M5	41 00N	73 00W
Conon Bridge Scotland	9	E2	57 33N	4 26W
Consett England	13	E3	54 51N	1 49W
Constanța Romania	53	P2	44 12N	28 40E
Conwy Wales	14	C3	53 17N	3 50W
Conwy *r.* Wales	14	C3	53 10N	3 49W
Conwy *u.a.* Wales	14	C3	53 10N	3 40W
Cookham England	16	C2	51 34N	0 43W
Cook, Mount NZ	73	P2	43 36S	170 09E
Cookstown *district* NI	10	C1	54 35N	6 55W
Coolgrange Rol	21	D2	53 38N	7 08W
Cootehill Rol	20	D4	54 04N	7 05W
Copeland Island NI	10	D1	54 40N	5 31W
Copenhagen Denmark	49	D2	55 43N	12 34E
Copper Harbor USA	91	J6	47 28N	87 54W
Coppull England	12	D2	53 37N	2 40W
Coquet *r.* England	11	G2	55 20N	2 05W
Corbally Rol	20	B4	54 10N	9 03W
Corbeil-Essonnes France	50	F5	48 36N	2 29E
Corbridge England	12	D3	54 58N	2 01W
Corby England	15	F2	52 49N	0 32W
Cordillera Cantabrica *mts.* Spain	51	B5/C5	43 00N	5 30W
Córdoba Mexico	94	E3	18 55N	96 55W
Córdoba Spain	51	C2	37 53N	4 46W
Corfe Castle England	19	E2	50 38N	2 04W
Corfu Greece	55	H3	39 38N	19 55E
Corinth USA	91	J3	34 58N	88 30W
Cork Rol	21	C1	51 54N	8 28W
Cork *co.* Rol	21	C1	51 58N	8 40W
Cork Harbour Rol	21	C1	51 50N	8 10W
Corraun Peninsula Rol	20	B3	53 54N	9 51W
Corsewall Point Scotland	10	D2	55 00N	5 10W
Corsham England	16	A2	51 26N	2 11W
Corsica *i.* France	50	J1/J2	42 00N	9 00E
Corwen Wales	14	C2	52 59N	3 22W
Cosenza Italy	54	G3	39 17N	16 16E
COSTA RICA	95	H1/2		
CÔTE D'IVOIRE	80	C3/D3		
Cotgrave England	15	E3	52 54N	1 03W
Cotopaxi *mt.* Ecuador	96	B13	0 40S	78 28W
Cotswold Hills England	15	D1/E1	51 40N	2 10W
Cottbus Germany	52	G5	51 43N	14 21E
Cottenham England	17	D3	52 18N	0 09E
Coulommiers France	50	F5	48 49N	3 05E
Countesthorpe England	15	E2	52 33N	1 09W
Coupar Angus Scotland	9	F1	56 33N	3 17W
Courtown Rol	21	E2	52 38N	6 13W
Cove Bay *tn.* Scotland	9	G2	57 05N	2 05W
Coventry England	15	E2	52 25N	1 30W
Coverack England	18	B2	50 01N	5 05W
Cowbridge Wales	14	C1	51 28N	3 27W
Cowdenbeath Scotland	11	F3	56 07N	3 21W
Cowes England	16	B1	50 45N	1 18W
Cox's Bazar Bangladesh	67	G4	21 25N	91 59E
Craigavon NI	10	C1	54 28N	6 25W
Craigavon *district* NI	10	C1	54 30N	6 30W
Craigellachie Scotland	9	F2	57 29N	3 12W
Craighouse Scotland	10	D2	55 51N	5 57W
Craignure Scotland	8	D1	56 28N	5 42W
Crail Scotland	11	G3	56 16N	2 38W
Craiova Romania	53	L2	44 18N	23 47E
Cramlington England	13	E4	55 05N	1 35W
Cranleigh England	16	C2	51 09N	0 30W
Crathie Scotland	9	F2	57 02N	3 12W
Craughwell Rol	20	C3	53 14N	8 44W
Craven Arms England	14	D2	52 26N	2 50W
Crawford Scotland	11	F2	55 28N	3 40W
Crawley England	16	C2	51 07N	0 12W
Credenhill England	14	D2	52 05N	2 48W
Crediton England	18	D2	50 47N	3 39W
Cree *r.* Scotland	11	E2	55 00N	4 30W
Creeslough Rol	20	D5	55 07N	7 55W
Creetown Scotland	11	E1	54 54N	4 23W
Cregganbaun Rol	20	B3	53 42N	9 51W
Cremona Italy	54	D6	45 08N	10 01E
Creswell England	13	E2	53 16N	1 12W
Crewe England	12	D2	53 05N	2 27W
Crewkerne England	19	E2	50 53N	2 48W
Crianlarich Scotland	9	E1	56 23N	4 37W
Criccieth Wales	14	B2	52 55N	4 14W
Crickhowell Wales	14	C1	51 53N	3 09W
Cricklade England	16	B2	51 39N	1 51W
Crieff Scotland	9	F1	56 23N	3 52W
Crinan Scotland	10	D2	56 06N	5 35W
CROATIA	55	G6		
Crofton England	13	E2	53 39N	1 26W
Cromarty Scotland	9	E2	57 40N	4 02W
Cromarty Firth Scotland	9	E2	57 40N	4 20W
Cromer England	17	E3	52 56N	1 18E
Crook England	13	E3	54 43N	1 44W
Crookhaven Rol	21	B1	51 28N	9 43W
Crookstown Rol	21	C1	51 50N	8 50W
Croom Rol	21	C2	52 31N	8 43W
Crosby England	12	C2	53 30N	3 02W
Cross Fell *mt.* England	12	D3	54 43N	2 29W
Crossgar NI	10	D1	54 24N	5 45W
Cross Hands Wales	14	B1	51 48N	4 05W
Crosshaven Rol	21	C1	51 48N	8 17W
Crossmaglen NI	10	C1	54 05N	6 37W
Crossmolina Rol	20	B4	54 06N	9 20W
Crouch *r.* England	17	D2	51 38N	0 42E
Crowborough England	17	D2	51 03N	0 09E
Crowland England	16	C3	52 41N	0 11W
Crowle England	13	F2	53 37N	0 49W
Crowthorne England	16	C2	51 23N	0 49W
Croyde England	18	C3	51 08N	4 15W
Croydon England	16	C2	51 23N	0 06W
Crumlin NI	10	C1	54 37N	6 14W
Crummock Water England	12	C3	54 34N	3 18W
Crusheen Rol	21	C2	52 56N	8 53W
Crymych Wales	14	B1	51 59N	4 40W
CUBA	95	J4		
Cuckfield England	16	C2	51 00N	0 09W
Cudworth England	13	E2	53 35N	1 25W
Cuenca Spain	51	D4	40 04N	2 07W
Cuiabá Brazil	96	F10	15 32S	56 05W
Cuillin Hills Scotland	8	C2	57 15N	6 15W
Culdaff Rol	20	D5	55 17N	7 10W
Cullen Scotland	9	G2	57 41N	2 49W
Cullompton England	18	D2	50 52N	3 24W
Cullybackey NI	10	C1	54 53N	6 21W
Culm *r.* England	19	D2	50 55N	3 13W
Culross Scotland	11	F3	56 03N	3 35W
Cumbernauld Scotland	11	E2	55 57N	4 00W
Cumbria *co.* England	12	C3/D3	54 35N	3 00W
Cumbrian Mountains England	12	C3/D3	54 30N	3 00W
Cumnock Scotland	11	E2	55 27N	4 16W
Cuneo Italy	54	B6	44 24N	7 33E
Cupar Scotland	9	F1	56 19N	3 01W
Curitiba Brazil	96	H8	25 25S	49 25W
Cushendall NI	10	C2	55 04N	6 04W
Cushendun NI	10	C2	55 07N	6 03W
Cuxhaven Germany	52	D6	53 52N	8 42E
Cuzco Peru	96	C11	13 32S	1 57W
Cwmbran Wales	14	C1	51 39N	3 00W
CYPRUS	57	D1/D2		
CZECH REPUBLIC	52/53	G4/H4		
Częstochowa Poland	53	J5	50 49N	19 07E

D

Place	Page	Grid	Lat.	Long.
Dachau Germany	52	E4	48 15N	11 26E
Daingean Rol	20	D3	53 17N	7 17W
Dakar Senegal	80	A4	14 38N	17 27W
Dalbeattie Scotland	11	F1	54 56N	3 49W
Dalby Isle of Man	12	B3	54 10N	4 44W
Dalgety Bay *tn.* Scotland	11	F3	56 03N	3 18W
Dalian China	69	M5	38 53N	121 37E
Dalkeith Scotland	11	F2	55 51N	3 04W
Dallas USA	91	G3	32 47N	96 48W
Dalmally Scotland	9	E1	56 24N	4 58W
Dalmellington Scotland	11	E2	55 19N	4 24W
Dalry Scotland	11	E2	55 43N	4 44W
Dalton USA	91	K3	34 46N	84 59W
Dalton-in-Furness England	12	C3	54 09N	3 11W
Dalwhinnie Scotland	9	E1	56 56N	4 14W
Damascus Syria	64	C5	33 30N	36 19E
Danbury England	17	D2	51 44N	0 33E
Danville USA	91	J5	40 09N	87 37W
Dardanelles *sd.* Turkey	57	C3	40 08N	26 10E
Dar es Salaam Tanzania	83	F1	6 51S	39 18E
Darfield England	13	E2	53 34N	1 22W
Darjiling India	67	F5	27 02N	88 20E
Darling *r.* Australia	73	H4	30 30S	144 00E
Darlington England	13	E3	54 31N	1 34W
Darlington *u.a.* England	13	E3	54 30N	1 30W
Darmstadt Germany	52	D4	49 52N	8 39E
Dart *r.* England	18	D2	50 30N	3 50W
Dartford England	17	D2	51 27N	0 13E
Dartmouth England	18	D2	50 21N	3 35W
Darton England	13	E2	53 36N	1 32W
Darvel Scotland	11	E2	55 37N	4 18W
Darwen England	12	D2	53 42N	2 28W
Darwin Australia	72	F8	12 23S	130 44E
Daugava *r.* Europe	49	F2	56 45N	24 30E
Daugavpils Latvia	49	G2	55 52N	26 31E
Davenport USA	91	H5	41 32N	90 36W
Daventry England	15	E2	52 16N	1 09W
Davis Strait Canada/Greenland	89	Y7/Z6	69 00N	60 00W
Davos Switz.	52	D3	46 47N	9 50E
Dawley England	15	D2	52 40N	2 28W
Dawlish England	18	D2	50 35N	3 28W
Dawros Head Rol	20	C4	54 49N	8 34W
Dead Sea Israel/Jordan	64	C5	31 35N	35 30E
Deal England	17	E2	51 14N	1 24E
Deel *r.* Rol	21	C2	52 32N	8 57W
Death Valley USA	90	C4	36 00N	117 00W
Deben *r.* England	17	E3	52 02N	1 25E
Debenham England	17	E3	52 13N	1 11E
Debrecen Hungary	53	K3	47 30N	21 37E
Decatur USA	91	J4	39 51N	89 32W
Deccan *plat.* India	66	D3	18 00N	78 00E
Deddington England	16	B2	51 59N	1 19W
Dee *r.* England/Wales	14	C3	53 15N	3 10W
Dee *r.* Rol	20	E3	53 49N	6 38W
Dee *r.* Aberdeenshire Scotland	9	G2	57 05N	2 10W
Deer Sound Scotland	7	B1	58 57N	2 47W
Delaware *state* USA	91	L4	39 00N	75 00W
Delft Neths	48	C5	52 00N	4 22E
Delfzijl Neths	48	E6	53 19N	6 56E
Delhi India	66	D5	28 40N	77 14E
Delvin Rol	20	D3	53 37N	7 05W
Denbigh Wales	14	C3	53 11N	3 25W
Denbighshire *u.a.* Wales	14	C3	53 05N	3 30W
Denby Dale *tn.* England	13	E2	53 35N	1 38W
Den Helder Neths	48	C5	52 58N	4 46E
Denholme England	13	E2	53 47N	1 55W
Denison USA	91	G3	33 47N	96 34W
Denizli Turkey	57	C2	37 46N	29 05E
DENMARK	49	C2/D2		
Denny Scotland	11	E3	56 02N	3 55W
Denpasar Indonesia	71	F2	8 40S	115 14E
Denton England	12	D2	53 27N	2 07W
Denver USA	90	E4	39 45N	105 00W
De Panne Belgium	48	A4	51 06N	2 35E
Derby England	15	E2	52 55N	1 30W
Derby City *u.a.* England	15	E2	52 50N	1 30W
Derbyshire *co.* England	13	E2	52 55N	1 30W
Derg *r.* NI	10	B1	54 45N	7 25W
Derriana Lough Rol	21	A1/B1	51 54N	10 01W
Derrybrien Rol	21	C3	53 04N	8 37W
Dersingham England	17	D3	52 51N	0 30E
Derwent *r.* North Yorkshire England	13	F3	54 10N	0 35W
Derwent *r.* Cumbria England	12	C3	54 40N	3 30W
Derwent *r.* Derbyshire England	13	E2	53 15N	1 30W
Derwent *r.* Durham England	13	D3	54 50N	2 05W
Derwent Reservoir England	13	E2	53 25N	1 45W
Derwent Water England	12	C3	54 35N	3 09W
Desborough England	15	F2	52 27N	0 49W
Desierto de Atacama Chile	96	C9/D10	22 30S	70 00W
Des Moines USA	91	H5	41 35N	93 35W
Dessau Germany	52	F5	51 51N	12 15E
Detroit USA	91	K5	42 23N	83 05W
Deveron *r.* Scotland	9	G2	57 35N	2 35W
Devil's Bridge Wales	14	C2	52 23N	3 51W
Devil's Lake *tn.* USA	91	G6	48 03N	98 57W
Devizes England	16	B2	51 22N	1 59W
Devon *co.* England	18	D2	50 45N	3 50W
Dewsbury England	13	E2	53 42N	1 37W
Dezfül Iran	65	E5	32 23N	48 28E
Dhaka Bangladesh	67	G4	23 42N	90 22E
Didcot England	16	B2	51 37N	1 15W
Dieppe France	50	E5	49 55N	1 05E
Digby Canada	89	X2	44 37N	65 47W
Digne-les-Bains France	50	H3	44 05N	6 14E
Dijon France	50	G4	47 20N	5 02E
Dili East Timor	71	H2	8 33S	125 34E
Dinan France	50	C5	48 27N	2 02W
Dinara Planina *mts.* Europe	55	G5	44 00N	17 00E
Dinard France	50	C5	48 38N	2 03W
Dinas-Mawddwy Wales	14	C2	52 43N	3 41W
Dinas Powys Wales	14	C1	51 25N	3 14W
Dingle Rol	21	A2	52 08N	10 15W
Dingle Bay Rol	21	A2	52 05N	10 15W
Dingle Peninsula Rol	21	A2	52 12N	10 15W
Dingwall Scotland	9	E2	57 35N	4 29W
Dinnington England	13	E2	53 22N	1 12W
Diss England	17	E3	52 23N	1 06W
DJIBOUTI	81	P4		
Djibouti Djibouti	81	P4	11 35N	43 11E
Dnestr *r.* Ukraine	57	C4	48 00N	27 30E
Dnipro *r.* Europe	57	D4	47 30N	33 00E
Dobrich Bulgaria	55	M5	43 34N	27 51E
Dochart *r.* Scotland	9	E1	56 25N	4 25W
Docking England	17	D3	52 55N	0 38E
Dodekánisos *is.* Greece	55	M2	37 00N	26 00E
Dodman Point England	18	C2	50 13N	4 48W
Dodoma Tanzania	83	D1	6 10S	35 40E
Doha Qatar	65	F4	25 15N	51 36E
Dôle France	50	G4	47 05N	5 30E
Dolgellau Wales	14	C2	52 44N	3 53W
Dollar Scotland	11	F3	56 09N	3 41W
Dombas Norway	49	C3	62 05N	9 07E
DOMINICA	94	Q8		
DOMINICAN REPUBLIC	95	L3		
Don *r.* England	13	E2	53 37N	1 02W
Don *r.* Russia	62	G7	50 00N	41 00E
Don *r.* Scotland	9	F2	57 15N	2 40W
Donabate Rol	20	E3	53 30N	6 09W
Donaghadee NI	10	D1	54 39N	5 33W
Donau *r.* Europe	52	D4	48 00N	16 00E
Doncaster England	13	E2	53 32N	1 07W
Donegal Rol	20	C4	54 39N	8 07W
Donegal *co.* Rol	20	C4	54 55N	8 00W
Donegal Bay Rol	20	C4	54 30N	8 30W
Donegal Point Rol	21	B2	52 44N	9 38W
Donets'k Ukraine	56	E4	48 00N	37 50E
Donington England	15	F2	52 53N	2 25W
Donoughmore Rol	21	C1	51 57N	8 45W
Dooagh Rol	20	A3	53 58N	10 07W
Doon *r.* Scotland	11	E2	55 20N	4 30W
Doonbeg Rol	21	B2	52 44N	9 32W
Dorchester England	19	E2	50 43N	2 26W
Dorchester England	16	B2	51 39N	1 10W
Dordogne *r.* France	50	E3	44 55N	0 30E
Dordrecht Neths	48	C4	51 48N	4 40E
Dorking England	16	C2	51 14N	0 20W
Dornie Scotland	8	D2	57 17N	5 31W
Dornoch Scotland	9	E2	57 52N	4 02W
Dornoch Firth Scotland	9	E2/F2	57 55N	3 55W
Dorset *co.* England	19	E2	50 50N	2 20W
Dortmund Germany	52	C5	51 32N	7 27E
Douai France	50	F6	50 22N	3 05E
Douala Cameroon	80	F2	4 04N	9 43E
Douglas Isle of Man	12	B3	54 09N	4 29W
Douglas Scotland	11	F2	55 33N	3 51W
Douglas *r.* England	12	D2	53 38N	2 48W
Doulus Head Rol	21	A1	51 57N	10 19W
Doune Scotland	11	E3	56 11N	4 04W
Douro *r.* Portugal/Spain	51	B4	41 00N	8 30W
Dove *r.* England	13	E2	53 05N	1 55W
Dove Dale *v.* England	13	E2	53 10N	1 45W
Dover England	17	E2	51 08N	1 19E
Dover USA	91	L4	39 10N	75 32W
Dover, Strait of English Channel	17	E1/E2	51 00N	1 20W
Dovrefjell *mts.* Norway	49	C3	62 15N	9 10E
Down *district* NI	10	D1	54 25N	5 55W
Downham Market England	17	D3	52 36N	0 23E
Downpatrick NI	10	D1	54 20N	5 43W
Downpatrick Head Rol	20	B4	54 20N	9 15W
Downton England	16	B2	51 00N	1 44W
Dowra Rol	20	C4	54 11N	8 02W
Draguignan France	50	H2	43 32N	6 28E
Drakensberg *mts.* RSA	82	E1/E2	30 00S	28 00E
Drammen Norway	49	C2	59 45N	10 15E
Draperstown NI	10	C1	54 48N	6 47W
Drava *r.* Europe	53	H3	46 00N	18 00E
Dreghorn Scotland	11	E2	55 37N	4 37W
Dresden Germany	52	F5	51 03N	13 45E
Drimoleague Rol	21	B1	51 40N	9 15W
Drobeta-Turnu-Severin Romania	53	L2	44 36N	22 39E
Drogheda Rol	20	E3	53 43N	6 21W
Droichead Nua Rol	20	E3	53 11N	6 45W
Droitwich England	15	D2	52 16N	2 09W
Dromcolliher Rol	21	C2	52 20N	8 55W
Dromore NI	10	B1	54 31N	7 28W

Dromore NI 10 C1 54 25N 6 09W
Dromore West RoI 20 C4 54 15N 8 53W
Dronfield England 13 E2 53 19N 1 27W
Drongan Scotland 11 E2 55 29N 4 30W
Drummore Scotland 10 E1 54 42N 4 54W
Drumnadrochit Scotland 9 E2 57 20N 4 30W
Drumshanbo RoI 20 C4 54 03N 8 02W
Drumsna RoI 20 D3 53 56N 8 00W
Dryden Canada 89 S3 49 48N 92 48W
Dubai UAE 65 G4 25 14N 55 17E
Dublin RoI 20 E3 53 20N 6 15W
Dublin co. RoI 20 E3 53 25N 6 10W
Dublin USA 91 K3 32 31N 82 54W
Dublin Bay RoI 20 E3 53 20N 6 05W
Dubrovnik Croatia 55 H5 42 40N 18 07E
Duddon r. England 12 C3 54 20N 3 20W
Dudley England 15 D2 52 30N 2 05W
Dudley England 13 E4 55 10N 1 20W
Duero r. Spain/Portugal 51 B4 41 25N 6 30W
Duffield England 15 E2 52 59N 1 29W
Duisburg Germany 52 C5 51 26N 6 45E
Duleek RoI 20 E3 53 39N 6 25W
Dulnain r. Scotland 9 F2 57 20N 3 57W
Duluth USA 91 H6 46 45N 92 10W
Dulverton England 18 D3 51 03N 3 33W
Dumbarton Scotland 11 E2 55 57N 4 35W
Dumfries Scotland 11 F2 55 04N 3 37W
Dumfries and Galloway u.a. Scotland 11 E2/F2 55 10N 4 10W
Duna r. Hungary 53 J2/J3 46 00N 19 00E
Dunany Point RoI 20 E3 53 51N 6 14W
Dunav r. Europe 55 K5 45 00N 20 00E
Dunbar Scotland 11 G2 56 00N 2 31W
Dunbeath Scotland 9 F3 58 15N 3 25W
Dunblane Scotland 11 F3 56 12N 3 59W
Dunboyne RoI 20 E3 53 25N 6 29W
Duncannon RoI 21 E2 51 13N 6 55W
Duncansby Head Scotland 9 F3 58 39N 3 01W
Dunchurch England 15 E2 52 20N 1 16W
Dundalk RoI 20 E4 54 01N 6 25W
Dundalk Bay RoI 20 E3 53 55N 6 15W
Dundee Scotland 9 G1 56 28N 3 00W
Dundee City u.a. Scotland 9 F1/G1 56 30N 2 55W
Dundonald NI 10 D1 54 36N 5 48W
Dundrennan Scotland 11 F1 54 49N 3 57W
Dundrum RoI 20 E3 53 17N 6 15W
Dundrum Bay NI 10 D1 54 13N 5 45W
Dunedin NZ 73 P1 45 53S 170 30E
Dunfermline Scotland 11 F3 56 04N 3 29W
Dungannon NI 10 C1 54 31N 6 46W
Dungannon district NI 10 B1/C1 54 30N 7 05W
Dungarvan RoI 21 D2 52 05N 7 37W
Dungarvan Harbour RoI 21 D2 52 04N 7 35W
Dungeness c. England 17 D1 50 55N 0 58E
Dungiven NI 10 C1 54 55N 6 55W
Dunglow RoI 20 C4 54 57N 8 22W
Dungourney RoI 21 C1 51 58N 8 05W
Dunholme England 13 F2 53 18N 0 29W
Dunkeld Scotland 9 F1 56 34N 3 35W
Dunkerque France 50 F6 51 02N 2 23E
Dunkery Beacon sum. England 18 D3 51 11N 3 35W
Dún Laoghaire RoI 20 E3 53 17N 6 08W
Dunleer RoI 20 E3 53 50N 6 24W
Dunmanus Bay RoI 21 B1 51 30N 9 50W
Dunmanway RoI 21 B1 51 43N 9 06W
Dunmore RoI 20 C3 53 37N 8 44W
Dunmurry NI 10 C1 54 33N 6 00W
Dunnamaggan RoI 21 D2 52 29N 7 17W
Dunnet Scotland 9 F3 58 37N 3 21W
Dunnet Bay Scotland 9 F3 58 36N 3 21W
Dunnett Head Scotland 9 F3 58 40N 3 25W
Dunoon Scotland 10 E2 55 57N 4 56W
Duns Scotland 11 G2 55 47N 2 20W
Dunshaughlin RoI 20 E3 53 31N 6 33W
Dunstable England 16 C2 51 53N 0 32W
Dunvegan Scotland 8 C2 57 26N 6 35W
Dunvegan Head Scotland 8 C2 57 30N 6 42W
Durban RSA 82 F2 29 53S 31 00E
Durham England 13 E3 54 47N 1 34W
Durham USA 91 L4 36 00N 78 54W
Durlston Head England 19 E2 50 35N 1 57W
Durness Scotland 8 E3 58 33N 4 45W
Durrington England 16 B2 51 12N 1 48W
Durrow RoI 21 D2 52 51N 7 23W
Dursey Head RoI 21 A1 51 20N 10 10W
Dursey Island RoI 21 A1 51 36N 10 12W
Dursley England 15 D1 51 42N 2 21W
Dushanbe Tajikistan 62 J4 38 38N 68 51E
Düsseldorf Germany 52 C5 51 13N 6 47E
Dyce Scotland 9 G2 57 12N 2 11W
Dyfi r. Wales 14 C2 52 38N 3 50W
Dyke Scotland 9 F2 57 35N 3 40W
Dymchurch England 17 D2 51 02N 1 00E
Dysart Scotland 11 F3 56 08N 3 08W

E

Eaglescliffe England 13 E3 54 31N 1 22W
Eaglesfield Scotland 11 F2 55 04N 3 12W
Ealing England 16 C2 51 31N 0 18W
Earby England 12 D2 53 56N 2 08W
Earls Colne England 17 D2 51 56N 0 42E
Earl Shilton England 15 E2 52 35N 1 18W
Earlston Scotland 11 G2 55 39N 2 40W
Earn r. Scotland 9 F1 56 20N 3 40W
Easington England 13 E3 54 47N 1 21W
Easington England 13 G2 53 40N 0 07E
Easingwold England 13 E3 54 07N 1 11W
Easky RoI 20 C4 54 17N 8 58W
East Ayrshire u.a. Scotland 11 E2 55 30N 4 30W
Eastbourne England 17 D1 50 46N 0 17E
East Burra i. Scotland 7 C3 60 04N 1 19W
East Cowes England 16 B1 50 45N 1 16W
East Dean England 17 D1 50 45N 0 13E
East Dereham England 17 D3 52 41N 0 56E
East Dunbartonshire u.a. Scotland 11 E2 55 55N 4 15W
Eastern Ghats mts. India 66 D2/E3 15 00N 80 00E
Eastfield England 13 F3 54 15N 0 25W
East Grand Forks USA 92 A3 47 56N 96 59W
East Ilsley England 16 B2 51 33N 1 17W
Eastington England 15 D1 51 45N 2 20W
East Kilbride Scotland 11 E2 55 46N 4 10W
East Leake England 15 E2 52 50N 1 11W
East Linton Scotland 11 G2 55 59N 2 39W
East Loch Tarbert Scotland 8 C2 57 53N 6 48W
East Lothian u.a. Scotland 11 G2 55 56N 2 42W
Eastmain Canada 89 V4 52 10N 78 30W
East Markham England 13 F2 53 15N 0 54W
Easton England 19 E2 50 32N 2 26W
East Renfrewshire u.a. Scotland 11 E2 55 45N 4 25E
East Riding of Yorkshire u.a. England 13 F2 53 54N 0 40W
Eastriggs Scotland 11 F1 54 59N 3 10W
East Suisnish Scotland 8 C2 57 21N 6 03W
East Sussex co. England 17 D1 50 55N 0 10E
EAST TIMOR 71 H2
East Wittering England 16 C1 50 41N 0 53W
Eastwood England 13 E2 53 01N 1 18W
Eaton Socon England 16 C2 52 13N 0 18W
Ebbw Vale Wales 14 C1 51 47N 3 12W
Ebro r. Spain 51 D5 43 00N 4 30W
Ecclefechan Scotland 11 F2 55 03N 3 17W
Eccles England 12 D2 53 29N 2 21W
Eccleshall England 15 D2 52 52N 2 15W
Eckington England 13 E2 53 19N 1 21W
ECUADOR 96 B13
Eday i. Scotland 7 B2 59 11N 2 47W
Eday Sound Scotland 7 B2 59 10N 2 43W
Ede Neths 48 D5 52 03N 5 40E
Eden r. Cumbria England 12 D3 54 50N 2 45W
Eden r. Kent England 16 C2 51 12N 0 06E
Eden r. Scotland 11 F3 56 20N 3 15W
Eden USA 91 L4 36 30N 79 46W
Edenbridge England 16 C2 51 12N 0 04E
Edenderry RoI 20 D3 53 21N 7 35W
Eden Mouth Scotland 9 G2 56 22N 2 36W
Edessa Greece 55 K4 40 48N 22 03E
Edgeworthstown RoI 20 D3 53 42N 7 36W
Edinburgh Scotland 11 F2 55 57N 3 13W
Edmonton Canada 88 N4 53 34N 113 25W
Eeklo Belgium 48 B4 51 11N 3 34E
Eems r. Neths/Germany 48 E6 53 25N 6 55E
Efyrnwy r. Wales 14 C2 52 40N 3 15W
Egham England 16 C2 51 26N 0 34W
Egilsay i. Scotland 7 B2 59 09N 2 56W
Eglinton NI 10 C1 55 01N 7 11W
Egremont England 12 C3 54 29N 3 33W
EGYPT 81 L7/M7
Eigg i. Scotland 8 C1 56 55N 6 10W
Eindhoven Neths 48 D4 51 26N 5 30E
Elat Israel 64 B4 29 33N 34 57E
Elâzığ Turkey 57 E2 38 41N 39 14E
Elbe est. Europe 52 E6 54 00N 9 00E
Elbeuf France 50 E5 49 17N 1 01E
Elbląg Poland 53 J7 54 10N 19 25E
El'brus mt. Russia 57 F3 43 21N 42 29E
Elburg Neths 48 D5 52 27N 5 50E
Elburz Mountains Iran 65 F6 36 15N 51 00E
Elche Spain 51 E3 38 16N 0 41W
El Dorado USA 91 H3 33 12N 92 40W
Elgin Scotland 9 F2 57 39N 3 20W
Elgol Scotland 8 C2 57 09N 6 06W
Elie Scotland 11 G3 56 12N 2 50W
Elland England 13 E2 53 41N 1 50W
Ellen r. England 12 C3 54 45N 3 25W
Ellesmere England 14 D2 52 54N 2 54W
Ellesmere Island Canada 89 U9/X10 77 30N 82 30W
Ellesmere Port England 12 D2 53 17N 2 54W
Ellon Scotland 9 G2 57 22N 2 05W
El Minya Egypt 81 M7 28 06N 30 45E
Elmira USA 91 L5 42 06N 76 50W
El Paso USA 90 E3 31 45N 106 30W

EL SALVADOR 94 G2
Ely England 17 D3 52 24N 0 16E
Elyria USA 91 K5 41 22N 82 06W
Embleton England 11 H2 55 30N 1 37W
Emden Germany 52 C6 53 23N 7 13E
Emmeloord Neths 48 D5 52 43N 5 46E
Emmen Neths 48 E5 52 47N 6 55E
Emsworth England 16 C1 50 51N 0 56W
Emyvale RoI 20 E4 54 21N 6 58W
Enard Bay Scotland 8 D3 58 10N 5 25W
Enfield England 16 C2 51 39N 0 05W
England country UK 6 53 00N 2 00W
English Channel UK/France 6 50 00N 2 00W
Enid USA 91 G4 36 24N 97 54W
Ennis RoI 21 C2 52 50N 8 59W
Enniscorthy RoI 21 E2 52 30N 6 34W
Enniskean RoI 21 C1 51 44N 8 56W
Enniskerry RoI 20 E3 53 12N 6 10W
Enniskillen NI 10 B1 54 21N 7 38W
Ennistimon RoI 21 B2 52 57N 9 15W
Enschede Neths 48 E5 52 13N 6 55E
Entebbe Uganda 83 C5 0 04N 32 27E
Épernay France 50 F5 49 02N 3 58E
Epping England 17 D2 51 42N 0 08E
Epsom England 16 C2 51 20N 0 16W
Epworth England 13 F2 53 31N 0 50W
EQUATORIAL GUINEA 80 F2/G2
Erfurt Germany 52 E5 50 58N 11 02E
Erie USA 91 K5 42 07N 80 05W
Erie, Lake Canada/USA 93 D2 42 15N 81 00W
Eriskay i. Scotland 8 B2 57 05N 7 10W
ERITREA 81 P4 14 40N 40 15E
Errigal Mountain RoI 20 C5 55 02N 8 07W
Errill RoI 21 D2 52 52N 7 40W
Erris Head RoI 20 A4 54 20N 10 00W
Erzgebirge mts. Europe 52 F5 50 00N 13 00E
Erzurum Turkey 57 F2 39 57N 41 17E
Esbjerg Denmark 49 C2 55 20N 8 20E
Escondido USA 90 C3 33 07N 117 05W
Esfahān Iran 65 F5 32 41N 51 41E
Esha Ness c. Scotland 7 C3 60 29N 1 37W
Esher England 16 C2 51 22N 0 22W
Esk r. North Yorkshire England 13 F3 54 25N 0 40W
Esk r. Cumbria England 12 C3 54 25N 3 10W
Esk r. Scotland/England 11 F2 55 10N 3 05W
Eskişehir Turkey 57 D2 39 46N 30 30E
Espoo Finland 49 F3 60 10N 24 40E
Essen Germany 52 C5 51 27N 6 57E
Essex co. England 17 D2 51 46N 0 30E
Eston England 13 E3 54 34N 1 07W
ESTONIA 49 G2
Estremoz Portugal 51 B3 38 50N 7 35W
Étampes France 50 F5 48 26N 2 10E
ETHIOPIA 81 N3/P3
Etna, Mount Italy 54 F2 37 45N 15 00E
Eton England 16 C2 51 31N 0 37W
Ettrick Scotland 11 F2 55 25N 3 05W
Ettrickbridge Scotland 11 G2 55 30N 2 58W
Eugene USA 90 B5 44 03N 123 04W
Euphrates r. Asia 64 D5 34 40N 42 00E
Europoort Neths 48 C4 51 55N 4 10E
Evanton Scotland 9 E2 57 40N 4 20W
Evercreech England 19 E3 51 09N 2 30W
Everest, Mount China/Nepal 67 F5 27 59N 86 56E
Evesham England 15 E2 52 06N 1 56W
Evora Portugal 51 B3 38 46N 7 41W
Evreux France 50 E5 49 03N 1 11E
Evvoia i. Greece 55 L3 38 00N 24 00E
Exe r. England 18 D3 51 08N 3 36
Exeter England 18 D2 50 43N 3 31W
Exmouth England 18 D2 50 37N 3 25W
Eyam England 13 E2 53 24N 1 42W
Eye England 17 E3 52 19N 1 09E
Eyemouth Scotland 11 G2 55 25N 2 06W
Eye Peninsula Scotland 8 C3 58 10N 6 10W
Eyeries RoI 21 B1 51 41N 9 57W
Eynsham England 16 B2 51 46N 1 28W

F

Fairbourne Wales 14 B2 52 41N 4 03W
Fair Head NI 10 C2 55 15N 6 10W
Fair Isle Scotland 7 C2 59 32N 1 38W
Fairlight England 17 D1 50 52N 0 38E
Fairmont USA 91 K4 39 28N 80 08W
Faisalabad Pakistan 66 C6 31 25N 73 09E
Fakenham England 17 D3 52 50N 0 51E
Fal r. England 18 C2 50 16N 4 56W
Falcarragh RoI 20 C5 55 08N 8 06W
Falfurrias USA 91 G2 27 17N 98 10W
Falkirk Scotland 11 F2 55 59N 3 48W
Falkirk u.a. Scotland 11 F2 55 59N 3 45W
Falkland Scotland 11 F3 56 15N 3 13W
Falkland Islands S Atlantic Ocean 97 E2/F2 52 30S 60 00W
Falmouth England 18 B2 50 08N 5 04W
Fanad Head RoI 20 D5 55 17N 7 38W
Fane r. RoI 20 E3 53 58N 6 28W
Fano Italy 54 E5 43 51N 13 01E
Fareham England 16 B1 50 51N 1 10W
Fargo USA 91 G6 46 52N 96 49W
Faringdon England 16 B2 51 40N 1 35W

Farnborough England 16 C2 51 17N 0 46W
Farne Islands England 11 H2 55 38N 1 38W
Farnham England 16 C2 51 13N 0 49W
Farnham Royal England 16 C2 51 33N 0 38W
Farnworth England 12 D2 53 33N 2 24W
Faro Portugal 51 B2 37 01N 7 56W
Farranfore RoI 21 B2 52 10N 9 33W
Farrar r. Scotland 9 E2 57 15N 4 41W
Faughan r. NI 10 B1 54 54N 7 09W
Faversham England 17 D2 51 20N 0 53E
Fawley England 16 B1 50 49N 1 20W
Feale r. RoI 21 B2 52 26N 9 22W
Featherstone England 13 E2 53 41N 1 21W
Fécamp France 50 E5 49 45N 0 23E
FEDERATED STATES OF MICRONESIA 100 F8
Feldkirch Austria 52 D3 47 15N 9 38E
Felixstowe England 17 E2 51 58N 1 20E
Felling tn. England 13 E3 54 57N 1 33W
Felton England 11 H2 55 18N 1 42W
Feltwell England 17 D3 52 29N 0 33E
Fens, The England 16 C3/D3 52 45N 0 05E
Feolin Ferry tn. Scotland 10 C2 55 51N 6 06W
Ferbane RoI 20 D3 53 15N 7 49W
Fermanagh district NI 10 B1 54 25N 7 45W
Fermo Italy 54 E5 43 09N 13 44E
Fermoy RoI 21 C2 52 08N 8 16W
Ferndown England 19 F2 50 48N 1 55W
Ferns RoI 21 E2 52 35N 6 30W
Ferrara Italy 54 E6 44 50N 11 38E
Ferryhill tn. England 13 E3 54 41N 1 33W
Fès Morocco 80 C8 34 05N 5 00W
Fethaland, Point of Scotland 7 C3 60 35N 1 18W
Fethard RoI 21 D2 52 27N 7 41W
Fethard RoI 21 E2 52 11N 6 50W
Fetlar i. Scotland 7 D3 60 37N 0 52W
Fettercairn Scotland 9 G1 56 51N 2 34W
Ffestiniog Wales 14 C2 52 58N 3 55W
Fforest Fawr Wales 14 C1 51 50N 3 40W
Ffostrasol Wales 14 B2 52 06N 4 23W
Fiddown RoI 21 D2 52 20N 7 19W
Fife u.a. Scotland 11 G3 56 10N 3 00W
Fife Ness c. Scotland 11 G3 56 17N 2 35W
Figeac France 50 F3 44 32N 2 01E
Figueira da Foz Portugal 51 A4 40 09N 8 51W
Figueres Spain 51 G5 42 16N 2 57E
FIJI 100 H6
Filey England 13 F3 54 12N 0 17W
Filton England 15 D1 51 31N 2 35W
Findhorn r. Scotland 9 F2 57 25N 3 55W
Findhorn Scotland 9 F2 57 39N 3 36W
Findhorn Bay Scotland 9 F2 57 39N 3 36W
Findochty Scotland 9 G2 57 42N 2 55W
Finglas RoI 20 E3 53 24N 6 18W
FINLAND 49 G3
Finland, Gulf of Finland 49 F2/G2 59 40N 23 30E
Finnea RoI 20 D3 53 47N 7 23W
Fintagh Bay RoI 20 C4 54 35N 8 33W
Fintona NI 10 B1 54 30N 7 19W
Fintown RoI 20 C4 54 52N 8 07W
Fionn Loch Scotland 8 D2 57 45N 5 25W
Fionnphort Scotland 8 C1 56 19N 6 23W
Firat r. Asia 57 E2 37 30N 38 00E
Firth of Clyde Scotland 10 D2/E2 55 30N 5 00W
Firth of Forth Scotland 11 F3/G3 56 05N 3 00W
Firth of Lorn Scotland 8 D1 56 15N 6 00W
Firth of Tay Scotland 9 F1 56 25N 3 00W
Fishbourne England 16 B1 50 44N 1 12W
Fishguard Wales 14 B1 51 59N 4 59W
Flagstaff USA 90 D4 35 12N 111 38W
Flamborough England 13 F3 54 07N 0 07W
Flamborough Head England 13 F3 54 06N 0 04W
Fleet England 16 C2 51 16N 0 50W
Fleetwood England 12 C2 53 56N 3 01W
Flekkefjord Norway 49 C2 58 17N 6 40E
Flimby England 12 C3 54 41N 3 31W
Flint Wales 14 C3 53 15N 3 07W
Flintshire u.a. Wales 14 C3 53 15N 3 10W
Flitwick England 16 C2 51 59N 0 29W
Florence Italy 54 D5 43 47N 11 15E
Florida state USA 91 K2 28 00N 82 00W
Florida Keys is. USA 91 K1 25 00N 80 00W
Flotta i. Scotland 7 A1 58 49N 3 07W
Fochabers Scotland 9 F2 57 37N 3 05W
Focșani Romania 53 N2 45 41N 27 12E
Fóggia Italy 55 F4 41 28N 15 33E
Folkestone England 17 E2 51 05N 1 11E
Folkingham England 16 C2 52 54N 0 24W
Fontainebleau France 50 F5 48 24N 2 42E
Fontstown RoI 21 E3 53 03N 6 53W
Fordham England 17 D3 52 19N 0 24E
Fordingbridge England 16 B1 50 56N 1 47W
Foreland p. England 16 B1 50 41N 1 04W
Foreland Point England 18 D3 51 16N 3 47W
Foreness Point England 17 E2 51 23N 1 27E
Forest Channel Islands 19 E1 49 25N 2 35W
Forest Row England 16 D2 51 06N 0 02E
Forfar Scotland 9 G1 56 38N 2 54W
Forlì Italy 54 E6 44 13N 12 02E
Formby England 12 C2 53 34N 3 05W
Formentera i. Spain 51 F3 38 41N 1 30E

Place	Page	Grid	Lat.	Long.
FORMER YUGOSLAV REPUBLIC OF MACEDONIA (FYROM)	55	J4/K4		
Forres Scotland	9	F2	57 37N	3 38W
Fortaleza Brazil	96	K13	3 45S	38 35W
Fort Augustus Scotland	9	E2	57 09N	4 41W
Fort George Scotland	9	E2	57 35N	4 05W
Forth r. Scotland	11	E3	56 05N	4 05W
Fort Lauderdale USA	91	K2	26 08N	80 08W
Fort Liard Canada	88	L6	60 14N	123 28W
Fortrose Scotland	9	E2	57 34N	4 09W
Fort Saskatchewan Canada	88	N4	53 42N	113 12W
Fortuneswell England	19	E2	50 33N	2 27W
Fort William Scotland	9	D1	56 49N	5 07W
Fort Worth USA	91	G3	32 45N	97 20W
Foula i. Scotland	7	B3	60 08N	2 05W
Foulness Island England	17	D2	51 35N	0 57E
Foulness Point England	17	D2	51 37N	0 57E
Fowey England	18	C2	50 20N	4 38W
Fowey r. England	18	C2	50 27N	4 38W
Foxford Rol	20	B3	53 58N	9 08W
Foyle r. NI/Rol	20	D4	54 55N	7 25W
Foynes Rol	21	B2	52 37N	9 06W
Foz Spain	51	B5	43 34N	7 15W
Framlingham England	17	E3	52 13N	1 21E
Frampton Cotterell England	15	D1	51 32N	2 30W
FRANCE	50			
Frankfurt am Main Germany	52	D5	50 06N	8 41E
Frankfurt an der Oder Germany	52	G6	52 20N	14 32E
Fraser r. Canada	88	L4	52 00N	122 00W
Fraserburgh Scotland	9	G2	57 42N	2 00W
Freckleton England	12	D2	53 46N	2 52W
Frederick USA	93	E1	39 25N	77 25W
Fredericksburg USA	91	L4	38 18N	77 30W
Frederikshavn Denmark	49	D2	57 28N	10 33E
Fredrikstad Norway	49	D2	59 20N	10 50E
Freemount Rol	21	C2	52 17N	8 51W
Freeport Canada	89	X2	44 17N	66 19W
Freetown Sierra Leone	80	B3	8 30N	13 17W
Freiburg im Breisgau Germany	52	C3	48 00N	7 52E
Fréjus France	50	H2	43 26N	6 44E
French Guiana territory France	96	G14	5 00N	53 00W
Frenchpark Rol	20	C3	53 53N	8 24W
Freshwater England	16	B1	50 40N	1 37W
Fresno USA	90	C4	36 41N	119 47W
Fribourg Switz.	52	C3	46 50N	7 10E
Friedrichshafen Germany	52	D3	47 39N	9 29E
Frinton on Sea England	17	E2	51 50N	1 14E
Frodsham England	12	D2	53 18N	2 44W
Frogmore England	16	C2	51 20N	0 50W
Frome England	19	E	51 14N	2 20W
Frome r. Herefordshire England	15	D2	52 05N	2 30W
Frome r. Somerset England	19	E3	51 10N	2 20W
Frome r. Dorset England	19	E2	50 42N	2 16W
Fuday i. Scotland	8	B2	57 05N	7 20W
Fuenlabrada Spain	51	D4	40 16N	3 49W
Fuerteventura i. Spain	80	B7	28 25N	14 00W
Fuji Japan	70	C2	35 10N	138 37E
Fuji-san mt. Japan	70	C2	35 23N	138 42E
Fukuoka Japan	70	B1	33 39N	130 21E
Furnace Scotland	10	D3	56 09N	5 12W
Fürth Germany	52	E4	49 28N	11 00E
Fushun China	69	M6	41 50N	123 54E
Fuzhou China	69	L3	26 09N	119 17E
G				
GABON	82	B7		
Gaborone Botswana	82	E3	24 45S	25 55E
Gadsden USA	91	J3	34 00N	86 00W
Gaeta Italy	54	E4	41 13N	13 36E
Gainsborough England	13	F2	53 24N	0 48W
Gairloch tn. Scotland	8	D2	57 42N	5 40W
Gairsay i. Scotland	7	B2	59 05N	2 58W
Galashiels Scotland	11	G2	55 37N	2 49W
Galați Romania	53	P2	45 27N	28 02E
Gallan Head Scotland	8	B3	58 14N	7 01W
Galley Head Rol	21	C1	51 35N	8 55W
Gallipoli Italy	55	H4	40 03N	17 59E
Gallup USA	90	E4	32 32N	108 46W
Galston Scotland	11	E2	55 36N	4 24W
Galveston USA	91	H2	29 17N	94 48W
Galway co. Rol	20	B3/C3	53 25N	8 45W
Galway Rol	20	B3	53 16N	9 03W
Galway Bay Rol	20	B3	53 15N	9 15W
Gambia r. Senegal/The Gambia	80	B4	13 45N	13 15W
GAMBIA, THE	80	A4		
Gandía Spain	51	E3	38 59N	0 11W
Ganga r. India	66	E5	25 00N	83 30E
Gangdisê Shan mts. China	68	D4	31 00N	82 30E
Gap France	50	H3	44 33N	6 05E
Garda Italy	54	D6	45 34N	10 43E
Garden City USA	90	F4	37 57N	100 54W
Gardenstown Scotland	9	G2	57 40N	2 20W
Gare Loch Scotland	11	E3	56 03N	4 39W
Garelochhead Scotland	11	E3	56 05N	4 50W
Garforth England	13	E2	53 48N	1 22W
Garlieston Scotland	11	E1	54 48N	4 22W
Garonne r. France	50	D3	44 45N	0 15E
Garrison NI	10	A1	54 25N	8 05W
Garron Point NI	10	D2	55 05N	6 00W
Garstang England	12	D2	53 55N	2 47W
Garth Wales	14	C2	52 08N	3 32W
Garthorpe England	13	F2	53 40N	0 42W
Garve Scotland	9	E2	57 37N	4 42W
Gaspé Canada	89	Y3	48 50N	64 30W
Gastonia USA	91	K4	35 14N	81 12W
Gatehouse of Fleet Scotland	11	E1	54 53N	4 11W
Gateshead England	13	E3	54 58N	1 35W
Gatty Mountains Rol	21	C2	52 21N	8 11W
Gaydon England	15	E2	52 45N	0 34E
Gaza Middle East	64	N10	31 30N	34 28E
Gaziantep Turkey	57	E2	37 04N	37 21E
Gdańsk Poland	53	J7	54 22N	18 41E
Gdynia Poland	53	J7	54 31N	18 30E
Geleen Neths	48	D3	50 58N	5 45E
Gelligaer Wales	14	C1	51 39N	3 15W
Gelsenkirchen Germany	52	C5	51 30N	7 05E
Geneva Switz.	52	C3	46 13N	6 09E
Genk Belgium	48	D3	50 58N	5 30E
Genova Italy	54	C6	44 24N	8 56E
Gent Belgium	48	B4	51 02N	3 42E
Georgetown Guyana	96	E5	6 46N	58 10W
George Town Malaysia	71	C5	5 25N	100 20E
GEORGIA	57	F3		
Georgia state USA	91	K3	33 00N	83 00W
Gera Germany	52	F5	50 51N	12 11E
GERMANY	52			
Gerona Spain	51	G4	41 59N	2 49E
Gerrards Cross England	16	C2	51 35N	0 34W
Getafe Spain	51	D4	40 18N	3 44W
GHANA	80	D3		
Giant's Causeway NI	10	C2	55 10N	6 30W
Gibraltar territory U.K.	51	C2	36 09N	5 21W
Gigha i. Scotland	10	D2	55 40N	5 45W
Gijón Spain	51	C5	43 32N	5 40W
Gila Bend USA	90	D3	32 56N	112 42W
Gilfach Goch Wales	14	C1	51 38N	3 30W
Gilford NI	10	C1	54 23N	6 22W
Gillingham Medway England	17	D2	51 24N	0 33E
Gillingham Dorset England	19	E3	51 02N	2 17W
Gilsland England	12	D3	55 00N	2 35W
Gironde r. France	50	D3	45 30N	0 45W
Girvan Scotland	10	E2	55 15N	4 51W
Givet Belgium	48	C3	50 08N	4 49E
Glanaman Wales	14	C1	51 47N	3 55W
Glanton England	13	E3	55 26N	1 54W
Glasgow Scotland	11	E2	55 53N	4 15W
Glasgow City u.a. Scotland	11	E2	55 52N	4 16W
Glass r. Scotland	9	E2	57 15N	4 40W
Glassan Rol	20	D3	53 28N	7 52W
Glasson England	12	D2	54 00N	2 51W
Glastonbury England	19	E3	51 09N	2 43W
Glenaffric r. Scotland	8	D2	57 15N	5 15W
Glenbeigh Rol	21	B2	52 03N	9 56W
Glencoe Scotland	8	D1	56 40N	5 04W
Glencolumbkille Rol	20	C4	54 42N	8 44W
Glenfinnan Scotland	8	D1	56 53N	5 27W
Glengad Head Rol	20	D5	55 20N	7 11W
Glengarriff Rol	21	B1	51 45N	9 33W
Glenluce Scotland	11	E1	54 53N	4 49W
Glenamaddy Rol	20	C3	53 37N	8 35W
Glenridding England	12	D3	54 33N	2 58W
Glenrothes Scotland	11	F3	56 12N	3 10W
Glen Shee r. Scotland	9	F1	46 45N	3 25W
Glenties Rol	20	C4	54 47N	8 17W
Glin Rol	21	B2	52 34N	9 17W
Glossop England	13	E2	53 27N	1 57W
Gloucester England	15	D1	51 53N	2 14W
Gloucestershire co. England	15	D1/E1	51 50N	2 20W
Glusburn England	12	D2	53 55N	2 01W
Glydar Fawr mt. Wales	14	B3	53 05N	4 03W
Glyncorrwg Wales	14	C1	51 41N	3 38W
Glyn-neath Wales	14	C1	51 46N	3 38W
Gniezno Poland	53	H6	52 32N	17 32E
Goat Fell mt. Scotland	10	D2	55 39N	5 11W
Gobi Desert Mongolia	68/69	G6/J6	48 30N	100 00E
Godalming England	16	C2	51 11N	0 37W
Godmanchester England	16	C3	52 19N	0 11W
Goiânia Brazil	96	H10	16 43S	49 18W
Goiás Brazil	96	G10	15 57S	50 07W
Golam Head Rol	20	B3	53 14N	9 44W
Golfo de California Mexico	94	B5	27 00N	111 00W
Golfo di Genova Italy	54	C6	44 00N	9 00E
Golfo di Táranto Italy	55	G3/G4	40 00N	17 00E
Golfo di Venézia Italy	54	E6	45 00N	13 00E
Golspie Scotland	9	F2	57 58N	3 58W
Gomera i. Spain	80	A7	28 08N	17 14W
Good Hope, Cape of RSA	82	C1	34 30S	19 00E
Goodland USA	90	F4	39 20N	101 43W
Goodwick Wales	14	B1	52 00N	5 00W
Goole England	13	F2	53 42N	0 52W
Gorebridge Scotland	11	F2	55 51N	3 02W
Gorey Rol	21	E2	52 40N	6 18W
Gorinchem Neths	48	C4	51 50N	4 59E
Goring England	16	B2	51 32N	1 09W
Gorizia Italy	54	E6	45 57N	13 37E
Gorseinon Wales	14	B1	51 41N	4 02W
Gort Rol	21	C3	53 04N	8 50W
Gorteen Rol	20	C3	53 22N	8 35W
Gortmore Rol	20	C3	53 36N	9 36W
Gorumna Island Rol	20	B3	53 15N	9 55W
Gosforth England	13	E4	55 01N	1 37W
Gosport England	16	B1	50 48N	1 08W
Göteborg Sweden	49	D2	57 45N	12 00E
Gotha Germany	52	E5	50 57N	10 43E
Gotland i. Sweden	49	E2	57 30N	18 40E
Göttingen Germany	52	D5	51 32N	9 57E
Gouda Neths	48	C5	52 00N	4 42E
Gourock Scotland	11	E2	55 58N	4 49W
Gower p. Wales	14	B1	51 35N	4 10W
Gowran Rol	21	D2	52 38N	7 04W
Graemsay i. Scotland	7	A1	58 56N	3 17W
Grafham Water England	16	C3	52 18N	0 20W
Graiguenamanagh Rol	21	E2	52 32N	6 56W
Grain England	17	D2	51 28N	0 43E
Grampian Mountains Scotland	9	E1/F1	56 45N	4 00W
Granada Spain	51	D2	37 10N	3 35W
Granard Rol	20	D3	53 47N	7 30W
Gran Canaria i. Spain	80	A7	28 00N	15 35W
Grand Canal Rol	20	D3	53 18N	7 15W
Grand Canyon USA	90	D4	36 04N	112 07W
Grand Cayman i. Caribbean Sea	95	H3	19 20N	81 15W
Grand Rapids tn. USA	91	J5	42 57N	86 40W
Grange Rol	20	C4	54 24N	8 31W
Grange-over-Sands tn. England	12	D3	54 33N	3 09W
Grantham England	15	F2	52 55N	0 39W
Grantown-on-Spey Scotland	9	F2	57 20N	3 58W
Granville France	50	D5	48 50N	1 35W
Grasmere England	12	D3	54 28N	3 02W
Grasse France	50	H2	43 40N	5 56E
Grassington England	12	E3	54 04N	1 59W
Gravelines France	48	A3	50 59N	2 08E
Gravesend England	17	D2	51 27N	0 24E
Gray France	50	G4	47 27N	5 35E
Grays England	17	D2	51 29N	0 20E
Graz Austria	52	G3	47 05N	15 22E
Greasby England	12	C2	53 23N	3 10W
Great Bardfield England	17	D2	51 57N	0 26E
Great Bear Lake Canada	88	L7/M7	66 00N	120 00W
Great Broughton England	13	E3	54 27N	1 10W
Great Chesterford England	17	D3	52 04N	0 11E
Great Coates England	13	F2	53 35N	0 08W
Great Cumbrae i. Scotland	10	E2	55 46N	4 55W
Great Dividing Range Australia	73	H8/J3	35 00N	148 00E
Great Driffield England	13	F3	54 01N	0 26W
Great Dunmow England	17	D2	51 53N	0 22E
Great Eccleston England	12	D2	53 51N	2 53W
Greater Antilles is. West Indies	95	H4/L3	19 00N	78 00W
Greater London co. England	16	C2	51 30N	0 10W
Greater Manchester co. England	12	D2	53 30N	2 15W
Great Harwood England	12	D2	53 48N	2 24W
Great Malvern England	15	D2	52 07N	2 19W
Great Missenden England	16	C2	51 43N	0 43W
Great Ormes Head Wales	14	C3	53 21N	3 53W
Great Ouse r. England	17	D3	52 40N	0 20E
Great Salt Lake USA	90	D5	41 10N	112 40W
Great Shelford England	17	D2	52 08N	0 09E
Great Slave Lake Canada	88	N6	62 00N	114 00W
Great Torrington England	18	C2	51 57N	4 09W
Great Victoria Desert Australia	72	E5/F5	28 00S	130 00E
Great Whernside sum. England	12	E3	54 10N	1 59W
Great Wyrley England	15	D2	52 27N	2 02W
Great Yarmouth England	17	E3	52 37N	1 44E
GREECE	55	J3/K3		
Greencastle NI	10	C1	54 02N	6 06W
Greenisland tn. NI	10	D1	54 42N	5 52W
GREENLAND	89	BB8/EE8		
Greenlaw Scotland	11	G2	55 43N	2 28W
Greenock Scotland	11	E2	55 57N	4 45W
Greenore Rol	20	E4	54 02N	6 08W
Greenore Point Rol	21	E2	52 15N	6 18W
Greenstone Point Scotland	8	D2	57 55N	5 37W
GRENADA	94	R11		
Grenoble France	50	G3	45 11N	5 43E
Greta r. England	12	D3	54 10N	2 30W
Gretna Scotland	11	F1	54 59N	3 04W
Gretna Green Scotland	11	F1	55 00N	3 04W
Greystones Rol	21	E3	53 09N	6 04W
Grimethorpe England	13	E2	53 34N	1 23W
Grimsby England	13	F2	53 35N	0 05W
Groningen Neths	48	E6	53 13N	6 35E
Grosseto Italy	54	D5	42 46N	11 07E
Grove England	16	B2	51 37N	1 26W
Groznyy Russia	62	G5	43 21N	45 42E
Gruinard Bay Scotland	8	D2	57 55N	5 30W
Guadalajara Mexico	94	D4	20 40N	103 20W
Guadalajara Spain	51	D4	40 37N	3 10W
Guadalquivir r. Spain	51	C2	37 45N	5 30W
Guadeloupe i. Lesser Antilles	94	Q9	16 30N	61 30W
Guadiana r. Spain/Portugal	51	B3	38 30N	7 30W
GUAM	100	E9		
Guangzhou China	69	K2	23 08N	113 20E
Guantánamo Cuba	95	J4	20 09N	75 14W
Guarda Portugal	51	B4	40 32N	7 17W
GUATEMALA	94	F3		
Guatemala City Guatemala	94	F2	14 38N	90 22W
Guayaquil Ecuador	96	A13	2 13S	79 54W
Guéret France	50	E4	46 10N	1 52E
Guernsey i. Channel Islands	19	E1	46 27N	2 35W
Guide Post England	13	E4	55 10N	1 36W
Guildford England	16	C2	51 14N	0 35W
Guimarães Portugal	51	A4	41 26N	8 19W
GUINEA	80	B4		
GUINEA-BISSAU	80	A4/B4		
Guisborough England	13	E3	54 32N	1 04W
Guiseley England	13	E2	53 53N	1 42W
Guiyang China	69	J3	26 35N	106 40E
Gujranwala Pakistan	66	C6	32 06N	74 11E
Gulf, The Middle East	65	F4	27 20N	51 00E
Gullane Scotland	11	G3	56 02N	2 50W
Gunnislake England	18	C2	50 31N	4 12W
Gutcher Scotland	7	C3	60 40N	1 00W
Guthrie USA	91	G4	35 53N	97 26W
GUYANA	96	F14		
Gweebarra Bay Rol	20	C4	54 55N	8 30W
Gweedore Rol	20	C5	55 03N	8 14W
Gwynedd u.a. Wales	14	C2	52 45N	3 55W
Győr Hungary	53	H3	47 41N	17 40E
H				
Haarlem Neths	48	C5	52 23N	4 39E
Hacketstown Rol	21	E2	52 52N	6 33W
Haddington Scotland	11	G2	55 58N	2 47W
Hadleigh England	17	D3	51 02N	0 57E
Hadleigh England	17	D2	51 34N	0 36E
Hadley England	15	D2	52 43N	2 28W
Hagen Germany	52	C5	51 22N	7 27E
Hagley England	15	D2	52 26N	2 08W
Hagondange France	50	H5	49 16N	6 11E
Hags Head Rol	21	B2	52 56N	9 30W
Haguenau France	50	H5	48 49N	7 47E
Haifa Israel	64	B5	32 49N	34 59E
Hailsham England	17	D1	50 52N	0 16E
Hainan Dao i. China	69	J1/K1	18 50N	109 50E
Hai Phong Vietnam	69	J2	20 50N	106 41E
HAITI	95	K3		
Hakodate Japan	70	D3	41 46N	140 44E
Hale England	15	D2	53 22N	2 20W
Halesowen England	15	D2	52 26N	2 05W
Halesworth England	17	E2	52 21N	1 30E
Halifax England	13	E2	53 44N	1 52W
Halifax Canada	89	Y2	44 38N	63 35W
Halkirk Scotland	9	F3	58 30N	3 30W
Halladale r. Scotland	9	F3	58 30N	3 55W
Halle Germany	52	E5	51 28N	11 58E
Hallein Austria	52	F3	47 41N	13 06E
Halmstad Sweden	49	D2	56 41N	12 55E
Halstead England	17	D2	51 57N	0 38E
Haltwhistle England	12	D3	54 58N	2 27W
Hamāh Syria	64	C6	35 10N	36 45E
Hamamatsu Japan	70	C1	34 42N	137 42E
Hamble-le-Rice England	16	B1	50 52N	1 19W
Hambleton Hills England	13	E3	54 15N	1 15W
Hamburg Germany	52	E6	53 33N	10 00E
Hämeenlinna Finland	49	F3	61 00N	24 25E
Hamilton Canada	89	U2	43 15N	79 50W
Hamilton NZ	73	Q3	37 47S	175 17E
Hamilton Scotland	11	E2	55 47N	4 03W
Hamm Germany	52	C5	51 40N	7 49E
Hammerfest Norway	49	F5	70 40N	23 44E
Hampshire co. England	16	B2	51 10N	1 15W
Hampshire Downs England	16	B2	51 15N	1 10W
Hamstreet England	17	D2	51 05N	0 52E
Hangzhou China	69	M4	30 18N	120 07E
Hanko Finland	49	E2	59 50N	23 00E
Hanley England	12	D2	53 01N	2 10W
Hannover Germany	52	D6	52 23N	9 44E
Hanoi Vietnam	69	J2	21 01N	105 52E
Harare Zimbabwe	82	F4	17 50S	31 03E
Harbin China	69	N7	45 45N	126 41E
Harlech Wales	14	B2	52 52N	4 07W

Harleston England 17 E3 52 24N 1 18E
Harlingen Neths 48 D6 53 10N 5 25E
Harlow England 17 D2 51 47N 0 08E
Haroldswick Scotland 7 D3 60 47N 0 50E
Harpenden England 16 C2 51 49N 0 22W
Harris i. Scotland 8 C2 57 50N 6 55W
Harris, Sound of
  Scotland 8 B2 57 40N 9 12W
Harrogate England 13 E2 54 00N 1 33W
Harrow England 16 C2 51 34N 0 20W
Hartford USA 91 M5 41 00N 72 00W
Hartington England 13 E2 53 09N 1 48W
Hartland England 18 C2 50 59N 4 29W
Hartland Point England 18 C3 51 02N 4 31W
Hartlepool England 13 E3 54 41N 1 13W
Hartlepool u.a. England 13 E3 54 41N 1 13W
Hartshill England 15 E2 52 33N 1 30W
Harwell England 16 C2 51 37N 1 18W
Harwich England 17 E2 51 57N 1 17E
Harworth England 13 E2 53 26N 1 04W
Harz mts. Europe 52 E5 52 00N 10 00E
Hascosay i. Scotland 7 D3 60 36N 1 00W
Haslemere England 16 C2 51 06N 0 44W
Haslingden England 12 D2 53 43N 2 18W
Hasselt Belgium 48 D3 50 56N 5 20E
Hastings England 17 D1 50 51N 0 36E
Hatfield South Yorkshire
  England 13 F2 53 36N 0 59W
Hatfield Hertfordshire
  England 16 C2 51 46N 0 13W
Hatherleigh England 18 C2 50 49N 4 04W
Hathersage England 13 E2 53 19N 1 38W
Hatton Scotland 9 H2 57 25N 1 55W
Haugesund Norway 49 C2 59 25N 5 16E
Haut Atlas mts.
  Morocco 80 C8 30 45N 6 50W
Havana Cuba 95 H4 23 07N 82 25W
Havant England 16 C1 50 51N 0 59W
Haverfordwest Wales 14 B1 51 49N 4 58W
Haverhill England 17 D3 52 05N 0 26E
Havering England 17 D2 51 34N 0 14E
Hawaiian Islands
  Pacific Ocean 100 J10/L9 25 00N 166 00W
Hawarden Wales 14 C3 53 11N 3 02W
Hawes England 12 D3 54 18N 2 12W
Hawick Scotland 11 G2 55 25N 2 47W
Hawkesbury Canada 89 W3 45 36N 74 38W
Hawkhurst England 17 D2 51 02N 0 30E
Haworth England 13 E2 53 50N 1 57W
Haxby England 13 E3 54 01N 1 05W
Haydon Bridge tn.
  England 12 D3 54 58N 21 4W
Hayle England 18 B2 50 10N 5 25W
Hay-on-Wye Wales 14 C2 52 04N 3 07W
Haywards Heath
  England 16 C2 51 00N 0 06W
Hazel Grove England 12 D2 53 23N 2 08W
Hazelmere England 16 C2 51 38N 0 44W
Heacham England 17 D3 52 55N 0 30E
Headford Rol 20 B3 53 28N 9 06W
Heanor England 13 E2 53 01N 1 22W
Heathfield England 17 D1 50 58N 0 15E
Hebden Bridge England 12 D2 53 45N 2 00W
Hebi China 69 K5 35 57N 114 08E
Heckington England 15 F2 52 59N 0 18W
Heckmondwike
  England 13 E2 53 43N 1 45W
Hedge End England 16 B1 50 55N 1 18W
Hednesford England 15 E2 52 43N 2 00W
Hedon England 13 F2 53 44N 0 12W
Heerenveen Neths 48 D5 52 57N 5 55E
Heerlen Neths 48 D3 50 53N 5 59E
Hefei China 69 L4 31 55N 117 18E
Heidelberg Germany 52 D4 49 25N 8 42E
Heighington England 13 E2 54 36N 1 37W
Heilbronn Germany 52 D4 49 08N 9 14E
Heisker is. Scotland 8 B2 57 30N 7 40W
Hekla mt. Iceland 49 L6 64 00N 19 41W
Helchteren Belgium 48 D4 51 03N 5 23E
Helena USA 90 D6 46 35N 112 00W
Helen's Bay tn. NI 10 D1 54 41N 5 50W
Helensburgh Scotland 11 E3 56 01N 4 44W
Hellifield England 12 D3 54 01N 2 12W
Helmsdale r. Scotland 9 F3 58 10N 3 50W
Helmsdale Scotland 9 F3 58 07N 3 40W
Helmsley England 13 E3 54 14N 1 04W
Helsingborg Sweden 49 D2 56 03N 12 43E
Helston England 18 B2 50 05N 5 16W
Helvellyn mt. England 12 D3 54 32N 3 02W
Hemel Hempstead
  England 16 C2 51 46N 0 28W
Hemsworth England 13 E2 53 38N 1 21W
Henfield England 16 C1 50 56N 0 17W
Hengelo Neths 48 E5 52 16N 6 46E
Henley-in-Arden
  England 15 E2 52 17N 1 46W
Henley-on-Thames
  England 16 C2 51 32N 0 56W
Herbertstown Rol 21 C2 52 32N 8 28W
Hereford England 14 D2 52 04N 2 43W
Herefordshire co.
  England 14/15 D2 52 10N 2 45W
Herentals Belgium 48 C4 51 11N 4 50E
Herm i. Channel Islands 19 E1 49 28N 2 27W
Herne Germany 48 F4 51 32N 7 12E
Herne Bay tn. England 17 E2 51 23N 1 08E

Herning Denmark 49 C2 56 08N 8 59E
Hertfordshire co.
  England 16 C2 51 50N 0 05W
Hessle England 13 F2 53 44N 0 26W
Hetton-le-Hole England 13 E3 54 50N 1 27W
Hexham England 12 D3 54 58N 2 06W
Heysham England 12 D3 54 02N 2 54W
Heywood England 12 D2 53 36N 2 13W
Higham Ferrers
  England 15 F2 52 18N 0 36W
High Bentham England 12 D3 54 08N 2 30W
Higher Walton England 12 D2 53 45N 2 37W
Highland u.a. Scotland 8/9 D2/E2 57 00N 5 00W
Highworth England 16 B2 51 38N 1 43W
High Wycombe England 16 C2 51 38N 0 46W
Hildesheim Germany 52 D6 52 09N 9 58E
Hillingdon England 16 C2 51 33N 0 27W
Hillsborough NI 10 C1 54 28N 6 05W
Hilversum Neths 48 D5 52 14N 5 10E
Hinckley England 15 E2 52 33N 1 21W
Hindhead England 16 C2 51 07N 0 44W
Hindley England 12 D2 53 32N 2 35W
Hindu Kush mts.
  Afghanistan 66 B7/C7 35 00N 70 00E
Hiroshima Japan 70 B1 34 23N 132 27E
Hirwaun Wales 14 C1 51 45N 3 30W
Histon England 17 D3 52 15N 0 06E
Hitachi Japan 70 D2 36 35N 140 40E
Hitchin England 16 C2 51 57N 0 17W
Hobart Australia 73 J2 42 54S 147 18E
Hô Chi Minh Vietnam 71 D6 10 46N 106 43E
Hockley England 17 D2 51 35N 0 39E
Hodder r. England 12 D3 53 55N 2 30W
Hoddesdon England 17 D2 51 46N 0 01W
Hodnet England 15 D2 52 51N 2 35W
Hoek van Holland
  Neths 48 C5 51 59N 4 08E
Hohhot China 69 K6 40 49N 117 37E
Hokkaidô i. Japan 70 D3 43 30N 143 00E
Holbeach England 15 D3 52 49N 0 01E
Holderness p. England 13 F2 53 45N 0 05W
Hollyford Rol 21 C2 52 38N 8 06W
Hollywood Rol 21 E3 53 06N 6 35W
Holmes Chapel tn.
  England 12 D2 53 12N 2 22W
Holme-on-Spalding-Moor
  England 13 F2 53 49N 0 46W
Holmfirth England 13 E2 53 35N 1 46W
Holmhead Scotland 11 E2 55 29N 4 17W
Holsworthy England 18 C2 50 49N 4 21W
Holt England 17 E3 52 55N 1 05E
Holycross Limerick Rol 21 C2 52 38N 7 52W
Holycross Tipperary Rol 21 D2 52 38N 7 52W
Holyhead Wales 14 B3 53 19N 4 38W
Holy Island England 11 H2 55 41N 1 48W
Holy Island Wales 14 B3 53 16N 4 39W
Holywell Wales 14 C3 53 17N 3 13W
Holywood NI 10 D1 54 38N 5 50W
Homs Syria 64 C5 34 42N 36 40E
Homyel' Belarus 53 Q6 52 25N 31 00E
Honddu r. Wales 14 C1 51 50N 2 50W
HONDURAS 94 G2
Hong Kong China 69 K2 23 00N 114 00E
Honiton England 19 D2 50 48N 3 13W
Honshû i. Japan 70 C2 37 15N 139 00E
Hoo England 17 D2 51 26N 0 34E
Hoogeveen Neths 48 E5 52 44N 6 29E
Hook England 16 C2 51 17N 0 58W
Hook Head Rol 21 E2 52 10N 6 55W
Hope Wales 14 C3 53 07N 3 03W
Hopton on Sea England 17 E3 52 33N 1 43E
Horbury England 13 E2 53 41N 1 33W
Horley England 16 C2 51 11N 0 11W
Horncastle England 13 F2 53 13N 0 07W
Horn Head Rol 20 D5 55 13N 7 59W
Hornsea England 13 F2 53 55N 0 10W
Horsforth England 13 E2 53 51N 1 39W
Horsham England 16 C2 51 04N 0 21W
Horwich England 12 D2 53 37N 2 33W
Hospital Rol 21 C2 52 29N 8 25W
Hospitalet Spain 51 G4 41 21N 2 06E
Houghton-le-Spring
  England 13 E3 54 51N 1 28W
Hounslow England 16 C2 51 28N 0 21W
Houston USA 91 G2 29 45N 95 25W
Hove England 16 C1 50 49N 0 11W
Hovingham England 13 F3 54 10N 0 59W
Howden England 13 F2 53 45N 0 52W
Howth Rol 20 E3 53 23N 6 04W
Hoy i. Scotland 7 A1 58 48N 3 20W
Hoylake England 12 C2 53 23N 3 11W
Hoyland England 13 E2 53 30N 1 27W
Hoy Sound Scotland 7 A1 58 56N 3 20W
Hrodna Belarus 53 L6 53 40N 23 50E
Huang He r. China 69 K5 38 00N 111 00E
Hucknall England 13 E2 53 02N 1 11W
Huddersfield England 13 E2 53 39N 1 47W
Hudson Bay Canada 89 T5/T6 60 00N 89 00W
Huelva Spain 51 C2 37 15N 6 56W
Huesca Spain 51 E5 42 08N 0 25W
Hugh Town England 18 A1 49 55N 6 19W
Hull r. England 13 F2 53 55N 0 20W
Hullbridge England 17 D2 51 37N 0 37E
Humberston England 13 F2 53 32N 0 02W
HUNGARY 53 H3/K3
Hungerford England 16 B2 51 26N 1 30W

Hunmanby England 13 F3 54 11N 0 19W
Hunstanton England 17 D3 52 57N 0 30E
Huntford Scotland 11 G2 55 22N 2 28W
Huntingdon England 16 C3 52 20N 0 12W
Huntington USA 91 K4 38 24N 82 26W
Huntly Scotland 9 G2 57 27N 2 47W
Huntsville USA 91 J3 34 44N 86 35W
Huron, Lake
  Canada/USA 93 D2/3 45 00N 83 00W
Hurstpierpoint England 16 C1 50 56N 0 11W
Husbands Bosworth
  England 15 E2 52 27N 1 03W
Husum Germany 52 D7 54 29N 9 04E
Hutton Cranswick
  England 13 F2 53 57N 0 27W
Hyde England 12 D2 53 27N 2 04W
Hyderabad India 66 D3 17 22N 78 26E
Hyderabad Pakistan 66 B5 25 23N 68 24E
Hythe Hampshire
  England 16 B1 50 51N 1 24W
Hythe Kent England 17 E2 51 05N 1 05E

I

Iaşi Romania 53 N3 47 09N 27 38E
Ibadan Nigeria 80 E3 7 23N 3 56E
Ibiza i. Spain 51 F3 39 00N 1 20E
Ibstock England 15 E2 52 42N 1 23W
ICELAND 49 L7
Idaho state USA 90 D5 44 00N 115 00W
Idrigill Point Scotland 8 C2 57 21N 6 35W
Ieper Belgium 48 A3 50 51N 2 53E
Iglesias Italy 54 C3 39 19N 8 32E
IJsselmeer l. Neths 48 D5 52 50N 5 15E
Ilam England 13 E2 53 04N 1 49W
Ilchester England 19 E2 51 00N 2 41W
Îles Loyauté is.
  Pacific Ocean 73 N6/N7 21 00S 167 00E
Ilfracombe England 18 C3 51 13N 4 08W
Ilhéus Brazil 96 K11 14 50S 39 06W
Ilkeston England 15 E2 52 59N 1 18W
Ilkley England 13 E2 53 55N 1 50W
Illinois state USA 91 J5 40 00N 89 00W
Ilminster England 19 E2 50 56N 2 55W
Immingham England 13 F2 53 36N 0 11W
Imola Italy 54 E6 44 22N 11 43E
Imperia Italy 54 C5 43 53N 8 03E
Imphal India 67 G4 24 47N 93 55E
Inch Island i. Rol 20 D5 55 04N 7 30W
Inchon S. Korea 69 N5 37 30N 126 38E
Independence USA 91 G4 37 13N 95 43W
INDIA 66/67
Indiana state USA 91 J5 40 00N 86 00W
Indianapolis USA 91 J4 39 45N 86 10W
Indian Ocean 105
INDONESIA 71 C3/H3
Indus r. Pakistan 66 B5 28 00N 69 00E
Ingatestone England 17 D2 51 41N 0 22E
Ingleborough sum.
  England 12 D3 54 10N 2 23W
Ingleton England 13 D3 54 10N 2 27W
Ingolstadt Germany 52 E4 48 46N 11 27E
Inishannon Rol 21 C1 51 45N 8 38W
Inishbofin i. Rol 20 A3 53 38N 10 12W
Inishcrone Rol 20 B4 54 13N 9 06W
Inisheer i. Rol 21 B3 53 03N 9 30W
Inishkea North i. Rol 20 A4 54 08N 10 11W
Inishkea South i. Rol 20 A4 54 08N 10 11W
Inishmaan i. Rol 21 B3 53 05N 9 35W
Inishmore i. Rol 21 B3 53 07N 9 45W
Inishmurray i. Rol 20 C4 54 25N 8 35W
Inishowen Peninsula
  Rol 20 D5 55 15N 7 15W
Inishshark i. Rol 20 A3 53 37N 10 16W
Inishturk i. Rol 20 A3 53 43N 10 05W
Inn r. Europe 52 E3 48 00N 12 00E
Inner Hebrides is. Scotland 8 C1/C2 56 45N 6 45W
Innerleithen Scotland 11 F2 55 38N 3 05W
Inner Sound Scotland 8 D2 57 25N 5 55W
Innfield Rol 20 D3 53 25N 6 50W
Innsbruck Austria 52 E3 47 17N 11 25E
Inny r. Rol 20 D3 53 35N 7 30W
Interlaken Switz. 52 C3 46 42N 7 52E
Inuvik Canada 88 J7 68 16N 133 40W
Inverary Scotland 10 D3 56 13N 5 05W
Inver Bay Rol 20 C4 54 36N 8 20W
Inverbervie Scotland 9 G1 56 51N 2 17W
Invercargill NZ 73 N1 46 25S 168 22E
Inverclyde u.a. Scotland 11 E2 55 50N 4 45W
Invergarry Scotland 9 E2 57 02N 4 47W
Invergordon Scotland 9 E2 57 13N 4 38W
Inverkeithing Scotland 11 F3 56 02N 3 25W
Invermoriston Scotland 9 E2 57 13N 4 38W
Inverness Scotland 9 E2 57 27N 4 15W
Inverquharity Scotland 9 G1 56 44N 2 59W
Inverurie Scotland 9 G2 57 17N 2 23W
Ioánnina Greece 55 J3 39 40N 20 51E
Iona i. Scotland 8 C1 56 19N 6 25W
Iónia Nisiá Greece 55 H3 39 00N 20 00E
Íos i. Greece 55 L2 36 00N 25 00E
Iowa state USA 91 H5 42 00N 94 00W
Iowa City USA 91 H5 41 39N 91 31W
Ipswich England 17 E3 52 04N 1 10E
IRAN 65 F5/G5
IRAQ 64 D5

Irbid Jordan 64 C5 32 33N 35 51E
Irfon r. Wales 14 C2 52 10N 3 25W
Irish Sea British Isles 6 53 30N 5 30W
Irkutsk Russia 63 N7 52 18N 104 15E
Ironbridge England 15 D2 52 38N 2 30W
Irrawaddy r. Myanmar 71 A8 20 00N 95 00E
Irthing r. England 12 D3 55 00N 2 40W
Irthlingborough
  England 15 F2 52 20N 0 37W
Irtysh r. Asia 62 K8 57 30N 72 30E
Irún Spain 51 E5 43 20N 1 48W
Irvine Scotland 11 E2 55 37N 4 40W
Irvinestown NI 10 B1 54 29N 7 38W
Irving USA 91 G3 32 49N 96 57W
Ise r. England 15 F2 52 25N 00 50W
Isernia Italy 54 F4 41 35N 14 14E
Iskenderun Turkey 57 E2 36 37N 36 08E
Isla r. Scotland 9 F1 56 35N 3 10W
Isla d'Elba Italy 54 D5 42 00N 10 00E
Isla Grande de Tierra del Fuego
  Chile/Argentina 97 D2 54 00S 67 30W
Islamabad Pakistan 66 C6 33 40N 73 08E
Island Magee NI 10 D1 54 45N 5 40W
Islay i. Scotland 10 C2 55 48N 6 12W
Isleham England 17 D3 52 21N 0 25E
Isle of Man British Isles 12 B3 54 15N 4 15W
Isle of Portland England 19 E2 50 33N 2 27W
Isle of Purbeck England 19 E2 50 38N 2 05W
Isle of Whithorn tn.
  Scotland 11 E1 54 42N 4 22W
Isle of Wight u.a.
  England 16 B1 50 40N 1 20W
ISRAEL 64 B5/C5
Istanbul Turkey 57 C3 41 02N 28 57E
Itabuna Brazil 96 K11 14 48S 39 18W
ITALY 54 D5/E5
Itchen r. England 16 B2 51 05N 1 15W
Ithon r. Wales 14 C2 52 20N 3 25W
Itzehoe Germany 52 D6 53 56N 9 32E
Ivybridge England 18 D2 50 23N 3 56W
Ixworth England 17 D3 52 18N 0 50E
Izhevsk Russia 62 H8 56 49N 53 11E
Izmir Turkey 57 C2 38 25N 27 10E

J

Jackson USA 91 H3 32 20N 90 11W
Jacksonville USA 91 K3 30 20N 81 40W
Jaén Spain 51 D2 37 46N 3 48W
Jaipur India 66 D5 26 53N 75 50E
Jakarta Indonesia 71 D2 6 08S 106 45E
Jakobstad Finland 49 F3 63 40N 22 42E
JAMAICA 95 J3
James Bay Canada 89 U4 53 45N 81 00W
Jamestown USA 91 G6 46 54N 98 42W
Jammu India 66 C6 32 43N 74 54E
JAPAN 70
Jarrow England 13 E3 54 59N 1 29W
Jasper Canada 88 M4 52 55N 118 05W
Jastrowie Poland 53 H6 53 25N 16 50E
Jawa i. Indonesia 71 D2/E2 7 00S 110 00E
Jedburgh Scotland 11 G2 55 29N 2 34W
Jedda Saudi Arabia 64 C3 21 30N 39 10E
Jefferson City USA 91 H4 38 33N 92 10W
Jena Germany 52 E5 50 56N 11 35E
Jerez de la Frontera
  Spain 51 C2 36 41N 6 08W
Jericho Middle East 64 N10 31 51N 35 27E
Jersey i.
  Channel Islands 19 E1 49 13N 2 07W
Jerusalem Israel/Jordan 64 C5 31 47N 35 13E
Jilin China 69 N6 43 53N 126 35E
Jinan China 69 L5 36 41N 117 00E
Jinja Uganda 83 C5 0 27N 33 14E
João Pessoa Brazil 96 K12 7 06S 34 53W
Jodhpur India 66 C5 26 18N 73 08E
Joensuu Finland 49 G3 62 35N 29 46E
Johannesburg RSA 82 E2 26 10S 28 02E
John o'Groats Scotland 9 F3 58 39N 3 05W
Johnstone Scotland 11 E2 55 50N 4 31W
Jönköping Sweden 49 D2 57 45N 14 10E
Jonquière Canada 89 W3 48 25N 71 16W
JORDAN 64 C5
Jordan r. Middle East 64 N11 32 15N 32 10E
Joyce Country Rol 20 B3 53 32N 9 33W
Juàzeiro Brazil 96 J12 9 25S 40 30W
Juneau USA 88 J5 58 20N 134 20W
Jungfrau mt. Switz. 52 C346 33N 7 58E
Junsele Sweden 49 E3 63 40N 16 55E
Jura mts. France/Switz. 52 G4/H4 46 30N 6 00E
Jura i. Scotland 10 D2/D3 55 55N 6 00W
Jura, Sound of
  Scotland 10 D2 55 45N 5 55W
Jylland p. Denmark 49 C2 55 00N 9 00E
Jyväskylä Finland 49 G3 62 16N 25 50E

K

K2 mt. China/India 68 C5 35 47N 76 30E
Kâbul Afghanistan 66 B6 34 30N 69 10E
Kagoshima Japan 70 B1 31 37N 130 32E
Kaiserslautern
  Germany 52 C4 49 27N 7 47E
Kajaani Finland 49 G3 64 14N 27 37E
Kalahari Desert
  Southern Africa 82 D3 23 30S 23 00E
Kalamáta Greece 55 K2 37 02N 22 07E

Kaliavesi *l.* Finland	49	G3	63 00N	27 20E
Kaliningrad Russia	49	F1	54 40N	20 30E
Kalmar Sweden	49	E2	56 39N	16 20E
Kalmthout Belgium	48	C4	51 23N	4 29E
Kamchatka *p.* Russia	63	T8	57 30N	160 00E
Kames Scotland	10	D2	55 54N	5 15W
Kamloops Canada	88	L4	50 39N	120 24W
Kampala Uganda	83	C5	0 19N	32 35E
Kankakee USA	91	J5	41 08N	87 52W
Kannapolis USA	91	K4	35 30N	80 36W
Kano Nigeria	80	F4	12 00N	8 31E
Kanpur India	66	E5	26 27N	80 14E
Kansas *state* USA	90/91	G4	38 00N	98 00W
Kansas City USA	91	H4	39 02N	94 33W
Kanturk Rol	21	C2	52 10N	8 55W
Kaohsiung Taiwan	69	M2	22 36N	120 17E
Kapukasing Canada	89	U3	49 25N	82 26W
Karachi Pakistan	66	B4	24 51N	67 02E
Kara Sea Russia	101		75 00N	70 00E
Karasjok Norway	49	G4	69 27N	25 30E
Karcag Hungary	53	K3	47 19N	20 53E
Karlovac Croatia	54	F6	45 30N	15 34E
Karlskoga Sweden	49	D2	59 19N	14 33E
Karlskrona Sweden	49	E2	56 10N	15 35E
Karlsruhe Germany	52	D4	49 00N	8 24E
Karlstad Sweden	49	D2	59 24N	13 32E
Kaskinen Finland	49	F3	62 23N	21 10E
Kassel Germany	52	D5	51 18N	9 30E
Kathmandu Nepal	67	F5	27 42N	85 19E
Katowice Poland	53	J5	50 15N	18 59E
Katrineholm Sweden	49	E2	58 59N	16 15E
Kattegat *sd.* Denmark/Sweden	49	D2	57 00N	11 00E
Kaunas Lithuania	49	F1	54 52N	23 55E
Kawasaki Japan	70	C2	35 30N	139 45E
Kayseri Turkey	57	E3	38 42N	35 28E
KAZAKHSTAN	62	H6/J6		
Kazan' Russia	62	G8	55 45N	49 10E
Keady NI	10	C1	54 15N	6 42W
Kealkill Rol	21	B1	51 45N	9 20W
Kecskemét Hungary	53	J3	46 56N	19 43E
Kefallonia *i.* Greece	55	J3	38 00N	20 00E
Keighley England	13	E2	53 52N	1 54W
Keith Scotland	9	G2	57 32N	2 57W
Kells Rol	20	E3	53 44N	6 53W
Kelowna Canada	88	M3	49 50N	119 29W
Kelso Scotland	11	G2	55 36N	2 25W
Kelvedon England	17	D2	51 51N	0 42E
Kemnay Scotland	9	G2	57 14N	2 27W
Kempston England	16	C3	52 07N	0 30W
Kempten Germany	52	E3	47 44N	10 19E
Kendal England	12	D3	54 20N	2 45W
Kenilworth England	15	E2	52 21N	1 34W
Kenmare Rol	21	B1	51 53N	9 35W
Kennacraig Scotland	10	C2	55 50N	5 27W
Kennet *r.* England	16	B2	51 30N	1 45W
Kennington England	17	D2	51 09N	0 55E
Kennoway Scotland	11	F3	56 12N	3 03W
Kenora Canada	89	S3	49 47N	94 26W
Kent *co.* England	17	D2	51 10N	0 45E
Kentford England	17	D3	52 16N	0 30E
Kentucky *state* USA	91	J4	37 00N	85 00W
KENYA	83	E5/F5		
Kerkrade Neths	48	E3	50 52N	6 04E
Kérkyra *i.* Greece	55	H3	39 00N	19 00E
Kerpen Germany	48	E3	50 52N	6 42E
Kerrera *i.* Scotland	8	D1	56 25N	5 34W
Kerry Rol	21	B2	52 10N	9 30W
Kerry Head Rol	21	B2	52 25N	9 55W
Kesh NI	10	B1	54 31N	7 43W
Kessingland England	17	E3	52 25N	1 42E
Keswick England	12	C3	54 37N	3 08W
Kettering England	15	F2	52 24N	0 44W
Keynsham England	19	E3	51 26N	2 30W
Key West USA	91	K1	24 34N	81 48W
Keyworth England	15	E2	52 52N	1 05W
Khabarovsk Russia	63	R6	48 32N	135 08E
Khartoum Sudan	81	M5	15 33N	32 35E
Kherson Ukraine	57	D4	46 39N	32 38E
Khmel'nyts'kyy Ukraine	53	N4	49 25N	26 59E
Khulna Bangladesh	67	F4	22 49N	89 34E
Khyber Pass Afghanistan/Pakistan	66	C6	34 06N	71 05E
Kidderminster England	15	D2	52 23N	2 14W
Kidlington England	16	B2	51 50N	1 17W
Kidsgrove England	12	D2	53 05N	2 14W
Kidwelly Wales	14	B1	51 45N	4 18W
Kiel Germany	52	E7	54 20N	10 08E
Kielce Poland	53	K5	50 51N	20 39E
Kielder Water England	12	D4	55 10N	2 30W
Kiev Ukraine	53	Q5	50 25N	30 30E
Kigali Rwanda	83	B4	1 56S	30 04E
Kilbaha Rol	21	B2	52 35N	9 52W
Kilbeggan Rol	20	D3	53 22N	7 30W
Kilberry Rol	20	E3	53 43N	6 41W
Kilbirnie Scotland	11	E2	55 46N	4 41W
Kilbrannan Sound Scotland	10	D2	55 30N	5 30W
Kilcavan Rol	20	D3	53 11N	7 21W
Kilchoan Scotland	8	C1	56 43N	6 06W
Kilcock Rol	20	E3	53 24N	6 40W
Kilcormac Rol	21	D3	53 10N	7 43W
Kilcreggan Scotland	11	E2	56 01N	4 48W
Kilcullen Rol	21	E3	53 08N	6 45W
Kildare Rol	21	E3	53 10N	6 55W
Kildare *co.* Rol	21	E3	53 10N	6 55W
Kildorrery Rol	21	C2	52 15N	8 20W
Kilfinnane Rol	21	C2	52 22N	8 28W
Kilgetty Wales	21	B1	51 45N	4 44W
Kinglass Lough Rol	20	C3	53 50N	8 01W
Kilimanjaro *mt.* Tanzania	83	E3	3 04S	37 22E
Kilkeary Rol	21	C2	52 50N	8 07W
Kilkee Rol	21	B2	52 41N	9 38W
Kilkeel NI	10	C1	54 04N	6 00W
Kilkelly Rol	20	C3	53 53N	8 51W
Kilkenny *co.* Rol	21	D2	52 30N	7 10W
Kilkenny Rol	21	D2	52 39N	7 15W
Kilkhampton England	18	C2	50 53N	4 29W
Kilkieran Bay Rol	20	B3	53 18N	9 41W
Kilkishen Rol	21	C2	52 48N	8 45W
Killala Rol	20	B4	54 13N	9 13W
Killaloe Rol	21	C2	52 48N	8 27W
Killamarsh England	13	E2	53 20N	1 20W
Killarney Rol	21	B2	52 03N	9 30W
Killary Harbour Rol	20	B3	53 38N	9 55W
Killeigh Rol	20	D3	53 13N	7 27W
Killenaule Rol	21	D2	52 34N	7 40W
Killimer Rol	21	B2	52 37N	9 24W
Killimor Rol	21	C3	53 10N	8 17W
Killin Scotland	9	E1	56 28N	4 19W
Killorglin Rol	21	B2	52 06N	9 47W
Killybegs Rol	20	C4	54 38N	8 27W
Killyleagh NI	10	D1	54 24N	5 39W
Kilmacolm Scotland	11	E2	55 54N	4 38W
Kilmacrenan Rol	20	D5	55 02N	7 47W
Kilmacthomas Rol	21	D2	52 12N	7 25W
Kilmallock Rol	21	C2	52 23N	8 34W
Kilmaluag Scotland	8	C2	57 41N	6 17W
Kilmarnock Scotland	11	E2	55 36N	4 30W
Kilmona Rol	21	C1	51 58N	8 33W
Kilmory Scotland	10	D2	55 55N	5 41W
Kilrea NI	10	C1	54 57N	6 33W
Kilrenny Scotland	11	G3	56 15N	2 41W
Kilrush Rol	21	B2	52 39N	9 30W
Kilsheelan Rol	21	D2	52 22N	7 35W
Kilsyth Scotland	11	E2	55 59N	4 04W
Kiltamagh Rol	20	B3	53 51N	9 00W
Kiltealy Rol	21	E2	52 34N	6 45W
Kiltullagh Rol	21	C3	53 35N	8 35W
Kilwinning Scotland	11	E2	55 40N	4 42W
Kimberley Canada	88	M3	49 40N	115 58W
Kimberley England	15	E2	53 00N	1 17W
Kimbolton England	16	C3	52 18N	0 24W
Kinbrace Scotland	9	F3	58 15N	3 56W
Kineton England	15	E2	52 10N	1 30W
Kingsbridge England	18	D2	50 17N	3 46W
Kingsclere England	16	B2	51 20N	1 14W
Kingscourt Rol	20	E3	53 53N	6 48W
Kingskerswell England	18	D2	50 30N	3 37W
Kings Langley England	16	C2	51 43N	0 28W
King's Lynn England	17	D3	52 45N	0 24E
Kings Muir Scotland	11	F2	55 40N	3 12W
Kingsport USA	91	K4	36 33N	82 34W
Kingsteignton England	18	D2	50 33N	3 35W
Kingston Jamaica	95	U13	17 58N	76 48W
Kingston upon Hull England	13	F2	53 45N	0 20W
Kingston-upon-Thames England	16	C2	51 25N	0 18W
Kingswood England	15	D1	51 28N	2 30W
Kington England	14	C2	52 12N	3 01W
Kingussie Scotland	9	E2	57 05N	4 03W
Kinloch Scotland	8	C1	57 01N	6 17W
Kinlocheil Scotland	8	D1	56 51N	5 20W
Kinlochewe Scotland	8	D2	57 36N	5 20W
Kinlochleven Scotland	9	E1	56 42N	4 58W
Kinloch Rannoch Scotland	9	E1	56 42N	4 11W
Kinloss Scotland	9	F2	57 38N	3 33W
Kinlough Rol	20	C4	54 27N	8 17W
Kinnaird Head Scotland	9	G2	57 40N	2 00W
Kinnegad Rol	20	D3	53 27N	7 05W
Kinnitty Rol	21	D3	53 06N	7 43W
Kinross Scotland	11	F3	56 13N	3 27W
Kinsale Rol	21	C1	51 42N	8 32W
Kinsale Harbour Rol	21	C1	51 40N	8 30W
Kinshasa CDR	82	C7	4 18S	15 18E
Kintore Scotland	9	G2	57 13N	2 21W
Kintyre *p.* Scotland	10	D2	55 30N	5 35W
Kinvarra Rol	21	C3	53 08N	8 56W
Kippax England	13	E2	53 46N	1 22W
Kippford Scotland	11	F1	54 52N	3 49W
Kirby Muxloe England	15	E2	52 38N	1 14W
Kircubbin NI	10	D1	54 29N	5 28W
KIRIBATI	100	K7		
Kirikkale Turkey	57	D2	39 51N	33 32E
Kirkbean Scotland	11	F1	54 55N	3 36W
Kirkburton England	13	E2	53 37N	1 42W
Kirkby England	12	D2	53 29N	2 54W
Kirkby in Ashfield England	13	E2	53 13N	1 15W
Kirkby Londsale England	12	D3	54 13N	2 36W
Kirkbymoorside England	13	F3	54 16N	0 55W
Kirkby Stephen England	12	D3	54 28N	2 20W
Kirkcaldy Scotland	11	F3	56 07N	3 10W
Kirkcolm Scotland	10	D1	54 58N	5 04W
Kirkconnel Scotland	11	F2	55 23N	4 00W
Kirkcowan Scotland	11	E1	54 55N	4 36W
Kirkcudbright Scotland	11	E1	54 50N	4 03W
Kirkgunzeon Scotland	11	F1	54 58N	3 46W
Kirkham England	12	D2	53 47N	2 53W
Kirkintilloch Scotland	11	F2	55 57N	4 10W
Kirkmuirhill Scotland	11	F2	55 39N	3 55W
Kirkpatrick Durham Scotland	11	F2	55 01N	3 54W
Kirk Sandall England	13	E2	53 34N	1 04W
Kirkwall Scotland	7	B1	58 59N	2 58W
Kirov Russia	62	G8	58 00N	49 38E
Kirovohrad Ukraine	56	D4	48 31N	32 15E
Kirriemuir Scotland	9	F1	56 41N	3 01W
Kirton England	16	C3	52 56N	0 04W
Kisumu Kenya	83	D4	0 08S	34 47E
Kita-Kyūshū Japan	70	B1	33 52N	130 49E
Kitami Japan	70	D3	43 51N	143 54E
Kitchener Canada	89	U2	43 27N	80 30W
Kitimat Canada	88	K4	54 05N	128 38W
Kitzbühel Austria	52	F3	47 27N	12 23E
Klaipėda Lithuania	49	F2	55 43N	21 07E
Klamath Falls *tn.* USA	90	B5	42 14N	121 47W
Klöfta Norway	49	D3	60 04N	11 06E
Knapdale Scotland	10	D2	55 52N	5 31W
Knaresborough England	13	E3	54 00N	1 27W
Knighton England	14	C2	52 21N	3 03W
Knock Rol	20	C3	53 47N	8 55W
Knockadoon Head Rol	21	D1	51 50N	7 50W
Knockanevin Rol	21	C2	52 17N	8 21W
Knockdrislagh Rol	21	C2	52 03N	8 41W
Knocktopher Rol	21	D2	52 29N	7 13W
Knokke-Heist Belgium	48	B4	51 21N	3 19E
Knottingley England	13	E2	53 43N	1 14W
Knowle England	15	E2	52 23N	1 43W
Knoxville USA	91	K4	36 00N	83 57W
Knutsford England	12	D2	53 18N	2 23W
Kōbe Japan	70	C1	34 40N	135 12E
Koblenz Germany	52	C5	50 21N	7 36E
Kōfu Japan	70	C2	35 42N	138 34E
Kokkola Finland	49	F3	62 45N	30 06E
Kolhapur India	66	C3	16 40N	74 20E
Kolkata India	67	F4	22 30N	88 20E
Komatsu Japan	70	C2	36 25N	136 27E
Komotiní Greece	55	L4	41 06N	25 25E
Kóniz Switz.	52	C3	46 56N	7 25E
Konstanz Germany	52	D3	47 40N	9 10E
Konz Germany	48	E2	49 42N	6 35E
Koper Slovenia	54	E6	45 31N	13 44E
Korbach Germany	52	D5	51 16N	8 53E
Korinthiakós Kólpos *g.* Greece	55	K3	38 00N	22 00E
Kórinthos Greece	55	K2	37 56N	22 55E
Kortrijk Belgium	48	B3	50 50N	3 17E
Kós *i.* Greece	55	M2	36 45N	27 10E
Košice Slovakia	53	K4	48 44N	21 15E
Koszalin Poland	53	H7	54 10N	16 10E
Kotka Finland	49	G3	60 26N	26 55E
Kovrov Russia	56	F6	56 23N	41 21E
Kozáni Greece	55	J4	40 18N	21 48E
Kragujevac Yugoslavia	55	J5	44 01N	20 55E
Kraków Poland	53	J5	50 03N	19 55E
Kranj Slovenia	54	F7	46 15N	14 20E
Krefeld Germany	52	C5	51 20N	6 32E
Krems Austria	52	G4	48 25N	15 36E
Kristiansand Norway	49	C2	58 08N	8 01E
Kristianstad Sweden	49	D2	56 02N	14 10E
Kriti *i.* Greece	55	L1	35 00N	25 00E
Kryvyy Roh Ukraine	56	D4	47 55N	33 24E
Kuala Lumpur Malaysia	71	C4	3 09N	101 42E
Kuching Malaysia	71	E4	1 35N	110 21E
Kufstein Austria	52	F3	47 36N	12 11E
Kumamoto Japan	70	B1	32 50N	130 42E
Kunlun Shan *mts.* China	68	D5/E5	36 30N	85 00E
Kunming China	69	H3	25 04N	102 41E
Kurashiki Japan	70	B1	34 36N	133 43E
Kurgan Russia	62	J8	55 30N	65 20E
Kuril Islands Russia	63	T6	50 00N	155 00E
Kursk Russia	62	F7	51 45N	36 14E
Kushiro Japan	70	D3	42 58N	144 24E
KUWAIT	65	E4		
Kuwait Kuwait	65	E4	29 20N	48 00E
Kuytun China	68	D6	44 30N	85 00E
Kwangju S. Korea	69	N5	35 07N	126 52E
Kyleakin Scotland	8	D2	57 16N	5 44W
Kyle of Lochalsh Scotland	8	D2	57 17N	5 43W
Kyles of Bute Scotland	10	D2	55 52N	5 13W
Kylestrome Scotland	9	D3	58 16N	5 02W
Kyōto Japan	70	C2	35 02N	135 45E
KYRGYZSTAN	62	K5		
Kythira *i.* Greece	55	K2	36 00N	23 00E
Kýthnos *i.* Greece	55	L2	37 25N	24 25E
Kyūshū *i.* Japan	70	B1	32 20N	131 00E

L

Laâyoune Western Sahara	80	B7	27 10N	13 11W
Labrador *geog. reg.* Canada	89	Y4	54 00N	63 00W
la Chaux-de-Fonds Switz.	52	C3	47 07N	6 51E
la Ciotat France	50	G2	43 10N	5 36E
Lac Léman Switzerland	52	C3	46 20N	6 20E
La Coruña Spain	51	A5	43 22N	8 24W
La Crosse USA	91	H5	43 48N	91 04W
Lacul Razim *l.* Romania	53	P2	45 00N	29 00E
Ladozhskoye Ozero *l.* Russia	62	F9	61 00N	30 00E
Ladybank Scotland	11	F3	56 17N	3 08W
Lagan *r.* NI	10	C1	54 30N	6 05W
Laggan Bay *b.* Scotland	10	C2	55 38N	6 17W
Lago di Como *l.* Italy	54	C6	46 00N	9 00E
Lago di Garda *l.* Italy	54	D6	45 00N	10 00E
Lago Maggiore *l.* Italy	54	C6	46 00N	8 00E
Lagos Nigeria	80	E3	6 27N	3 28E
Lagos Portugal	51	A2	37 05N	8 40W
Lago Titicaca *l.* Peru/Bolivia	96	C10/D10	16 00S	69 30W
La Grande USA	90	C6	45 21N	118 05W
La Grande Rivière Canada	89	W4	54 00N	74 00W
Lahore Pakistan	66	C6	31 34N	74 22E
Lahti Finland	49	G3	61 00N	25 40E
Lairg Scotland	9	E3	58 01N	4 25W
Lakenheath England	17	D3	52 25N	0 31E
La Línea de la Concepción Spain	51	C2	36 10N	5 21W
La Maddalena Italy	54	C4	41 13N	9 25E
Lamar USA	90	F4	38 04N	102 37W
Lambay Island Rol	20	E3	53 29N	6 01W
Lambourn England	16	B2	51 31N	1 31W
Lambourn *r.* England	16	B2	51 27N	1 28W
Lamego Portugal	51	B4	41 05N	7 49W
Lamia Greece	55	K3	38 55N	22 26E
Lamlash Scotland	10	D2	55 32N	5 08W
Lammermuir Hills Scotland	11	G2	55 50N	2 45W
Lampeter Wales	14	B2	52 07N	4 05W
Lanark Scotland	11	F2	55 41N	3 48W
Lancashire *co.* England	12	D2	53 50N	2 30W
Lancaster England	12	D3	54 03N	2 48W
Lanchester England	13	E3	54 50N	1 44W
Lancing England	16	C1	50 50N	0 19W
Landerneau France	50	B5	48 27N	4 16W
Land's End *c.* England	18	B2	50 03N	5 44W
Landshut Germany	52	F4	48 31N	12 10E
Landskrona Sweden	49	D2	55 53N	12 50E
Langdon USA	92	A3	48 46N	98 21W
Langholm Scotland	11	F2	55 09N	3 00W
Langport England	19	E3	51 02N	2 50W
Langres France	50	G4	47 53N	5 20E
Lannion France	50	C5	48 44N	3 27W
L'Anse USA	92	C3	46 45N	88 27W
Lansing USA	91	K5	42 44N	85 34W
Lanzarote *i.* Spain	80	B7	29 00N	13 38W
Lanzhou China	69	H5	36 01N	103 45E
Laois *co.* Rol	21	D2	52 59N	7 25W
Laon France	50	F5	49 34N	3 37E
LAOS	71	C7/D7		
La Paz Bolivia	96	D10	16 30S	68 10W
Lapford England	18	D2	50 52N	3 47W
Lappland *geog. reg.* Finland/Sweden	49	F4/G4	67 30N	20 05E
Lapua Finland	49	F3	62 57N	23 00E
L'Aquila Italy	54	E4	42 22N	13 24E
Laragh Rol	21	E3	53 00N	6 18W
Laredo USA	90	G2	27 32N	99 22W
Largs Scotland	11	E2	55 48N	4 52W
Lárisa Greece	55	K3	39 38N	22 25E
Larkhall Scotland	11	F2	55 45N	3 59W
Larne NI	10	D1	54 51N	5 49W
Larne *district* NI	10	D1	54 50N	6 00W
Larne Lough *b.* NI	10	D1	54 49N	5 49W
la Rochelle France	50	D4	46 10N	1 10W
la Roche-sur-Yon France	50	D4	46 40N	1 25W
La Roda Spain	51	D3	39 13N	2 15W
La Seo d'Urgel Spain	51	F5	42 22N	1 27E
la Seyne-sur-Mer France	50	G2	43 06N	5 53E
Las Palmas Spain	80	A7	28 08N	15 27W
La Spézia Italy	54	C6	44 07N	9 48E
Las Vegas USA	90	C4	36 10N	115 10W
Latakia Syria	64	C6	35 31N	35 47E
Latheron Scotland	9	F3	58 17N	3 22W
Latina Italy	54	E4	41 28N	12 53E
LATVIA	49	G2		
Lauder Scotland	11	G2	55 43N	2 45W
Laugharne Wales	14	B1	51 47N	4 28W
Launceston Australia	73	J2	41 25N	147 07E
Launceston England	18	C2	50 38N	4 21W
Lauragh Rol	21	B1	51 46N	9 46W
Laurel USA	91	J3	31 41N	89 09W
Laurencekirk Scotland	9	G1	56 50N	2 29W
Laurencetown Rol	21	C3	53 14N	8 10W
Lauria Italy	54	F4	40 03N	15 50E
Laurieston Scotland	11	E1	54 57N	4 03W
Laurieston Scotland	11	F2	55 59N	3 45W
Lausanne Switz.	52	C3	46 32N	6 39E
Laval France	50	D5	48 04N	0 45W
Lavenham England	17	D2	52 06N	0 47E
Lawrence USA	91	G4	38 58N	95 15W
Lawton USA	91	G3	34 36N	98 25W
Laxey Isle of Man	12	B3	54 14N	4 24W
Laxford Bridge *tn.* Scotland	9	D3	58 22N	5 01W
Lay *r.* France	50	D4	46 32N	1 15W
Lazonby England	12	D3	54 46N	2 41W
Lea *r.* England	16	C2	51 47N	0 17W
Leach *r.* England	16	B2	51 46N	1 41W
Leadhills Scotland	11	F2	55 25N	3 47W
Leadon *r.* England	15	D1	51 57N	2 21W
Leatherhead England	16	C2	51 18N	0 20W

LEBANON 64 C5
Lebanon USA 91 H4 37 40N 92 40W
le Blanc France 50 E4 46 38N 1 04E
Lebrija Spain 51 B2 36 55N 6 10W
Lecarrow Rol 20 C3 53 33N 8 02W
Lecce Italy 55 H4 40 21N 18 11E
Lechlade England 15 E1 51 43N 1 41W
le Creusot France 50 G4 46 48N 4 27E
Ledbury England 15 D2 52 02N 2 25W
Ledmore Scotland 9 E3 58 03N 4 58W
Leeds England 13 E2 53 50N 1 35W
Leek England 12 D2 53 06N 2 01W
Leenaun Rol 20 B3 53 36N 9 41W
Leeuwarden Neths 48 D6 53 12N 5 48E
Leeward Islands
  Lesser Antilles 95 M3 17 30N 64 00W
Lefkáda i. Greece 55 J3 38 45N 20 40E
Leganés Spain 51 D4 40 20N 3 46WE
Legnica Poland 53 H5 51 12N 16 10E
le Havre France 50 E5 49 30N 0 06E
Leicester England 15 E2 52 38N 1 05W
Leicester City u.a. England 15 E2 52 38N 1 05W
Leicestershire co. England 15 E2 52 40N 1 20W
Leiden Neths 48 C5 52 10N 4 30E
Leigh England 12 D2 53 30N 2 33W
Leighton Buzzard England 16 C2 51 55N 0 41W
Leipzig Germany 52 F5 51 20N 12 25E
Leiria Portugal 51 A3 39 45N 8 49W
Leiston England 17 E3 52 13N 1 34E
Leith Hill tn. England 16 C2 51 11N 0 23W
Leitrim co. Rol 20 C4 54 05N 8 00W
Leivadiá Greece 55 K3 38 26N 22 53E
Leixlip Rol 20 E3 53 22N 6 30W
le Mans France 50 E4 48 00N 0 12E
Lemybrien Rol 21 D2 52 10N 7 31W
Lena r. Russia 63 Q10 70 00N 125 00E
Lens France 50 F6 50 26N 2 50E
Leoben Austria 52 G3 47 23N 15 06E
Leominster England 14 D2 52 14N 2 45W
León Mexico 94 D4 21 10N 101 42W
León Spain 51 C5 42 35N 5 34W
Leonding Austria 52 G4 48 19N 14 17E
le Puy France 50 F3 45 03N 3 53E
Lerwick Scotland 7 C3 60 09N 1 09W
Lesmahagow Scotland 11 F2 55 38N 3 54W
LESOTHO 82 E2
les Sables-d'Olonne France 50 D4 46 30N 1 47W
Lesser Antilles is. W. Indies 95 M2/M3 18 00N 65 00W
Lesser Slave Lake Canada 88 M5 55 25N 115 30W
Lésvos i. Greece 55 M3 39 00N 26 00E
Leswalt Scotland 10 D1 54 46N 5 05W
Letchworth England 16 C2 51 58N 0 14W
le Touquet-Paris-Plage France 50 E6 50 13N 1 36E
le Tréport France 50 E6 50 04N 1 22E
Letterfrack Rol 20 B3 53 33N 9 57W
Letterkenny Rol 20 D4 54 57N 7 44W
Leuchars Scotland 9 G1 56 23N 2 53W
Levanto Italy 54 C6 44 10N 9 37E
Leven England 13 F2 53 54N 0 19W
Leven Scotland 11 G3 56 11N 3 00W
Leverburgh Scotland 8 B2 57 45N 7 00W
Leverkusen Germany 52 C5 51 02N 6 59E
Lewes England 16 D1 50 52N 0 01E
Lewis i. Scotland 8 C3 58 15N 6 30W
Lexington USA 91 K4 38 03N 84 30W
Lexington USA 93 E1 37 47N 79 27W
Leyburn England 13 E3 54 19N 1 49W
Leyland England 12 D2 53 42N 2 42W
Leysdown on Sea England 17 D2 51 24N 0 55E
Lhasa China 68 F3 29 41N 91 10E
LIBERIA 80 B3/C3
Libourne France 50 D3 44 55N 0 14W
Libreville Gabon 80 F2 0 30N 9 25E
LIBYA 81 G7/K7
Libyan Desert North Africa 81 K7/L6 25 00N 25 00E
Lichfield England 15 E2 52 42N 1 48W
LIECHTENSTEIN 52 D3
Liège Belgium 48 D3 50 38N 5 35E
Lienz Austria 52 F3 46 51N 12 50E
Liepāja Latvia 49 F2 56 30N 21 00E
Liffey r. Rol 20 E3 53 16N 6 37W
Lifford Rol 20 D4 54 50N 7 29W
Lille France 50 F6 50 39N 3 05E
Lillehammer Norway 49 D3 61 06N 10 27E
Lilongwe Malawi 82 F5 13 58S 33 49E
Lima Peru 96 B11 12 06S 8 40W
Limavady NI 10 C2 55 03N 6 57W
Limavady district NI 10 B1/C1 54 50N 7 00W
Limburg Germany 52 D5 50 23N 8 04E
Limerick Rol 21 C2 52 04N 8 38W
Limerick co. Rol 21 C2 52 30N 8 40W
Limoges France 50 E3 45 50N 1 15E
Limoux France 50 F2 43 03N 2 13E
Limpopo r. Southern Africa 82 F3 22 30S 32 00E
Linares Spain 51 D3 38 05N 3 38W
Lincoln England 13 F2 53 14N 0 33W
Lincoln USA 91 G5 40 49N 96 41W

Lincolnshire co. England 13 F2 53 10N 0 20W
Lincoln Wolds England 13 F2 53 25N 0 05W
Lingen Germany 52 C6 52 32N 7 19E
Lingfield England 16 C2 51 11N 0 01W
Linköping Sweden 49 E2 58 25N 15 35E
Linlithgow Scotland 11 F2 55 59N 3 37W
Linslade England 16 C2 51 55N 0 42W
Linton England 17 D3 52 06N 0 17E
Linz Austria 52 G4 48 19N 14 18E
Liphook England 16 C2 51 05N 0 49W
Lippstadt Germany 52 D5 51 41N 8 20E
Lisbellaw NI 10 B1 54 19N 7 32W
Lisbon Portugal 51 A3 38 44N 9 08W
Lisburn NI 10 C1 54 31N 6 03W
Lisburn co. NI 10 C1 54 35N 6 10W
Liscannor Bay Rol 21 B2 52 55N 9 30W
Lisdoonvarna Rol 21 B3 53 02N 9 17W
Lisieux France 50 E5 49 09N 0 14E
Liskeard England 18 C2 50 28N 4 28W
Lismore Rol 21 D2 52 08N 7 55W
Lismore i. Scotland 8 D1 56 30N 5 30W
Lisnaskea NI 10 B1 54 15N 7 27W
Liss England 16 C2 51 03N 0 55W
Lisse Neths 48 C5 52 16N 4 34E
Lissycasey Rol 21 B2 52 44N 9 12W
Listowel Rol 21 B2 52 27N 9 29W
Litherland England 12 D2 53 28N 2 59W
LITHUANIA 49 F2
Littleborough England 12 D2 53 39N 2 05W
Littlehampton England 16 C1 50 48N 0 33W
Little Minch sd. Scotland 8 C2 57 45N 6 30W
Little Ouse r. England 17 D3 52 30N 0 30E
Littleport England 17 D3 52 28N 0 19E
Liverpool England 12 D2 53 25N 2 55W
Liverpool Bay England 12 C2 53 28N 3 15W
Liversedge England 13 E2 53 43N 1 41W
Livingston Scotland 11 F2 55 53N 3 32W
Livorno Italy 54 D5 43 33N 10 18E
Lizard England 18 B1 49 57N 5 13W
Lizard Point England 18 B1 49 56N 5 13W
Ljubljana Slovenia 54 F7 46 04N 14 30E
Ljusdal Sweden 49 E3 61 57N 16 05E
Llanberis Wales 14 B3 53 07N 4 06W
Llanbister Wales 14 C2 52 21N 3 19W
Llandeilo Wales 14 C1 51 53N 3 59W
Llandovery Wales 14 C1 51 59N 3 48W
Llandrindod Wells Wales 14 C2 52 15N 3 23W
Llandudno Wales 14 C3 53 19N 3 49W
Llandysul Wales 14 B2 52 02N 4 19W
Llanelli Wales 14 B1 51 42N 4 10W
Llanerchymedd Wales 14 B3 53 20N 4 22W
Llanes Spain 51 C3 43 25N 4 45W
Llanfair Caereinion Wales 14 C2 52 15N 3 20W
Llanfairfechan Wales 14 C3 53 15N 3 58W
Llanfyllin Wales 14 C2 52 46N 3 17W
Llangadfan Wales 14 C2 52 41N 3 28W
Llangadog Wales 14 C1 51 57N 3 53W
Llangefni Wales 14 B3 53 16N 4 18W
Llangollen Wales 14 C2 52 58N 3 10W
Llangurig Wales 14 C2 52 25N 3 36W
Llangynog Wales 14 C2 52 50N 3 25W
Llanharan Wales 14 C1 51 32N 3 28W
Llanidloes Wales 14 C2 52 27N 3 32W
Llanrhystud Wales 14 B2 52 18N 4 09W
Llanrwst Wales 14 C3 53 08N 3 48W
Llantrisant Wales 14 C1 51 33N 3 23W
Llantwit Major Wales 14 C1 51 25N 3 30W
Llanuwchllyn Wales 14 C2 52 52N 3 41W
Llanwrtyd Wells Wales 14 C2 52 07N 3 38W
Llanybydder Wales 14 B2 52 04N 4 09W
Lleida Spain 51 F4 41 37N 0 38E
Lleyn Peninsula Wales 14 B3 52 53N 4 30W
Llyn Brianne Resevoir Wales 14 C2 52 09N 3 43W
Llyn Celyn Wales 14 C2 53 04N 4 10W
Llyn Efyrnwy Wales 14 C2 52 50N 3 30W
Llyn Tegid Wales 14 C2 52 53N 3 38W
Loanhead Scotland 11 F2 55 53N 3 09W
Loch Affric Scotland 9 D2 57 15N 5 02W
Lochailort tn. Scotland 8 D1 56 53N 5 40W
Lochaline tn. Scotland 8 D1 56 32N 5 47W
Loch Alsh Scotland 8 D2 57 15N 5 35W
Locharbriggs Scotland 11 F2 55 06N 3 35W
Loch Assynt Scotland 9 D3/E3 58 05N 5 00W
Lochboisdale tn. Scotland 8 B2 57 09N 7 19W
Loch Bracadale Scotland 8 C2 57 20N 6 30W
Loch Broom Scotland 8 D2 57 52N 5 08W
Loch Caolisport Scotland 10 D2 55 53N 5 38W
Lochcarron tn. Scotland 8 D2 57 24N 5 30W
Loch Carron Scotland 8 D2 57 40N 5 45W
Loch Chroisg Scotland 8 D2 57 30N 5 10W
Loch Craignish Scotland 10 D3 56 05N 5 30W
Loch Creran Scotland 8 D1 56 30N 5 20W
Lochdon tn. Scotland 8 D1 56 35N 5 35W
Loch Duich Scotland 8 D2 57 15N 5 30W
Loch Earn Scotland 9 F1 56 25N 4 10W
Lochearnhead Scotland 9 E1 56 23N 4 18W
Loch Eil Scotland 8 D1 56 50N 5 25W
Loch Eishort Scotland 8 C2/D2 57 08N 6 00W
Loch Eriboll Scotland 9 E3 58 31N 4 41W

Loch Ericht Scotland 9 E1 56 48N 4 25W
Loch Erisort Scotland 8 C3 58 05N 6 30W
Loches France 50 E4 47 08N 1 00E
Loch Etive Scotland 8 D1 56 30N 5 10W
Loch Ewe Scotland 8 D2 57 50N 5 40W
Loch Eynort Scotland 8 B2 57 10N 7 15W
Loch Fannich Scotland 9 D2 57 40N 5 00W
Loch Fyne Scotland 10 D3 56 00N 5 20W
Loch Gairloch Scotland 8 D2 57 45N 5 45W
Loch Garry Scotland 9 D2 57 05N 5 00W
Lochgelly Scotland 11 F3 56 08N 3 19W
Lochgilphead Scotland 10 D3 56 03N 5 26W
Loch Glass Scotland 9 E2 57 40N 4 30W
Loch Goil Scotland 10 E3 56 05N 4 55W
Loch Gorm Scotland 10 C2 55 49N 6 30W
Loch Gruinart Scotland 10 C2 55 51N 6 21W
Loch Hope Scotland 9 E3 58 25N 4 37W
Loch Indaal Scotland 10 C2 55 45N 6 21W
Lochinver tn. Scotland 8 D3 58 09N 5 15W
Loch Katrine Scotland 11 E3 56 16N 4 30W
Loch Ken Scotland 11 E2 55 02N 4 07W
Loch Laggan Scotland 9 E1 56 55N 4 30W
Loch Langavet Scotland 8 C3 58 05N 6 50W
Loch Leven Scotland 9 D1/E1 56 45N 5 05W
Loch Leven Scotland 11 F3 56 15N 3 23W
Loch Linnhe Scotland 8 D1 56 35N 5 25W
Loch Lochy Scotland 9 E1 56 58N 4 55W
Loch Lomond Scotland 11 E3 56 10N 4 35W
Loch Long Scotland 10 E3 56 05N 4 55W
Loch Lyon Scotland 9 E1 56 30N 4 35W
Lochmaben Scotland 11 F2 55 08N 3 27W
Lochmaddy Scotland 8 B2 57 36N 7 08W
Loch Maree Scotland 8 D2 57 40N 5 30W
Loch Meig Scotland 9 E2 57 05N 4 45W
Loch Melfort Scotland 10 D3 56 10N 5 30W
Loch Monar Scotland 9 D2 57 25N 5 02W
Loch Morar Scotland 8 D1 57 55N 5 45W
Loch More Scotland 9 E3 58 15N 4 55W
Loch Mullardoch Scotland 9 D2 57 27N 4 58W
Lochnagar mt. Scotland 9 F1 56 57N 3 16W
Loch Nan Clar Scotland 9 E2 58 15N 4 05W
Loch Ness Scotland 9 E2 57 02N 4 30W
Loch Nevis Scotland 8 D1/D2 57 00N 5 40W
Loch of Harray Scotland 7 A2 59 02N 3 14W
Loch Rannoch Scotland 9 E1 56 41N 4 18W
Lochranza tn. Scotland 10 D2 55 42N 5 18W
Loch Roag Scotland 8 C3 58 10N 6 50W
Loch Ryan Scotland 10 D2 55 00N 5 05W
Loch Scridain Scotland 8 C1 56 20N 6 05W
Loch Seaforth Scotland 8 C3 58 00N 6 40W
Loch Shell Scotland 8 C2 58 00N 6 25W
Loch Shiel Scotland 8 D1 56 45N 5 35W
Loch Shin Scotland 9 E3 58 05N 4 30W
Loch Snizort Scotland 8 C2 57 30N 6 30W
Loch Striven Scotland 10 D2 55 58N 5 07W
Loch Sunart Scotland 8 D1 56 40N 5 45W
Loch Sween Scotland 10 D2 55 58N 5 38W
Loch Tarbert Scotland 10 D2 55 57N 5 55W
Loch Tay Scotland 9 E1 56 31N 4 10W
Loch Torridon Scotland 8 D2 57 35N 5 46W
Lockerbie Scotland 11 F2 55 07N 3 22W
Lockhart USA 91 G2 29 54N 97 14W
Locks Heath England 16 B1 50 52N 1 17W
Loddon England 17 E2 52 32N 1 29E
Lofoten Islands Norway 49 D4 68 30N 15 00E
Lofthouse Gate England 13 E2 53 44N 1 30W
Loftus England 13 F3 54 33N 0 53W
Logan, Mount Canada 88 G6 60 34N 140 25W
Logroño Spain 51 D5 42 28N 2 26W
Loire r. France 50 D4 47 20N 1 20W
Loja Spain 51 C2 37 10N 4 09W
Lolland i. Denmark 49 D1 54 45N 12 20E
Lomé Togo 80 E3 6 10N 1 21E
London Canada 89 U2 42 58N 81 15W
London England 16 C2 51 30N 0 10W
Londonderry NI 10 B1 54 59N 7 19W
Londonderry district NI 10 B1 54 55N 7 20W
Londrina Brazil 96 G9 23 18S 51 13W
Long Beach tn. USA 90 C3 33 47N 118 15W
Longbenton England 13 E4 55 02N 1 35W
Long Crendon England 16 C2 51 47N 0 59W
Long Eaton England 15 E2 52 54N 1 15W
Longford Rol 20 D3 53 44N 7 47W
Longford co. Rol 20 D3 53 40N 7 50W
Longhorsley England 11 H2 55 15N 1 46W
Longhoughton England 11 H2 55 26N 1 36W
Long Melford England 17 D3 52 05N 0 43E
Longridge England 12 D2 53 51N 2 36W
Long Sutton England 17 D3 52 47N 0 08E
Longuyon France 50 G5 49 27N 5 36E
Longwy France 50 G5 49 32N 5 46E
Lons-le-Saunier France 50 G4 46 41N 5 33E
Looe England 18 C2 50 21N 4 27W
Loop Head Rol 21 B2 52 30N 9 55W
Lora del Rio Spain 51 C2 37 39N 5 32W
Lorca Spain 51 E2 37 40N 1 41W
Loreto Italy 54 E5 43 26N 13 36E
Lorient France 50 C4 47 45N 3 21W
Los Angeles USA 90 C3 34 00N 118 15W
Lossiemouth Scotland 9 F2 57 43N 3 18W
Lostwithiel England 18 C2 50 25N 4 40W
Loudéac France 50 C5 48 11N 2 45W

Lough Allen Rol 20 C4/D4 54 15N 8 00W
Lough Arrow Rol 20 C4 54 05N 8 15W
Lough Beg NI 10 C1 54 48N 6 30W
Loughborough England 15 E2 52 47N 1 11W
Lough Carra Rol 20 B3 53 40N 9 15W
Lough Conn Rol 20 B4 54 05N 9 10W
Lough Corrib Rol 20 B3 53 10N 9 10W
Lough Cullin Rol 20 B3 53 58N 9 10W
Lough Dan Rol 21 E3 53 05N 6 17W
Lough Derg Donegal Rol 20 D4 54 35N 7 55W
Lough Derg Tipperary Rol 21 C2 52 55N 8 15W
Lough Derravaragh Rol 20 D3 53 40N 7 22W
Lough Ennell Rol 20 D3 53 28N 7 24W
Lough Eske Rol 20 C4 54 41N 8 05W
Lough Feeagh Rol 20 B3 53 57N 9 35W
Lough Finn Rol 20 C4 54 51N 8 08W
Lough Graney Rol 21 C2 52 59N 8 40W
Lough Kinale Rol 20 D3 53 46N 7 25W
Lough Leane Rol 21 B2 52 03N 9 33W
Lough Macnean Lower NI 10 B1 54 17N 7 50W
Lough Macnean Upper NI/Rol 10 B1 54 18N 7 55W
Lough Mask Rol 20 B3 53 40N 9 30W
Lough Melvin Rol/NI 20 C4 54 25N 8 05W
Lough Neagh NI 10 C1 54 35N 6 30W
Lough Oughter Rol 20 D4 54 00N 7 30W
Loughrea tn. Rol 20 C3 53 12N 8 34W
Lough Rea Rol 20 C3 53 11N 8 05W
Lough Ree Rol 20 D3 53 35N 8 00W
Lough Sheelin Rol 20 D3 53 48N 7 20W
Lough Swilly Rol 20 D5 55 20N 7 35W
Loughton England 16 D2 51 39N 0 03E
Louisburgh Rol 20 B3 53 46N 9 48W
Louisiana state USA 91 H3 32 00N 92 00W
Louisville USA 91 J4 38 13N 85 48W
Lourdes France 50 D2 43 06N 0 02W
Louth England 13 F2 53 22N 0 01W
Louth Rol 20 E3 53 57N 6 33W
Louth co. Rol 20 E3 53 55N 6 25W
Louviers France 50 E5 49 13N 1 11E
Lower Lough Erne NI 10 B1 54 30N 7 45W
Lowestoft England 17 E3 52 29N 1 45E
Lowick England 11 H2 55 38N 1 58W
Lowther Hills Scotland 11 F2 55 25N 3 45W
Luanda Angola 82 B6 8 50S 13 15E
Luarca Spain 51 B5 43 33N 6 31W
Lubbock USA 90 F3 33 35N 101 53W
Lübeck Germany 52 E6 53 52N 10 40E
Lublin Poland 53 L5 51 18N 22 31E
Lubumbashi CDR 82 E5 11 41S 27 29E
Lucan Rol 20 E3 53 22N 6 27W
Lucca Italy 54 D5 43 50N 10 30E
Luce Bay Scotland 11 E1 54 47N 4 50W
Lucena Spain 51 C2 37 25N 4 29W
Luckenwalde Germany 52 F6 52 05N 13 11E
Lucknow India 66 E5 26 50N 80 54E
Ludgershall England 16 B2 51 16N 1 37W
Ludlow England 14 D2 52 22N 2 43W
Ludwigshafen Germany 52 D4 49 29N 8 27E
Ludwigslust Germany 52 E6 53 20N 11 30E
Lugano Switz. 52 D3 46 01N 8 57E
Lugnaquillia mt. Rol 21 E2 52 58N 6 27W
Lugo Spain 51 B5 43 00N 7 33W
Luhans'k Ukraine 56 E4 48 35N 39 20E
Luleå Sweden 49 F4 65 35N 22 10E
Lundy i. England 18 C3 51 11N 4 40W
Lüneburg Germany 52 E6 53 15N 10 24E
Lunéville France 50 H5 48 35N 6 30E
Lurgan NI 10 C1 54 28N 6 20W
Lusaka Zambia 82 E4 15 26S 28 20E
Lusk Rol 20 E3 53 32N 6 10W
Lustenau Austria 52 D3 47 26N 9 42E
Luton England 16 C2 51 53N 0 25W
Luton u.a. England 16 C2 51 53N 0 25W
Lutterworth England 15 E2 52 28N 1 10W
LUXEMBOURG 48 D2/E2
Luxembourg Luxembourg 48 E2 49 37N 6 08E
Luxor Egypt 81 M7 25 41N 32 24E
Luzern Switz. 52 D3 47 03N 8 18E
Luzhou China 69 J3 28 55N 105 25E
Luzon i. Philippines 71 G7 15 00N 122 00E
L'viv Ukraine 53 M4 49 50N 24 00E
Lybster Scotland 9 F3 58 18N 3 13W
Lydd England 17 D1 50 57N 0 55E
Lydham England 15 D2 52 31N 2 59W
Lydney England 15 D1 51 43N 2 32W
Lyme Bay England 19 D2 50 40N 2 55W
Lyme Regis England 19 D2 50 44N 2 57W
Lyminge England 17 E2 51 08N 1 05E
Lymington England 16 B1 50 46N 1 33W
Lymm England 12 D2 53 23N 2 28W
Lyndhurst England 16 B1 50 52N 1 34W
Lynher r. England 18 C2 50 33N 4 25W
Lynmouth England 18 C3 51 15N 3 50W
Lynn Lake tn. Canada 89 Q5 56 51N 101 01W
Lynton England 18 C3 51 15N 3 50W
Lyon France 50 G3 45 46N 4 50E
Lytham St. Anne's England 12 C2 53 45N 3 01W

M

Name		Page	Grid	Lat	Long
Maam Cross Rol		20	B3	53 27N	9 33W
Maas r. Neths		48	E4	51 50N	5 32E
Maastricht Neths		48	D3	50 51N	5 42E
Mablethorpe England		13	G2	53 21N	0 15E
Macao China		69	K2	22 10N	113 40E
Macapá Brazil		96	G14	0 04N	51 04W
Macarata Italy		54	E5	43 18N	13 27E
Macclesfield England		12	D2	53 16N	2 07W
Macdonnell Ranges					
Australia		72	F6	24 00S	132 30E
Macduff Scotland		9	G2	57 40N	2 29W
Maceió Brazil		96	K12	9 40S	35 44W
Macgillycuddy's Reeks					
mts. Rol		21	B2	52 00N	9 27W
The Machars Scotland		11	E1	54 49N	4 31W
Machrihanish Scotland		10	D2	55 26N	5 44W
Machynlleth Wales		14	C2	52 35N	3 51W
Mackenzie r. Canada		88	J7	67 00N	132 00W
Mackenzie Mountains					
Canada		88	J7/L6	66 00N	130 00W
McKinley, Mount USA		88	E6	62 02N	151 01W
McKinney USA		91	G3	33 14N	96 37W
Mâcon France		50	G4	46 18N	4 50E
Macon USA		91	K3	32 49N	83 37W
Macroom Rol		21	C1	51 54N	8 57W
MADAGASCAR		82	H2/J5		
Madeira r. Brazil		96	E12	6 00S	61 30W
Madeira Islands					
Atlantic Ocean		80	A8	32 45N	17 00W
Madison USA		91	J5	43 04N	89 22W
Madrid Spain		51	D4	40 25N	3 43W
Maesteg Wales		14	C1	51 37N	3 40W
Magadan Russia		63	T8	59 38N	150 50E
Magdeburg Germany		52	E6	52 08N	11 37E
Maghera NI		10	C1	54 51N	6 40W
Magherafelt NI		10	C1	54 45N	6 36W
Magherafelt district NI		10	C1	54 45N	6 50W
Maghull England		12	D2	55 32N	2 57W
Mahilyow Belarus		53	Q6	53 54N	30 20E
Mahón Spain		51	H3	39 54N	4 15E
Maidenhead England		16	C2	51 32N	0 44W
Maiden Newton					
England		19	E2	50 46N	2 35W
Maidstone England		17	D2	51 17N	0 32E
Main r. NI		10	C1	54 50N	6 20W
Maine state USA		91	N6	45 00N	70 00W
Mainz Germany		52	D4	50 00N	8 16E
Málaga Spain		51	C2	36 43N	4 25W
Malahide Rol		20	E3	53 27N	6 09W
Malatya Turkey		57	E2	38 22N	38 18E
MALAWI		82	F6		
MALAYSIA		71	C5/E5		
MALDIVES		103			
Maldon England		17	D2	51 45N	0 40E
MALI		80	C4/D5		
Malin Head Rol		20	D5	55 30N	7 20W
Malin More Rol		20	C4	54 41N	8 46W
Mallaig Scotland		8	D2	57 00N	5 50W
Mallorca i. Spain		51	G3	39 50N	2 30E
Mallow Rol		21	C2	52 08N	8 39W
Malmesbury England		16	A2	51 36N	2 06W
Malmö Sweden		49	D2	55 35N	13 00E
Malpas England		12	D2	53 01N	2 46W
MALTA		54	F1		
Maltby England		13	E2	53 26N	1 11W
Malton England		13	F3	54 08N	0 48W
Malvern Hills England		15	D2	52 05N	2 22W
Manacor Spain		51	G3	39 35N	3 12E
Managua Nicaragua		94	G2	12 06N	86 18W
Manama Bahrain		65	F4	26 12N	50 38E
Manaus Brazil		96	F13	3 06S	60 00W
Manchester England		12	D2	53 30N	2 15W
Manfredonia Italy		54	F4	41 37N	15 55E
Mangotsfield England		15	D1	51 29N	2 31W
Manhattan USA		93	F2	40 48N	73 58W
Manila Philippines		71	G6	14 37N	120 58E
Manitoba prov. Canada		89	R5	55 15N	100 00W
Manitoba, Lake Canada		89	R4	50 30N	98 15W
Mannheim Germany		52	D4	49 30N	8 28E
Manningtree England		17	E2	51 57N	1 04E
Manorhamilton Rol		20	C4	54 18N	8 10W
Manresa Spain		51	F4	41 43N	1 50E
Mansfield England		13	E2	53 09N	1 11W
Mansfield Woodhouse					
England		13	E2	53 10N	1 11W
Mantes-la-Jolie France		50	E5	48 59N	1 43E
Manuta Italy		54	D6	45 10N	10 47E
Manzanares Spain		51	D3	39 00N	3 23W
Maputo Mozambique		82	F2	25 58S	32 35E
Marabá Brazil		96	H12	5 23S	49 10W
Maracaibo Venezuela		96	C16	10 44N	71 37W
Marbella Spain		51	C2	36 31N	4 53W
Marburg Germany		52	D5	50 49N	8 36E
March England		17	D3	52 33N	0 06E
Mar del Plata Argentina		97	F6	38 00S	57 32W
Marden England		17	D2	51 11N	0 30E
Maresfield England		17	D2	51 00N	0 05E
Margam Wales		14	C1	51 34N	3 44W
Margate England		17	E2	51 24N	1 24E
Maribor Slovenia		54	F7	46 34N	15 38E
Marignane France		50	G2	43 25N	5 12E
Mariupol' Ukraine		57	E2	47 05N	37 34E
Market Deeping					
England		15	F2	52 41N	0 19W

Name		Page	Grid	Lat	Long
Market Drayton					
England		15	D2	52 54N	2 29W
Market Harborough					
England		15	F2	52 29N	0 55W
Markethill NI		10	C1	54 18N	6 31W
Market Rasen England		13	F2	53 24N	0 21W
Market Weighton					
England		13	F2	53 52N	0 40W
Markinch Scotland		11	F3	56 12N	3 09W
Marlborough England		16	B2	51 26N	1 43W
Marlborough Downs					
England		16	B2	51 28N	1 50W
Marlow England		16	C2	51 35N	0 48W
Marmande France		50	E3	44 30N	0 10E
Marple England		12	D2	53 24N	2 03W
Marrakesh Morocco		80	C8	31 49N	8 00W
Marsala Italy		54	E2	37 48N	12 27E
Marsden West Yorkshire					
England		13	E2	53 36N	1 55W
Marsden Tyne and Wear					
England		13	E3	54 58N	1 21W
Marseille France		50	G2	43 18N	5 22E
MARSHALL ISLANDS		100	G9/H8		
Marshfield England		15	D1	51 28N	2 19W
Marske-by-the-Sea					
England		13	E3	54 36N	1 01W
Martigny Switz.		52	C3	46 07N	7 05E
Martigues France		50	G2	43 24N	5 03E
Martinique i.					
Lesser Antilles		94	R12	14 30N	61 00W
Martos Spain		51	C2	37 44N	3 58W
Maryland state USA		91	L4	39 00N	77 00W
Maryport England		12	C3	54 43N	3 30W
Maryport Scotland		10	E1	54 43N	3 30W
Maseru Lesotho		82	E2	29 19S	27 29E
Masham England		13	E3	54 13N	1 40W
Mashhad Iran		65	G6	36 16N	59 34E
Massa Italy		54	D5	44 02N	10 09E
Massachusetts state					
USA		91	M5	42 00N	72 00W
Massif Central France		50	F3	45 00N	3 30E
Massif de la Vanoise					
France		50	H3	45 20N	6 20E
Mataró Spain		51	G4	41 32N	2 27E
Matera Italy		55	G4	40 40N	16 37E
Matlock England		13	E2	53 08N	1 32W
Matterhorn mt. Switz.		52	C3/C4	45 59N	7 39E
Maubeuge France		50	F6	50 17N	3 58E
Mauchline Scotland		11	E2	55 31N	4 24W
MAURITANIA		80	B5/C6C		
MAURITIUS		103			
Maybole Scotland		11	E2	55 21N	4 41W
Mayenne France		50	D5	48 18N	0 37W
Maykop Russia		62	G5	44 37N	40 48E
Maynooth Rol		20	E3	53 23N	6 35W
Mayo NI		20	B3	54 35N	9 07W
Mayo co. Rol		20	B3	53 55N	9 20W
Mazamet France		50	F2	43 29N	2 22E
Mazara del Vallo Italy		54	E2	37 40N	12 34E
Mazarrón Spain		51	E2	37 36N	1 19W
Mazatlán Mexico		94	C4	23 11N	106 25W
Mazirbe Latvia		49	F2	57 40N	22 21E
Meath co. Rol		20	E3	35 35N	6 30W
Meaux France		50	F5	48 58N	2 54E
Mecca Saudi Arabia		64	C3	21 26N	39 49E
Medan Indonesia		71	B4	3 35N	98 39E
Medellín Colombia		96	B15	6 15N	75 36W
Mediterranean Sea		54	B2/E2	35 00N	15 00E
Medway r. England		17	D2	51 24N	0 40E
Medway u.a. England		17	D2	51 25N	0 35E
Meig r. Scotland		9	E2	57 35N	4 50W
Mekong r. Asia		71	C8	16 00N	105 00E
Melbourn England		16	D3	52 05N	0 01E
Melbourne Australia		73	H3	37 45S	144 58E
Melbourne England		13	E2	52 49N	1 25W
Melilla territory Spain		51	D1	35 17N	2 57W
Melitopol' Ukraine		57	E4	46 51N	35 22E
Melksham England		16	A2	51 23N	2 09W
Melrose Scotland		11	G2	55 36N	2 44W
Meltham England		13	E2	53 36N	1 52W
Melton Mowbray					
England		15	F2	52 46N	0 53W
Melun France		50	F5	48 32N	2 40E
Melvich Scotland		9	F3	58 33N	3 55W
Memmingen Germany		52	E3	47 59N	10 11E
Memphis USA		91	J4	35 10N	90 00W
Menai Bridge tn. Wales		14	B3	53 14N	4 10W
Menai Strait Wales		14	B3	53 14N	4 10W
Mende France		50	F3	44 32N	3 30E
Mendip Hills England		19	E3	51 18N	2 45W
Menorca i. Spain		51	G4/H3	39 45N	4 15E
Menton France		50	H2	43 47N	7 30E
Meppel Neths		48	E5	52 42N	6 12E
Merano Italy		54	D7	46 41N	11 10E
Mere England		19	E2	51 06N	2 16W
Mérida Mexico		94	G4	20 59N	89 39W
Mérida Spain		51	B3	38 55N	6 20W
Mérignac France		50	D3	44 50N	0 36W
Merrick mt. Scotland		11	E2	55 08N	4 29W
Merriott England		19	E2	50 55N	2 49W
Mersea Island England		17	D2	51 46N	0 57
Mersey r. England		12	D2	53 20N	2 53W
Merseyside co.					
England		12	D2	53 30N	3 00W
Merthyr Tydfil Wales		14	C1	51 46N	3 23W
Merthyr Tydfil u.a.					
Wales		14	C1	51 48N	3 20W

Name		Page	Grid	Lat	Long
Merton England		16	C2	51 25N	0 12W
Messina Italy		54	F3	38 13N	15 33E
Metheringham England		13	F2	53 08N	0 25W
Methil Scotland		11	F3	56 12N	3 01W
Metz France		50	H5	49 07N	6 11E
Meuse r.					
Belgium/France		48	D3	50 03N	4 40E
Mevagissey England		18	C2	50 16N	4 48W
Mexborough England		13	E2	53 30N	1 17W
MEXICO		94	C5/E3		
Mexico City Mexico		94	E3	19 25N	99 10W
Mexico, Gulf of Mexico		94	F4/G4	25 00N	90 00W
Miami USA		91	K2	25 45N	80 15W
Michigan state USA		91	J5/K5	45 00N	85 00W
Michigan, Lake					
Canada/USA		92	C2/C3	45 00N	87 00W
Middlesbrough					
England		13	E3	54 35N	1 14W
Middlesbrough u.a.					
England		13	E3	54 33N	1 04W
Middleton England		12	D2	53 33N	2 12W
Middleton-in-Teesdale					
England		12	D3	54 38N	2 04W
Middleton-on-the-Wolds					
England		13	F2	53 56N	0 33W
Middlewich England		12	D2	53 11N	2 27W
Midhurst England		16	C1	50 59N	0 45W
Midleton Rol		21	C1	51 55N	8 10W
Midlothian u.a.					
Scotland		11	F2	55 50N	3 05W
Midsomer Norton					
England		19	E3	51 17N	2 30W
Mieres Spain		51	C5	43 15N	5 46W
Mikkeli Finland		49	G3	61 44N	27 15E
Milano Italy		54	C6	45 28N	9 12E
Milborne Port England		19	E2	50 58N	2 29W
Mildenhall England		17	D3	52 21N	0 30E
Milestone Rol		21	C2	52 40N	8 05W
Milford Rol		20	D5	55 07N	7 43W
Milford Haven Wales		14	A1	51 44N	5 02W
Millau France		50	F3	44 06N	3 05E
Millisle NI		10	D1	54 37N	5 30W
Millom England		12	C3	54 13N	3 18W
Millport Scotland		10	E2	55 46N	4 55W
Millstreet Rol		21	B2	52 03N	9 04W
Milltown Malbay Rol		21	B2	52 52N	9 23W
Milngavie Scotland		11	E2	55 57N	4 19W
Milnthorpe England		12	D3	54 14N	2 46W
Milton Keynes England		16	C3	52 02N	0 42W
Milton Keynes u.a.					
England		16	C3	52 02N	0 42W
Milverton England		19	D3	51 02N	3 16W
Milwaukee USA		91	J5	43 03N	87 56W
Mimizan France		50	D3	44 12N	1 14W
Minch, The sd. Scotland		8	C3/D3	58 00N	6 00W
Mindanao i. Philippines		71	G5/H5	8 00N	125 00E
Minden Germany		52	D6	52 18N	8 54E
Mindoro i. Philippines		71	G6	13 00N	121 00E
Minehead England		18	D3	51 13N	3 29W
Mine Head Rol		21	D1	52 00N	7 35W
Mingulay i. Scotland		8	B1	56 49N	7 38W
Minneapolis USA		91	H5	45 00N	93 15W
Minnedosa Canada		89	R4	50 14N	99 50W
Minnesota state USA		91	H6	47 00N	95 00W
Minsk Belarus		56	C5	53 51N	27 30E
Minster England		17	D2	51 26N	0 49E
Minster England		17	E2	51 20N	1 19E
Minsterley England		14	D2	52 39N	2 55W
Mintlaw Scotland		9	G2	57 31N	2 00W
Mirfield England		13	E2	53 41N	1 42W
Mirnyy Russia					
Miskolc Hungary		53	K4	48 07N	20 47E
Mississippi r. USA		91	H3	35 00N	90 00W
Mississippi state USA		91	H3/J3	32 00N	90 00W
Missouri r. USA		91	H4	39 00N	93 00W
Missouri state USA		91	H4	38 00N	93 00W
Mitchelstown Rol		21	C2	52 16N	8 16W
Mito Japan		70	D2	36 22N	140 29E
Mizen Head Rol		21	B1	51 30N	9 50W
Moate Rol		20	D3	53 24N	7 43W
Mobile USA		91	J3	30 40N	88 05W
Modbury England		18	D2	50 21N	3 53W
Módena Italy		54	D6	44 39N	10 55E
Modesto USA		90	B4	37 37N	121 00W
Mödling Austria		53	H4	48 06N	16 18E
Moelfre Wales		14	B3	53 21N	4 14W
Moffat Scotland		11	F2	55 20N	3 27W
Mogadishu Somalia		81	Q2	2 02N	45 21E
Mohill Rol		20	D3	53 54N	7 52W
Mo-i-Rana Norway		49	D4	66 18N	14 00E
Mold Wales		14	C3	53 10N	3 08W
MOLDOVA		53	P3		
Mole r. England		16	C2	51 15N	0 20W
Molfetta Italy		55	G4	41 12N	16 36E
Mölndal Sweden		49	D2	57 40N	12 00E
Mombasa Kenya		83	F2	4 04S	39 40E
MONACO		50	H2		
Monadhliath Mountains					
Scotland		9	E2	57 10N	4 00W
Monaghan Rol		20	E4	54 15N	6 58W
Monaghan co. Rol		20	D4/E4	54 10N	7 00W
Monasterevin Rol		21	D3	53 07N	7 02W
Mönchengladbach					
Germany		52	C5	51 12N	6 25E
Moncton Canada		89	Y3	46 04N	64 50W
Mondovi Italy		54	B6	44 23N	7 49E
Moneen Rol		20	C3	53 26N	8 54W

Name		Page	Grid	Lat	Long
Monfalcone Italy		54	E6	45 49N	13 32E
MONGOLIA		68/69	G7/K7		
Moniaive Scotland		11	F2	55 12N	3 55W
Monifieth Scotland		9	G1	56 29N	2 49W
Monmouth Wales		14	D1	51 50N	2 43W
Monmouthshire u.a.					
Wales		14	D1	51 47N	2 55W
Monopoli Italy		55	G4	40 57N	17 18E
Monrovia Liberia		80	B3	6 20N	10 46W
Montana Bulgaria		55	K5	43 25N	23 11E
Montana state USA		90	E6	47 00N	111 00W
Montargis France		50	F4	48 00N	2 44E
Montauban France		50	E3	44 01N	1 20E
Montbéliard France		50	H4	47 31N	6 48E
Mont Blanc France/Italy		50	H3	45 50N	6 52E
Montceau-les-Mines					
France		50	G4	46 40N	4 23E
Mont-de-Marsan					
France		50	D2	43 54N	0 30W
Montdidier France		50	F5	49 39N	2 35E
Monte Carlo Monaco		50	H2	43 44N	7 25E
Montélimar France		50	G3	44 33N	4 45E
Montenegro admin.					
Yugoslavia		55	H5	42 30N	19 00E
Montepulciano Italy		54	D5	43 05N	11 46E
Monterrey Mexico		94	D5	25 40N	100 20W
Montevideo Uruguay		97	F6	34 55S	56 10W
Montgomery USA		91	J3	32 22N	86 20W
Montgomery Wales		14	C2	52 34N	3 10W
Montlçon France		50	F4	46 20N	2 36E
Montmirail France		50	F5	48 52N	3 34E
Montmorillon France		50	E4	46 26N	0 52E
Montoro Spain		51	C3	38 02N	4 23W
Montpelier USA		21	C2	52 45N	8 30W
Montpellier France		50	F2	43 36N	3 53E
Montréal Canada		89	W3	45 32N	73 36W
Montreux Switz.		52	C3	46 27N	6 55E
Montrose Scotland		9	G1	56 43N	2 29W
Montserrat i.					
Lesser Antilles		94	P9	16 45N	62 14W
Monza Italy		54	C6	45 35N	9 16E
Mooncoin Rol		21	D2	52 17N	7 15W
Moone Rol		21	D2	52 58N	6 49W
Moorfoot Hills Scotland		11	F2/G2	55 50N	3 00W
Moosonee Canada		89	U4	51 18N	80 39W
Mora Sweden		49	D3	61 00N	14 30E
Moray u.a. Scotland		9	F2	57 20N	3 10W
Moray Firth Scotland		9	F2	57 45N	3 45W
Morcenx France		50	D3	44 02N	0 55W
Morecambe England		12	D3	54 04N	2 53W
Morecambe Bay					
England		12	D3	54 10N	2 55W
Morelia Mexico		94	D3	19 40N	101 11W
Moreton England		12	C2	53 24N	3 07W
Moretonhampstead					
England		18	D2	50 40N	3 45W
Moreton-in-Marsh					
England		15	E1	51 59N	1 42W
Morlaix France		50	C5	48 35N	3 50W
Morley England		13	E2	53 46N	1 36W
MOROCCO		80	C8/D8		
Morón de la Frontera					
Spain		51	C2	37 07N	5 27W
Morpeth England		13	E4	55 10N	1 41W
Morte Point England		18	C3	51 10N	4 15W
Mosborough England		13	E2	53 19N	1 22W
Moscow Russia		62	F8	55 45N	37 42E
Mosel r.					
Germany/France		52	C4	50 00N	7 00E
Mossley NI		10	D1	54 42N	5 57W
Mossoró Brazil		96	K12	5 10S	37 18W
Mostar					
Bosnia-Herzegovina		55	G5	43 20N	17 50E
Móstoles Spain		51	D4	40 19N	3 53W
Mosul Iraq		64	D6	36 21N	43 08E
Motherwell Scotland		11	F2	55 48N	3 59W
Motril Spain		51	D2	36 45N	3 31W
Moulins France		50	F4	47 00N	3 48E
Mountain Ash Wales		14	C1	51 42N	3 24W
Mount Bellew Rol		20	C3	53 28N	8 30W
Mount Leinster Rol		21	E2	52 36N	6 42W
Mountmellick tn. Rol		21	D3	53 07N	7 20W
Mountrath Rol		21	D3	53 00N	7 27W
Mounts Bay England		18	B2	50 05N	5 30W
Mountshannon Rol		21	C2	52 56N	8 26W
Mountsorrel England		15	E2	52 44N	1 07W
Moura Portugal		51	B3	38 08N	7 27W
Mourne Mountains NI		10	C1	54 05N	6 05W
Mousehole England		18	B2	50 04N	5 33W
Moville Rol		20	D5	55 11N	7 03W
Moy NI		10	C1	54 27N	6 42W
Moycullen Rol		20	B3	53 20N	9 10W
Moygashel NI		10	C1	54 31N	6 46W
Moyle district NI		10	C1	55 06N	6 10W
Moyvore Rol		20	D3	53 22N	7 37W
MOZAMBIQUE		82	F3/G5		
Much Wenlock England		15	D2	52 36N	2 34W
Muck i. Scotland		8	C1	56 50N	6 15W
Muckross Rol		21	B2	52 01N	9 29W
Muff Rol		20	D5	55 04N	7 16W
Muine Bheag Rol		21	E2	52 41N	6 58W
Muirkirk Scotland		11	F2	55 31N	4 04W
Muir of Ord Scotland		9	E2	57 31N	4 27W
Mulhacén mt. Spain		51	D2	37 04N	3 19W
Mülheim an der Ruhr					
Germany		48	E4	51 25N	6 50E

Mulhouse France 50 H4 47 45N 7 21E
Mulhuddart Rol 20 E3 53 24N 6 24W
Mulkear r. Rol 21 C2 52 38N 8 24W
Mull i. Scotland 8 D1 56 25N 6 00W
Mullet Peninsula Rol 20 A4 54 07N 10 05W
Mull Head Scotland 7 B2 59 20N 2 58W
Mullinahone Rol 21 D2 52 30N 7 30W
Mullinavat Rol 21 D2 52 22N 7 10W
Mullingar Rol 20 D3 53 32N 7 20W
Mullion England 18 B2 50 01N 5 14W
Mull of Galloway
   Scotland 10 E1 54 38N 4 55W
Mull of Kintyre Scotland 10 D2 55 17N 5 55W
Mull of Oa Scotland 10 C2 55 35N 6 20W
Mull, Sound of Scotland 8 D1 56 30N 6 00W
Multan Pakistan 66 C6 30 10N 71 36E
Mumbai India 66 C3 18 56N 72 51E
Mundesley England 17 E3 52 53N 1 26E
Munich Germany 52 E4 48 08N 11 35E
Münster Germany 52 C5 51 58N 7 37E
Murcia Spain 51 E2 37 59N 1 08W
Murmansk Russia 62 F10 68 59N 33 08E
Murray r. Australia 73 H3 35 30S 144 00E
Murray Bridge Australia 73 G3 35 10S 139 17E
Murton England 13 E3 54 49N 1 23W
Muş Turkey 57 F2 38 45N 41 30E
Muscat Oman 65 G3 23 37N 58 38E
Mushin Nigeria 80 E3 6 30N 3 15E
Musselburgh Scotland 11 F2 55 57N 3 04W
Mutare Zimbabwe 82 F4 18 58N 32 40E
Mutton Island i. Rol 21 B2 52 49N 9 31W
MYANMAR 71 B7
Mybster Scotland 9 F3 58 27N 3 25W
Mykolayiv Ukraine 57 D4 46 57N 32 00E
Mynydd Eppynt Wales 14 C2 52 02N 3 35W
Mynydd Preseli Wales 14 B1 51 58N 4 45W
Mytilini Greece 55 M3 39 06N 26 34E
Mytishchi Russia 56 E6 55 54N 37 47E

N

Naas Rol 20 E3 53 13N 6 39W
Naestved Denmark 49 D2 55 14N 11 47E
Náfplio Greece 55 K2 37 34N 22 48E
Nagano Japan 70 C2 36 39N 138 10E
Nagasaki Japan 70 A1 32 45N 129 52E
Nagles Mountains Rol 21 C2 52 10N 8 25W
Nagoya Japan 70 C2 35 08N 136 53E
Nagpur India 66 D4 21 10N 79 12E
Nailsea England 19 E3 51 26N 2 46W
Nailsworth England 15 D1 51 42N 2 14W
Nairn Scotland 9 F2 57 35N 3 53W
Nairobi Kenya 83 E4 1 17S 36 50E
Namib Desert Namibia 82 B3/C2 22 00S 14 00E
NAMIBIA 82 C3
Namur Belgium 48 C3 50 28N 4 52E
Nanchang China 69 L3 28 33N 115 58E
Nancy France 50 H5 48 42N 6 12E
Nanjing China 69 L4 32 03N 118 47E
Nantes France 50 D4 47 14N 1 35W
Nantwich England 12 D2 53 04N 2 32W
Naples Italy 54 F4 40 50N 14 15E
Naples USA 91 K2 26 09N 81 48W
Narberth Wales 14 B1 51 48N 4 45W
Narbonne France 50 F2 43 11N 3 00E
Narborough England 15 E2 52 35N 1 11W
Narvik Norway 49 E4 68 26N 17 25E
Naseby England 15 F2 52 23N 0 59W
Nashville USA 91 J4 36 10N 86 50W
Nassau Bahamas 95 J5 25 05N 77 20W
Nasser, Lake Egypt 81 M6 22 35N 31 40E
Nässjö Sweden 49 D2 57 40N 14 40E
Natal Brazil 96 K12 5 46S 35 15W
Natchez USA 91 H3 31 32N 91 24W
Naul Rol 20 E3 53 35N 6 17W
NAURU 100 G7
Navan Rol 20 E3 53 39N 6 41W
Navenby England 13 F2 53 06N 0 32W
Naver r. Scotland 9 E3 58 30N 4 10W
Ndjamena Chad 81 J4 12 10N 14 59E
Néapoli Greece 55 K2 36 31N 23 03E
Neath Wales 14 C1 51 40N 3 48W
Neath Port Talbot u.a.
   Wales 14 C1 51 37N 3 43W
Nebraska state USA 90 F5 42 00N 102 00W
Needham Market
   England 17 E3 52 09N 1 03E
Needles, The England 16 B1 50 39N 1 35W
Nefyn Wales 14 B2 52 56N 4 32W
Negro r. Brazil 96 D13 0 05S 67 00W
Nelson England 12 D2 53 51N 2 13W
Neman r.
   Lithuania/Russia 56 C5 55 00N 22 00E
Nenagh Rol 21 C2 52 52N 8 12W
Nene r. England 16 D2 52 35N 0 30W
Nene r. England 17 D3 52 45N 0 10E
NEPAL 66/67 E5/F5
Nephin mt. Rol 20 B4 54 01N 9 22W
Nephin Beg Range Rol 20 B3/B4 54 00N 9 34W
Nerva Spain 51 B2 37 41N 6 33W
Neston England 12 C2 53 18N 3 03W
NETHERLANDS 48 D5/E5
Nether Stowey
   England 19 D3 51 09N 3 10W
Netzahualcóyotl
   Mexico 94 E3 19 24N 99 02W

Neubrandenburg
   Germany 52 F6 53 33N 13 16E
Neuchâtel Switz. 52 C3 46 55N 6 56E
Neufchâteau France 50 G5 48 21N 5 42E
Neufchâtel-en-Bray
   France 50 E5 49 44N 1 26E
Neumünster Germany 52 D7 54 05N 9 59E
Neuruppin Germany 52 F6 52 56N 12 49E
Neuss Germany 52 C5 51 12N 6 42E
Neustrelitz Germany 52 F6 53 22N 13 05E
Nevada state USA 90 C4 39 00N 118 00W
Nevers France 50 F4 47 00N 3 09E
New Abbey Scotland 11 F1 54 59N 3 38W
New Alresford England 16 B2 51 06N 1 10W
Newark USA 91 M5 40 44N 74 24W
Newark-on-Trent
   England 13 F2 53 05N 0 49W
New Ash Green
   England 17 D2 51 21N 0 18E
Newbiggin-by-the-Sea
   England 13 E4 55 11N 1 30W
Newbridge Wales 14 C1 51 41N 3 09W
Newbridge-on-Wye
   Wales 14 C2 52 13N 3 27W
New Brunswick prov.
   Canada 89 X3 47 30N 66 00W
New Buildings NI 10 B1 54 56N 7 21W
Newburgh Scotland 9 F1 56 21N 3 15W
Newburn England 13 E3 54 59N 1 43W
Newbury England 16 B2 51 25N 1 20W
New Caledonia i.
   Pacific Ocean 73 M6/N6 22 00S 165 00E
Newcastle NI 10 D1 54 12N 5 54W
Newcastle Emlyn
   Wales 14 B2 52 02N 4 28W
Newcastle-under-Lyme
   England 12 D2 53 00N 2 14W
Newcastle upon Tyne
   England 13 E3 54 59N 1 35W
Newcastle West Rol 21 B2 52 27N 9 03W
New Cumnock
   Scotland 11 E2 55 24N 4 12W
New Deer Scotland 9 G2 57 30N 2 12W
New Delhi India 66 D5 28 37N 77 14E
Newfoundland i.
   Canada 89 Z3 48 15N 57 00W
Newfoundland prov.
   Canada 89 Y5/AA3 52 30N 62 30W
New Galloway
   Scotland 11 E2 55 05N 4 10W
New Guinea i.
   Pacific Ocean 72/73 F10/J9 5 00S 141 00E
New Hampshire state
   USA 91 M5 43 00N 72 00W
New Haven USA 91 M5 41 18N 72 55W
New Holland England 13 F2 53 42N 0 22W
Newick England 16 D1 50 58N 0 01E
New Jersey state USA 91 M4 40 00N 75 00W
New Liskeard Canada 89 V3 47 31N 79 41W
Newlyn England 18 B2 50 06N 5 34W
Newmachar Scotland 9 G2 57 16N 2 10W
Newmains Scotland 11 F2 55 47N 3 53W
Newmarket England 17 D3 52 15N 0 25E
Newmarket Rol 21 C2 52 13N 9 00W
Newmarket-on-Fergus
   Rol 21 C2 52 45N 8 53W
New Mexico state USA 90 E3 35 00N 107 00W
New Milton England 16 B1 50 46N 1 40W
New Orleans USA 91 H2 30 00N 90 03W
Newport Telford and Wrekin
   England 15 D2 52 47N 2 22W
Newport Isle of Wight
   England 16 B1 50 42N 1 18W
Newport Essex England 17 D2 51 58N 0 13E
Newport Mayo Rol 20 B3 53 53N 9 32W
Newport Tipperary Rol 21 C2 52 43N 8 25W
Newport Pembrokeshire
   Wales 14 B2 52 01N 4 50W
Newport Newport
   Wales 14 C1 51 35N 3 00W
Newport u.a. Wales 14 C1/D1 51 33N 3 00W
Newport Bay Rol 20 B3 53 51N 9 41W
Newport News USA 91 L4 36 59N 76 26W
Newport-on-Tay
   Scotland 9 G1 56 27N 2 56W
Newport Pagnell
   England 16 C3 52 05N 0 44W
Newquay England 18 B2 50 25N 5 05W
New Quay Wales 14 B2 52 13N 4 22W
New Radnor Wales 14 C2 52 15N 3 10W
New Romney England 17 D1 50 59N 0 57E
New Ross Rol 21 D2 52 24N 6 56W
New Rossington
   England 13 E2 53 29N 1 04W
Newry NI 10 C1 54 11N 6 20W
Newry and Mourne
   district NI 10 C1 54 10N 6 35W
New Sauchie Scotland 11 F3 56 08N 3 41W
New Scone Scotland 9 F1 56 25N 3 25W
Newton Abbot
   England 18 D2 50 32N 3 36W
Newton Aycliffe
   England 13 E3 54 37N 1 34W
Newton Mearns
   Scotland 11 E2 55 45N 4 18W
Newtonmore Scotland 9 E2 57 04N 4 08W

Newton Stewart
   Scotland 11 E1 54 57N 4 29W
Newtown Rol 21 D2 52 52N 7 07W
Newtown Wales 14 C2 52 32N 3 19W
Newtownabbey NI 10 D1 54 40N 5 54W
Newtownabbey
   district NI 10 C1/D1 54 40N 6 05W
Newtownards NI 10 D1 54 36N 5 41W
Newtown Cunningham
   Rol 20 D4 54 59N 7 31W
Newtownhamilton NI 10 C1 54 12N 6 35W
Newtownmountkennedy
   Rol 21 E3 53 06N 6 07W
Newtown St. Boswells
   Scotland 11 G2 55 34N 2 40W
Newtownstewart NI 10 B1 54 43N 7 24W
New Tredegar Wales 14 C1 51 44N 3 15W
New York USA 91 M5 40 40N 73 50W
New York state USA 91 L5 43 00N 76 00W
NEW ZEALAND 73
Neyland Wales 14 B1 51 43N 4 57W
Niagara Falls tn.
   Canada 93 E2 43 05N 79 06W
Niamey Niger 80 E4 13 32N 2 05E
NICARAGUA 95 G2
Nice France 50 H2 43 42N 7 16E
Nicobar Islands India 67 G1 8 30N 94 00E
Nicosia Cyprus 57 D2 35 11N 33 23E
Nienburg Germany 52 D6 52 38N 9 13E
NIGER 80 E5/G5
Niger r. West Africa 80 E5 5 30N 6 15E
NIGERIA 80 F4/G4
Nigg Scotland 9 G2 57 08N 2 03W
Nigg Bay Highland
   Scotland 9 E2 57 42N 4 01W
Nigg Bay Aberdeenshire
   Scotland 9 G2 57 08N 2 03W
Nijmegen Neths 48 D4 51 50N 5 52E
Nikopol' Ukraine 56 D4 45 34N 34 25E
Nile r. Sudan/Egypt 81 M7 27 30N 31 40E
Nîmes France 50 G2 43 50N 4 21E
Niort France 50 D4 46 19N 0 27W
Nizhniy Novgorod
   Russia 62 G8 56 20N 44 00E
Nordhausen Germany 52 E5 51 31N 10 48E
North Cape Norway 49 F5 71 11N 25 40E
Norfolk co. England 17 D3 52 45N 1 00E
Norfolk USA 91 L4 36 54N 76 18W
Norham England 11 G2 55 43N 2 10W
Normanton England 13 E2 53 42N 1 25W
Norrköping Sweden 49 E2 58 35N 16 10E
Northallerton England 13 E3 54 20N 1 26W
Northam England 18 C3 51 02N 4 14W
Northampton England 15 F2 52 14N 0 54W
Northamptonshire co.
   England 15 E2/F2 52 20N 1 00W
North Ayrshire u.a.
   Scotland 11 E2 55 30N 5 05W
North Baddesley
   England 16 B1 50 58N 1 27W
North Ballachulish
   Scotland 8 D1 56 42N 5 11W
North Berwick Scotland 11 G3 56 04N 2 44W
North Carolina state
   USA 91 L4 36 00N 80 00W
North Channel
   British Isles 10 D1/D2 55 20N 5 50W
North Dakota state
   USA 90/91 F6/G6 47 00N 102 00W
North Dorset Downs
   England 19 E2 50 40N 2 30W
North Down co. NI 10 D1 54 40N 5 40W
North Downs England 16 C2 51 13N 0 30W
North East Lincolnshire
   u.a. England 13 F2 53 30N 0 10W
Northern Ireland UK 10 B1/C1 54 40N 7 00W
NORTHERN MARIANAS
   100 F9
North Foreland England 17 E2 51 23N 1 27E
North Hykeham
   England 13 F2 53 12N 0 34W
North Island NZ 73 P3/Q3 39 00N §76 00E
North Kessock Scotland 9 E2 57 30N 4 15W
North Lanarkshire u.a.
   Scotland 11 E2/F2 55 50N 3 55W
Northleach England 15 E1 51 51N 1 50W
North Lincolnshire u.a.
   England 13 F2 53 40N 0 40W
North Petherton
   England 19 D3 51 06N 3 01W
North Pole
   Arctic Ocean 101 90 00N
North Ronaldsay i.
   Scotland 7 B2 59 23N 2 26W
North Shields England 13 E4 55 01N 1 26W
North Somercotes
   England 13 G2 53 28N 0 08E
North Somerset u.a.
   England 19 E3 51 15N 2 50W
North Sound Rol 21 B3 53 11N 9 43W
North Sound, The
   Scotland 7 B2 59 17N 2 45W
North Tawton England 18 D2 50 48N 3 53W

North Tidworth
   England 16 B2 51 16N 1 40W
North Uist i. Scotland 8 B2 57 04N 7 15W
Northumberland co.
   England 12 D4 55 10N 2 05W
North Walsham
   England 17 E3 52 50N 1 24E
Northwest Highlands
   Scotland 8/9 D2/E3 58 00N 5 00W
Northwest Territories
   territory Canada 88 L6/N6 65 15N 115 00W
North Wheatley
   England 13 F2 53 22N 0 52W
Northwich England 12 D2 53 16N 2 32W
North Wingfield
   England 13 E2 53 09N 1 24W
North York Moors
   England 13 F3 55 22N 0 45W
North Yorkshire co.
   England 13 E3/F3 54 10N 2 10W
Norton England 13 F3 54 08N 0 48W
NORWAY 49 C2/F4
Norwich England 17 E3 52 38N 1 18E
Norwich USA 93 F2 41 32N 72 05W
Noss Head Scotland 9 F3 58 28N 3 04W
Nottingham England 15 E2 52 58N 1 10W
Nottinghamshire co.
   England 13 E2/F2 53 20N 1 00W
Nouakchott Mauritania 80 A5 18 09N 15 58W
Novara Italy 54 C6 45 27N 8 37E
Nova Scotia prov.
   Canada 89 Y2/Y3 44 30N 65 00W
Novgorod Russia 62 F8 58 30N 31 20E
Novi Sad Yugoslavia 55 H6 45 15N 19 51E
Novosibirsk Russia 63 L8 55 04N 83 05E
Nubian Desert Sudan 81 M6 21 00N 33 00E
Nullarbor Plain
   Australia 72 E4 32 00S 128 00E
Nuneaton England 15 E2 52 32N 1 28W
Nuoro Italy 54 C4 40 20N 9 21E
Nuremberg Germany 52 E4 49 27N 11 05E
Nuuk Greenland 89 AA6 64 10N 51 40W
Nyasa, Lake
   Southern Africa 82 F5 12 00S 35 00E
Nykøbing Denmark 49 D1 54 47N 11 53E
Nyköping Sweden 49 E2 58 45N 17 03E
Nyons France 50 G3 44 22N 5 08E

O

Oadby England 15 E2 52 36N 1 04W
Oakengates England 15 D2 52 42N 2 28W
Oakham England 16 F2 52 40N 00 43W
Oakland USA 90 B4 37 50N 122 15W
Oakley England 16 B2 51 15N 1 11W
Oakley Scotland 11 F3 56 05N 3 35W
Ob' r. Russia 62 J10 65 30N 66 00E
Oban Scotland 8 D1 56 25N 5 29W
Oberhausen Germany 52 C5 51 27N 6 50E
Ob', Gulf of Russia 62 K10 68 00N 74 00E
O'Briensbridge Rol 21 C2 52 45N 8 30W
Ochil Hills Scotland 11 F3 56 15N 3 30W
Odda Norway 49 C3 60 03N 6 34E
Oddsta Scotland 7 D3 60 37N 0 59W
Odense Denmark 49 D2 55 24N 10 25E
Oder r. Germany 52 G6 52 00N 15 30E
Odessa Ukraine 57 D4 46 30N 30 46E
Offaly co. Rol 20 D3 53 15N 7 35W
Offenbach am Main
   Germany 52 D5 50 06N 8 46E
Offenburg Germany 52 C4 48 29N 7 57E
Ohio state USA 91 K5 40 00N 83 00W
Ohio r. USA 91 J4 38 00N 86 00W
Oilgate Rol 21 E2 52 25N 6 32W
Ōita Japan 70 B1 33 15N 131 36E
Okehampton England 18 C2 50 44N 4 00W
Oklahoma state USA 91 G4 36 00N 98 00W
Oklahoma City USA 91 G4 35 28N 97 33W
Öland i. Sweden 49 E2 56 45N 16 50E
Olbia Italy 54 C4 40 56N 9 30E
Oldbury England 15 D2 52 30N 2 00W
Oldcastle Rol 20 D3 53 46N 7 10W
Oldenburg Germany 52 D6 53 08N 8 13E
Old Fletton England 16 C2 52 34N 0 12W
Oldham England 12 D2 53 33N 2 07W
Old Head of Kinsale c.
   Rol 21 C1 51 40N 8 30W
Oldmeldrum Scotland 9 G2 57 20N 2 20W
Olhão Portugal 51 B2 37 01N 7 50W
Ollerton England 13 E2 53 12N 1 00W
Olney England 16 C3 52 09N 0 43W
Olsztyn Poland 53 K6 53 48N 20 29E
Olten Switz. 52 C3 47 22N 7 55E
Ólympos mt. Greece 55 J4 40 05N 22 21E
Omagh NI 10 B1 54 36N 7 18W
Omagh district NI 10 B1 54 36N 7 30W
Omaha USA 91 G5 41 15N 96 00W
OMAN 65 F2/G3
Oman, Gulf of
   Iran/Oman 65 G3 24 30N 58 30E
Omdurman Sudan 81 M5 15 37N 32 29E
Omeath Rol 20 E4 54 06N 6 17W
Omsk Russia 62 K8 55 00N 73 22E
Ōmuta Japan 70 B1 33 02N 130 26E
Onezhskoye Ozero l.
   Russia 62 F9 62 00N 40 00E
Ontario prov. Canada 89 S4/U4 51 00N 91 00W

Ontario, Lake Canada/USA 93 E2 43 45N 78 00W
Oola Rol 21 C2 52 33N 8 16W
Oostende Belgium 48 A4 51 13N 2 55E
Opava Czech Rep. 53 H4 49 58N 17 55E
Opole Poland 53 H5 50 40N 17 56E
Oporto Portugal 51 A4 41 09N 8 37W
Oran Algeria 80 D9 35 45N 0 38W
Orange France 50 G3 44 08N 4 48E
Oranmore Rol 20 C3 53 16N 8 54W
Orbetello Italy 54 D5 42 27N 11 07E
Örebro Sweden 49 E2 59 17N 15 13E
Oregon state USA 90 B5/C5 44 00N 120 00W
Oregon City USA 90 B6 45 21N 122 36W
Orel Russia 62 F7 52 58N 36 04E
Orenburg Russia 62 H7 51 50N 55 00E
Orense Spain 51 B5 42 20N 7 52W
Orford England 17 E3 52 06N 1 31E
Orihuela Spain 51 E3 38 05N 0 56W
Orinoco r. Venezuela 96 E15 8 00N 64 00W
Oristano Italy 54 C3 39 54N 8 36E
Orkney Islands u.a. Scotland 7 A1/B2 59 00N 3 00W
Orlando USA 91 K2 28 33N 81 21W
Orléans France 50 E4 47 54N 1 54E
Ormskirk England 12 D2 53 35N 2 54W
Oronsay i. Scotland 10 C3 56 00N 6 15W
Orrell England 12 D2 53 33N 2 45W
Orsha Belarus 56 D5 54 30N 30 23E
Orthez France 50 D2 43 29N 0 46W
Ortigueira Spain 51 B5 43 43N 8 13W
Ortona Italy 54 F5 42 21N 14 24E
Orvieto Italy 54 E5 42 43N 12 06E
Orwell r. England 17 E3 52 00N 1 15E
Ōsaka Japan 70 C1 34 40N 135 30E
Oshawa Canada 89 V2 43 53N 78 51W
Oslo Norway 49 D2 59 56N 10 45E
Osmaniye Turkey 57 E2 37 04N 36 15E
Osnabrück Germany 52 D6 52 17N 8 03E
Ossett England 13 E2 53 41N 1 35W
Östersund Sweden 49 D3 63 10N 14 40E
Östervall Sweden 49 E2 62 20N 15 20E
Ostrava Czech Rep. 53 J4 49 50N 18 15E
Oswaldtwistle England 12 D2 53 44N 2 24W
Oswestry England 14 C2 52 52N 3 03W
Otford England 17 D2 51 19N 0 12E
Otley England 13 E2 53 54N 1 41W
Otranto Italy 55 H4 40 08N 18 30E
Ottawa Canada 89 V3 45 24N 75 38W
Otterburn England 12 D4 55 14N 2 10W
Ottery St. Mary England 19 D2 50 45N 3 17W
Ouagadougou Burkina 80 D4 12 20N 1 40W
Oughterard Rol 20 B3 53 26N 9 19W
Oulart Rol 21 E2 53 30N 6 23W
Oulu Finland 49 G4 65 02N 25 27E
Oundle England 15 F2 52 29N 0 29W
Ouse r. North Yorkshire England 13 E3 54 05N 1 15W
Ouse r. East Sussex England 16 D1 50 55N 0 03E
Outer Hebrides is. Scotland 8 B2/B3 58 00N 7 00W
Outwell England 17 D3 52 37N 0 14E
Overton England 16 B2 51 15N 1 15W
Overton Wales 14 D2 52 58N 2 56W
Oviedo Spain 51 C5 43 21N 7 18W
Owen Sound Canada 89 U2 44 3N 80 56W
Oxford England 16 B2 51 46N 1 15W
Oxfordshire co. England 16 B2 51 50N 1 25W
Oxted England 16 C2 51 15N 0 01W
Oysterhaven Rol 21 C1 51 41N 8 26W
Ozero Balkhash l. Kazakhstan 62 K6 46 00N 75 00E
Ozero Baykal l. Russia 63 N7 54 00N 109 00E
Ozieri Italy 54 C4 40 35N 9 01E

P
Pacific Ocean 100
Padang Indonesia 71 C3 1 00S 100 21E
Paddock Wood tn. England 17 D2 51 11N 0 23E
Paderborn Germany 52 D5 51 43N 8 44E
Padiham England 12 D2 53 49N 2 19W
Padstow England 18 C2 50 33N 4 56W
Padua Italy 54 D6 45 24N 11 53E
Paisley Scotland 11 E2 55 50N 4 26W
PAKISTAN 66 B5/C5
PALAU 100 D8 7 30N 134 30E
Palawan i. Philippines 71 F5/F6 10 00N 119 00E
Palembang Indonesia 71 C3 2 55S 104 45E
Palencia Spain 51 C3 41 01N 4 32W
Palermo Italy 54 E3 38 08N 13 23E
Palma de Mallorca Spain 51 G3 39 35N 2 39E
Palmer USA 88 F6 61 35N 149 10W
Palmyra Syria 64 C3 34 40N 38 10E
Pamiers France 50 E2 43 07N 1 36E
Pampas geog. reg. Argentina 97 E6 36 00S 63 00W
Pamplona Spain 51 E5 42 49N 1 39W
PANAMA 95 H1/J1
Panama Canal Panama 95 J1 9 00N 80 00W
Panama City Panama 95 J1 8 57N 79 30W
Pangbourne England 16 B2 51 29N 1 05W

Papa Sound Scotland 7 B2 59 20N 2 54W
Papa, Sound of Scotland 7 C3 60 37N 1 40W
Papa Stour i. Scotland 7 C3 60 20N 1 42W
Papa Westray i. Scotland 7 B2 59 22N 2 54W
PAPUA NEW GUINEA 73 H9/K9
PARAGUAY 96 F9
Paraguay r. Paraguay/Argentina 96 F8 26 30S 58 00W
Paramaribo Suriname 96 F15 5 52N 55 14W
Paraná r. Paraguay/Argentina 96 F7 27 00S 56 00W
Paris France 50 F5 48 52N 2 20E
Parkano Finland 49 F3 62 03N 23 00E
Parma Italy 54 D6 44 48N 10 19E
Parnaiba Brazil 96 J13 2 58S 41 46W
Páros Greece 55 L2 37 04N 25 06E
Parrett r. England 19 E3 51 05N 2 54W
Parthenay France 50 D4 46 39N 0 14W
Partry Rol 20 B3 53 42N 9 16W
Partry Mountains Rol 20 B3 53 39N 9 27W
Paşcani Romania 53 N3 47 14N 26 46E
Passage East Rol 21 E2 52 13N 6 59W
Passage West tn. Rol 21 C1 51 52N 8 20W
Passau Germany 52 F4 48 35N 13 28E
Patagonia geog. reg. Argentina 97 C2/D4 48 00S 70 00W
Pateley Bridge tn. England 13 E3 54 05N 1 45W
Patna Scotland 11 E2 55 20N 4 30W
Patras Greece 55 J3 38 14N 21 44E
Patrickswell Rol 21 C2 52 36N 8 42W
Patrington England 13 F2 53 41N 0 02W
Pau France 50 D2 43 18N 0 22W
Pavia Italy 54 C6 45 12N 9 09E
Pavullo nel Frignano Italy 54 D6 44 20N 10 49E
Peacehaven England 16 C1 50 47N 0 01E
Peč Yugoslavia 55 J5 42 40N 20 19E
Pécs Hungary 53 J3 46 04N 18 15E
Peebles Scotland 11 F2 55 39N 3 12W
Peel Isle of Man 12 B3 54 14N 4 42W
Peloponnisos geog. reg. Greece 55 J2/K2 37 00N 22 00E
Pembridge England 14 D2 52 14N 2 53W
Pembroke Wales 14 B1 51 41N 4 55W
Pembroke Dock Wales 14 B1 51 42N 4 56W
Pembrokeshire u.a. Wales 14 A1/B1 51 50N 5 00W
Pembury England 17 D2 51 08N 0 19E
Penarth Wales 14 C1 51 27N 3 11W
Pencoed Wales 14 C1 51 31N 3 30W
Pendine Wales 14 B1 51 34N 4 35W
Penicuik Scotland 11 F2 55 50N 3 14W
Penistone England 13 E2 53 32N 1 37W
Penkridge England 15 D2 52 44N 2 07W
Penmaenmawr Wales 14 C3 53 16N 3 54W
Pennines 12/13 D3/E2 54 30N 2 10W
Penrhyndeudraeth Wales 14 B2 52 56N 4 04W
Penrith England 12 D3 54 40N 2 44W
Penryn England 18 B2 50 09N 5 06W
Pensilva England 18 C2 50 30N 4 25W
Pentland Firth Scotland 7 A1 58 45N 3 10W
Pentland Hills Scotland 11 F2 55 45N 3 30W
Pen-y-ghent sum. England 12 D3 54 10N 2 14W
Penygroes Wales 14 B2 53 04N 4 17W
Penzance England 18 B2 50 07N 5 33W
Périgueux France 50 E3 45 12N 0 44E
Perm' Russia 62 H8 58 01N 56 10E
Pernik Bulgaria 55 K5 42 36N 23 03E
Péronne France 50 F5 49 56N 2 57E
Perpignan France 50 F2 42 42N 2 54E
Perranporth England 18 B2 50 20N 5 09W
Perth Australia 72 A3 31 58S 115 49E
Perth Scotland 9 F1 56 42N 3 28W
Perth and Kinross u.a. Scotland 9 F1 56 45N 3 50W
PERU 96 B11/C11
Perugia Italy 54 E5 43 07N 12 23E
Pesaro Italy 54 E5 43 54N 12 54E
Pescara Italy 54 F5 42 27N 14 13E
Peshawar Pakistan 66 C6 34 01N 71 40E
Pessac France 50 D3 44 49N 0 37W
Peterborough England 16 C2 52 35N 0 15W
Peterculter Scotland 9 G2 57 05N 2 16W
Peterhead Scotland 9 H2 57 30N 1 46W
Peterlee England 13 E3 54 46N 1 19W
Petersfield England 16 C2 51 00N 0 56W
Petrolina Brazil 96 J12 9 22S 40 30W
Petworth England 16 C1 50 59N 0 38W
Pevensey England 17 D1 50 49N 0 20E
Pewsey England 16 B2 51 21N 1 46W
Pforzheim Germany 52 D4 48 53N 8 41E
Phenix City USA 91 J3 32 28N 85 01W
Philadelphia USA 91 L4 40 00N 75 10W
PHILIPPINES, THE 71 G7/H5
Phnom Penh Cambodia 71 C6 11 35N 104 55E
Phoenix USA 90 D3 33 30N 112 03W
Piacenza Italy 54 C6 45 03N 9 41E
Pickering England 13 F3 54 14N 0 46W
Píndhos mts. Greece 55 J3 40 00N 21 00E
Pinsk Belarus 57 C5 52 08N 26 01E
Pinwherry Scotland 10 E1 55 09N 4 50W
Piombino Italy 54 D5 42 56N 10 32E

Pýrgos Greece 55 J2 37 40N 21 27E
Pirineos mts. Spain/France 51 E5/F5 42 50N 0 30E
Pirmasens Germany 52 C4 49 12N 7 37E
Pisa Italy 54 D5 43 43N 10 24E
Pistoia Italy 54 D5 43 56N 10 55E
Piteå Sweden 49 F4 65 19N 21 30E
Pitești Romania 53 M2 44 51N 24 51E
Pitlochry Scotland 9 F1 56 43N 3 45W
Pitmedden Scotland 9 G2 57 19N 2 11W
Pittenweem Scotland 11 G3 56 13N 2 44W
Pittsburgh USA 91 L5 40 26N 80 00W
Planalto de Mato Grosso geog. reg. Brazil 96 F11/G11 13 00S 56 00W
Plasencia Spain 51 B4 40 02N 6 05W
Platte r. USA 90 F5 41 00N 100 00W
Plauen Germany 52 F5 50 29N 12 08E
Pleven Bulgaria 55 L5 43 25N 24 37E
Płock Poland 53 J6 52 32N 19 40E
Plockton Scotland 8 D2 57 20N 5 40W
Ploiești Romania 53 M2 44 57N 26 01E
Plovdiv Bulgaria 55 L5 42 08N 24 45E
Plymouth England 18 C2 50 23N 4 10W
Plympton England 18 C2 50 23N 4 03W
Plymstock England 18 C2 50 21N 4 07W
Plynlimon mt. Wales 14 C2 52 28N 3 47W
Plzeň Czech Rep. 52 F4 49 45N 13 25E
Po r. Italy 54 D6 45 00N 10 00E
Pocklington England 13 F2 53 56N 0 46W
Podgorica Yugoslavia 55 H5 42 28N 19 17E
Point-Noire tn. Congo 82 B7 4 46S 11 53E
Poitiers France 50 E4 46 35N 0 20E
POLAND 53 J6/K6
Polegate England 17 D1 50 50N 0 15E
Polesworth England 15 E2 52 44N 1 36W
Policoro Italy 55 G4 40 12N 16 40E
Pollensa Spain 51 G3 39 52N 3 01E
Polperro England 18 C2 50 19N 4 31W
Polýgyros Greece 55 K4 40 23N 23 25E
Pondicherry India 66 D2 11 59N 79 50E
Ponferrada Spain 51 B5 42 33N 6 35W
Pont r. England 12 E4 55 02N 1 55W
Ponta Grossa Brazil 96 G8 25 07S 50 09W
Pont-à-Mousson France 50 H5 48 55N 6 03E
Pontardawe Wales 14 C1 51 44N 3 52W
Pontardulais Wales 14 B1 51 43N 4 02W
Pontefract England 13 E2 53 42N 1 18W
Ponteland England 13 E4 55 03N 1 44W
Ponte Leccia France 50 J2 42 28N 9 12E
Ponterwyd Wales 14 C2 52 25N 3 50W
Pontevedra Spain 51 A5 42 25N 8 39W
Pontivy France 50 C5 48 04N 2 58W
Pontrilas England 14 D1 51 57N 2 53W
Pontyclun Wales 14 C1 51 33N 3 23W
Pontycymer Wales 14 C1 51 36N 3 35W
Pontypool Wales 14 C1 51 43N 3 02W
Pontypridd Wales 14 C1 51 37N 3 22W
Poole England 19 F2 50 43N 1 59W
Poole u.a. England 19 F2 50 43N 1 59W
Poole Bay b. England 19 F3 50 41N 1 52W
Poolewe Scotland 8 D2 57 45N 5 37W
Pooley Bridge tn. England 12 D3 54 38N 2 49W
Popacatepetl mt. Mexico 94 E3 19 02N 98 38W
Pordenone Italy 54 E6 45 58N 12 39E
Pori Finland 49 F3 61 28N 21 45E
Porlock England 18 D3 51 14N 3 36W
Portadown NI 10 C1 54 26N 6 27W
Portaferry NI 10 D1 54 23N 5 33W
Portalegre Portugal 51 B3 39 17N 7 25W
Portarlington Rol 21 D3 53 10N 7 11W
Port Askaig Scotland 10 C2 55 51N 6 07W
Port-au-Prince Haiti 95 K3 18 33N 72 20W
Portavogie NI 10 D1 54 28N 5 25W
Port Ellen Scotland 10 C2 55 39N 6 12W
Port-Eynon Wales 14 B1 51 28N 4 12W
Port Gentil Gabon 82 A7 0 40S 8 50E
Port Glasgow Scotland 11 E2 55 56N 4 41W
Portglenone NI 10 C1 54 52N 6 29W
Port Harcourt Nigeria 80 F2 4 43N 7 05E
Porthcawl Wales 14 C1 51 29N 3 43W
Porthleven England 18 B2 50 30N 5 21W
Porthmadog Wales 14 B2 52 56N 4 08W
Portimão Portugal 51 A2 37 08N 8 32W
Port Isaac England 18 C2 50 35N 4 49W
Portishead England 19 E3 51 30N 2 46W
Portknockie Scotland 9 G2 57 42N 2 52W
Portland USA 90 B6 45 32N 122 40W
Portlaoise Rol 21 D3 53 02N 7 17W
Portlaw Rol 21 D2 52 17N 7 19W
Portlethen Scotland 9 G2 57 03N 2 07W
Portmahomack Scotland 9 F2 57 49N 3 50W
Portmadoc Wales 14 B2 52 55N 4 08W
Port Moresby PNG 73 J9 9 30S 147 07E
Portnaguran Scotland 8 C3 58 17N 6 13W
Portnahaven Scotland 10 B2 55 41N 6 31W
Porto Alegre Brazil 97 G7 30 03S 51 10W
Port of Ness Scotland 8 C3 58 29N 6 13W
Port-of-Spain Trinidad and Tobago 95 V15 10 38N 61 31W
Porto Novo Benin 80 E3 6 30N 2 47E
Porto Tórres Italy 54 C4 40 51N 8 24E
Porto-Vecchio France 50 J1 41 35N 9 16E
Pôrto Velho Brazil 96 E12 8 45S 63 54W
Portpatrick Scotland 10 D1 54 51N 5 07W

Portreath England 18 B2 50 51N 5 17W
Portree Scotland 8 C2 57 24N 6 12W
Portrush NI 10 C2 55 12N 6 40W
Portskerra Scotland 9 F3 58 33N 3 55W
Portsmouth England 16 B1 50 48N 1 05W
Portsmouth u.a. England 16 B1 50 48N 1 05W
Portsmouth USA 91 L4 36 50N 76 20W
Portsoy Scotland 9 G2 57 41N 2 41W
Portstewart NI 10 C2 55 11N 6 43W
Port Talbot Wales 14 C1 51 36N 3 47W
PORTUGAL 51 A3/B3
Portumna Rol 21 C3 53 06N 8 13W
Port Wemyss Scotland 10 C2 55 42N 6 29W
Port William Scotland 11 E1 54 46N 4 35W
Potenza Italy 54 F4 40 38N 15 48E
Potomac r. USA 91 L4 39 10N 77 30W
Potsdam Germany 52 F6 52 24N 13 04E
Potter's Bar England 16 C2 51 42N 0 11W
Potton England 16 C3 52 08N 0 14W
Poulton-le-Fylde England 12 D2 53 51N 3 00W
Powell River tn. Canada 88 L3 49 54N 124 34W
Power Head Rol 21 C1 51 47N 8 10W
Powfoot Scotland 11 F1 54 59N 3 20W
Powys u.a. Wales 14 C2 52 10N 3 30W
Poznań Poland 53 H6 52 25N 16 53E
Prague Czech Rep. 52 G5 50 06N 14 26E
Prato Italy 54 D5 43 53N 11 06E
Prawle Point England 18 D2 50 12N 3 44W
Preesall England 12 D2 53 55N 2 57W
Prešov Slovakia 53 K4 49 00N 21 10E
Prestatyn Wales 14 C3 53 20N 3 24W
Presteigne Wales 14 C2 52 17N 3 00W
Preston England 12 D2 53 46N 2 42W
Prestonpans Scotland 11 G2 55 57N 3 00W
Prestwich England 12 D2 53 32N 2 17W
Prestwick Scotland 11 E2 55 30N 4 37W
Pretoria RSA 82 E2 25 45S 28 12E
Přibram Czech Rep. 52 G4 49 42N 14 01E
Prince Albert Canada 89 P4 53 13N 105 45W
Prince Edward Island prov. Canada 89 Y3 46 30N 63 00W
Prince Rupert Canada 88 J4 54 09N 130 20W
Princes Risborough England 16 C2 51 44N 0 51W
Princetown England 18 D2 50 33N 3 59W
Pripyats' r. Belarus 56 B5/C5 52 30N 27 00E
Priština Yugoslavia 55 J5 42 39N 21 20E
Privas France 50 F5 44 44N 4 36E
Prokop'yevsk Russia 63 L7 53 55N 86 45E
Providence USA 91 M5 41 50N 71 28W
Provins France 50 F5 48 34N 3 18E
Prudhoe England 13 E3 54 58N 1 51W
Prudhoe Bay tn. USA 88 F8 70 05N 148 20W
Pruszków Poland 53 K6 52 10N 20 47E
Prut r. Romania 53 N2 47 00N 28 00E
Pskov Russia 62 E8 57 48N 28 26E
Puddletown England 19 E2 50 45N 2 21W
Pudsey England 13 E2 53 48N 1 40W
Puebla Mexico 94 E3 19 03N 98 10W
Pueblo USA 90 F4 38 17N 104 38W
Puertollano Spain 51 C3 38 41N 4 07W
PUERTO RICO 95 L3
Pulborough England 16 C1 50 58N 0 30W
Pumsaint Wales 14 C2 52 03N 3 58W
Pune India 66 C3 18 34N 73 58E
Punta Arenas Chile 97 C3 53 10S 70 56W
Purfleet England 17 D2 51 29N 0 14E
Puri India 67 F3 19 49N 85 54E
Puulavesi l. Finland 49 G3 61 50N 26 40E
Pwllheli Wales 14 B2 52 53N 4 25W
Pyle Wales 14 C1 51 32N 3 42W
Pyongyang N. Korea 69 N5 39 00N 125 47E
Pyrénées mts. France/Spain 50 E2 42 50N 0 30E
Pýrgos Greece 55 L1 35 00N 25 10E

Q
QATAR 65 F4
Qingdao China 69 M5 36 04N 120 22E
Qiqihar China 69 M7 47 23N 124 00E
Quantock Hills England 19 D3 51 10N 3 15W
Québec prov. Canada 89 V4/X4 50 00N 75 00W
Québec Canada 89 W3 46 50N 71 15W
Queenborough England 17 D2 51 26N 0 45E
Queen Charlotte Islands Canada 88 J4 53 00N 132 30W
Queen Elizabeth Islands Canada 89 N9/S9 77 30N 105 00W
Queensbury England 13 E2 53 46N 1 50W
Queenstown Australia 73 J2 42 07S 145 33E
Querétaro Mexico 94 D4 20 38N 100 23W
Quetta Pakistan 66 B6 30 15N 67 00E
Quezon City Philippines 71 G6 14 39N 121 02E
Quiberon France 50 C4 47 29N 3 07W
Quigley's Point Rol 20 D5 55 17N 7 08W
Quimper France 50 B4 48 00N 4 06W
Quito Ecuador 96 B13 0 14S 78 30W
Quorn England 15 E2 52 45N 1 10W

R
Raahe Finland 49 F3 64 42N 24 30E
Raasay i. Scotland 8 C2 57 25N 6 05W
Rabat-Salé Morocco 80 C8 34 02N 6 51W

Radcliffe England 12 D2 53 34N 2 20W
Radcliffe on Trent England 15 E3 52 57N 1 03W
Radlett England 16 C2 51 41N 0 19W
Radom Poland 53 K5 51 26N 21 10E
Radstadt Austria 52 F3 47 23N 13 28E
Radstock England 19 E3 51 18N 2 28W
Raglan Wales 14 D1 51 47N 2 51W
Ragusa Italy 54 F2 36 56N 14 44E
Rainford England 12 D2 53 30N 2 48W
Rainier, Mount USA 90 B6 46 25N 121 45W
Rainworth England 13 E2 53 08N 1 08W
Raipur India 66 E4 21 16N 81 42E
Rame Head England 18 C2 50 19N 4 13W
Ramore Head NI 10 C2 55 13N 6 39W
Ramsbottom England 12 D2 53 39N 2 19W
Ramsey England 16 C3 52 27N 0 07W
Ramsey Isle of Man 12 B3 54 19N 4 23W
Ramsey Island Wales 14 A1 51 53N 5 20W
Ramsgate England 17 E2 51 20N 1 25E
Randalstown NI 10 C1 54 45N 6 19W
Rangpur Bangladesh 67 F5 25 45N 89 21E
Rannoch Moor Scotland 9 E1 56 35N 4 50W
Rannoch Station Scotland 9 E1 5642N 4 34W
Rapallo Italy 54 C6 44 21N 9 13E
Raphoe Rol 20 D4 54 52N 7 36W
Rastatt Germany 52 D4 48 51N 8 13E
Rathangan Rol 20 E3 53 12N 6 59W
Rathcoole Rol 20 E3 53 17N 6 28W
Rathcormack Rol 21 C2 52 05N 8 17W
Rathdowney Rol 21 D2 52 51N 7 35W
Rathdrum Rol 21 E2 52 56N 6 13W
Rathfriland NI 10 C1 54 14N 6 10W
Rathkeale Rol 21 C2 52 32N 8 56W
Rathlackan Rol 20 B4 54 18N 9 15W
Rathlin Sound NI 10 C2 55 20N 6 25W
Rath Luirc Rol 21 C2 52 21N 8 41W
Rathmelton Rol 20 D5 55 02N 7 38W
Rathmore Rol 21 B2 52 05N 9 13W
Rathnew Rol 21 E2 52 58N 6 05W
Rathvilly Rol 21 E2 52 53N 6 41W
Ratoath Rol 20 E3 53 31N 6 24W
Raton USA 90 F4 36 45N 104 27W
Rattray Scotland 9 F1 56 36N 3 20W
Rattray Head Scotland 9 H2 57 38N 1 45W
Rauma Finland 49 F3 61 09N 21 30E
Raunds England 15 F2 52 21N 0 33W
Ravenglass England 12 C3 54 21N 3 24W
Ravenna Italy 54 E6 44 25N 12 12E
Ravensburg Germany 52 D3 47 47N 9 37E
Ravenshead England 13 E2 53 40N 1 10W
Rawalpindi Pakistan 66 C6 33 40N 73 08E
Rawmarsh England 13 E2 53 27N 1 21W
Rawtenstall England 12 D2 53 42N 2 18W
Rayleigh England 17 D2 51 36N 0 36E
Reading England 16 C2 51 28N 0 59W
Reading u.a. England 16 B1/C1 50 25N 1 00W
Reay Forest Scotland 9 E3 58 30N 4 55W
Recife Brazil 96 L12 8 06S 34 53W
Recklinghausen Germany 52 C5 51 37N 7 11E
Red Bay NI 10 C2 55 04N 6 01W
Redbourn England 16 C2 51 48N 0 24W
Redbridge England 16 D2 51 34N 0 05E
Redcar England 13 E3 54 37N 1 04W
Redcar and Cleveland u.a. England 13 E3/F3 54 30N 1 00W
Redditch England 15 E2 52 19N 1 56W
Redhill tn. England 16 C2 51 14N 0 11W
Redon France 50 C4 47 39N 2 05W
Redruth England 18 B2 50 13N 5 14W
Red Sea Middle East 64 C4/C2 27 00N 35 00E
Reepham England 17 E3 52 46N 1 07E
Regensburg Germany 52 F4 49 01N 12 07E
Reggio di Calabria Italy 54 F3 38 06N 15 39E
Regina Canada 89 Q4 50 30N 104 38W
Reigate England 16 C2 51 14N 0 13W
Reims France 50 G5 49 15N 4 02E
Reinosa Spain 51 C3 43 01N 4 09W
Rendsburg Germany 52 D7 54 19N 9 39E
Renfrew Canada 89 V3 45 28N 76 44W
Renfrew Scotland 11 E2 55 53N 4 24W
Renfrewshire u.a. Scotland 11 E2 55 50N 4 40W
Rennes France 50 D5 48 06N 1 40W
Reno USA 90 C4 39 32N 119 49W
REPUBLIC OF IRELAND 20/21
REPUBLIC OF SOUTH AFRICA 82 D1/D2
Requena Spain 51 E3 39 29N 1 08W
Resolute Canada 89 S8 74 40N 95 00W
Retford England 13 F2 53 19N 0 56W
Rethel France 50 G5 49 31N 4 22E
Reus Spain 51 F4 41 10N 1 06E
Reutlingen Germany 52 D4 48 30N 9 13E
Reykjavik Iceland 49 K6 64 09N 21 58W
Rhayader Wales 14 C2 52 18N 3 30W
Rheden Neths 48 E5 52 01N 6 02E
Rheidol r. Wales 14 C2 52 32N 3 55W
Rhein r. Germany 52 C6 50 30N 8 00E
Rheine Germany 52 C6 52 17N 7 26E
Rhode Island state USA 91 M5 41 00N 71 00W
Rhondda Wales 14 C1 51 40N 3 30W
Rhondda Cynon Taff u.a. Wales 14 C1 51 40N 3 30W

Rhône r. Switz./France 50 G3 45 00N 4 50E
Rhoose Wales 14 C1 51 26N 3 22W
Rhosllanerchrugog Wales 14 C3 53 01N 3 04W
Rhosneigr Wales 14 B3 53 14N 4 31W
Rhossili Wales 14 B1 51 34N 4 17W
Rhubodach Scotland 10 D2 55 56N 5 09W
Rhum i. Scotland 8 C2 57 00N 6 20W
Rhyl Wales 14 C3 53 19N 3 29W
Rhymney Wales 14 C1 51 46N 3 18W
Rhynie Scotland 9 G2 57 19N 2 50W
Ribble r. England 12 D2 53 45N 2 30W
Riccall England 13 E2 53 51N 1 04W
Richhill NI 10 C1 54 22N 6 33W
Richmond England 13 E3 54 24N 1 44W
Richmond upon Thames England 16 C2 51 28N 0 19W
Rickmansworth England 16 C2 51 38N 0 29W
Ried Austria 52 F4 48 13N 13 29E
Riesa Germany 52 F5 51 18N 13 18E
Rieti Italy 54 E5 42 24N 12 51E
Riga Latvia 49 F2 56 53N 24 08E
Rimini Italy 54 E6 44 03N 12 34E
Ringabella Bay Rol 21 C1 51 46N 8 13W
Ringaskiddy Rol 21 C1 51 49N 8 18W
Ringwood England 16 B1 50 51N 1 47W
Rio de Janeiro tn. Brazil 96 I8 22 53S 43 17W
Rio de la Plata est. Uruguay/Argentina 97 F5 35 00S 57 00W
Rio Grande tn. Brazil 97 G7 32 03S 52 08W
Río Grande r. Mexico/USA 90 E3/F3 30 00N 105 00W
Ripley England 13 E2 53 03N 1 24W
Ripon England 13 E3 54 08N 1 31W
Risca Wales 14 C1 51 37N 3 07W
Rishton England 12 D2 53 47N 2 24W
Riva del Garda Italy 54 D6 45 53N 10 50E
Riverton Canada 89 R4 51 00N 97 00W
Rivne Ukraine 53 M5 50 39N 26 10E
Riyadh Saudi Arabia 65 E3 24 39N 46 46E
Roanne France 50 G4 46 02N 4 05E
Robin Hood's Bay tn. England 13 F3 54 25N 0 33W
Rochdale England 12 D2 53 38N 2 09W
Rochefort France 50 D3 45 57N 0 58W
Rochester Northamptonshire England 12 D4 55 16N 2 16W
Rochester Medway England 17 D2 51 24N 0 30E
Rochester USA 91 L5 43 12N 77 37W
Rochford England 17 D2 51 36N 0 43E
Rochfortbridge Rol 20 D3 53 25N 7 18W
Rockhampton Australia 73 K6 23 22S 150 32E
Rocky Mountains Canada/USA 88 K5/P2 55 00N 125 00W
Rodel Scotland 8 C2 57 41N 7 05W
Rodez France 50 F3 44 21N 2 34E
Roding r. England 17 D2 51 45N 0 15E
Roermond Neths 48 D4 51 12N 6 00E
ROMANIA 53 L2/M2
Romans-sur-Isère France 50 G3 45 03N 5 03E
Rome Italy 54 E4 41 53N 12 30E
Romney Marsh England 17 D2 51 03N 0 58E
Romorantin-Lanthenay France 50 E4 47 22N 1 44E
Romsey England 16 B1 50 59N 1 30W
Rona i. Scotland 8 D2 57 32N 5 59W
Ronda Spain 51 C2 36 45N 5 10W
Ronse Belgium 48 B3 50 45N 3 36E
Roosendaal Neths 48 C4 51 32N 4 28E
Roosky Rol 20 D3 53 50N 7 55W
Roquetas de Mar Spain 51 D2 36 46N 2 35W
Rora Head Scotland 7 A1 58 52N 3 25W
Rosarno Italy 54 F3 38 29N 15 59E
Roscoff France 50 C5 48 43N 3 59W
Roscommon Rol 20 C3 53 38N 8 11W
Roscommon co. Rol 20 C3 53 45N 8 10W
Roscrea Rol 21 D2 52 57N 7 47W
Rosehearty Scotland 9 G2 57 42N 2 07W
Rosenheim Germany 52 F3 47 51N 12 09E
Roskilde Denmark 49 D2 55 39N 12 07E
Rossano Italy 54 G3 39 35N 16 38E
Rossan Point Rol 20 C4 54 40N 8 50W
Ross Carbery Rol 21 B1 51 35N 9 02W
Rosscarbery Bay Rol 21 B1 51 32N 9 00W
Rosslare Rol 21 E2 52 15N 6 22W
Rosslare Harbour tn. Rol 21 E2 52 15N 6 22W
Rosslare Point Rol 21 E2 52 19N 6 21W
Ross-on-Wye England 15 D1 51 55N 2 35W
Rostock Germany 52 F7 54 06N 12 09E
Rostov-na-Donu Russia 62 F6 47 15N 39 45E
Rostrevor NI 10 C1 54 06N 6 12W
Rothbury England 11 H2 55 19N 1 55W
Rother r. England 16 C1 51 00N 0 50W
Rother r. England 17 D1 51 00N 0 17E
Rotherham England 13 E2 53 26N 1 20W
Rothes Scotland 9 F2 57 31N 3 13W
Rothesay Scotland 10 D2 55 51N 5 03W
Rothwell West Yorkshire England 13 E2 53 45N 1 29W
Rothwell Northamptonshire England 15 F2 52 25N 0 48W
Rotterdam Neths 48 C4 51 54N 4 28E

Rottingdean England 16 C1 50 48N 0 04W
Roubaix France 50 F6 50 42N 3 10E
Rouen France 50 E5 49 26N 1 05E
Roundwood Rol 21 E3 53 04N 6 13W
Rousay i. Scotland 7 A2 59 10N 3 00W
Rovigo Italy 54 D6 45 04N 11 47E
Rowlands Gill England 13 E3 54 54N 1 45W
Royal Leamington Spa England 15 E2 52 18N 1 31W
Royal Tunbridge Wells England 17 D2 51 08N 0 16E
Royan France 50 D3 45 38N 1 02W
Royston South Yorkshire England 13 E2 53 37N 1 27W
Royston Hertfordshire England 16 C3 52 03N 0 01W
Royton England 12 D2 53 34N 2 08W
Ruabon Wales 14 C2 52 59N 3 02W
Ruddington England 15 E2 52 54N 1 09W
Rufford England 12 D2 53 39N 2 49W
Rugby England 15 E2 52 23N 1 15W
Rugeley England 15 E2 52 46N 1 55W
Ruhr r. Germany 52 D5 51 00N 7 00E
Rumney Wales 14 C1 51 30N 3 10W
Runcorn England 12 D2 53 20N 2 44W
Ruse Bulgaria 55 M5 43 50N 25 59E
Rush Rol 20 E3 53 32N 6 06W
Rushden England 15 F2 52 17N 0 36W
RUSSIAN FEDERATION 62/63
Ruthin Wales 14 C3 53 07N 3 18W
Rutland u.a. England 15 F2 5241N 00 39W
Rutland Water England 15 F2 52 40N 0 37W
RWANDA 83 A3/B3
Ryazan' Russia 62 F7 54 37N 39 43E
Rybinsk Russia 62 F8 58 03N 38 50E
Rybnik Poland 53 J5 50 07N 18 30E
Ryde England 16 B1 50 44N 1 10W
Rye r. England 16 C5 54 15N 1 10W
Rye England 17 D1 50 57N 0 44E
Ryton England 13 E3 54 59N 1 57W
Ryukyu Islands Japan 69 N3 27 30N 127 30E

S

Saalfeld Germany 52 E5 50 39N 11 22E
Saarbrücken Germany 52 C4 49 15N 6 58E
Sabadell Spain 51 G4 41 33N 2 07E
Sacramento USA 90 B4 38 32N 121 30W
Sacriston England 13 E3 54 50N 1 38W
Saffron Walden England 17 D3 52 01N 0 15E
Saga Japan 70 B1 33 16N 130 18E
Sagunto Spain 51 E3 39 40N 0 17W
Sahagún Spain 51 C3 42 23N 5 02W
St. Abbs Scotland 11 G2 55 54N 2 08W
St. Abb's Head Scotland 11 G2 55 55N 2 09W
St. Agnes England 18 B2 50 18N 5 13W
St. Albans England 16 C2 51 46N 0 21W
St Alban's or St Aldheim's Head England 16 B1 50 34N 2 04W
St. Andrews Scotland 9 G1 56 20N 2 48W
St Anne Channel Islands 19 E1 49 43N 2 12W
St. Asaph Wales 14 C3 53 15N 3 26W
St. Austell England 18 C2 50 20N 4 48W
St. Bees England 12 C3 54 29N 3 35W
St. Blazey England 18 C2 50 22N 4 43W
St. Bride's Bay Wales 14 A1 51 50N 5 15W
St-Brieuc France 50 C5 48 31N 2 45W
St. Catharines Canada 89 V2 43 10N 79 15W
St-Chamond France 50 G3 45 29N 4 32E
St. Clears Wales 14 B1 51 50N 4 30W
St. Columb Major England 18 C2 50 26N 4 56W
St. David's Wales 14 A1 51 54N 5 16W
St. David's Head Wales 14 A1 51 55N 5 19W
St.-Dié France 50 H5 48 17N 6 57E
St.-Dizier France 50 G5 48 38N 4 58E
Saintes France 50 D3 45 44N 0 38W
St.-Étienne France 50 G3 45 26N 4 23E
Saintfield NI 10 D1 54 28N 5 50W
St. Finnan's Bay Rol 21 A1 51 50N 10 23W
St. Gallen Switz. 52 D3 47 25N 9 23E
St.-Gaudens France 50 E2 43 07N 0 44E
St. George's Grenada 94 R11 12 04N 61 44W
St. George's Channel British Isles 21 E2 52 00N 6 00W
St.-German en-Laye France 50 F5 48 54N 2 04E
St-Girons France 50 E2 42 59N 1 08E
St. Helens England 12 D2 53 28N 2 44W
St. Helier Channel Islands 19 E1 49 12N 2 07W
St. Ives England 16 C3 52 20N 0 05W
St. Ives England 18 B2 50 12N 5 29W
St. Jean-de-Luz France 50 D2 43 23N 1 39W
Saint John Canada 89 X3 45 16N 66 03W
St. John's Canada 89 AA3 47 34N 52 41W
St. John's Point NI 10 D1 54 15N 5 35W
St. Johnstown Rol 20 D4 54 56N 7 28W
St. John's Town of Dalry Scotland 11 E2 55 07N 4 10W
St. Just England 18 B2 50 07N 5 41W
St. Keverne England 18 B2 50 03N 5 06W
St. Kilda i. Scotland 7 A3 57 49N 8 34W
ST. KITTS AND NEVIS 94 P9

St. Lawrence r. Canada/USA 89 X3 46 55N 55 24W
St. Leonards England 19 F2 50 50N 1 50W
St-Lô France 50 D5 49 07N 1 05W
St. Louis USA 91 H4 38 40N 90 15W
ST. LUCIA 94 R11/R12
St. Malo France 50 C5 48 39N 2 00W
St. Margaret's at Cliffe England 17 E2 51 10N 1 23E
St. Mawes England 18 B2 50 09N 5 01W
St. Monance Scotland 11 G1 56 13N 2 46W
St. Moritz Switz. 52 D3 46 30N 9 51E
St.-Nazaire France 50 C4 47 17N 2 12W
St. Neots England 16 C3 52 14N 0 17W
St.-Omer France 50 F6 50 45N 2 15E
St. Paul USA 91 H5 45 00N 93 10W
St. Peter Port Channel Islands 19 E1 49 27N 3 32W
St. Petersburg Russia 62 F8 59 55N 30 25E
Saint-Pierre & Miquelon is. Atlantic Ocean 89 Z3 47 00N 56 20W
St. Pölten Austria 53 G4 48 13N 15 37E
St.-Quentin France 50 F5 49 51N 3 17E
St.-Tropez France 50 H2 43 16N 6 39E
ST. VINCENT AND THE GRENADINES 94 R11
Sakhalin i. Russia 63 S7 50 00N 143 00E
Salamanca Spain 51 C4 40 58N 5 40W
Salcombe England 18 D2 50 13N 3 47W
Sale England 12 D2 53 26N 2 19W
Salen Scotland 8 D1 56 43N 5 47W
Salen Scotland 8 D1 56 31N 5 57W
Salerno Italy 54 F4 40 40N 14 46E
Salford England 12 D2 53 30N 2 16W
Salisbury England 16 B2 51 05N 1 48W
Salisbury Plain England 16 B2 51 10N 1 55W
Salmon USA 90 D6 45 11N 113 55W
Salo Finland 49 F3 60 23N 23 10E
Salò Italy 54 D6 45 37N 10 31E
Salon-de-Provence France 50 G2 43 38N 5 06E
Salt Jordan 64 N11 32 03N 35 44E
Saltash England 18 C2 50 24N 4 12W
Saltburn-by-the-Sea England 13 F3 54 35N 0 58W
Saltcoats Scotland 11 E2 55 38N 4 47W
Saltdal Norway 49 E4 67 06N 15 25E
Saltdean England 16 C1 50 49N 0 02W
Saltfleet England 13 G2 53 26N 0 10E
Saltillo Mexico 94 D5 25 30N 101 00W
Salt Lake City USA 90 D5 40 45N 111 55W
Salvador Brazil 96 K11 12 58S 38 29W
Salween r. China/Myanmar 71 B8 20 00N 103 00E
Salzburg Austria 52 F3 47 48N 13 03E
Salzgitter Germany 52 E6 52 13N 10 20E
Samara Russia 62 H7 53 10N 50 10E
SAMOA 100 J6
Samsun Turkey 57 E3 41 17N 36 22E
San Antonio USA 91 G2 29 25N 98 30W
Sanda Island Scotland 10 D2 55 18N 5 35W
Sanday i. Scotland 7 B2 59 15N 2 30W
Sandbach England 12 D2 53 09N 2 22W
Sandhead Scotland 10 E1 54 48N 4 58W
Sandhurst England 16 C2 51 21N 0 48W
San Diego USA 90 C3 32 45N 117 10W
Sandown England 16 B1 50 39N 1 09W
Sandray i. Scotland 8 B1 56 53N 7 30W
Sandringham England 17 D3 52 50N 0 31E
Sandwich England 17 E2 51 17N 1 20E
Sandy England 16 C3 52 08N 0 18W
San Fernando Spain 51 B2 36 28N 6 12W
San Francisco USA 90 B4 37 45N 122 27W
San José Costa Rica 95 H1 9 59N 84 04W
San José USA 90 B4 37 20N 121 55W
San Juan Puerto Rico 95 L3 18 29N 66 08W
San Juan Bautista Spain 51 F3 39 05N 1 31E
SAN MARINO 54 E5 44 00N 12 00E
Sanmenxia China 69 K4 34 46N 111 17E
Sanming China 69 L3 26 16N 117 35E
Sannox Scotland 10 D2 55 41N 5 08W
Sanquhar Scotland 11 F2 55 22N 3 56W
San Remo Italy 54 B5 43 48N 7 46E
San Salvador El Salvador 94 G2 13 40N 89 10W
San Sebastián Spain 51 E5 43 19N 1 59W
San Severo Italy 54 F4 41 41N 15 23E
Santa Barbara USA 90 C3 33 29N 119 01W
Santa Cruz Spain 80 A7 28 28N 16 15W
Santa Cruz USA 90 E4 35 41N 105 57W
Santander Spain 51 D5 43 28N 3 48W
Sant'Antioco Italy 54 C3 39 04N 8 27E
Santarém Brazil 96 G13 2 26S 54 41W
Santarém Portugal 51 A3 39 14N 8 40W
Santa Teresa Gallura Italy 54 C4 41 14N 9 12E
Santiago Chile 97 C6 33 30S 70 40W
Santiago de Compostela Spain 51 A5 42 52N 8 33W
Santo Andre Brazil 96 H9 23 39S 46 29W
Santo Domingo Dom. Rep. 95 L3 18 30N 69 57W
Santoña Spain 51 D5 43 27N 3 26W
São Francisco r. Brazil 96 J11 15 00S 44 00W

São Luís Brazil 96 J13 2 34S 44 16W
Saône r. France 50 G4 46 28N 4 55E
São Paulo Brazil 96 H9 23 33S 46 39W
SÃO TOMÉ AND PRINCIPE 80 F2
Sapporo Japan 70 D3 43 05N 141 21E
Sarajevo Bosnia-Herzegovina 55 H5 43 52N 18 26E
Saratov Russia 62 G7 51 30N 45 55E
Sardinia i. Italy 54 C3/C4 40 00N 9 00E
Sark i. Channel Islands 19 E1 49 26N 2 22W
Sarnia Canada 89 U2 42 58N 82 23W
Sarrebourg France 50 H5 48 43N 7 03E
Sarreguemines France 50 H5 49 06N 6 55E
Sartène France 50 J1 41 37N 8 58E
Saskatchewan prov. Canada 88/89 P5/Q5 53 50N 109 00W
Saskatoon Canada 88 P4 52 10N 106 40W
Sassari Italy 54 C4 40 43N 8 34E
Sassnitz Germany 52 F7 54 32N 13 40E
Sassuolo Italy 54 D6 44 32N 10 47E
Satu Mare Romania 53 L3 47 48N 22 52E
SAUDI ARABIA 64/65 D3/F3
Sault Ste. Marie Canada 89 U3 46 31N 84 20W
Saumur France 50 D4 47 16N 0 05W
Saundersfoot Wales 14 B1 51 43N 4 43W
Savannah USA 91 K3 32 04N 81 07W
Savona Italy 54 C6 44 18N 8 28E
Sawbridgeworth England 17 D2 51 50N 0 09E
Sawel mt. NI 10 B1 54 49N 7 02W
Sawston England 17 D2 52 07N 0 10E
Saxilby England 13 F2 53 17N 0 40W
Saxmundham England 17 E3 52 13N 1 29E
Saxthorpe England 17 E3 52 50N 1 09E
Scafell Pike mt. England 12 C3 54 27N 3 14W
Scalasaig Scotland 10 C3 56 04N 6 12W
Scalby England 13 F3 54 18N 0 27W
Scalloway Scotland 7 C3 60 08N 1 17W
Scalpay i. Scotland 8 C2 57 52N 6 40W
Scalpay i. Scotland 8 D2 57 15N 6 00W
Scapa Scotland 7 B1 58 58N 2 59W
Scapa Flow sd. Scotland 7 A1 58 55N 3 00W
Scarborough England 13 F3 54 17N 0 24W
Scarinish Scotland 8 C1 56 29N 6 48W
Scarp i. Scotland 8 B3 58 02N 7 08W
Scarriff Rol 21 C2 52 55N 8 37W
Scartaglin Rol 21 B2 52 10N 9 26W
Schaffhausen Switz. 52 D3 47 42N 8 38E
Schefferville Canada 89 X4 54 50N 67 00W
Schleswig Germany 52 D7 54 32N 9 34E
Schwäbisch Gmünd Germany 52 D4 48 49N 9 48E
Schwarzwald mts. Germany 52 D4 47 00N 8 00E
Schwaz Austria 52 E3 47 21N 11 44E
Schwechat Austria 53 H4 48 09N 16 27E
Schweinfurt Germany 52 E5 50 03N 10 16E
Schwerin Germany 52 E6 53 38N 11 25E
Schwyz Switz. 52 D3 47 02N 8 39E
Sciacca Italy 54 E2 37 31N 13 05E
Scilly, Isles of England 18 A1 49 56N 6 20W
Sconser Scotland 8 C2 57 18N 6 07W
Scotland UK 6 56 00N 4 00W
Scottish Borders u.a. Scotland 11 F2/G2 55 30N 2 55W
Scourie Scotland 8 D3 58 20N 5 08W
Scrabster Scotland 9 F3 58 37N 3 34W
Scunthorpe England 13 F2 53 35N 0 39W
Seaford England 17 D1 50 46N 0 06E
Seaham England 13 E3 54 50N 1 20W
Seahouses England 11 H2 55 35N 1 38W
Seascale England 12 C3 54 24N 3 29W
Seaton Devon England 19 D2 50 43N 3 05W
Seaton Cumbria England 12 C3 54 40N 3 30W
Seaton Delaval England 13 E4 55 04N 1 31W
Seattle USA 90 B6 47 35N 122 20W
Sedan France 50 G5 49 42N 4 57E
Sedbergh England 12 D3 54 20N 2 31W
Segovia Spain 51 C4 40 57N 4 07W
Seine r. France 50 E5 49 15N 1 15E
Selborne England 16 C2 51 06N 0 56W
Selby England 13 E2 53 48N 1 04W
Sélestat France 50 H5 48 16N 7 28E
Selkirk Scotland 11 G2 55 33N 2 50W
Selsey England 16 C1 50 44N 0 48W
Selsey Bill p. England 16 C1 50 43N 0 48W
Semarang Indonesia 71 E2 6 58S 110 29E
Sendai Japan 70 D2 38 16N 140 52E
SENEGAL 80 A4/B4
Senlis France 50 F5 49 12N 2 35E
Sennen England 18 B2 50 03N 5 42W
Sennybridge Wales 14 C1 51 57N 3 34W
Sens France 50 F5 48 12N 3 18E
Seoul S. Korea 69 N5 37 32N 127 00E
Sept-Îles tn. Canada 89 X4 50 10N 66 00W
Serbia admin. Yugoslavia 55 J5/J6 44 50N 21 00E
Serov Russia 62 J8 59 42N 60 32E
Serra Brazil 96 J10 20 06S 40 16W
Sérres Greece 55 K4 41 03N 23 33E
Sète France 50 F3 43 25N 3 43E
Settle England 12 D3 54 04N 2 16W
Setúbal Portugal 51 A3 38 31N 8 54W

Sevastopol' Ukraine 57 D3 44 36N 33 31E
Seven Head c. Rol 21 C1 51 34N 8 42W
Severn r. England/Wales 14 C2 52 30N 3 15W
Severodvinsk Russia 62 F9 64 35N 39 50E
Sevilla Spain 51 C2 37 24N 5 59W
Seward USA 88 F6 60 05N 149 34W
SEYCHELLES 103
Sézannes France 50 F5 48 44N 3 44E
Sfântu Gheorghe Romania 53 M2 45 51N 25 48E
Sfax Tunisia 80 G8 34 45N 10 43E
Sgurr Mór mt. Scotland 9 D2 57 42N 5 03W
Shaftesbury England 19 E3 51 01N 2 12W
Shaldon England 18 D2 51 35N 3 30W
Shanghai China 69 M4 31 06N 121 22E
Shanklin England 16 B1 50 38N 1 10W
Shannon Rol 21 C2 52 41N 8 55W
Shannon r. Rol 21 C2/B2 52 45N 8 57W
Shap England 12 D3 54 32N 2 41W
Shapinsay i. Scotland 7 B2 59 03N 2 51W
Sheerness England 17 D2 51 27N 0 45E
Sheffield England 13 E2 53 23N 1 30W
Shefford England 16 C3 52 02N 0 20W
Shelburne Canada 89 X2 43 37N 65 20W
Shenandoah USA 91 G5 40 48N 95 22W
Shenyang China 69 M6 41 50N 123 26E
Shepetovka Ukraine 53 N5 50 12N 27 01E
Shepperton England 16 C2 51 23N 0 28W
Sheppey, Isle of England 17 D2 51 25N 0 50E
Shepshed England 15 E2 52 47N 1 18W
Shepton Mallet England 19 E3 51 12N 2 33W
Sherborne England 19 E2 50 57N 2 31W
Sherbrooke Canada 89 W3 45 24N 71 54W
Shercock Rol 20 E3 53 59N 6 54W
Sheringham England 17 E3 52 57N 1 12E
Sherkin Island Rol 21 B1 51 28N 9 25W
's-Hertogenbosch Neths 48 D4 51 41N 5 19E
Shetland Islands u.a. Scotland 7 C2/D3 60 00N 1 15W
Shieldaig Scotland 8 D2 57 31N 5 39W
Shifnal England 15 D2 52 41N 2 22W
Shijiazhuang China 69 K5 38 04N 114 28E
Shilbottle England 11 H2 55 23N 1 42W
Shildon England 13 E3 54 38N 1 39W
Shilelagh Rol 21 E2 52 45N 6 32W
Shipley England 13 E2 53 50N 1 47W
Shipston-on-Stour England 15 E2 52 04N 1 37W
Shipton England 13 E2 54 01N 1 09W
Shiraz Iran 65 F4 29 38N 52 34E
Shirebrook England 13 E2 53 13N 1 13W
Shoeburyness England 17 D2 51 32N 0 48E
Shoreham-by-Sea England 16 C1 50 49N 0 16W
Shotton Wales 14 C3 53 12N 3 02W
Shotts Scotland 11 F2 55 49N 3 48W
Shrewsbury England 14 D2 52 43N 2 45W
Shrewton England 16 B2 51 12N 1 55W
Shropshire co. England 14/15 D2 52 35N 2 25W
Shumen Bulgaria 55 M5 43 17N 26 55E
Sible Hedingham England 17 D2 51 58N 0 35E
Sicily i. Italy 54 E2/F2 37 00N 14 00E
Siderno Italy 54 G3 38 16N 16 17E
Sidi Bel Abbès Algeria 80 D9 35 15N 0 39W
Sidlaw Hills Scotland 9 F1/G1 56 30N 3 10W
Sidmouth England 19 D2 50 41N 3 15W
Siegen Germany 52 D5 50 52N 8 02E
Siena Italy 54 D5 43 19N 11 19E
SIERRA LEONE 80 B3
Sierra Madre Occidental mts. Mexico 94 C5/D4 26 00N 107 00W
Sierra Nevada mts. Spain 51 D2 37 00N 3 20W
Sierra Nevada mts. USA 90 C4 37 00N 119 00W
Sighişoara Romania 53 M3 46 12N 24 48E
Sigüenza Spain 51 D4 41 04N 2 38W
Sileby England 15 E2 52 44N 1 05W
Silistra Bulgaria 55 M6 44 06N 27 17E
Silloth England 12 C3 54 52N 3 23W
Silverton England 18 D2 50 48N 3 30W
Silves Portugal 51 A2 37 11N 8 26W
Simferopol' Ukraine 57 D3 44 57N 34 05E
Simonsbath England 18 D3 51 09N 3 45W
Sinclair's Bay Scotland 9 F3 58 30N 3 07
Sines Portugal 51 A2 37 58N 8 52W
SINGAPORE 71 C4
Sintra Portugal 51 A3 38 48N 9 22W
Sion Switz. 52 C3 46 14N 7 22E
Sion Mills NI 10 B1 54 47N 7 28W
Siracusa Italy 54 F2 37 04N 15 19E
Sisak Croatia 54 G6 45 30N 16 22E
Sisteron France 50 G3 44 16N 5 56E
Sittingbourne England 17 D2 51 21N 0 44E
Sixmilebridge Rol 21 C2 52 45N 8 46W
Sjaelland i. Denmark 49 D2 55 15N 11 30E
Skagerrak sd. Denmark/Norway 49 C2 57 30N 8 00E
Skegness England 13 G2 53 10N 0 21E
Skelleftea Sweden 49 F3 64 45N 21 00E
Skellingthorpe England 13 F2 53 14N 0 37W

Skelmanthorpe England 13 E2 53 36N 1 40W
Skelmersdale England 12 D2 53 55N 2 48W
Skelmorlie Scotland 10 E2 55 51N 4 53W
Skelton England 13 F3 54 33N 0 59W
Skerries Rol 20 E3 53 35N 6 07W
Skiddaw mt. England 12 C3 54 40N 3 08W
Skien Norway 49 C2 59 14N 9 37E
Skipton England 12 D2 53 58N 2 01W
Skokholm Island Wales 14 A1 51 41N 5 16W
Skomer Island Wales 14 A1 51 45N 5 18W
Skopje FYROM 55 J4 42 00N 21 28E
Skövde Sweden 49 D2 58 24N 13 52E
Skull Rol 21 B1 51 32N 9 40W
Skye i. Scotland 8 C2 57 20N 6 15W
Slaidburn England 12 D2 54 00N 2 26W
Slane Rol 20 E3 54 43N 6 33W
Slaney r. Rol 21 E2 52 24N 6 33W
Slatina Romania 53 M2 44 26N 24 22E
Slave r. Canada 88 N5 59 20N 111 10W
Slavonski Brod Croatia 55 G6 45 09N 18 02E
Sleaford England 13 F2 53 00N 0 24W
Sleat, Point of Scotland 8 C2 57 01N 6 01W
Sleat, Sound of Scotland 8 D2 57 00N 5 55W
Sledmere England 13 F3 54 04N 0 35W
Sleights England 13 F3 54 26N 0 40W
Slieve Donard mt. NI 10 D1 54 11N 5 55W
Slieve Gamph hills Rol 20 C4 54 11N 8 53W
Slieve Mish Mountains Rol 21 B2 51 12N 10 00W
Sligo Rol 20 C4 54 17N 8 28W
Sligo co. Rol 20 C4 54 10N 8 40W
Sligo Bay b. Rol 20 C4 54 15N 8 55W
Sliven Bulgaria 55 M5 42 40N 26 19E
Slough England 16 C2 51 31N 0 36W
Slough u.a. England 16 C1 50 25N 0 40W
SLOVAKIA 53 J4/K4
SLOVENIA 54 F6
Smethwick England 15 E2 52 30N 1 58W
Smolensk Russia 62 F7 54 49N 32 04E
Smolyan Bulgaria 55 L4 41 34N 24 42E
Snaefell mt. Isle of Man 12 B3 54 16N 4 28W
Snake r. USA 90 C5 44 00N 118 00W
Sneek Neths 48 D6 53 02N 5 40E
Sneem Rol 21 B1 51 50N 9 45W
Snodland England 17 D2 51 20N 0 27E
Snowdon mt. Wales 14 B3 53 04N 4 05W
Snowy Mountains Australia 73 J3 36 50S 147 00E
Soar r. England 15 E2 52 50N 1 15W
Soay i. Scotland 8 C2 57 08N 6 14W
Socotra i. Yemen 65 F1 12 55N 54 00E
Söderhamn Sweden 49 E3 61 19N 17 10E
Sodertälje Sweden 49 E2 59 11N 17 39E
Sofia Bulgaria 55 K5 42 40N 23 18E
Soham England 17 D3 52 20N 0 20E
Soissons France 50 F5 49 23N 3 20E
Solapur India 66 D3 17 43N 75 56E
Solent, The sd. England 16 B1 50 45N 1 25W
Soligorsk Belarus 53 N6 52 50N 27 32E
Solihull England 15 E2 52 25N 1 45W
Sollefteå Sweden 49 E3 63 09N 17 15E
Sóller Spain 51 G3 39 46N 2 42E
SOLOMON ISLANDS 73 L9/M9
Solothurn Switz. 52 C3 47 13N 7 32E
Soltau Germany 52 D6 52 59N 9 50E
Solway Firth Scotland 11 F1 54 45N 3 40W
SOMALIA 81 Q2/Q3
Somerset co. England 19 D3/E3 51 10N 3 00W
Somerton England 19 E3 51 03N 2 44W
Sompting England 16 C1 50 50N 0 21W
Sønderborg Denmark 49 C1 54 55N 9 48E
Sondrio Italy 54 C7 46 11N 9 52E
Sonning Common tn. England 16 C2 51 31N 0 59W
Sopron Hungary 53 H3 47 40N 16 35E
Sora Italy 54 E4 41 43N 13 37E
Soria Spain 51 D4 41 46N 2 28W
Soroca Moldova 53 P4 48 08N 28 17E
Sosnowiec Poland 53 J5 50 16N 19 07E
Souillac France 50 E3 44 53N 1 29E
Southam England 15 E2 52 15N 1 23W
Southampton England 16 B1 50 55N 1 25W
Southampton u.a. England 16 B1 50 50N 1 20W
Southampton Water sd. England 16 B1 50 50N 1 20W
South Ayrshire u.a. Scotland 11 E2 55 20N 4 40W
South Ballachulish Scotland 8 D1 56 42N 5 09W
South Bank tn. England 13 E3 54 35N 1 10W
South Benfleet England 17 D2 51 33N 0 34E
Southborough England 17 D2 51 10N 0 15E
South Brent England 18 D2 50 25N 3 50W
South Carolina state USA 91 K3 34 00N 81 00W
South Cave tn. England 13 F2 53 46N 0 35W
South Cerney England 15 E1 51 41N 1 57W
South Dakota state USA 90 F5 45 00N 102 00W
South Dorset Downs England 19 E2 50 40N 2 30W
South Downs England 16 C1 50 50N 0 30W
Southend u.a. England 17 D2 51 32N 0 50E
Southend Scotland 10 D2 55 20N 5 38W

Southend-on-Sea England 17 D2 51 33N 0 43E
Southerness Point Scotland 11 F1 54 53N 3 37W
Southern Ocean 101
South Esk r. Scotland 9 F1 56 50N 3 10W
South Foreland c. England 17 E2 51 09N 1 23E
South Gloucestershire u.a. England 15 D1 51 30N 2 30W
South Hayling England 16 C1 50 47N 0 59W
South Island NZ 73 N1/P2 42 30S 172 00E
SOUTH KOREA 69 N5
South Kirkby England 13 E2 53 34N 1 20W
South Lanarkshire u.a. Scotland 11 E2/F2 55 35N 3 55W
Southminster England 17 D2 51 40N 0 50E
South Molton England 18 D3 51 01N 3 50W
South Normanton England 13 E2 53 06N 1 20W
South Ockendon England 17 D2 51 32N 0 18E
South Petherton England 19 E2 50 58N 2 49W
South Pole Antarctica 101 90 00S
Southport England 12 C2 53 39N 3 01W
South Queensferry Scotland 11 F2 55 59N 3 25W
South Shields England 13 E3 55 00N 1 25W
South Tyne r. England 12 D3 54 52N 2 30W
South Uist i. Scotland 8 B2 57 20N 7 15W
South Walls i. Scotland 7 A1 58 47N 3 11W
Southwick England 16 C1 51 01N 0 14W
Southwold England 17 E3 52 20N 1 40E
South Woodham Ferrers England 17 D2 51 38N 0 38E
South Yorkshire co. England 13 E2 53 30N 1 30W
Sowerby Bridge England 13 E2 53 43N 1 54W
SPAIN 51 C3/E3
Spalding England 13 F2 52 47N 0 10W
Spárti Greece 55 K2 37 05N 22 25E
Spean Bridge tn. Scotland 9 E1 56 53N 4 54W
Spennymoor England 13 E3 54 42N 1 35W
Sperrin Mountains NI 10 B1 54 49N 7 06W
Spey r. Scotland 9 F2 57 15N 3 45W
Spiddle Rol 20 B3 53 15N 9 18W
Spilsby England 13 G2 53 11N 0 05E
Spink Rol 21 D2 52 53N 7 12W
Spithead sd. England 16 B1 50 45N 1 10W
Spitsbergen i. Arctic Ocean 62 D12 79 00N 15 00E
Spittal an der Drau Austria 52 F3 46 48N 13 30E
Split Croatia 55 G5 43 31N 16 28E
Spokane USA 90 C6 47 40N 117 25W
Spoleto Italy 54 E4 42 44N 12 44E
Springfield Illinois USA 91 J4 39 49N 89 39W
Springfield Masachusetts USA 91 M5 42 07N 72 35W
Spurn Head England 13 G2 53 36N 0 07E
SRI LANKA 66 E1
Srinagar Kashmir 66 C6 34 08N 74 50E
Stacks Mountains Rol 21 B2 52 19N 9 33W
Staffa i. Scotland 8 C1 56 30N 6 15W
Stafford England 15 D2 52 48N 2 07W
Staffordshire co. England 15 D2/E2 52 50N 2 00W
Staines England 16 C2 51 26N 0 30W
Stainforth England 13 E2 53 36N 1 01W
Stalbridge England 19 E2 50 58N 2 23W
Stalybridge England 12 D3 53 29N 2 04W
Stamford Bridge tn. England 13 F2 53 59N 0 55W
Standish USA 93 D2 43 59N 83 58W
Stane Scotland 11 F2 55 50N 3 47W
Stanhope England 12 D3 54 45N 2 01W
Stanley England 13 E3 54 53N 1 42W
Stansted Mountfitchet England 17 D2 51 54N 0 12E
Stapleford England 17 D2 52 56N 1 15W
Staplehurst England 17 D2 51 10N 0 33E
Starachowice Poland 53 K5 51 03N 21 00E
Stara Zagora Bulgaria 55 L5 42 25N 25 37E
Start Bay England 18 D2 50 16N 3 35W
Start Point England 18 D2 50 13N 3 38W
Staunton USA 91 L4 38 10N 79 05W
Stavanger Norway 49 C2 58 58N 5 45E
Staveley England 13 E2 53 16N 1 20W
Stavropol' Russia 62 G6 45 03N 41 59E
Staxton England 13 F3 54 11N 0 26W
Steeping r. England 13 F2 53 10N 0 15E
Stendal Germany 52 E6 52 36N 11 52E
Stenhousemuir Scotland 11 F3 56 02N 3 49W
Stevenage England 16 C2 51 55N 0 14W
Stevenston Scotland 11 E2 55 39N 4 45W
Stewart Canada 88 J5 55 56N 130 01W
Stewarton Scotland 11 E2 55 41N 4 31W
Stewartstown NI 10 C1 54 35N 6 41W
Steyning England 16 C1 50 54N 0 20W
Steyr Austria 52 G3 48 04N 14 25E
Stilton England 16 C3 52 29N 0 17W
Stinchar r. Scotland 11 E2 55 10N 4 50W

Stirling Canada 88 N3 49 34N 112 30W
Stirling u.a. Scotland 11 E3 56 10N 4 15W
Stirling Scotland 11 F3 56 07N 3 57W
Stockbridge England 16 B2 51 07N 1 29W
Stockerau Austria 53 H4 48 24N 16 13E
Stockholm Sweden 49 59 20N 18 05E
Stockport England 12 D2 53 25N 2 10W
Stocksbridge England 13 E2 53 27N 1 34W
Stockton-on-Tees England 13 E3 54 34N 1 19W
Stockton-on-Tees u.a. England 13 E3 54 33N 1 24W
Stoer, Point of Scotland 8 D3 58 25N 5 25W
Stoke-on-Trent u.a. England 12 D2 53 00N 2 10W
Stokenchurch England 16 C2 51 40N 0 55W
Stoke-on-Trent England 12 D2 53 00N 2 10W
Stoke Poges England 16 C2 51 33N 0 35W
Stokesley England 13 E3 54 28N 1 11W
Stone England 15 D2 52 54N 2 10W
Stonehaven Scotland 9 G1 56 58N 2 13W
Stonehouse Scotland 11 F2 55 43N 3 59W
Stony Stratford England 16 C3 52 04N 0 52W
Størdal Norway 49 D3 63 18N 11 48E
Støren Norway 49 D3 63 03N 10 16E
Stornoway Scotland 8 C3 58 12N 6 23W
Storrington England 16 C1 50 55N 0 28W
Storr, The mt. Scotland 8 57 30N 6 11W
Storuman Sweden 49 E4 65 05N 17 10E
Stotfold England 16 C3 52 01N 0 15W
Stour r. Warwickshire England 15 E2 52 05N 1 45E
Stour r. Suffolk England 17 D3 52 10N 0 30E
Stour r. Kent England 17 E2 51 10N 1 10E
Stour r. Dorset England 19 E2 50 50N 2 10W
Stourbridge tn. England 15 D2 52 27N 2 09W
Stourport-on-Severn England 15 D2 52 21N 2 16W
Stow Scotland 11 G2 55 42N 2 51W
Stowmarket England 17 E3 52 11N 1 00E
Stow-on-the-Wold England 15 E1 51 56N 1 44W
Strabane NI 10 B1 54 49N 7 27W
Strabane district NI 10 B1 54 45N 7 30W
Strachur Scotland 10 D3 56 10N 5 04W
Stradbally Rol 21 D3 53 00N 7 08W
Stradone Rol 20 D3 53 59N 7 14W
Stralsund Germany 52 F7 54 18N 13 06E
Strangford Lough NI 10 D1 54 30N 5 35W
Stranorlar Rol 20 D4 54 48N 7 46W
Stranraer Scotland 10 D2 54 55N 5 02W
Strasbourg France 50 H5 48 35N 7 45E
Stratford-upon-Avon England 15 E2 52 12N 1 41W
Strathaven Scotland 11 E2 55 41N 4 05W
Strathcarron Scotland 8 D2 57 26N 5 27W
Strathpeffer Scotland 9 E2 57 35N 4 33W
Strathy Scotland 9 F3 58 33N 3 59W
Strathy r. Scotland 9 F3 58 30N 4 00W
Strathy Point Scotland 9 E3 58 35N 4 02W
Stratton England 18 C2 50 50N 4 31W
Straubing Germany 52 F4 48 53N 12 35E
Street England 19 3 51 03N 2 45W
Stretford England 12 D2 53 27N 2 19W
Strimonas r. Greece 55 K4 41 00N 23 00E
Strokestown Rol 20 C3 53 47N 8 06W
Stroma i. Scotland 7 A1 58 40N 3 08W
Stromboli mt. Italy 54 F3 38 48N 15 15E
Stromeferry Scotland 8 D2 57 21N 5 34W
Stromness Scotland 7 A1 58 57N 3 18W
Stronsay i. Scotland 7 59 07N 2 37W
Stronsay Firth Scotland 7 B2 59 00N 2 55W
Strontian Scotland 8 D1 56 41N 5 34W
Strood England 17 D2 51 24N 0 28E
Stroud England 15 D1 51 45N 2 12W
Strumble Head Wales 14 A2 52 02N 5 04W
Stryy Ukraine 53 L4 49 16N 23 51E
Stubbington England 16 B1 50 49N 1 13W
Studley England 15 E2 52 16N 1 52W
Sturminster Marshall England 19 E2 50 48N 2 04W
Sturminster Newton England 19 E2 50 55N 2 18W
Stuttgart Germany 52 D4 48 47N 9 12E
Subotica Yugoslavia 55 H7 46 04N 19 41E
SUDAN 81 L4/M4
Sudbury Canada 89 U3 46 30N 81 01W
Sudbury England 17 D2 52 02N 0 44E
Suffolk co. England 17 D3/E3 52 10N 1 00E
Suhl Germany 52 E5 50 37N 10 43E
Sulawesi i. Indonesia 71 F3/G3 2 00S 120 00E
Sumatera i. Indonesia 71 B4/C3 0 00 100 00E
Sumburgh Head Scotland 7 59 51N 1 16W
Summerhill Rol 20 E3 53 29N 6 44W
Sumy Ukraine 56 D5 50 55N 34 49E
Sunderland England 13 E3 54 55N 1 23W
Sundsvall Sweden 49 E3 62 22N 17 20E
Sunningdale England 16 C2 51 24N 0 37W
Superior, Lake Canada/USA 92 C3 48 00N 88 00W
Surabaya Indonesia 71 E2 7 14S 112 45E
Surat India 66 C4 21 10N 72 54E
SURINAME 96 F14
Surrey co. England 16 C2 51 15N 0 30W
Sutton England 16 C2 51 22N 0 12W

Sutton Coldfield England 15 E2 52 34N 1 48W
Sutton in Ashfield England 13 E2 53 08N 1 15W
Sutton on Sea England 13 G2 53 19N 0 17E
Suwalki Poland 53 L7 54 06N 22 56E
Suzhou China 69 M4 31 21N 120 40E
Svilengrad Bulgaria 55 M4 41 45N 26 14E
Swadlincote England 15 E2 52 46N 1 33W
Swaffham England 17 D3 52 39N 0 41E
Swale r. England 12 D3 54 20N 2 00W
Swanage England 19 F2 50 37N 1 58W
Swanley England 17 D2 51 24N 0 12E
Swanlinbar Rol 20 D4 54 12N 7 42W
Swanscombe England 17 D2 51 26N 0 18E
Swansea Wales 14 C1 51 38N 3 57W
Swansea Bay Wales 14 C1 51 35N 3 55W
Swansea u.a. Wales 14 B1/C1 51 35N 4 10W
SWAZILAND 82 F2
SWEDEN 49 D2/E4
Swiebodzin Poland 53 G6 52 15N 15 31E
Swilly r. Rol 20 D4 54 55N 7 45W
Swindon England 16 B2 51 34N 1 47W
Swindon u.a. England 16 B2 51 34N 1 47W
Swinford Rol 20 C3 53 57N 8 57W
Swinoujście Poland 52 G6 53 55N 14 18E
Swinton England 13 E2 53 30N 1 19W
SWITZERLAND 52 C3/D3
Swords Rol 20 E3 53 28N 6 13W
Sydney Australia 73 K4 33 55S 151 10E
Sylt Germany 52 D7 54 00N 8 00E
Symbister Scotland 7 C3 60 21N 1 02W
Symington Scotland 11 F2 55 37N 3 35W
Syracuse USA 91 L5 43 03N 76 10W
SYRIA 64 C6
Syzran' Russia 62 G7 53 10N 48 29E
Szczecin Poland 52 G6 53 25N 14 32E
Szeged Hungary 53 K3 46 15N 20 09E
Szombathely Hungary 53 H3 47 14N 16 38E

T

Tábor Czech Rep. 52 G4 49 25N 14 39E
Tabriz Iran 65 E6 38 05N 46 18E
Tacoma USA 90 B6 47 16N 122 30W
Tadcaster England 13 E2 53 53N 1 16W
Tadley England 16 B2 51 21N 1 08W
Taegu S. Korea 69 N5 35 52N 128 36E
Taejon S. Korea 69 N5 36 20N 127 26E
Tafalla Spain 51 E5 42 32N 1 41W
Taff r. Wales 14 C1 51 30N 3 10W
Taghmon Rol 21 E2 52 19N 6 39W
Taibei Taiwan 69 M3 25 05N 121 32E
Tain Scotland 9 E2 57 48N 4 04W
TAIWAN 69 M2
Taiyuan China 69 K5 37 50N 112 30E
TAJIKISTAN 62 J4/K4
Tajo r. Spain/Portugal 51 B3 39 00N 7 00W
Takamatsu Japan 70 B1 34 20N 134 01E
Talgarth Wales 14 C2 52 00N 3 15W
Tallaght Rol 20 E3 53 17N 6 21W
Tallahassee USA 91 K3 30 26N 84 16W
Tallinn Estonia 49 F2 59 22N 24 48E
Tallow Rol 21 C2 52 05N 8 01W
Tal-y-bont Wales 14 C2 52 39N 3 59W
Tamanrasset Algeria 80 F6 22 50N 5 28E
Tamar r. England 18 C2 50 32N 4 13W
Tambov Russia 62 G7 52 44N 41 28E
Tame r. England 15 D2 52 40N 1 45W
Tampa USA 91 K2 27 58N 82 38W
Tampere Finland 49 F3 61 32N 23 45E
Tamworth England 15 E2 52 39N 1 40W
Tandragee NI 10 C1 54 22N 6 25W
Tanganyika, Lake East Africa 83 B1 7 00S 30 00E
Tangier Morocco 80 C9 35 48N 5 45W
Tangshan China 69 L5 39 37N 118 05E
TANZANIA 83 B1/D1
Tapachula Mexico 94 F2 14 54N 92 15W
Taransay i. Scotland 8 B2 57 55N 7 00W
Táranto Italy 55 G4 40 28N 17 15E
Tarazona Spain 51 E4 41 54N 1 44W
Tarbat Ness c. Scotland 9 F2 57 50N 3 45W
Tarbert Rol 21 B2 52 32N 9 23W
Tarbert Western Isles Scotland 8 C2 57 54N 6 49W
Tarbert Argyle and Bute Scotland 10 D2 55 52N 5 26W
Tarbes France 50 E2 43 14N 0 05E
Tarbet Scotland 11 E3 56 12N 4 43W
Tarbolton Scotland 11 E2 55 31N 4 29W
Târgoviște Romania 53 M2 44 56N 25 27E
Târgu Mureș Romania 53 M3 46 33N 24 34E
Tarleton England 12 D2 53 41N 2 50W
Tarporley England 12 D2 53 10N 2 40W
Tarragona Spain 51 F4 41 07N 1 15E
Tarrasa Spain 51 G4 41 34N 2 00E
Tarsus Turkey 57 D2 36 25N 34 52E
Tartu Estonia 49 G2 58 20N 26 44E
Tashkent Uzbekistan 62 J5 41 16N 69 13E
Taunton England 19 D3 51 01N 3 06W
Taunus mts. Germany 52 D5 50 00N 8 00E
Tauranga NZ 73 Q3 37 41S 176 10E
Taverham England 17 E3 52 41N 1 10E
Tavira Portugal 51 B2 37 07N 7 39W
Tavistock England 18 C2 50 33N 4 08W
Tavy r. England 18 C2 50 36N 4 04W

Taw r. England 18 D2 50 46N 3 55W
Tay r. Scotland 9 F1 56 30N 3 25W
Taynuilt Scotland 8 D1 56 25N 5 14W
Tayport Scotland 9 G1 56 27N 2 53W
T'bilisi Georgia 57 F3 41 43N 44 48E
Tczew Poland 53 J7 54 05N 18 46E
Tebay England 12 D3 54 26N 2 35W
Tees r. England 12 D3 54 40N 1 20W
Tegucigalpa Honduras 94 G2 14 05N 87 14W
Tehran Iran 65 F6 35 40N 51 26E
Teifi r. Wales 14 B2 52 03N 4 30W
Teign r. England 18 D2 50 42N 3 48W
Teignmouth England 18 D2 50 33N 3 30W
Teith r. Scotland 11 E3 56 10N 4 00W
Tejo r. Portugal 51 B3 39 30N 8 15W
Tel Aviv-Yafo Israel 64 B5 32 05N 34 46E
Telford England 15 D2 52 42N 2 28W
Teme r. England 15 D2 52 15N 2 25W
Tempio Pausania Italy 54 C4 40 54N 9 07E
Templemore Rol 21 D2 52 48N 7 50W
Templenoe Rol 21 B1 51 51N 9 41W
Tenbury Wells England 15 D2 52 19N 2 35W
Tenby Wales 14 B1 51 41N 4 43W
Tenerife i. Spain 80 A7 28 15N 16 35W
Tennessee r. USA 91 J4 35 00N 88 00W
Tennessee state USA 91 J4 35 00N 87 00W
Tenterden England 17 D2 51 05N 0 41E
Teramo Italy 54 E5 42 40N 13 43E
Teresina Brazil 96 J12 5 09S 42 46W
Termim Imerese Italy 54 E2 27 59N 13 42E
Termoli Italy 54 F4 42 00N 15 00E
Terni Italy 54 E4 42 34N 12 39E
Terracina Italy 54 E4 41 17N 13 15E
Terrasini Italy 54 E3 38 09N 13 05E
Terre Haute USA 91 J4 39 27N 87 24W
Teruel Spain 51 E4 40 21N 1 06W
Teslin Canada 88 J6 60 10N 132 42W
Test r. England 16 B2 51 05N 1 30W
Tetbury England 15 D1 51 39N 2 10W
Tetney England 13 F2 53 30N 0 01W
Tétouan Morocco 80 C9 35 34N 5 22W
Teviotdale Scotland 11 G2 55 20N 3 00W
Teviothead Scotland 11 G2 55 19N 2 56W
Tewkesbury England 15 D1 51 59N 2 09W
Texas state USA 90 G3 31 00N 100 00W
THAILAND 71 B7/C7
Thame r. England 16 B2 51 45N 1 05W
Thame England 16 B2 51 45N 0 59W
Thames r. England 16 C2 51 32N 0 50W
Thar Desert India 66 C5 27 30N 72 00E
Thatcham England 16 B2 51 25N 1 15W
Thaxted England 17 D2 51 57N 0 20E
The Downs tn. Rol 20 D3 53 30N 7 14W
The Everglades USA 91 K2 26 00N 81 00W
The Mumbles tn. Wales 14 C1 51 35N 3 59W
The Peak mt. England 13 E2 53 24N 1 51W
Thermaïkós Kólpos g. Greece 55 K3/K4 40 00N 22 50E
The Rower tn. Rol 21 E2 52 29N 6 57W
Thessaloníki Greece 55 K4 40 38N 22 58E
Thetford England 17 D3 52 25N 0 45E
Thiers France 50 F3 45 51N 3 33E
Thimphu Bhutan 67 F5 27 32N 89 43E
Thionville France 50 H5 49 22N 6 11E
Thíra i. Greece 55 L2 36 00N 25 00E
Thirsk England 13 E3 54 14N 1 20W
Thíva Greece 55 K3 38 19N 23 19E
Thomastown Rol 21 D2 52 31N 7 08W
Thompson Canada 89 R5 55 45N 97 54W
Thornaby-on-Tees England 13 E3 54 34N 1 18W
Thornbury England 15 D1 51 37N 2 32W
Thorne England 13 F2 53 37N 0 58W
Thorney England 16 C3 52 37N 0 07W
Thornhill Scotland 11 F2 55 15N 3 46W
Thornton England 12 D2 53 53N 3 00W
Thorpe-le-Soken England 17 E2 51 52N 1 10E
Thouars France 50 D4 46 59N 0 13W
Thrapston England 16 C2 52 24N 0 32W
Thuin Belgium 48 C3 50 21N 4 18E
Thun Switz. 52 C3 46 46N 7 38E
Thurcroft England 13 E2 53 24N 1 16W
Thurles Rol 21 D2 52 41N 7 49W
Thurrock u.a. England 17 D2 51 30N 0 25E
Thursby England 12 C3 54 51N 3 03W
Thurso Scotland 9 F3 58 35N 3 32W
Thurso r. Scotland 9 F3 58 20N 3 40W
Thurso Bay Scotland 9 F3 58 37N 3 34W
Tianjin China 69 L5 39 08N 117 12E
Tiberias, Lake Israel 64 N11 32 45N 35 30E
Tibesti mts. Chad 81 J6 21 00N 17 00E
Tickhill England 13 E2 53 26N 1 06W
Tighnabruaich Scotland 10 D2 55 56N 5 14W
Tigris r. Turkey/Iraq 65 D5 32 00N 46 00E
Tijuana Mexico 94 A6 32 29N 117 10W
Tilburg Neths 48 D4 51 34N 5 05E
Tilbury England 17 D2 51 28N 0 23E
Till r. England 11 G2 55 38N 2 08W
Till r. England 13 F2 53 20N 0 40W
Tillicoultry Scotland 11 F3 56 09N 3 45W
Tilt r. Scotland 9 F1 56 50N 3 45W
Timișoara Romania 53 K2 45 45N 21 15E
Timor i. Indonesia 71 G1/H2 9 00S 125 00E
Tinahely Rol 21 E2 52 48N 6 28W
Tingwall Scotland 7 A2 59 04N 3 03W
Tintagel England 18 C2 50 40N 4 45W

Tintagel Head England 18 C2 50 41N 4 46W
Tipperary Rol 21 C2 52 29N 8 10W
Tipperary co. Rol 21 D2 52 30N 8 00W
Tiptree England 17 D2 51 49N 0 45E
Tiranë Albania 55 H4 41 20N 19 49E
Tiree i. Scotland 8 C1 56 30N 6 55W
Titu Romania 53 M2 44 40N 25 32E
Tiverton England 18 D2 50 55N 3 29W
Tivoli Italy 54 E4 41 58N 12 48E
Tlemcen Algeria 80 D8 34 53N 1 21W
Tobercurry Rol 20 C4 54 03N 8 43W
Tobermore NI 10 C1 54 48N 6 42W
Tobermory Scotland 8 C1 56 37N 6 05W
Todmorden England 12 D2 53 43N 2 05W
Toe Head r. Rol 21 B1 51 30N 9 12W
Toe Head Scotland 8 B2 57 50N 7 07W
TOGO 80 E3
Tokelau Islands Pacific Ocean 100 J7 9 00S 168 00W
Tokyo Japan 70 C2 35 40N 139 45E
Toledo Spain 51 C3 39 52N 4 02W
Toledo USA 91 K5 41 40N 83 35W
Tolmezzo Italy 54 E7 46 24N 13 01E
Tolosa Spain 51 D5 43 09N 2 04W
Tolsta Head Scotland 8 C3 58 20N 6 10W
Toluca Mexico 94 E3 19 20N 99 40W
Tomar Portugal 51 A3 39 36N 8 25W
Tomatin Scotland 9 F2 57 20N 3 59W
Tomelloso Spain 51 D3 39 09N 3 01W
Tomintoul Scotland 9 F2 57 14N 3 22W
Tomsk Russia 63 L8 56 30N 85 05E
Tonbridge England 17 D2 51 12N 0 16E
TONGA 100 J5
Tongue Scotland 9 E3 58 28N 4 25W
Tønsberg Norway 49 D2 59 16N 10 25E
Tonyrefail Wales 14 C1 51 36N 3 25W
Toomyvara Rol 21 C2 52 51N 8 02W
Topsham England 18 D2 50 42N 3 27W
Tor Bay England 18 D2 50 25N 3 30W
Torbay England 18 D2 50 27N 3 30W
Torbay u.a. England 18 D2 50 27N 3 30W
Tordesillas Spain 51 C4 41 30N 5 00W
Tore Scotland 9 E2 57 37N 4 21W
Torfaen u.a. Wales 14 C1 51 38N 3 04W
Tornio Finland 49 F4 65 50N 24 10E
Toronto Canada 89 V2 43 42N 79 46W
Torpoint tn. England 18 C2 50 22N 4 11W
Torre del Greco Italy 54 F4 40 46N 14 22E
Torrelavega Spain 51 C5 43 21N 4 03W
Torremolinos Spain 51 C2 36 38N 4 30W
Torrente Spain 51 E3 39 27N 0 28W
Torres Vedras Portugal 51 A3 39 05N 9 15W
Torrevieja Spain 51 E2 37 59N 0 40W
Torridge r. England 18 C2 50 56N 4 22W
Torridon Scotland 8 D2 57 33N 5 31W
Tortosa Spain 51 F4 40 49N 0 31E
Toruń Poland 53 J6 53 01N 18 35E
Tory Island Rol 20 C5 55 16N 8 14W
Tory Sound Rol 20 C5 55 15N 8 05W
Totland England 16 B1 50 40N 1 32W
Totnes England 18 D2 50 25N 3 41W
Tottington England 12 D2 53 37N 2 20W
Totton England 16 B1 50 56N 1 29W
Touggourt Algeria 80 F8 33 08N 6 04E
Toul France 50 G5 48 41N 5 54E
Toulon France 50 G2 43 07N 5 55E
Toulouse France 50 E2 43 33N 1 24E
Tourcoing France 50 F6 50 44N 310E
Tours France 50 E4 47 23N 0 42E
Toward Scotland 10 D2 55 51N 4 58W
Towcester England 15 F2 52 08N 1 00W
Townsville Australia 73 J7 19 13S 146 48E
Toyama Japan 70 C2 36 42N 137 14E
Toyota Japan 70 C2 35 05N 137 09E
Tralee Rol 21 B2 52 16N 9 42W
Tralee Bay Rol 21 B2 52 20N 9 55W
Tramore Rol 21 D2 52 10N 7 10W
Tramore Bay Rol 21 D2 52 10N 7 08W
Tranent Scotland 11 G2 55 57N 2 57W
Trani Italy 55 G4 41 17N 16 25E
Trápani Italy 54 E3 38 02N 12 32E
Traun Austria 52 G4 48 14N 14 15E
Trawsfynydd Wales 14 C2 52 54N 3 55W
Tredegar Wales 14 C1 51 47N 3 16W
Tregaron Wales 14 C2 52 13N 3 55W
Tregony England 18 C2 50 16N 4 55W
Tremadog Bay Wales 14 B2 52 54N 4 15W
Trent r. England 13 F2 53 30N 0 50W
Trento Italy 54 D7 46 04N 11 08E
Tresco i. England 18 A1 49 57N 6 20W
Treviso Italy 54 E6 45 40N 12 15E
Trier Germany 52 C4 49 45N 6 39E
Trieste Italy 54 E6 45 39N 13 47E
Tríkala Greece 55 J3 39 33N 21 46E
Trim Rol 20 E3 53 34N 6 47W
Tring England 16 C2 51 48N 0 40W
TRINIDAD AND TOBAGO 95 M2
Trípoli Greece 55 K2 37 31N 22 22E
Tripoli Lebanon 64 C5 34 27N 35 50E
Tripoli Libya 81 G8 32 54N 13 11E
Trois-Rivières tn. Canada 89 W3 46 21N 72 34W
Trollhättan Sweden 49 D2 58 17N 12 20E
Tromsø Norway 49 E4 69 42N 19 00E
Trondheim Norway 49 D3 63 36N 10 23E
Troon Scotland 11 E2 55 32N 4 40W

Place	Page	Grid	Lat	Long
Trotternish p. Scotland	8	C2	57 00N	6 00W
Troup Head Scotland	9	G2	57 41N	2 19W
Trouville France	50	E5	49 22N	0 05E
Trowbridge England	16	A2	51 20N	2 13W
Troyes France	50	G5	48 18N	4 05E
Trujillo Spain	51	C3	39 28N	5 53W
Truro England	18	B2	50 16N	5 03W
Tuam RoI	20	C3	53 31N	8 50W
Tübingen Germany	52	D4	48 32N	9 04E
Tubruq Libya	81	K8	32 05N	23 59E
Tucson USA	90	D3	32 15N	110 57W
Tudela Spain	51	E5	42 04N	1 37W
Tudweiliog Wales	14	B2	52 55N	4 39W
Tula Russia	62	F7	54 11N	37 38E
Tulcea Romania	53	P2	45 10N	28 50E
Tulla RoI	21	C2	52 52N	8 45W
Tullamore RoI	20	D3	53 16N	7 30W
Tulle France	50	E3	45 16N	1 46E
Tullow RoI	21	E2	52 48N	6 44W
Tulsa USA	91	G4	36 07N	95 58W
Tulsk RoI	20	C3	53 47N	8 15W
Tummel r. Scotland	9	E1	56 40N	4 00W
Tummel Bridge Scotland	9	F1	56 43N	3 58W
Tunis Tunisia	80	G9	36 50N	10 13E
TUNISIA	80	F8/G8		
Türgovishte Bulgaria	55	M5	43 14N	26 37E
Turgutlu Turkey	55	M3	38 30N	27 43E
Turin Italy	54	B6	45 04N	7 40E
Turkana, Lake Ethiopia/Kenya	83	D6/E6	4 00N	36 00E
TURKEY	57	C2/E2		
TURKMENISTAN	62	H4/J4		
Turks and Caicos Islands W. Indies	95	K4	21 30N	72 00W
Turku Finland	49	F3	60 27N	22 15E
Turnberry Scotland	10	E2	55 20N	4 50W
Turriff Scotland	9	G2	57 32N	2 28W
Tutbury England	15	E2	52 52N	1 40W
Tuttlingen Germany	52	D4	47 59N	8 49E
TUVALU	100	H7		
Túy Spain	51	A5	42 03N	8 39W
Tuz Gölü l. Turkey	57	D2	38 40N	33 35E
Tuzla Bosnia-Herzegovina	55	H6	44 33N	18 41E
Tver' Russia	62	F8	56 49N	35 57E
Tweed r. Scotland/England	11	G2	55 45N	2 10W
Tweedmouth England	11	G2	55 47N	2 00W
Twin Falls tn. USA	90	D5	42 34N	114 30W
Twyford England	16	C2	51 29N	0 53W
Twyford England	16	B2	51 01N	1 19W
Tyldesley England	12	D2	53 32N	2 29W
Tylers Green England	16	C2	51 37N	0 42W
Tyndrum Scotland	9	E1	57 27N	4 44W
Tyne r. Scotland	11	G2	55 58N	2 43W
Tyne and Wear co. England	13	E3	55 00N	1 10W
Tynemouth tn. England	13	E4	55 01N	1 24W
Tynset Norway	49	D3	62 17N	10 47E
Tywi r. Wales	14	B1	51 50N	4 25W
Tywyn Wales	14	B2	52 35N	4 05W

U

Place	Page	Grid	Lat	Long
Uaupés Brazil	96	D13	0 07S	67 05W
Uberaba Brazil	96	H10	19 47S	47 57W
Uckfield England	17	D1	50 58N	0 05E
Uddevalla Sweden	49	D2	58 20N	11 56E
Udine Italy	54	E7	46 04N	13 14E
Uelzen Germany	52	E6	52 58N	10 34E
Ufa Russia	62	H7	54 45N	55 58E
Uffculme England	19	D2	50 54N	3 21W
UGANDA	83	B6/C6		
Ugie r.	9	G2	57 31N	1 55W
Uig Scotland	8	C2	57 35N	6 22W
Uithuizen Neths	48	E6	53 24N	6 41E
UKRAINE	56	C4/D4		
Ulan Bator Mongolia	69	J7	47 54N	106 52E
Ulan-Ude Russia	63	N7	51 55N	107 40E
Ullapool Scotland	8	D2	57 54N	5 10W
Ullswater l. England	12	D3	54 35N	2 55W
Ulm Germany	52	D4	48 24N	10 00E
Ulva i. Scotland	8	C1	56 30N	6 15W
Ulverston England	12	C3	54 12N	3 06W
Umeå Sweden	49	F3	63 50N	20 15E
Unapool Scotland	9	D3	58 14N	5 01W
Ungava Bay Canada	89	X5	59 00N	67 30W
Unimak Island USA	88	C4	55 00N	164 00W
UNITED ARAB EMIRATES	65	F3		
UNITED KINGDOM	6			
UNITED STATES OF AMERICA	90/91			
Unst i. Scotland	7	D3	60 45N	0 55W
Upavon England	16	B2	51 18N	1 49W
Upper Lough Erne NI	10	B1	54 15N	7 30W
Upper Team England	15	E2	52 57N	0 43W
Uppingham England	15	F2	52 35N	0 43W
Uppsala Sweden	49	E2	59 55N	17 38E
Upton West Yorkshire England	13	E2	53 37N	1 17W
Upton Dorset England	19	E2	50 42N	2 02W
Ural r. Asia	62	H6	48 00N	52 00E
Ural Mountains Russia	62	H7/H9	57 00N	60 00E
Ure r. England	13	E3	54 20N	1 55W
Urlingford RoI	21	D2	52 43N	7 35W
Urmston England	12	D2	53 27N	2 21W
Urr r. Scotland	11	F2	55 05N	3 57W
URUGUAY	97	F6		
Uruguay r. Uruguay/Argentina	97	F6	32 00S	57 40W
Ürümqi China	68	E6	43 43N	87 38E
Ushaw Moor tn. England	13	E3	54 47N	1 39W
Usk r. Wales	14	C1	51 55N	3 40W
Ussel France	50	F3	45 32N	2 18E
Ust'-Ilimsk Russia	63	N8	58 03N	102 39E
Utah state USA	90	D4	39 00N	112 00W
Utah Lake USA	90	D5	40 10N	111 50W
Utrecht Neths	48	D5	52 05N	5 07E
Utrera Spain	51	C2	37 10N	5 47W
Uttoxeter England	15	E2	52 54N	1 52W
UZBEKISTAN	62	J5		

V

Place	Page	Grid	Lat	Long
Vác Hungary	53	J3	47 46N	19 08E
Valdepeñas Spain	51	D3	38 46N	3 24W
Val-d'Or Canada	89	V3	48 07N	77 47W
Valence France	50	G3	44 56N	4 54E
Valencia Spain	51	E3	39 29N	0 24W
Valencia Venezuela	96	D16	10 14N	67 59W
Valencia, Gulf of Spain	51	F3	39 30N	0 20E
Valencia Island i. RoI	21	A1	51 52N	10 20W
Valenciennes France	50	F6	50 22N	3 32E
Vale of Glamorgan, The u.a. Wales	14	C1	51 30N	3 30W
Valladolid Mexico	94	G4	20 40N	88 11W
Valladolid Spain	51	C4	41 39N	4 45W
Valletta Malta	54	F1	35 54N	14 32E
Valley r. Wales	14	B3	53 17N	4 34W
Valverde del Camino Spain	51	B2	37 35N	6 45W
Vanadzor Armenia	57	F3	40 49N	44 30E
Vancouver Canada	88	L3	49 13N	123 06W
Vancouver USA	90	B6	45 38N	122 40W
Vänern l. Sweden	49	D2	59 00N	13 30E
Van Gölü l. Turkey	57	F2	38 33N	42 46E
Vanna i. Norway	49	E5	70 05N	19 50E
Vännäs Sweden	49	E3	63 56N	19 50E
Vannes France	50	C4	47 40N	2 44W
Vantaa Finland	49	F3	60 20N	24 50E
VANUATU	73	N7		
Varanasi India	66	E5	25 20N	83 00E
Vardø Norway	49	K6	70 22N	31 06E
Varese Italy	54	C6	45 49N	8 49E
Varkhaus Finland	49	G3	62 20N	27 50E
Varna Bulgaria	55	M5	43 12N	27 57E
Värnamo Sweden	49	D2	57 11N	14 03E
Vaslui Romania	53	N3	46 37N	27 46E
Västerås Sweden	49	E2	59 36N	16 32E
Västervik Sweden	49	E2	57 45N	16 40E
Vasto Italy	54	F5	42 07N	14 43E
Vatersay i. Scotland	8	B1	56 55N	7 32W
Vatra Dornei Romania	53	M3	47 20N	25 21E
Vättern l. Sweden	49	D2	58 20N	14 20E
Växjö Sweden	49	D2	56 52N	14 50E
Vejle Denmark	49	C2	55 43N	9 33E
Velebit mts. Croatia	54	F6	44 00N	15 00E
Vélez-Málaga Spain	51	C2	36 47N	4 06W
Vélez Rubio Spain	51	D2	37 39N	2 04W
Vementry i. Scotland	7	C3	60 20N	1 28W
Vendôme France	50	E4	47 48N	1 04E
VENEZUELA	96	D15		
Venice Italy	54	E6	45 26N	12 20E
Venissieux France	50	G3	45 42N	4 46E
Venlo Netherland	48	E4	51 22N	6 10E
Ventnor England	16	B1	50 36N	1 11W
Ventura USA	90	C3	34 16N	119 18W
Vera Spain	51	E2	37 15N	1 51W
Veracruz Mexico	94	E3	19 11N	96 10W
Vercelli Italy	54	CC6	45 19N	8 26E
Verdun-sur-Meuse France	50	G5	49 10N	5 24E
Verín Spain	51	B4	41 55N	7 26W
Vermont state USA	91	M5	44 00N	73 00W
Verona Italy	54	D6	45 26N	11 00E
Versailles France	50	F5	48 48N	2 07E
Verviers Belgium	48	D3	50 36N	5 52E
Verwood England	19	F2	50 53N	1 52W
Vesoul France	50	H4	47 38N	6 09E
Vesuvius vol. Italy	54	F4	40 49N	14 26E
Veszprém Hungary	53	H3	47 06N	17 54E
Vetlanda Sweden	49	E2	57 26N	15 05E
Vevey Switz.	52	C3	46 28N	6 51E
Viana do Castelo Portugal	51	A4	41 41N	8 50W
Viareggio Italy	54	D5	43 52N	10 15E
Viborg Denmark	49	C2	56 28N	9 25E
Vibo Valentia Italy	54	G3	38 40N	16 06E
Vicenza Italy	54	D6	45 33N	11 32E
Vichy France	50	F4	46 07N	3 25E
Victoria Canada	88	L3	48 26N	123 20W
Victoria, Lake East Africa	83	C4	2 00S	33 00E
Vienna Austria	53	H4	48 13N	16 22E
Vienne France	50	G3	45 32N	4 54E
Vientiane Laos	71	C7	17 59N	102 38E
Vierzon France	50	F4	47 14N	2 03E
VIETNAM	71	D7		
Vigo Spain	51	A5	42 15N	8 44W
Vila Nova de Gaia Portugal	51	A4	41 08N	8 37W
Vila Real Portugal	51	B4	41 17N	7 45W
Vilhelmina Sweden	49	E3	64 38N	16 40E
Villach Austria	52	F3	46 37N	13 51E
Villalba Spain	51	B5	43 17N	7 41W
Villarrobledo Spain	51	D3	39 16N	2 36W
Villefranche-sur-Saône France	50	G3	46 00N	4 43E
Villena Spain	51	E3	38 39N	0 52W
Villeneuve-sur-Lot France	50	E3	44 25N	0 43E
Villeurbanne France	50	G3	45 46N	4 54E
Vilnius Lithuania	49	G1	54 40N	25 19E
Vinaroz Spain	51	F4	40 29N	0 28E
Vipiteno Italy	54	D7	46 54N	11 27E
Virginia RoI	20	D3	53 49N	7 04W
Virginia USA	91	H6	47 30N	92 28W
Virginia state USA	91	L4	38 00N	77 00W
Virginia Water tn. England	16	C2	51 24N	0 34W
Virgin Islands W. Indies	95	M3	18 00N	64 30W
Visby Sweden	49	E2	57 32N	18 15E
Viseu Portugal	51	B4	40 40N	7 55W
Viterbo Italy	54	E5	42 26N	12 06E
Vitória Brazil	96	J9	20 20S	40 18W
Vitoria Gasteiz Spain	51	D5	42 51N	2 40W
Vitry-le-François France	50	G5	48 44N	4 36E
Vitsyebsk Belarus	56	D6	55 10N	30 14E
Vittoria Italy	54	F2	36 58N	14 32E
Vladimir Russia	62	G8	56 08N	40 25E
Vladivostok Russia	63	R5	43 09N	131 53E
Vlissingen Neths	48	B4	51 27N	3 35E
Voitsberg Austria	52	G3	47 04N	15 09E
Volga r. Russia	62	G6	50 00N	45 00E
Volgograd Russia	62	G6	48 45N	44 30E
Volta, Lake Ghana	80	D3	7 30N	0 30W
Vóreioi Sporádes is. Greece	55	K3/L3	39 00N	24 00E
Vosges mts. France	50	H5	48 10N	6 50E
Voss Norway	49	C3	60 38N	6 25E
Voxnan Sweden	49	E3	61 22N	15 39E
Vukovar Croatia	55	H6	45 19N	19 01E

W

Place	Page	Grid	Lat	Long
Waal r. Neths	48	D4	51 50N	5 07E
Waalwijk Neths	48	D4	51 42N	5 04E
Waddesdon England	16	C2	51 51N	0 56W
Waddington England	13	F2	53 10N	0 32W
Wadebridge England	18	C2	50 32N	4 50W
Wadhurst England	17	D2	51 04N	0 21E
Wainfleet All Saints England	13	G2	53 06N	0 15E
Wakefield England	13	E2	53 42N	1 29W
Wales UK	14	C2	52 40N	3 30W
Wallasey England	12	C2	53 26N	3 03W
Wallingford England	16	B2	51 37N	1 08W
Wallis and Futuna is. Pacific Ocean	100	J6	13 16S	176 15W
Walls Scotland	7	C3	60 14N	1 34W
Wallsend England	13	E3	55 00N	1 31W
Walney, Isle of England	12	C3	54 05N	3 10W
Walsall England	15	E2	52 35N	1 58W
Waltham Abbey England	16	D2	51 41N	0 00
Waltham Forest England	16	C2	51 36N	0 00
Waltham on the Wolds England	15	F2	52 49N	0 49W
Walton-le-Dale England	12	D2	53 45N	2 41W
Walton-on-the-Naze England	17	E2	51 51N	1 16E
Walvis Bay tn. Namibia	82	B3	22 59S	14 31E
Wanganui NZ	73	P3	39 56S	175 03E
Wanlockhead Scotland	11	F2	55 24N	3 47W
Wantage England	16	B2	51 36N	1 25W
Warboys England	16	C2	52 24N	0 06W
Ward Hill Scotland	7	A1	58 54N	3 20W
Ware England	16	C2	51 49N	0 02W
Wareham England	19	E2	50 41N	2 07W
Warley England	15	E2	52 30N	1 59W
Warlingham England	16	C2	51 19N	0 04W
Warminster England	16	A2	51 13N	2 12W
Warrenpoint tn. NI	10	C1	54 06N	6 15W
Warrington England	12	D2	53 24N	2 37W
Warsaw Poland	53	K6	52 15N	21 00E
Warsop England	13	E2	53 13N	1 10W
Warton England	12	D3	53 46N	2 54W
Warwick England	15	E2	52 17N	1 34W
Warwickshire co. England	15	E2	52 15N	1 40W
Washborough England	13	F2	53 14N	0 28W
Washington England	13	E3	54 54N	1 31W
Washington state USA	90	B6/C6	47 00N	120 00W
Washington D.C. USA	91	L4	38 55N	77 00W
Wash, The b. England	17	D3	52 55N	0 10E
Watchet England	19	D3	51 12N	3 20W
Waterbeach England	17	D3	52 16N	0 11E
Waterford RoI	21	D2	52 15N	7 06W
Waterford co. RoI	21	D2	52 10N	7 30W
Waterford Harbour RoI	21	E2	52 10N	6 57W
Watergrasshill RoI	21	C2	52 00N	8 20W
Waterlooville England	16	B1	50 53N	1 02W
Waterville RoI	21	A1	51 50N	10 10W
Watford England	16	C2	51 39N	0 24W
Wath upon Dearne England	13	E2	53 31N	1 21W
Watlington England	16	C2	51 39N	1 00W
Watton England	17	D3	52 34N	0 50E
Waveney r. England	17	E2	52 30N	1 30E
Wavre Belgium	48	C3	50 43N	4 37E
Wear r. England	12	D3	54 45N	2 05W
Weaverham England	12	D2	53 16N	2 35W
Wedmore England	19	E3	51 14N	2 49W
Weedon Bec England	15	E2	52 14N	1 05W
Weiden Germany	52	F4	49 40N	12 10E
Weimar Germany	52	E5	50 59N	11 20E
Weissenfels Germany	52	E5	51 12N	11 58E
Welland r. England	15	C3	52 50N	0 10
Welland r. England	15	F2	52 30N	0 50W
Wellingborough England	15	F2	52 19N	0 42W
Wellington Telford and Wrekin England	15	D2	52 43N	2 31W
Wellington Somerset England	19	D2	50 59N	3 15W
Wellington NZ	73	P2	41 17S	174 46E
Wells England	19	E3	51 13N	2 39W
Wells-next-the-Sea England	17	D3	52 58N	0 51E
Wels Austria	52	F4	48 10N	14 02E
Welshpool Wales	14	C2	52 40N	3 09W
Welton England	13	F2	54 47N	3 00W
Welwyn Garden City England	16	C2	51 48N	0 13W
Wem England	14	D2	52 51N	2 44W
Wemyss Bay Scotland	10	E2	55 55N	4 53W
Wendover England	16	C2	51 46N	0 46W
Wensum r. England	17	D3	52 45N	1 10E
Wenzhou China	69	M3	28 02N	120 40E
West Berkshire u.a. England	16	B2	51 28N	1 00W
West Bridgford England	15	E2	52 56N	1 08W
West Bromwich England	15	E2	52 31N	1 59W
Westbury England	16	A2	51 16N	2 11W
West Dunbartonshire u.a. Scotland	11	E3	56 02N	4 39W
Westerham England	16	D2	51 16N	0 05E
Western Ghats mts. India	66	C3/D2	15 30N	74 00E
Western Isles u.a. Scotland	8	B2/B3	57 45N	7 30W
WESTERN SAHARA	80	B6/B7		
Western Sayan mts. Russia	63	M7	52 30N	92 30E
West Felton England	14	D2	52 49N	2 58W
West Haddon England	15	E2	52 20N	1 04W
Westhill Scotland	9	G2	57 11N	2 16W
West Horsley England	16	C2	51 16N	0 26W
West Indies is. Caribbean Sea	95	K4/L4	22 00N	69 00W
West Kilbride Scotland	10	E2	55 42N	4 51W
West Kirby England	12	C2	53 22N	3 10W
West Loch Tarbert Western Isles Scotland	8	B2/C2	57 55N	6 52W
West Loch Tarbert Argyll and Bute Scotland	10	D2	55 48N	5 31W
West Lothian u.a. Scotland	11	F2	55 50N	3 36W
Westmeath co. RoI	20	D3	53 30N	7 30W
West Mersea England	17	D2	51 47N	0 55E
West Midlands co. England	15	D2	52 35N	2 00W
Weston-super-Mare England	19	E3	51 21N	2 59W
Westport RoI	20	B3	53 48N	9 32W
Westport Bay RoI	20	B3	53 49N	9 37W
Westray i. Scotland	7	A2	59 18N	3 00W
West Sussex co. England	16	C1	51 00N	0 25W
West Thurrock England	17	D2	51 28N	0 20E
West Virginia state USA	91	K4	39 00N	81 00W
Westward Ho! England	18	C3	51 02N	4 15W
West Wittering England	16	C1	50 47N	0 54W
West Yorkshire co. England	13	E2	53 50N	1 30W
Wetherby England	13	E2	53 56N	1 23W
Wetzlar Germany	52	D5	50 33N	8 30E
Wexford co. RoI	21	E2	52 20N	6 35W
Wexford RoI	21	E2	52 20N	6 27W
Wexford Bay RoI	21	E2	52 20N	6 10W
Wexford Harbour RoI	21	E2	52 20N	6 25W
Wey r. England	16	C2	51 18N	0 30W
Weybridge England	16	C2	51 22N	0 28W
Weyburn Canada	89	Q3	49 39N	103 51W
Weymouth England	19	E2	50 37N	2 25W
Whaley Bridge England	12	D2	53 20N	1 59W
Whalley England	12	D2	53 50N	2 24W
Wharfe r. England	13	E3	54 10N	2 05W
Wharfedale v. England	12	D3	54 10N	2 00W
Wheatley England	16	B2	53 22N	0 52W
Whernside sum. England	12	D3	54 14N	2 23W
Whickham England	13	E3	54 57N	1 41W
Whitburn England	13	E3	54 57N	1 21W
Whitburn Scotland	11	F2	55 52N	3 42W
Whitby England	13	F3	54 29N	0 37W
Whitchurch Shropshire England	15	D2	52 58N	2 41W

Whitchurch Buckinghamshire
England 16 C2 51 53N 0 51W
Whitchurch Hampshire
England 16 B2 51 14N 1 20W
Whitefield England 12 D2 53 34N 2 18W
Whitegate RoI 21 C1 51 50N 8 14W
Whitehaven England 12 C3 54 33N 3 35W
Whitehead NI 10 D1 54 45N 5 43W
Whitehills Scotland 9 G2 57 40N 2 35W
White Horse, Vale of
England 16 B2 51 35N 1 30W
Whiten Head Scotland 9 E3 58 34N 4 32W
Whiteparish England 16 B2 51 01N 1 39W
Whitfield England 17 E2 51 09N 1 17E
Whithorn Scotland 11 E1 54 44N 4 25W
Whitland Wales 14 B1 51 50N 4 37W
Whitley Bay tn. England13 E4 55 03N 1 25W
Whitney, Mount USA 90 C4 36 35N 118 17W
Whitsand Bay England 18 C2 50 20N 4 25W
Whitstable England 17 E2 51 22N 1 02E
Whittington England 14 C2 52 52N 3 00W
Whittlesey England 16 C3 52 34N 0 08W
Whitton England 13 F2 53 43N 0 38W
Whitworth England 12 D2 53 40N 2 10W
Wichita USA 91 G4 37 43N 97 20W
Wick Scotland 9 F3 58 26N 3 06W
Wick r. Scotland 9 F3 58 26N 3 10W
Wickford England 17 D2 51 38N 0 31E
Wickham England 16 B1 50 54N 1 10W
Wickham Market
England 17 E3 52 09N 1 22E
Wicklow RoI 21 E2 52 59N 6 03W
Wicklow co. RoI 21 E2 52 55N 6 25W
Wicklow Mountains
RoI 21 E2/E3 53 00N 6 20W
Widnes England 12 D2 53 22N 2 44W
Wiener Neustadt
Austria 53 H3 47 49N 16 15E
Wierden Neths 48 E5 52 21N 6 35E
Wiesbaden Germany 52 D5 50 05N 8 15E
Wigan England 12 D2 53 33N 2 38W
Wigston England 15 E2 52 36N 1 05W
Wigton England 12 C3 54 49N 3 09W
Wigtown Scotland 11 E1 54 52N 4 26W
Wigtown Bay Scotland 11 E1 54 45N 4 20W
Wil Switzerland 52 D3 47 28N 9 03E
Wilberfoss England 13 F2 53 57N 0 53W
Wilhelmshaven
Germany 52 D6 53 32N 8 07E
Willington England 13 E3 54 43N 1 41W
Williton England 19 D3 51 10N 3 20W
Wilmslow England 12 D2 53 20N 2 15W
Wilton England 16 B2 51 05N 1 52W
Wiltshire co. England 16 A2/B2 51 30N 2 00W
Wimborne Minster
England 19 F2 50 48N 1 59W
Wincanton England 19 E3 51 04N 2 25W
Winchelsea England 17 D1 50 55N 0 42E
Winchester England 16 B2 51 04N 1 19W
Windermere tn England12 D3 54 23N 2 54W
Windermere l. England 12 D3 54 20N 3 10W
Windhoek Namibia 82 C3 22 34S 17 06E
Windsor Canada 89 U2 42 18N 83 00W
Windsor England 16 C2 51 29N 0 38W
Windsor and Maidenhead
u.a. England 16 C1 50 25N 0 50W
Windward Islands
Lesser Antilles 95 M2 12 30N 62 00W
Wingate England 13 E3 54 55N 1 23W
Wingerworth England 13 E2 53 13N 1 28W
Winkleigh England 18 D2 50 51N 3 56W
Winnipeg Canada 89 R3 49 53N 97 10W
Winnipeg, Lake Canada89 R4 52 30N 97 30W
Winnipegosis, Lake
Canada 89 Q4 52 10N 100 00W
Winschoten Neths 48 F6 53 07N 7 02E
Winscombe England 19 E3 51 28N 2 52W
Winsford England 12 D2 53 11N 2 31W
Winslow England 16 C2 51 57N 0 54W
Winterbourne England 15 D1 51 30N 2 31W
Winterthur Switz. 52 D3 47 30N 8 45E
Winterton-on-Sea
England 17 E3 52 43N 1 42E
Wirksworth England 13 E2 53 05N 1 34W
Wisbech England 17 D3 52 40N 0 10E
Wisconsin state USA 91 H6/J6 45 00N 90 00W
Wishaw Scotland 11 F2 55 47N 3 56W
Wisła r. Poland 53 J6 53 00N 19 00E
Wismar Germany 52 E6 53 54N 11 28E
Wissembourg France 50 H5 49 02N 7 57E
Witham r. England 13 F2 53 05N 0 40W
Witham England 17 D2 51 48N 0 38E
Witheridge England 18 D2 50 55N 3 42W
Withernsea England 13 G2 53 44N 0 02E
Witley England 16 C2 51 08N 0 39W
Witney England 16 B2 51 48N 1 29W
Wittenberg Germany 52 F5 51 53N 12 39E
Wittenberge Germany 52 E6 52 59N 11 45E
Wittlich Germany 52 C4 49 59N 6 54E
Wiveliscombe England 19 D3 51 03N 3 19W
Wivenhoe England 17 D2 51 52N 0 58E
Woburn Sands tn.
England 16 C3 52 01N 0 39W
Woking England 16 C2 51 20N 0 34W
Wokingham England 16 C2 51 25N 0 51W
Wokingham u.a.
England 16 C1 50 25N 0 55W

Wolfsberg Austria 52 G3 46 50N 14 50E
Wolfsburg Germany 52 E6 52 27N 10 49E
Wollaston England 15 F2 52 16N 0 41W
Wollongong Australia 73 K4 34 25S 150 52E
Wolsingham England 13 E3 54 44N 1 52W
Wolverhampton
England 15 D2 52 36N 2 08W
Wolverton England 16 C3 52 04N 0 50W
Wombourne England 15 D2 52 32N 2 11W
Wombwell England 13 E2 53 32N 1 24W
Woodbridge England 17 E3 52 06N 1 19E
Woodford Halse
England 15 E2 52 10N 1 13W
Woodhall Spa England 13 F2 53 09N 0 14W
Woodlands tn. Canada 92 A4 50 12N 97 40W
Woodstock England 16 B2 51 52N 1 21W
Wool England 19 E2 50 41N 2 14W
Woolacombe England 18 C3 51 10N 4 13W
Wooler England 11 G2 55 33N 2 01W
Wootton Bassett
England 16 B2 51 33N 1 54W
Worcester England 15 D2 52 11N 2 13W
Worcester USA 91 M5 42 17N 71 48W
Worcestershire co.
England 15 D2 52 15N 2 15W
Workington England 12 C3 54 39N 3 33W
Worksop England 13 E2 53 18N 1 07W
Worms Germany 52 D4 49 38N 8 23E
Worms Head Wales 14 B1 51 34N 4 20W
Worsbrough England 13 E2 53 33N 1 29W
Worthing England 16 C1 50 48N 0 23W
Wotton-under-Edge
England 15 D1 51 39N 2 21W
Wrangle England 13 G2 53 02N 0 07E
Wrath, Cape Scotland 9 D3/E3 58 37N 5 01W
Wrexham tn Wales 14 C3 53 03N 3 00W
Wrexham u.a. Wales 14 C3/D3 53 00N 3 00W
Writtle England 17 D2 51 44N 0 26E
Wrocław Poland 53 H5 51 05N 17 00E
Wrotham England 17 D2 51 19N 0 19E
Wroughton England 16 B2 51 31N 1 48W
Wroxham England 17 E3 52 42N 1 24E
Wuhan China 69 K4 30 35N 114 19E
Wuppertal Germany 52 C5 51 15N 7 10E
Würzburg Germany 52 D4 49 48N 9 57E
Wuxi China 69 M4 31 35N 120 19E
Wye England 17 D2 51 11N 0 56E
Wylye England 16 B2 51 08N 2 01W
Wylye r. England 16 A2 51 08N 2 13W
Wymondham England 17 E3 52 34N 1 07E
Wyoming state USA 90 E5 43 00N 108 00W

X
Xi'an China 69 J4 34 16N 108 54E

Y
Yakutsk Russia 63 Q9 62 10N 129 50E
Yamoussoukro Côte d'Ivoire 80 C3 6 50N 5 20W
Yangon Myanmar 71 B7 16 47N 96 10E
Yaoundé Cameroon 80 G2 3 51N 11 31E
Yarmouth England 16 B1 50 42N 1 29W
Yaroslavl' Russia 62 F8 57 34N 39 52E
Yate England 15 D1 51 32N 2 25W
Yateley England 16 C2 51 20N 0 51W
Yatsushiro Japan 70 B1 32 32N 130 35E
Yatton England 19 E3 51 24N 2 49W
Yaxley England 16 C3 52 31N 0 16W
Yeadon England 13 E2 53 52N 1 41W
Yealmpton England 18 D2 50 21N 3 59W
Yekaterinburg Russia 62 J8 56 52N 60 35E
Yell i. Scotland 7 C3 60 35N 1 10W
Yellowknife Canada 88 N6 62 30N 114 29W
Yelverton England 18 C2 50 30N 4 05W
YEMEN REPUBLIC 64/65 D2/E2
Yeovil England 19 E2 50 57N 2 39W
Yerevan Armenia 57 F3 40 10N 44 31E
Yokohama Japan 70 C2 35 27N 139 38E
York England 13 E2 53 58N 1 05W
York u.a. England 13 E2 53 56N 1 02W
York, Cape Australia 73 H8 10 42S 142 32E
Yorkshire Wolds
England 13 F3 54 00N 0 45W
York, Vale of England 13 E3 54 10N 1 20W
Youghal RoI 21 D1 51 51N 7 50W
Youghal Bay RoI 21 D1 51 55N 7 48W
Yoxford England 17 E3 52 16N 1 30E
Ystalyfera Wales 14 C1 51 47N 3 47W
Ystrad Aeron Wales 14 B2 52 10N 4 10W
Ystradgnlais Wales 14 C1 51 47N 3 45W
Ystwyth r. Wales 14 C2 52 20N 3 55W
Ytterhogdal Sweden 49 D3 62 10N 14 55E
Yucatan p. Mexico 94 G3 19 00N 89 00W
Yuci China 69 K5 37 40N 112 44E
YUGOSLAVIA 55 H6/K6
Yukon r. Canada/USA 88 D6 63 30N 159 40W
Yukon Territory territory
Canada 88 H6/J6 64 15N 135 00W
Yumen China 68 G5 39 54N 97 43E
Yverdon Switz. 52 C3 46 47N 6 38E
Yvetot France 50 E5 49 37N 0 45E

Z
Zaanstad Neths 48 C5 52 27N 4 49E
Zadar Croatia 54 F6 44 07N 15 14E
Zafra Spain 51 B3 38 25N 6 25W
Żagań Poland 52 G5 51 37N 15 20E
Zagreb Croatia 54 F6 45 48N 15 58E
Zagros Mountains Iran 65 E5/F5 32 45N 48 50E
Zakopane Poland 53 J4 49 17N 19 54E
Zákynthos i. Greece 55 J2 37 45N 20 50E
Zambezi r.
Zambia/Zimbabwe 82 D4 16 00S 23 00E
ZAMBIA 82 D5/E5
Zamora Spain 51 C4 41 30N 5 45W
Zanzibar Tanzania 83 F1 6 10S 39 12E
Zaragoza Spain 51 E4 41 39N 0 54W
Zeebrugge Belgium 48 B4 51 20N 3 13E
Zell-am-See tn. Austria 52 F3 47 19N 12 47E
Zenica
Bosnia-Herzegovina 55 G6 44 11N 17 53E
Zermatt Switz. 52 C3 46 01N 7 45E
Zhengzhou China 69 K4 34 45N 113 38E
Zhmerynka Ukraine 53 P4 49 00N 28 02E
Zhytomyr Ukraine 53 P5 50 18N 28 40E
Zibo China 69 L5 36 51N 118 01E
Zielona Góra Poland 53 G5 51 57N 15 30E
ZIMBABWE 82 E4/F4
Zlín Czech Rep. 53 H4 49 14N 17 40E
Zug Switz. 52 D3 47 10N 8 31E
Zugspitze mt. Austria 52 E3 47 25N 11 00E
Zürich Switz. 52 D3 47 23N 8 33E
Zvolen Slovakia 53 J4 48 34N 19 08E
Zwettl Austria 52 G4 48 37N 15 11E
Zwickau Germany 52 F5 50 43N 12 30E
Zwolle Neths 48 E5 52 31N 6 06E

Acknowledgements

The publishers would like to thank the following for permission to reproduce photographs:

Corbis UK Ltd, p.15; FAO-UN, p.76; NASA, p.76, 84, 97, 106, 113, 127; Oxford Scientific Films, p.114, 115; spaceimaging.com, p.87; Science Photo Library, p.108, 113, 114; US Geological Survey, p.126; Visual Insights, p.131.

Cover image:
Visible Earth / Rich Irish, Landsat 7 Team, NASA GSFC; data provided by EROS Data Center. Globes / GEOATLAS.

The page design is by Adrian Smith.

The publishers are grateful to the following colleagues in geography education for their helpful comments and advice during the development stages of this atlas:

Pam Boardman, Graham Butt, Kathryn Clayton, Alan Cottle, Ruth Crossley, Rachel Dean, Bob Digby, Ian Douglass, Tony Field, Martyn Gill, Joel Griffiths, Matthew Gunn, Gareth Huws, Kathryn Jones, Irfon Morris Jones, David Langham, Patrick Lewis, Bob Newman, Andrew Parkinson, Liz Roodhouse, John Sadler, Toni Schiavone, Natasha Sirin, Andrea Wade, Patrick Wherity, Steve Wilkes, and Malcolm Yates.

The publishers would also like to thank the many individuals, companies, societies, and institutions who gave assistance in the gathering of data.